The Composition of Everyday Life
A Guide to Writing

John Mauk
Northwestern Michigan College

John Metz
The University of Toledo

THOMSON
WADSWORTH

Australia   Canada   Mexico   Singapore   Spain   United Kingdom   United States

The Composition of Everyday Life
A Guide to Writing
Mauk / Metz

Publisher: Michael Rosenberg
Acquisitions Editor: Dickson Musslewhite
Development Editor: Julie McBurney
Senior Production Editor: Esther Marshall
Editorial Assistant: Stephen Marsi
Marketing Director: Lisa Kimball

Manufacturing Manager: Marcia Locke
Compositor/Project Management: Pre-Press Company, Inc.
Photo Researcher Manager: Sheri Blaney
Cover/Text Designer: Will Tenney, Perspectives
Cover Photo: ©Karen Moskowitz/GETTY IMAGES
Printer: QuebecorWorld

For permission to use material from this text or product contact us:
Tel   1-800-730-2214
Fax   1-800-730-2215
Web   www.thomsonrights.com

Library of Congress Cataloging-in-Publication Data
Mauk, John
   The composition of everyday life: a guide to writing/ John Mauk, John Metz.
      p. cm.
   Includes index.
   1. English language--Rhetoric--Handbooks, manuals, etc. 2. Manners and customs--Problems, exercises, etc. 3. Report writing--Handbooks, manuals, etc. 4. Readers--Manners and customs. 5. College readers. I. Metz, John (John W.) II. Title.

PE1408.M3869 2003
808'.042--dc21

2003049999

Acknowledgments

The *Composition of Everyday Life* embodies a widely held belief in composition studies: that any piece of writing grows out of a large context of voices. Over the past three years, during the invention, revision, development, revision, writing, and revision of the text, a number of important writers, thinkers, teachers and students informed our decisions. Particularly, we are thankful to:

Steve Mockensturm at Studio Vent, not only for originating the book's layout and the cover design but also for teaching us how to think visually; Michael Morgan at Bemidji State University for insights and Web site contributions; our colleagues (and comrades) at Owens Community College, who talked openly with us about their pedagogy and contributed their writing and energy to the project; our colleagues at The University of Toledo and Northwestern Michigan College, who have been a source of energy; Alice Calderonello, Patricia Harkin, and Joan Mullin for a deeper understanding of composition and for hints on being writers.

We are deeply indebted to our development editor, Julie McBurney, whose consistent wisdom brought us from the inception of this project to its final chapter. Thanks also to Dickson Musslewhite for his constant advocacy, to Esther Marshall for ably shepherding the book through the production process, and to all the energetic and visionary folks at Wadsworth, as well as all the freelancers and in particular: Janet McCartney; Pre-Press Company: Elsa van Bergen, Katy Faria, and Christopher Forestieri; Peggy Hines and Patrice Titterington. Bravo. Finally, thanks to the reviewers, whose opinions added layers and dimensions to our work:

Cathryn Amdahl, *Harrisburg Area Community College*
Sheila Booth, *Quinsigamond Community College*
Jennifer Brezina, *College of the Canyons*
Rebecca L. Busker, *Arizona State University*
Maria Clayton, *Middle Tennessee State University*
Chidsey Dickson, *Christopher Newport University*
Michael Donnelly, *Temple University*
Jhon Gilroy, *Albuquerque Technical Vocational Institute*
Greg Glau, *Arizona State University*
Dave Golden, *Casper College*
Wesley Hellman, *University of Mary*
Maurice Hunt, *Baylor University*
Sharla Hutchison, *University of Oklahoma*
Carolyn J. Kelly, *Iowa State University*
Virginia Kuhn, *University of Wisconsin, Milwaukee*
Susan Lang, *Texas Tech University*
Jeremy Meyer, *Arizona State University*
Richard McLamore, *McMurry Univerisity*
Gloria McMillan, *University of Arizona*
Michael Morgan, *Bemidji State University*
Maureen Placilla, *Finger Lakes Community College*
Diane Orsini, *Valencia Community College*
Michael Roos, *University of Cincinnati*
Lisa Schneider, *Columbus State Community College*
Lou Thomson, *Texas Women's University*

A Note to Instructors

This text emerged out of our own pedagogical crises. After years of teaching at two-year and four-year colleges, we realized that our students were having the most difficulty with invention—the act of generating ideas. For many of our students, especially novice and apprehensive writers, invention meant grabbing onto the first topic that felt comfortable (that would most likely generate several pages), and these topics (such as abortion, capital punishment, legalization of marijuana, etc.), most often did not propel students into vital intellectual space. Generally, we discovered that students become bored by their own topic choices, and instructors become frustrated at the lack of invention.

So after a collective 32 years of teaching college composition courses, we found ourselves asking a basic question: *how does one teach invention?* For many years, invention has been wrapped in vague terms for students. Writing tricks such as webbing, brainstorming, and the like have been offered to students as tools for generating ideas. Beyond those tools, which imply that invention is merely a lucky accident of the synapses, we were wondering how to teach *inventive perspectives*— to help students see their lives and the world around them as realms of possibilities and to re-see the famliar aspects of everyday life.

We also thought about the changing student demographics in higher education. At the universities and community colleges where we have taught, the student body has included the traditional 18-20-year-olds who leave behind hometowns to reside within collegiate space. But we have also seen the steady rise of 20-, 30-, 40-somethings, with jobs and families, looking for an additional layer in their lives. And our experience is not unique. Increasingly, college students are less apt to leave behind familiar lives and steep themselves in school. They are increasingly more apt to attend school part-time, hold jobs (sometimes more than one), and have children. And even the students attending four-year residential campuses are increasingly more likely to read, study, and carry on everyday life off-campus.

Because students are spending less time on campus, less time in traditional academic space, they need a pedagogy they can carry with them into everyday life, one that actually depends on and uses everyday life beyond the classroom. To address these needs, each chapter in *Composition of Everyday Life* prompts students through a rigorous invention process, which begins in life beyond the classroom and goes beyond the actual assignment itself. In other words, each chapter casts the *invention process* as a broader, more expansive and encompassing, process than the actual act of writing. Each chapter promotes consistent inquiry, so that the student writer does not leave invention behind at the drafting/writing phase, but continues to re-write, and be re-written by, increasingly complex ideas. In other words, as the chapters proceed, they call students further into their own topics. Even when they are considering voice or organization or revision, students are prompted to create by inquiring—by looking at the gaps in their own texts and their own understanding. *CEL,* then, does not simply teach students how to write, or even how to invent ideas, but how to *be inventive thinkers and writers.* Invention, we believe, is not merely a skill, but an intellectual posture that transfers to and develops within disciplines across the curriculum.

From our experience as composition teachers, we have come to believe that invention lies at the center of the composition enterprise, and is fundamental to transforming students from apprehensive first-year college writers to curious intellectuals. Although not necessarily taught explicitly in other courses, invention is often the skill that most first-year college students need as they develop a genuine sense of inquiry. And contrary to its sublimated placement in "the writing process," the complicated act of invention is not merely an initial phase of writing. It is a perspective that gives way to inquiry. Learning how to invent involves re-learning the possibilities of everyday life and being *re-written* as a thinker.

Beyond Dualisms

Many students have been led to believe in two unhelpful dualisms: (1) *personal vs. private life* and (2) *non-academic vs. academic life.* When students cling to these, they are often unable to grow as writers and thinkers. But *CEL* attempts to break down these dualisms, explicitly and implicitly, throughout the chapters. First, although *CEL* focuses on students' abilities to invent ideas, the approach does not emphasize the internal or intimately personal. In fact, the chapters prompt students to see invention as an intellectual-social act—one in which the thinker/writer is steeped in public/civic affairs. The Point of Contact sections prompt topics to emerge not from the writer's enclosed consciousness, but from the writer's interactions in everyday life. The Public Resonance sections help students to see how ideas emerge and develop from layers of social connectedness. Second, the chapters teach students to see writing (which they often designate as an exclusively academic behavior) as an academic-public-personal behavior. All the chapter sections, in some way, teach students to take writing outside of the classroom—and to bring everyday life into the classroom (or the academic consciousness).

The Layout

For the last year of the book's development, we attempted to create a layout that would visually appeal to students. As incoming college students are increasingly steeped in a culture of visually sophisticated appeals for their attention, they require textbooks that speak with equal sophistication. *CEL* chapters speak with written text and with images, and at the end of each chapter, students are prompted to analyze the images in light of the chapter's focus. Our goal was not to simply appeal to a "visual generation," but to teach a generation that is constantly bombarded with images to see rhetorically.

Also, you may notice that the sections in each chapter appear on two-page spreads. With this design, we hoped to create a new textbook space—a new geography—for students to enter. Because *CEL* is focused on creating a new student perspective about writing, it also encourages students to approach textbook pages as spaces. Our intention in clumping information (into chapter sections) was not to "package" ideas for students, but to invite them *into* the pages—rather than *through* them. Though this may seem like a subtle difference from other textbooks, we have been convinced that such small details may further prompt students to constantly make connections between the rhetorical strategies offered in the pages and the material world around them.

What is Third Space?

Third space has been a controlling idea for the pedagogy of *CEL*. Borrowed from critical geographer Edward Soja, third space is the collision of the "real and the imagined." We see it as the collision of traditional academic space (books, classrooms, desks) and the everywhere-else of student life. *CEL* invites students to carry academia out, to smear school across everyday life and to bring everyday life into the classroom. Of course textbooks have been doing this for years, but *CEL* focuses on this intersection as the primary tool of invention. This approach is developed throughout *CEL*: The Point of Contact sections, for instance, prompt students to *go, do,* and *ask*. Third space is created in that moment when the student, in some place beyond traditional academia, embodies critical inquiry. And as we suggest throughout the chapters, this moment is *writing* as much as keying words into a computer.

A Final Note

When we began writing *The Composition of Everyday Life,* we imagined a textbook that demystifies the acts of writing, and *teaches* the acts of invention. We imagined a book that students could use as an exciting reader and a powerful rhetorical heuristic. And in considering the instructional realities of the field, we imagined a book that would be valuable for part-time instructors, who often work without a network of support.

While we considered the more explicit objectives of composition studies (statements by NCTE and WPA), we also studied the undercurrents of the field to detect the underlying crises of typical classrooms and the inclinations of typical (and not-so-typical) students. We found that students are increasingly more transient, intellectually tied to life beyond traditional academic space. This growing body of students (and their instructors), we imagined, need a textbook that engages (rather than ignores) the complexities of everyday life. We hope this textbook achieves, at least to some degree, our original hopes.

Brief Contents

Contents

Chapter 1
Remembering Who You Were   2

Chapter 2
Explaining Relationships   58

Chapter 8
Searching for Causes 370

Chapter 9
Proposing Solutions 418

Chapter 14
Rhetorical Handbook 704

Using *CEL* as a Thematic Reader

Readings throughout this book can be grouped thematically—according to subject matter. Here, we suggest how readings from different chapters might be grouped together thematically. As you explore a particular subject (Education and Learning, for example), you might focus on a particular rhetorical aim (such as Evaluating or Proposing a Solution). Or you might explore a subject area without a particular aim in mind, eventually discovering not only a writing topic but also the rhetorical aim into which it falls. The common subjects are: Education and Learning, Justice and Equality, Environment and Animals, Consumerism and Economy, America, The World, Self, Others (Community), Language and Culture, Gender and Identity, Parents and Family, Popular Culture, Technology. More complete lists of readings for each subject are available in the *Survival Guide for Instructors* and on the *CEL* Web site: http://english.wadsworth.com/maukmetz/.

Education and Learning:
How do people view education in both formal and informal settings? What is the role of education in our lives, and how might we view that role differently? A variety of readings explore Education and Learning from a variety of viewpoints. Through reading, writing, and discussion, you might explore Education and Learning to the extent that you come to think differently about it and can participate in an ongoing dialogue about its role in people's lives. You might discover an important point about education by exploring a memory, identifying a less-usual relationship, making sense out of an observation, redefining a key term, and so on.

"The Grapes of Mrs. Rath," Steve Mockensturm
"A *Beat* Education," Leonard Kress
"The Aloha Spirit: A Reminiscence," Aunty D.
"What the Honey Meant," Cindy Bosley
"Have It Your Way," Simon Benlow
"College: What's in It for Me?" Steven M. Richardson
"Why We No Longer Use the 'H' Word," Dan Wilkins
"Why a Great Books Education Is the Most Practical," David Crabtree
"Entitlement Education," Daniel Bruno
"When Bright Girls Decide That Math Is a 'Waste of Time,'" Susan Jacoby
"How to Say Nothing in 500 Words," Paul Roberts
"Television: Destroying Childhood," Rose Batchel
"The Menstrual Cycle," Christiane Northrup, M.D.

Justice and Equality:
A quick survey of the readings about Justice and Equality listed below suggests a range of areas: Native American rights, body type, legal drugs, the mentally and physically challenged, wildlife, and so on. These readings can help you identify and explain a relationship, analyze a concept (such as "justice" or "equality"), respond to an argument, identify a cause or propose a solution, and so on. What is justice, and how might exploring the concept of justice in today's world be of value? What interesting idea about justice and equality might you discover and share with others?

"Why We No Longer Use the 'H' Word," Dan Wilkins
"Crimes Against Humanity," Ward Churchill
"Cruelty, Civility, and Other Weighty Matters," Ann Marie Paulin
"Beware of Drug Sales," Therese Cherry
"Is Hunting Ethical?" Ann F. Causey

"The New Politics of Consumption," Juliet Schor
"Why Doesn't GM.Sell Crack?" Michael Moore
"The Menstrual Cycle," Christiane Northrup, M.D.
"An Apology to Future Generations," Simon Benlow

Environment and Animals:
Land, trees, weasels, chimps, porches, smoking, hunting—and the role that we as consumers play in it all. These readings, which offer different ways of looking at Environment and Animals, encourage you to explore ideas beyond your initial thoughts and beyond conventional beliefs. What is your relationship to the land? To the air? To the animals? How might you think differently about that relationship? And what might be the consequence of your new way of thinking?

"Americans and the Land," John Steinbeck
"Living Like Weasels," Annie Dillard
"Planting a Tree," Edward Abbey
"Gombe," Jane Goodall
"The Front Porch," Chester McCovey
"My Daughter Smokes," Alice Walker
"Is Hunting Ethical?" Ann F. Causey
"The New Politics of Consumption," Juliet Schor
"The Obligation to Endure," Rachel Carson
"Technology, Movement, and Sound," Ed Bell
"The Parting Breath of the Now Perfect Woman," Chester McCovey
"Farming and the Global Economy," Wendell Berry
"The Menstrual Cycle," Christiane Northrup, M.D.
"An Apology to Future Generations," Simon Benlow

Consumerism and Economy: Several readings in this book encourage you to think about yourself as a consumer. What, and how, do you consume? And what, if anything, do you produce by consuming? As with other subjects in CEL, you might spend an entire semester exploring this one subject area, or you might explore it for just one assignment. Perhaps it would be of great value to spend an entire semester exploring just this question: What does it mean to be a consumer?

"The Front Porch," Chester McCovey
"Have It Your Way," Simon Benlow
"Response to Juliet Schor," Betsy Taylor
"Entitlement Education," Daniel Bruno
"Whales R Us," Jayme Stayer
"Rethinking Divorce," Barbara Dafoe Whitehead
"The New Politics of Consumption," Juliet Schor
"Sex, Lies, and Advertising," Deborah Tannen
"Technology, Movement, and Sound," Ed Bell
"Television: Destroying Childhood," Rose Batchel
"Farming and the Global Economy," Wendell Berry
"An Apology to Future Generations," Simon Benlow

America: What does it mean to be an American?

What is "America"? Are beauty pageants American? And what about The Aloha Spirit? These readings deal with America and being American. They allow you to explore the relationship between yourself and your country. (International students may find this subject to be especially interesting as they bring a unique perspective.) To what degree do the two—individual and country—influence each other? You can make observations, evaluate, identify causes, propose solutions, and so on. And, you can explore how America communicates with you.

"The Grapes of Mrs. Rath," Steve Mockensturm
"Americans and the Land," John Steinbeck
"Planting a Tree," Edward Abbey
"Crimes Against Humanity," Ward Churchill
"Cruelty, Civility, and Other Weighty Matters,"
  Ann Marie Paulin
"My Daughter Smokes," Alice Walker
"Whales R Us," Jayme Stayer
"The New Politics of Consumption," Juliet Schor
"The Plight of High-Status Women," Barbara Dafoe
  Whitehead
"Hip-Hop: A Roadblock or Pathway to Black
  Empowerment?" Geoffrey Bennett
"Why Doesn't GM Sell Crack?" Michael Moore

The World: This book encourages you to look out-

ward—from self, to tribe, to nation, to world. The readings below allow you to think about your role in the world.

How do your actions impact the world, and what is the world's impact on you? From "The Aloha Spirit" (hello) to "An Apology to Future Generations" (I'm sorry), you can read about and discuss a very interesting relationship—the one you have with the world.

"Aloha Spirit: A Reminiscence," Aunty D.
"Planting a Tree," Edward Abbey
"Gombe," Jane Goodall
"The New Politics of Consumption," Juliet Schor
"When Bright Girls Decide That Math Is a 'Waste of
  Time,'" Susan Jacoby
"Farming and the Global Economy," Wendell Berry
"Why Doesn't GM Sell Crack?" Michael Moore
"The Menstrual Cycle," Christiane Northrup, M.D.
"An Apology to Future Generations," Simon Benlow

Self: Looking at self can be fascinating and worth-

while. The readings in this book encourage you to explore your own life in a way you have, perhaps, not done before. These readings about Self go beyond mere expressive writing. They encourage you to connect with others, even though—or perhaps, *especially when*—you are looking inward, at yourself. You can explore how these readings, your own writing, and focused discussion with others helps you to see differently—to learn something about yourself and connect it to the world around you.

"How I Lost the Junior Miss Pageant," Cindy Bosley
"A *Beat* Education," Leonard Kress
"Thrill of Victory, Agony of Parents," Jennifer
  Schwind-Pawlak
"What the Honey Meant," Cindy Bosley
"Friend or Foe," Dean A. Meek
"What it Means to be Creative," S.I. Hayakawa
"Cruelty, Civility, and Other Weighty Matters,"
  Ann Marie Paulin
"My Daughter Smokes," Alice Walker
The Andy Griffith Show: Return to Normal," Ed Bell
"Rethinking Divorce," Barbara Dafoe Whitehead
"The New Politics of Consumption," Juliet Schor
"Throwing Up Childhood," Leonard Kress
"In Bed," Joan Didion
"The Plight of High-Status Women," Barbara Dafoe
  Whitehead
"The Menstrual Cycle," Christiane Northrup, M.D.

Others (Community): Can we look at our-

selves without looking at our community? Both subjects (Self and Others) explore relationships between the individual and his or her surroundings. What is community? How is community created? These readings will help you to explore what we commonly call *community,* to consider how it works, and to examine your place in it. An entire writing course might be an exploration of one very important question: What is the relationship between community and communication?

"The Aloha Spirit: A Reminiscence," Aunty D.
"Dog-Tied," David Hawes
"Living Like Weasels," Annie Dillard
"A Building of Mailboxes," Dean Meek
"Cruelty, Civility, and Other Weighty Matters," Ann Marie Paulin
"Is Hunting Ethical?" Ann F. Causey
"Rethinking Divorce," Barbara Dafoe Whitehead
"Technology, Movement, and Sound," Ed Bell
"Thoughts on the International Access Symbol," Dan Wilkins
"Television: Destroying Childhood," Rose Batchel
"The Parting Breath of the Now Perfect Woman," Chester McCovey
"Hip-Hop: A Roadblock or Pathway to Black Empowerment?" Geoffrey Bennett
"Farming and the Global Economy," Wendell Berry
"Why Doesn't GM.Sell Crack?" Michael Moore
"An Apology to Future Generations," Simon Benlow

Language and Culture: How is language
important in culture? How is language important in the way a person thinks? These readings deal with the relationship between language and culture—between words and ideas. For example, "Aloha" is a word, but it is also a concept—a very important one in Hawaii! There is an Aloha Spirit, a culture of "Aloha"—not just a word. This reading and others will help you step back and explore the relationship between words, ideas and actions. Through exploration of this subject, you might discover that your college writing class is something more than you had originally imagined it to be.

"The Aloha Spirit: A Reminiscence," Aunty D.
"The Grapes of Mrs. Rath," Steve Mockensturm
"In Praise of the Humble Comma," Pico Iyer
"Why We No Longer Use the 'H' Word," Dan Wilkins
"Crimes Against Humanity," Ward Churchill
"Why a Great Books Education Is the Most Practical," David Crabtree
"Whales R Us," Jayme Stayer
"Pulp Fiction: Valuable Critique or Use Titillation?" Simon Benlow
"Rethinking Divorce," Barbara Dafoe Whitehead
"Sex, Lies, and Advertising," Deborah Tannen
"When Bright Girls Decide That Math Is a 'Waste of Time,'" Susan Jacoby
"The Plight of High-Status Women," Barbara Dafoe Whitehead

"Hip-Hop: A Roadblock or Pathway to Black Empowerment?" Geoffrey Bennett
"Why Doesn't GM.Sell Crack?" Michael Moore
"The Menstrual Cycle," Christiane Northrup, M.D.

Gender and Identity: What role does Gender
play in our lives? What does it mean to be male or female? How does gender affect our identities? And what influence can we have on issues of gender and identity? This group of readings, like the others, can be used in combination with other reading groups—from America or Pop Culture, for example. Instead of exploring just Gender and Identity, you might narrow your focus to readings that relate to Gender and Identify and Pop Culture.

"How I Lost the Junior Miss Pageant," Cindy Bosley
"TheThrill of Victory . . . The Agony of Parents," Jennifer Schwind-Pawlak
"The Ring of Truth: My Child Is Growing Up," Jessie Thuma
"Cruelty, Civility, and Other Weighty Matters," Ann Marie Paulin
"My Daughter Smokes," Alice Walker
"Rethinking Divorce," Barbara Dafoe Whitehead
"Throwing Up Childhood," Leonard Kress
"Sex, Lies, and Advertising," Deborah Tannen
"When Bright Girls Decide That Math Is a 'Waste of Time,'" Susan Jacoby
"In Bed," Joan Didion
"The Plight of High-Status Women," Barbara Dafoe Whitehead
"The Menstrual Cycle," Christiane Northrup, M.D.

Parents and Family: What role do our parents
play in our lives? Such a question might be explored endlessly with interesting results for both writer and reader. You might spend an entire semester exploring issues about Parents and Family. (Such a simple subject area can prove to be far more complicated—and interesting—than you first imagined.) What might be the value of thinking analytically and finding public resonance regarding the subject of parents and family?

"How I Lost the Junior Miss Pageant," Cindy Bosley
"The Aloha Spirit: A Reminiscence," Aunty D.
"Thrill of Victory, Agony of Parents," Jennifer Schwind-Pawlak
"The Ring of Truth: My Child Is Growing Up," Jessie Thuma
"What the Honey Meant," Cindy Bosley
"Friend or Foe," Dean A. Meek
"Gombe," Jane Goodall
"The Front Porch," Chester McCovey
"A Building of Mailboxes," Dean Meek
"My Daughter Smokes," Alice Walker

"*The Andy Griffith Show:* Return to Normal," Ed Bell
"Rethinking Divorce," Barbara Dafoe Whitehead
"Throwing Up Childhood," Leonard Kress
"An Apology to Future Generations," Simon Benlow

Popular Culture: What is the relationship between the individual and his or her pop culture? In what ways are we products of our own popular culture? From beauty pageants to hopping trains, from belly rings to dogs and beer, the readings dealing with popular culture allow you to consider the world that surrounds you from a fresh perspective. You can explore the *why* of your own behavior, considering how you—and others—are influenced by pressures of which you are both very aware and barely aware.

"How I Lost the Junior Miss Pageant," Cindy Bosley
"A *Beat* Education," Leonard Kress
"The Front Porch," Chester McCovey
"Have It Your Way," Simon Benlow
"Crimes Against Humanity," Ward Churchill
"Cruelty, Civility, and Other Weighty Matters,"
   Ann Marie Paulin
"Entitlement Education," Daniel Bruno
"Is Hunting Ethical?" Ann F. Causey
"*Star Wars,*" Roger Ebert
"Whales R Us," Jayme Stayer
"*The Andy Griffith Show*: Return to Normal," Ed Bell
"*Pulp Fiction:* Valuable Critique or Use Titillation?"
   Simon Benlow
"Rethinking Divorce," Barbara Dafoe Whitehead
"The New Politics of Consumption," Juliet Schor
"Sex, Lies, and Advertising," Deborah Tannen
"Television: Destroying Childhood," Rose Batchel
"The Plight of High-Status Women," Barbara Dafoe
   Whitehead
"The Parting Breath of the Now Perfect Woman,"
   Chester McCovey
"Hip-Hop: A Roadblock or Pathway to Black
   Empowerment?" Geoffrey Bennett

Technology: We cannot overlook technology. How does it influence the way we live? Through reading, writing, and discussion, you can explore beyond your initial thoughts and perceptions. You can consider the complex relationship in today's world between the individual and technology—or between one individual and another *because of technology.* What idea about technology might you discover and share with others, helping them to think or act differently?

"Americans and the Land," John Steinbeck
"Planting a Tree," Edward Abbey
"The Front Porch," Chester McCovey
"Cruelty, Civility, and Other Weighty Matters,"
   Ann Marie Paulin
"Beware of Drug Sales," Therese Cherry
"Whales R Us," Jayme Stayer
"*The Andy Griffith Show:* Return to Normal," Ed Bell
"The New Politics of Consumption," Juliet Schor
"Technology, Movement, and Sound," Ed Bell
"Television: Destroying Childhood," Rose Batchel
"The Parting Breath of the Now Perfect Woman,"
   Chester McCovey
"Farming and the Global Economy," Wendell Berry
"Why Doesn't GM Sell Crack?" Michael Moore
"The Menstrual Cycle," Christiane Northrup, M.D.
"An Apology to Future Generations," Simon Benlow

The first and most important principle of this book is that writing is deeply connected to everyday life. A writer develops ideas and revises thoughts simply by living life. If we see writing as something that only occurs during a few short hours before a paper is due, we shrink the processes and layers of writing into a single isolated act. Granted, some isolated typing, drafting, and editing is necessary for academic writing. But such work is actually only a portion of the real-life activities of a writer. Real writing occurs long before the computer is turned on or the pen is in hand. Real writing involves a perspective that informs what and how we see on a daily basis:

- We come in contact with something (an aluminum can on the sidewalk, for example).
- This bothers us (not just intellectually, but even physically—perhaps we feel anger, sorrow, frustration, or a sense of being alone in the world).
- This matters to us, so we pursue it intellectually (we think about it).
- We ask questions to sort it all out (why do people litter? what are the causes? what, if anything, can be done about it? what are the solutions? and so on).
- We keep it to ourselves, or we deliver our thoughts to others.

The point here is that writers often get ideas (and revise old ones) when they are away from the keyboard and outside the classroom: in a movie theatre, a city park, Venice Beach, their parents' dinner table, Interstate 80, Mud Hens Stadium, or Paris, France. This may seem absurd—but the important point is that writing is an extension of living and being curious. Writing is not the performance of something we know; rather, it is *the act of inventing, developing, and reinventing what can be known.* The entire process extends in all directions beyond the act of typing on the keyboard or writing with a pen; it begins with the act of living and extends past an assignment deadline. Writing also changes everyday life: it changes the individual consciousness of the writer, the reader(s), and the people who interact with both of them.

How to Use *The Composition of Everyday Life*

CEL offers the student several possibilities for inventing and developing writing topics. (1) The Point of Contact sections in chapters 1–11 are designed to launch you into an exploration of everyday behaviors, policies, situations, attitudes, and arguments, which you can then develop into a topic. Following the Point of Contact sections, the Analysis and Public Resonance sections in each chapter will help you examine the topic and extend your own thinking. (2) Chapters 1–11 contain several readings that exemplify writing and thinking strategies. After each reading, questions follow that will help you to analyze the issues and the actual writing techniques of the authors. Each reading also offers several "Ideas for Writing," which are designed to generate potential topics. (3) The readings throughout the book can be categorized according to certain themes (see p. xvi). Rather than focus on one chapter at a time, students can read several (or all) content-related essays in a category, and then use the Invention section from one of the chapters (1–11) to develop a particular topic.

Chapter Readings

Reading in academia is different from casual reading. When we read a newspaper, magazine, or popular literature casually, we breeze through paragraphs and over the top of ideas. Such material is filled with familiar ideas, common phrases, and even predictable transitions and conclusions. When we read such material, often we expect only to pick up some basic information or follow a fairly simple plot. Of course, this is not altogether bad. Such reading serves a purpose. We may need to pick up ideas quickly or even follow a plot without our critical radar on. But such reading has its downside: we tend not to learn much or to rethink issues in any significant way because we expect to encounter ideas and words that echo our own preconceptions and prejudices.

However, in academia, we read for different reasons: to rethink issues, to discover positions we had not previously imagined, to revise common perceptions. To fulfill such goals, we cannot breeze through paragraphs. We must expect to work through ideas, even to struggle at times. And most importantly, we must expect to be surprised, to have our comfortable mental rooms messed up occasionally. Reading in academia means being intellectually adventurous and expecting something new or radically different. It also means reading actively: always analyzing and refiguring ideas as they develop throughout a text.

To help you read actively and critically, each chapter of *CEL* features an *annotated* essay (an essay with comments and analysis in the margins). The annotations have two primary purposes: (1) to point out particular writing strategies, and (2) to illustrate how one might actively read and respond to a written text. As you will notice, the annotations vary from chapter to chapter to illustrate a range of possible strategies for active reading. You might see the annotations as an active reader walking

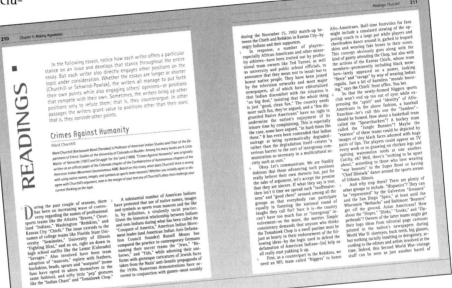

through the essays. They show the reader stopping at certain places, noticing particular claims, and speaking back to ideas. Readers who engage a text in this fashion gain a deep awareness of writing and are more likely to extract writing techniques than are those who quickly read through a text. As you read all the texts in *CEL,* try these active reading strategies on your own.

Each reading begins with a brief author bio and offers a reading strategy or two, something to help you read with curiosity and focus. Each reading is followed by a series of "Exploring Ideas" questions, which pick up where the reading strategies left off. These questions encourage you to explore the author's ideas in a way that an inquisitive thinker might.

The readings are placed between a reading strategy and several "Exploring Ideas" questions to encourage you to actively explore the ideas expressed in the reading. This way, even though the readings

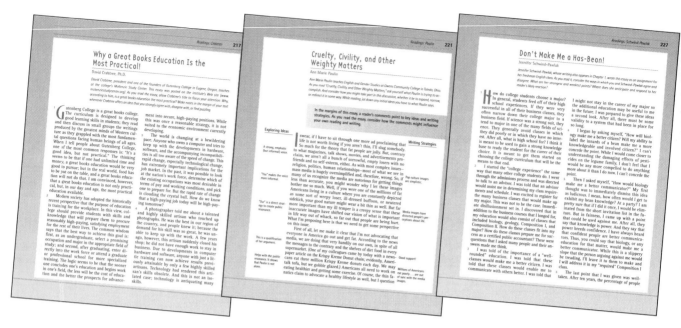

precede the **Invention** section of the chapter, they become an important part of your invention process. How? The "Exploring Ideas" questions usually begin by asking you what the author said and meant, thus "testing" your reading comprehension. Then they ask you to consider how your thinking is similar to or different from the author's. You are then prompted to explore these ideas both inside and outside the classroom through discussion with others, and to consider how other people's thoughts are similar to or different from your own. Finally, you are asked to write in response to your exploration, explaining how your ideas have changed or developed. Responding to these questions can be quite an experience (as it is meant to be), helping you to move through a process of exploration, driven by writing and discussion and intended to create *new ideas!*

The "Exploring Ideas" questions (which correspond to the **Invention** section of the chapter) are followed by "Technique and Style" questions (which correspond to the **Delivery** section). And finally, each reading is followed by several "Ideas for Writing." These "Ideas for Writing" are not called "Writing Topics" because you shouldn't see them as final topics about which to write, but instead as starting points for exploration, which ultimately help you to discover—after much exploration through writing and discussion—your own main idea.

The readings throughout *CEL* come from writers who represent a variety of disciplines and career fields, such as history, economics, business, computer graphics, literature, and the sciences. Despite the different disciplines and fields, they all seek to communicate a point that involves and impacts the world around them. And while writing techniques and personal styles differ, some qualities are constant: valuable insights, well-supported ideas, and appropriate tone. As you read through the chapters and encounter professionals from different disciplines, keep in mind that these essays were not written for a college writing textbook. The essays are a sample of the real writing that gets done in the public sphere; they show real economists, real scientists, real philosophers, real people talking to their colleagues and to the public, trying to change the world for the better. These are not writers locked inside an academic tower; rather, they are people who are deeply connected to, and intellectually stimulated by, the world around them.

CEL also invites you to find reading material on your own. After the chapter readings, each chapter contains an Outside Reading activity, which asks you to search the Internet, library databases, Infotrac, or print journals and magazines for a relevant article. This can be an opportunity to explore a vast amount of writing that is both valuable and easily accessible.

Invention

Have you ever wondered why some writers draw you in with new ideas and others seem like they are merely rehearsing their thoughts? What causes the difference? You might be inclined to believe that some people are simply better writers than others; however, good writing comes as a result of particular strategies, not innate mental capacity, and there is no more important writing strategy than *invention*.

Invention, or what is sometimes called *pre-writing*, is the process of discovering some idea you are not presently thinking. It is the activity of developing points and thinking through potential topics. Often it is associated with only one particular activity: coming up with an idea to write about. However, invention is a complex activity that extends far beyond the initial topic idea. It involves committing to an idea, exploring it in depth, and discovering its worth. When writers take the time to explore topics, they discover what is beyond their own biases or preconceptions—and even beyond the common beliefs of their potential audiences. They discover something worth telling, something that is not already floating around in everyone's minds. In short, invention makes all the difference between powerful, engaging writing that introduces new ideas and dull, lifeless writing that offers nothing but a writer's attempt to fulfill an assignment.

When college instructors assign writing, they are not expecting students to type the first thoughts that enter their minds and then go to spell check. Instructors want students to explore, to seek out ideas and extend their thinking. Instructors want students to discover new ideas for themselves and to communicate those ideas well. And without invention,

without the tools of discovery, such expectations are nearly impossible to meet.

The following three sections, which appear in each chapter, are designed to help you through the invention process. The first section, Point of Contact,

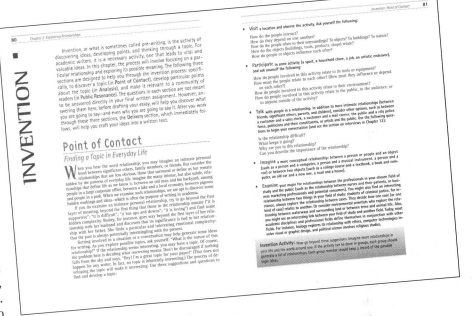

will help you discover a topic from everyday life; the second, Analysis, will help you explore the topic and develop particular points for writing assignments; and the third section, Public Resonance, will help you to make the topic relevant to a community of readers. The questions in each section are not meant to be answered directly in your final written assignment. Answering them before you start drafting will, however, help you discover ideas.

We also suggest that you go beyond the questions in each section. While we hope that these particular questions help to generate ideas for your writing projects, nothing is more valuable to a writer than generating her or his own questions. As you proceed through *CEL*, we hope you will find yourself asking your own invention questions.

Point of Contact

As we go through our daily lives, we pass by countless situations, disregard unlimited issues, and ignore crowds of people. We overlook them to get through life and carry on with our daily routines and rituals. To stay focused on our daily goals (going to work, getting groceries, driving in the right lane, staying relatively sane), we have to ignore much of what goes on around us. However, a writer (or someone developing a writer's perspective) stops in the middle of life's hustle and bustle and notices the potential meaning and significance in things; that is, the writer looks into what others disregard and sees the extraordinary in the ordinary. A writer finds the significance in an abandoned building, a busy shopping mall, or a group of young children. Before a writer can start writing, he or she must see life.

The Point of Contact section, after the readings in each chapter, invites the writer to slow down, to stop, to notice common and not-so-common aspects of life. The *point of contact* refers to the intersection of the writer's perspective and the real world. It is where the writer's vision collides with issues, events, situations, behaviors, and people. The idea here is that writing is more than simply arranging preconceived ideas—writing is about discovering something that might otherwise go unnoticed. Therefore, writers have to be ready; their radar must be on.

As you go through the Point of Contact sections, you will notice lists of questions, which are designed to generate possibilities for writing topics. Think of the questions as exploration tools, raising possible points of interest for writing. The lists are by no means exhaustive; they are simply examples of what can be asked. Follow up (in peer groups or alone) to generate more questions. (And if you are outside of an academic setting, at home, for instance, it is certainly fair play to borrow a family member or friend to help with the brainstorming.)

Analysis

We are all familiar with analysis. We participate in it constantly. We see auto mechanics analyze our cars to discover the cause of the knocking sound. We see our doctors analyze our condition to understand why we have those chronic headaches. Basically put, such analysis is a process of discovering *why* and/or *how* something occurs. But analysis also involves discovering meaning. Writers are not content to simply see a person or situation or object. They explore the *significance;* that is, they imagine what ideas a thing might suggest. For instance, a writer sees an empty storefront in a strip mall and imagines that it suggests corporate irresponsibility, or a declining economic system, or even the end of an era when businesses lasted for several years before leaving a community. In other words, the storefront has potential meaning when analyzed (and often that analysis, as we will make clear in the next section, can make a topic relevant to a broader community).

The questions in each **Analysis** section are designed to help you explore your topics and can be answered in a variety of ways. As in the Point of Contact sections, they should be approached as tools of exploration. Answering them quickly and moving on will not yield valuable analysis. We suggest imagining various answers, thereby expanding the possibilities for your topic. And even though the Analysis sections directly follow Point of Contact, do not assume that analysis ends early on in the writing process. Writers must analyze and reanalyze the way their topics evolve as their texts evolve.

For instance, let us use the aluminum can example. Imagine a discarded soda can on the side of the road. Why do people throw trash out car windows? What kind of thinking drives people to do this? But beyond discovering why something occurs, remember that analysis also involves an exploration of significance (what ideas the soda can suggests). For example:

> It may have something to do with Americans' assumption that we have unlimited space, that with all this land and open highways we cannot possibly clutter up our living space. This assumption is also apparent in the way we build new homes and neighborhoods—sprawling outward at every opportunity.

> It could also have something to do with people's sense of property. In the United States, we stress the idea of personal property (with fences, "Keep Out" and "No Trespassing" signs) but we have very little to say about collective property. The idea is almost foreign. Most people don't consider the highways, the forests, the fields outside their own backyards to be theirs, so they feel no remorse in polluting. The aluminum can, then, represents an entire way of thinking in the United States.

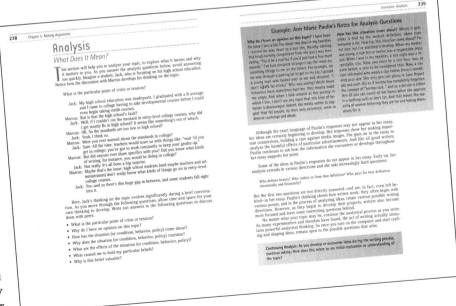

Analysis is an important part of the invention process. However, it is also the part that some students skip over, thus leading them to express ideas that will not engage their reader (or listener)—whether that person is a professor, an employer, a stranger, or a friend. Consider the following two paragraphs from a somewhat typical rough draft.

> I feel that a major problem in today's world is the fact that 18–20-year olds can't purchase or consume alcoholic beverages. Many people feel that this is not right and would like to see it changed. An 18-year-old is considered an adult, but why can't an adult drink alcohol?
>
> An adult, a person who is 18 years old, should be able to drink alcohol. If people think that an 18-year-old isn't responsible, then why does he have to register for a draft, and if drafted, go off to war and defend your country? An 18-year-old is also allowed to vote, and decide on who is going to run the country. This has a major effect on the country. Another reason that the age should be lowered is that people are doing it anyways, and it might cut back on costs for the police. It would be one less thing they have to worry about.

We do not dispute the writer's claim that a citizen who risks life for country ought to be allowed to legally drink a beer at the local pub. Our concern here is that this exact argument, acceptable as it may be, has been made countless times before. It has been around since the 1960s, and our writer is merely getting in a long line to restate it again. But good invention strategies, including analysis, help the writer to think beyond this standard approach—to think more adventurously, to venture into the frontier of ideas.

The writer of our typical rough draft asks, *"If people think that an 18-year-old isn't responsible, then why does he have to register for a draft, and if drafted, go off to war and defend your country?"* Then the writer moves on to another point. But what would happen if, instead of employing this tried-and-true approach, he analyzed and tried to answer his own question? First, he might ask, what *are* the reasons that 18-year-olds cannot legally drink? Instead of assuming there is no good reason for this (that it's just absurd and unfair), our writer might try getting at the reasons. He might start by imagining that elected officials would not discriminate against young eligible voters for no reason at all. He might suspect that the laws are the result of traffic accidents (or he might have some other theory), and he might research the issue for more information. In short, a little analysis may lead our writer to a better understanding of the issue—perhaps even changing his own mind about it.

He then might go on to the second part of his question: Why must 18-year-olds (instead of 40-year-olds, for example) have to register for a draft? The possible answers might be enlightening: because 18-year-olds are less likely to be married and have children; because they are less likely to own businesses, employ others, and pay taxes; because they are more physically fit; because they are more willing to take risks; because they have less political power and less financial influence; because in the past (and perhaps in the future) the United States fought wars that required the sacrifice of many thousands of lives, and for the reasons just mentioned (and probably many more), 18-year-old lives can be sacrificed as well as any. These answers are harsh and bleak. You may disagree and come up with your own ideas about why 18-year-olds are more likely to be drafted as soldiers, and you may be right. The point is: analysis leads to the complexities of issues, and revealing those complexities, rather than avoiding them, is at the heart of college writing.

The Analysis questions in each chapter are designed to help you explore the complexities of your topic. Use these questions as starting points and then try to develop your own, more particular, questions.

Public Resonance

Perhaps the most important feature of writing is that it matters to a reader. This may sound obvious, but topics are not necessarily, in and of themselves, relevant to people's lives. They need to be made relevant. They need to be expressed in a way that involves readers.

Consider capital punishment. It is not, in itself, a relevant topic to the average college student—or even the average American citizen. That is, most people have not had a personal experience with the death penalty, but many people still have much to say about it. Why? The answer is rather simple: Capital punishment has been made relevant. Human rights activists, civil liberties groups, and religious groups have spoken or written the relevance of capital punishment into being. They have made the life of a death-row inmate in Texas relevant to a suburban schoolteacher in Minnesota or a biology major at UCLA.

Good writers can make an issue resonate with their readers' feelings, thoughts, and situations. They can make their own personal situations resonate with their readers. They can transform a bad day at the office into an important efficiency issue for all workers. Or they can make a seemingly distant event, such as the deforestation of rainforests or the death of a prison inmate, real and immediate. They make a connection between two things: (1) what they see, know, do, believe, and feel, and (2) how that matters to other people. It may not matter to every other person (in fact, it need not and could not matter to everyone), but generally it *resonates* with the public. It speaks to and engages the members of a community who, like the writer, are able to look beyond themselves (beyond the "me") and into the public arena (the "we").

Take, for example, an abandoned car on the side of a road. In itself, it does not mean anything. But in a writer's vision, the car might raise the issue of maintenance (the owner may have not been able to afford maintenance); highway safety (the car may pose a threat to motorists); hitchhiking (the driver may have had to hitchhike to get help); abduction (people fear strangers in cars more than being stranded); cell phones (although people often use them thoughtlessly, they are helpful and even life-saving in certain situations); or consumer society (many people are incensed over the throwaway economy, in which entire cars are merely tossed out like an old pair of shoes).

The assumption behind public resonance is that we are deeply connected to others in our communities—and even beyond those communities. Our very identities are bound to a complex system of rela-

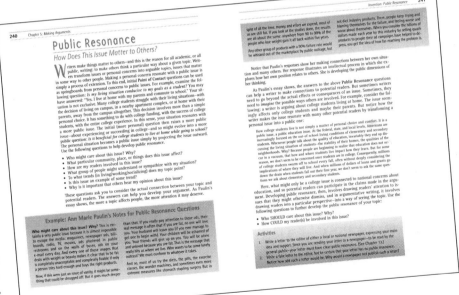

tionships that extend into all different realms of social life. We are tied by economic, social, institutional, political, familial, religious, and even psychological connections. We share laws, fears, dreams, and hopes. And when writers tap into those connections, when they make topics part of that large social network, they achieve public resonance.

Delivery

Although *CEL* chapters separate delivery from invention, the two are intertwined. In fact, the act of developing (supporting, illustrating, counterarguing) ideas and writing them down is very much an inventive process. Writers do not stop inventing when they begin drafting, and drafting actually begins long before the pen or computer keyboard is at hand. However, there is also an important distinction between invention and delivery. In initial invention stages, writers try to develop their own thinking. In delivery, writers must consider strategies for shaping the reader's consciousness. In short, *writers must think of strategies for making readers share their own vision,* and this involves many strategies, such as exemplifying ideas, ordering information, offering evidence, and creating a voice.

As you work through this book, your delivery strategies should evolve. What you learn in earlier chapters can certainly be applied to writing done in later chapters, but you will also encounter increasingly sophisticated delivery strategies as you advance through the book. All writers benefit from a large collection of strategies for building texts. To that end, **Delivery** is broken into several

sections in each chapter: Rhetorical Tools, Organizational Strategies, Writer's Voice, and Revision Strategies. Consider these sections as guides for developing, arranging, and revising ideas in each particular chapter and for expanding your overall abilities to build texts for other chapters and situations. And even though these sections come toward the end of the chapters, after Invention and after the chapter readings, they are not less important, nor do they necessarily come at the end of a sequence. For instance, as you will discover, a writer's voice is always being developed—he or she does not start thinking about it *only* after organizational issues.

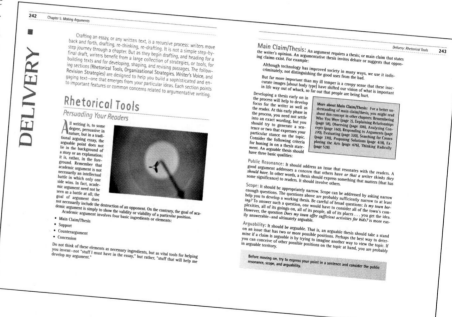

Rhetorical Tools

The term **rhetoric** comes from ancient Greece, where philosophers such as Aristotle studied the acts of persuasion and the role of language in public affairs.

A *rhetorical* tool is a technique of persuasion, a strategy for making people believe or accept an idea. Throughout *CEL,* we will refer to writers' rhetorical strategies—the techniques they use to convey their ideas to others and to attempt to convince others to accept their positions. Good writers use good rhetorical tools. If they are remembering, explaining, observing, or arguing, writers need to convince readers that the ideas being presented are worthy. They come in many forms, including traditional modes:

Narration is the act of storytelling. Stories are often used to persuade people, to help them appreciate the value of an idea.

Description involves giving specific details to the reader. Sensory details (sounds, smells, sights, tastes, touches) prompt a reader to experience a topic—and so accept the ideas the writer offers.

Illustration is the graphic depiction of an idea. While illustration certainly suggests pictures and charts, it can also be accomplished with words.

Comparison involves showing similarities between one topic and another.

Definition is the act of outlining or clarifying exact meaning. We might imagine giving the definition of a word or phrase, but writers also define acts, situations, and even behaviors.

Classification is the act of determining the group or category to which a thing or idea belongs.

Rhetorical tools also include *allusions* (references to history, popular culture, literature, news events) and *figurative language* (any device that goes beyond the basic definitions of words and uses them to suggest imaginative connections between ideas). Figurative language includes *metaphor* (a comparison in which one thang takes on the qualities of another) and *simile* (a comparison which uses *like* or *as*).

Any one piece of writing involves many different rhetorical tools. Notice how Annie Dillard uses a variety to communicate ideas:

Then I cut down through the woods to the mossy fallen tree where I sit. This tree is excellent. It makes a dry upholstered bench at the upper, marshy end of the pond, a plush jetty raised from the thorny shore between a shallow blue body of water and a deep blue body of sky.

The sun had just set. I was relaxed on the tree trunk, ensconced in the lap of lichen, watching the lily pads at my feet tremble and part dreamily over the thrusting path of a carp. A yellow bird appeared to my right and flew behind me. It caught my eye; I swiveled around—and the next instant, inexplicably, I was looking down at a weasel, who was looking up at me.

Weasel! I'd never seen one in the wild before. He was ten inches long, thin as a curve, a muscled ribbon, brown as fruitwood, soft-furred, alert. His face was fierce, small and pointed as a lizard's; he would have a good arrowhead. There was just a dot of a chin, maybe two brown hairs' worth, and then the pure white fur began that spread down his underside. He had two black eyes I didn't see, any more than you see a window.

Here, Dillard uses narrative to tell the reader the sequence of events, and description to help the reader experience important details. This passage also depends on figurative language, a metaphor to suggest the transparency of the weasel's eyes, and a simile ("pointed as a lizard's") to portray the shape of his face. All of these tools help Dillard engage the reader's consciousness.

Keep in mind that no strategy belongs exclusively to a particular kind of writing. The strategies introduced throughout the book can be used for unlimited writing situations. For example, starting in Chapter 5: Making Arguments, the rhetorical tools become a bit more complicated. Prompting readers to accept argumentative ideas involves some direct intervention with readers' assumptions, biases, and possible rebuttals. As you will see, the latter chapters of the book (from Chapter 5 on) all involve argumentative rhetorical tools; however, rhetorical tools introduced earlier in the book (such as narration, description, figurative language, etc.) are also applicable to argumentative writing. As you move through the book, think of your collection of rhetorical tools growing.

Organizational Strategies

Organization is the arrangement of ideas. Writers must decide when and where they will use different rhetorical tools. The most common strategy for planning the arrangement of ideas is outlining. Outlines range from very formal (with full sentences expressing each main idea) to informal (with main ideas represented by phrases or words). Notice the informal or rough outline for an evaluating essay:

Working Thesis: *Pulp Fiction* points out, reveals, and even turns upside down American moviegoers' fascination with violent characters.

The American film tradition of violent male characters (*Terminator, First Blood, Dirty Harry*): We see violence without consequences and cheer for the revenge-seeking hero.

Pulp Fiction: Scenes that portray the consequences of violence. The American film tradition of glorified gangsters (*Good Fellows, Godfather and Godfather II, Billy Bathgate, Hoffa, Donnie Brasco, The Untouchables, Capone*)

Pulp Fiction: Scenes that portray the gangster getting duped—or killed.

Conclusion: The traditional American violent dramas make us crave violence, but *Pulp Fiction* creates discomfort about watching violence.

This is a very rough outline. It simply charts out a plan for the writer, who knows, at the very least, the main points to be achieved in each section of the essay. (See this essay, "*Pulp Fiction:* Valuable Critique or Useless Titillation?" in Chapter 7: Evaluating.) With such an outline, the writer will know what's coming next. Of course, writers always look back once they are started down a path and often change directions. But with a rough outline, a writer knows the basic course. And without any direction, writers often go in circles, paragraphs meander, and essays become disjointed and hard to follow.

While writers have to consider the overall arrangement of their ideas, they also must focus on smaller

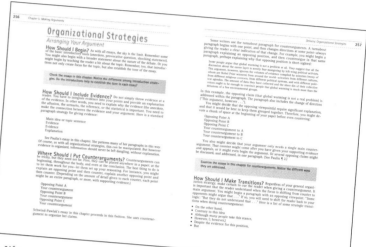

units of text: paragraphs and transitions between points. Paragraphs are arranged according to their purpose: narrating an event, describing a scene, offering evidence, making an allusion, and so on, and they can be arranged in an unlimited number of ways, depending on the amount of support and detail the writer desires. (See paragraph patterns in the *Handbook*, pp. 740–743.) And within and between paragraphs, writers must connect individual points with transitional expressions (see p. 257). If a writer has succeeded, a completed text should read like a coherent journey: the reader begins with some sense of direction (a good introduction), passes through various locations and over different terrain (in separate paragraphs), which are all connected by road signs (transitions). And finally, having traveled through a country of ideas, the reader should feel as though he or she has arrived somewhere unique and valuable (a good conclusion).

The Organizational Strategies sections do not prescribe particular frameworks for essays; rather, they suggest various possible strategies for arranging ideas. They present common (and sometimes not-so-common) options for shaping essays, ordering points, and connecting ideas. As with many of the **Delivery** strategies in the chapters, these should be seen as hints or tools that can be used in various writing situations.

Writer's Voice

When we talk, we project a character or mood, not only by choosing certain words, but also by how we say them: the sound, the pitch and pace, of our voices. (Some people talk with dramatic ups and downs; others blab at us in a single-note dirge.) When we talk, we also use physical gestures. We can swing our hands around wildly, or bow our heads, or open our eyes very wide—all at different moments of a sentence—simply to project an attitude. As writers, we have just as many strategies at our disposal. We may not be able to use our hands and eyeballs to gesture to the reader, but we have plenty of *writerly* tools.

Every writer, for each writing event, creates a voice, the character that is projected by the language and style of that essay. Writers use a vast array of techniques to create voices. Sometimes those voices are sober and formal. Other voices are comedic, even hilarious. This does not mean that the topic itself is funny; it simply means that the way in which the writer presents ideas is humorous. Some of the best writers can make a potentially dull topic feel quirky or a light topic have depth and profound significance.

Of course, most writers fall somewhere in the middle between serious and comic, between utterly stiff and totally untamed. You will ultimately create a voice whether you know it or not: simply by writing a sentence, in some small way, you create a voice. And since a writerly voice will emerge from your essays, it's certainly better to be crafty; otherwise, your voice might very well come off as . . . well . . . boring.

The **Writer's Voice** sections in each chapter will help you shape an appropriate voice or explore different voices. While it is valuable to develop a personal voice (a style that feels unique or somehow genuinely more *you*), it is perhaps even more valuable to experiment with voices. Because we often have to write in different contexts, for different audiences, and on different occasions, we need to be flexible, able to fit into audiences' conventions and expectations. (A radically informal, knee-slappin' voice would not go over well in a formal report to a government agency, nor would an overly-somber voice be appropriate for a public invitation to a community event.) Learning how to stylize voice according to the audience and situation is certainly one of the most valuable skills for a writer.

Revision Strategies

Revision is about reapproaching ideas and is essential to the act of writing. As academic writers work, they are constantly rethinking their original ideas. To some degree, revision is fused into every act of the writing process. Writers are constantly asking questions: "Is this the best way to do this?" "Is there a better way to engage my reader?" Writers also benefit from a holistic rereading of their work, a process that first involves stepping away from the text for a period of time, and then refocusing on everything (the main ideas, the supporting points, the organization, and even the voice). This probably sounds intimidating—rethinking *everything* after a significant amount of work has already gone into a draft. But revision is where a writer can make a text function as a whole by making important connections and adding necessary detail. It is often only through revision that a text comes to life.

The Global Revision Questions ask you to consider important points not just about **Delivery**, but about **Invention** as well. For example, as you revise you are asked to discuss *in writing* what other ideas you considered writing about and to explain why you ultimately chose the one you did. You are also asked to explain how your ideas developed beyond your initial thinking and beyond the common beliefs of your reader. And you are asked to explain how your ideas matter, or might matter, to someone else. Thus, CEL encourages you to see revision as something more than providing more details or organizing your ideas differently. Global Revision gets to the root of good writing: How might what you say actually matter? And how does it go beyond your initial ideas and attempt to make a reader think, and possibly act, differently?

After Global Revision, each chapter guides students through Peer Revision, a process of collaborative analysis and re-thinking. Editing concerns (focus on small, sentence-level issues) are dealt with in Chapter 14: Rhetorical Handbook.

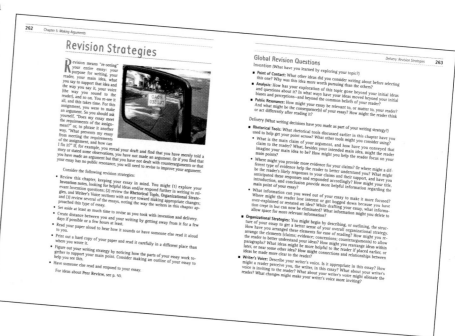

Considering Consequences

One look at history tells us that writing changes the world. It provokes people to think differently and, ultimately, to act differently. As one writer explained: "People do not operate based on reality, but on their perceptions of reality, and with writing, we can change people's perceptions." This is an amazing piece of knowledge. And of course, people who wish to change the world (in big and small ways) throughout history have used writing, and many people would argue that the consequences of texts in world history far outlast the effects of more physical means of persuasion (like bombs and guns). Consider, for example, the Declaration of Independence: Jefferson's declaration helped a group of diverse colonies imagine themselves as a unified people against a tyrannical king. Or consider Mary Wollstonecraft's *Vindication of the Rights of Woman,* which prompted increasingly more public debate about the role of women in everyday life. Of course, many women before Wollstonecraft deeply understood what it meant to have their rights ignored, but the book resonated with their concerns and helped energize political action.

The above examples, you might think, are *big* documents; they were, in many respects, presumed to be important and to have significant consequences. But consider more recent texts that only gained status once they were within the realm of public debate, for example: tobacco companies' reports on nicotine, NASA's reports from the Hubble telescope, or even the diary of Anne Frank (presumably a personal text that, as it turned out, helped to show the world the effects of Nazism). It is not only these momentous historical texts that have consequences. Everyday writing, the kind that gets done in offices and homes and schools, also changes the world. Memos about office meetings or new policies directly impact people's behaviors.

Letters (or e-mails) to friends and relatives can profoundly influence their behaviors and their attitudes. Advertising changes how we think about ourselves and the world around us; the constant presence of particular words and slogans eventually prompts us to think (even desire) in certain ways. And we all use written instructions to get us through complicated tasks (such as hooking up the stereo).

But on a deeper level, beyond hooking up a CD player, academia depends very much on the idea that writing affects how people think. Certainly, professionals in the various disciplines do not assume people will change their minds about topics based on a single essay or report. However, the entire academic community works on the assumption that writing can motivate people to reconsider ideas or even consider something totally novel. The practice of writing, then, is deeply connected to the act of influencing thought.

Each chapter in *CEL* contains questions about the consequences of your writing, the chapter readings, and the chapter images. These questions can help you understand the complexities of written and visual rhetoric. The section points to ways that public texts, written or visual, work in the world.

Everyday Rhetoric

Most of the sample texts in *CEL* are essays. It is the most common format used in English and humanities courses. And professionals in many disciplines across the curriculum use the essay to explore new ideas, revise old ones, and communicate to their peers. However, the essay is only one particular means of delivery. Like any format, it has limitations. Complex ideas can be developed and communicated through various means outside of the traditional academic essay: in writing (through memos, letters, flyers, pamphlets, etc.); by speech (through formal speeches, debates, briefings, small group discussions, etc.); with action (through protests, parades, sit-ins, strikes, buying choices, etc.); with graphics (through art, advertisements, Web sites, and videos).

A means of delivery is not simply a channel of communication; it is also a means of invention. In other words, the type of delivery influences the ideas that are generated. The process of writing an essay prompts writers to develop or associate ideas in particular ways. Likewise, the act of protesting generates certain thoughts and ideas that may not come to mind while writing an essay. However, to a large degree, the ideas that are developed (in the Invention sections in each chapter) can evolve into many different forms—many different kinds of delivery. Therefore, each chapter suggests particular alternatives beyond the essay.

In each chapter, you will encounter several options for delivering your ideas: during **Invention** and **Delivery** exercises, and at the end of the chapter. The assumption is that your ideas can be communicated in a variety of ways, in writing, speech, and action, and that alternative forms of delivery (like making a poster or a pamphlet) can be part of a bigger invention process. Depending on your instructor or class requirements, you might deliver your ideas in one of these forms in addition to or instead of an essay.

The final section of each chapter includes an exploration of *visual rhetoric,* in which we will draw attention to the persuasion techniques of photographs, images, and artwork. Just as written texts (essays, letters, etc.) employ rhetorical tools, so do visual texts. For instance, the photographs or images beginning the chapters have certain rhetorical aspects, and questions at the end of each chapter will prompt you to explore those aspects. Working through *CEL,* you will begin to see how images can function as rhetorically as the most sophisticated essay.

As you explore the various possibilities of writing, speech, action, and visual rhetoric, see Chapter 13: Everyday Rhetoric for examples and guidelines. This chapter explores various possibilities for interacting with the world. The idea throughout the chapter is that language works in various, even countless, ways. Because language is omnipresent (all around us), we should study how it works in various contexts. We should know how to develop ideas and how to compress complex ideas into engaging soundbites. We should explore how to craft our thoughts and how to envision them working in the practical world. We should know how to develop ideas for a general audience and how to communicate directly with a particular group of people. Finally, we should know how to use public language and public documents. All of these are discussed in Chapter 13.

Everyday Life and the Writer: A Final Thought

The act of writing is often frustrating. It is an intellectual struggle—shaping thoughts and making connections that seem, at first, totally impossible. Writers do not look for the easy topics (ones they can write about most quickly); they understand that valuable ideas are not those that simply fall out of the brain and onto the page. And in the most difficult moments, they remember that difficulty is an essential part of the process. Because the human brain is not a *linear* machine (it does not necessarily produce thoughts that go from left to right and then down a page), writers understand that their ideas have to be formed and re-formed. And in that long, and sometimes exhausting, process, they turn frustration into inquiry. They hope to find the most valuable insights in the moments of uncertainty.

Finally, as you begin *CEL,* remember that a writer not only engages everyday life, but also stops consistently amidst the hustle and bustle to discover meaning. Remember that a writer is not divorced from everyday life; isolation only occurs when the writer has to draft text. While participating in the daily chaos, the writer also goes beneath the surface, looks behind the wall, digs up personal biases. The writer is an intellectual excavator, looking to discover what would otherwise be overlooked, left behind, or discarded. From this point on, when you are working or socializing, when you are steeped in everyday life, consider yourself a writer.

1

Chapter Contents

Remembering Who You Were

What specific memories does this image bring to mind? What does the image say about childhood?

—*George Santayana*

You have probably heard Santayana's famous statement—perhaps when someone in a history class asked plaintively, "Why do we have to learn this stuff?" Santayana's point, of course, is that the past is filled with situations that teach us about ourselves, and that ignoring the past results in blindness to the present and future. While Santayana's statement is most often applied to a collective history (e.g., American or world history), it also suggests something for the individual. In the same way that countries learn from their pasts, individuals also come to new insights because of their experiences. Obviously, we learn basic *dos* and *don'ts* from experience (not to ride a bike over the icy patch in the driveway, not to talk during math class, not to indulge too much the night before an exam). But our pasts are filled with more opportunity for insight beyond simple I'll-never-do-that-again situations. A vast array of moments lurks in the past, moments that may mean far more than what we have always assumed.

Writers looking into their pasts attempt to learn something new, to understand the importance of some moment, or to understand the significance of a situation. They are retrieving an event or situation, uncovering a moment, and examining it from the present perspective. The hope is that the writer will see more about the situation than he or she could have possibly seen in the past. Imagine an adult writer looking back at a childhood baseball game: as a child, he could fret over striking out in the last inning. But as an adult, he sees how important that moment of failure was to his life, to his intellectual and spiritual growth. The present (adult) writer is able to see this because the elapsed time has allowed him emotional and intellectual distance.

In academia, writers often look to the past for insight:

- In a sociology course, students recall their childhood communities; they pay close attention to the institutions (churches and schools) they attended, and include their memories in a theory about institutional affiliation.
- A psychology professor prompts students to recall their early experiences with nonparental authority (such as teachers, extended family, and babysitters) and form a theory of authority based on those experiences.
- In a Western Civilization course, students recall their early experiences with organized religion. They include their experiences in their collective examination of religious principles.

Memories do not, in themselves, teach us anything. We must create the lesson. We must look back at the past with a certain perspective: one of curiosity and possibility. Although we have lived through the past, we must entirely rediscover it if we are to learn.

1 This chapter will help you rediscover a specific situation or event from your past, explore it in depth, develop a particular point about it, and communicate your ideas in writing. The following essays will provide insight to various writing strategies. After you read the essays, you can find a topic in one of two ways:

1. Go to the **Point of Contact** section to find a topic from your everyday life.
2. Choose one of the **Ideas for Writing** that follow the essays.

After you find a topic, go to the **Analysis** section to begin developing your ideas.

READINGS

■

Each essay in this chapter takes the reader back in time to a particular event or set of events from the writer's life. However, the essays are not merely memories; rather, they are reflections on the past that give way to new insights about family, education, growing up, parents, or even America. In each, the past is used to learn something, and to share new insights with readers. In Bosley's essay, for example, the writer goes back into the past to find meaning and to dig up the origin of her own feelings in the present. Mockensturm's essay seems to exist at the intersection of his past and his daughters' present, where he rediscovers dimensions of his life. All the authors use their own experiences to show us some point that is bigger and more public than their own lives. That point, the idea that can be extracted from the personal and delivered to the public, is most often the main idea of these essays.

How I Lost the Junior Miss Pageant

Cindy Bosley

Cindy Bosley, whose writing also appears in Chapter 2, has taught literature and writing and has published poems in various journals including North American Review, Prairie Schooner, Willow Springs, Midwest Quarterly, *and* The Alsop Review *online. As you read "How I Lost the Junior Miss Pageant," think about how Bosley views beauty pageants and how her views on pageants speak to a larger issue. Jot down your initial reactions to Bosley's ideas as you read.*

1 Every evening of the annual broadcast of the Miss America Pageant, I, from the age of seven or so, carefully laid out an elaborate chart so that I might also participate as an independent judge of the most important beauty contest in the world. From my viewing seat on a green striped couch in my parents' smoky living room where the carpet, a collage of white, brown, and black mixed-shag, contrasted so loudly with the cheap 70's furnishings that it threatened my attention to the television set, I sat with popcorn and soda, pen in hand, thrilled at the oncoming parade of the most beautiful women in the world.

2 In the hours before the show began, I'd carefully written out in ink, sometimes over and over again to be free of errors and scribbles, the names of all 50 states, Washington, D.C., and Puerto Rico along the y axis of my paper. And my categories of evaluation of the contestants ribbed themselves along the x axis—beauty, poise, swimsuit, evening gown—plus categories of my own—hair, likability, teeth. Over the years, an increasingly complex system of points and penalties evolved: an extra point for being tan, a loss of points for sucking up, more points for breasts, more points for unpainted nails, fewer points for big noses, fewer points for skinny lips, an extra point for smartness, subtraction of a point for playing the piano. Who wants to hear a sonata? Dance for me, bounce your bootie.

3   My mother had secret hopes. Finally divorced for the second time from the same man, my father, she sat with me and gave her own running commentary about who was cute, who smiled too much, who would find a handsome husband. My mother, having always been a little to a lot overweight, excelled at swimming, and she told me much later that she chose swimming because she didn't feel fat in the water. Her sister was the cheerleader, but she was a swimmer, too heavy for a short skirt of her own, she said. My mother's secret was that she wanted the winner to be her daughter. Sitting with me on the couch at 137 North Willard Street, she already knew I wasn't tall enough or pretty enough in the way of models and movie stars to ever stand a chance, but her real fear, which I only became aware of as an older teen, was that I would always be too chubby and too backward and too different and too poor, for which she blamed herself, to win a beauty pageant. Still, there were always those surprises of the contests—Miss Utah? She was no good! Why did *she* win? What were those judges thinking! It should have been Miss Alabama, anyone can see that. Who would have guessed Miss Utah, with that mole on her shoulder?

4   After my mother's never-subtle hints that if I'd just lose 20 pounds boys would like me and I might even win a beauty contest, it was my friend Bridget who wanted us to enter the Ottumwa (pronounced Uh-TUM-wuh) Junior Miss Pageant together. I secretly believed that I stood a better chance than Bridget did, though she had the right name and the right body, though she wore the right clothes and was more magazine-beautiful than I. I had *some* hope for the contest: I had *some* talents and a kind of baby-cute innocence complete with blond hair and blue eyes that I was sure the judges would find "charming and fresh." Yeah, okay, so I was already engaged to be married—so what—I was still on my way to college, and Bridget was not. And Judy was funny but had a flat face. Marcy was smart but had no breasts or hips. Carol was pretty but totally uncoordinated and her knees came together when she jumped. Desirea had enviable boobs, almost as nice as mine and probably firmer, but her chin did weird things when she smiled and her eyes were brown.

5   We practiced, all of us together, several times a week with a lithe woman—somebody's mom with good hair and body—getting us into form for the stage. This was the era of *Flashdance*, so we all wore our own leg warmers and torn sweatclothes and fancy headband scarves. If you were one of the north-side girls (that meant your daddy was a businessman or doctor), you had gotten your leg warmers from Marshall Fields in Chicago. If you were Bridget, your dad worked at John Deere like mine but was in management and not out in the factory threading bolts on a greasy, noisy machine, so you got your leg warmers from the mall in Des Moines. If you were me, with a factory dad who didn't even live in the same house, you got your leg warmers from Kmart down the road because Target was all the way across town and too expensive, and Wal-Mart hadn't yet been born as far as we knew. The fancy mom-lady made sure everyone had a brochure about her charm school (this is small-town Iowa, mind you, so anyone operating a charm school and modeling agency in this town was kidding themselves. But making lots of money.).

6   So 14 of us, nervous, jealous, ears ringing with Mirror-Mirror-on-the-Wall, met daily for two weeks prior to the pageant to go over our choreographed group fitness routine to be performed, not in swimsuits, but in short-shorts and white T-shirts, Hooters-style (also not invented yet as far as we knew), and to discuss such techniques as Vaseline along the teeth and gum lines to promote smooth smiles, lest our lips dry out and get stuck in a grin during discussions with the judges of the agonies of world hunger. We were each responsible for our own talent routines and props, and each one of us had to provide a 5x7 black-and-white photo for the spread in the town paper.

7   The photographs were a problem. My father did not believe in such things for girls as shoes,

clothes, haircuts, college, or photographs for Junior Miss, and so there was no way he was going to give a penny for a pageant-worthy dress or a professional photographer's 10-min-utes-plus-proofs. I believe my mother even hu-miliated herself enough to ask. This was hard for her, since he'd admitted before leaving to a five-year affair with a woman who looked sur-prisingly like my mother but heavier. So Mom and I tried some Polaroid headshots against the side of the house, but me dressed up in my pret-tiest sailor blouse couldn't counteract the hos-pital green of the aluminum siding. We moved up to our only other option, which was my mother's flash camera with Instamatic film, and still nothing suitable (I could have agreed on one of the Polaroid shots, but my mother knew it would knock me out of the contest for sure even before the night itself).

8 I don't know who she borrowed the money from or what she did to get the favor, but my mother had me down at Lee's Photography the very next afternoon, and he took one shot and offered us the one proof. Abracadabra, there was my face among all the other faces as a contes-tant in the Uh-TUM-wuh Junior Miss Pageant. From the layout in the paper, it looked to me, and to my flushed mother, as though I had as good a shot as any.

9 The contest night went quickly: my foot, couched, pinched, and Band-Aided uncomfort-ably in a neighbor's hand-me-down high heels, slipped (hear the auditorium's quick and loud intake of breath in horror!) as I walked forward to say my name with a strong, vibrant hello just like I'd been coached by the fancy-mom; my dress was last year's prom dress, which earned me no cool points with my peers but didn't lose me any either since I had none to subtract; I managed not to land on my bottom (as I had in every practice before the contest) in my gym-nastics routine, self-choreographed with my own robot-style moves to the synthesizer-heavy tune, "Electricity," by a band that was popular in Sacramento, California, in that year, 1985, but not yet in my hometown. (The cassette tape had

been given to me by my Hispanic, juvenile delin-quent, just-released-from-young-boy-prison-in-California ex-boyfriend Jim.)

10 My exercise routine went off very well in front of the crowd, and I don't think anyone could even tell that my shorts were soaking wet from having been dropped by me into the toilet just an hour before as I arranged my items for quick-change. My mother and fiancé were actu-ally sitting together, their mutual hatred of each other squeezed like a child between them. I'd even kept myself from leaving my mother behind when, backstage after the contest as I hugged and cried in joy for the co-winners and out of desper-ate relief that it was over now, my mother, beside herself with embarrassment for me and disap-pointment for herself, and misunderstanding my tears, hissed loudly enough for the benefit of everyone, "STOP your crying, they'll think you're not a nice LOSER!"

11 So I had done it: I had been a contestant in the Junior Miss Pageant and my mother had the snapshots to prove it.

12 I'd lost the contest because I didn't yet know how to tell people what they wanted to hear. The small girl that boys secretly liked but wouldn't date doesn't win Miss America. The girl hiding in her room reading and writing poetry doesn't win Miss America. The girl playing violin de-spite her mother's anxiousness that other people will think she's weird doesn't win Miss America. The girl on Willard Street doesn't ever win Miss America.

13 But the truth is that I'd lost the contest when I told the judges, when they asked, that my most personal concern was my mother's loneliness, and if I could change anything at all, I would give her something—a man, God, anything to free her from that loneliness.

14 Clearly, I lacked the save-the-whales-and-rainforest civic-mindedness required not only of Miss America, but of Junior Miss America, too. Even, although one wouldn't think it, in Ottumwa, Iowa, where my mother would go on to work in a bathtub factory, and then a glue factory, and then an electrical connectors factory (the factory

worker's version of upward mobility), and finally, a watch factory where they shipped and received not just watches but cocaine in our town that at that time had more FBI agents in it than railroad engineers. And even in this town where my sister would go to work the kill floor of the pork plant where, for fun, the workers shot inspection dye at each other and threatened each other's throats with hack-knives. And even in this town where my cousin, age 13, would bring a bomb to seventh grade for show-and-tell, and get caught and evacuated, and be given community service to do because the public-school-as-terrorist-ground phenomena hadn't yet been born. And even in this town where if you want to go to college, you better know someone who knows how to get you there because otherwise it's too far away and too much money and too much trouble and way, way, way beyond your own intellect and sense of self to do it alone. How scary (get married). How wasteful (get married). How expensive (get married). How strange (get married). How pretentious (get married). How escapist (get married).

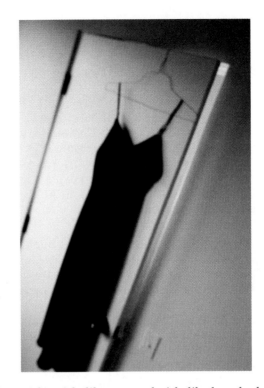

15   If your parents are crazy and poor, and if you can't win the Junior Miss Pageant, and if it's the kind of town where you stay or they don't ever want you coming back, you get married, you move to Texas where your husband sells drugs, you hide away from the world until your self grows enough to break you out, and then you leave and you pray for your mother's loneliness and you spend your life learning to come to terms with your own, and you are smart and willful and strong, and you don't ever have to draw another chart before the pageant begins.

16   My mother told me later that she was just sure I would have won the Junior Miss contest if I hadn't made that awful mistake in my gymnastics routine (I don't know what mistake she was talking about—it was the least flawed part of the evening), but I knew the truth about why I'd lost, and I knew I'd lost even before the contest or the practices began. I'd lost this contest at birth, probably, to be born to my father who had a date that night, and to my mother who believed some girls—girls like me, and girls like her—had to try very hard to catch and keep a boy's attention. I'd lost the contest in borrowed shoes and an out-of-date dress. I'd lost the contest with the engagement ring on my seventeen-year-old finger. I'd lost the contest with wet shorts and too funky music. I'd lost the contest with a bargain photograph and Kmart legwarmers. I'd lost the contest with an orange Honda Express moped parked between the other girls' cars. I'd lost the contest in a falling-down green house. I'd lost the contest in the grease on my father's hands and hair and the taste of grease in his lunchbox leftovers. I'd lost the contest in my growingly cynical evaluation of Miss America as I'd gotten older—"chubby thighs touching, minus five points," "big hair, minus three points," "too small nipples, minus two," "flabby arms, minus five," and subtract and subtract and subtract. It's a contest no one should want to win. Our mothers should not have such dreams for us. Our mothers should not have such loneliness.

Exploring Ideas

1. How is the way that you view beauty pageants similar to or different from the way Bosley does?

2. Interview several classmates to find out how they view beauty pageants (or interview several people outside of class to find out their views). Accurately record their responses (refer to the Field Notes section of this text on pages 580–581 for help) and then explain in writing what viewpoints seemed to be the most common, most unusual, most interesting, most thought-provoking.

3. As a way to stimulate further thinking on the topic, e-mail to at least three people your initial reaction to Bosley's essay. Be sure to provide enough background for them to understand it. Then share the most thought-provoking response to your e-mail with your classmates or use the response as a springboard into your own essay, crediting your source as you write.

4. How does Bosley's point about beauty pageants speak to a larger (more general) issue, such as competition, class, tradition, media, and so on?

5. What do you think is the most important or interesting thing about Bosley's viewpoint?

6. How might you participate in the discussion Bosley has initiated? What memories of your own might you call upon to generate ideas for a response or to use as support for a response?

Writing Strategies

1. Bosley provides details throughout her essay. Which ones work best for you? Select several details and compare them to the ones your classmates selected. Attempt to explain why certain details made the essay more engaging to you.

2. What is the public resonance of Bosley's essay? That is, how does it matter to others? How does it matter to someone who doesn't care at all about such pageants?

3. If workshopping Bosley's essay, complete the following statements:

   a. What I like most about your essay is _____.

   b. The main suggestion I have about your essay is _____.

4. Bosley's title suggests that she will tell us how she lost the Junior Miss pageant. Does she deliver? What is the point of her essay? How did she lose the pageant?

Ideas for Writing

1. Discover the significance of an experience or activity you participated in with disappointing results. Perhaps it was sitting on the bench for an entire season in a sport, running for student council and not winning, pursuing a certain girl or boy without luck, or something else.

2. Recall an experience or activity at which you exceeded your own expectations. What, now, is the significance of that experience to you?

If responding to one of these ideas, go to the **Analysis** section of this chapter to begin developing ideas for your essay.

A *Beat* Education

Leonard Kress

Len Kress, whose writing also appears in Chapter 7, teaches humanities and writing courses at Owens Community College and has published three collections of poetry. His fourth, Orphics, *was published in 2003 by Kent State University Press. He rode the rails because he was writing a research paper on 1930s hobo/tramp writer Harry Kemp (*Tramping on Life*) and wanted to begin his paper with a personal experience. He never completed the research paper, but he did create "A Beat Education." Based on this essay, what does Kress think is valuable? Consider ways that you might participate in, or contribute to, the discussion.*

1   At 20 I was convinced that the single most important experience, without which my education would remain shamefully incomplete, was that of hopping a freight. Doubtless, my sense of education at that time (as well as my sense of what constituted good writing) was more than mildly seasoned by huge doses of the Beats—Allen Ginsberg, Gregory Corso, William Burroughs, Kenneth Patchen, Leroi Jones, and, of course, Jack Kerouac. That these writers were at the time considered non-scholarly, marginal, and were all but vilified by my literature teachers made them, I'm sure, that much more irresistible. I would merely open a page at random—a short story, say Kerouac's "Railroad Earth"—and find myself filled with wonder and admiration and conviction: this was sacramental:

> Remembering my wonder at the slow grinding movement and squee of gigantic boxcars and flats and gons rolling by with that overpowering steel and dust clenching closh and clack of steel on steel, the shudder of the whole steely proposition, a car going by . . . the frightening fog nights in California when you can see thru the mists the monsters slowly passing . . . when those wheels go over your leg they don't care about you.

2   I did manage, once at least, to imitate the Beats. I was staying with some friends in Grand Rapids, Michigan, when I decided, receiving little or no discouragement from them, to seek out the local freight yard. I figured I would ride the rails in whichever direction they took me—unconcerned as I was with notions of destination and arrival. Unable to summon up any practical or procedural advice on how to begin from Kerouac's disjointed and out-of-control prose, I simply searched for a site full of boxcars and cabooses and lanes upon lanes of tracks.

3   It was early morning and the yard seemed deserted, so I brazenly set forth. I had no fear of the dreaded railway dicks, no sense of the danger of heavy machinery, but I did carry with me a bright blue rucksack, a sense that all would go well if I only abandoned myself to the open road. As hoped for and expected, a figure appeared out of nowhere. I assumed he was something of a tramp or hobo—I had the sense at least not to ask him about his vocation—and he quickly took me under his grimy wing. With no exchange of words, we managed to cross over several tracks, duck out of sight of the hollering

switchers, and second-guess the direction of cars clanking over shuntings. He knew which trains were already made up and ready to pull out, and which might sit for hours filling up with unbearable heat from the morning sun. He led me to one, sitting on the outer tracks, mostly a string of lime-dusty hoppers interspersed with empty boxcars—doors flung invitingly wide open! I rushed in front of him, tossed my rucksack in, and was about to hoist myself inside, when he grabbed my leg and tackled me down to the rails. I was too shocked to resist; he pinned me to the railroad ties and moved his head in real close to mine. Just when I was sure that he was about to slit my throat, he released his grip and delivered what seemed to be a prepared speech about hopping freights. "Don't never board a still train," I remember him saying, "they shut them doors when the train's pulling out. You get stuck in there, you roast, you just roast, that's all there is to it."

4   Although I was a bit chastened from the stern warning, which at the time didn't seem to be warranted, and covered with brush and gravel burns from the take-down, I felt that I had just participated in some arcane initiation rite and passed through it successfully, the bearer of some sort of *tramp-gnosis*. If I were to characterize it now, I might say that it seemed to be a particular mix of the medieval Franciscan ideal, International Workers of the World notions of brotherhood and solidarity . . . and my own middle class suburban naïveté.

5   We strode together—in some sort of unacknowledged sync—farther down the line, to a spot beyond the cluster of workers' shacks and railroad paraphernalia. Ducking in a trackside ravine almost as if we were kids playing backyard war, we waited until the freight began its slow grinding movement, almost overwhelmed by what Kerouac called that *overpowering steel dust and clenching closh and clack of steel on steel, the shudder of the whole steely proposition. . . .* We waited, nodding as each car rolled past, until a boxcar with unshut doors presented itself to us. Then we sprung up, tossed our packs inside, and scissor-jumped our way in.

6   While I was making myself comfortable, shifting around on a sift of rust and pebbles, dangling my legs over the side, my companion leaped off, barely losing his footing, and rushed off. I didn't know why he left. I thought at first that he had forgotten something, later that he was trying to set me up—for what, though, I couldn't imagine. He just disappeared, and though the train was barely snailing along, I was afraid to jump down after him. As it picked up speed, however, I regretted not taking that chance, as my dangling legs were almost sheared off by a switching signal the boxcar curved past.

7   The ride itself was unbelievably jittery and uncomfortable. I couldn't open the can of beans I'd brought along, and the slices of bread I'd stuffed into my rucksack fell onto the floor and coated themselves in rust-flecked grease. The freight did, however, grant me a spectacular view of the setting sun as it ambled ever so slowly along the banks of Lake Michigan. And it did ease through innumerable small town backyards where children ran alongside, not easily winded, cheering both the train and me on. Even young mothers waved shyly while they pinned banner-like sheets onto their clotheslines.

8   Almost half a day later, around midnight, the train crunched into Chicago, where I hopped off, exhausted and exhilarated. As my shaky train-legs hit the gravel of the roadbed, I thought I heard a threatening shout, so I ran, tripped mostly, over the 50 or so tracks and platforms and switchings, down a steep embankment. Right into the middle of some run-down neon-shod shopping strip near 95th Street on the South Side—bars and liquor stores and boarded-up groceries, card readers, barber colleges, and storefront churches, groups of men hanging on the corners drinking from passed-around rumpled paper bags. Here was a whole gallery of street life like nothing I'd ever seen. Somehow the rickety freight ride and all that drama and lure of the past two days quickly dissipated, replaced by an urgent sense of new gaps in my learning, of new educational possibilities.

Exploring Ideas

1. How does the way Kress talks about education invite the reader to think differently about the subject?

2. How is Kress's essay part of a larger discussion? What is the general subject matter—or issue—of that larger discussion?

3. What educational experiences can you remember that might help you think further, and differently, about this topic?

4. Ask at least five people, not including your classmates, about an important learning experience of their own. Phrase your question to them carefully and be certain to accurately record their responses. (Asking the question via e-mail will give you a written e-mail record of the response.)

5. Examine the responses you received from #4. How many people's experiences included formal education settings? How many didn't? How were others' experiences similar to or different from Kress's or your own? How might these responses help you better understand and write about an educational experience of your own?

6. How might you respond to Kress's essay and thus take part in that ongoing discussion? What memories of your own can you use to illustrate your main idea?

Writing Strategies

1. Through his use of vivid language, Kress shows himself riding the rails. Identify several fresh expressions that appealed to you. Was it "shifting around on a sift of rust and pebbles" or "he grabbed my leg and tackled me down to the rails"? Find several expressions that brought his experience to life for you.

2. How else might Kress have vividly described his experience for the reader? Write two or three additional sentences of description and explain why each one is successful at describing the scene.

3. Describe Kress's voice as a writer. What does he sound like? Provide several examples from the essay (particular word choice, for example) that support your description. Is Kress's voice appropriate for an essay about hopping a freight train?

4. If workshopping Kress's essay, how would you answer the following questions: What do you like most about the essay? What do you like the least about it? What suggestion do you have for the writer?

5. Kress refers (or alludes) to several poets and writers in the essay. Explain the effect of these *allusions*: how they help to illustrate a point, how they influenced you as you read.

Ideas for Writing

1. Have you had an experience without which your education would be shamefully incomplete?

2. Kress's train ride leaves him ready to learn. Recall an experience from your own life that had a positive impact on your education—not just that you learned something, but that your overall attitude about learning changed. Of course, a certain teacher might come to mind. If so, try to focus not on the teacher, but on the experience (the train ride)—a very specific moment perhaps—that left you ready to learn.

> If responding to one of these ideas, go to the **Analysis** section of this chapter to begin developing ideas for your essay.

The Aloha Spirit: A Reminiscence

Aunty D.

"The Aloha Spirit: A Reminiscence" was published on "The Hawaiian Home Page" Web site where you can read more about Hawaii, the Hawaiian language, and the Aloha spirit. After reading this essay, write down in your own words what "Aloha spirit" means.

1   Last night, I listened, REALLY listened, to The Aloha Chant by Mel Amina on his CD, *KŪ HAʻ AHEO KÂKOU, E NÂ HAWAIʻI (Let Us Stand Proudly, Hawaiians)*. Mel begins it with this narrative:

> To the Hawaiʻi of Old, The Spirit of Aloha was a concept REAL and vital to the existence of her people. Aloha was the spiritual essence of life. Aloha was a philosophy, a way of living, a code in life. The Aloha Chant defines and expresses the characteristics and traits of that Spirit. These words were not composed by, but conveyed, to Pilahi Pakî, a makua (parent/elder) with a purpose and responsibility . . . a kuleana. That kuleana was to carry and pass on the message of Aloha.

2   The Aloha Chant captured my full attention, and evoked a warm reminiscence: With crystal clarity, I remember the day the Aloha Spirit became REAL for me. I was maybe four years old, because at age five, I was no longer living in my parents' home but at Gramma's. (Gramma and Grampa lost their home on the Kalapana Road, when a volcanic cone erupted in the middle of their cucumber patch! Pele, the volcano goddess, didn't bury their home with lava, but nearby brush caught fire and flying embers ignited their home, burning it to the ground. Grampa died soon thereafter, when I was five. True to our ways of taking care of our kupuna [elders], Dad built Gramma a cottage behind our house, and I went to live with her.)

3   If you're ever Kalapana way in the southeast quadrant of the Big Island, look for a King Kamehameha tourist marker on the left side, about a mile down the road (Hwy 130) from Pâhoa Elementary School. It points to Gramma's & Grampa's volcanic cone. If you take a short walk to the sleeping, steaming cone, you'll come across shards of Gramma's porcelain china.

4   But I digress. I'll get back to that red-letter day: I was stirred out of my slumber by unaccustomed sounds. Outside, it was still dark, as it always was when Mom and Dad quietly breakfasted together before he left at daybreak to tend to his Puna papaya fields, the seminal beginnings of a fresh fruit industry. The usual morning sounds were their hushed, pidgin-speaking voices and the soft clatter of chopsticks against everyday melamine dishes.

5   The sounds emanating from the kitchen were decidedly different that morning. Maybe it was the voice of a stranger that awakened me. Or, perhaps the harsh clinking of silverware against fine china. Or, it might have been my parents speaking in "good" English. Or, perhaps their hearty laughter, uncharacteristic so early in the morning. Whatever it was, it was enough to rouse me from deep sleep.

6   Curiosity overcame the inertia of my eyelids, and I crept into the dark hallway and squinted into the kitchen's harsh fluorescent glare. There was a stranger at the kitchen table! With his back to me, he was eating bacon and eggs—with a fork! And off my parents' wedding china, so exquisitely special that this was the first time that I had ever seen those purple-flowered plates out of the far reaches of the uppermost kitchen cabinets!

7   Most unusual of all was the color of the stranger's hair. It was yellow! The word "blonde" was neither in my vocabulary, nor in my expe-

rience, as those "wonder years" were T.V.-less. Signals from O'ahu never made it past the majestic Mauna Kea (the tallest mountain in the world, half of it below sea level). That famous blond, Dennis the Menace (hô, da kolohe dat boy!), was not yet, in our electronically remote corner of the island, a part of our experience.

8   Noiselessly, I crawled on all fours down the hall to the living room. In the middle of the floor was an empty, rumpled bed, fashioned with Mom's best (guest) sheets, stiffly starched and ironed, between silk-covered futons.

9   Shy as little country girls are wont to be, I chose to forego meeting the stranger, but the novel, billowy bed was too much to resist. I slipped between the sheet-lined depths of the futon bed, luxuriating in its smooth, stiff coolness before sleep came sweetly. When I awakened to the brightness of the morning sunlight streaming through the living room's broad windows, the stranger was gone.

10   Over supper that day, Dad explained the unusual events of the morning. The night before, as he drove home from a Young Farmers' meeting at a beach pavilion in Kalapana, he had spotted a lone figure's silhouette among the coconut trees at Kaimû, the most beautiful and famous black sand beach in Hawai'i.

11   He backed up his jeep, hailed the figure toward him. It turned out to be a mainland tourist who had wandered too far, missing the bus back to Hilo.

Dad, ever the teaser, asked him, "Eh, where you planning to sleep tonight?"

"I guess right here on the beach," the stranger replied, sheepishly.

"I don't t'ink so," said Dad, motioning him into the jeep. With that simple invitation, the stranger hopped in. Dad brought him home, just a few miles up that windy road, lined by pristine rainforests.

12   So that was how that stranger became our impromptu overnight houseguest. And so it was that morning that their houseguest was recounting the panic felt when he realized that the bus had taken off for Hilo without him. He had resigned himself to spending a chilly, hungry night under the coconut trees on the beach, arranging coconut fronds into a "bed." Dad had pulled over to rescue him from his predicament, just as he was futilely attempting to extract some supper from fallen coconuts: "Just how are you s'posed to crack one of those @#$! things open?!"

13   So it was the laughter that had awakened me. Mom's and Dad's hearty laughter! Fortified with a good night's sleep and a hearty breakfast, the stranger was dropped off at the village's post office, the village's bus stop. Although we never heard from the stranger again, the memories of that wonder morning—and that yellow hair—remain indelibly vibrant. With no small influence from these words of wisdom:

"Do not neglect to show hospitality to strangers,
    for by doing that,
    some have entertained angels unawares."

I have fancied that stranger to be an angel-in-disguise, who alighted but briefly, so by their own examples of spontaneous, "go for broke" hospitality, a father and mother taught their child an abiding life lesson about The Aloha Spirit:

"O ke aloha ke kuleana o kâhi malihini."
    "Love is the host of strange places."
In old Hawai'i, every passerby was greeted
    and offered hospitality whether
    a total stranger or acquaintance.

14   While *Wonder Years'* kids vicariously experienced how a Velveteen Rabbit became Real, that day in Hawai'i, for a little island girl, The Aloha Spirit became REAL. The little girl grew up, and she and her three siblings left their safe corner of the world. All four chose careers of service and (Hawaiian) hospitality, infusing perfect strangers with The Aloha Spirit. These career choices are direct testaments to the power of examples set by two parents, a mom, a friendly soul who easily turned strangers into friends, and a dad, an impulsive softie who turned strangers into houseguests, with their indwelling Aloha Spirit.

15   A year ago, almost to the day, my brother, Dad, and I took a drive down to Kalapana. I shared my reminiscence of that morning, but Dad seemed to have completely forgotten it. As I recalled more and more details, Dad riffled through the memories of a lifetime, then his face lit up. Nodding slowly, he said, "Yeah, yeah, I remember da guy . . . he was going (to) sleep on da beach." He closed his eyes and smiled, savoring the recalling of that distant, innocent time.

16   Kissing him on the cheek, I said to him, "Thanks, Dad, for making The Aloha Spirit REAL for me that day."

17   I shared with him how that morning had made all the difference in the world for me. Because of his kindness to a perfect stranger, I realized, at an early age, how easy it is to take a moment out of a busy life to show Aloha with a word, a smile, a note, a card, a treat, an ice cream cone . . . an invitation.

18   That morning, I saw firsthand how a day was made brighter for a stranger to whom Aloha was given, for my parents, who laughingly shared their Aloha with him, and for a little girl in a dark hallway, who was lucky enough to witness the light of The Aloha Spirit. Those seconds created a lifelong habit of sharing The Aloha Spirit, even if it is just a humble act, for someone else every day. After all, no action, big or small, is insignificant when we allow The Aloha Spirit to move us to be unexpectedly kind toward those around us. My father's recent passing, as well as his two sisters' (my aunties) and my favorite uncle's, all within the year, has thrust me into fledgling "kupuna-ship" (eldership). Over the past year, what is important in life has stood out in bold relief:

> In the end, what is most important is that we have loved, have been loved . . . and that we have invited The Aloha Spirit to dwell within.

> And to laugh. To heartily laugh.

19   Mahalo for REALLY listening, for by listening with your heart, may The Aloha Spirit become REAL for you, and in turn, help you make it REAL for those who enter your life's sphere as perfect strangers.

Exploring Ideas

1. Research "Aloha Spirit." Find several other sources, besides Aunty D., who talk about what The Aloha Spirit is. In your own words, define "Aloha Spirit" in a paragraph or so.

2. How might others benefit by reading Aunty D.'s reminiscence?

3. Aunty D. makes a connection between childhood experience and who she is today. That is, she and her siblings all experienced The Aloha Spirit as children and all chose careers in service and (Hawaiian) hospitality. What experiences have influenced your career choice or the type of person you are? Explore your own beliefs, the way you treat others, what you think is important, your own major and career goals. What experiences growing up might have influenced them?

4. Ask several people what childhood experiences they think influenced their career choices or way of living. Ask them *why* they think one experience was more influential than others.

5. Reconsider your own experiences (#3) and explore why your experience was so influential in your later life. Consider not just the experience, but the surrounding circumstances as well. What allowed that experience to be so influential?

Writing Strategies

1. How does Aunty D.'s essay develop? That is, what does she do to keep her point growing throughout the essay?

2. How does Aunty D. express her main idea? Does she state it or does she imply it?

3. What details help to bring the essay to life for you?

4. Describe Aunty D.'s voice. Is she formal, abrasive, gentle, conversational, mushy, bullying, or something else? Find a word or a phrase that you think best describes her voice and then refer to at least three sentences and explain how they support your description.

5. How does Aunty D. conclude her essay—with a summary, a restatement of the thesis, a call to action, or in some other way? Is her conclusion successful? How else might she have concluded?

Ideas for Writing

1. What moment (such as the one described in "The Aloha Spirit: A Reminiscence") represents an important aspect of your upbringing? For example, the stranger's visit in this essay is representative of the spirit with which the writer saw her parents treating others throughout her life.

2. How have the actions of some adult(s) influenced the person you are today?

If responding to one of these ideas, go to the **Analysis** section in this chapter to begin developing ideas for your essay.

The Thrill of Victory . . .
The Agony of Parents

Jennifer Schwind-Pawlak

Jennifer Schwind-Pawlak, whose writing also appears in Chapter 5, wrote "The Thrill of Victory . . . The Agony of Parents" for her freshman English class. As you read, think about why Schwind-Pawlak felt this experience was worth writing about. What message is she trying to convey to her reader? List your own experiences that this essay brings to mind.

In the margins of this essay, a reader's comments point to key ideas and writing strategies. As you read the essay, consider how the comments might influence your own reading and writing.

Exploring Ideas

worth writing about?

trying to convey?

my own experiences?

Writing Strategies

Parents—one word that can strike many emotions in children when said aloud. Some children will smile and think about how silly their dad looked when he put carrot sticks up his nose that very morning, while others will cringe when they think about how their mother picked them up from school last week wearing orange polyester pants and a green shirt, oblivious to the hard work that some fellow went through to create the color wheel. My own emotional state of mind seemed to run the gamut throughout childhood. I chose to blame my parents for all of the traumatic events that unfolded but took pride in my obvious independence during the successes. One of the most heinous crimes that my parents committed was "the soccer foul." If I could have ejected them from the game of life at that point, I would have.

Introduces general subject matter leading up to main idea: parent/child dynamics.

Ironically, I was not particularly fond of soccer. Being the youngest of four children, I often chose to run around the field with friends while my brothers and sisters performed feats of soccer, the likes of which had only been seen during the World Cup. I would happily contort my fingers into chubby pretzels while singing "The Itsy Bitsy Spider" as the game's events were recounted on the drives home. Still, whether by guilt or by the need to belong, I joined the team when I became of age.

Develops essay through narration and description.

The team that I played on was designed to turn the young and awkward into the swans of the soccer field. My father (a one-time soccer coach) explained several times that this was the time that I would learn the rules and workings of the game and that I shouldn't expect much more than that. Since it was a child's league, learning and the team experience were the focuses. Winning was a pleasant bonus but should not have

Exploring Ideas

We have all partici-
pated in these child-
hood activities that
were supposed to
teach us lessons,
about sportsmanship,
teamwork, etc.

been achieved at the cost of the main objectives. This litany was taken and stored somewhere in the recesses of my brain. For me, however, the main objective was looking cool while running down the field chasing a spotted ball. Everything else seemed secondary.

Due to the family history, I attended every Tuesday and Thursday practice and managed to make each a social occasion while going through the motions of the game. I succeeded in understanding the game and, though not the most skilled of players, began to enjoy the half game of playing time that was required by the league for each player. Though I was far from a star player, I felt that my contribution mattered to the overall outcomes of the games, all of which had been lost to this point.

Sunday, the morning of the fifth game of the season, came with no warning. I got up, went to church with the family, then came home to suit up for the game. Upon arrival at the field, I was greeted by the coach and went to take my place along the sidelines with the rest of my team. There was a buzz of excitement that left me with the feeling that I would get when my brother would poke me with his fingertip after dragging his stocking feet across the carpet. The team that we were playing had a record identical to ours. We could win this game. I didn't care what the parents said. Winning would be a blast.

We all—most of us—
have not gotten to
play at some point:
common experience?

The coach kept me on the sidelines the entire first half of the game, which my pre-adolescent mind attributed to my obviously increasing skill at the game. He was saving his trump card, me, for the last half of the game. I knew this was rare, but I was sure that his reason was to bedazzle the crowd and the other team with my pure firepower on the field. The other players, except one other girl, continued to cycle in and out of the game. While I was excited because we were winning the game, I was concerned that the coach had forgotten about me. I inched, ever so slowly, toward him and started mindless conversation to let him know that I was there. He spoke to me, so I knew that he could not have forgotten about me. As the game was winding down, I was sure that he must have decided to put me in for the last play of the game.

The game ended.

I was horrified to realize that I had not played one moment of the first win of the season. After all of that practice and the ugly uniform, I was deemed such a poor player that I was not even good enough to play one moment of that game. How would I ever live this down at school? How would I face all of my classmates on Monday? My stomach began to churn, the way that it does when you are going down the first hill of any great roller coaster. I looked to my parents for support, which only added to the horror of that day.

Writing Strategies

Details are carefully
selected: Father's
explanation becomes
key later in the essay.

Three-word paragraph
has dramatic effect.

Exploring Ideas

Worth writing about: because it's a common feeling growing up?

We have all, I guess, been embarrassed by our parents, though maybe not in this way.

Worth writing about because she sees the experience differently now. Sometimes—many times—we see experiences differently when they're occurring than we do later on.

She might want us to see this: parents do things FOR us even though we not only don't appreciate it, but are embarrassed. My experiences:
1) my own flipping out and yelling at umpire in Little League.
2) my father's short pants.
3) Dad asking basketball referee after the game why he threw me out, then taking the referee's side.
4) Mom working at the gas station.

Joann (the name I call my mother when she does something embarrassing) was screaming at the coach. In a voice so screeching that it rivaled fingernails on a blackboard, she told him that he was a disgraceful coach and that he should be ashamed of himself. She continued to point out the error of his ways by reminding him that I had not played at all in the game. How could she do this to me? My mother had managed to enlighten the few people that hadn't noticed on their own that I had not played at all. What was she thinking? She might as well have rented billboard space saying, "So what if Jeni sucks at soccer? The coach wouldn't let her play." My only thought was, "I don't want to go to school tomorrow!"

Looking back, I realize that it wasn't so bad the next day at school. I walked out to recess and talked about how nuts my mother was and everyone seemed to agree, sympathize, and get on with the important task of freeze tag. At that moment I wasn't sure that I would ever be able to forgive my parents for what happened that day, but, as far as I can recall, I began loving her again within the week. I am sure that she either cooked my favorite dinner, told a corny joke, or told me how much she loved me to make that lump of anger fade away.

I never went to soccer again. As a matter of fact, I never played another organized sport again. Maybe it was the fear of rejection. Maybe it was the uncertainty of my talent. Maybe I was just too busy with other things. I never really felt the urge to compete on that level after that day.

The relationship that I have with my parents has changed very much throughout the years. The polyester pants don't bother me anymore, but the carrot sticks still make me laugh. While their "soccer foul" embarrassed and angered me at the time, I understand and appreciate it now. My mother was angry <u>FOR</u> me. She was hurt <u>FOR</u> me. Through the pages of time, I can look back and see that, more often than not, I embarrassed her. She never stopped feeling for me, loving me, or protecting me. I have grown enough to realize that, though I often pointed out my parent's fouls, they scored countless goals that I didn't even notice.

Writing Strategies

Reflects on her experience: What it means "looking back."

Mentions possible impact of this experience.

Finds meaning through reflection.

Exploring Ideas

1. What experiences of your own did Schwind-Pawlak's essay bring to mind? How were they similar to or different from her own?

2. Explore an experience that you remember being very embarrassing but aren't embarrassed by now. When and why did you get over the embarrassment? How was your experience similar to or different from Schwind-Pawlak's?

3. Describe a particular childhood experience that you view differently now than you did at the time. You might, like Schwind-Pawlak, remember an experience involving a parent and yourself in a public setting.

4. Consider Schwind-Pawlak's essay from her parents' point of view. Have you embarrassed your child, a parent, or a friend? Explore the experience in writing until you understand what happened and why.

5. Share your writing from #4 with several others, asking them how they think someone might benefit from reading about your experience. After recording their responses, explain in a paragraph or two how your experience has public resonance—that is, how it might relate to and matter to others.

Writing Strategies

1. Describe Schwind-Pawlak's opening strategy. Does it work for you? Do you want to read on? How else might Schwind-Pawlak have begun her essay?

2. Why does Schwind-Pawlak tell us that her father "explained several times that this was the time that [she] would learn the rules and workings of the game and that [she] shouldn't expect much more than that"? Why does she place this information in her third paragraph? Where else might she have placed this information, and how would that placement affect her essay?

3. Describe the tone of Schwind-Pawlak's essay. Is it funny, serious, pensive, silly? Describe it with your own one-word description and then refer to three sentences that support your decision.

4. Explain the effect of Schwind-Pawlak's one-sentence paragraph: "The game ended."

5. Schwind-Pawlak now realizes her mother was angry for her, hurt for her. She says, "My mother was angry <u>FOR</u> me. She was hurt <u>FOR</u> me." Why do you think she decides to both underline and all-cap the word "for"?

Ideas for Writing

1. What is the significance of a big game or event from your past?

2. What emotional or intellectual experience has prevented you from ever doing something again? How has the experience influenced your later decisions?

If responding to one of these ideas, go to the Analysis section in this chapter to begin developing ideas for your essay.

The Grapes of Mrs. Rath

Steve Mockensturm

Steve Mockensturm is an artist, musician, and graphic designer. He wrote "The Grapes of Mrs. Rath" after visiting his old high school. As you read his essay, think about what Mockensturm is trying to accomplish. What might be his purpose in writing? How might this essay about his high school English teacher and himself matter to others?

1   I wonder if Mrs. Hulda Rath ever realized how much she affected my life. Probably not. It's funny how a teacher gets stuck in your head and you find yourself referencing that for the rest of your life.

2   Mrs. Rath taught English at DeVilbiss High School in 1975—my junior year. I say taught, but she didn't really teach. Didn't even talk that much, just gave us a lot of stories to read. She said they were classic, important books, but I'd never heard of any of them: *Animal Farm, Lord of the Flies, 1984, The Crucible, Cry the Beloved Country.*

3   DeVilbiss was a rough and rowdy school (inner city, a thousand kids, half black, half white) with a lot of distractions. During the '40s and '50s it was THE high school to attend, very academic, but by the mid-70s it was starting to run down, perhaps stigmatized by a few race riots in '68.

4   Mrs. Rath had an ability to recognize the kids that actually wanted to read and learn and, often times, would send a few of us down to the library where it was quiet and we could have some sanctuary from the usual classroom shenanigans. Looking back, I realize how amazing and grand this school library was. It was bigger than the local public branch and very church-like with its vaulted ceiling and tall windows. Everything was made of wood—the chairs, the tables, the shelves, the big librarian's station in the middle—and it was always full of light, the windows exposed to the south and west. Three sets of large mahogany doors would clang and creak, echoing down the hall, up around the stairwell, and into our classroom.

5   It was in this environment that I was introduced to the work of John Steinbeck. Two of the books assigned were *The Grapes of Wrath* and *Of Mice and Men.* I was smitten with these masterpieces and savored Steinbeck's work like a rich meal. Reading these stories in the great, holy library of my young life is one of the happiest memories I have. These were stories about my country and my people. Flawed yet beautiful people in tough situations in an imperfect land. I was discovering America. I suddenly wanted to read everything Steinbeck had ever written.

6   I checked out *Tortilla Flat* and *The Wayward Bus* from the library and asked Mrs. Rath what else he wrote and where I could get it. She loaned me her copy of "In Dubious Battle." Soon, I wanted to own all of Steinbeck's books. I scoured the bookstores to complete the collection, a collection that has traveled with me for 25 years.

7   The city sadly closed down DeVilbiss High School a few years after I graduated. It was too big and too expensive to maintain. Thankfully, they never tore it down and trimmed only a few trees from the large oak grove lining the front walkway. For years it sat empty, the massive entrance looking out on Upton Avenue with no expression.

8   Then, a few years ago, some parts of it reopened for special programs and the industrial skills center was transformed into a technology academy. My children were enrolled in the Horizons program at the old school. From time to time, during open house, I'll wan-

der the halls and conjure up old voices. Many areas of the building are unsafe; the library is almost unrecognizable. It's a massive storage room now, crap piled to the ceiling, desks and shelves torn out and not a book in sight.

9   The girls have Russian language lessons in Mrs. Rath's old room at the top of the stairwell.

Sometimes I'll stand in the doorway and picture the room as it was back in '75, gazing around, putting old friends in their seats. Whenever I'm reading Steinbeck, my memory goes back to this classroom, the library, and Mrs. Hulda Rath's quiet ways and I get the urge to plop down and read *Cannery Row*.

Exploring Ideas

1. How is the way Mockensturm sees high school English different from the way you see it?

2. Based on this essay, how are Mockensturm's thoughts, values, beliefs, or feelings different from yours?

3. Visit your old school, an old playground, park, or some other place. Write down any memories that come to mind.

4. Explore the memories that came to mind for #3. What connection can you make between an old memory and who you are today? What memory that came to mind recalls an experience or aspect of your youth that influenced who you are today?

5. As a way to stimulate your thinking, ask others to name an important activity in their life (reading, being hospitable, etc.) and a person from their childhood who encouraged them in that activity. That is, ask them to connect who they are now to their past. Then consider your own activities and attitudes and who was important in shaping them. Write at least a paragraph about one such individual's influence on you.

Writing Strategies

1. Describe Mockensturm's voice as a writer. That is, how does he come across sounding

to the reader? Refer to three specific passages to support your description.

2. If workshopping Mockensturm's essay, how would you answer the following questions: What do you like most about the essay? What suggestion do you have for the writer?

3. What would you say is Mockensturm's main idea? How does he convey it to the reader?

4. Identify the most effective uses of narration (or storytelling) and description in Mockensturm's essay and explain why they work well.

Ideas for Writing

1. What high school experience do you view differently—for example, seeing it as more valuable—than most of your peers do?

2. What individual influenced you growing up and may not realize it?

> If responding to one of these ideas, go to the **Analysis** section in this chapter to begin developing ideas for your essay.

Outside Reading

Find a written text about a memory and print it out or make a photocopy. In journals or magazines, these are often called *memoirs*. You might find a memoir in a general readership publication (such as *Time, Newsweek, Reader's Digest*, or the *New York Times*). Some publications feature writers who tell their own stories. Enthusiast magazines (about various hobbies and travel) often feature personal memoirs as well. (Check the table of contents for story titles with first-person pronouns *I* or *my*.) To conduct an electronic search of journals and magazines, go to your library's periodical database or to InfoTrac (http://infotrac.galegroup.com/itweb/). For your library database, perform a keyword search, or go to the main search box for InfoTrac and click on "keywords." Enter word combinations that interest you, such as *memoir and Jewish and women, memoir and Japan and war, memoir and soccer, memoir and punk rock*. (When performing keyword searches, avoid using phrases or articles *a, an, the*; instead, use nouns separated by *and*.) The search results will yield lists of journal and magazine articles.

You can also search the Internet. Try the search engine Altavista.com. Like most Internet search engines, Altavista.com combines words using *and*. In the search box, try various combinations, such as those above.

The purpose of this assignment is to broaden the range of possibilities; that is, to help you discover more strategies for writing about the past. As you are probably discovering, this kind of writing varies widely (in organization, voice, and even length). As you read through this chapter and begin your own writing, keep the memoir you have discovered close by and notice the elements and strategies the writer uses. Depending on your instructor's suggestions, do one or more of the following:

1. Notice how the writer applies various strategies from this chapter. On the hard copy or photocopy:
   - Highlight the thesis (or main idea about the memory) if it is stated. If the thesis is implied, write it in your own words.
   - Highlight the most descriptive or detailed passage(s).
   - Highlight any passages that suggest a connection between the writer's memory and the reader's (your) life. In the margin, write "public resonance."

2. Write an essay that discusses the strategies employed by the writer. The following questions may be helpful.
   - How does the writer's approach differ from the readings in this chapter?
   - How does the writer connect his or her own experience to potential readers?
   - Who is the audience for this text?
   - How does the audience impact the kinds of things said in the memoir?

3. Write at least three "Exploring Ideas" questions for the text you found.

4. Write at least three "Writing Strategies" questions for the text you found.

5. Write two "Ideas for Writing" questions, such as the ones following the essays in this book, for the text you found.

Biographies and Autobiographies:

An *autobiography* is an account of a person's life, told by that person. A *biography* is an account of a person's life told by someone else. While we generally think of biographies as written works, films or television shows can also be *biographical*. For example, each weeknight the television series "Biography" on *A&E* gives an account of a series of events making up a person's life. Films, too, such as *Ali* or *Man on the Moon* tell a person's life story by relating a series of events.

Biographies and autobiographies are like remembering essays in that they do not merely report what happened. Instead, they present certain events in a particular light so as to tell a story or make a point. For example, two different biographies of Muhammad Ali might present Ali quite differently. One might show him as a great American hero by focusing on his role as an activist or humanitarian. The other might show him as a great heavyweight boxer, focusing on his career as a fighter. Both biographies could be accurate and interesting, yet quite different. The selection and arrangement of details would present two different Alis.

Because a remembering essay is quite short, it will not present a series of events, or as many events, but will instead focus on one event or several closely related events. Still, both remembering essay and biography/autobiography seek to make a point and not just convey facts.

How true, or accurate, is a biography or autobiography? Although based on fact, any representation of history depends on the teller's interpretation. For example, a person might purposely misrepresent the truth in an autobiography or a person might add a historically inaccurate detail as a result of a false memory or a misinterpretation. As you explore your own past in order to write a remembering essay for this chapter, you might consider biographies and autobiographies you are familiar with and the way in which they not only present details, but selectively present details in order to make a point.

You can read the autobiographies of a wide range of people, from sports and popular culture figures—such as Vanna White or Dennis Rodman—to political and religious figures—such as Benjamin Franklin and St. Augustine. If you have not read many biographies or autobiographies yourself, ask others which ones they have read, why they found them to be interesting, and how the books presented the particular individuals.

Activities

1. Make a list of biographies and autobiographies that you have read. How did they present a person's life through a series of events? What point were they making about the person's life?

2. Make a list of biographical television shows and movies you have seen. How did they present a person's life through a series of events? What point were they making about the person's life?

3. Watch one episode of *Biography* on A &E. How did the show present a person's life through a series of events? What point was the show making about the person's life? What other perspective might the biography have taken?

INVENTION

> " **I**'m digging in the dirt
>
> to find the places I got hurt
>
> to open up the places I got hurt. "
>
> —"Digging in the Dirt," *Peter Gabriel*

Remember that invention is not simply about finding a topic. It also involves exploring and analyzing that topic, analyzing your thoughts and developing points. For a remembering essay, the process will be rather self-reflective. The following three sections are designed to help you through invention: specifically, to discover a particular topic, a situation or event from your past (in **Point of Contact**), develop points about the topic (in **Analysis**), and make it relevant to a community of readers (in **Public Resonance**). The questions in each section are not meant to be answered directly in your final written assignment. Answering them before you begin drafting will, however, help you discover what you are going to say—and even why you are going to say it. The **Delivery** section, which immediately follows **Invention**, will help you craft your ideas into a written text.

Point of Contact

Looking Back

You might think that nothing interesting has ever happened to you. But even if you have lived in one place your whole life, never won the lottery, never wrestled an alligator, never written a top ten song, or never been on a first date, your life is still filled with thousands of situations and moments that can reveal something to you and to your audience.

Remembering is a process of digging up the past, unearthing moments that have been buried. You should begin by looking back and trying to find a specific situation, event, or set of events from your life. The situation or event you choose for your topic you will analyze and develop throughout this chapter. Use the suggestions and questions below for your exploration. As you move through the questions, do not hold out for a huge moment (the time an earthquake hit your town, or when you crashed your parents' car into the local mall). Remember that interesting moments occur constantly—and sometimes the most interesting and valuable insights come from a particularly small and seemingly unimportant moment.

Using Images as a Point of Contact: Images can jar the memory and prompt you to recall something significant about your past. Examine the images on this page, or images you find in everyday life (a newspaper, magazine, billboard, etc.) and ask yourself: what situation or thought from my past does this image raise? Be careful not to dismiss an image if it does not immediately stir up a "big" moment in your life. Remember that some of the most interesting and valuable memories are those that linger quietly in the past. If an image strikes you, move to the **Analysis** section to explore it in depth. (Or use the questions on the next two pages to explore different memories.)

Activity: Find an image of your own that prompts you to remember. Or, find any image and show it to a friend, then discuss what memories come to mind.

- **Visit a place** from your past (a schoolyard, a house, an apartment building, an old neighborhood, a workplace, etc.). Once there, ask yourself the following:

    What memories or feelings are most prominent?

    How have my feelings about the place changed?

    What do I see now that I did not see then?

    What is the meaning or value of this place in my life?

- **You might also do something** that you have not done for many years: go fishing, play baseball, listen to a particular song, reread a particular book, do nothing. Afterwards, consider the following:

    How was the activity different from the past?

    What did it mean to me back then?

    Does it mean the same now? Why or why not?

- **If you are geographically too far away from your past, try to call or write someone from your past. Ask him or her about your shared history. Begin with the following questions:**

    What do you remember most about our lives back then?

    What was the best part of our lives? The worst?

    How have we both changed since then?

    Why did we change?

    What forces/feelings/situations kept us together?

Example: Cindy Bosley's Responses to the Point of Contact Questions

Did I ever win or lose a big sporting event? The Junior Miss Pageant!

Did I have a crush on someone? I had crushes on everyone.

Have I ever embarrassed the family? Now THERE's a question. I am certain that I often humiliated my mother (I was not the daughter she wanted me to be), but not so much as the night of the Ottumwa Junior Miss Pageant when I shared happy tears with my fellow contestants, and she misinterpreted them as sad tears, and snapped at me the moment she saw me backstage to "stop crying, they'll think you're not a nice loser." I have always mar-

veled at the misunderstanding evident there. For years, she talked about my talent routine, and maybe if I hadn't made the mistakes I'd made in it, I'd have been the sure winner. The only problem is that I didn't remember any mistakes! And I knew exactly when I'd lost the pageant, and it was way before the contest started—I believe I lost the pageant with the judges in the interview segment of the contest, but also before that, just by the facts of my birth in terms of place/time/expectation/socio-economic status. I've never known how to tell my mother what really lost me (her) the contest in my conversation with the judges, and it really encapsulates so much—the atmosphere of my town, my family, my mother, and all we don't talk about.

- **You might recall an event from your past life. To do so, consider the following questions:**

School

Did I ever get beat up? Did I ever beat up someone else?

Was I ever embarrassed by a teacher or classmate?

Did I ever win or lose a big sporting event?

Was I popular, unpopular, or normal?

Was I one of the "smart" kids? Was I one of the "normal" kids?

Did I fit into a particular clique (jocks, hoods, hippies, punks, nerds, etc.)?

Did I come out of my shell a particular year?

Work

What was my first job? Did I like or dislike it?

Why did I quit?

How did I get along with my peers? My boss?

Did the job put me in any weird situations?

Social Life

When and with whom was my first date?

When did I first stay out late?

Did I have a lot of friends? No friends?

What situation led to my first friendship?

When did I first learn about the differences between girls and boys?

Was I ever asked to drink or try drugs? (Did I?)

When did I first drive a car (illegally or legally)?

Did I ever change my hair or image drastically?

Family Life

Did I experience a sibling being born?

Have I experienced a child of my own being born?

Did we have a pet? (Did it pass away?)

Did we take any family vacations?

Have I ever embarrassed my family? (Has my family ever embarrassed me?)

What did we do on Sundays?

Did we eat dinner, watch television, or attend religious services together?

Invention Activity: Of course, these questions only hint at the many possible topics. In groups or alone, generate another five to ten questions until one has triggered something for you (and/or everyone in your group).

Keep in mind that answering "no" to any of the above (or similar) questions is ultimately as interesting as answering "yes." Consider, for example, the question: *Did I ever change my hair or image drastically?* Answering "no" could provide interesting insight into someone's self-image—into the way someone grew gradually through adolescence, a time often marked by drastic and chaotic change. Such an insight could develop into an interesting essay about image and adolescence.

Analysis

Finding the Significance

Now that you have a topic (a particular event or situation from your past), you should try to find the significance. What do we mean by *significance*? Basically put, *significance* refers to why something is important for the both the writer and the reader. Consider Kress's essay about his education. The essay focuses on a particular trip he took (by jumping a freight train) to Chicago. The significance, though, is apparent in the conclusion:

> Somehow the rickety freight ride and all that drama and lure of the past two days quickly dissipated, replaced by an urgent sense of new gaps in my learning, of new educational possibilities.

Kress discovers that the freight train ride was more than an adventure, but was something that showed him "the gaps" and opened new possibilities for learning. Although it was probably not apparent at the time (when Kress was younger), the meaning of the situation comes to him later. Similarly, Schwind-Pawlak discovers the significance of a particular soccer game:

> The relationship that I have with my parents has changed very much throughout the years. The polyester pants don't bother me anymore, but the carrot sticks still make me laugh. While their "soccer foul" embarrassed and angered me at the time, I understand and appreciate it now. My mother was angry <u>FOR</u> me. She was hurt <u>FOR</u> me. Through the pages of time, I can look back and see that, more often than not, I embarrassed her. She never stopped feeling for me, loving me, or protecting me. I have grown enough to realize that, though I often pointed out my parent's fouls, they scored countless goals that I didn't even notice.

For her, the significance lies in the difference between her past and present perspectives. Her present perspective allows her to see the soccer game ("foul") differently than her childhood self did. This realization is valuable because it shows the stark differences between childhood and adult perspectives, and even the evolution of parent/child relationships.

Discovering the significance of the past can be tricky because it is not obvious. In fact, the most significant events might be those that seem totally normal or insignificant. Certainly, a single soccer game spent standing on the sidelines would seem to have no meaning, other than frustration, for the younger Schwind-Pawlak; but to the older writer looking back, the game reveals something about her relationship with her parents.

As you consider your own topic (memory), remember that the goal is not simply to tell a story about your past, but to discover something meaningful about the past—something that can be shared with and valued by others.

Use the following questions to find the significance of your topic:

- How did I change? (Who was I before and after the situation?)
- Why did the event or situation occur?
- Did I realize the significance of the event at the time? Why or why not?
- What do I see now that I didn't see then?
- Why was the event or situation important to me?

  Did it help me to understand myself as a man or woman?
  Did it help me to grow intellectually? Spiritually? Socially?
  Did it help me to see myself in a different way?

- What does the memory reveal about communities? Children? Teenagers? Towns? Families? Schools? Teachers? Churches? Neighborhoods?

Activity: In small groups, choose Bosley's, Mockensturm's, or Aunty D.'s essay, and discover the significance of the memory. First, each group member should explain the significance in writing. The following questions may be helpful:

- What is the importance of the memory?
- What point does the memory show?
- What passage best reveals the significance of the memory?

Among group members, discuss the differences and similarities of your responses. Then share the group's discoveries with the rest of the class.

As you analyze your own past, avoid moving too quickly. Imagine a student, Jack, who visited his old elementary school:

What do I see now that I didn't see then?
I see that school is important, and back then I didn't.

Jack certainly answers the question and begins walking the path of analysis, but his brief answer may not go far enough. It probably does not reveal the complexity of his experience. He says that "school is important," but such a phrase is broad and hollow. What particular aspect of school, we might ask, is important? What specific moments or situations are valuable to a growing individual? Struggling through impossibly difficult classes? The reward of a good grade? Being prompted to read material he would otherwise ignore? Or maybe what's important is the slow and charted evolution of one's identity through various classes, teachers, friends, and hallways. Jack's answer blankets such rich possibilities, covering them up with a broad sweeping phrase, and if he sought out the particulars, he might, in fact, learn something about his own understanding.

Another student, Diana, goes further in her thinking:

What do I see now that I didn't see then?
When I was younger, I didn't see the big picture, how my life in school connected to anything outside of school. I went, did the work, and came home, but mostly daydreamed about the time I'd spend away from schoolwork. For me, and probably most of my friends, life was separate from schoolwork. Every day, the goal was to get it done so we could be away from it. I remember the feeling of freedom in running out the door after school or during recess, but what I was running toward was a bunch of silly games, posing, and meaningless searches for excitement. I never thought, maybe I was never taught, that learning is really what makes life worth anything, that an intellectual challenge is real excitement. When I was a teenager, I was focused on the surface—the shallow giddiness of thrills and "parties." I thought school was a drag—and I looked for every possible excuse to be bored. I actually *convinced* myself to be bored. But now that I am older, I realize that school is the only place where people actually care about your mind—where they want you to grow, imagine, and experience new ideas. These are the things that make life outside of school worth living. I see that now.

All the jobs I had after high school just wanted me to perform a certain duty. No one wanted me to explore my intellectual potential. And unfortunately, I see a lot of younger college students still thinking the way I did in high school. They moan at challenging assignments; they just want to duck out of everything. Today, a boy said to me, "Can you believe how long that reading took?" as though the goal was to get through it. What's that about? Well, I know what it's about—blindness to the big picture.

Diana's thoughts are beginning to develop here. She is making powerful and specific distinctions between her present and her past understanding. She is analyzing—not simply answering **Analysis** questions.

Example: Cindy Bosley's Responses
to the Analysis Questions

Why did the event or situation occur? If I isolate the event or situation as the gulf between my own grasp of fun and happiness and my mother's severe disappointment and embarrassment, her concern that others would think I was not a "nice loser" in that small moment, I think it clearly speaks so much more about my mother—as though I saw her, her disappointments and worries about image and desirability in herself through me. She was no stage mother, not at all, but she must have had these fears about how people in the town looked at her, and at us, her three children, because of my father to a certain extent, but also just because she herself was a woman who'd grown up to some degree "unacceptable" in her and her family's eyes because she was heavy, or because she liked lots of boys, or because she got pregnant and married, or because she moved so far away. My mother was and is a creative, talented, vibrant woman, and she worked very hard, and very successfully, sacrificing so much for herself so my sister, brother, and I could have the things that we wanted like the other kids, things that might help us break out of our own family's economic situation. Things like acrobat lessons, and cheerleading camp, and swimming lessons, and overnight birthday parties. I have absolutely no idea how she pulled all those things off.

The Junior Miss thing is just a moment, just a slice of a moment, that helped me see my mother more clearly, and rightly or wrongly, caused me to gulp down my confusion and anger, and just see her fresh, vulnerable, scared, and lonelier than anyone I knew. I think, though, this essay isn't about my mother so much as it is about women more generally, and the images we're given through history at birth and before, and never ever really break. I always felt shame after what I told the judges about wanting my mother to not have to be so lonely—how narrow of me, how far I missed the point—and yet, now I feel the truth of it, and I hope if I could go back, I'd still tell them that's the one thing I'd want to be able to change—for my mother to be able to feel beautiful and free and lovely and bright, overweight or not, advanced education or not, and with or without a man.

Notice how Bosley's notes are exploratory. They are not simple answers to questions. Much of the language in her response does not appear in her final essay, but what is important is the level of thinking, the degree to which she is willing to explore and stretch her reasoning. Notice how the ideas evolve into her essay:

> But the truth is that I'd lost the contest when I told the judges, when they asked, that my most personal concern was my mother's loneliness, and if I could change anything at all, I would give her something—a man, God, anything to free her from that loneliness.

We do not imagine Bosley articulating these thoughts as a young girl at the pageant—at least not with such elegance. But as she looks back, as a reflective writer, she understands and communicates the significance of the memory.

Public Resonance

Involving Others

Even though this writing assignment focuses primarily on your past, the ideas should also have meaning for others. That is, what you discover should in some way suggest something for the lives of your readers. Such writing uses the personal to highlight a particular aspect of everyday life. Notice how Aunty D. makes her memory extend beyond the personal, how she makes her memory resonate with her audience by relating it to The Aloha Spirit—something that includes but also extends beyond her personal memory:

> That morning, I saw first-hand how a day was made brighter for a stranger to whom Aloha was given, for my parents, who laughingly shared their Aloha with him, and for a little girl in a dark hallway, who was lucky enough to witness the light of The Aloha Spirit. Those seconds created a lifelong habit of sharing The Aloha Spirit, even if it is just a humble act, for someone else every day. After all, no action, big or small, is insignificant when we allow The Aloha Spirit to move us to be unexpectedly kind toward those around us. My father's recent passing, as well as his two sisters' (my aunties) and my favorite uncle's, all within the year, has thrust me into fledgling "kupuna-ship" (eldership). Over the past year, what is important in life has stood out in bold relief:
>
> > In the end, what is most important is that we have loved, have been loved . . . and that we have invited The Aloha Spirit to dwell within.

Her personal memory is not simply a revelation about her own life; it communicates a broader, shared concept: The Aloha Spirit. To make the connection even more pronounced, Aunty D. changes to the plural pronoun *we*.

The public resonance in Mockensturm's writing is a bit subtler. Early in the essay, he describes the social world around his personal experiences:

> DeVilbiss was a rough and rowdy school (inner city, a thousand kids, half black, half white) with a lot of distractions. During the '40s and '50s it was THE high school to attend, very academic, but by the mid-70s it was starting to run down, perhaps stigmatized by a few race riots in '68.

While this bit of information seems only incidental, it prompts the reader to see a connection between the individual experience and broader societal experience. Later in the essay, Mockensturm makes that connection more directly:

> I was smitten with these masterpieces and savored Steinbeck's work like a rich meal. Reading these stories in the great, holy library of my young life is one of the happiest memories I have. These were stories about my country and my people. Flawed yet beautiful people in tough situations in an imperfect land. I was discovering America.

These passages connect Mockensturm's memory to the social world around him, to a world the reader can also envision. His intellectual growth is not exclusively personal. It is a developing recognition of the social world—the "flawed yet beautiful people" that surround him. (In some ways, then, Mockensturm's essay reveals the process of a student realizing the public resonance of literature.)

Discuss the Public Resonance of the other essays in this chapter.

Dealing with public resonance is simply a process of addressing the connection between your particular memory and its relation to a public or shared issue. You may have already found public resonance by answering the **Analysis** questions. But closely consider your response to the following:

- What public issue is related to my memory?
- What does my memory reveal or show about the nature of _____? (Childhood? Teenagers? Towns? Families? Schools? Teachers? Churches? Education? Parenthood? Growing up? Failing? Succeeding? Suffering? Dying? Healing?)
- What general behavior or condition does my memory bring to mind?
- Who else, what type of person, might relate to my memory?

If you cannot imagine how your topic resonates with others' experiences, ask a classmate or friend outside of class how your experience (your memory) relates to him or her—or to the world around both of you.

Example: Cindy Bosley's Response to Public Resonance Questions

What public issue is related to my memory? This isn't about my mother so much as it is about women more generally, and the images we're given through history at birth and before and never ever really break. I always felt shame after what I told the judges about wanting my mother to not have to be so lonely—how narrow of me, how far I missed the point—and yet, now I feel the truth of it, and I hope if I could go back, I'd still tell them that's the one thing I'd want to be able to change—for my mother to be able to feel beautiful and free and lovely and bright, overweight or not, advanced education or not, and with or without a man.

I remember my joy in graduate school when my friend Karen hosted a Miss America party the night of the pageant, and maybe my essay began to grow here. It was that night that I discovered I wasn't the ONLY little girl making up my own score sheets for the contest, hoping to predict who would win, and always imagining, because we thought it was the thing to wish for, that we could someday be Miss America. And all the usual stuff about women's narrow, "perfected" images in the media, Barbie dolls, fairy tales, all of it comes to bear here. There's such a feeling of shame and degradation (I don't think it is too big a word to describe it) in allowing oneself to be judged in this way, whether literally in a contest, or even just by agreeing to play, which we all do, by all the ancient rules of "fitting in" whether you're male or female. And there seems to be this desperate hole of loneliness and fear that seems anchored to it all. We often recognize it first in other people.

As in the **Analysis** section, your answers to the **Public Resonance** questions may not appear directly in your final writing. However, they may generate focused thinking about your topic that, eventually, may find its way into your final draft. For example, in Bosley's conclusion, her initial thoughts show up. They do not come word-for-word from her notes, but it is easy to see the connection. In her notes, she understands that her situation (and her mother's loneliness) is not unique. And in her conclusion, she makes this evident by changing the personal pronoun from *I* to *our*, thereby including others in her thinking. She attempts to link her realization about beauty pageants and mother/daughter relationships to others, so that her essay is not simply about herself, but about people who grew up in similar conditions. Bosley shows us how a potentially unusual memory can resonate with readers. The importance and meaning of the memory translates into something beyond her personal feelings.

DELIVERY

> "**Q**uite often you want to tell somebody your
> dream, your nightmare. Well, nobody wants
> to hear about someone else's dream, good
> or bad; nobody wants to walk around with it.
> The writer is always tricking the
> reader into listening to the dream."
>
> —*Joan Didion*

The writing for this chapter, perhaps more than any other, is rather personal in nature. It involves reflections from your past alone. However, such personal writing still needs to involve an audience. It needs to extend beyond the personal, develop into a point that connects to the public. And to do this, writers need to explore various tools. The following sections (**Rhetorical Tools, Organizational Strategies, Writer's Voice,** and **Revision Strategies**) are designed to help you build a sophisticated and engaging text—one that emerges from your particular ideas. Each section points to important features or common concerns related to evaluative writing.

Rhetorical Tools
Focusing and Developing the Idea

Considering Your Thesis: Like any essay, even one that is based on a personal experience should have a main point or thesis. The thesis of a remembering essay is a statement that suggests the significance of the memory. The thesis is *not* simply a description of the memory. Notice how the thesis develops or evolves from a description of the memory to a statement about the meaning.

Evolution of a Thesis

The writer responds to a Point of Contact question:	*I remember as a kid sitting in my grandparents' backyard listening to them and my parents tell boring family stories.*
The writer focuses on a particular moment:	*I remember when I was ten years old and my parents made me visit my grandparents with them and wouldn't let me stay home and play outside with my friends.*
The writer responds to Analysis questions to find the significance:	*I realize now that I learned a lot about my family history from sitting around as a kid listening to my grandparents and parents tell family stories.*
Public Resonance questions help extend the writer's thinking:	*We learn important things about who we are and where we came from by listening to family stories.*
The writer integrates personal insights and public resonance:	*Though we might prefer not to hear them, we can better understand who we are and why by taking in family stories as children.*

A thesis statement that is stated directly in the essay is **explicit**; an **implied** thesis is suggested by the details of the text, but is not directly stated. Notice, for instance, Mockensturm's essay: the details and events suggest a main point, but that point is not stated directly. Having an implied thesis does not mean a writer can simply wander through many different ideas. The details throughout the essay must be focused and coherent enough to suggest a main point—for both the writer and the reader.

Because you have already explored the significance and public resonance of your memory, you may already have a thesis. Ask yourself: *What is the most important point about this memory that should be communicated?* Try to express that point in one statement. (Even if you have an implied thesis, stating the main idea will help you develop the essay.)

Ask yourself: What is the most important point about this memory that should be communicated?

Developing Support: As in any essay, you have to support your thesis and illustrate it for the reader. And because this is a rather personal essay (about a personal history), most of the support will involve the following:

Narration is a retelling of events or a story. All of the essays in this chapter depend heavily on narration. That is, they all tell stories. The art of storytelling involves pace, or the movement of events. At important points in a narrative, the amount of detail tends to increase, and so the reader slows down and experiences each moment. But good storytellers also move quickly through unimportant events. It might be helpful to think of this strategy as it works in movies: At the climax of an adventure movie, the events slow down (we see the lead character's hand grasping for the light saber; we hear each breath of the character as she walks down the hallway), but during less important moments, an entire day or week can flash by in a second.

Notice how Schwind-Pawlak moves quickly through unimportant events:

> Sunday, the morning of the fifth game of the season, came with no warning. I got up, went to church with the family, then came home to suit up for the game. Upon arrival at the field, I was greeted by the coach and went to take my place along the sidelines with the rest of my team.

She quickly relates the pregame events (going to church and suiting up) because they do not have a significant impact on the main idea of the essay. However, notice how the narrative slows down (and offers more details) at important moments:

> Joann (the name I call my mother when she does something embarrassing) was screaming at the coach. In a voice so screeching that it rivaled fingernails on a blackboard, she told him that he was a disgraceful coach and that he should be ashamed of himself. She continued to point out the error of his ways by reminding him that I had not played at all in the game. How could she do this to me? My mother had managed to enlighten the few people that hadn't noticed on their own that I had not played at all. What was she thinking? She might as well have rented billboard space saying, "So what if Jeni sucks at soccer? The coach wouldn't let her play." My only thought was, "I don't want to go to school tomorrow!"

As you consider your own narrative, slow the pace when relaying events that are directly related to your main idea.

Allusions are references to some public bit of knowledge (such as a historical event, a political situation, or a popular culture figure). An allusion can give a personal essay a more public and broader feeling; that is, it can make the ideas and events of a personal situation relate to a reader through a shared culture. Mockensturm's brief allusion to the race riots of the 1960s, for instance, helps create public resonance. And Leonard Kress relates his personal experience to us by pointing to the Beat writers, Kerouac specifically. By alluding to these writers, he reinforces the intensity of the experience. In simply mentioning Kerouac, Kress turns the train ride into an important educational moment, one that relates to travel and experience. In other words, the allusion expands the meaning of Kress's narrative. In considering your essay, ask yourself: *Does my situation relate to any historical situations, figures, or events? Any popular culture figures or fictional characters?*

Dialogue is discussion between two or more people. Portraying dialogue in an essay can make an event (or memory in this case) more real and engaging to the reader. Dialogue is most valuable when it is used to emphasize a main point in an essay, not simply to convey events. Conveying general events is better left to narration. But dialogue is useful when a particular exchange of words shows something significant.

Because dialogue slows the reader down, it is best to use it when making an important point. For instance, Aunty D. uses dialogue to show her father's interaction with the stranger. Because the dialogue illustrates The Aloha Spirit, it helps to support the main point of the essay. If you are considering dialogue for your essay, ask yourself: *Does the dialogue help to show something in support of the main idea?*

Formatting for dialogue involves several steps:

- Use quotation marks before and after the actual spoken words.
- Put end punctuation (such as a period) inside the end quotation marks.
- Indent when a new speaker begins.

Integrating a speaker's words can be accomplished in several ways:

- Use a comma between the quotation and the speaking verb (explained, asked, said, yelled, proclaimed, etc.).

    Louisa asked, "What are we going to do now?"

- Use a colon before the speaker's words. In this case, the narrator usually forecasts the ideas or mood of the speaker in a sentence preceding the colon.

    I was clearly agitated at her question: "How in the heck should I know?"

- Work the sentence directly into the grammar of your sentence.

    But Louisa was convinced that our decision would "hurt us either way."

See all of these rules operating in the following exchange:

> "Come on in," Mr. Smith said.
> "Hey, something smells great," I said as I walked into his lamp-lit living room. The small terrier looked up out of its lazy place on the sofa as Mr. Smith reached to get his wallet.
> "Yep, I've been cookin' my chili again. It's Max's favorite." He gestured at the complacent blurry-eyed dog. "So, is the price of papers still the same?"
> "Well, as far as I know, it's still $4.25 for the month." And then without considering the consequences, I asked the wrong question: "How have you been, Mr. Smith?" It took him 45 minutes to explain his "return to normal" after a long spell of stomach flu.

In this example, notice how attributive phrases (such as *he said*), which give ownership to the spoken words, are absent after the second indentation. Generally, after the dialogue pattern is established and the reader can easily tell who is speaking at each indentation, attributive phrases are unnecessary.

Organizational Strategies
Addressing Common Concerns

What Details Should I Include? Sometimes when we tell stories (especially our own), they take over, and cause us to wander through irrelevant details. If this happens you might consider two primary strategies: leave out irrelevant details that distract the reader, and emphasize those details that help illustrate your main idea. For instance, in Aunty D.'s essay, we do not learn about the furniture in her childhood home; such information would not be important for her main point about the Aloha spirit. We do, however, learn about the color of the houseguest's hair. This is important because his blond hair signifies his foreign quality and her parents' decision to welcome the man despite his difference:

> Most unusual of all was the color of the stranger's hair. It was yellow! The word "blonde" was neither in my vocabulary, nor in my experience, as those "wonder years" were T.V.-less. Signals from O`ahu never made it past the majestic Mauna Kea (the tallest mountain in the world, half of it below sea level). That famous blond, Dennis the Menace (hô, da kolohe dat boy!), was not yet, in our electronically remote corner of the island, a part of our experience.

In Mockensturm's essay, we are not told about the antics of his school buddies or the long walk to school in the mornings. But we do hear about the library:

> Looking back, I realize how amazing and grand this school library was. It was bigger than the local public branch and very church-like with its vaulted ceiling and tall windows. Everything was made of wood—the chairs, the tables, the shelves, the big librarian's station in the middle—and it was always full of light, the windows exposed to the south and west. Three sets of large mahogany doors would clang and creak, echoing down the hall, up around the stairwell, and into our classroom.

Such details convey Mockensturm's feelings of awe as he looks back. The grand description helps portray the environment in which he encountered literature and America. In Kress's essay, he does not tell us about the day before his journey; he even excludes how he made it home from Chicago. But he uses details strategically to show us all the "gaps" in his learning:

> He led me to one, sitting on the outer tracks, mostly a string of lime-dusty hoppers interspersed with empty boxcars—doors flung invitingly wide open! I rushed in front of him, tossed my rucksack in, and was about to hoist myself inside, when he grabbed my leg and tackled me down to the rails. I was too shocked to resist; he pinned me to the railroad ties and moved his head in real close to mine. Just when I was sure that he was about to slit my throat, he released his grip and delivered what seemed to be a prepared speech about hopping freights. "Don't never board a still train," I remember him saying, "they shut them doors when the train's pulling out. You get stuck in there, you roast, you just roast, that's all there is to it."

These details ultimately link to Kress's main point about the gaps in his learning. The dramatic scene here illustrates the first of several educational moments that lead to his final point. And because the scene helps the reader witness the main idea, Kress includes minute details (such as the closeness of the stranger's head). Like a good filmmaker, Kress slows down time and brings the memory into sharp focus:

> The ride itself was unbelievably jittery and uncomfortable. I couldn't open the can of beans I'd brought along, and the slices of bread I'd stuffed into my rucksack fell onto the floor and coated themselves in rust-flecked grease. The freight did, however, grant me a spectacular view of the setting sun as it ambled ever so slowly along the banks of Lake Michigan.

If anything illustrates Kress's gaps in learning, it is certainly the image of his bread slices lying on the rusty floor of a train car, coated in goo.

As in these essays, details should add up to the main point. That is, as readers work through the text, gathering details along the way, they should be led to the main idea; they should, in fact, experience the deep complexity of living in a particular moment. And without those details, the reader will merely experience being told something about a distant time and place. As you consider your own narrative, think of the details that can help illustrate your point. If the moment is important, do not hold any detail back. If you were, for instance, sitting in an alley, explain the color of the empty bottles and the smell of the damp brick. If you were standing in a classroom at the end of a day, explain the placement of the desks and dying fern by the window. If you were swimming in a pond, explain how the weeds waved back and forth from the impact of your movements. But only focus on such particulars when they help get your reader closer to the main idea. Ask yourself: *What details from the past will help the reader to fully understand my point?*

How Should I Begin? As with any essay, introduction strategies are limitless. A favorite strategy among writers (especially those in this chapter) is to begin in the past, taking the readers back in time from the first sentence. Some of the writers in this chapter (such as Kress) not only start in the past, but also give the reader a general statement about the past:

> At 20 I was convinced that the single most important experience, without which my education would remain shamefully incomplete, was that of hopping a freight. Doubtless, my sense of education at that time (as well as my sense of what constituted good writing) was more than mildly seasoned by huge doses of the Beats—Allen Ginsberg, Gregory Corso, William Burroughs, Kenneth Patchen, Leroi Jones, and, of course, Jack Kerouac. That these writers were at the time considered non-scholarly, marginal, and were all but vilified by my literature teachers made them, I'm sure, that much more irresistible.

Other writers (such as Bosley) begin narrating and wait to characterize or give meaning to the events until later in their essays. Still another option is to make a general statement about the subject, and then begin narrating events. Notice Schwind-Pawlak's strategy:

> Parents—one word that can strike many emotions in children when said aloud. Some children will smile and think about how silly their dad looked when he put carrot sticks up his nose that very morning, while others will cringe when they think about how their mother picked them up from school last week wearing orange polyester pants and a green shirt, oblivious to the hard work that some fellow went through to create the color wheel. My own emotional state of mind seemed to run the gamut throughout childhood. I chose to blame my parents for all of the traumatic events that unfolded but took pride in my obvious independence during the successes. One of the most heinous crimes that my parents committed was "the soccer foul." If I could have ejected them from the game of life at that point, I would have.

She begins with a statement that has public resonance; that is, she makes a point that readers can immediately share, and then integrates her own particular experience.

Activity: After writing an introduction for your essay, share it with two classmates (either in class or by e-mail). Each classmate should write an alternative introduction using an entirely different strategy. Do the same for each classmate. After each writer has seen the others' alternatives to his or her introduction, discuss the strategies and decide if they might inspire changes. (Do not be afraid to borrow ideas from your peers. The best writers take inspiration from others: J. R. R. Tolkien, author of *The Lord of the Rings*, consistently took advice from his friend C. S. Lewis, author of many books, including *The Chronicles of Narnia*.)

How Should I Conclude?

Perhaps the most popular strategy for concluding a remembering essay is to explain the significance and/or public resonance in the last paragraph. All the writers in this chapter end their essays by explaining the importance of their memory, and some writers, such as Bosley, even suggest that others can share the personal significance:

> It's a contest no one should want to win. Our mothers should not have such dreams for us. Our mothers should not have such loneliness.

Here, Bosley offers her own discovery, the truth of why she did not win the Junior Miss contest, a conclusion that is both deeply personal and shared. Schwind-Pawlak also explains the significance of her memory in her conclusion:

> The relationship that I have with my parents has changed very much throughout the years. The polyester pants don't bother me anymore, but the carrot sticks still make me laugh. While their "soccer foul" embarrassed and angered me at the time, I understand and appreciate it now. My mother was angry <u>FOR</u> me. She was hurt <u>FOR</u> me. Through the pages of time, I can look back and see that, more often than not, I embarrassed her. She never stopped feeling for me, loving me, or protecting me. I have grown enough to realize that, though I often pointed out my parent's fouls, they scored countless goals that I didn't even notice.

Most of the conclusions in the chapter readings work similarly. In some way, they all communicate the main idea, the significance of their memories. For example, in Mockensturm's essay, the conclusion brings together his own memories and his girls' education:

> The girls have Russian language lessons in Mrs. Rath's old room at the top of the stairwell. Sometimes I'll stand in the doorway and picture the room as it was back in '75, gazing around, putting old friends in their seats. Whenever I'm reading Steinbeck, my memory goes back to this classroom, the library, and Mrs. Hulda Rath's quiet ways and I get the urge to plop down and read *Cannery Row*.

Kress's conclusion follows suit, but is perhaps more subtle than the others:

> Almost half a day later, around midnight, the train crunched into Chicago, where I hopped off, exhausted and exhilarated. As my shaky train-legs hit the gravel of the roadbed, I thought I heard a threatening shout, so I ran, tripped mostly, over the 50 or so tracks and platforms and switchings, down a steep embankment. Right into the middle of some run-down neon-shod shopping strip near 95th Street on the South Side—bars and liquor stores and boarded-up groceries, card readers, barber colleges, and storefront churches, groups of men hanging on the corners drinking from passed-around rumpled paper bags. Here was a whole gallery of street life like nothing I'd ever seen. Somehow the rickety freight ride and all that drama and lure of the past two days quickly dissipated, replaced by an urgent sense of new gaps in my learning, of new educational possibilities.

Notice that he does not explain specifically what he learned, nor does he draw attention to his present perspective ("looking back, I now realize . . . "). Instead, he leaves his readers in the past, alone in Chicago. The conclusion actually dramatizes his main point: along with the younger, more naïve Kress, we are left in the gaps of his learning.

Writer's Voice

Exploring Options

As we explain in the **Introduction,** writers all have voices—whether they know it or not. Some voices are extravagant; others are simple. Some are solemn, others light or even comedic. Most, however, are somewhere between these extremes.

Creating a voice involves both choosing what to say and how to say it: a writer with a sober voice would probably not make several allusions to a silly television show (unless she was suggesting something about its value). However, good writers can characterize the content of their texts by creating a certain voice. For example, a good humorist can make a solemn occasion feel light—even giddy. And a writer with a strong, sober voice can make us look seriously at frivolous subjects like teen magazines.

A writer's voice, then, characterizes the ideas in a text. It creates the mood in which the reader will approach the ideas. Imagine walking into a party and the host greets you at the door: "Hey! Look what the cat dragged in!" Her interaction would prompt you to assume that the party is rather informal and festive. But the host could also greet you more soberly: "Hello. Please come in. May I please take your coat?" In this case, you would probably assume the affair is formal. In other words, the host creates a particular mood for the incoming guests. Likewise, a writer creates the mood in which readers will enter the text. And this can be accomplished in a variety of ways.

In general, you might ask yourself how you feel about the memory—and how, in turn, you want the reader to feel about the point you are making. Do you want the reader to enter your text (and walk away from your text) feeling solemn, giddy, or something in between? Here are some general strategies to consider.

Using Figurative Language: Figurative language is nonliteral. It goes beyond the basic definitions of words and uses them to suggest imaginative connections between ideas. We will discuss four types of figurative language here.

Metaphor: A comparison of one thing to another in which one thing is made to share the characteristics of another: Her home was a sanctuary, where we felt healed spiritually and psychologically.

Simile: A comparison of two seemingly unrelated things using *like* or *as*: "Life is like a box of chocolates."

With simile and metaphor, the nature of the comparisons can help create voice. For example, Forrest Gump's simile, above, fits with his uncomplicated and easygoing character. A box of chocolates is a simple, pleasant surprise, and so it equates with his character. (It certainly would not be fitting for Gump to say, "Life is like a raging volcanic explosion bursting forth from the fires of the earth.") Notice how Schwind-Pawlak uses a metaphor:

> At that moment I wasn't sure that I would ever be able to forgive my parents for what happened that day, but, as far as I can recall, I began loving her again within the week. I am sure that she either cooked my favorite dinner, told a corny joke, or told me how much she loved me to make that lump of anger fade away.

Several features of this passage help create Schwind-Pawlak's voice. Among them is the metaphor "lump of anger." It is important that her anger is portrayed as a lump and not a mountain or a raging river. The smaller, more manageable, lump fits the mood of a small child. We get the sense from her language (as well as her point in the conclusion) that she is effectively over the childhood emotions the situation brought on.

> **Understatement:** A claim that is deliberately less forceful or dramatic than reality: Hurricanes tend to create a little wind.

> **Hyperbole:** A deliberate exaggeration: I'm so hungry, I could eat a horse.

These strategies lend a certain layer of informality to writing. That is, writers who are attempting to lay low, to remain seemingly invisible, or to remain sober and formal usually refrain from hyperbole and understatement.

Choosing Details: The details one chooses help create voice. Both Bosley and Schwind-Pawlak focus on their mothers, but notice the different details we get about them:

> Some children will smile and think about how silly their dad looked when he put carrot sticks up his nose that very morning, while others will cringe when they think about how their mother picked them up from school last week wearing orange polyester pants and a green shirt, oblivious to the hard work that some fellow went through to create the color wheel.

Schwind-Pawlak's details about her parents create a comedic voice. While her subject could be approached with gravity (she does, after all, give up on competitive sports), she casts the situation, and her own state of mind, lightly. However, Bosley's voice is not comedic. The details create a more solemn writerly presence:

> My mother had secret hopes. Finally divorced for the second time from the same man, my father, she sat with me and gave her own running commentary about who was cute, who smiled too much, who would find a handsome husband. My mother, having always been a little to a lot overweight, excelled at swimming, and she told me much later that she chose swimming because she didn't feel fat in the water. Her sister was the cheerleader, but she was a swimmer, too heavy for a short skirt of her own, she said.

Bosley's details create a different voice. This is not someone looking back with ease or with laughter. Her voice is more melancholy. Because she offers more sensitive information than Schwind-Pawlak (her mother's self-consciousness and rocky marital history rather than orange polyester pants), the reader is apt to experience the memory with more sensitivity, even with sadness.

As you consider your own writing, ask yourself how you want to project yourself: darkly reflective, comfortable, learned, free-spirited? Your decision will, then, influence what details you mention and what moments you emphasize. The details will affect how the reader understands you (as a writer) and the ideas you communicate. (And this is a powerful lesson about writing: it not only conveys ideas, but also shapes how people feel about those ideas.)

Choosing Allusions:

An allusion is a reference to some cultural or historical text, person, figure, or event: The high school's sit-in was not necessarily a Boston Tea Party. As with figurative language, the nature of an allusion can help create voice. Notice Aunty D.'s allusion:

> While *Wonder Years'* kids vicariously experienced how a Velveteen Rabbit became Real, that day in Hawai'i, for a little island girl, The Aloha Spirit became REAL. The little girl grew up, and she and her three siblings left their safe corner of the world. All four chose careers of service and (Hawaiian) hospitality, infusing perfect strangers with The Aloha Spirit.

The reference to *Wonder Years*, a light family television sitcom, adds to Aunty D.'s informal and inviting voice. You can imagine how allusions to more serious subjects (such as a war) might create a different kind of voice. Kress's allusion to the Beat writers of the mid-twentieth century also creates a particular voice—one that is reflective, curious, and literary.

Using Sentence Length:

Sentence structure is perhaps the most powerful, yet most invisible, tool a writer has for creating voice. Sentence length, specifically, can create a wide variety of different effects, depending on the context (or material surrounding the sentence). Long, winding sentences, which travel in and out of various ideas before returning the reader to the original path, can create a self-reflective and sophisticated voice, one that seems thoughtful of the complexities. Short sentences can create a determined voice. Notice the difference between the following:

> Childhood was a gas.
>
> Childhood was a raucous journey of twists and turns in which each moment was its own forever and every day a monument.

While the metaphors used certainly help create distinct voices, the sentence length also helps characterize the writer. (How would you characterize each writer?)

Although sentence length alone does not automatically create a particular voice, it figures into the process. Notice, again, Bosley's passage and how the sentence length tugs and pulls at the reader:

> My mother had secret hopes. Finally divorced for the second time from the same man, my father, she sat with me and gave her own running commentary about who was cute, who smiled too much, who would find a handsome husband.

The first sentence is short—and because of the content, it is almost a whisper. The second, longer sentence takes the reader further into the idea. Both sentences, working together, create the sensation of a living person telling a story. The movement, the back and forth between long and short sentences, helps conjure the sense of a real human telling a real story. The content of those sentences, then, helps communicate the feelings and emotional complexities of that human.

Learning about Voice: To become more aware of writer's voice, make a study of various written texts in your everyday life. Over the next few days, as you read newspaper or magazine articles, textbooks, syllabi, and advertisements, describe in a few words the voice of the writer and then explain in a sentence or two what particulars from the written text helped to create that voice. For example, did the writer use figurative language in a particular way? Did he or she include certain details that helped create a certain mood or feeling? And so on.

Activities

1. Bring several paragraphs of any written text (such as an advertisement, a newspaper article, etc.) to class. Describe the writer's voice in a few words, then write a paragraph in which you explain what particular aspects of the writing (figurative language, details, word choice, sentence structure, and so on) helped to create that voice.

2. Share your written text for #1 with several classmates, asking them to describe its voice and explain, in writing, what particular aspects of the text helped to create its voice. Then in groups, discuss the similarities and differences in your responses.

3. After your discussion (for #2), write a paragraph or two explaining how you now perceive the voice of the written text. How did your ideas change as a result of the discussion?

4. Rewrite the text you found for #1, changing its voice. Be certain that you express the same ideas while changing the writer's voice. Then describe the new voice in a few words and explain what specific changes in the writing (figurative language, details, word choice, and so on) created the new voice.

5. Rewrite the text you found for #1 above again, this time creating a third voice. If you created a drastically different voice for #4, make the voice only slightly different this time. If you created a slightly different voice, make this one drastically different. Then describe the new voice and explain what specific changes in the writing created it.

6. Ask several other people to read the original text (#1) and your rewrites (#4 or #5) and to describe the voice(s) of each. How are their descriptions similar to or different from your own?

7. Do images have a voice? Find an image, without words, and describe its voice. Then ask others to describe the voice of the same image. Discuss the reasons for similarities and differences in your descriptions.

8. Three of the writers in this chapter also appear in later chapters. Of the three, choose your favorite (Cindy Bosley, Leonard Kress, or Jennifer Schwind-Pawlak) and read his or her essay in another chapter. In your own words, describe the writer's voice. Does it change from essay to essay or is it the same? How? Illustrate your points with particular examples from the two essays. Bosley appears again in Chapter 2, Kress in Chapter 8, and Schwind-Pawlak in Chapter 5.

Revision Strategies

In revising an essay about remembering, you will need to focus on the significance of the memory. Just telling the reader what you remember is not enough. Your reader will be more engaged if you describe the experience with vivid details, yet too many details—and not enough significance—will bore the reader. These and other concerns must be addressed through revision.

Consider the following revision strategies:

- Review this chapter, keeping your essay in mind. You might (1) explore your Invention notes, looking for helpful ideas and/or respond further in writing to relevant Invention questions; (2) review the **Rhetorical Tools, Organizational Strategies,** and **Writer's Voice** sections with an eye toward making appropriate changes; and (3) review several of the essays, noting the way the writers in this chapter approached this type of essay.

- Set aside at least as much time to revise as you took with invention and delivery.

- Create distance between you and your writing by getting away from it for a few days if possible or a few hours at least.

- Read your paper aloud to hear how it sounds or have someone else read it aloud to you.

- Print out a hard copy of your paper and read it carefully in a place different from where you wrote it.

- Figure out your writing strategy by noticing how the parts of your essay work together to support your main point. Consider making an outline of your essay to help you see this.

- Have someone else read and respond to your essay.

Global Revision Questions

Invention (What have you learned by exploring your topic?)

- **Point of Contact:** What other ideas did you consider writing about before selecting this one? Why was this idea more worth pursuing than the others?

- **Analysis:** How has your exploration of this topic gone beyond your initial ideas and questions about it? In what ways have your ideas moved beyond your initial biases and perceptions—and beyond the common beliefs of your reader?

- **Public Resonance:** How might your essay be relevant to, or matter to, your reader? And what might be the consequence(s) of your essay? How might the reader think or act differently after reading it?

Delivery (What writing decisions have you made as part of your writing strategy?)

- **Rhetorical Tools:** The purpose of your remembering essay should be more than just recalling a memory: you should find meaning in the memory. The rhetorical tools discussed earlier in this chapter will help you go beyond the personal, thus engaging the reader with the significance of the past experience.

  - What is the main idea of your essay, and how have you conveyed that idea to the reader? What, besides your *intended* main idea, might the reader imagine your main idea to be? How might you help the reader hear what you are trying to say?

  - What gaps might you fill in to help your reader understand the significance of your memory? What additional details might bring the memory to life for the reader? How might your title, introduction, and conclusion provide more helpful information regarding the main point of your essay?

  - One of the most important elements of revision is deleting superfluous information. Where might the reader lose interest or get bogged down because you have overexplained an idea or provided too much detail? What words, sentences, or paragraphs can be safely deleted from your essay?

- **Organizational Strategies:** You might begin by describing, or outlining, the structure of your essay to get a better sense of your overall organizational strategy. Then consider the following questions: How might you rearrange sections to allow the reader to better understand your ideas? How might you rearrange ideas within paragraphs? What ideas might be more helpful to the reader if placed earlier, or later, or near some other idea? How might connections and relationships between ideas be made more clear to the reader?

- **Writer's Voice:** Describe your writer's voice. In revision, writers consider the way they sound to the reader. While writers consider their voice as they compose, revising allows them to take a step back and re-see (or re-hear) the way they might sound to others. Is your writer's voice appropriate to your subject matter? What about your writer's voice is inviting to the reader? What about your writer's voice might alienate the reader? What changes might make your writer's voice more inviting?

Peer Review: Your instructor may arrange for someone else to read your essay—and for you to read someone else's. Or it may be up to you to arrange this on your own. Any interested person can provide helpful feedback, but working with a conscientious classmate may be especially helpful—to both of you. Peer review can be done in various ways. Your instructor may provide specific guidelines and, of course, you are always free to try different approaches outside the classroom. Some general advice, however, can be given to ensure that you work efficiently and get positive results.

The Writer Should

- Provide the reader with a readable copy of the rough draft.
- Help to focus the reader by asking questions about several major concerns you have. Write down your questions, wording them carefully.

The Reader Should

- Carefully read the draft at least twice, then respond in writing (not just verbally) to the writer's main concerns.
- Be specific. In addition to saying what you think, say *why* you think it.
- Be encouraging *and* honest. Providing only praise will not help the writer, yet phrasing your comments in too negative terms might be discouraging.

1. Write down your overall impression of the essay.

2. Write down a summary of the writer's main points. (For example, instead of saying, "I understood what you were saying," say, "I think you were saying. . . ." Then, if the writer was not trying to say that at all, he or she knows that in this case the point was not successfully communicated.)

3. Write down specific responses to the writer's questions about the essay.

4. Write down any major concerns that you feel the writer should have raised but didn't.

The Writer Should

- Not defend his or her essay, but instead view it as a work in progress.
- Listen carefully, ask questions only to clarify what the reviewer means, take notes on *all* verbal comments for later reference, and thank the reader for his or her help.
- Later, carefully consider all comments and make only the changes that he or she considers to be appropriate.

You might do peer review face to face, discussing the papers as you go; or you might read and write comments without any verbal discussion between writer and reader. You might even do peer review over the Internet. If you are pressed for time, or if you have difficulty staying focused on the work at hand, exchanging written comments without discussion can be an efficient peer review strategy.

Exploring Ideas in Groups (Peer Review)

Prepare a Briefing: For this activity prepare a written briefing of your essay ideas. Your briefing should be less than 100 words long and include the following: a summary of your essay ideas thus far, including a statement of your main, the main support for your main idea, and an explanation of why your ideas matter. In addition to the 100-word briefing, for your own benefit you should also list: at least one (and preferably three) strengths of your essay, at least one (and preferably three) weaknesses of your essay, questions that you have for your group members about your essay.

Brief Classmates Orally and Everyone Take Notes: Do not pass around your briefing for others to read. Instead, use it (along with your strengths, weaknesses, and questions) for your own reference as you orally brief your classmates on your ideas. Also, take notes throughout the briefing/discussion process. Whether talking about your ideas or someone else's, take notes to stay focused, to generate ideas, and to record ideas that you can refer to and consider further later on.

Work Efficiently through the Briefing/Discussion Process

- A briefing should provide the audience with necessary information in a concise manner.
- Work in groups of three or four; be focused and work efficiently.
- One person goes first, briefing other group members on his or her essay ideas, concluding the briefing by asking, and/or inviting others to ask, questions.
- Explore ideas through focused and educationally valuable discussion for ten minutes.
- Then repeat the briefing and discussion procedure with another student until everyone has had a chance to brief his or her group members and explore his or her essay ideas for ten minutes.

Explore Further following the Discussion: Following the briefing/discussion, spend ten minutes reflecting, through writing, on your exploratory discussion. Do not merely write down things that jump out at you, but use this writing time to explore further, noticing important points that might not be so obvious.

- How do you think differently now than you did before your group discussion?
- What new ideas did you consider that you had not thought about before?
- How does your thinking now go beyond your initial ideas, biases, perceptions, beliefs, and the common beliefs of the reader?
- What idea might you talk about that would change the way someone thinks or acts, how might someone think or act differently, and what might be the positive consequence to others if someone thought or acted in this new way?

Explore Further outside of Class: Go home and explore further. Reflect on your original briefing, the subsequent discussion, and the writing you did afterward. Look for engaging ideas. Try to identify areas where your thinking changed. Do more writing as a way of exploring ideas.

Name the Fruit of Your Exploration: In writing, explain the most significant way(s) that your thinking changed as a result of all the steps above. (Turn this writing in next class period.)

CONSIDERING CONSEQUENCES

While writers consider consequences throughout the writing process, this text draws attention to them here as a post-writing activity, to remind you that after an idea is communicated, consequences follow. The act of writing does not end with turning in an essay or writing a letter. Instead, that is just the beginning.

Finding meaning in past experience can have interesting consequences, both for the writer and for the reader. Writers often discover as they write; they don't just write down what they already know. And if the writer finds meaning, the reader is likely to find meaning, too. What might be the consequences of your essay for this chapter? That is, what effect might your ideas have on your reader's thoughts and actions? Consider these questions:

- Will the reader better understand the issue about which you wrote?
- Is the reader likely to think or behave differently?
- What might be the benefits to others? How might others be harmed?
- Who besides your instructor might benefit from your ideas?
- What might be the effect of these consequences on you, the writer?

Activities

The Consequences of Your Essay

1. List as many individuals as you can imagine whose thinking and/or actions might change if they were to read the essay you wrote for this chapter. For each individual you list, name the possible change in his or her thinking and/or action. (As you consider consequences upon your reader, consider the "ripple effect" of those consequences. If your reader thinks or behaves differently, what is the impact of that thinking or behavior on others?)

2. Discuss the possible consequences of your essay with others. Explain what your essay is about and then ask for feedback. You might ask the following questions: What impact might this essay have on the reader? How might this essay change the way someone thinks or acts? How did it make you think differently? How might it make you act differently?

3. List three other forms of delivery that you might have used to express your idea (report, letter, poster, screenplay, Web site, speech, song, poem, action). How might the consequences of your message have been different if delivered by way of these other forms?

The Consequences of the Chapter Readings

1. What reading in this chapter might actually influence you to think or act differently? What specific part of the essay influenced you the most, and why? Explain what element of the reading helped to change your mind, or explain how certain elements worked together to help change your mind.

2. How might *you* think and/or behave differently because of one of the readings? And, how might *others* benefit, or be harmed, by your new way of thinking and/or acting?

3. How might *the writers* in this chapter be influenced by what they write? How might they think or act differently? How might they be treated differently by others?

Considering Images

1. Explain how someone might view one of the following images differently after reading the related essay. Be specific when you describe the way in which someone might view the image before reading the essay, and how it might be viewed differently after the reading.

   A. The "No Trespassing" sign (page 55) after reading Len Kress's "A *Beat* Education."
   B. The evening gown (page 9) after reading Cindy Bosley's "How I Lost the Junior Miss Pageant."
   C. The "No Trespassing" sign (page 55) after reading "How I Lost the Junior Miss Pageant," Jennifer Schwind-Pawlak's "The Thrill of Victory . . . The Agony of Parents," or Steve Mockensturm's "The Grapes of Mrs. Rath."

2. Find an image not in this book and explain how someone might view it differently after having read one of the essays in this chapter.

3. Take a snapshot of life, either with a camera or describing it in a paragraph or two, and then write an essay explaining how a person might view that snapshot differently after reading one of the essays in this chapter or your own essay.

The Consequences of Everyday Writing

1. Identify one written work besides an essay (for example, a novel, short story, screenplay, the text of a speech, and so on) that conveys to its audience the significance of some past experience. Explain how a memory is used to convey the point (the significance) and how the audience might as a result think or act differently.

2. Respond to questions 1–3 under "The Consequences of the Chapter Readings" for the work you named in #1 above.

Considering Images

Find an image that encourages viewers to look into their pasts, retrieve an event or situation, and examine it from the present perspective. In a paragraph, explain how the image encourages the viewer to do this and how the viewer *might* think or act differently as a result. Attach a copy of the image to your paragraph.

EVERYDAY RHETORIC

Writing, Speech, and Action

The invention and delivery strategies discussed earlier in this chapter apply to other forms of communication as well. Chapter 13 discusses other forms of communication that can be used to make an argument. For practice applying this chapter's rhetorical tools and strategies to other forms, you might do one of the following activities.

Write a Letter: Communicate your main idea and support in the form of a letter. Select a specific and appropriate individual to receive your letter. But do not merely put your essay in a letter format. Instead, revise it so that your content and style match the letter-writing situation, in which the writer and reader share a somewhat different relationship than they do in an essay.

Give a Speech: Communicate the idea from your essay in the form of a speech to your classmates. Instead of merely reading your essay, which will bore the audience, prepare note cards and practice your delivery. Remember to provide verbal cues, use visual aids if helpful, and *present* the argument without arguing *with* or *at* your listeners.

Discuss: Explain your essay to a group of classmates, then open the floor to discussion. Notice how the discussion evolves. Then summarize the discussion in a paragraph or two and explain why it was or was not fruitful.

Design a Bumper Sticker: Design a bumper sticker expressing the point of your remembering essay. Get others' responses to it, then write an essay explaining how successful you think the bumper sticker is.

Take Action: In addition to speaking and writing, you might convey your idea by taking action. For example, if you see a problem with beauty pageants, you might protest one; or if you see the benefits of beauty pageants, you might organize one. Action can attempt to influence government policy; it can attempt to get others involved; it can be individual—such as riding a train as a life/learning experience or being hospitable to others. Then, in an essay, discuss the action you took, why you took it, and what its consequences were.

Exploring Visual Rhetoric

It can be argued that images, too, use rhetoric. And by looking at how images work, we can apply some of the important concepts of rhetoric, not just to writing and speaking, but to images as well. Looking at visual rhetoric can also help us to better understand how rhetoric is used in writing and speech.

Consider All the Images in This Chapter: The images in this text are often subtle; their meaning is not always obvious at first glance. (A subtle smile, for example, might go unnoticed by a less observant person, while a hearty laugh is hard to miss.) These subtle images encourage different ways of thinking. They invite the reader to look closely, not just at the elements of the particular image, but also at the way those elements relate to each other to create meaning—and at the way they relate to the written text. Throughout the chapter, the written text and the images sometimes interact to create interesting ideas.

1. How does the image of an evening gown relate to Cindy Bosley's essay "How I Lost the Junior Miss Pageant"? How do the specific elements of that particular image relate to Bosley's essay and more specifically to the significance of her essay?

2. How *might* the image of a "No Trespassing" sign relate to each of the following written texts?
   - "A *Beat* Education" by Len Kress
   - "How I Lost the Junior Miss Pageant" by Cindy Bosley
   - "The Grapes of Mrs. Rath" by Steve Mockensturm
   - The **Point of Contact** section of this chapter
   - The **Public Resonance** section of this chapter
   - The **Writer's Voice** section of this chapter
   - The **Considering Consequences** section of this chapter
   - Some other section of this chapter

As you consider these various possible relationships between image and written text, remember that subtleties can be difficult to detect—and to describe. These subtle relationships encourage you to develop different ways of thinking. As you explore these relationships, keep in mind the significance of the written text ("A *Beat* Education" by Leonard Kress, for example) and the significance, or point of, the image. Also keep in mind the particulars of both written text and visual image that lead you to understanding their significance.

Find an Image That Relates to Your Essay: What image might you use in conjunction with the essay you wrote for this chapter?

1. Write a caption for the image.

2. In writing, explain the relationship between the image and your text. Consider the following ideas:

    - How does the image support or help to explain the text of the essay?
    - What is the theme of the image? What idea does it convey?
    - What specific elements of the image convey the main idea and the support for that idea?
    - How might the reader view the image differently after having read your essay?
    - How might the reader be confused by the relationship of your essay and image?

3. Show the image to several people, then ask each person to read your explanation. Then ask them how they now view the image differently.

4. Describe the rhetoric of your own photograph, or image, using the "Analyzing an Image" questions in Chapter 13 on page 694.

Find Your Own Remembering Image: Most people have quite a few remembering images of their own. Look through family photo albums, your high school yearbook, and so on in search of a few good remembering photographs.

1. Find one photo that you would say has a theme. What is the theme and what particular elements of the photo help to convey it?

2. Give your photo from #1 to several people, asking them what they think the photograph says. Then compare their way of seeing the image to your own way of seeing it. How and why do you see it differently from them? How and why do you see it similarly?

3. Find several images (at least five) that can be seen as the parts of a larger photo essay. What is the main idea of the photo essay, and how do the individual photographs work together to convey that idea? In an essay explain how particular elements of individual images and the relationship of the images to each other work to express an overall main idea.

4. What is the significance of the photo essay you created for #3 above? How might arranging the photographs differently change the significance of the photo essay?

Images in the Media

1. Find several old magazines, preferably from when you were in elementary school, and study the images. Note at least three images that stand out in each magazine—perhaps the cover image, advertisements, or photographs accompanying stories. Using the "Analyzing an Image" questions in Chapter 13 to help you explore, explain what ideas these images convey about the time period in which the magazine was published.

   A. Select the most striking image you found and analyze it carefully. What seems to be the main idea of the image? How do content, framing, composition, focus, lighting, texture, angle, and vantage point help to convey the idea? What public concern does the image speak to? To whom might this concern matter? How might people benefit by exploring the photograph's possible meanings?

   B. Does one of the images you found look as if it is from a different time period? Going beyond obvious matters of content, how do visual elements such as framing, composition, focus, lighting, texture, angle, and vantage point suggest that the image is not from a magazine published more recently?

   C. Based on the images you studied in old magazines, what conclusions can you draw about the time period in which they were published? Write an essay explaining your conclusions, being specific about how the particular elements of certain images convey important information about an earlier time.

2. Find an old or recent comic strip that speaks to your past. What elements of the comic strip, including both visual image and written text, capture something from your past?

3. Compare several old comic strips to several current ones, noticing differences that are a result of their time periods. What conclusions can you draw? Are the visual elements of the comic strips significantly different, somewhat different, or the same? Be specific in discussing their visual elements.

4. Find any old image from your past, whether it be from a board game, a children's book, a TV show, or something else. What particular elements of that image are unique to that time period? What elements of that image, if any, are uncommon in images produced today? What conclusions about the past can you draw based on the image?

Chapter Contents

Explaining
Relationships

What relationship do you see in this image?
What is the nature of that relationship?

The human beings depended on the aid and charity of the animals. Only through interdependence could the human beings survive. Families belonged to clans, and it was by the clan that the human being joined with the animal and plant world. Life on the high arid plateau became viable when the human beings were able to imagine

In the above passage, from "Landscape, History, and the Pueblo Imagination," Silko explains the conceptual and physical relationship between the pueblo Native Americans and their surrounding landscape. It was a subtle and complex relationship, one that went far beyond harvesting crops and extracting resources. The land, for the Pueblo people, helped them to know who they were; it helped them to have a particular identity and culture. Silko's explanation sheds light on this particular relationship.

Explaining relationships is common everyday work: People on city councils explore the relationship between neighborhoods to help the cities better understand ethnic diversity; corporate executives constantly try to understand the nature of the relationship between their own companies and their competitors; and certainly, everyone is aware of the ongoing attempts by political leaders to explain the relationships between countries or religions. In a shrinking world in which people of vastly different value systems attempt to coexist, explaining relationships is more than an exercise—it is an act of survival.

The value of discovering meaning in relationships is immeasurable. In fact, many writers, theorists, and scientists suggest that discovering the nature of any one thing is only possible through the examination of its relationships. It might even be argued that the greatest philosophical and scientific discoveries have involved the discovery of relationships—between, for example, atomic elements, religious practices, geological events, historical figures, or heavenly bodies.

themselves as sisters and brothers to the badger, antelope, clay, yucca, and sun. Not until they could find a viable relationship to the terrain, the landscape they found themselves in, could they emerge. **"**

—*Leslie Marmon Silko*

In all academic disciplines, people work to understand and communicate the nature of relationships:

- In a computer technology course, students study the relationship between an individual computer and a network of computers, or between a group of users and the Internet.
- In an anthropology course, students explore the relationship between a particular waterway and the ruins of a past civilization.
- In a biology course, students and faculty work to see the relationship between two forms of bacteria.
- In an interior design course, students examine the relationship between a large interior office space and a front entrance to a particular building.

This chapter explores relationships—between places, things, events, people, and even ideas. The goal here is to investigate, to seek out some of the hidden dynamics of relationships, to discover the nature of a relationship, or even to discover a relationship where one is not necessarily seen.

2 This chapter will help you discover a topic (a particular relationship), explore that relationship in depth, and explain the nature of the relationship in writing. The following essays will provide valuable insight and necessary strategies for exploring relationships. After reading the essays, you can begin looking for a particular relationship in one of two ways:

1. Go to the **Point of Contact** section to find a relationship from your everyday life.
2. Choose one of the **Ideas for Writing** that follow the essays.

After finding a topic, go to the **Analysis** section to begin developing the evaluation.

READINGS

■

In the following essays, the authors deal with various possible relationships. While their ideas and stylistic strategies vary, these essays also share some features. Notice, for instance, that the writers offer very specific details about the relationship—sometimes through narrative, sometimes through description. Some writers, such as Meek and Thuma, also use dialogue to emphasize key moments and better illustrate the nature of the relationship. All the writers do more than simply relay details about a relationship; instead, they use particular details to make an interesting point that the reader can carry away from the essay, a point that has public resonance. In other words, each writer makes a point about relationships that is bigger than any one particular detail—or any one relationship. In some essays, such as Steinbeck's, that point is obvious. In others, such as Thuma's, it is subtle, hidden inside the details of the essay.

The Ring of Truth: My Child Is Growing Up

Jessie Thuma

"The Ring of Truth: My Child Is Growing Up" appeared in the March 5, 2001 issue of Newsweek. *How does this essay not only speak to the particular relationship between Thuma and her daughter but also to a larger relationship issue? As you read, consider how you might participate in Thuma's discussion of relationships.*

1 "Mom, can I get a belly ring?" My 14-year-old daughter plunks the *Newsweek* magazine down on the kitchen table and points to the picture of a young woman's taut, tan stomach. Nestled in her bellybutton is a sparkling white stone. And radiating outward from the stone is a sun-shaped tattoo.

2 "IT'S SO . . ." my daughter searches for the right word.

3 "Cool," she finishes lamely. What she really means is "sexy." That chip of crystal begs to be framed by a top that barely covers a girl's ribcage and by jeans that barely cover her hips.

4 "No," I tell her, handing back the magazine. "Absolutely not!"

5 "And I hope that's the end of it," I say to my husband while he makes his coffee the next morning.

6 But that isn't the end of it. My daughter stands next to me doing the dishes, or putting away the groceries, or arguing about why her brother should be given up for adoption, when suddenly she'll pop the question again: "Can I get a belly ring?"

7 Sometimes we're lucky. Requests vanish into thin air, bumped off the list by a newer fad, a lesser evil. But other requests—the ones that force us to confront our children's emerging sexuality and drive for independence—echo in our ears long after we answer them. Like many

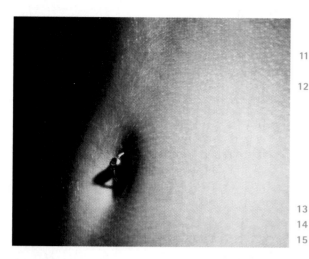

cine. "And her bottom line on bellybutton piercing? It hurts!"

11   "I don't care," my daughter says, tossing her hair. "I want to suffer!"

12   It turns out my daughter has already visited the local tattoo parlor and picked up an information sheet on the postoperative care of navel piercing. I am speechless. I cannot believe that a child of mine has set foot into that store, with its window displays of a pierced head and eviscerated corpse. "Mom," my daughter sniffs. "Those are just decorations!"

13   "You're not to go in there," I tell her. "Ever!"

14   So this is where belly rings lead.

15   "It costs $40." My daughter presses on. "But I could go somewhere else and get Novocain so it won't hurt at all. Look!" she says, lifting up her shirt to reveal her flat stomach and the narrow curve of her waist. "I need a belly ring!" She grins.

things that teenagers want, this request brings me and my husband face to face with the larger questions that vex parents of adolescents: What to give? What to withhold?

8   My daughter doesn't ask for $42 pants from the Gap or $38 shirts from Abercrombie & Fitch. She doesn't wear makeup, unless you count the dozen pots of flavored lip gloss that rattle around the bottom of her orange book bag. She gets straight A's. My daughter doesn't have a boyfriend; she isn't obsessed with boys. She dreams about meeting a "totally hot guy" when we go camping for a week at a deserted state forest, but she is prepared to settle for reading a stack of books next to the lake if the boy thing doesn't work out. The extent of her rebellion is to sneak into the occasional R-rated movie. I have much to be grateful for.

9   So because it is something my daughter really wants, I wrestle with the question of the belly ring. And each time I argue against it, my daughter senses my ambivalence.

10   "There is," I tell her (stretching the truth), "a young woman at work who has pierces in places you don't even want to know about." I am sitting at the computer, and my daughter, tall and slender, is leaning against the door frame. Maybe I can frighten her out of wanting a belly ring. After all, this is the same teenager who cried hysterically when she got her hepatitis B vac-

16   I look at my daughter. Despite the time she spends in front of the mirror doing an inventory of phantom blemishes, imagining how her hair would look if she dyed it pink like Gwen Stefani, she is still oblivious to the fact that already she is beautiful. Men in passing cars stare at her. When she walks with my husband down the hallway at his work, her arm hooked through his, older women narrow their eyes in disapproval, thinking that my husband has himself a young, trophy girlfriend.

17   Within the small circle of the contested belly ring, my daughter and I see the same things: sexual allure, boyfriends, the instant acquisition of a Daring New Persona. I find the prospects alarming. There is part of me that would stop time here if I could, on the very edge of the changes I know are in store for my daughter, whether she gets a belly ring or not. "Come on, Mom," she says, laughing, leaning down to give me a kiss. "It's just a ring. I could always take it off."

18   She smells clean, like cucumbers and watermelon. I catch her hand, feeling the bones in her long fingers. Once acquired, knowledge and experience are hard to shed. "No," I tell her, "you only think you can take it off."

Exploring Ideas

1. Describe the relationship between Thuma and her daughter. Based on Thuma's essay, does it seem like a relationship you would enjoy having?

2. What is Thuma trying to achieve in this essay? Refer to specific passages from her essay to support your response.

3. If you were Thuma—and your daughter wanted a belly ring—would you let her get one? Explain why or why not.

4. Survey classmates, friends, co-workers, parents, and complete strangers (if you feel comfortable doing so) about belly rings. What do others think about the subject? Go beyond mere fashion ("They look nice." "I think they're disgusting.") and explore why some people are for or against them. Expand your survey to other piercings and even tattoos if you'd like. Then analyze your field research and report your findings. What can you conclude about the public's attitude toward belly rings, other piercings, and so on?

5. How might you respond to Thuma's essay, or how might you contribute to the discussion about belly rings? What interesting light can you shed on the issue?

Writing Strategies

1. Does the writer's daughter seem real to you? Why or why not?

2. What is most appealing about Thuma's essay? Is it the content, her word choice, the organization, her sentences, or a combination of these?

3. Does Thuma state her main idea? If so, identify her statement. If not, write your own thesis statement for this essay. Is the point clear to her reader?

4. Thuma uses small paragraphs. What is the effect of smaller paragraphs?

5. If you were workshopping Thuma's essay, would you suggest she cut anything? What, if anything, would you suggest that she add? Would you say she should start her last paragraph by writing "In conclusion" or by summarizing her main points?

Ideas for Writing

1. What relationship between two people can you discuss, focusing on a change taking place in the relationship? For example, you might show how two friends slowly drifted apart, how one person came to love another, how two people changed roles, or something else.

2. Recall an important point in a relationship you had with a parent or an older relative. What is the significance of the point both to you and to others?

> If responding to one of these ideas, go to the Analysis section of this chapter to begin developing ideas for your essay.

Americans and the Land

John Steinbeck

John Steinbeck wrote many novels and short stories including Of Mice and Men *(1937) and* The Grapes of Wrath, *which won a Pulitzer Prize in 1939. He was awarded the Nobel Prize for Literature in 1962. As you read "Americans and the Land," highlight or underline passages that help you understand Steinbeck's view on this topic, and jot down in the margin your initial reaction to Steinbeck's ideas.*

1   I have often wondered at the savagery and thoughtlessness with which our early settlers approached this rich continent. They came at it as though it were an enemy, which of course it was. They burned the forests and changed the rainfall; they swept the buffalo from the plains, blasted the streams, set fire to the grass, and ran a reckless scythe through the virgin and noble timber. Perhaps they felt that it was limitless and could never be exhausted and that a man could move on to new wonders endlessly. Certainly there are many examples to the contrary, but to a large extent the early people pillaged the country as though they hated it, as though they held it temporarily and might be driven off at any time.

2   This tendency toward irresponsibility persists in very many of us today; our rivers are poisoned by reckless dumping of sewage and toxic industrial wastes, the air of our cities is filthy and dangerous to breathe from the belching of uncontrolled products from combustion of coal, coke, oil, and gasoline. Our towns are girdled with wreckage and the debris of our toys—our automobiles and our packaged pleasures. Through uninhibited spraying against one enemy we have destroyed the natural balances our survival requires. All these evils can and must be overcome if America and Americans are to survive; but many of us still conduct ourselves as our ancestors did, stealing from the future for our clear and present profit.

3   Since the river-polluters and the air-poisoners are not criminal or even bad people, we must presume that they are heirs to the early conviction that sky and water are unowned and that they are limitless. In the light of our practices here at home it is very interesting to me to

read of the care taken with the carriers of our probes into space, to make utterly sure that they are free of pollution of any kind. We would not think of doing to the moon what we do every day to our own dear country.

4   When the first settlers came to America and dug in on the coast, they huddled in defending villages hemmed in by the sea on one side and by endless forests on the other, by Red Indians and, most frightening, the mystery of an unknown land extending nobody knew how far. And for a time very few cared or dared to find out. Our first Americans organized themselves and lived in a state of military alertness; every community built its blockhouse for defense. By law the men went armed and were required to keep their weapons ready and available. Many of them wore armor, made here or imported; on the East Coast, they wore the cuirass and helmet, and the Spaniards on the West Coast wore both steel armor and heavy leather to turn arrows.

5   On the East Coast, and particularly in New England, the colonists farmed meager lands close to their communities and to safety. Every man was permanently on duty for the defense of his family and his village; even the hunting parties went into the forest in force, rather like raiders than hunters, and their subsequent quarrels with the Indians, resulting in forays and even massacres, remind us that the danger was very real. A man took his gun along when he worked the land, and the women stayed close to their thick-walled houses and listened day and night for the signal of alarm. The towns they settled were permanent, and most of them exist today with their records of Indian raids, of slaughter, of scalpings, and of punitive counter-raids. The military leader of the community became the chief authority in time of trouble, and it was a long time before danger receded and the mystery could be explored.

6   After a time, however, brave and forest-wise men drifted westward to hunt, to trap, and eventually to bargain for the furs which were the first precious negotiable wealth America produced for trade and export. Then trading posts were set up as centers of collection and the exploring men moved up and down the rivers and crossed the mountains, made friends for mutual profit with the Indians, learned the wilderness techniques, so that these explorer-traders soon dressed, ate, and generally acted like the indigenous people around them. Suspicion lasted a long time, and was fed by clashes sometimes amounting to full-fledged warfare; but by now these Americans attacked and defended as the Indians did.

7   For a goodly time the Americans were travelers, moving about the country collecting its valuables, but with little idea of permanence; their roots and their hearts were in the towns and the growing cities along the eastern edge. The few who stayed, who lived among the Indians, adopted their customs and some took Indian wives and were regarded as strange and somehow treasonable creatures. As for their half-breed children, while the tribe sometimes adopted them they were unacceptable as equals in the eastern settlements.

8   Then the trickle of immigrants became a stream, and the population began to move westward—not to grab and leave but to settle and live, they thought. The newcomers were of peasant stock, and they had their roots in a Europe where they had been landless, for the possession of land was the requirement and the proof of a higher social class than they had known. In America they found beautiful and boundless land for the taking—and they took it.

9   It is little wonder that they went land-mad, because there was so much of it. They cut and burned the forests to make room for crops; they abandoned their knowledge of kindness to the land in order to maintain its usefulness. When they had cropped out a piece they moved on, raping the country like invaders. The topsoil, held by roots and freshened by leaf-fall, was left helpless to the spring freshets, stripped and eroded with the naked bones of clay and rock exposed. The destruction of the forests changed the rainfall, for the searching clouds could find no green and beckoning woods to draw them on and milk them. The merciless nineteenth century was like a hostile expedition for loot that seemed limitless. Uncountable buffalo were killed, stripped of their hides, and left to rot, a reservoir of permanent food supply eliminated. More than that, the land of the Great Plains was robbed of the manure of the herds. Then the plows went in and ripped off the protection of the buffalo grass and opened the helpless soil to quick water and slow drought and the mischievous winds that roamed through the Great Central Plains. There has always been more than enough desert in America; the new settlers, like overindulged children, created even more.

10   The railroads brought new hordes of land-crazy people, and the new Americans moved like locusts across the continent until the western sea put a boundary to their movements. Coal and copper and gold drew them on; they savaged the land, gold-dredged the rivers to skeletons of pebbles and debris. An aroused and

fearful government made laws for the distribution of public lands—a quarter section, one hundred and sixty acres, per person—and a claim had to be proved and improved; but there were ways of getting around this, and legally. My own grandfather proved out a quarter section for himself, one for his wife, one for each of his children, and, I suspect, acreage for children he hoped and expected to have. Marginal lands, of course, suitable only for grazing, went in larger pieces. One of the largest land-holding families in California took its richest holdings by a trick: By law a man could take up all the swamp or water-covered land he wanted. The founder of this great holding mounted a scow on wheels and drove his horses over thousands of acres of the best bottomland, then reported that he had explored it in a boat, which was true, and confirmed his title. I need not mention his name; his descendants will remember.

11   Another joker with a name still remembered in the West worked out a scheme copied many times in after years. Proving a quarter section required a year of residence and some kind of improvement—a fence, a shack—but once the land was proved the owner was free to sell it. This particular princely character went to the stews and skid rows of the towns and found a small army of hopeless alcoholics who lived for whisky and nothing else. He put these men on land he wanted to own, grubstaked them and kept them in cheap liquor until the acreage was proved, then went through the motions of buying it from his protégés and moved them and their one-room shacks on sled runners on to new quarter sections. Bums of strong constitution might prove out five or six homesteads for this acquisitive hero before they died of drunkenness.

12   It was full late when we began to realize that the continent did not stretch out to infinity; that there were limits to the indignities to which we could subject it. Engines and heavy mechanical equipment were allowing us to ravage it even more effectively than we had with fire, dynamite, and gang plows. Conservation came to us slowly, and much of it hasn't arrived yet. Having killed the whales and wiped out the sea otters and most of the beavers, the market hunters went to work on game birds; ducks and quail were decimated, and the passenger pigeon eliminated. In my youth I remember seeing a market hunter's gun, a three-gauge shotgun bolted to a frame and loaded to the muzzle with shingle nails. Aimed at a lake and the trigger pulled with a string, it slaughtered every living thing on the lake. The Pacific Coast pilchards were once the raw material for a great and continuing industry. We hunted them with aircraft far at sea until they were gone and the canneries had to be closed. In some of the valleys of the West, where the climate makes several crops a year available, which the water supply will not justify, wells were driven deeper and deeper for irrigation, so that in one great valley a million acre feet more of water was taken out than rain and melting snow could replace, and the water table went down and a few more years may give us a new desert.

13   The great redwood forests of the western mountains early attracted attention. These ancient trees, which once grew everywhere, now exist only where the last Ice Age did not wipe them out. And they were found to have value. The Sempervirens and the Gigantea, the two remaining species, make soft, straight-grained timber. They are easy to split into planks, shakes, fenceposts, and railroad ties, and they have a unique virtue: they resist decay, both wet and dry rot, and an inherent acid in them repels termites. The loggers went through the great groves like a barrage, toppling the trees—some of which were two thousand years old—and leaving no maidens, no seedlings or saplings on the denuded hills.

14   Quite a few years ago when I was living in my little town on the coast of California a stranger came in and bought a small valley where the Sempervirens redwoods grew, some of them three hundred feet high. We used to walk among these trees, and the light colored as though the great glass of the Cathedral at Chartres had strained and sanctified the sunlight. The emotion we felt in this grove was one

of awe and humility and joy; and then one day it was gone, slaughtered, and the sad wreckage of boughs and broken saplings left like nonsensical spoilage of the battle-ruined countryside. And I remember that after our rage there was sadness, and when we passed the man who had done this we looked away, because we were ashamed for him.

15   From early times we were impressed and awed by the fantastic accidents of nature, like the Grand Canyon and Yosemite and Yellowstone Park. The Indians had revered them as holy places, visited by the gods, and all of us came to have somewhat the same feeling about them. Thus we set aside many areas of astonishment as publicly owned parks; and though this may to a certain extent have been because there was no other way to use them, as the feelings of preciousness of the things we had been destroying grew in Americans, more and more areas were set aside as national and state parks, to be looked at but not injured. Many people loved and were in awe of the redwoods; societies and individuals bought groves of these wonderful trees and presented them to the state for preservation.

16   No longer do we Americans want to destroy wantonly, but our new-found sources of power—to take the burden of work from our shoulders, to warm us, and cool us, and give us light, to transport us quickly, and to make the things we use and wear and eat—these power sources spew pollution on our country, so that the rivers and streams are becoming poisonous and lifeless. The birds die for the lack of food; a noxious cloud hangs over our cities that burns our lungs and reddens our eyes. Our ability to conserve has not grown with our power to create, but this slow and sullen poisoning is no longer ignored or justified. Almost daily, the pressure of outrage among Americans grows. We are no longer content to destroy our beloved country. We are slow to learn; but we learn. When a super-highway was proposed in California which would trample the redwood trees in its path, an outcry arose all over the land, so strident and fierce that the plan was put aside. And we no longer believe that a man, by owning a piece of America, is free to outrage it.

17   But we are an exuberant people, careless and destructive as active children. We make strong and potent tools and then have to use them to prove that they exist. Under the pressure of war we finally made the atom bomb, and for reasons which seemed justifiable at the time we dropped it on two Japanese cities—and I think we finally frightened ourselves. In such things, one must consult himself because there is no other point of reference. I did not know about the bomb, and certainly I had nothing to do with its use, but I am horrified and ashamed; and nearly everyone I know feels the same thing. And those who loudly and angrily justify Hiroshima and Nagasaki—why, they must be the most ashamed of all.

Exploring Ideas

1. What does Steinbeck say about Americans and the land? What is he trying to accomplish in this essay?

2. What does your response to the reading tell you about the way that you view "the land" or "the environment"?

3. What is your relationship with the land? What everyday actions of your own have a positive impact on the land? What everyday actions of your own have a negative impact on the land?

4. Observe the way land is used in your community. Take field notes. Then organize the data you have collected into two categories: observations that support what Steinbeck says, and observations that refute what he says.

5. Discuss your observations (#4) with others, looking for ways that you might participate in Steinbeck's discussion of Americans and the land. How might you contribute to this discussion? What idea, for example, could use further explanation or clarification?

Writing Strategies

1. Evaluate Steinbeck's opening paragraph. How does it function? Does it state or imply the main idea? Does it establish tone? Does it invite the reader into the essay? If so, how?

2. Study Steinbeck's use of subjects and verbs. Write down at least ten lively action verbs Steinbeck uses. Then go through an old piece of your own writing, redrafting sentences with more lively action verbs.

3. In paragraph 10, Steinbeck describes the people that the railroad brought west as "land-crazy" and says they moved "like locusts." Identify other expressions he uses to describe the people. Which expressions are especially effective? Think of several appropriate expressions that Steinbeck might have used, but didn't.

4. Describe Steinbeck's tone. Is his essay inviting to the reader, or does it put the reader off? Support your response with specific references to the text.

5. Describe Steinbeck's conclusion. Where does he end up—that is, where does he ultimately take the reader? Is his conclusion effective or not? What seems to be his concluding strategy?

Ideas for Writing

1. What is the relationship of Americans and the land today?

2. Describe your relationship with your immediate surroundings (your house, bedroom, apartment, dorm, etc.). How is it typical (or not typical) of your broader attitude concerning the relationship of humans to the land?

If responding to one of these ideas, go to the **Analysis** section of this chapter to begin developing ideas for your essay.

What the Honey Meant

Cindy Bosley

Cindy Bosley, whose writing also appears in Chapter 1, has taught literature and writing and has had poems published in various journals, including North American Review, Prairie Schooner, Willow Springs, Midwest Quarterly, *and* The Alsop Review *online. As you read, consider Bosley's title. What, in her essay, does the honey mean? And how did she discover that meaning? How does the essay ask the reader to further explore everyday things such as honey?*

In the margins of this essay, a reader's comments point to key ideas and writing strategies. As you read the essay, consider how the comments might influence your own reading and writing.

Exploring Ideas

Writing Strategies

My husband disappeared out the back door with an empty bowl in his hand. I did not see him leave, but a few moments later, he came back in and asked me to shut my eyes. I did as he asked. When I opened them, he stood in front of me holding out a bowl of fresh honey and a piece of the comb which had been pulled away from the hive and was still running with the buttery sweet liquid of all my best memories. My husband might as well have gone out just then and shoved his hand, in brown bear fashion, through the stinging, angry bees to release this small brick of honeycomb for all the love and gratitude I felt toward him at that moment. He stood there holding out to me a bowl filled with my life as it should have been, and I wept.

Begins with an anecdote

The metaphor sets up the rest of the essay.

When I think of honeycomb, I think of my father. I first tried a small bite, and then more and more by the spoonful, the day before my father left. He had brought the honey home from a guy at work, he said, and so he set the brick in its jar onto the counter, and found a spoon for himself, plunged the spoon into the hexagon cells and pulled it away with a *suck*. And then he went back for more. I stood over the jar of honeycomb marveling at it—the many sections of honey, the yellowish layer of beeswax sealing the liquid in, the small brown and black flecks of flower remnant, or bee poop, I guessed. My father said nothing to me, and he did not offer me his spoon, but when I got off my chair to get one from the drawer, I stood over the honey jar again waiting for permission, and he said, "Wanna try it?" with surprise and, I think, a little joy, as if it hadn't occurred to him before to offer some to others. That was the way he was.

Honeycomb is the link to understanding her relationship with her father.

We're gaining insight into his character. He seems the opposite of the husband, who brings her the honey without notice.

The degree and level of detail suggest that this is an important situation.

Exploring Ideas

The honey is related to sharing.

And I ate and ate and ate. I loved the wax like gum, how it stayed behind in my mouth long after the honey part was gone, swallowed, tasted, and replaced with another spoonful.

Writing Strategies

When my father left that night, I was sleeping and he did not say good-bye. In the years to come as he came and went, moving in and out like a college boy from a dormitory, I would learn that this was how he did things. That first morning, though, I did not know anything had happened, but like a too bulky winter coat a kid inherits from an older sibling, that morning when I woke, the house just *felt* different—a little bigger, a little old. The rooms were quieter. It's hard to believe that was possible, the new quiet, since my father was a too quiet man to begin with, but it was *quiet*. And the browns and golds of our '70's decor were browner, and deeper gold. And my mother was in her bedroom on the phone trying to muffle hard crying. And my younger sister was watching *Land of the Lost*, while my brother played with his Tinker Toys. Something had happened, and I didn't have to ask anyone what that was. The sun was a sawblade in the sky.

Life changes here. The father is gone. This is the beginning of something— a "new quiet."

She uses paragraph changes as shifts in time.

The allusions to popular culture give the essay a context— help the reader to experience the situation in time.

The metaphor of the sun creates a feeling of hardness—cutting.

I didn't quite know what to feel about this. Part of what I felt was certainly excitement. *Wow. Our dad's gone. Wow.* I also felt a puncture, very small like a needle, that I couldn't locate inside me. And I was, I think now, terrified at the new development that no one had yet explained to me though it was nearing lunch time, though it was time for someone to talk.

Another painful or hard metaphor.

I finally had to ask the obvious question, but I didn't know how these things were supposed to go—I had imagined other families, more loving families, sitting down together to talk over the coming changes with the children well before they happened, or maybe even a day before they happened. I had imagined other families dealing with it in other ways—the father kissing the children a special goodnight when he knew he would not be there the next day when they woke up, or maybe he would not save the trauma for the night or morning, but ease out in the smooth part of the afternoon, lots of hugs and tears, but at least the witnessing of leave-taking. And then I remembered the honeycomb.

The honey is about hope—a hope for sharing in something meaningful?

She tends to use short sentences to shift the reader back into her reflections.

The situation has different possible meanings. Every event has different possible outcomes. The outcome of this event creates a particular reality—and set of relationships.

And if I say: I went to the kitchen to look for something. Like a small and pitiful gesture of his helplessness and regret, there on the counter was a spoon he'd left beside the jar of honey, and I knew he meant it for me.

It feels one way.

But if I say: I went to the kitchen to look for the jar of honey. When I saw the counter, I saw there was nothing there, and I suppose I expected that. He must have taken it with him.

That feels another way.

The one-sentence paragraphs slow everything down. They make this section feel very reflective—almost meditative.

Exploring Ideas

But what really happened is that I did not have to ask my obvious question, "What happened with Dad?" And I did not have to bother looking for the honey because, yes, he left it—it simply wasn't that important to him. And no, there was no symbolic spoon or other invitation, *Eldest Daughter, please eat,* nearby. What happened was that I took a bite of honey and then I joined my sister and brother, two and ten years younger, watching Saturday morning cartoons together on the black, brown, white carpet, patterned in such a wild way that it was quickly making my head ache.

Writing Strategies

I heard my mother tell the story five or six times that morning, with different details and emphasis, to the people she talked to most easily. She had moved from the heavy weight of the red and black paisley bedroom to the dimness of the kitchen, a room the sun rarely ventured into, like all the dark rooms of our house. She told Aunt Edith that he better damn well get his stereo cabinet out of this house today. She moaned her money fears to Patty, and there was a hitch in my heart when I heard her mention my violin lessons. While she talked to Marlene, I heard several female names come flying, and with Darla, I understood more clearly that there was somehow another woman involved. What had happened I never did learn exactly, but my father had moved out overnight. Everything felt brand new. And there was a jar half-full of honey in the kitchen that no one but me wanted to eat.

Same as the honey jar in the kitchen: situations have different psychological layers, and they come out in different tellings—or stories.

The facts aren't important. The psychological consequences are. (They impact her future.)

When my husband brought his bowl of honeycomb to me that bright, grown-up day in the kitchen, I did not think *Father.* I did not think *Childhood.* I did not think *Old Pain.* But my husband knows my stories well enough to understand what it might mean to me, and when he heard our neighbor at the door that morning telling him to come get some of this amazing honey someone had given him, my husband knew enough to grab a bowl and bring me some.

The short, almost poem-like, sentences bring the reader into her feelings. (The brevity = intimate realizations.)

Again, the various possibilities create complexity. Her emotions emerge from a long complex history, and we cannot pin down, exactly, what makes her (us?) feel a certain way.

Everyone I know has aches so deep that small triggers bring tears to their eyes. The honey gift was clearly that trigger for me. I like to think I cried because seeing that bowl of honey made me miss my father. Or maybe I cried because I don't yet understand all that happened in my life back then, or why people can do the things they do to each other. Maybe I cried because my husband loves me that much, enough to know what the honey would mean. But I do know one thing: I sure do like honey. I wept to see that honey just for me.

Here's the public resonance.

She's returning to the original scene.

Exploring Ideas

1. In a paragraph, explain what the honey means to Bosley. Include in your explanation how the honey comes to have the meaning for her that it does.

2. Revise the paragraph you wrote for #1 and e-mail it (or show it) to several people who have not read Bosley's essay, asking them what object (such as honey) has special meaning to them and why. Use their responses to help you explore this discussion further.

3. How does Bosley's essay encourage the reader to think about everyday things, such as honey?

4. In what ways might you respond to Bosley's essay? That is, what kinds of responses does it invite? List several possibilities and discuss them with your peers.

5. Talk to old friends and relatives and visit places from your past (a playground, old school, church, and so on). Take note of any strong memories or emotions you experience. Jot them down and explore them through writing. Later, explore your initial writing through discussion with others and further writing. Explore until you discover the reason for your strong reaction.

Writing Strategies

1. In paragraph #3, Bosley offers the reader details about physical goings-on:

> And the browns and golds of our '70's decor were browner, and deeper gold. And my mother was in her bedroom on the phone trying to muffle hard crying. And my younger sister was watching *Land of the Lost,* while my brother played with his Tinker Toys. Something had happened, and I didn't have to ask anyone what that was. The sun was a sawblade in the sky.

What purpose do these details serve? What point, if any, might they communicate to the reader?

2. Notice how Bosley uses her introduction and conclusion (about honey) to frame her essay. Is her framing technique effective? What are such a technique's effect on the reader? Can you think of any situations in which this framing technique would be ineffective?

3. Paragraphs #7 and #9 are very short—one sentence each. What effect does their brevity have on the reading of the essay? Why does she offer these particular ideas in one-sentence paragraphs?

4. How does Bosley develop her main idea—with narration (story telling), description, or both? In what other ways does she develop it?

5. Identify at least one use of figurative language such as hyperbole, metaphor, understatement, or allusion and explain why it is effective.

Ideas for Writing

1. Bosley begins her second paragraph, "When I think of honeycomb, I think of my father." What relationship are you reminded of by honeycomb or some other thing?

2. What have you figured out about a relationship you had with a parent, grandparent, or significant adult figure growing up?

> If responding to one of these ideas, go to the **Analysis** section of this chapter to begin developing ideas for your essay.

Dog-Tied

David Hawes

Dave Hawes, who teaches literature and writing, wrote "Dog-Tied" when the authors of this text asked him to write an essay about relationships. As you read, think about how Hawes's ideas fit into a larger discussion. How, for example, might Hawes's essay relate to some other idea about, let's say, dogs and humans, pets and humans, animals, other life forms, or the environment and humans?

1   I realize this is an odd paraphrase of the Beatles, but it certainly seems fitting: I have a dog, or should I say, my dog has me? Often it seems unclear which of us is in charge in this arrangement. As I once explained to a non–dog owner, "Logan and I have a symbiotic relationship: I feed him, walk him, bathe him, take him to the vet, give him his heartworm and flea-and-tick medicines, buy him treats, pet him, and play with him. And what does he do? He lets me." This past summer I even bought him a kiddie pool to lay in when he got too hot. He is, after all, a retriever, so he likes water. Not to mention that he has this hairy coat on all the time that he can't take off when he's too warm. Do I spoil him? Of course I do. Isn't that the whole point of having a dog?

2   On the other hand, I realize some people don't see things the way I do. Just this morning I saw a man walking his dog past the front of my house. In a loud and commanding voice he kept saying, "Heel! Heel!" Obviously he wanted his dog to make no mistake about who was in charge. However, I did notice that the man kept up his commands all the way down the street. Maybe the dog's name is "Heel." I think most people, though, have a tendency to spoil their dogs. Just go to any pet store and look at the vast array of foods, toys, beds, and treats, not to mention the shampoos and skin treatments.

3   It wasn't always this way, of course. Dogs were originally domesticated so they could help with the work. And some dogs are still workers, helping herd the sheep or bring in the cattle. But I have to believe these true "working dogs" are a small minority. I think most dogs these days, at least in this country, lead a fairly pampered life, so it certainly gives a different meaning to the old sayings about "a dog's life" and "working like a dog." Personally, I'd love to work as much as my dog does.

4   Sometimes, though, I have to wonder about him liking his pampered life. Sometimes when he's in a really deep sleep, his legs jerk violently, like he's running. Is he dreaming about retrieving ducks and quail? When fall comes, do those longing looks he gives me mean he's wondering when I'm going to get the shotgun out so he can do what he was bred to do? When he lies down with his head between his paws and heaves one of the heavy dog sighs, is he wishing he could be running through a field somewhere, sniffing out the game? Does he feel like something is missing from his life, but he's not sure what it is? And worst of all, does he blame me for what's missing?

5   I worry about these things sometimes, but not too much, I guess, because when I leave for work in the morning and he looks very sad, or when I get home from work and he wiggles all over the place in his happiness to see me, or when he comes into the bedroom and lies beside me first thing in the morning waiting for his wake-me-up belly rub, it seems like maybe this relationship is working out OK.

Exploring Ideas

1. Describe the relationship between Hawes and his dog.

2. Describe the relationship you have with a dog, some other pet, a stray or wild animal, or some other life form, such as your prize orchids, herb garden, and such.

3. To further explore people's relationships with other life, interview at least five people about their relationship with any nonhuman life form.

   A. Begin by considering what you want to know. For example, you might ask them to describe the relationship in general, explain what they find rewarding about it, explain what they find frustrating about it, and so on. In groups or alone, compose several clear and purposeful questions that will encourage informative responses.

   B. Conduct the interviews, being certain to accurately record the responses. Then look for interesting ideas that help you to learn something new about people's relationships with other life. Write down the two or three most interesting ideas you discovered and explain what you think is interesting about them.

4. How might you respond to Hawes's essay without writing about dogs and pets? What relationships can you use to illustrate your main idea?

Writing Strategies

1. How does Hawes convey his main idea? Does he state it explicitly or imply it? Does he develop it through narration, description, explanation, or a combination of the three?

2. Hawes describes his relationship with Logan as "symbiotic." Is this a good word choice? Explain. If it is not, what one word would you use to describe their relationship?

3. Is Hawes's essay engaging—that is, do you as a reader become interested and want to read on? If so, carefully consider why. If not, why not?

4. If workshopping Hawes's essay, how would you answer the following questions: What is the essay's biggest strength? What is the essay's biggest weakness? What one recommendation would you make?

5. Write a new introduction and conclusion for Hawes's essay, and then compare it with one a classmate wrote. Discuss the different strategies you chose and the advantages and disadvantages of both.

Ideas for Writing

1. What relationship of your own is symbiotic, though it may not appear to others to be so?

2. Using Hawes's essay for inspiration, what else is interesting about human/animal relationships in general?

> If responding to one of these ideas, go to the Analysis section of this chapter to begin developing ideas for your essay.

Friend or Foe?

Dean A. Meek

Dean Meek, whose writing also appears in Chapter 3, wrote "Friend or Foe?" as an assignment for his first-year writing class. As you read this essay, think about Meek's purpose in writing, beyond completing a requirement for a class. What other purpose might Meek's essay serve? What else might he be trying to accomplish?

1   As a boy growing up in suburban Indiana, I still remember the feelings of loneliness and alienation. I was always bigger than the other children in my class and they often made fun of my husky build. This was a feeling that I would carry with me through my teenage years, a feeling of not fitting in and being ashamed of the way I looked. However, this would all change once I was introduced to that great healer of all, the one thing that could right all wrongs and change my life forever. From the moment I took my first drink of alcohol, it was obvious we were meant to be together. We were akin to the likes of Steve Yzerman and Brendan Shanahan or Terry Bradshaw and Lynn Swann. Together we were unstoppable and feared nothing.

2   It all started on a lovely fall day my freshman year of high school. Although this day started no different than all the previous, it would drastically change all the days to come. Prior to school I was standing outside and was approached by Cool Jim. Cool Jim was a very popular kid in school; he was happy-go-lucky and very outgoing. He wasn't afraid of anyone or anything and really had a way with the ladies.

3   "Would you like to buy a bottle of wine?" said Cool Jim.

4   "No, I'm not into that," I replied, while leaning against the building and smoking a cigarette.

5   "That's cool," commented Jim as he made his way down the side of the school.

6   Finishing my smoke, I watched Jim stop and talk to all the people; he had so many friends. On the way to my first class, I still recall thinking to myself, 'how lucky Cool Jim was to have so many friends and such self-esteem. If I could only be more like him, life would be great!'

7   Later that morning, I passed Jim in the hall between periods.

8   "Still got that wine!" Jim said.

9   Before I could respond, a thought came over me: 'If I want to be more like Jim, then maybe this was one way to get started.'

"How much?" I replied.

"Five dollars, it's top shelf," said Jim.

"I'll take it!"

10   During lunch, I went for a walk with my newfound friend, a bottle of Mad Dog 20/20. As I opened that classy metal cap, it was as if I had transformed into manhood. At first the taste was quite bitter but the more I indulged, the better the flavor became. Walking back to school, my face seemed to become numb and that numbness continued throughout my entire body. 'That's it!' I thought. This is what I had been searching for all my life. This new comrade of mine would shelter me from those unbearable feelings of loneliness and disgust.

11   That evening while lying in bed, I had a strange feeling come over me. In a matter of seconds it was obvious to me that my new friend would revisit me. In the bathroom praying at the porcelain altar, I somehow had the crazy notion this was all worthwhile. This physical pain was nothing compared to the emotional turmoil I endured. Kindly, I would trade an upset stomach for the feeling of fearlessness.

12   Through the years we stuck together and were completely inseparable. Occasionally we would find ourselves in a sticky situation but nonetheless we were best of friends.

13   Then came the day that would begin an unexpected metamorphosis. It was Sunday morning and I bowled on a league at 11:00 A.M. As with every Sunday, soon as the clock hit 12:00 noon, it was party time. The bar would start selling alcohol and more importantly, I would begin coming out of my shell. By the middle of the second game, I was back on top and feeling good. Sure, my bowling would suffer but who cares? It was just for fun and lots of it. Then after bowling, we headed into the bar and continued throwing down the suds. Shortly after that, I have no memory of what was to come.

14   The next morning as I opened my eyes, the glare of bright lights blinded me. The glare magnified the pounding in my head, which had become as certain as the rising of the morning sun. While rubbing my eyes, I noticed a shadow hanging over me. Startled by the image, I fought to gain my faculties. As my eyes began to focus, the image became clear. It was that of a rather large police officer. Overwhelmed by the fear and confusion of not knowing what had happened, I visually scanned the room for answers. I was in a hospital room and at the foot of my bed stood my parents: they were clearly upset and on edge. Placing her hand on my leg, Mom said: "Just relax. You are going to be all right." I tried to speak but could not. It felt as if my heart was pounding in my throat and I was trembling in fear. Then the officer said: "The charges are DUI and leaving the scene of an accident."

15   "DUI, for what?" I exclaimed.

16   "Just keep your mouth shut," replied my mother forcefully.

17   After the officer had left the room, my parents informed me that I had hit three cars in the parking lot of the bowling alley. Then, I had continued on to hit two more parked cars and a telephone pole: thankfully no one was hurt.

This was where the police and EMTs had found me. Furthermore, the 1965 Mustang that I had cherished was totaled and I was facing some very serious legal issues. 'How could this be?' I thought. The one thing that had removed my emotional turbulence was now the cause of all this. Well, that thought was short-lived. Maybe I overdid it a little and needed to exercise some control, but quitting was definitely out of the question!

18   Several months had passed and I lay awake in bed suffering from an anxiety attack. Feelings of loneliness and disgust flowed through me like the Maumee River through Toledo, Ohio. How could I be lonely? After all, I had a wife and four daughters. How could anyone be lonely? Nevertheless, I was and the one true friend that could always be counted on was failing me. Those same emotions of that teenage schoolboy came rushing back. Where drinking once removed them, it now magnified those demons. I could run no more. Those emotions now compounded with alcoholism would be the end of me. I only had two choices left: I would either get help or commit suicide and there were no other options. Thankfully, I chose treatment and, with the help of my wife, was admitted to a program that same day.

19   That was a few 24 hours ago and life is much better today. That once shy high school boy has matured into a recovering alcoholic. After giving up the alcohol, I again faced those evil emotions but this time I faced them head-on. You see, nothing external could mend this torn soul. It had to be fixed internally. As for my old friend, he is now my foe. I see him around but only from a distance. Sometimes, I think he would like us to rekindle those burning desires we once shared but I refuse. As for those schoolboy feelings of loneliness and shamefulness, gratitude and pride have since replaced them and the yearning to be a part of the crowd is no more.

Exploring Ideas

1. Briefly summarize Meek's relationship with alcohol, including how/why it began, the nature of the relationship, and its current status.

2. How does Meek's essay encourage the reader to think about alcohol?

3. What "Friend or Foe" relationships have you had or do you have? Consider, but do not limit yourself to, substances, activities, habits, people, thoughts, and so on. You might discover less-obvious relationships through discussion with relatives, friends, classmates, and co-workers, or by looking through personal belongings.

4. How might writing about one of your "Friend or Foe" relationships (#3) help you or others? What might be the consequence of such an essay?

Writing Strategies

1. Describe Meek's voice and identify several passages to support your description. How does Meek's voice influence your response to his essay?

2. In your own words, write down what you think Meek's main idea is, and then discuss what you wrote down with several classmates. How were your understandings of the main idea similar or different?

3. Identify several passages in which Meek personifies (gives human characteristics to) his foe. What is the effect of these passages? How are they, or aren't they, successful?

4. How else might Meek have begun and ended his essay? Discuss different approaches with a group of classmates, considering the advantages and disadvantages of each.

Ideas for Writing

1. What "Friend or Foe" relationship have you experienced yourself, or seen others experience?

2. What "Friend or Foe" relationship can you think of that doesn't involve humans?

If responding to one of these ideas, go to the **Analysis** section of this chapter to begin developing ideas for your essay.

Outside Reading

ind a written text that explains or points out an unordinary relationship. Go to a library database or search engine and experiment by typing in combinations of words (joined by *and*). To conduct an electronic search through journals and magazines, go to your library's periodical database or to InfoTrac (http://infotrac.galegroup. com/itweb/). For your library database, perform a keyword search, or for InfoTrac, go to the main search box and select *keywords*. In the search box, enter word combinations, such as *water and politics, lakes and engineering, nursing and chemistry*. (When performing keyword searches, avoid using phrases or articles *(a, an, the)*; instead, use nouns separated by *and*.) The search results will yield lists of journal and magazine articles. The same strategy can be used with an Internet search. Try Google.com and enter various word combinations. Once you find an interesting text, print it out.

The purpose of this assignment is to explore a broad spectrum of possible relationships and to discover more about explanatory writing. You may discover relationships you never imagined, and will probably witness a variety of writing strategies. As you read through this chapter, keep the document you have discovered close by and notice the elements and strategies the writer uses. Depending on your instructor's suggestions, do one or more of the following:

1. Notice how the writer applies various strategies from this chapter. On the hard copy:

   - Highlight the thesis (main point about the relationship) if it is stated. If the thesis is implied, write it in your own words.
   - Identify the major rhetorical tools (narrative, description, allusion).
   - Identify any passages that show public resonance (in which the writer makes the relationship a public issue or concern).

2. Write an essay that discusses the strategies employed by the writer. The following questions may be helpful.

   - How is the writer's voice different from the essays in this chapter?
   - How does the writer support or illustrate his or her thesis?
   - Who is the audience for this text?
   - How does the audience impact the kinds of things said in the text?

3. Write at least three "Exploring Ideas" questions for the text you found.

4. Write at least three "Writing Strategies" questions for the text you found.

5. Write two "Ideas for Writing," such as the ones following the essays in this book, for the text you found.

■

INVENTION

Invention, or what is sometimes called *pre-writing*, is the activity of discovering ideas, developing points, and thinking through a topic. For academic writers, it is a necessary activity, one that leads to vital and valuable ideas. In this chapter, the process will involve focusing on a particular relationship and exploring its possible meaning. The following three sections are designed to help you through the invention process: specifically, to discover a topic (in **Point of Contact**), develop particular points about the topic (in **Analysis**), and make it relevant to a community of readers (in **Public Resonance**). The questions in each section are not meant to be answered directly in your final written assignment. However, answering them here, before drafting your essay, will help you discover what you are going to say—and even why you are going to say it. After you work through these three sections, the **Delivery** section, which immediately follows, will help you craft your ideas into a written text.

Point of Contact
Finding a Topic in Everyday Life

When you hear the word *relationship*, you may imagine an intimate personal bond between significant others, family members, or friends. But consider the relationships that are less obvious, those that surround or define us but remain hidden by the patterns of everyday life. Imagine the many intense, but also subtle, relationships that define life as we know it: between an old man and his backyard, among people in a large corporate office, between a lake and a local economy, between pigeons and people in a park. When we examine such relationships, we are apt to discover some hidden workings and ideas—which is often the purpose of writing in academia.

If you do examine an intimate personal relationship, try to go beyond the first layer of meaning, beyond the first thing that those in the relationship assume ("it is supportive"; "it is difficult"; "it has ups and downs"; "it is loving") and find some hidden complexity. Bosley, for instance, goes way beyond the first layer of her relationship with her husband and discovers that its significance is tied to her relationship with her father. She finds a particular and interesting emotional complexity: that the past is always potentially intermingling with the present.

Getting involved in a situation or a conversation may help generate some ideas for writing. As you explore possible topics, ask yourself: "What is the nature of this relationship?" If the relationship seems interesting, you may have a topic. Of course, the problem here is deciding what *interesting* means. Don't be discouraged if nothing falls from the sky and says, "Hey! I'm a great topic for your paper!" (That does not happen for any writer. In fact, no topic is inherently interesting.) The process of developing the topic will make it interesting. Use these suggestions and questions to find and develop a topic:

- Visit a location and observe the activity. Ask yourself the following:

  How do the people interact?
  How do they depend on one another?
  How do the people relate to their surroundings? To objects? To buildings? To nature?
  How do the objects (buildings, tools, products, shops) relate?
  How do people or objects influence each other?

- Participate in some activity (a sport, a household chore, a job, an artistic endeavor), and ask yourself the following:

  How do people involved in this activity relate to its tools or equipment?
  How must the people relate to each other? (How must they influence or depend on each other?)
  How do people involved in this activity relate to their environment?
  How do people involved in this activity relate to the public, to the audience, or to anyone outside of the activity?

- Talk with people in a relationship. In addition to more intimate relationships (between friends, significant others, parents, and children), consider other options, such as between a customer and a sales clerk, a customer and a mail carrier, the public and a city police force, politicians and their constituents, or artists and the public. Use the following questions to begin your conversation (and see the section on interviews in Chapter 12):

  Is the relationship difficult?
  What keeps it going?
  Why are you in this relationship?
  Can you describe the importance of the relationship?

- Imagine a more conceptual relationship: between a person or people and an object (such as a person and a computer, a person and a musical instrument, a person and a car) or between two objects (such as a college course and a textbook, a book and computer, an old car and a new one, a road and a house).

- Examine your major for relationships between the professionals in your chosen field of study and the public (such as the relationship between nurses and their patients, or business marketing professionals and potential consumers). You might also find an interesting relationship between two things in your field of study: students of criminal justice, for instance, always explore the relationship between cases. They decide how one case (or one kind of case) relates to another. Or consider environmental scientists who explore the relationship between waterways and surrounding land or between trees and animal life. Also, you might see an interesting link between your field of study and another field. Today, most academic disciplines and professional fields define themselves in conjunction with other fields. For instance, biology explores its relationship with ethics, computer technologies involve visual or graphic design, and political science involves religious studies.

Invention Activity: Now go beyond these suggestions. Imagine more relationships in your life and the world around you. If the activity can be done in groups, each group should generate a list of relationships. Each group member should keep a record of the possible topic ideas.

Example: Dean Meek's Response to Point of Contact Questions

Talk with people in a relationship. In addition to more intimate relationships (between friends, significant others, parents, and children), consider other options: Between alcohol and me.

Is the relationship difficult? The relationship in the beginning seemed to be a good one. However, the longer the relationship lasted the worse it became. It was a constant struggle between facing my inner fears or taking the chance of drinking without knowing the final results. Today it is a relationship I treasure in the aspect that I never want to forget where it took me, and the consequences I had to face.

What keeps it going? I believe that what keeps it going is my nature to want everything the easy way. As long as the relationship continued, I never really had to look at the real problem, myself and my thinking.

Why are you in this relationship? The reason I was initially in this relationship was to hide from the real world and all its shortcomings. Yet today I realize that it is because I am an alcoholic and more than likely always have been, but more importantly I know I always will be an alcoholic.

Notice how Meek's responses begin in an interesting place: he is treating his alcoholism as an intimate relationship. Already, his exploration of the topic is yielding important insights. While the relationship may be a troubled one, it is one he *treasures* because it constantly shows him truths about himself. This degree of honesty reveals valuable ideas, ones that can engage and extend others' thinking.

Imagine another writer, Marcus, answering the same questions about a relationship between a local police department and the surrounding community.

Is the relationship difficult? Yes. My father is a police officer, and he is constantly stressed about the work. Patrolling in some neighborhoods is hard work—and dangerous. And even though many officers face dangerous situations, they are expected, by people in the community, to be totally passive. It's nearly impossible work.

What keeps it going? People stay in the job for obvious reasons: they need money, they have the training, they get some satisfaction out of the job (most of them still assume that they are "protecting and serving"). But the real question is: what keeps the tension going? And that's a mixture of things: on one side, economic problems in the city create bad neighborhoods where people are desperate. On the other side, every time the news reports anything involving the police, it's going to be bad, so people learn to associate police cars and uniforms with negative feelings.

Why are you in this relationship? Technically, I'm not in it. Or maybe I am. I am "the community." But I guess most people probably don't think they are in the relationship until they see the flashing lights behind them. That's also part of the reason that the tension keeps going. People in the community don't see themselves as part of the relationship—maybe they don't even see a relationship.

Notice that Marcus's answer to the last question actually takes him further into his own thinking. Although it would seem that the question is not applicable to his topic, it actually prompts him to see an essential point. (In this way, make sure to use the questions to seek out potential in your topic.)

Using Images as a Point of Contact

In addition to the questions on page 81, images can be used as springboards for ideas. The images on this page (as well as others in this text or from everyday life) can be used along with the questions on page 81 to help you identify a relationship that is worth further exploration. For example, when prompted to "visit a location and observe the activity," you can visit any location, but you can also "visit" the locations (such as a college campus or Venice Beach) through images such as those below.

Analysis

Exploring the Relationship

Analysis is the process of inspecting how or why something works, but analysis also involves discovering what something means. In this chapter, analysis involves investigating all the possible ways two entities relate to each other. It means going beyond the obvious relationship and exploring the hidden or abstract connections. The following questions will help you to explore your chosen relationship in depth.

- How does the presence of one influence the other?
- What would occur to one if the other were gone?
- What qualities or characteristics do they share?
- Is one dependent on the other?
- What qualities, things, or characteristics does one give to the other?
- Do they depend on each other?
- Does your idea about one involve the other? How?
- How does the nature of the relationship change one or both subjects?

The above questions can help to generate a main idea. That is, if one of these questions generates any response at all, you can probably turn that response into a main idea. For example, imagine a writer looking at the relationship between a mountain and a town. She might discover that the mountain gives the small valley town a certain humble quality. In other words, the idea of the town is influenced by the presence of the mountain. Or perhaps another writer, exploring the relationship between two restaurants, discovers that they highlight the other's particular cuisine. The Italian restaurant, on one side of the street, highlights the character of the Mexican restaurant on the other side, and vice versa. The writer might find, then, that the two depend on one another's differences. Or notice Steinbeck's analysis at the beginning of his essay:

> I have often wondered at the savagery and thoughtlessness with which our early settlers approached this rich continent. They came at it as though it were an enemy, which of course it was. They burned the forests and changed the rainfall; they swept the buffalo from the plains, blasted the streams, set fire to the grass, and ran a reckless scythe through the virgin and noble timber.

In analyzing the relationship between early American settlers and the North American continent, Steinbeck discovers a particular kind of relationship, one of aggression. It is his analysis of the relationship that allows him to characterize it in this way.

Important Questions for Human Relationships: Consult the section on interviews in Chapter 12, and then use the following to generate your notes:

- In what ways do I communicate with this person?
- To what degree do I share in his or her personal crises?
- How much do I depend on talking with or seeing this person?
- How often do I need or want to communicate with this person?
- Do I ever feel obligated to do, think, or say something for this person?
- What do each of us expect from the other without asking?
- What are the consequences of not meeting each other's personal needs?
- What kinds of disagreements arise in the relationship?
- Do they become sources of debate and tension, or do they fade away?
- If there is a disagreement, how is it solved?

As you analyze your topic, avoid moving to conclusions too quickly. Share your answers to the **Analysis** questions with another student or with a small group. In your conversation, try to get beyond the easy answers. Imagine that two students, Diana and Linda, are discussing a topic (the relationship between a coffee shop and its customers, who are primarily students). Notice how the brief conversation actually transforms a rather simple idea into a more sophisticated one:

What would occur to one if the other were gone?

Linda: Well . . . the coffee shop wouldn't get very much business, and the students wouldn't have their favorite coffee.

Diana: OK . . . but I wonder what else the coffee shop does for the students. I mean, maybe the coffee shop provides something besides coffee and a place to go.

Linda: It also provides a place to study, doesn't it? A lot of students go there to read. And a few people even bring laptops and write.

Diana: And last semester, in psychology, we had group projects, and our group met there twice to work out our presentation.

Linda: I guess people also go there to study and be seen, to do some work, but also to get out a little. Students can go with their books and not feel weird about it. They can do some reading and feel like they're surrounded by college activity.

Diana: Maybe that's important, too. Maybe going to the coffee shop gives students something, the feeling of *being* students. They come here to think and act and talk like college students—and that's pretty important.

Linda: Yeah . . . I think you're right. When I go there, I actually feel more like a college student, and I'm able to concentrate on things and feel more intellectual. It's odd how a building can actually change how people approach their work. The coffee shop actually makes many of us more able to focus, and in the big picture take studying more seriously.

Notice that Linda and Diana go beyond the first response, the first and most obvious layer to the relationship between the coffee shop and the students. As they discuss the relationship, they discover a more subtle, and perhaps more interesting, layer to the relationship. Their conversation shows how the **Analysis** questions can be used to explore a topic. They go beyond simply answering the question: they use the question to launch an analysis.

Example: Dean Meek's Response to Analysis Questions

What qualities/characteristics does one give the other? The relationship that I have/had with alcohol was one that initially started out as what I perceived to be a positive one. In my mind alcohol allowed me to be everything I wasn't. Alcohol allowed me to be fun-loving, outgoing, personable and an all-around better person, or so I thought. Alcohol took me places where I would never go sober and introduced me to many people. Because of alcohol I was able to be the life of the party and was a real ladies' man. It was all these thoughts and feelings that were actually preying on my poor self-esteem. By initially attacking my self-esteem the alcohol was eventually able to consume the rest of my being. It was only at the point that alcohol caused me enormous pain and confusion that I would even half-heartedly look at it as a problem. Yet it still took more pain for me to realize that not only was it a problem, it was the problem.

Not all of Meek's ideas, as they are expressed here, find their way into his essay. However, in his response to the **Analysis** questions, we can see important concepts that seem to lay the groundwork for his essay: the acknowledgment of his low self-esteem, the description of himself as a drinker, and the manner in which alcohol manipulated his sense of identity. In the essay, these ideas are treated as part of the narrative:

> As a boy growing up in suburban Indiana, I still remember the feelings of loneliness and alienation. I was always bigger than the other children in my class and they often made fun of my husky build. This was a feeling that I would carry with me through my teenage years, a feeling of not fitting in and being ashamed of the way I looked. However, this would all change once I was introduced to that great healer of all, the one thing that could right all wrongs and change my life forever. From the moment I took my first drink of alcohol, it was obvious we were meant to be together.

Even though Meek's essay reads easily like a simple narrative, it is full of analysis: it shows a complex relationship between public identity, substance abuse, and esteem. The other chapter readings also depend heavily on analysis. Bosley's essay, for instance, is also a narrative, but calls the reader into an analysis of past and present:

> When my husband brought his bowl of honeycomb to me that bright, grown-up day in the kitchen, I did not think *Father*. I did not think *Childhood*. I did not think *Old Pain*. But my husband knows my stories well enough to understand what it might mean to me, and when he heard our neighbor at the door that morning telling him to come get some of this amazing honey someone had given him, my husband knew enough to grab a bowl and bring me some.

Steinbeck's essay contains more obvious analytical passages in which he details the nature of the relationship between modern American people and the land:

> The merciless nineteenth century was like a hostile expedition for loot that seemed limitless. Uncountable buffalo were killed, stripped of their hides, and left to rot, a reservoir of permanent food supply eliminated. More than that, the land of the Great Plains was robbed of the manure of the herds. Then the plows went in and ripped off the protection of the buffalo grass and opened the helpless soil to quick water and slow drought and the mischievous winds that roamed through the Great Central Plains. There has always been more than enough desert in America; the new settlers, like overindulged children, created even more.

   As you develop your own topic, go beyond what you have always assumed and what most people overlook about the nature of the relationship. Look into the deep connections of present and past; look at the consequences of actions; consider the effects of attitudes. Let no thought, policy, or behavior go unnoticed.

1. According to this cartoon, what is the relationship between Native Americans and European settlers?

2. According to this cartoon, what is the relationship between present American citizens and illegal immigrants?

3. What is an *illegal immigrant?*

Public Resonance

Why Does This Topic Matter to Others?

Remember that you are not only writing for yourself. You are writing to explain something for others. The particular relationship you are explaining may be specific and narrow (perhaps between two people), but it may suggest something beyond the particular—something that is relevant or important to your readers. For example, notice how Bosley's very personal discoveries extend outward to others:

> Everyone I know has aches so deep that small triggers bring tears to their eyes. The honey gift was clearly that trigger for me. I like to think I cried because seeing that bowl of honey made me miss my father. Or maybe I cried because I don't yet understand all that happened in my life back then, or why people can do the things they do to each other. Maybe I cried because my husband loves me that much, enough to know what the honey would mean. But I do know one thing: I sure do like honey. I wept to see that honey just for me.

In this, her final paragraph, Bosley makes a simple but powerful gesture to include others. Her point is not simply *honey reminds me of my father*. It is far more complex and rich; it is about the painful memories that are folded quietly away into our histories and how they sometimes emerge. With only one sentence Bosley extends the explanation of her own relationships to others. Thuma makes a similar move in the middle of her essay:

> Sometimes we're lucky. Requests vanish into thin air, bumped off the list by a newer fad, a lesser evil. But other requests—the ones that force us to confront our children's emerging sexuality and drive for independence—echo in our ears long after we answer them. Like many things that teenagers want, this request brings me and my husband face to face with the larger questions that vex parents of adolescents: What to give? What to withhold?

Certainly, many parents and their children debate the value of belly rings, so Thuma's topic has public resonance, but she also extends her situation outward. She not only uses the first person plural pronoun *we*; she also broadens the scope of the crisis, pointing to a bigger issue: children's "drive for independence." Thuma invites other parents to share not simply the crisis about belly rings, but the *nature of the crisis*.

This gets to an important aspect of public resonance: a particular topic may not resonate with potential readers, but the nature or essence of that topic will. In other words, a particular relationship (for instance, between a teenage daughter and her mother) is not necessarily a public issue; however, teenagers' drive for independence concerns many people. When a writer discovers the nature of an issue (such as the core of a relationship crisis), he or she discovers the quality that may resonate with others.

As you consider your own topic, ask the following questions:

- Does the relationship reveal something about people's strengths or weaknesses?
- Does the relationship reveal something about the nature of the subject?
- Why is it important that people see the meaning of the relationship?

- Is there something unusual about this relationship? (If so, what is it, and why is it so unusual?)

- Is there something usual about this relationship? (If so, what is it, and why is it so usual? That is, why do most relationships seem to function this way?)

- Does this relationship show how difficult or easy human relationships can be?

- Does this relationship show how rewarding or valuable a particular kind of relationship can be?

Now try integrating some of the questions above. That is, see what happens when you bring two of the above questions into play:

- How does the unusual nature of this relationship reveal something about the subjects?

- What does the unusual (or usual) nature of this relationship reveal about people's needs?

- Why is such a relationship necessary or valuable?

Example: Dean Meek's Response to Public Resonance Questions

Does the relationship reveal something about people's strengths or weaknesses? I feel this relationship does because it is my belief that people in general would rather look at others or at circumstances as the cause of their problems. None of us want to look within ourselves and admit that the answer to our problems is within our own being. This is a confusing and sometimes painful process of soul-searching that even the toughest of us will avoid if possible. We will blame others, blame circumstances, blame our parents or our upbringing. But not once will we think that the problem is in our own emotions, personality, and fears.

I also feel that ultimately most of us come to a dead end. At this dead end we are alone and have no one or thing left to blame. It is at this point that we have only two choices left. One, we give up and live the rest of our lives in pain and turmoil or two, we ask someone for help, seek treatment, and honestly make a decision to fix the real problem. This is true whether it be with alcohol or spiritual, social, or economic concerns. Our concerns and issues may vary and some of us may be better off than others. But none of us are superhuman and all need a little help from time to time living life on its terms.

Activity: Discuss your topic with a friend or family member. Ask about his or her take on the topic: "Have you ever thought about the relationship between _____ and _____?" Then, write a memo to your instructor about the discussion. Explain how your understanding of the topic may have changed because of the discussion. (See Chapter 13 for more information on memos.)

■

DELIVERY

The next step is to develop these ideas into a text—an invitation to the reader to learn something about relationships. An essay can illustrate a simple fact (about relationships, for instance), revive an old-fashioned way of thinking, or revise an idea completely. Remember that a potential reader already knows about relationships in general. (He or she is certainly mired in several.) But in your essay you have the opportunity to shed light, to go beyond ordinary thinking, and to reveal something that most people (maybe including yourself) do not necessarily consider. Regardless of the particular topic, good essay writing is not simply a report about what you or your audience already knows. It is a discovery of something new.

The following sections (**Rhetorical Tools, Organizational Strategies, Writer's Voice,** and **Revision Strategies**) are designed to help you build a sophisticated and engaging text—one that emerges from your particular ideas. Each section points to important features or common concerns related to explanatory writing.

Rhetorical Tools

Focusing and Developing the Idea

Considering Your Thesis: As you focus on a topic, you will also be narrowing in on a thesis statement or main idea. Of course, you may write your way to a thesis (in a discovery draft), but ultimately, you need to have a single statement that

not only gives focus to your topic, but also gives your stance (your particular view) on that topic. As in any essay, the narrower and more particular your thesis, the more engaging the paper is for the writer and the reader. For example, a thesis statement that claims *biology is connected to many fields* is rather broad and probably uninteresting. Such a statement also does not really offer a particular insight. It does not rediscover or recharacterize relationships. However, notice a more focused version of the idea: *Stem cell research has prompted a complex marriage*

of law and biology that will continue to impact careers in both fields. This statement offers a more particular point. As you narrow in on a topic, make certain you offer a particular insight. Go beyond nonspecific nouns, such as *many fields.* Go beyond simple descriptors such as *connected.* Before moving on, try to articulate your main point (your take on the nature of the relationship).

Evolution of a Thesis	
For Point of Contact, the writer explores her major:	*What is the relationship between my major, biology, and law?*
Writer responds to Analysis question: How does the nature of the relationship change one or both subjects?	*Stem cell research has changed the way biologists think about law.*
Public Resonance questions extend the point outward: Why is it important that people see the meaning of the relationship?	*As stem cell research continues to develop, biologists and lawyers will both need to develop an understanding of the other's field.*
The writer refines the point:	*Stem cell research has prompted a complex marriage of law and biology that will continue to impact careers in both fields.*

Your project might do one of the following:

- Explain the significant qualities of a particular kind of relationship.
- Explain what is sometimes hidden in a particular kind of relationship.
- Explain the difficulties or problems of being a child or friend or parent or significant other.
- Explain all the qualities necessary for being a good _____ (friend, sibling, child, parent, and so on).
- Explain how a particular relationship (say, with a pet) is much like something else (say, an accidental fall down a mountain side).
- Explain how a particular relationship reveals something important about a subject.

Using Narration: Narration, or storytelling, is appropriate for many kinds of writing. It is not simply relegated for remembering events. You might consider beginning your essay with a brief retelling of a situation regarding the relationship, or using a brief account to illustrate something about the relationship (notice Thuma and Bosley). Meek's essay depends almost entirely on narration.

If you decide to use narration, make good choices:

1. Start the narrative at an appropriate place. That is, limit your story to include only relevant parts of the situation.

2. Focus on only the relevant details of the events.

3. Use consistent verb tense. (In most cases, past or present tense can work in retelling a story. However, you must be consistent throughout the narrative.)

4. Make sure, at some point, to explain the significance or relevance of the narrative to the reader.

5. Refer to Chapter 1 for other valuable narrative strategies.

Using Description: Readers like details. The more detailed the images, the more the reader will experience them. In this essay, you might decide to describe the people involved in the relationship—their particular postures, facial expressions, and gestures. Or you might need to detail more abstract qualities—their imaginations, their appetites, their pride, their esteem, their effect on strangers. Imagine a writer, Linda, explaining the relationship between a coffee shop and its student customers:

> The coffee shop makes them feel more academic. It is more than a location to do homework and drink caffeine. It is a place where students totally surround themselves in college work.

These are valuable statements, but they remain abstract and general. They would come to life more with details:

> The coffee shop is more than a location for doing homework. It is like a satellite campus where students and professors alike work, talk, reflect. On any given day, several tables will be pushed together while a group of students work together on a project, their papers and notebooks scattered between coffee cups and half-eaten bagels. Invariably, a professor, graduate student, or staff member from the college will sit in one of the corner tables reading a newspaper. Several students will be perched on the windowsill, their backs against the outside world as they read through textbook chapters.

You might need to describe a particular situation in detail. In that case, narration and description will work together. Notice Bosley's strategy:

> When I think of honeycomb, I think of my father. I first tried a small bite, and then more and more by the spoonful, the day before my father left. He had brought the honey home from a guy at work, he said, and so he set the brick in its jar onto the counter, and found a spoon for himself, plunged the spoon into the hexagon cells and pulled it away with a *suck*. And then he went back for more. I stood over the jar of honeycomb marveling at it—the many sections of honey, the yellowish layer of beeswax sealing the liquid in, the small brown and black flecks of flower remnant, or bee poop, I guessed. My father said nothing to me, and he did not offer me his spoon, but when I got off my chair to get one from the drawer, I stood over the honey jar again waiting for permission, and he said, "Wanna try it?" with surprise and, I think, a little joy, as if it hadn't occurred to him before to offer some to others. That was the way he was. And I ate and ate and ate. I loved the wax like gum, how it stayed behind in my mouth long after the honey part was gone, swallowed, tasted, and replaced with another spoonful.

Here, Bosley narrates a past event while delivering very particular details. This is how she captures her readers, how she draws us in. And once we are seeing the relationship along with her, we participate more easily in the meaning she gives it later in the essay. Also, notice how Steinbeck offers detailed description:

> When they had cropped out a piece they moved on, raping the country like invaders. The topsoil, held by roots and freshened by leaf-fall, was left helpless to the spring freshets, stripped and eroded with the naked bones of clay and rock exposed. The destruction of the forests changed the rainfall, for the searching clouds could find no green and beckoning woods to draw them on and milk them. The merciless nineteenth century was like a hostile expedition for loot that seemed limitless.

The description in this passage (and others like it) allows the reader to accept and understand Steinbeck's main idea. Without such details, the essay would not achieve its purpose and communicate its point.

Activity: Choose another essay from this chapter or the text you found for the **Outside Reading** assignment and point to the most detailed passage. In a paragraph, explain how the details of the passage help to support the main idea. That is, explain the significance and value of the details.

Using Figurative Language: Any explanatory essay can benefit from figurative language, which is any language that goes beyond the basic definitions of words and uses them to suggest imaginative connections between ideas.

Metaphor: A metaphor is a comparison of one thing to another in which one thing is made to share the characteristics of another. Notice Bosley's metaphor of the sun and how it helps deliver the gravity of the situation:

> And the browns and golds of our '70's decor were browner, and deeper gold. And my mother was in her bedroom on the phone trying to muffle hard crying. And my younger sister was watching *Land of the Lost*, while my brother played with his Tinker Toys. Something had happened, and I didn't have to ask anyone what that was. The sun was a sawblade in the sky.

Simile: A simile is a comparison that uses *like* or *as*. Notice Steinbeck's similes:

> I have often wondered at the savagery and thoughtlessness with which our early settlers approached this rich continent. They came at it as though it were an enemy, which of course it was.

> There has always been more than enough desert in America; the new settlers, like overindulged children, created even more.

Metaphors and similes can help to characterize situations; in this case, they can lend a quality to a relationship. As you consider your own topic, create metaphors and similes if they help to develop a key point. (And remember that too much figurative language can distract the reader.) The following questions can help you develop metaphors and similes for your own writing:

- Can I compare the relationship (or the entities in the relationship) to an animal? A thing? A place? A person?
- What purpose would this comparison serve?

Organizational Strategies
Addressing Common Concerns

How Should I Begin? As we will suggest throughout this book, the possibilities for introductions are boundless. For this particular paper, you might:

- Begin with a general statement about the relationship. Steinbeck begins with a general statement about American settlers and the land:

  I have often wondered at the savagery and thoughtlessness with which our early settlers approached this rich continent. They came at it as though it were an enemy, which of course it was. They burned the forests and changed the rainfall; they swept the buffalo from the plains, blasted the streams, set fire to the grass, and ran a reckless scythe through the virgin and noble timber.

- Begin with a brief story or anecdote about the relationship. Bosley and Thuma both begin with stories that they develop throughout their essays. (But also notice that the stories eventually give way to some analysis, some explanation of the meaning in the events.)

- Begin with a typical belief or stereotype about the relationship and then turn to your particular insight. Imagine a writer focusing on the relationship between the police and the surrounding community:

  Most people assume they have no relationship with their local police departments. Other than an emergency situation, most are even reluctant to acknowledge police officers. They often treat them as uniformed specters lurking on the roads of their towns. But the police of any community are deeply connected to the everyday patterns of life. They are serving their communities and participating in daily routines at all levels.

- Begin with a fictional account, or scenario, of a relationship. Imagine the same topic about police and communities beginning differently:

  Imagine a community in which the police only appeared for emergencies, in which people had to make a 911 call simply to get a police car to visit the area. Imagine the streets of a crowded city without the occasional police cruiser. Imagine the downtown stores without the presence of a city officer.

> **When to Write the Introduction:** If a good introduction comes to mind, by all means, write it down. But if one doesn't, don't worry. Go ahead and write the essay without an introduction. Once you have a draft (without the introduction), you'll have a better idea what you are introducing; thus, the introduction should be easier to write.

Where Should My Thesis or Main Point Go? Remember that a
thesis can be explicitly stated or it can be implied (that is, suggested by the content but not stated in the essay). Of course, even if a thesis is implied, the author needs to know the main idea. A thesis for this essay might go:

- At the very beginning—the first sentence of the first paragraph
- At the end of the first paragraph
- In the conclusion
- After a brief account that illustrates the main idea

> Examine the introduction of each chapter reading. Decide on the thesis statement or main idea. Is it stated? Is it implied?

What Should I Include? This essay bases itself on personal insights about
a particular relationship. In addition to details about that relationship, consider using the following:

- Particular anecdotes or narratives. This strategy is the most common in the chapter readings. Bosley, for instance, focuses her entire essay on a particular anecdote. Meek uses two primary anecdotes of his relationship with alcohol to illustrate his point.
- Details about other, similar, relationships. Although you are focusing on a particular relationship, other relationships from the past or present can help round out your ideas. Bosley's point depends on her use of the past. Hawes refers briefly to another dog/human relationship to illustrate his point.

Remember that the information throughout the essay should work to support a main idea. Consider Meek's essay. Because the main point of his essay involves his relationship with alcohol, we learn primarily of his feelings and behaviors associated with drinking. We do not, however, see details about his mother or the furniture in his home. Such information would not be important to his point.

> Reexamine the chapter readings. Do they include other kinds of ideas or information?

When Should I Change Paragraphs? Remember that paragraphs are
tools for focusing and refocusing your readers' attention. Paragraph breaks stop readers and signal them to refocus their attention. Particularly, for this paper, you might change paragraphs:

- When beginning a scenario or narrative
- When offering a memory
- When changing scenes or time in the middle of a longer narrative
- When offering a detailed allusion

How Should I Make Transitions?

You might think of paragraph transitions in two ways. Sometimes making paragraph transitions is as easy as choosing the right information to come next—that is, choosing the most appropriate information to begin the paragraph. In these cases, the content of the paragraphs works to bridge the gap between them. (See Steinbeck ¶ 7–9. The content of each paragraph follows logically from the preceding paragraph. Steinbeck uses a time sequence to move from one point to the next, and so explicit transitions are unnecessary.)

Often, however, the writer needs to create a phrase, sentence, or sentences at the beginning of the new paragraph so that the relationship between the old and the new is clear. This sentence or phrase helps to bridge the gap between points. Notice how Hawes bridges his gaps:

> On the other hand, I realize some people don't see things the way I do. Just this morning I saw a man walking his dog past the front of my house. In a loud and commanding voice he kept saying, "Heel! Heel!" Obviously he wanted his dog to make no mistake about who was in charge. However, I did notice that the man kept up his commands all the way down the street. Maybe the dog's name is "Heel." I think most people, though, have a tendency to spoil their dogs. Just go to any pet store and look at the vast array of foods, toys, beds, and treats, not to mention the shampoos and skin treatments.
>
> It wasn't always this way, of course. Dogs were originally domesticated so they could help with the work. And some dogs are still workers, helping herd the sheep or bring in the cattle. But I have to believe these true "working dogs" are a small minority. I think most dogs these days, at least in this country, lead a fairly pampered life, so it certainly gives a different meaning to the old sayings about "a dog's life" and "working like a dog." Personally, I'd love to work as much as my dog does.

Here, both paragraphs begin with statements showing the logical shift from the preceding paragraphs.

Examine the sample essays in this chapter. Can you discover other phrases or sentences that function as transitions?

How Should I Conclude? As with introductions, the possibilities for conclusions are limitless. Usually, short explanatory essays (such as those under 1000 words) do not need to summarize main points. Instead, writers often use conclusions to suggest the significance of the ideas expressed in the body of the essay. For this essay, you might consider concluding with:

- The overall statement on, and particular meaning of, the relationship (the thesis). Notice Bosley's conclusion:

    > Everyone I know has aches so deep that small triggers bring tears to their eyes. The honey gift was clearly that trigger for me. I like to think I cried because seeing that bowl of honey made me miss my father. Or maybe I cried because I don't yet understand all that happened in my life back then, or why people can do the things they do to each other. Maybe I cried because my husband loves me that much, enough to know what the honey would mean. But I do know one thing: I sure do like honey. I wept to see that honey just for me.

- An allusion that best illustrates your points about the relationship. An allusion can be a powerful conclusion strategy because it projects the point of the essay onto some other subject or idea. It extends the essay's reach outward. Notice Steinbeck's use of a historical allusion:

    > But we are an exuberant people, careless and destructive as active children. We make strong and potent tools and then have to use them to prove that they exist. Under the pressure of war we finally made the atom bomb, and for reasons which seemed justifiable at the time we dropped it on two Japanese cities—and I think we finally frightened ourselves. In such things, one must consult himself because there is no other point of reference. I did not know about the bomb, and certainly I had nothing to do with its use, but I am horrified and ashamed; and nearly everyone I know feels the same thing. And those who loudly and angrily justify Hiroshima and Nagasaki—why, they must be the most ashamed of all.

- A return to an introductory image or scene that reveals something significant about that image. This strategy is often called "framing." (See Bosley's conclusion above.)

- A message about or concern for particular kinds of relationships. Notice Thuma's subtle strategy:

    > Within the small circle of the contested belly ring, my daughter and I see the same things: sexual allure, boyfriends, the instant acquisition of a Daring New Persona. I find the prospects alarming. There is part of me that would stop time here if I could, on the very edge of the changes I know are in store for my daughter, whether she gets a belly ring or not. "Come on, Mom," she says, laughing, leaning down to give me a kiss. "It's just a ring. I could always take it off."
    >
    > She smells clean, like cucumbers and watermelon. I catch her hand, feeling the bones in her long fingers. Once acquired, knowledge and experience are hard to shed. "No," I tell her, "you only think you can take it off."

Here, Thuma extends the scope of the essay. Although it primarily focuses on the belly ring crisis, Thuma admits that it is a "small circle," which is presumably surrounded by a larger circle.

Writer's Voice

Exploring Options

ome writers create very serious, sober voices. They offer claims with the utmost formality. Sentences may be consistent in length and structure. Slang words and contractions are often absent. Notice Steinbeck's sobering voice:

> This tendency toward irresponsibility persists in very many of us today; our rivers are poisoned by reckless dumping of sewage and toxic industrial wastes, the air of our cities is filthy and dangerous to breathe from the belching of uncontrolled products from combustion of coal, coke, oil, and gasoline.

Other writers create more relaxed or even humorous voices; they offer asides (in parenthetical statements) and fun metaphors. Their allusions, also, might be informal, such as Hawes's allusion to the Beatles.

> I realize this is an odd paraphrase of the Beatles, but it certainly seems fitting: I have a dog, or should I say, my dog has me? Often it seems unclear which of us is in charge in this arrangement.

As you write, decide how you want to come off to the reader, how you want to posture yourself. The following strategies can be used for various kinds of voices. Whether formal or comedic (or somewhere in between), these strategies help make any voice more engaging.

Writerly Whispers (Ways to Draw Readers in Closer)

- Parenthetical statements can offer gentle asides. Notice Schwind-Pawlak's strategy (from her essay in Chapter 1):

> Joann (the name I call my mother when she does something embarrassing) was screaming at the coach. In a voice so screeching that it rivaled fingernails on a blackboard, she told him that he was a disgraceful coach and that he should be ashamed of himself.

- Longer sentences with long phrases can create a sense of delicacy and can bring the reader into the subtleties of a thought. Notice, in Bosley's opening paragraph, the intricacy of the final two sentences and the corresponding intimacy of the ideas:

> When I opened them, he stood in front of me holding out a bowl of fresh honey and a piece of the comb which had been pulled away from the hive and was still running with the buttery sweet liquid of all my best memories. My husband might as well have gone out just then and shoved his hand, in brown bear fashion, through the stinging, angry bees to release this small brick of honeycomb for all the love and gratitude I felt toward him at that moment. He stood there holding out to me a bowl filled with my life as it should have been, and I wept.

Writerly Yells (Ways to Give Emphasis)

- Interrupting the natural flow of a sentence with a phrase or clause can draw attention to an idea. This does not mean that the writer is angry or shouting at the reader; rather, it allows the writer to guide the reader's attention to particular ideas. This is often done, as in Thuma's paragraph, with appositive phrases, set off by commas—or even dashes.

Sometimes we're lucky. Requests vanish into thing air, bumped off the list by a new fad, a lesser evil. But other requests—the ones that force us to confront our children's emerging sexuality and drive for independence—echo in our ears long after we answer them.

- Repeating words, phrases, or clauses can highlight an idea. Notice Steinbeck's use of *us* to highlight the collective nature of the issue:

  No longer do we Americans want to destroy wantonly, but our new-found sources of power—to take the burden of work from our shoulders, to warm us, and cool us, and give us light, to transport us quickly, and to make the things we use and wear and eat—these power sources spew pollution on our country, so that the rivers and streams are becoming poisonous and lifeless.

- Very short, even one-sentence, paragraphs can highlight an important point. Notice Bosley's use of two one-sentence paragraphs:

  And if I say: I went to the kitchen to look for something. Like a small and pitiful gesture of his helplessness and regret, there on the counter was a spoon he'd left beside the jar of honey, and I knew he meant it for me.
  It feels one way.
  But if I say: I went to the kitchen to look for the jar of honey. When I saw the counter, I saw there was nothing there, and I suppose I expected that. He must have taken it with him.
  That feels another way.

- Short sentences can work many ways. Paradoxically, they can work as whispers or as yells, depending on the content and the context. They sometimes create emphasis because of their placement after longer sentences or after questions. Notice Hawes's strategy:

  Do I spoil him? Of course I do. Isn't that the whole point of having a dog?

- Exclamation points . . . of course!

Writerly Pace (Ways to Control Speed and Time)

- Having more details slows down time for the reader. Like in a film, time slows down when a writer (or producer) focuses in on many particular details. Notice how Steinbeck uses details throughout his essay to focus on particular moments in history:

  Quite a few years ago when I was living in my little town on the coast of California a stranger came in and bought a small valley where the Sempervirens redwoods grew, some of them three hundred feet high. We used to walk among these trees, and the light colored as though the great glass of the Cathedral at Chartres had strained and sanctified the sunlight. The emotion we felt in this grove was one of awe and humility and joy; and then one day it was gone, slaughtered, and the sad wreckage of boughs and broken saplings left like nonsensical spoilage of the battle-ruined countryside.

- Having fewer details speeds up time for the reader. The fewer details a reader gets, the more quickly he or she moves through the events or thoughts in a text. Certainly, it is important to decide which ideas you want the reader to slow down for—and which ideas you want the reader to move quickly through. For example, Bosley moves slowly through key events (such as tasting honey for the first time or finding out about her father's departure). However, she moves quickly through less important events (such as her neighbor's being given some honey).

Revision Strategies

Now that you have a rough draft, you're halfway there. It's time to rethink. At a broad level, you should ask yourself if your essay accomplishes its goal: to discover and communicate something valuable about relationships. You especially want to make sure that you are not merely describing a relationship, but that you have investigated and sought out some of the hidden workings of relationships, or even discovered a relationship where one is not necessarily seen. In revising your essay, keep in mind the difference between revising and editing. Don't just edit, which involves correcting spelling, punctuation, and grammar (editing is important too, but it alone is not enough). To write a good essay, you may need to make big, or global, changes regarding content and organization.

Consider the following revision strategies:

- Review this chapter, keeping your essay in mind. You might (1) explore your **Invention** notes, looking for helpful ideas and/or respond further in writing to relevant Invention questions; (2) review the **Rhetorical Tools, Organizational Strategies,** and **Writer's Voice** sections with an eye toward making appropriate changes; and (3) review several of the essays, noting the way the writers in this chapter approached this type of essay.

- Set aside at least as much time to revise as you took with invention and delivery.

- Create distance between you and your writing by getting away from it for a few days if possible or a few hours at least.

- Read your paper aloud to hear how it sounds, or have someone else read it aloud to you.

- Print out a hard copy of your paper and read it carefully in a different place than where you wrote it.

- Figure out your writing strategy by noticing how the parts of your essay work together to support your main point. Consider making an outline of your essay to help you see this.

- Have someone else read and respond to your essay.

For ideas about **Peer Review,** see page 50.

Global Revision Questions

Invention (What have you learned by exploring your topic?)

- **Point of Contact:** What other ideas did you consider writing about before selecting this one? Why was this idea more worth pursuing than the others?

- **Analysis:** How has your exploration of this topic gone beyond your initial ideas and questions about it? In what ways have your ideas moved beyond your initial biases and perceptions—and beyond the common beliefs of your reader?

- **Public Resonance:** How might your essay be relevant to, or matter to, your reader? And what might be the consequence(s) of your essay? How might the reader think or act differently after reading it?

Delivery (What writing decisions have you made as part of your writing strategy?)

- **Rhetorical Tools:** Revising your rough draft while considering the rhetorical tools discussed earlier in this chapter will help the reader to understand the significance of the relationship you discovered.

  - What is the main idea of your essay, and how have you conveyed that idea to the reader? What, besides your *intended* main idea, might the reader imagine your main idea to be? How might you help the reader hear what you are trying to say?

  - What might be added to help your reader understand what your essay reveals about the relationship, the people, or the subjects involved? Where might you provide more evidence? Or where might a different type of evidence help the reader understand? How might your title, introduction, and conclusion provide more helpful information regarding the main point of your essay?

  - One of the most important elements of revision is deleting superfluous information. Where might the reader lose interest or get bogged down because you have overexplained an idea or provided too much detail? What words, sentences, or paragraphs can be safely deleted from your essay?

- **Organizational Strategies:** You might begin by describing, or outlining, the structure of your essay to get a better sense of your overall organizational strategy. Then consider the following questions: How might you rearrange sections to allow the reader to better understand your ideas? How might you rearrange ideas within paragraphs? What ideas might be more helpful to the reader if placed earlier, or later, or near some other idea? How might connections and relationships between ideas be made clearer to the reader?

- **Writer's Voice:** Describe your writer's voice. Is it appropriate to your subject matter? What about your writer's voice is inviting to the reader? What about your writer's voice might alienate the reader? What changes might make your writer's voice more inviting?

■

CONSIDERING CONSEQUENCES

While writers consider consequences throughout the writing process, this text draws attention to them here as a post-writing activity, to remind you that after an idea is communicated, consequences follow. The act of writing does not end with turning in an essay or writing a letter. Instead, that is just the beginning.

What might be the consequences of your essay for this chapter? That is, what effect might your ideas have on your reader's thoughts and actions? Consider these questions:

- Will the reader better understand the relationship about which you wrote?
- Is the reader likely to think or behave differently?
- What might be the benefits to others? How might others be harmed?
- Who besides your instructor might benefit from your ideas?
- What might be the effect of these consequences on you, the writer?

Activities

The Consequences of Your Essay

1. List as many individuals as you can imagine whose thinking and/or actions might change if they were to read the essay you wrote for this chapter. For each individual you list, name the possible change in his or her thinking and/or action. (As you consider consequences upon your reader, consider the "ripple effect" of those consequences. If your reader thinks or behaves differently, what is the impact of that thinking or behavior on others?)

2. Identify someone you know who might think or act differently as a result of reading your essay. Ask this person to read your essay and suggest what he or she thinks the consequences of it might be on him or her and on others.

3. List three other forms of delivery that you might have used to express your idea (report, letter, poster, screenplay, Web site, speech, song, poem, action). How might the consequences of your message have been different if delivered by way of these other forms?

The Consequences of the Chapter Readings

1. What reading in this chapter helped you to better understand a relationship? Might you think or act differently after having read the essay? What specific part of the essay influenced you the most and why? Try to pinpoint an element of the reading that helped you to better understand a relationship, or explain how certain elements worked together to help you understand it.

2. How might you think and/or behave differently because of one of the readings? And, how might others benefit, or be harmed, by your new way of thinking and/or acting?

3. How might *the writers* in this chapter be influenced by what they write? How might they think or act differently? How might they be treated differently by others?

Considering Images

1. Find an image and explain how someone might view it differently after having read one of the essays in this chapter.

2. Take a snapshot of life, either with a camera or describing it in a paragraph or two, and write an essay explaining how a person might view that snapshot differently after reading one of the essays in this chapter or your own essay.

The Consequences of Everyday Writing

1. Make a list of important written works that help to explain some relationship. As you generate ideas, think in categories and make connections. For example, you might think of relationships between people and people, people and places, people and things; or relationships between men and women, adults and children, workers and employees. Thinking in categories and making connections between one idea and another are helpful tools for focusing and organizing your ideas.

2. Write an essay explaining which work from your list for #1 above has had the most significant consequence on its readers.

Considering Images

1. Find an image that encourages viewers to think differently about some relationship. In a paragraph, explain how the image encourages the viewer to do this and how the viewer *might* think or act differently as a result. Attach a copy of the image to your paragraph.

2. What image has had a significant impact on those who have seen it? Generate a list of images that have had a significant impact on people, then choose one image and explain how it has influenced people to think or act differently.

3. What image has had an unintended and negative consequence? Explain.

4. What image has had an unintended and positive consequence? Explain.

EVERYDAY RHETORIC

Writing, Speech, and Action

9/27/03

Dear Students,

Now that you have written an "Explaining Relationships" essay, you might consider delivering those same ideas in some other form, such as a letter or a speech. You see, the invention and delivery strategies discussed in this chapter are good for not only writing an essay, but for communicating your ideas in various other ways. We write essays in classes like this because the essay is a good practice field. It's a good place to learn about invention and delivery. But the strategies you learned earlier in this chapter work for other forms of communication as well.

Throughout this text, we suggest in the **Everyday Rhetoric** section of each chapter that you take your ideas and write a letter. There are different kinds of letters, of course—some of which you can read about in Chapter 13. Your instructor may have you write a particular type of letter: a professional letter, a personal letter, a letter to the editor. Or he or she may ask you to write a letter, leaving the type of letter up to you.

If you do write a letter, you should not merely copy your essay into letter form, but instead rewrite it entirely. Keeping in mind the specific audience for the letter will influence the decisions you make, from matters of word choice and sentence structure to organization and content. Your writer's voice is likely to change. Taking the ideas from your essay and expressing them anew, in a letter, will help you to experience these differences.

You might also deliver your ideas in the form of a speech, or you might discuss your ideas with a small group of classmates. Refer to pages 672 and 682 if your instructor asks you to do either of these. It might also be fun to create a poster that expresses the main idea and support of your essay. You've all seen posters. They present information in a more visual manner, thus grabbing the reader's (or viewer's) attention. Creating a poster will require you to convey your ideas quickly, and will allow you to incorporate visual elements into your message.

As in the other chapters of this text, you can also *act* on your ideas. For example, had you written John Steinbeck's essay "Americans and the Land," you might then act in various ways, from recycling your own bottles to organizing an environmental protest.

Your instructor may assign one of these activities, or you may take it upon yourself to convey your idea—for example, in an e-mail to a friend. Either way, realize that the invention and delivery activities in this chapter apply to other forms of communication, as well as to essays.

Enjoy,
John and John

Exploring Visual Rhetoric

I t can be argued that images, too, use rhetoric. And by looking at how images work, we can apply some of the important concepts of rhetoric, not just to writing and speaking, but to images as well. Looking at visual rhetoric can also help us to better understand how rhetoric is used in writing and speech.

Analyzing Images: Analyze one of this chapter's images using the "Analyzing an Image" questions in Chapter 13 on page 694. As you explore the image, notice how its details work to express an idea about a relationship.

1. Write an essay explaining your analysis of one of this chapter's images. Be sure that your analysis focuses on how the details of the image work together to convey a significant point about a relationship. You should not answer every "Analyzing an Image" question in your essay, but you should consider each one as you analytically explore the image.

2. Discuss your analysis with several people, exploring through discussion how your understanding of the image is similar to or different from their own. Following the discussion, write down the main similarities and differences in your viewpoints, and explain how your ideas about the image developed or changed through discussion. What did you learn, or how did you come to think differently about the image because of the discussion?

Find an Image That Relates to Your Essay: What image might

you use in conjunction with the essay you wrote for this chapter?

1. Write a caption for the image.

2. Write an essay explaining the relationship between the image and your text. Consider the following questions:

   - How does the image support or help to explain the text of the essay?
   - What is the theme of the image? What idea does it convey?
   - What specific elements of the image convey the main idea and the support for that idea?
   - How might the reader view the image differently after having read your essay?
   - How might the reader be confused by the relationship of your essay and image?

3. Show the image to several people, and ask each person to read your essay. Then ask them how they view the image differently now.

4. Describe the rhetoric of your own photograph or image, using the "Analyzing an Image" questions on page 694.

Find an Everyday Image about a Relationship

1. Explain the relationship between some common image and American culture. Consider images you see often in the course of everyday life, whether on television, in magazines, on billboards, or elsewhere. What is the relationship between the image and American culture?

2. What image does your school use to promote itself? Consider your school's logo, mascot, or any other school-supported image. What is the relationship between school and image? What does the image say about your school?

3. What image does your community use to promote itself? What does the image say about your community?

4. Find an image that could be used with one of the essays you read for this chapter. Using the "Analyzing an Image" questions in Chapter 13 to help you support your decision, write an essay explaining why the image you chose works well with the written text.

5. Find an image in a newspaper or magazine that makes a point about a relationship. What point does the image make and what particular elements of the image convey that point?

6. Using the image you found for #5 above, what is the relationship between the image (and the point it makes) and the publication you found it in? That is, does it support some political view held by the publisher? Is it counter to the publisher's likely political view? (If you found the image in your college newspaper, how does the image relate to the views of students on your campus? How does it relate to the views of those who publish the college newspaper?)

Consider the Images in This Chapter: As stated in the previous chapter, the images in this text are often subtle; their meaning is not always obvious at first glance. Looking carefully at these subtle images encourages different ways of thinking. While each image alone conveys an idea through the way its elements relate to each other, the images also relate in various ways to the written text.

1. Look at this chapter's images, noticing the relationship between image and written text. Think in ways that connect images to nearby text as well as to text in other parts of the chapter. What interesting relationship can you find between an image and some written text in this chapter?

2. Explore the relationship, or interaction, between one of the images in the **Invention** or **Delivery** section of this chapter and one of the chapter readings. Write down your responses to the following:

   - What specific elements of the image support the text?
   - How might the image contradict the text?
   - How might the reader view this image differently after reading the essay?
   - How might the reader understand the text differently after analyzing the image

3. How does each image on this page encourage you to think differently about a relationship? Don't expect an idea to jump out at you; instead explore each image to discover or create an interesting relationship.

3

Chapter Contents

■ **Readings**

Outside Reading

Observing

How is seeing something different from observing it? What can be learned through observation?

> **A**s I sat there I felt the expectant thrill that, for me, always precedes a day with the chimpanzees, a day roaming the forests and mountains of Gombe, a day for new discoveries, new insights.

—Jane Goodall

Jane Goodall, world-renowned ethologist, has made a life of observing. She also has shown the academic community what can be learned through close attention to the living world. As Goodall suggests in the passage above, observing is about discovery—about finding something unique and particular about a subject. It involves more than simply describing a subject. Careful observers go beyond the casual glance; they study their subjects, and learn something by seeing them in a particular way. In some ways, then, learning how to observe involves learning how to see things, how to notice what is beneath the surface.

We casually observe our daily lives constantly. We watch our communities carrying on with life; we watch our co-workers, friends, children, and families. Occasionally, we take time to study, to focus on subjects and take in something beyond surface meanings: at those times we go beyond what something means to us and discover something outside of our expectations and biases. We see, for instance, how a man sitting on a street corner means something to the city that surrounds him; we suddenly see the systematic design in the movements of a seemingly chaotic crowd of people. Such seeing involves more than open eyes; it involves an open consciousness.

Observation is an essential strategy in academic life:

- Child psychology students observe the behaviors of young teens at a video arcade.
- Education students observe the interaction between high school teachers and their students.

- Biology students study the growth of bacteria over a 24-hour period.
- Chemistry students observe the effects of mixing different compounds.
- Sociology graduate students and faculty observe the language habits of a small island town.

Observers find the hidden meaning, the significant issues, and the important aspects of a particular subject. They point out how and why a particular subject is of interest to a broader public. We experience this kind of observing and reporting when we watch news programs or nature specials. Writers and researchers for such programs first make general observations. Then they focus their perspective on a particular issue or subject. They analyze that issue or subject to find the most important or valuable thing to say—to find the significance for their audience. Throughout this process, the observing writer is always looking to discover, to find and communicate a fresh and interesting idea.

3 This chapter will help you choose a subject to observe, discover something particular about that subject, and communicate your findings in writing. The following essays will provide insight to various strategies for observing. After reading the essays, you can find a topic in one of two ways:

1. Go to the **Point of Contact** section to find a topic from your everyday life.
2. Choose one of the **Ideas for Writing** that follow each essay.

After you find a topic, go to the **Analysis** section to begin developing your observation.

READINGS

The readings in this chapter all go beyond the quick glance, even beyond common sense perspectives. Each offers a new way to see a subject, whether it is a weasel or a porch. It is almost as if each essay calls on us to re-see the subject by asking us: *Have you ever thought about weasels (or front porches, etc.) this way?* Notice, also, that these essays are not mere laundry lists of details. Instead, they each offer a particular point about the subject at hand and use extensive details to support that point. In other words, each essay is a unified whole: unnecessary details (those that do not support the main point) are minimized or absent altogether.

Living Like Weasels

Annie Dillard

Annie Dillard is a Pulitzer Prize–winning author and has published many books, including Pilgrim at Tinker Creek *(1974). "Living like Weasels" first appeared in Dillard's book* Teaching a Stone to Talk *(1982). As you read this essay, jot down your thoughts about how Dillard encourages the reader to think about life.*

1   A weasel is wild. Who knows what he thinks? He sleeps in his underground den, his tail draped over his nose. Sometimes he lives in his den for two days without leaving. Outside, he stalks rabbits, mice, muskrats, and birds, killing more bodies than he can eat warm, and often dragging the carcasses home. Obedient to instinct, he bites his prey at the neck, either splitting the jugular vein at the throat or crunching the brain at the base of the skull, and he does not let go. One naturalist refused to kill a weasel who was socketed into his hand deeply as a rattlesnake. The man could in no way pry the tiny weasel off, and he had to walk half a mile to water, the weasel dangling from his palm, and soak him off like a stubborn label.

2   And once, says Ernest Thompson Seton—once, a man shot an eagle out of the sky. He examined the eagle and found the dry skull of a weasel fixed by the jaws to his throat. The supposition is that the eagle had pounced on the weasel and the weasel swiveled and bit as instinct taught him, tooth to neck, and nearly won. I would like to have seen that eagle from the air a few weeks or months before he was shot: was the whole weasel still attached to his feathered throat, a fur pendant? Or did the eagle eat what he could reach, gutting the living weasel with his talons before his breast, bend-

ing his beak, cleaning the beautiful airborne bones?

3   I have been reading about weasels because I saw one last week. I startled a weasel who startled me, and we exchanged a long glance.

4   Twenty minutes from my house, through the woods by the quarry and across the highway, is Hollins Pond, a remarkable piece of shallowness, where I like to go at sunset and sit on a tree trunk. Hollins Pond is also called Murray's Pond; it covers two acres of bottomland near Tinker Creek with six inches of water and six thousand lily pads. In winter, brown-and-white steers stand in the middle of it, merely dampening their hooves; from the distant shore they look like miracle itself, complete with miracle's nonchalance. Now, in summer, the steers are gone. The water lilies have blossomed and spread to a green horizontal plane that is terra firma to plodding blackbirds, and tremulous ceiling to black leeches, crayfish, and carp.

5   This is, mind you, suburbia. It is a five-minute walk in three directions to rows of houses, though none is visible here. There's a 55 mph highway at one end of the pond, and a nesting pair of wood ducks at the other. Under every bush is a muskrat hole or a beer can. The far end is an alternating series of fields and woods, fields and woods, threaded everywhere with motorcycle tracks—in whose bare clay wild turtles lay eggs.

6   So. I had crossed the highway, stepped over two low barbed-wire fences, and traced the motorcycle path in all gratitude through the wild rose and poison ivy of the pond's shoreline up into high grassy fields. Then I cut down through the woods to the mossy fallen tree where I sit. This tree is excellent. It makes a dry, upholstered bench at the upper, marshy end of the pond, a plush jetty raised from the thorny shore between a shallow blue body of water and a deep blue body of sky.

7   The sun had just set. I was relaxed on the tree trunk, ensconced in the lap of lichen, watching the lily pads at my feet tremble and part dreamily over the thrusting path of a carp. A yellow bird appeared to my right and flew behind me. It caught my eye; I swiveled around—and the next instant, inexplicably, I was looking down at a weasel, who was looking up at me.

8   Weasel! I'd never seen one wild before. He was ten inches long, thin as a curve, a muscled ribbon, brown as fruitwood, soft-furred, alert. His face was fierce, small and pointed as a lizard's; he would have made a good arrowhead. There was just a dot of chin, maybe two brown hairs' worth, and then the pure white fur began that spread down his underside. He had two black eyes I didn't see, any more than you see a window.

9   The weasel was stunned into stillness as he was emerging from beneath an enormous shaggy wild rose bush four feet away. I was stunned into stillness twisted backward on the tree trunk. Our eyes locked, and someone threw away the key.

10   Our look was as if two lovers, or deadly enemies, met unexpectedly on an overgrown path when each had been thinking of something else: a clearing blow to the gut. It was also a bright blow to the brain, or a sudden beating of brains, with all the charge and intimate grate of rubbed balloons. It emptied our lungs. It felled the forest, moved the fields, and drained the pond; the world dismantled and tumbled into that black hole of eyes. If you and I looked at each other that way, our skulls would split and drop to our shoulders. But we don't. We keep our skulls. So.

11   He disappeared. This was only last week, and already I don't remember what shattered the enchantment. I think I blinked, I think I retrieved my brain from the weasel's brain, and tried to memorize what I was seeing, and the weasel felt the yank of separation, the careening splashdown into real life and the urgent current of instinct. He vanished under the wild rose. I waited motionless, my mind suddenly full of data and my spirit with pleadings, but he didn't return.

12   Please do not tell me about "approach-avoidance conflicts." I tell you I've been in that weasel's brain for sixty seconds, and he was in mine. Brains are private places, muttering through unique and secret tapes—but the weasel and I both plugged into another tape simultaneously, for a sweet and shocking time. Can I help it if it was a blank?

13   What goes on in his brain the rest of the time? What does a weasel think about? He won't say. His journal is tracks in clay, a spray of feathers, mouse blood and bone: uncollected, unconnected, loose-leaf, and blown.

14   I would like to learn, or remember, how to live. I come to Hollins Pond not so much to learn how to live as, frankly, to forget about it. That is, I don't think I can learn from a wild animal how to live in particular—shall I suck warm blood, hold my tail high, walk with my footprints precisely over the prints of my hands?—but I might learn something of mindlessness, something of the purity of living in the physical senses and the dignity of living without bias or motive. The weasel lives in necessity and we live in choice, hating necessity and dying at the last ignobly in its talons. I would like to live as I should, as the weasel lives as he should. And I suspect that for me the way is like the weasel's: open to time and death painlessly, noticing everything, remembering nothing, choosing the given with a fierce and pointed will.

15   I missed my chance. I should have gone for the throat. I should have lunged for that streak of white under the weasel's chin and held on, held on through mud and into the wild rose, held on for a dearer life. We could live under the wild rose wild as weasels, mute and uncomprehending. I could very calmly go wild. I could live two days in the den, curled, leaning on mouse fur, sniffing bird bones, blinking, licking, breathing musk, my hair tangled in the roots of grasses. Down is a good place to go, where the mind is single. Down is out, out of your ever-loving mind and back to your careless senses. I remember muteness as a prolonged and giddy fast, where every moment is a feast of utterance received. Time and events are merely poured, unremarked, and ingested directly, like blood pulsed into my gut through a jugular vein. Could two live that way? Could two live under the wild rose, and explore by the pond, so that the smooth mind of each is as everywhere present to the other, and as received and as unchallenged, as falling snow?

16   We could, you know. We can live any way we want. People take vows of poverty, chastity, and obedience—even of silence—by choice. The thing is to stalk your calling in a certain skilled and supple way, to locate the most tender and live spot and plug into that pulse. This is yielding, not fighting. A weasel doesn't "attack" anything; a weasel lives as he's meant to, yielding at every moment to the perfect freedom of single necessity.

17   I think it would be well, and proper, and obedient, and pure, to grasp your one necessity and not let it go, to dangle from it limp wherever it takes you. Then even death, where you're going no matter how you live, cannot you part. Seize it and let it seize you up aloft even, till your eyes burn out and drop; let your musky flesh fall off in shreds, and let your very bones unhinge and scatter, loosened over fields, over fields and woods, lightly, thoughtless, from any height at all, from as high as eagles.

Exploring Ideas

1. What is Dillard trying to accomplish in this essay?

2. What change does Dillard's essay call for? How does she ask the reader to think or live differently?

3. Dillard's experience with the weasel affected her strongly, thus prompting her to explore her thoughts on how she lives. What similar personal experiences have prompted you to think differently about how you, and others, live?

4. Interview others, asking them what small experiences made them think differently about their lives. Ask them to describe the experience and how it influenced their thinking.

5. Discuss your interview responses from #4 above with classmates. Which responses were most common? Which were most unusual? Which would make for the most interesting essay and why?

Writing Strategies

1. What might Dillard be trying to achieve with her introduction? Does she achieve it? Does her introduction make you want to read on? Why or why not?

2. How did you react when Dillard addressed you directly in paragraph 8? ("*He had two black eyes I didn't see, any more than you see a window.*") Were you startled? Did you know what she meant? When you write, do you sometimes speak more directly to the reader than at other times? Provide a few examples of how the writing situation influences how directly you speak to the reader.

3. Dillard describes the weasel's face as being "fierce." Is this a good description? What are the characteristics of a fierce-looking face? Did her description, or word choice, help you get a better mental image of a weasel? How else might she have described the weasel?

4. What point is Dillard making in her concluding paragraph? How might she have stated her main point in a less poetic essay?

Ideas for Writing

1. What person, place, or thing can you describe as a way of making an interesting point?

2. Have you interacted with an animal in the way Dillard has or in some other thought-provoking way?

> If responding to one of these ideas, go to the **Analysis** section of this chapter to begin developing ideas for your essay.

Planting a Tree

Edward Abbey

Edward Abbey wrote many books, mostly semi-autobiographical novels and personal nonfiction, including Desert Solitaire *(1968) and* Down the River *(1982), in which "Planting a Tree" was originally published. Based on this essay, what does Abbey think is valuable? Identify the key passages that state or suggest what Abbey is trying to achieve.*

1   My wife and I and my daughter live (for the moment) in a little house near the bright, doomed city of Tucson, Arizona. We like it here. Most of the time. Our backyard includes a portion of the Sonoran Desert, extending from here to the California border and down into Mexico. Mesquite trees grow nearby, enough to supply fuel for the Franklin stove when the nights are cold, enough to cook the occasional pork chop, or toast the tortilla, on the grill under the decaying Chinese elm.

2   Out back is the dry creekbed, full of sand, called a "wash" in this country, winding through the trees and cactus toward the Tucson Mountains five miles away. We'll climb those hills yet, maybe. Rattlesnakes live in the rocky grottoes along the wash. Sometimes they come to the house for a social call. We found one coiled on the *Welcome* mat by the front door Sunday evening. Our cat has disappeared.

3   There are still a few bands of javelina—wild semi-pigs—out there. They come by at night, driving the dogs into hysterics of outrage, which the javelinas ignore. Coyotes howl at us when they feel like it, usually in the mornings and again around sundown, when I rile them some with my flute—they seem partial to "Greensleeves," played on the upper register. We have an elf owl living in a hole in the big saguaro cactus by the driveway, and three pygmy owls, bobbing and weaving like boxers, up in the palm at evening. There are packrats in the woodpile and scorpions under the bark of the logs; I usually find one when I'm splitting firewood.

4   So it's pretty nice here. We'd like to stay for a while, a lifetime or two, before trying something else. But we probably won't. We came down here from Utah four years ago, for practical reasons, now satisfied. We are free to leave whenever we wish.

5   The city remains at a comfortable distance. We hear the murmur of it by day, when the wind is from the east, and see its campfires glow by night—those dying embers. The police helicopters circle like fireflies above Tucson, Arizona, all night long, maintaining order. The homicide rate hangs steady at 3.2 per diem per 1,000,000, including lowriders, dope peddlers, and defenseless winos. All is well. Eighteen Titan missile bases ring the city, guarding us from their enemies. The life expectancy of the average Tucsonan, therefore, is thirty minutes—or whatever it takes for an ICBM to shuttle from there to here. Everything is A-OK. We sleep good.

6   Still, the city creeps closer, day by day. While the two great contemporary empires are dying—one in Afghanistan and Poland, the other in Vietnam, Iran, Nicaragua, El Salvador. And though I welcome their defeat, their pain and fear make them more dangerous than ever. Like mortally wounded tyrannosaurs, they thrash about in frenzy, seeking enemies, destroying thousands of innocent lives with each blind spasm of reaction. And still the city creeps closer. I find a correlation in these movements. I foresee the day when we shall be obliged to strike camp, once again.

7   Where to this time? Home to Utah? Back to Appalachia? On to Australia? Down the river of eternal recurrence? It doesn't matter too much. There is no final escape, merely a series of tactical retreats, until we find the stone wall at our backs, bedrock beneath our feet.

8   Ah well, enough of this skulking rhetoric. Before we go we will plant a tree. I cleared away some ragweed yesterday, dug a thigh-deep hole this morning, and planted a young budding cottonwood this afternoon. We soaked the hole with well water, mixed in the peat moss and the carefully set-aside topsoil, and lowered the root ball of the sapling into its new home. The tree shivered as I packed the earth around its base. A shiver of pleasure. A good omen. A few weeks of warm weather and the little green leaves will be trembling in the sunlight. A few good years and the tree will be shading the front porch and then the roof of the house. If the house is still here. If someone, or something, as I hope, is still enjoying this house, this place, this garden of rock and sand and paloverde, of sunshine and delight.

9   We ourselves may never see this cottonwood reach maturity, probably will never take pleasure in its shade or birds or witness the pale gold of its autumn leaves. But somebody will. Something will. In fifty years Tucson will have shrunk back to what it once was, a town of adobe huts by the trickling Santa Cruz, a happier place than it is now, and our tree will be here, with or without us. In that anticipation I find satisfaction enough.

Exploring Ideas

1. In one paragraph, summarize what Abbey is saying in this essay.

2. How is the way that you see "the city" similar to or different from the way Abbey sees it? How is the way you see "planting a tree" similar to or different from the way Abbey sees it?

3. What does your response to this essay tell you about the way you see things? That is, whether you agree with Abbey, disagree, or have some other response, what does that response tell you about your own outlook on the world?

4. Why are your ideas different from or similar to Abbey's? What in your life has most directly influenced your outlook?

5. Get reactions to Abbey's essay from several classmates, friends, or relatives. Which reaction do you find to be most interesting and why? Why would that reaction be worth pursuing in an essay?

Writing Strategies

1. How does Abbey convey his main idea? Does he state it explicitly or imply it? In your own words, write a thesis statement (a statement of the main idea) for "Planting a Tree."

2. Notice Abbey's use of concrete language ("Tucson, Arizona"; "mesquite trees"; "Franklin stove"; "pork chop"; "tortilla"; "decaying Chinese elm"). Identify specific language that you found to be effective or ineffective in his essay. Explain why the specific language did or did not work.

3. Abbey describes his own rhetoric as "skulking." What does he mean? What, if anything, does the writer's own commentary about his rhetoric tell you about the writer?

4. Abbey uses figurative language throughout his essay; for example, he compares the city lights to campfires glowing and police helicopters to fireflies. How are these comparisons consistent with the overall content and tone of "Planting a Tree"?

Ideas for Writing

1. Recall the details of a place you once lived or still live. Pay special attention to the tone of your essay, including details and using language that helps to develop, or support, the purpose of your description.

2. Observe a specific tree—one you have long been familiar with or one you have not noticed until now. Observe it carefully and also read to learn more about that type of tree.

If responding to one of these ideas, go to the Analysis section of this chapter to begin developing ideas for your essay.

Gombe

Jane Goodall

Jane Goodall, an ethologist, is a pioneer in primatology and has written a number of books about her experiences with chimpanzees. "Gombe" was originally published in her book Through a Window *(1990). As you read, consider the purpose of Goodall's observation. What does her observation tell you about the way that she views the world? And what is her purpose in sharing this experience with others?*

1 I rolled over and looked at the time—5.44 a.m. Long years of early rising have led to an ability to wake just before the unpleasant clamour of an alarm clock. Soon I was sitting on the steps of my house looking out over Lake Tanganyika. The waning moon, in her last quarter, was suspended above the horizon, where the mountainous shoreline of Zaire fringed Lake Tanganyika. It was a still night, and the moon's path danced and sparkled towards me across the gently moving water. My breakfast—a banana and a cup of coffee from the thermos flask—was soon finished, and ten minutes later I was climbing the steep slope behind the house, my miniature binoculars and camera stuffed into my pockets along with notebook, pencil stubs, a handful of raisins for my lunch, and plastic bags in which to put everything should it rain. The faint light from the moon, shining on the dew-laden grass, enabled me to find my way without difficulty and presently I arrived at the place where, the evening before, I had watched eighteen chimpanzees settle down for the night. I sat to wait until they woke.

2 All around, the trees were still shrouded with the last mysteries of the night's dreaming. It was very quiet, utterly peaceful. The only sounds were the occasional chirp of a cricket, and the soft murmur where the lake caressed the shingle, way below. As I sat there I felt the expectant thrill that, for me, always precedes a day with the chimpanzees, a day roaming the forests and mountains of Gombe, a day of new discoveries, new insights.

3 Then came a sudden burst of song, the duet of a pair of robin chats, hauntingly beautiful. I realized that the intensity of light had changed: dawn had crept upon me unawares. The coming brightness of the sun had all but vanquished the silvery, indefinite illumination of its own radiance reflected by the moon. The chimpanzees still slept.

4 Five minutes later came a rustling of leaves above. I looked up and saw branches moving against the lightening sky. That was where Goblin, top-ranking male of the community, had made his nest. Then stillness again. He must have turned over, then settled down for a last snooze. Soon after this there was movement from another nest to my right, then from one behind me, further up the slope. Rustlings of leaves, the cracking of a little twig. The group was waking up. Peering through my binoculars into the tree where Fifi had made a nest for herself and her infant Flossi, I saw the silhouette of her foot. A moment later Fanni, her eight-year-old daughter, climbed up from her nest nearby and sat just above her mother, a small dark shape against the sky. Fifi's other two offspring, adult Freud and adolescent Frodo, had nested further up the slope.

5 Nine minutes after he had first moved, Goblin abruptly sat up and, almost at once, left his nest and began to leap wildly through the tree, vigorously swaying the branches. Instant pandemonium broke out. The chimpanzees closest to Goblin left their nests and rushed out of his way. Others sat up to watch, tense and ready for flight. The early morning peace was shattered by frenzied grunts and screams as Goblin's subordinates voiced their respect or fear. A few moments later, the arboreal part of his display over, Goblin leapt down and charged past me, slapping and stamping on the

wet ground, rearing up and shaking the vegetation, picking up and hurling a rock, an old piece of wood, another rock. Then he sat, hair bristling, some fifteen feet away. He was breathing heavily. My own heart was beating fast. As he swung down, I had stood up and held onto a tree, praying that he would not pound on me as he sometimes does. But, to my relief, he had ignored me, and I sat down again.

6   With soft, panting grunts Goblin's young brother Gimble climbed down and came to greet the alpha or top-ranking male, touching his face with his lips. Then, as another adult male approached Goblin, Gimble moved hastily out of the way. This was my old friend Evered. As he approached, with loud, submissive grunts, Goblin slowly raised one arm in salutation and Evered rushed forward. The two males embraced, grinning widely in the excitement of this morning reunion so that their teeth flashed white in the semi-darkness. For a few moments they groomed each other and then, calmed, Evered moved away and sat quietly nearby.

7   The only other adult who climbed down then was Fifi, with Flossi clinging to her belly. She avoided Goblin, but approached Evered, grunting softly, reached out her hand and touched his arm. Then she began to groom him. Flossi climbed into Evered's lap and looked up into his face. He glanced at her, groomed her head intently for a few moments, then turned to reciprocate Fifi's attentions. Flossi moved halfway towards where Goblin sat—but his hair was still bristling, and she thought better of it and, instead, climbed a tree near Fifi. Soon she began to play with Fanni, her sister.

8   Once again peace returned to the morning, though not the silence of dawn. Up in the trees the other chimpanzees of the group were moving about, getting ready for the new day. Some began to feed, and I heard the occasional soft thud as skins and seeds of figs were dropped to the ground. I sat, utterly content to be back at Gombe after an unusually long time away—almost three months of lectures, meetings, and lobbying in the USA and Europe. This would be my first day with the chimps and I planned to enjoy it to the full, just getting reacquainted with my old friends, taking pictures, getting my climbing legs back.

9   It was Evered who led off, thirty minutes later, twice pausing and looking back to make sure that Goblin was coming too. Fifi followed, Flossi perched on her back like a small jockey, Fanni close behind. Now the other chimps climbed down and wandered after us. Freud and Frodo, adult males Atlas and Beethoven, the magnificent adolescent Wilkie, and two females, Patti and Kidevu, with their infants. There were others, but they were travelling higher up the slope, and I didn't see them then. We headed north, parallel with the beach below, then plunged down into Kasakela Valley and, with frequent pauses for feeding, made our way up the opposite slope. The eastern sky grew bright, but not until 8.30 a.m. did the sun itself finally peep over the peaks of the rift escarpment. By this time we were high above the lake. The chimpanzees stopped and groomed for a while, enjoying the warmth of the morning sunshine.

10   About twenty minutes later there was a sudden outbreak of chimpanzee calls ahead—a mixture of pant-hoots, as we call the loud distance calls, and screams. I could hear the distinctive voice of the large, sterile female Gigi among a medley of females and youngsters. Goblin and Evered stopped grooming and all the chimps stared towards the sounds. Then, with Goblin now in the lead, most of the group moved off in that direction.

11   Fifi, however, stayed behind and continued to groom Fanni while Flossi played by herself, dangling from a low branch near her mother and elder sister. I decided to stay too, delighted that Frodo had moved on with the others for he so often pesters me. He wants me to play, and, because I will not, he becomes aggressive. At twelve years of age he is much stronger than I am, and this behavior is dangerous. Once he stamped so hard on my head that my neck was nearly broken. And on another occasion he

pushed me down a steep slope. I can only hope that, as he matures and leaves childhood behind him, he will grow out of these irritating habits.

12   I spent the rest of the morning wandering peacefully with Fifi and her daughters, moving from one food tree to the next. The chimps fed on several different kinds of fruit and once on some young shoots. For about forty-five minutes they pulled apart the leaves of low shrubs which had been rolled into tubes held closely by sticky threads, then munched on the caterpillars that wriggled inside. Once we passed another female—Gremlin and her infant, little Galahad. Fanni and Flossi ran over to greet them, but Fifi barely glanced in their direction.

13   All the time we were climbing higher and higher. Presently, on an open grassy ridge we came upon another small group of chimps: the adult male Prof, his young brother Pax, and two rather shy females with their infants. They were feeding on the leaves of a massive *mbula* tree. There were a few quiet grunts of greeting as Fifi and her youngsters joined the group, then they also began to feed. Presently the others moved on, Fanni with them. But Fifi made herself a nest and stretched out for a midday siesta. Flossi stayed too, climbing about, swinging, amusing herself near her mother. And then she joined Fifi in her nest, lay close and suckled.

14   From where I sat, below Fifi, I could look out over the Kasakela Valley. Opposite, to the south, was the Peak. A surge of warm memories flooded through me as I saw it, a rounded shoulder perched above the long grassy ridge that separates Kasakela from the home valley, Kakombe. In the early days of the study at Gombe, in 1960 and 1961, I had spent day after day watching the chimpanzees, through my binoculars, from the superb vantage point. I had taken a little tin trunk up to the Peak, with a kettle, some coffee and sugar, and a blanket. Sometimes, when the chimps had slept nearby, I had stayed up there with them, wrapped in my blanket against the chill of the night air. Gradually I had pieced together something of their daily life, learned about their feeding habits and

travel routes, and begun to understand their unique social structure—small groups joining to form larger ones, large groups splitting into smaller ones, single chimpanzees roaming, for a while, on their own.

15   From the Peak I had seen, for the first time, a chimpanzee eating meat: David Greybeard. I had watched him leap up into tree clutching the carcass of an infant bushpig, which he shared with a female while the adult pigs charged about below. And only about a hundred yards from the Peak, on a never-to-be-forgotten day in October, 1960, I had watched David Greybeard, along with his close friend Goliath, fishing for termites with stems of grass. Thinking back to that far-off time I re-lived the thrill I had felt when I saw David reach out, pick a wide blade of grass and trim it carefully so that it could more easily be poked into the narrow passage in the termite mound. Not only was he using the grass as a tool—he was, by modifying it to suit a special purpose, actually showing the crude beginnings of tool-*making*. What excited telegrams I had sent off to Louis Leakey, that far-sighted genius who had instigated the research at Gombe. Humans were not, after all, the *only* tool-making animals. Nor were chimpanzees the placid vegetarians that people had supposed.

16   That was just after my mother, Vanne, had left to return to her other responsibilities in England. During her four-month stay she had made an invaluable contribution to the success of the project: she had set up a clinic—four poles and a thatched roof—where she had provided medicines to the local people, mostly fishermen and their families. Although her remedies had been simple—aspirin, Epsom salts, iodine, Band-Aids and so on—her concern and patience had been unlimited, and her cures often worked. Much later we learned that many people had thought that she possessed magic powers for healing. Thus she had secured for me the goodwill of the local human population.

17   Above me, Fifi stirred, cradling little Flossi more comfortably as she suckled. Then her eyes

closed again. The infant nursed for a few more minutes, then the nipple slipped from her mouth as she too slept. I continued to daydream, re-living in my mind some of the more memorable events of the past.

18   I remembered the day when David Greybeard had first visited my camp by the lakeshore. He had come to feed on the ripe fruits of an oil-nut palm that grew there, spied some bananas on the table outside my tent, and taken them off to eat in the bush. Once he had discovered bananas he had returned for more and gradually other chimpanzees had followed him to my camp.

19   One of the females who became a regular visitor in 1963 was Fifi's mother, old Flo of the ragged ears and bulbous nose. What an exciting day when, after five years of maternal preoccupation with her infant daughter, Flo had become sexually attractive again. Flaunting her shell-pink sexual swelling she had attracted a whole retinue of suitors. Many of them had never been to camp, but they had followed Flo there, sexual passions overriding natural caution. And, once they had discovered bananas, they had joined the rapidly growing group of regular camp visitors. And so I had become more and more familiar with the whole host of unforgettable chimpanzee characters who are described in my first book, *In the Shadow of Man.*

20   Fifi, lying so peacefully above me now, was one of the few survivors of those early days. She had been an infant when first I knew her in 1961. She had weathered the terrible polio epidemic that had swept through the population—chimpanzee and human alike—in 1966. Ten of the chimpanzees of the study group had died or vanished. Another five had been crippled, including her eldest brother, Faben, who had lost the use of one arm.

21   At the time of that epidemic the Gombe Stream Research Centre was in its infancy. The first two research assistants were helping to collect and type out notes on chimp behavior. Some twenty-five chimpanzees were regularly

visiting camp by then, and so there had been more than enough work for all of us. After watching the chimps all day we had often transcribed notes from our tape recorders until late at night.

22   My mother Vanne had made two other visits to Gombe during the sixties. One of those had been when the National Geographic Society sent Hugo van Lawick to film the study—which, by then, they were financing. Louis Leakey had wangled Vanne's fare and expenses, insisting that it would not be right for me to be alone in the bush with a young man. How different the moral standards of a quarter of a century ago! Hugo and I had married anyway, and Vanne's third visit, in 1967, had been to share with me, for a couple of months, the task of raising my son, Grub (his real name is Hugo Eric Louis) in the bush.

23   There was a slight movement from Fifi's nest and I saw that she had turned and was looking down at me. What was she thinking? How much of the past did she remember? Did she ever think of her old mother, Flo? Had she followed the desperate struggle of her brother, Figan, to rise to the top-ranking, alpha position? Had she even been aware of the grim years when the males of her community, often led by Figan, had waged a sort of primitive war against their neighbours, assaulting them, one after the other, with shocking brutality? Had she known about the gruesome cannibalistic attacks made by Passion and her adult daughter Pom on newborn infants of the community?

24   Again my attention was jerked back to the present, this time by the sound of a chimpanzee crying. I smiled. That would be Fanni. She had reached the adventurous age when a young female often moves away from her mother to travel with the adults. Then, suddenly, she wants mother desperately, leaves the group, and sets off to search for her. The crying grew louder and soon Fanni came into sight. Fifi paid no attention, but Flossi jumped out of the nest and scrambled down to embrace her elder sister. And Fanni, finding Fifi where she had left her, stopped her childish crying.

25 Clearly Fifi had been waiting for Fanni—now she climbed down and set off, and the children followed after, playing as they went. The family moved rapidly down the steep slope to the south. As I scrambled after them, every branch seemed to catch in my hair or my shirt. Frantically I crawled and wriggled through a terrible tangle of undergrowth. Ahead of me the chimpanzees, fluid black shadows, moved effortlessly. The distance between us increased. The vines curled around the buckles of my shoes and the strap of my camera, the thorns caught in the flesh of my arms, my eyes smarted till the tears flowed as I yanked my hair from the snags that reached out from all around. After ten minutes I was drenched in sweat, my shirt was torn, my knees bruised from crawling on the stony ground—and the chimps had vanished. I kept quite still, trying to listen above the pounding of my heart, peering in all directions through the thicket around me. But I heard nothing.

26 For the next thirty-five minutes I wandered along the rocky bed of the Kasakela Stream, pausing to listen, to scan the branches above me. I passed below a troop of red colobus monkeys, leaping through the tree tops, uttering their strange, high-pitched, twittering calls. I encountered some baboons of D troop, including old Fred with his one blind eye and the double kink in his tail. And then, as I was wondering where to go next, I heard the scream of a young chimp further up the valley. Ten minutes later I had joined Gremlin with little Galahad, Gigi and two of Gombe's youngest and most recent orphans, Mel and Darbee, both of whom had lost their mothers when they were only just over three years old. Gigi, as she so often does these days, was 'auntying' them both. They were all feeding in a tall tree above the almost dry stream and I stretched out on the rocks to watch them. During my scramble after Fifi the sun had vanished, and now, as I looked up through the canopy, I could see the sky, grey and heavy with rain. With a growing darkness came the stillness, the hush, that so often pre-cedes hard rain. Only the rumbling of the thunder, moving ever closer, broke this stillness; the thunder and the rustling movements of the chimpanzees.

27 When the rain began Galahad, who had been dangling and patting at his toes near his mother, quickly climbed to the shelter of her arms. And the two orphans hurried to sit, close together, near Gigi. But Gimble started leaping about in the tree tops, swinging vigorously from one branch to the next, climbing up then jumping down to catch himself on a bough below. As the rain got heavier, as more and more drops found their way through the dense canopy, so his leaps became wilder and ever more daring, his swaying of the branches more vigorous. This behaviour would, when he was older, express itself in the magnificent rain display, or rain dance, of the adult male.

28 Suddenly, just after three o'clock, heralded by a blinding flash of lightning and a thunder-clap that shook the mountains and growled on and on, bouncing from peak to peak, the grey-black clouds let loose such torrential rain that sky and earth seemed joined by moving water. Gimble stopped playing then, and he, like the others, sat hunched and still, close to the trunk of the tree. I pressed myself against a palm, sheltering as best I could under its overhanging fronds. As the rain poured down endlessly I got colder and colder. Soon, turned in upon myself, I lost all track of time. I was no longer recording—there was nothing to record except silent, patient and uncomplaining endurance.

29 It must have taken about an hour before the rain began to ease off as the heart of the storm swept away to the south. At 4.30 the chimps climbed down, and moved off through the soaked, dripping vegetation. I followed, walking awkwardly, my wet clothes hindering movement. We travelled along the stream bed then up the other side of the valley, heading south. Presently we arrived on a grassy ridge overlooking the lake. A pale, watery sun had appeared and its light caught the raindrops so that the world seemed hung with diamonds,

31   There are many windows through which we can look out into the world, searching for meaning. There are those opened up by science, their panes polished by a succession of brilliant, penetrating minds. Through these we can see ever further, ever more clearly, into areas that once lay beyond human knowledge. Gazing through such a window I have, over the years, learned much about chimpanzee behaviour and their place in the nature of things. And this, in turn, has helped us to understand a little better some aspects of human behaviour, our own place in nature.

32   But there are other windows; windows that have been unshuttered by the logic of philosophers; windows through which the mystics seek their visions of the truth; windows from which the leaders of the great religions have peered as they searched for purpose not only in the wondrous beauty of the world, but also in its darkness and ugliness. Most of us, when we ponder on the mystery of our existence, peer through but one of these windows onto the world. And even that one is often misted over by the breath of our finite humanity. We clear a tiny peephole and stare through. No wonder we are confused by the tiny fraction of a whole that we see. It is, after all, like trying to comprehend the panorama of the desert or the sea through a rolled-up newspaper.

sparkling on every leaf, every blade of grass. I crouched low to avoid destroying a jewelled spider's web that stretched, exquisite and fragile, across the trail.

30   The chimpanzees climbed into a low tree to feed on fresh young leaves. I moved to a place where I could stand and watch as they enjoyed their last meal of the day. The scene was breathtaking in its beauty. The leaves were brilliant, a pale, vivid green in the soft sunlight; the wet trunk and branches were like ebony; the black coats of the chimps were shot with flashes of coppery-brown. And behind this vivid tableau was the dramatic backcloth of the indigo-black sky where the lightning still flickered and flashed, and the distant thunder rumbled.

33   As I stood quietly in the pale sunshine, so much a part of the rain-washed forests and the creatures that lived there, I saw for a brief moment through another window and with other vision. It is an experience that comes, unbidden, to some of us who spend time alone in nature. The air was filled with a feathered symphony, the evensong of birds. I heard new frequencies in their music and, too, in the singing of insect voices, notes so high and sweet that I was amazed. I was intensely aware of the shape, the colour, of individual leaves, the varied patterns of the veins that made each one unique. Scents were clear, easily identifiable—fermenting, over-ripe fruit; water-logged earth; cold, wet bark; the damp odour of chimpanzee hair and, yes, my own too. And the aro-

matic scent of young, crushed leaves was almost overpowering. I sensed the presence of a bushbuck, then saw him, quietly browsing upwind, his spiralled horns dark with rain. And I was utterly filled with that peace 'which passeth all understanding.'

34   Then came far-off pant-hoots from a group of chimpanzees to the north. The trance-like mood was shattered. Gigi and Gremlin replied, uttering their distinctive pant-hoots. Mel, Darbee and little Galahad joined in the chorus.

35   I stayed with the chimps until they nested— early, after the rain. And when they had settled down, Galahad cosy beside his mother, Mel and Darbi each in their own small nests close to the big one of auntie Gigi, I left them and walked back along the forest trail to the lakeshore. I passed the D troop baboons again. They were gathered around their sleeping trees, squabbling, playing, grooming together, in the soft light of evening. My walking feet crunched the shingle of the beach, and the sun was a huge red orb above the lake. As it lit the clouds for yet another magnificent display, the water became golden, shot with gleaming ripples of violet and red below the flaming sky.

36   Later, as I crouched over my little wood fire outside the house, where I had cooked, then eaten, beans and tomatoes and an egg, I was still lost in the wonder of my experience that afternoon. It was, I thought, as though I had looked onto the world through such a window as a chimpanzee might know. I dreamed, by the flickering flames. If only we could, however briefly, see the world through the eyes of a chimpanzee, what a lot we should learn.

37   A last cup of coffee and then I would go inside, light the hurricane lamp, and write out my notes of the day, the wonderful day. For, since we cannot know with the mind of a chimpanzee we must proceed laboriously, meticulously, as I

have for thirty years. We must continue to collect anecdotes and, slowly, compile life histories. We must continue, over the years, to observe, record and interpret. We have, already, learned much. Gradually, as knowledge accumulates, as more and more people work together and pool their information, we are raising the blind of the window through which, one day, we shall be able to see even more clearly into the mind of the chimpanzee.

Exploring Ideas

1. What is Goodall trying to accomplish by sharing her observation with others?

2. How does Goodall's essay invite you to think differently?

3. In your own words, summarize Goodall's point. Then ask a variety of people what they think about it. Record and examine their responses, looking for ideas that can be explored through further thinking, writing, and discussion.

4. Is observing chimpanzees a worthwhile way to spend one's time? Consider various ways in which people spend their time (observing chimpanzees, playing basketball, writing songs, selling cars, waiting tables, and so on). What determines your answer to the question?

5. How might you participate in Goodall's discussion? Ask yourself what you think is most important and/or interesting about it and how you might contribute some worthwhile thought.

Writing Strategies

1. Carefully read Goodall's introduction several times. How does it function in her essay? Does it set the tone, establish her voice, suggest her thesis, state her thesis? What else does it do?

2. Find at least one example of each sense (taste, touch, sight, sound, smell) that Goodall appeals to.

3. How does Goodall convey her main idea to the reader?

4. Provide an example of good narration (storytelling) and good description in Goodall's essay. How does each example relate to or support Goodall's main idea?

5. What is Goodall's concluding strategy? What is she hoping to achieve in her conclusion? Is she successful? Why or why not?

Ideas for Writing

1. What is the value of an activity to which you have dedicated yourself (a sport, a hobby, a profession, and so on)? How might you illustrate the value of that activity through purposeful description?

2. What interesting point can you make by describing a quiet scene that becomes chaotic (a party just getting started and then in full swing; a course that begins well but then deteriorates; Thanksgiving dinner before and during; and so on).

If responding to one of these ideas, go to the **Analysis** section of this chapter to begin developing ideas for your essay.

The Front Porch

Chester McCovey

Chester McCovey, a teacher and student of writing, wrote "The Front Porch" about an observation he made of the new homes being built in his community. Based on this essay, what does McCovey value? How does his discussion of front porches fit into a larger issue about life? Jot down your initial reactions to McCovey's ideas and consider how you might participate in this discussion.

1 If you walk through my neighborhood, you won't see many porches, at least not the kind people sit on in the evenings. Those days are gone where I live, and likely where you live, too.

2 The front porch has been replaced—by the two-car garage. Both sets of my grandparents, who lived in the same small town, had big front porches, and summer visits often meant sitting on the porch, talking, and watching cars and people out walking. After a while someone might have suggested getting some ice cream. The adult conversation was often dull, sometimes painfully so for a child, but sometimes it was interesting. The everyday people a child sees in church or at the Little League field in a small town have a few years behind them, and what person who has lived a little doesn't have a story to tell—or a story to be told about them? Sometimes those stories would come out and bring to life a previously uninteresting Frank or Gretchen. Small towns are full of life's everyday dramas. A child hears and figures out many things on a place like a front porch on a thing like a warm summer night.

3 My grandparents' garages were small, just enough for one car and a few tools—not much of a garage for today's homeowner. In those days the garage kept a car and a small lawnmower, some rakes, and so on. The garage today must keep much more. One can see, then, how the exchange occurred. Like an old-fashioned trade in baseball, gone is the home team's beloved front porch, replaced by a big, new garage. Of course the trade is much more interesting than that. And a look at how it occurred enlightens us a little about the world in which we live. More importantly, it tells us not so much about how life is now but about how it came to be. And, I would argue, it shows us the way in which things will continue to change.

4 Back then, our own garage held two cars, a riding lawnmower, a push mower, bicycles, and lots of tools. We had a front porch and sat on it, but mostly just when we had company. Our house, then, represents the transition between two generations: my grandparents' generation that traveled less, received only three television stations (*sans* remote control), and didn't have

air conditioning *and* my own generation that is more likely to be on the go (driving from one place to another) or sitting inside, on the computer or watching TV.

5   The front porch fell victim to its two natural enemies: the internal-combustion engine (automobiles) and electricity (air conditioning, lights, and TV). Now, instead of gathering on our front porch as our grandparents did, we are either gone somewhere thanks to our transportation or we are at home but indoors.

> how life must have splashed
> out of the cup
> on warm summer nights
> before the cool air
> of electricity
> urged us all to relax
> in the fluttering glow
> of color tv

We have traded sitting on the front porch for sitting in traffic, or to be more positive about it, for sitting in our automobile as we speed along to some very important place to be. The shift from porch to garage is beautifully simple. It goes like this: I need a place to park my transportation machine (car, truck, SUV) and I don't need a large, outdoor room for sitting. The reasoning (the reality of the situation) is just as simple: There's not as much action on the sidewalk as there once was (the neighbors are indoors or driving somewhere) and I don't need to sit outdoors to stay cool on muggy nights (the air conditioning indoors takes care of that). So, a need or desire—to stay cool, to be entertained, to keep up with what's going on— is replaced not by a different need or desire but instead by a new way of meeting it.

> Need or Desire—To Stay Cool
> Previously met by evening breeze; now met by air conditioning
>
> Need or Desire—To Be Entertained
> Previously met by conversation with neighbors; now met by TV, computer, shopping at the mall, conversation with friends who we drive to see

> Need or Desire—To Keep Up with What's Going On
> Previously met by discussion with neighbors and friends; now met through national media (TV and Internet)

6   I am not saying there are no front porches. Obviously there are. And I am not saying everyone has a two-car garage instead. In my neighborhood, small garages not connected to the house still reign. But obviously, their days are numbered. The new houses sometimes look as much like a house attached to a garage as a garage attached to a house. Today's garage often dominates the house.

7   Finally, the careful reader is insisting that I deal with the backyard patio deck. What about *it*? When we do sit outdoors, we choose to do it out back, away from the rest of the world. This is interesting. We need a break, I would suggest, from the hustle and bustle of daily life, so we retreat to our own backyard to be left alone with our families. But that hustle and bustle is mostly the hustle and bustle of traffic, radio, television, and a few quick transactions with total strangers. Of course another reason for opting to relax in the backyard is that, as previously mentioned, there just isn't that much going on out front these days. (If there were, I wonder if we would sit on the front porch and watch it . . . *and* contribute to it.) I am arguing that we lose something very basic—very fundamental—when we lose the front porch culture.

8   On Sunday drives through the country, I see big new houses with big new porches. As Americans we can have it all—the house with the big front porch *and* the big garage. But I never (I am tempted to qualify this statement and say "almost never" or "rarely" but I have been thinking about it and I do mean "never")—I never see anyone out sitting on those porches. I am not prepared here to argue that we are a civilization in deep trouble because of this, though it does seem to me appropriate that we should lament, at least a little, the loss of the front porch.

9   Imagine: being entertained by sitting on a porch and talking.

Exploring Ideas

1. What point is McCovey making about front porches, and what larger point, beyond porches, is he making?

2. Based on this essay, what does McCovey value? To what degree do you value the same thing?

3. In your own words, summarize McCovey's main idea. Then share your summary with several classmates who have also read the essay. Discuss your understanding of what McCovey is getting at, then reread his essay and revise your summary as necessary.

4. To further explore this issue, share your summary (via e-mail or otherwise) with people of various age groups, asking them to respond to McCovey's ideas. Then, describe in a few paragraphs how their views are similar to or different from McCovey's.

5. Return to the initial ideas you wrote down while reading McCovey's essay. How have you gone (or how might you go) beyond those initial reactions? Through writing and discussion, explore your ideas on this issue, and in a paragraph or two describe how they have developed.

Writing Strategies

1. Why might McCovey address his reader directly in his first paragraph? Is this strategy effective? What effect does it have on you?

2. McCovey uses the first person "I" in his essay, referring to his grandparents' houses, his own childhood house, and the houses in his neighborhood today. How might his essay be different had he avoided using "I"? Would it be better? Worse? No different?

3. McCovey deals in his second-to-last paragraph with the backyard patio deck. Why? Is this an essential part of his essay? What else might he have dealt with that he didn't?

4. Identify McCovey's use of one metaphor or simile (comparing two unlike things such as *The clerk was a bear* [metaphor]; *The clerk was like a bear* [simile]). Think of a metaphor or simile of your own that might work well in this essay.

5. Imagine that you are helping McCovey revise his essay and he is not happy with his conclusion. What suggestions would you make?

Ideas for Writing

1. Besides the move from *porch* to *garage*, what other change has taken place? How has that change impacted everyday life?

2. Observe some difference in a way of living, whether it be the result of time (your grandparents and you, for example) or location (southern Californians and Midwesterners). Do not be afraid to generalize, as long as you do it thoughtfully and are mindful of exceptions.

If responding to one of these ideas, go to the **Analysis** section of this chapter to begin developing ideas for your essay.

A Building of Mailboxes

Dean A. Meek

Dean Meek, whose writing also appears in Chapter 2, wrote "A Building of Mailboxes" for his freshman English class. What is the purpose of Meek's essay? As you read, think about what Meek values. How might his essay invite a reader to think differently?

In the margins of this essay, a reader's comments point to key ideas and writing strategies. As you read the essay, consider how the comments might influence your own reading and writing.

Exploring Ideas

Writing Strategies

My wife and I, along with our four daughters, live in a doublewide mobile home on the outskirts of Perrysburg, Ohio. We have lived in this quiet community since we were married and find it quite comfortable. About six years ago we received the news of the upcoming arrival of our third child. While ecstatic over the opportunity of being parents to another child, we were also faced with a major concern. At the time we were living in a standard two-bedroom trailer that simply would not satisfy the needs of a couple and three small children. It was obvious to us that we would have to sell our home while simultaneously looking for a larger one. Neither my wife nor I were happy with the thought of having to leave the first home we shared together and were saddened by the thought of leaving the community we had grown to love.

Description and details establish need to move.

As for the people of the community, we're very close and protective of one another. If ever faced with the need for something, one would only have to take fifteen paces or so to the next home for assistance. If the residents are faced with a tragedy in their lives, neighbors flock to them to be of help. Security is never an issue due to the vigorous efforts of the neighborhood block watch committee. Any would-be crooks would rather face the township police than risk apprehension by an angry neighbor.

He values community.

Explains the benefits of his community.

So it was a blessing that we were able to find a much larger home in the community, right down the street. Such a short distance made the moving much easier. Then all we were faced with was transferring the utilities and changing the keys and slots at the mailbox building. To some this small, ten-by-six foot building is just a cost-effective means of delivering the mail, but to us it's much more. This small building on an island all its own, in the center of the park, is the heart and soul of the community.

He does not want a fancier home; he values this community!

Describes the move in general terms, focusing on "changing the keys and slots at the mailbox building."

Exploring Ideas

Writing Strategies

The walls of the building are made up of hundreds of six-by-four-inch metal doors. Each of these doors has a number engraved in it that corresponds with a lot in the community. Some of the doors are very shiny and others have tarnished with age. These doors bear resemblance to the homes in the area. While some of the residences are shiny and new, others seem to have been present for the last 30 years or more. A few of the doors are broken and in need of repair and so goes the same for some of the trailers. A couple of the doors are even missing, and in the community there is also a vacant lot or two. These doors are lined in rows, one on top of the other like the squares on a checkerboard, and that is exactly how the homes are arranged.

Physical description of the mailbox building and comparison to the mobile homes.

He invites the reader to look closely at ordinary things. To see what they mean or represent. To find meaning in them.

In addition, the small building housing the mailboxes serves as a bus stop for the many children who live here. At certain times throughout the day the children gather and await their ride to school. As they run and play around the building, one of them catches a glance of the big yellow bus coming in the entrance and yells out, "Here comes the bus," and they begin to line up. This is the beginning of the shoving match to see which child will be the lucky one on first. Then the bus driver opens the door and they file on, bound for one of the many local schools. At the end of the school day, the parents gather at the same building to welcome their children home.

Explains the functions of the mailboxes:

1) children gather to go to school

Also for the retirees, unemployed, or those on public assistance, this building secures their sole means of financial support on certain days of the month. On those important days of the month, the relief and happiness can be seen in their eyes as they retrieve their check from the building.

2) some people get sole means of financial support there

It is also the center for daily conversation as the residents pick up the mail. Everyone speaks to one another; whether it's a casual "hello" or a social exchange lasting an hour or more, they are sure to speak. To the elderly it is a place to reminisce with those of their own generation or the opportunity to tell a story to a member of a younger generation. Time after time they are seen braving the weather for their daily dose of socializing. The small overhang of this building provides them shelter to do so.

3) center for daily conversation

He invites us to see how something small, like mailboxes, can mean more than just a place to pick up mail.

And yet to others it is so much more. It is the source of their daily activity. To those who are physically challenged by tragedy or merely by old age, the daily walk or drive to this building for the mail is the highlight of their day.

4) source of daily activity for some

Thus this small building of mailboxes sitting on an island all its own, surrounded by homes that are encompassed by open fields, still enriched by wildlife, yet only 30 miles from a major city, is more than a convenience for the postal service. It has more meaning to this community than any outsider could ever imagine.

Exploring Ideas

As for my family and me, this small building of mailboxes represents all of this and still more. It's a constant reminder that, like each individual mailbox, our small family is a blessing unto its own. But also like those mailboxes when put together to form this special building, our families are joined together as a strong and loving community. Therefore, we are glad that we were able to find a larger home (mailbox) in this quiet community.

He values family and community.

Writing Strategies

Concludes with general statement of main idea: the mailbox building has much meaning. And it represents community.

Exploring Ideas

1. Based on this essay, what does Meek seem to care about?

2. Observe the mailboxes in your community. What do they tell you about the way people live individually and as members of a community?

3. What, besides mailboxes and front porches (see Chester McCovey's essay "The Front Porch"), can you observe in order to gain insight into the way we live? List as many objects as you can and then consider how they might be clues to understanding the way people live. (For example, malls, interstates, front yards, trash cans, cell phones, and so on.)

4. Ask several people to name three things they notice about their neighborhood. Then ask them what each observation says about their neighborhood. Discuss their observations with them until you create, or discover, meaning . . . or until they start getting annoyed with you.

5. What observation can you make to express an idea that you care about and would like to share with others? How might others benefit from reading your observation?

Writing Strategies

1. What details are most effective in getting Meek's point across?

2. If helping Meek with his essay, what suggestion would you make and why?

3. Discuss the suggestions that you and your classmates would make to Meek, listing the advantages and disadvantages of each suggestion.

4. Experiment with introductions and conclusions by writing a new one of each for Meek's essay. Then explain in a paragraph or two your introductory and concluding strategies.

Ideas for Writing

1. What physical characteristic of your community sheds light on the way the community members relate to each other?

2. What do you care deeply about, wish were different, or think is detrimental? What observation led you to your belief?

If responding to one of these ideas, go to the Analysis section of this chapter to begin developing ideas for your essay.

Outside Reading

Find a written observation and print it out or make a photocopy. You might find observing essays in nature or travel periodicals (such as *National Geographic*) or you might find an observation related to your major or a major that you are considering. In that case, explore a professional journal such as *Journal of Clinical Psychology in Medical Settings, Soil Biology & Biochemistry,* or *American Architect and Engineer.* You might also explore your library's electronic database or InfoTrac (http://infotrac.galegroup.com/itweb), an electronic database of journal and magazine articles. If you are using your library's database, go to "periodicals" or "articles" and then do a keyword search. If you are using InfoTrac, go to the main search box and click on "keywords." Type in *observing* or *observation* with other words that interest you, using *and* between them, such as *observing and animals, observing and wildlife, observation and city and life, observing and everyday life.* The search results will yield lists of articles in academic journals and magazines.

You might also use the Internet to find Web sites or articles that feature observations. Try a meta-search engine (a search engine that scans several other search engines) such as Webcrawler.com. As with the above searches, type in *observing* or *observation* and combinations of words that interest you. (Be careful of Web sites that are selling merchandise.)

The purpose of this assignment is to further your understanding of observation and to introduce a broad range of writing strategies. As you can see by the essays in this chapter, any imaginable subject can be rediscovered through close observation. As you read through this chapter, keep the observation you have discovered close by and notice the strategies the writer uses. Depending on your instructor's suggestions, do one or more of the following:

1. Notice how the writer applies various strategies from this chapter. On the hardcopy or photocopy:

   - Highlight the thesis if it is stated. If the thesis is implied, write it in your own words.
   - Highlight any passages that suggest the public resonance of the subject. Write "pr" in the margin.
   - Identify any narrative passages (those that tell a story). Write "narrative" in the margin.

2. Write an essay that discusses the strategies employed by the writer. The following questions may be helpful.

   - How is this observation different from the observations in this chapter?
   - How does the writer support his or her thesis?
   - Who is the audience for this argument?
   - How does the audience impact the kinds of things said in the argument?

3. Write at least three "Exploring Ideas" questions for the observation.

4. Write at least three "Writing Strategies" questions for the observation.

5. Write two "Ideas for Writing," such as the ones following the essays in this book, for the observation.

As you can probably infer from the chapter readings, observation requires a good deal of analysis and planning. It goes far beyond simply choosing a subject and writing down details. Writers usually go through a cyclical invention process, in which they return repeatedly to their original notes to find patterns and significant points. The following three sections are designed to help you through this process: specifically, to discover a topic (in **Point of Contact**), develop particular points about the topic (in **Analysis**), and make it relevant to a community of readers (in **Public Resonance**). The questions in each section are not meant to be answered directly in your final written assignment. However, answering them here, before you begin drafting, will help you discover what you are going to say—and even why you are going to say it. After you work through these three sections, the **Delivery** section, which immediately follows, will help you craft your ideas into a written text.

Point of Contact

Finding a Subject to Observe

To explore the questions that follow, actually go to a place and/or participate in an activity (ride a city bus or take a cab, buy something at a store, serve meals at a homeless shelter, recycle your trash, do your job, etc.). You may choose to visit places and do things you have never done before, or you may visit the usual places and participate in your usual activities—but with focused attention. Or you might interview people in that place. Use the following as possible starting places for your observation.

Observing a Place: a job site, family restaurant, factory, office, break room, playground, park, movie theater, shopping mall, school playground, college hall, college club, campground, woods. Use notes, audio and video recorders, and/or photographs to gather details about the place. (Some of the following questions will be more relevant to your subject than others.)

- What does the outside of the building(s) look like? What's the style of architecture?
- How is the inside of the building(s) organized?
- How is the lighting? (Where does light come from? What kind of mood does it create?)
- Besides buildings, what kinds of structures are here? How are they arranged?
- What other areas constitute the place (yards, fields, paths, walks, roads, etc.)? Are they maintained or decorated a particular way?
- What activities occur here?
- Who or what comes to this place? (Observe the demographics.)
- How are people dressed?
- What is the mood of the people or animals?
- Are people free to do as they please, or does something restrain them?

- How do people communicate? (Do they talk loudly? Intimately?)
- What kinds of sounds occur here?
- How does the place smell? (Are there many smells?)
- Is the place bright or dull in color?
- Do many colors, shapes, styles, and things clash?
- Is it messy or ordered?
- Is it warm or cold? Damp or dry? Stagnant, smoky, or fresh?
- Are the sights and sounds confusing or calming?
- What do people taste in this place?

Example: Chester McCovey's Response to Point of Contact Question

What does the outside of the building(s) look like?
New houses, built in developments or alone in fields: many are very large, some excessively. No trees, but that's understandable. Lots of different styles. Some look nice—others look plastic. Big garages, sometimes even jutting out in front of the living quarters. The garage often is a prominent part of the design, it seems. Though not flashy or stylish or aesthetically pleasing, the garage dominates, sticks out, is big. Some houses have porches; some don't. Some have big yards; some don't. But garages tend to be prominent (*tend* to be).

Observing a Person: regular at a bar or club, supervisor or manager, line worker, server, minister or priest, teacher or professor, principal, athlete, bingo player. Use notes, audio and video recorders, and/or photographs to gather details about the person. You might also interview the subject. (See the section on interviews in Chapter 12.) However, remember that a person's own words cannot reveal everything. In fact, you might find that your own observations reveal much more about this person than what his or her own perspective allows. Make certain that this person's words do not constitute the entire observing experience. Rather, use an interview as part of the observation. Use the following questions to gather information.

- How does the person dress?
- Does he or she talk loudly or quietly?
- What level of formality does he or she use?
- Does this person use figurative language (metaphors or similes)?
- What kinds of gestures does he or she use?
- What kinds of facial expressions does this person have?
- Does he or she look at people when conversing with them? What kinds of things does this person say to people?
- Does he or she ask questions?
- Does he or she make requests or give orders?
- Is this person willing to listen to people? For how long?
- What does he or she do while listening to someone?
- How do people respond or react to this person?
- Are people comfortable around this person?

Observing an Animal: family pet, friend's or neighborhood pet, stray cat or dog, birds, animals at a park or zoo, wild animals, farm animals. Observing an animal (or animals) may take significant patience. They are often unpredictable, so it may take some time to collect information. Also, animals act in more subtle ways than people do. That is, they might show anger, happiness, or other feelings with particularly small gestures. Watch carefully.

- How does this animal spend most of its time?
- How does it eat?
- How does it signal its mood?
- Does it have dramatic mood changes?
- How familiar with humans is it?
- How much does it like, or need attention from, humans?
- Does it prefer to be outside or inside?
- Does it respond differently to different people?
- How does this animal smell?
- How does it get clean?
- What rituals or habits does it have?
- Do these rituals involve humans or human materials?

Observing a Person or Object Involved in Your Major

- Use any of the above questions to help gather information, but also develop more questions to help you gain insight to the particular subject.

Invention Activity: Now that you have seen these questions, you can create more questions—and more possible topics. In groups, choose a category (a place, person, animal) and develop five to ten more questions. Try to think of questions that will reveal something interesting or valuable about a subject. Go beyond the above categories and generate questions for other categories. For example, develop questions for observing an object (a tree, a factory, a computer, and so on).

Exploring Your Invention Process:

Writers do not simply communicate something they know. Instead, they see the writing as an on-going act of discovery. Writers are always searching, always curious, always wondering about ideas or issues that might otherwise go unnoticed, and they use writing as a search tool. (And this is why writers often generate far more text than they actually submit or make public.)

As you respond to the **Point of contact** questions, always go further than your first intellectual reaction. Explore your own thoughts for hidden meaning. Develop an eye for noticing small points that might otherwise go unnoticed. You are looking for something normally dismissed, ignored, invisible, or oversimplified. You are also searching for something that you might pursue further—not necessarily a formed idea. If you begin with this sense of curiosity, the ideas you develop through the writing process will feel engaging to you, and will probably be valued by others.

Notice McCovey's initial response to one of the **Point of Contact** questions:

Example: Chester McCovey's Notes for Point of Contact Questions

What does the outside of the building(s) look like? New houses, built in developments or alone in fields: many are very large, some excessively. No trees, but that's understandable. Lots of different styles. Some look nice—others look plastic. Big garages, sometimes even jutting out in front of the living quarters. The garage often is a prominent part of the design, it seems. Though not flashy or stylish or aesthetically pleasing, the garage dominates, sticks out, is big. Some have porches; some don't. Some have big yards; some don't. But garages tend to be prominent (*tend* to be).

McCovey explores his **Point of Contact** writing further by listing points that emerged through his writing:

- New houses are excessively large (not all, but many).
- No trees
- Different styles
- Some look nice; some look plastic.
- Appearance
- Big garages, often in front of the house
- Garage often dominates the house—the living space.
- Porches—some have them; some don't.
- Yards

McCovey explores what might be interesting about the points that he listed:

- Why are houses so large? With a growing population, should we be building bigger houses? Who's building these big houses? Can they afford them? What about the animals that lived in those fields?
- No trees. What about the animals that lived there? Where do they go?
- Different styles. This may be a matter of personal taste. What does the style of these houses say about us? What do we like? Space—what do we do with it? How do we shape it and why?
- Big garages for big cars. Lots of driving. Not much walking. Big lawnmowers. Things to put in the garage. Ours is a garage/driving culture.

McCovey continues exploring his ideas this way, exploring his own writing/thinking in order to discover what is interesting about it. Then he moves to the **Analysis** and **Public Resonance** questions doing the same with them.

Analysis

What Meaning Can I Discover?

Of course, details do not simply mean things on their own. It is up to people to make meaning from details. As we analyze, we make the move from observation notes to focused ideas, from a collection of potentially unrelated details to a set of particular points. Analysis prompts us to see patterns, connections, and paths within the particulars. Jane Goodall, for example, has studied chimpanzees for years, observing minute details of their daily existence. And from her observations, she has made discoveries about chimp behavior. Goodall had to see the connections in her observational notes; she had to discover meaning behind the rituals of the chimps and make meaning out of her own observations. In her writing, she does not simply report details about chimp behavior; she analyzes and discovers meaning within the details. She makes meaning out of the experience and communicates it to her audience.

While focusing on and gathering details may be a challenging aspect of observation, analyzing those details poses a difficulty of its own. Because a list of details offers so many options, and no obvious path, for making meaning, the process can be uncertain and confusing. However, it can also be an intensive and valuable process. Imagine a student, Linda, who observed people at her place of work, a small factory. Her observation notes include long lists of details about the environment, the lighting, the physical actions of the workers, their interaction with the machines and with each other. But as she begins to analyze, using one of the **Analysis** questions (on the next page), she finds connections in those details. Notice how she goes beyond her first simplistic answer to a more complex idea:

> *What does a close examination of this subject show (about life, human interaction, social behavior, institutions, nature, and so on)?* At first, I thought that my co-workers were just miserable people at a job. They work at their individual stations, occasionally interact to communicate something about a machine part or materials, and then go to breaks—or home. But outside of that, I couldn't see anything important. But the more I looked over my notes, I realized something was going on in those small and infrequent interactions between people. While they might seem miserable and disconnected at times (maybe even most of the time), they all offer some support to one another: a small glance, a shared roll of the eyes when the supervisor inspects one person's work, the way Rob, the oldest in the shop, actually runs over to someone who needs help with something, the extra cup of coffee Bob got Maria because she didn't have time during break. All these things mean something— the underground, almost secretive, strategies to keep each other afloat in their shared situation. After I realized this, I went back over all my notes, and remembered things I had not written down. The days are actually filled with these little gestures; they happen at all times: at breaks, on the way into the shop in the morning, while the machines are operating.

Activity: Observe the activities in your classroom. Consider actions and behaviors among work groups, among demographic groups, before the instructor arrives, or as the class ends. As a class or in groups, discuss the possible meaning or significance of particular events, behaviors, or interactions.

Linda could then go on to develop this point in her writing. In fact, the idea may even develop into a thesis statement. This would mean that many other details (about physical structure, about the machines themselves) might be pushed aside—unless they have some significance for worker interaction. In this way, Linda's observation goes from a list of seemingly unrelated details to a focused idea.

The following questions can help you make meaning out of your observation notes, and to look at the subject as something more than its physical characteristics. This is where you think beyond the physical description and discover meaning. Attempt to gain insight beyond the simple glance, beyond the drive-by appearance of things. As you answer these questions, look for patterns or connections:

- What is unique about this subject? (How is it different from similar places, people, or animals?) And what does that quality show?
- What is ordinary about this subject? (How are its qualities common to other places, people, or animals?) And what does that quality show?
- What ideas or things are associated with the subject? Why?
- Is this subject symbolic of something? (Does it stand for some idea or ideal?)
- Does the subject seem different after the observation (more complicated, less intimidating, more human, less human, more predictable, and so on)?
- How is the subject different than my first impression? (And why was that impression wrong or inaccurate?)
- What does a close examination of this subject show (about life, human interaction, social behavior, institutions, nature, and so on)?

As you analyze your notes and consider the analysis questions, avoid answering too quickly. (Linda's insights come after a long examination of her ideas.) Notice McCovey's response.

Example: Chester McCovey's Response to Analysis Question

Is this subject symbolic of something? (Does it stand for some idea or ideal?) It is, perhaps. These big garages are obviously a necessity for today's homeowner. I mean, most of these homes are not within walking distance of where the owner works. Many, I suspect, can only be afforded if both husband and wife work—two cars! Now, fill the garage up with all the other machinery you need to maintain the yard. The garage quite simply says "go," "drive," "automobile," "transportation." I am at home, but not for long. No doubt the cars have air; as does the house. One need never be hot (or cold). The garage has replaced the porch. You pull into the garage and go inside and stay inside the house. Then get in the air-conditioned space bubble car when you want to leave. Of course there is recreation, but recreation is getting away from life and not a part of it. Let's take a break in our day and burn some calories, not let's burn some calories in the natural course of our day. The garage symbolizes driving, moving, loss of neighborhood, community, wealth, poverty . . .

Public Resonance

How Does This Matter to Others?

Making a subject resonate with a broader audience involves making the subject relevant to readers and helping them to see their own place in the world around them. When we read Annie Dillard or Jane Goodall, for instance, they prompt us to consider our connection to the natural world and the essence of our own lives. When we read Edward Abbey or Chester McCovey, we consider how the world around us is changing, and the effects those changes have on our lives.

Some subjects seem to have public resonance automatically. The initial steps of analysis involve making connections to broader cultural trends. For instance, McCovey's focus on porches resonates as a public trend. Some subjects, perhaps most, need to be made relevant to the audience, and it is up to a writer or speaker to make the connection. Consider Jane Goodall's strategies. She extends her personal observations into a broader intellectual world:

> There are many windows through which we can look out into the world, searching for meaning. There are those opened by science, their panes polished by a succession of brilliant, penetrating minds. Through these we can see ever further, ever more clearly, into areas that once lay beyond human knowledge. Gazing through such a window I have, over the years, learned much about chimpanzee behaviour and their place in the nature of things.

Annie Dillard makes a similar move in her essay. The stare of a weasel, one might think, has nothing whatsoever to do with the life of humans (or, specifically, the life of Dillard's readers), but she makes a connection. She prompts the readers to compare their own ordered and calculated lives to the pure moment-by-moment life of the weasel:

> We could, you know. We can live any way we want. People take vows of poverty, chastity, and obedience—even of silence—by choice. The thing is to stalk your calling in a certain skilled and supple way, to locate the most tender and live spot and plug into that pulse. This is yielding, not fighting. A weasel doesn't "attack" anything; a weasel lives as he's meant to, yielding at every moment to the perfect freedom of single necessity.

As Dillard shows, even the most personal observations can have public resonance; even the stare between one woman and one weasel can be connected to the lives of others.

Edward Abbey focuses on the connection between his own backyard and the lurking city beyond it:

> My wife and I and my daughter live (for the moment) in a little house near the bright, doomed city of Tucson, Arizona. We like it here. Most of the time.

He then goes on to explain the constant intrusion of the city (and its attendant qualities) into intimate and serene life. But he also takes an extra step to show the connection to others:

> Still, the city creeps closer, day by day. While the two great contemporary empires are dying—one in Afghanistan and Poland, the other in Vietnam, Iran, Nicaragua, El Salvador. And though I welcome their defeat, their pain and fear make them more dangerous than

ever. Like mortally wounded tyrannosaurs, they thrash about in frenzy, seeking enemies, destroying thousands of innocent lives with each blind spasm of reaction. And still the city creeps closer. I find a correlation in these movements. I foresee the day when we shall be obliged to strike camp, once again.

With this correlation, he suggests that his retreat from Tucson is like that of many people throughout the world who are running from the oppression of massive civilizations.

The following questions will help broaden the perspective and make the subject resonate with a potential audience:

- Who should know about this subject (what particular group or community)? Why?
- Should your peers know about this subject? Why?
- What do people normally experience, understand, or assume about the subject?
- Does the presence or action of this subject teach people something—about themselves, about life, about work, about happiness, about materialism, about sincerity, about identity, about relationships, about the past, about the future, about death?
- Why is this subject important to people? (Why is its uniqueness important?)

Example: Chester McCovey's Response to Public Resonance Question

Does the presence or action of this subject teach people something—about themselves, about life, about work, about happiness, about materialism, about sincerity, about identity, about relationships, about the past, about the future, about death? What we see is a loss of community. The big garage shows us we're leaving our own neighborhood a lot. The fact that the garage is connected to the living space shows us that we go from our living area directly, by pushing a button that opens the door, into the street and to another community far enough away that we drive to it. We don't interact with our neighbors (we might not even know their names). We drive past them with our windows rolled up. We maybe don't even smell or feel our neighborhood (I guess that's an exaggeration, but there's something there). Remember, we're not talking about all houses. We're talking about the ones built today. Is loss of neighborhood a loss to the people who live in those neighborhoods? Does big garage/no front porch mean loss of neighborliness? Yes, these relationships—or ones like them—can exist outside one's own neighborhood. But, what is the effect of this? What is a neighbor anymore?

Activities

1. If you can take a photograph of the subject of your essay, take one. Keep it in front of you when you write, and try to include any relevant details such as colors or its surroundings in your essay. Then, use the photograph as a visual aid, attaching it to and referring to it in your final essay.
2. Write a memo to your instructor informing him or her of your observation. In it, ask any questions that you have about your topic. (See Chapter 13 for information about memos.)

DELIVERY

Crafting an observing essay is a recursive process: writers often return to their field notes for a deeper understanding of the subject. And after they focus on a main idea, many of their initial thoughts (or notes) may be left behind because they would simply distract readers. The first step, of course, is to develop a main idea, and then to begin developing a text that supports it. The following sections (**Rhetorical Tools, Organizational Strategies, Writer's Voice,** and **Revision Strategies**) are designed to help you focus your observation notes into a sophisticated and engaging text. As you work through them, keep your notes and answers to the Invention questions close by.

Rhetorical Tools
Focusing and Developing the Idea

An observing essay seeks to show a reader something new about a particular subject and to lead a reader to an insightful conclusion about that subject. That insight, the writer's particular understanding about the subject, is the value for the reader—the thing he or she will carry away from the essay. So an observing essay goes far beyond offering details; it offers a unique awareness about a subject and its significance, an awareness that the writer has gained through careful study and examination.

Articulating Your Thesis: The thesis of an essay is not simply what the essay is "about" but is, rather, the writer's specific insight on the subject. Remember that a thesis can be *explicit* (stated directly) or *implied* (unstated but suggested by the details). But whether a thesis is stated directly or implied, a writer benefits from having a single focused statement to guide the process.

For example, imagine a writer is observing students at a community college. She notices many things about the students: their clothes, their age differences, and so on. But she decides to focus on a particular point: *The students at Beach Community College spend their time coming and going primarily alone.* Such a statement offers a particular idea about the college students. The essay, then, would focus on the solitary nature of the students. Notice how the point might develop layers throughout the invention process:

Evolution of a Thesis

The writer responds to a Point of Contact question: How do people communicate? (Do they talk loudly? Intimately?)	*The majority of the students coming in and out of the buildings are alone; they do not talk together or in groups. If people are talking, they are talking on cell phones.*
The writer responds to Analysis questions to find the significance: How is the subject different from my first impression? (And why was that impression wrong or inaccurate?)	*Although I have always associated college with social life, the students at Beach Community College show that college is often a solitary experience.*
Public Resonance questions help extend the writer's thinking: How do people normally experience or understand the subject?	*When most people talk about college, they inevitably bring up campus life: the parties, the Greek system, the study groups, etc. They think of all the movies and stories about those crazy college years, but the reality may be fundamentally different for many students.*
The writer refocuses the idea:	*Although college is often portrayed as a time of intense socializing and camaraderie, the students at Beach Community College suggest that it can be a solitary experience.*

Use the **Analysis** and/or **Public Resonance** questions to help develop the thesis of your essay. Or you might examine your notes and find one common idea or thread of details, which can lead to a general statement about the subject.

Activity: Develop a chart that shows the evolution of your thesis. Try to represent the way your thesis gains focus and depth. As in the above example, you might refer to specific Invention questions that help generate and focus your ideas.

Using Details: Remember that the details of the essay should lead the reader to the same conclusion that the writer makes. Refer to your notes from the **Point of Contact** section and find all the specific details to support your main point. Your essay, then, should be generated from *only* the details that help to show that point. Many unrelated details may be left behind. For example, consider Annie Dillard's observation of a weasel. Her main point focuses on the weasel's "purity of living." She gives us details and images that communicate that idea. You can imagine many other details (such as where the weasel went after the encounter or general information about weasel life), but such information would not necessarily support the main idea. The essay includes details that show the contrast between Dillard's life of motive and the weasel's life of purity.

Abbey's essay is filled with many details that might seem disconnected outside of his framework. We might, for instance, wonder how an "elf owl" and police helicopters are related. Although at first glance, they might seem like rambling details, Abbey's point depends on them. Because he is explaining the way the city creeps outward into the surrounding serenity, he uses details that illustrate the distinction between the chaotic city and the peaceful natural world.

Using Narrative: Many writers choose to narrate the events of an observation—to explain events leading up to a particular moment of discovery. Such narration can help to place the observation in time and help to situate the reader. Dillard uses narration particularly well at the beginning of her essay. She takes the reader through several paragraphs that lead up to the moment of her encounter with the weasel:

> The sun had just set. I was relaxed on the tree trunk, ensconced in the lap of lichen, watching the lily pads at my feet tremble and part dreamily over the thrusting path of a carp. A yellow bird appeared to my right and flew behind me. It caught my eye; I swiveled around—and the next instant, inexplicably, I was looking down at a weasel, who was looking up at me.

Here, Dillard takes the reader to a particular moment. She uses narration to focus the reader—from a broader view of the natural surroundings to a particular animal. The narration also creates a powerful contrast between the nonchalant, relaxed feeling of the surroundings and the weasel's intense stare. (Also notice Goodall's use of narrative throughout her essay. She uses narrative to explain her own preparation for the chimpanzees.)

If you are considering using narration in your writing, ask yourself the following questions:

- Would narrating the events leading up to the observation help engage the reader?
- Would narrating part of the observation help to engage the reader?

Caution: Using narrative can make an observation less formal. Some instructors in some disciplines may want you to avoid narration. Always consider your audience when planning such strategies. You might even ask your instructor about narrative.

Using Allusions: Allusions are references to bits of public knowledge, to things, events, or people outside of the main subject being observed. Writers use allusions to help illustrate a point or create a feeling. Notice Abbey's use of allusion:

> Still, the city creeps closer, day by day. While the two great contemporary empires are dying—one in Afghanistan and Poland, the other in Vietnam, Iran, Nicaragua, El Salvador. And though I welcome their defeat, their pain and fear make them more dangerous than ever. Like mortally wounded tyrannosaurs, they thrash about in frenzy, seeking enemies, destroying thousands of innocent lives with each blind spasm of reaction. And still the city creeps closer. I find a correlation in these movements. I foresee the day when we shall be obliged to strike camp, once again.

Abbey is up to some pretty serious business here. His main focus is the natural area around his home in Arizona, but he alludes to a global political crisis in which the Soviet Union and the United States (the two "empires") persistently wreaked havoc on people of the world, presumably, the rural, village-centered peoples of smaller countries. His allusion helps to create a point: that the serene beauty of his natural surroundings is jeopardized by the looming presence of an expanding city, one without knowledge or concern of its destructive power.

The following questions will help you develop allusions for your own writing.

- Does my subject relate to any political event or situation?
- Does my subject relate to any social or cultural event or situation?
- Does my subject relate to any person or event in history? In literature? In popular culture (movies, television, music)?

Using Simile and Metaphor:
Similes and metaphors are comparisons that point out or create similarities between two or more seemingly different things. (A simile uses "like" or "as.") Writers use them to help create pictures for readers, to make points more engaging and intense. Goodall uses the window metaphor in her essay to explain how human perception is framed. The metaphor helps make a potentially abstract point very tangible. Likewise, Abbey uses a simile to characterize the behavior of two countries, comparing two empires to wounded dinosaurs:

> Like mortally wounded tyrannosaurs, they thrash about in frenzy, seeking enemies, destroying thousands of innocent lives with each blind spasm of reaction.

While Abbey could have simply characterized the empires as "destructive," the simile adds an important notion: that the empires are living, breathing organisms, huge, monstrous, and even helpless.

As you consider your own writing, remember that figurative language such as similes and metaphors should be used to direct the reader's perception toward your main ideas. Such figurative language should be used sparingly. The following questions will help you develop similes and metaphors for your own writing:

- Can I compare my subject to an animal? A thing? A place? A person?
- What purpose would this comparison serve?

Activity: Find other similes or metaphors in the chapter readings and explain how they help extend the writer's thinking or support the writer's points.

Organizational Strategies

Addressing Common Concerns

How Should I Deal with Public Resonance? The questions relating to public resonance might simply help the writer develop a sense of mission. However, writers sometimes choose to make an explicit appeal to the audience; that is, they invite the reader directly into the issue at hand. Dillard's strategy, of course, is to explicitly state the relationship between her subject and her audience:

> We could, you know. We can live any way we want. People take vows of poverty, chastity, and obedience—even of silence—by choice. The thing is to stalk your calling in a certain skilled and supple way, to locate the most tender and live spot and plug into that pulse. This is not yielding, not fighting. A weasel doesn't "attack" anything; a weasel lives as he's meant to, yielding at every moment to the perfect freedom of single necessity.

Also notice Chester McCovey's opening paragraph:

> If you walk through my neighborhood, you won't see many porches, at least not the kind people sit on in the evenings. Those days are gone where I live, and likely where you live, too.

McCovey extends his observation to the reader's situation. This is an explicit strategy to make the subject relate to the reader. As the essay develops, McCovey makes his observation a public concern, and by the concluding paragraph, suggests something about the nature of American public life:

> On Sunday drives through the country, I see big new houses with big new porches. As Americans we can have it all—the house with the big front porch *and* the big garage. But I never (I am tempted to qualify this statement and say "almost never" or "rarely" but I have been thinking about it and I do mean "never")—I never see anyone out sitting on those porches. I am not prepared here to argue that we are as a civilization in deep trouble because of this, though it does seem to me appropriate that we should lament, at least a little, the loss of the front porch.

In Edward Abbey's essay, the main focus, the landscape surrounding his own home, does not necessarily have public resonance, but his strategy in paragraph 6 (referred to in the previous section) raises a public issue: the preservation of land and, for that matter, a way of life. Abbey's essay expands slowly as it progresses: beginning in his yard, opening up to include the looming city of Tucson, and even going beyond the United States to include international politics. The essay, then, becomes increasingly more public, and even more political, as it progresses. At the end, Abbey returns to his particular situation, but because the essay journeys outward, the return to the narrowed focus is layered with meaning. (Also, notice how Jane Goodall develops the public resonance in paragraphs 31 and 32 of her essay.)

How Should I Arrange Details?

Of course, arrangement depends upon the subject to some degree, but writers make deliberate choices about the placement of details. You might decide on a *chronological* strategy (presenting details through time), such as Dillard or Goodall. This strategy depends on narrative. But notice that both Dillard's and Goodall's essays do not depend entirely on narrative. For instance, Dillard begins with general reflections and a related account about weasels before offering a brief narrative. After the narrative, she explains the meaning and significance of her observation. The narrative is only a strategy to relay the details of her observation. You might also arrange the details *spatially*. Abbey, for example, organizes the first three paragraphs of his essay by discussing the spatial layout of his yard. As the essay develops, he uses paragraphs to shift from the rural setting to the city.

But chronological and spatial organization do not work for all topics. Often, writers must consider how the details of an observation can be arranged so that the reader can come to a similar conclusion as the writer. For instance, Meek organizes his essay according to the different people who use the mailbox building (devoting a section of his essay to each group of people). Each section, then, adds up to the final point about the mailbox building.

Chester McCovey's essay illustrates still another set of strategies for arranging details. Like Dillard, McCovey devotes much of his essay to a discussion about the significance or meaning of his observation. But where Dillard gives a narrative of her observation, McCovey shrinks the observation into a short introductory paragraph. (In other words, we do not witness McCovey encountering porches the way we witness Dillard encountering the weasel.) Because McCovey's point involves history (front porches are no longer central to our way of life), he moves to the past in the second paragraph. His essay, then, is arranged to illustrate the difference between the past and the present.

When Should I Change Paragraphs?

You might think of paragraph changes as camera shifts. That is, if you have a subject that allows spatial arrangement, change paragraphs whenever you want to create a new field of vision—whenever you want the reader to "see" a new thing or imagine a new scene. Notice, for example, Dillard's strategy:

> Then I cut down through the woods to the mossy fallen tree where I sit. This tree is excellent. It makes a dry, upholstered bench at the upper, marshy end of the pond, a plush jetty raised from the thorny shore between a shallow blue body of water and a deep blue body of sky.
>
> The sun had just set. I was relaxed on the tree trunk, ensconced in the lap of lichen, watching the lily pads at my feet tremble and part dreamily over the thrusting path of a carp. A yellow bird appeared to my right and flew behind me. It caught my eye; I swiveled around—and the next instant, inexplicably, I was looking down at a weasel, who was looking up at me.
>
> Weasel! I'd never seen one wild before. He was ten inches long, thin as a curve, a muscled ribbon, brown as fruitwood, soft-furred, alert.

Here, Dillard uses the first paragraph break to bring our attention away from the tree to a broader look at the scene, and then a second paragraph break to draw a narrow and intense focus on the weasel. (Notice, also, the extra space that Dillard inserts before the paragraph about the weasel. Some writers do this occasionally to create a more emphatic break in the action.)

Paragraphs can also be used to separate different aspects or qualities of a subject. Notice the first sentence (or two) of the following paragraphs in Meek's essay:

> In addition, the small building housing the mailboxes serves as a bus stop for the many children who live here.
>
> Also for the retirees, unemployed, or those on public assistance, this building secures their sole means of financial support on certain days of the month.
>
> It is also the center for daily conversation as the residents pick up the mail.
>
> And yet to others it is so much more. It is the source of their daily activity.
>
> Thus this small building of mailboxes sitting on an island all its own, surrounded by homes that are encompassed by open fields, still enriched by wildlife, yet only 30 miles from a major city, is more than a convenience for the postal service.
>
> As for my family and me, this small building of mailboxes represents all of this and still more. It's a constant reminder that, like each individual mailbox, our small family is a blessing unto its own.

Each paragraph break draws attention to another quality or purpose of the mailbox building, and to another group of people. Meek uses paragraphs to help the reader stay focused on each point.

Activity: Make a poster or flier expressing the main idea and support of your essay. Try to represent the relationships among your ideas. (See the section on posters in Chapter 13.)

Writer's Voice
Exploring Options

The Present "I": Some writers choose to make themselves visible in the text. They refer to themselves and their interactions with the subject. Dillard, Goodall, Abbey, and McCovey all include themselves in their observations and refer to their presence in the scenes or situations. This strategy obviously works for them. But they do not simply inject the "I" without good cause. Goodall draws attention to her own presence because the essay is as much about the processes of observation as about the chimpanzees themselves. The presence of the writerly "I" illustrates her point about seeing "through a window." McCovey's presence helps to show the lack of front porches in a particular area, but his personal history (such as his recollections of his grandparents) helps to make a point about changes that have occurred in American society. His use of the personal and of the present "I" gives support to his more general claims.

The present "I" can also be used to illustrate important human responses to a situation. For Dillard, the actual encounter between herself and the weasel is vital to the point of her essay. The stare between them provides insight into the weasel's life—and into Dillard's own connection to such a life. In Abbey's case, the "I" is used to show the real human role in the retreat from civilization. Both writers attempt to show the deep connection between human life and life beyond us. Without the "I" in these essays, the natural world (the world of the weasel and the desert) would seem more disconnected to people.

Activity: Rewrite the opening paragraph of either Abbey's or Dillard's essay without using the "I." Try to convey the information without attention to the writer. Then discuss how the change might influence how the essay is read.

The Invisible "I": In observation, the writer is sometimes invisible. That is, the writerly "I" never appears; instead, the text focuses entirely on the subject. In John Steinbeck's "Americans and the Land" (in Chapter 2: Explaining Relationships), the "I" is present only periodically. While the "I" surfaces to present a remembered observation, much of the text offers information without drawing attention to the personal observer. This does not mean the essay lacks a voice or that the essay is not based on Steinbeck's perspective. Like Steinbeck, Meek inserts the "I" only in key places. Although the introduction and conclusion of his essay draw attention to the "I" and to Meek's own presence and participation in the place, "I" is invisible throughout the body of his essay, as in the following passage:

> It is also the center for daily conversation as the residents pick up the mail. Everyone speaks to one another; whether it's a casual "hello" or a social exchange lasting an hour or more, they are sure to speak. To the elderly it is a place to reminisce with those of their own generation or the opportunity to tell a story to a member of a younger generation. Time after time they are seen braving the weather for their daily dose of socializing. The small overhang of this building provides them shelter to do so.

This passage reminds us that writing without the "I" does not mean writing without an interesting voice and a personal feel. Although "I" is absent, the sentences still project a voice and attract the reader. Even though Meek does not draw attention to his own feelings and thoughts (by inserting phrases such as "I think"), an individual writer, making personal choices, is behind each sentence.

You might ask your instructor if he or she finds the writerly "I" valuable, but every writer should also ask some basic questions:

- Should I put myself in the observation?
- If "I" am in the observation, what purpose does it serve?

Level of Formality: Formality is the adherence to an established convention. A formal text is one that closely follows expectations and avoids slipping out of conventional language and organizational patterns. A business memo, for instance, has certain conventions or guidelines, and memo writers rarely deviate from them because of *context,* the situation in which they are written and received. (Readers of memos in professional situations do not expect to follow a writer outside of the conventions.) Scientific reports also have conventions that vary, depending on the discipline. The scientist follows the discipline's conventions so that the writing does not interfere with the ideas being communicated. A text that strictly follows conventions is usually considered formal, while a text that deviates is considered informal.

Because essays are used in a number of situations and academic disciplines, the conventions vary, and so does the expected level of formality. Generally, writing with little or no attention to the writer's particular presence or writing style is considered more formal, while writing that draws attention to the writer's presence and style is less formal. (Of course, this is a general rule, and it does not apply to all writing situations.)

In her essay, Dillard illustrates a variety of informal strategies. At the heart of the essay is her own reflective state of mind:

> If you and I looked at each other that way, our skulls would split and drop to our shoulders. But we don't. We keep our skulls. So.

Here, Dillard constructs an elaborate metaphor and speaks directly to the reader (usually a more informal strategy). She not only draws attention to her own presence (and state of mind), but invites the reader into her thinking as well. She also draws attention to herself and her particular style with unconventional sentence structure. (Notice the one-word sentence, "So.") Much of Dillard's essay, in fact, is a study in breaking conventions of formality. Consider the following passage:

> I would like to learn, or remember, how to live. I come to Hollins Pond not so much to learn how to live as, frankly, to forget about it. That is, I don't think I can learn from a wild animal how to live in particular—shall I suck warm blood, hold my tail high, walk with my footprints precisely over the prints of my hands?—but I might learn something of mindlessness, something of the purity of living in the physical senses and the dignity of living without bias or motive.

In showing us the details of a weasel's life, Dillard goes beyond simply informing us. She does not say, "Weasels live in the purity of physical senses. They suck their prey's warm blood." She imagines herself in that purity ("Shall I suck warm blood?") and puts herself in the center of those details. Her sentence structure, which varies from very short, one-word sentences, to long, multi-layered musings, draw more attention to the writer's presence. In other words, as we read Dillard we experience her particular style, her writerly strategies and intimate thoughts, as part of the essay. "Annie Dillard" is not simply a name inscribed at the top of the page. It is an identity competing for our attention and sharing her meditations on the essence of life.

Activity: Try to rewrite any paragraph in Dillard's essay using a very formal style that does not draw attention to the presence of the writer or the sentence structure. How does the level of formality affect the meaning?

Chester McCovey also uses unconventional strategies to communicate his ideas and, in doing so, draws attention to his own thought processes. Notice how McCovey breaks entirely from essay conventions and inserts a poetic stanza. The move characterizes the essay's informality, but as with Dillard's informality, the essay does not suffer in its sophistication and complexity. In fact, the informal or unconventional moves promote sophisticated ideas. McCovey goes on to draw attention to his relationship with the readers. McCovey's and Dillard's unconventional strategies are purposeful. They are not breaking rules for the sake of breaking rules. As you consider your own writing, ask yourself if breaking conventions or exploring informality is helpful in communicating the main ideas.

Revision Strategies

Once you have completed your essay, going back through this chapter as a review will help you to better understand the finer points of communicating an observation. What is the point of your observation? Is your reader likely to find it interesting? Does it have public resonance?

Consider the following revision strategies:

- Review this chapter, keeping your essay in mind. You might (1) explore your Invention notes looking for helpful ideas and/or respond further in writing to relevant **Invention** questions; (2) review the **Rhetorical Tools, Organizational Strategies,** and **Writer's Voice** sections with an eye toward making appropriate changes; and (3) review several of the essays, noting the way the writers in this chapter approached this type of essay.

- Set aside at least as much time to revise as you took with invention and delivery.

- Create distance between you and your writing by getting away from it for a few days if possible or a few hours at least.

- Read your paper aloud to hear how it sounds, or have someone else read it aloud to you.

- Print out a hard copy of your paper and read it carefully in a different place than where you wrote it.

- Figure out your writing strategy by noticing how the parts of your essay work together to support your main point. Consider making an outline of your essay to help you see this.

- Have someone else read and respond to your essay.

For ideas about **Peer Review,** see page 50.

Global Revision Questions

Invention (What have you learned by exploring your topic?)

- **Point of Contact:** What other ideas did you consider writing about before selecting this one? Why was this idea more worth pursuing than the others?

- **Analysis:** How has your exploration of this topic gone beyond your initial ideas and questions about it? In what ways have your ideas moved beyond your initial biases and perceptions—and beyond the common beliefs of your reader?

- **Public Resonance:** How might your essay be relevant to, or matter to, your reader? And what might be the consequence(s) of your essay? How might the reader think or act differently after reading it?

Delivery (What writing decisions have you made as part of your writing strategy?)

- **Rhetorical Tools:** What rhetorical tools discussed earlier in this chapter have you used to convey the point of your observation? What other tools might be helpful?

  - What is the main idea of your essay, and how have you conveyed that idea to the reader? What, besides your *intended* main idea, might the reader imagine your main idea to be? How might you help the reader stay focused on your main idea?

  - What information might you provide to better help your reader understand the purpose of your observation? Where might you provide more evidence? Or where might a different type of evidence help the reader to better understand? How might your title, introduction, and conclusion provide more helpful information regarding the main point of your essay?

  - Drafts can be wordy or repetitious, and can contain unnecessary or irrelevant information. An essay about an observation runs the risk of boring the reader with too much description. The extra information can be a distraction, often slowing the pace of the essay to a crawl. What words, sentences, or entire paragraphs slow the pace of your writing without adding helpful information?

- **Organizational Strategies:** You might begin by describing, or outlining, the structure of your essay to get a better sense of your overall organizational strategy. How might you rearrange elements to help the reader see your main ideas more clearly? How might you rearrange ideas within paragraphs? What ideas might be more helpful to the reader if placed earlier, or later, or near some other idea? How might connections and relationships between ideas be made more clear to the reader?

- **Writer's Voice:** Describe your writer's voice. Then consider how the reader might perceive you, the writer, in this essay. What about your writer's voice is inviting to the reader? What about your writer's voice might alienate the reader? What changes might make your writer's voice more inviting?

■

CONSIDERING CONSEQUENCES

While writers consider consequences throughout the writing process, this text draws attention to them here as a post-writing activity, to remind you that after an idea is communicated, consequences follow. The act of writing does not end with turning in an essay or writing a letter. Instead, that is just the beginning.

How might an essay based on an observation influence the way someone thinks or acts? Chester McCovey might imagine that his essay gets readers to think about their interaction with people who live next door. He might also imagine that because of his essay, someone (a classmate, a professor, a friend) might decide to live in a neighborhood where front porches and walking about are still common. Thinking more radically, he might imagine that a classmate will some day become an influential architect or developer and will bring back walking neighborhoods and the "front porch culture." Essays need not—and rarely do—have such dramatic consequences. Yet they can have big consequences and certainly do have smaller ones. What might be the consequences of your essay for this chapter? That is, what effect might your ideas have on your reader's thoughts and actions? Consider these questions:

- Will the reader better understand the issue about which you wrote?
- Is the reader likely to think or behave differently?
- What might be the benefits to others? How might others be harmed?
- Who besides your instructor might benefit from your ideas?
- How might what you wrote about be affected?
- What might be the effect of these consequences on you, the writer?

Activities

The Consequences of Your Essay

1. List as many individuals as you can imagine whose thinking and/or actions might change if they were to read the essay you wrote for this chapter. For each individual you list, name the possible change in his or her thinking and/or action. (As you consider consequences upon your reader, consider the "ripple effect" of those consequences. If your reader thinks or behaves differently, what is the impact of that thinking or behavior on others?)

2. Ask someone to read your essay and to then write down what he or she thinks its consequences might be on various readers. Then discuss, in person or in writing, how the potential consequences of your ideas contribute to the overall quality of the essay.

The Consequences of the Chapter Readings

1. Which reading in this chapter caused you to think or act differently? Respond to the following questions: How did you think and/or act before reading the essay? How might you think and/or act differently after having read it? How did the reading influence your understanding? That is, did a particular example strike you? Did one sentence or paragraph stand out? Try to name the element or elements of the reading that contributed most to changing your mind. Or, explain how certain elements worked together to help change your mind.

2. How might *the writers* in this chapter be influenced by what they wrote? How might they think or act differently? How might they be treated differently by others?

Considering Images

1. Explain how someone might view one of the images in this chapter differently after reading one of the chapter essays. Be specific and describe how someone might view the image before and then after reading the essay.

2. Find an outside image (that is, one not from this book) and explain how someone might view it differently after reading one of the essays in this chapter.

3. After reading one of the essays in this chapter, how might someone view a person, place, or thing differently? Take a snapshot of life, either with a camera or by describing it in a paragraph or two. Then write an essay explaining how a person might view that snapshot differently after reading your own essay or one of the essays in this chapter.

The Consequences of Everyday Observations

1. Consider how your own careful observations have affected the lives of others. What observation have you made and acted upon that resulted in a benefit to other people? Avoid merely pointing out a casual or obvious observation you made, but think of one in which you studied the matter, discovering some significance beneath the surface. In writing, explain the important consequences of your careful observation.

2. With a group of classmates, develop a list of written texts that make observations. Consider all sorts of writing, including books, magazines, newspapers, Web sites, and so on. Then explore your list for the texts that go beneath the surface and point out the significance of the observation. After discussing the consequences of each text, summarize your group's discussion in several paragraphs.

3. Think of any written document that makes an important point—one that has successfully encouraged others to think and act differently. What observations led the writer to his or her point?

Considering Images Find an image that encourages people to observe more carefully. Write several paragraphs explaining how the image does this. Also explain the possible influence or effect the image might have on its viewers. (Be sure to attach a copy of the image to your paragraph.)

Writing, Speech, and Action

The **Invention** and **Delivery** strategies discussed earlier in this chapter apply to other forms of communication as well. Chapter 13 discusses other forms of communication that can be used to convey the point of an observation.

EVERYDAY RHETORIC

Exploring Visual Rhetoric

I t can be argued that images, too, use rhetoric. And by looking at how images "work," we can apply some of the important concepts of rhetoric, not just to writing and speaking, but to images. Looking at visual rhetoric can also help us to better understand how rhetoric is used in writing and speech.

Consider This Chapter's Opening Image: Analyze this chapter's opening image, using the "Analyzing an Image" questions in Chapter 13 on page 694 for help.

1. In writing, explain how the particular elements of the image work together to convey some main idea.

2. With a group of peers, discuss this chapter's opening image. What does it show about life, social behavior, or nature? After the discussion, write several paragraphs explaining how your understanding of the opening image has changed.

3. Write a letter to the authors of this text, sharing your views about this chapter's opening image. To support your opinion, refer to your "Analyzing an Image" responses as well as to your classmates' ideas, as appropriate.

Find or Create an Image That Relates to Your Essay: What image might you use in conjunction with the essay you wrote for this chapter?

1. Write a caption for the image.

2. Write an essay explaining the relationship between the image and your text. Consider the following questions:

   - How does the image support or help to explain the ideas of the essay?

   - What specific elements of the image convey the main idea?

   - How might the reader view the image differently after having read your essay?

   - How might the reader be confused by the relationship of your essay and image?

3. Show the image to several people, and ask each person to read your essay. Then ask them how they view the image differently now.

4. Describe the rhetoric of your own photograph or image, using the "Analyzing an Image" questions on page 694.

Consider Other Images in This Text:
As Jane Goodall's quote at the beginning of this chapter illustrates, observing is about discovery—about finding something unique and particular about a subject: "As I sat there I felt the expectant thrill that, for me, always precedes a day with the chimpanzees, a day roaming the forests and mountains of Gombe, a day for new discoveries, new insights."

1. How do the images in this chapter (and throughout this book) encourage you to see something unique and particular about a subject? Use the "Analyzing an Image" questions on page 694 to help you discover how the images throughout this text communicate ideas. Consider the following possibilities as you analyze an image:

   A. Explain how one of the images in this book shows something unique about its subject, draws attention to what is beyond the surface, and/or communicates a fresh and interesting idea.

   B. Explain how one of the images in this book takes the viewer beyond his or her expectations and biases.

   C. Explain how one of the images in this book makes a connection between a subject and the public.

   D. Explain how one of the images in this book suggests a systematic design where people commonly see chaos.

2. With a group of peers, discuss this chapter's opening image. How is or isn't it a good opening image for this chapter? What other images might have been better? After the discussion, write several paragraphs explaining how your understanding of this chapter's opening image has changed.

3. Write a letter to the authors of this text, sharing your views about this chapter's opening image. To support your opinion, refer to your "Analyzing an Image" responses as well as to your classmates' ideas, as appropriate.

Images in Everyday Life:
Find images in everyday life that draw attention to and make some point about an observation.

1. Pay special attention to images in the media that encourage the viewer to think beyond his or her expectations and biases. Identify one image, and in writing explain what observation it draws attention to and how its particular elements encourage the reader to think differently.

2. Notice an image in some public area such as a shopping mall, a government building, a library, or a city park. As you look at it, ask yourself what the image is asking you to think about. For example, the image on page 125—a chimpanzee observing Jane Goodall—might invite someone to think about the relationship between chimpanzees and Goodall, or about the more general relationship between animals and humans, or about the nature of observing in general.

   Describe the image in writing and analyze how the elements of the image work to express some main idea. What seems to be the main point of the image? How do content, framing, composition, focus, lighting, texture, angle, and vantage point help to convey that point? What public concern does the image speak to?

3. Analyze a space as you might an image. To better understand what it might be saying, try reading some public space with the help of the "Analyzing an Image" questions on page 694.

A. View some public space as an image, and analyze it. Can you, based on its visual elements, suggest what that space is saying, or trying to say, to people? You might, for example, consider a church chapel, a park, shopping mall, store, restaurant, and so on. What is the visual content of the space, and how are the specific objects in that space arranged? How is the space lit, and at what angle can different objects be viewed? What is the effect of this lighting and perspective on the people in that space? Was the effect intended or accidental?

B. Compare several spaces to discover how they speak differently based on visual elements. For example, you might look carefully at several churches, parks, or restaurants. Then in writing, explain how particular elements are used within the spaces to convey an idea or feeling.

C. What elements in addition to the visual ones communicate an idea about a space? Consider the space(s) you wrote about for A or B above. How, for example, do sound, smell, touch, and taste convey an idea about the space, and what is their influence on the people in that space?

4

Chapter Contents

Analyzing
Concepts

*What does this image say about the
process of analysis?
What does it suggest about vision or
perception?*

> "This is the whole point of technology. It creates an appetite for immortality on the one hand. It threatens universal extinction on the other. Technology is lust removed from nature."
>
> —Don DeLillo

Concepts are ideas or abstract formulations. They are generalized notions beyond specifics. For example, we have concepts of education, college, marriage, friendship, or technology that go beyond any particular college, spouse, friend, or piece of equipment. And when our colleges, spouses, friends, and machines do not measure up to our concepts, we get frustrated, and we may even alter our concepts.

Concepts are open to change and variation. Even within a particular culture, concepts change, sometimes drastically. Consider how *president*, as a concept, has changed for many people. Before the Watergate scandal (involving President Nixon), the Iran Contra scandal (involving President Reagan), and the Monica Lewinsky affair (involving President Clinton), most Americans' conception of *president* probably did not include scandal. But in the wake of such events, the concept has changed for many people. Or consider how the idea of *America* changed after September 11, 2001. Most Americans probably did not consider how their country related to the concerns of people in the Middle East before September 11; however, after the terrorist attacks, the concept of *America* shifted to accommodate our role in global politics.

Of course, people do not always agree on concepts. A dispute over a concept is often, in fact, the catalyst to major conflict between people, cultures, and countries. Think about the intense and extended battles brought on by differing notions of God or of the political struggles brought on by differing conceptions of *woman, man, family,* or *life*. Analyzing concepts turns out to be a rather important and sticky business.

In academia, students and professors are mired in the process of analyzing, discussing, and arguing about concepts. Consider, for example, sex:

- In a biology course, students discuss sex as reproduction. The concept in biology involves the study of hormones and reproductive systems (egg, sperm, gestation periods, embryo, and so on).
- In psychology, sex might be understood as a complex of drives. Students explore it using Freud's understanding of sexual development, repression, and parental affiliation.
- In sociology, students might approach sex as socially patterned behavior. A sociological understanding of sex may involve the study of social customs (such as dancing, clothing, dating, and marriage).

These concepts of sex are obviously different; in fact, many people claim that a discipline's take on a concept partly defines that discipline. (In other words, part of what defines a sociologist is how he or she understands sex or community or family.) Disciplines also focus on and develop their own concepts (ego, for instance, is a concept developed by psychology). And much of your college career will involve exploring and analyzing the main concepts of different disciplines and ultimately a long list of concepts in your chosen field.

4 This chapter will help you analyze a particular concept, develop focused explanation, and communicate your ideas in writing. The following essays will provide valuable insight into various analytical strategies. After reading the essays, you can find a concept in one of two ways:

1. Go to the **Point of Contact** section to find a topic from your everyday life.

2. Choose one of the **Ideas for Writing** that follow the essays.

After finding a subject, go to the **Analysis** section to begin developing the evaluation.

READINGS

The authors in this chapter analyze concepts (such as *college, student, creativity*). But notice, also, that each has a purpose beyond analysis. That is, each author offers the analysis as a contribution to our understanding. Iyer's discussion of punctuation, for example, sheds new light on language, and Hayakawa helps us to understand the meaning of creativity. Some analyses can even impact the way we live. Richardson's essay, for example, might influence someone's decision to attend college, and Benlow's essay might change how students take on their academic responsibilities.

In Praise of the Humble Comma

Pico Iyer

Pico Iyer has written many articles and books, often about his travels. His books include Video Night in Kathmandu: And Other Reports from the Not-so-far-East *(1988) and* The Global Soul: Jet Lag, Shopping Malls, and the Search for Home *(2000). Based on "In Praise of the Humble Comma," how does Iyer see punctuation? How does he invite the reader to view punctuation (writing, and/or language) differently?*

1   The gods, they say, give breath, and they take it away. But the same could be said—could it not?—of the humble comma. Add it to the present clause and, of a sudden, the mind is, quite literally, given pause to think; take it out if you wish or forget it and the mind is deprived of a resting place. Yet still the comma gets no respect. It seems just a slip of a thing, a pedant's tick, a blip on the edge of our consciousness, a kind of printer's smudge almost. Small, we claim, is beautiful (especially in the age of the microchip). Yet what is so often used, and so rarely recalled, as the comma—unless it be breath itself?

2   Punctuation, one is taught, has a point: to keep up law and order. Punctuation marks are the road signs placed along the highway of our communication—to control speeds, provide directions, and prevent head-on collisions. A period has the unblinking finality of a red light; the comma is a flashing yellow light that asks us only to slow down; and the semicolon is a Stop sign that tells us to ease gradually to a halt, before gradually starting up again. By establishing the relations between words, punctuation establishes the relations between the people using words. That may be one reason why schoolteachers exalt it, and lovers defy it ("We love each other and belong to each other let's don't ever hurt each other Nicole let's don't ever hurt each other," wrote Gary Gilmore to his girlfriend.) A comma, he must have known, "separates inseparables," in the clinching words of H. W. Fowler, king of English Usage.

3   Punctuation, then, is a civic prop, a pillar that holds society upright. (A run-on sentence, its phrases piling up without division, is as unsightly as a sink piled high with dirty dishes.) Small wonder, then, that punctuation was one of the first proprieties of the Victorian Age, the age of the corset, that the modernists threw off: the sexual revolution might be said to have begun when Joyce's Molly Bloom spilled out all her private thoughts in thirty-six pages of panting, unperioded, and officially censored prose; and another rebellion was surely marked when e. e. cummings first committed "god" to the lower case.

4   Punctuation thus becomes the signature of cultures. The hot-blooded Spaniard seems to be revealed in the passion and urgency of his doubled exclamation points and question marks (*"¡Caramba! ¿Quién sabe?"*), while the impassive Chinese traditionally added to his so-called inscrutability by omitting all directions from his ideograms. The anarchy and commotion of the sixties were given voice in the exploding exclamation marks, riotous capital letters, and Day-Glo italics of Tom Wolfe's spray-paint prose; and in Communist societies, where the State is absolute, the dignity—and divinity—of capital letters is reserved for Ministries, Subcommittees and Secretariats.

5   Yet punctuation is something more than a culture's birthmark; it scores the music in our minds, gets our thoughts moving to the rhythm of our hearts. Punctuation is the notation in the sheet music of our words, telling us when to rest, or when to raise our voices; it acknowledges that the meaning of our discourse, as of any symphonic composition, lies not in the units but in the pauses, the pacing, and the phrasing. Punctuation is the way one bats one's eyes, lowers one's voice, or blushes demurely. Punctuation adjusts color and tone and volume till the feeling comes into perfect focus: not disgust exactly, but distaste; not lust, or like, but love.

6   Punctuation, in short, gives us the human voice, and all the meanings that lie between the words. "You aren't young, are you?" loses its innocence when it loses the question mark.

Every child knows the menace of a dropped apostrophe (the parent's "Don't do that" shifting into the more slowly enunciated "Do not do that") and every believer the ignominy of having his faith reduced to "faith." Add an exclamation point to "To be or not to be . . ." and the gloomy Dane has all the resolve he needs; add a comma, and the noble sobriety of "God save the Queen" becomes a cry of desperation bordering on double sacrilege.

7   Sometimes, of course, our markings may be simply a matter of aesthetics. Popping in a comma can be like slipping on the necklace that gives an outfit quiet elegance, or like catching the sound of running water that complements, as it completes, the silence of a Japanese landscape. When V. S. Naipaul, in his latest novel, writes, "He was a middle-aged man, with glasses," the first comma can seem a little precious. Yet it gives the description a spin, as well as a subtlety, that it otherwise lacks, and it shows that the glasses are not part of the middle-agedness, but something else.

8   Thus all these tiny scratches give us breadth and heft and depth. A world that has only periods is a world without inflections. It is a world without shade. It has a music without sharps and flats. It is a martial music. It has a jackboot rhythm. Words cannot bend and curve. A comma, by comparison, catches the gentle drift of the mind in thought, turning in on itself and back on itself, reversing, redoubling, and returning along the course of its own sweet river music; while the semicolon brings clauses and thoughts together with all the silent discretion of a hostess arranging guests around her dinner table.

9   Punctuation, then, is a matter of care. Care for words, yes, but also, and more important, for what the words imply. Only a lover notices the small things: the way the afternoon light catches the nape of a neck, or how a strand of hair slips out from behind an ear, or the way a finger curls around a cup. And no one scans a letter so closely as a lover, searching for the small print, straining to hear its nuances, its

gasps, its sighs and hesitations, poring over the secret messages that lie in every cadence. The difference between "Jane (whom I adore)" and "Jane, whom I adore," and the difference between them both and "Jane—whom I adore," marks all the distance between ecstasy and heartache. "No iron can pierce the heart with such force as a period put at just the right place," in Isaac Babel's lovely words; a comma can let us hear a voice break, or a heart. Punctuation, in fact, is a labor of love. Which brings us back, in a way, to gods.

Exploring Ideas

1. What is Iyer trying to accomplish in this essay?

2. How does Iyer encourage the reader to think differently about commas? How might Iyer's essay encourage the reader to think differently about bigger issues than commas?

3. Examine syllabi from several classes that you and/or others are taking. Compare the way different professors use commas and other forms of punctuation. What, if anything, might the writer's punctuation say about the writer?

4. Look further at your study of professors' syllabi begun in #3 above, this time including word choice, sentence structure, and document design in your analysis. Aside from the content expressed in the syllabus, what message do you get from the way the writer expresses that content? Explain your analysis in several paragraphs.

5. Analyze the same syllabus as a classmate (doing #3 and #4 above), and then compare your analyses. To compare them, write down your and your classmate's main ideas and note how they are similar or different. Then take each main idea and write down how it was supported. That is, what evidence was provided to support or explain that idea? Note the similar or different support. Summarize your analysis comparison in several paragraphs.

Writing Strategies

1. How does Iyer invite the reader to his text? That is, how does Iyer make his text inviting to the reader?

2. Iyer uses figurative language such as metaphors (punctuation is a pillar) and similes (using a comma is *like* slipping on a necklace). Find several other uses of figurative language in Iyer's essay. Are they successful? How does his use of figurative language help the reader to understand his point?

3. Iyer says punctuation "gives us the human voice, and all the meanings that lie between the words." Identify one sentence in any essay besides Iyer's and punctuate it in three different ways, each way suggesting a different meaning.

4. Study Iyer's organization. How does he introduce new topics in his essay? What strategy does he use to connect one idea to another?

Ideas for Writing

1. What common object or familiar event can you define in a new and helpful way?

2. What everyday object or event deserves more respect than it gets? Consider objects and events that are so common (such as the comma) that they get overlooked.

> If responding to one of these ideas, go to the **Analysis** section of this chapter to begin developing ideas for your essay.

What It Means to Be Creative

S. I. Hayakawa

S. I. Hayakawa was a scholar of general semantics, a college president, and a United States senator. He wrote several books, including Language in Thought and Action *and* Through the Communication Barrier: On Speaking, Listening, and Understanding, *in which "What It Means to Be Creative" was first published. Before you read this essay, write down what you think it means to be creative. Then as you read, underline or highlight any ideas that are new to you. After reading the essay, write down how Hayakawa encourages the reader to think differently about creativity.*

1 What distinguishes the creative person? By creative person I don't mean only the great painter or poet or musician. I also want to include the creative housewife, teacher, warehouseman, sales manager—anyone who is able to break through habitual routines and invent new solutions to old problems, solutions that strike people with their appropriateness as well as originality, so that they say, "Why didn't I think of that?"

2 A creative person, first, is not limited in his thinking to "what everyone knows." "Everyone knows" that trees are green. The creative artist is able to see that in certain lights some trees look blue or purple or yellow. The creative person looks at the world with his or her own eyes, not with the eyes of others. The creative individual also knows his or her own feelings better than the average person. Most people don't know the answer to the question, "How are you? How do you feel?" The reason they don't know is that they are so busy feeling what they are supposed to feel, thinking what they are supposed to think, that they never get down to examining their own deepest feelings.

3 "How did you like the play?" "Oh, it was a fine play. It was well reviewed in *The New Yorker.*"

4 With authority figures like drama critics and book reviewers and teachers and professors telling us what to think and how to feel, many of us are busy playing roles, fulfilling other people's expectations. As Republicans, we think what other Republicans think. As Catholics, we think what other Catholics think. And so on. Not many of us ask ourselves, "How do I feel? What do I think?"—and wait for answers.

5 Another characteristic of the creative person is that he is able to entertain and play with ideas that the average person may regard as silly, mistaken, or downright dangerous. All new ideas sound foolish at first, because they are new. (In the early days of the railroad, it was argued that speeds of twenty-five mph or over were impractical because people's brains would burst.) A person who is afraid of being laughed at or disapproved of for having "foolish" or "unsound" ideas will have the satisfaction of having everyone agree with him, but he will never be creative, because creativity means being willing to take a chance—to go out on a limb.

6 The person who would be creative must be able to endure loneliness—even ridicule. If he has a great and original idea that others are not yet ready to accept, there will be long periods of loneliness. There will be times when his friends and relatives think he is crazy, and he'll begin to wonder if they are right. A genuinely creative person, believing in his creation, is able to endure this loneliness—for years if necessary.

7 Another trait of the creative person is idle curiosity. Such a person asks questions, reads books, conducts investigations into matters apparently unrelated to job or profession—just for the fun of knowing. It is from these apparently unrelated sources that brilliant ideas often emerge to enrich one's own field of work.

8 Finally, the creative person plays hunches. "Pure intellect," says Dr. Hans Selye, the great medical researcher at the University of Montreal, "is largely a quality of the middle-class mind. The lowliest hooligan and the greatest creator in

the fields of science are activated mainly by imponderable instincts and emotions, especially faith. Curiously, even scientific research, the most intellectual creative effort of which man is capable, is no exception in this respect."

9   Alfred Korzybski also understood well the role of undefinable emotions in the creative life. He wrote, "Creative scientists know very well from observation of themselves that all creative work starts as a feeling, inclination, suspicion, intuition, hunch, or some other nonverbal affective state, which only at a later date, after a sort of nursing, takes the shape of verbal expression worked out later in a rationalized, coherent . . . theory."

10   Creativity is the act of bringing something new into the world, whether a symphony, a novel, an improved layout for a supermarket, a new and unexpected casserole dish. It is based first on communication with oneself, then testing that communication with experience and the realities one has to contend with. The result is the highest, most exciting kind of learning.

Exploring Ideas

1. What does Hayakawa mean by "creative"?

2. How is Hayakawa's concept of creativity different from your own? How did your concept change after reading the essay?

3. Rate yourself on your own creativity scale. Be ready to support your claim.

4. Hayakawa says that one trait of the creative person is "idle curiosity"—asking questions, reading books, conducting investigations into matters "apparently unrelated to job or profession—just for the fun of knowing." Ask others to list several traits of the creative person, and then explain how their ideas about creativity are similar to or different from Hayakawa's.

5. In what ways is writing an essay an act of "creativity"? List Hayakawa's main points (or characteristics) of creativity and apply them to writing an essay. Which ones apply? Which ones don't?

6. Ask several people that you consider to be creative why they do certain creative things—those things that make you consider them to be creative. Explore their creative history and what continues to stimulate their creativity.

Writing Strategies

1. Describe the strategy Hayakawa uses to help the reader to understand the term "creative."
That is, how specifically does he make the term clear to the reader?

2. Describe Hayakawa's voice—the way he sounds to the reader.

3. Would you describe Hayakawa's writing as creative? Explain what is or is not creative about his writing.

4. How does Hayakawa lead the reader from one paragraph to another? Select several paragraphs as examples for your explanation.

Ideas for Writing

1. Based on Hayakawa's definition of "creative," who is not generally considered creative but in fact is?

2. Hayakawa's essay analyzes the concept of "creativity" or "the creative person." What other concepts might you analyze?

good teacher	great rock band
Thanksgiving dinner	good sermon
best friend	humanitarian
snappy dresser	nice day
bad waitress	good president
rewarding experience	parent

If responding to one of these ideas, go to the Analysis section of this chapter to begin developing ideas for your essay.

College? What's in It for Me?

Steven M. Richardson

Steven M. Richardson is Vice President for Academic Affairs at Winona State University in Winona, Minnesota. Based on this essay, how is Richardson's view of college (his understanding of the concept of college) different from the usual view that many of his readers have? What might Richardson be trying to achieve in this essay? When this essay was written, Richardson was a dean at Bowling Green State University, in Ohio. A version of this essay appeared in the Toledo Blade *on Saturday, February 7, 1998 under the title* College Not for Everyone, but It Can Open Doors.

1   There are lots of reasons not to go to college. If you and I sat down to make a list, I'll bet mine would be the longer one. You see, I have an advantage: I'm a college administrator. More importantly, I have two college-age children, one of whom is halfway to graduation and the other of whom has decided not to go to college. We've sat around the dining room table and made our lists many times. It's scary, let me tell you.

2   The biggest reason for not going, probably, is that college costs money. There are a lot of misconceptions about how much it costs, but everyone knows the bottom line: education is expensive. In a national survey in 1997, randomly selected adults estimated that the tuition and fees at a public community college averaged $6,295 per year and that the cost at public universities was $9,599. These guesses are both way over the mark. Owens Community College charged $1,896 that year, and Bowling Green State University cost $4,204. Nationally, the majority (54.1%) of students at public universities pay less than $4,000 a year. Nearly three quarters of all full-time undergraduates attending four-year colleges and universities pay less than $8,000 a year for tuition and fees. That's not as bad as most people think, by far, but it still isn't chicken feed.

3   So even after you clear away the fog, college isn't cheap. Housing and food add to the cost of taking classes, and so do books, transportation to and from campus, and a host of incidentals. I've been paying my daughter's bills for two and a half years, and it's like carrying a second mortgage. Financial aid helps a bit, but today that usually means low-interest loans instead of the scholarships that were available 20 years ago.

4   When the economy is in good shape and unemployment is low, as it is now, another reason not to attend college is that you can get a decent job without a college education. College admissions officers have known for a long time that student enrollment and the health of the economy move in opposite directions, so they joke about praying for economic disaster. It takes guts to turn down a chance to earn big bucks now and to hold out for a better job in four years, especially if you know that you'll be piling up college debts in the meantime.

5   A lot of students enter college without knowing what they want to study. About a quarter of Bowling Green's freshmen are unsure about what to major in, and that's true in most colleges and universities. Would they be better off not going to college? That's another reason that some high school graduates give for not applying. At age 18, students get a lot of pressure from family and friends to focus on a career. Sitting in classes without having career plans can seem like a colossal waste of time.

6   When all of the logical reasons for not going to college are exhausted—and I've only pointed to three so far—the fact remains that quite a number of people just don't like to go to school. It's hard work and, my son says, "It's BORING." If college looks like four more years of the routine you've seen since kindergarten, only tougher, you might start thinking about softer options, like enlisting in the Marines.

7   I told you this was a scary exercise, didn't I? Now that we are both discouraged, let me paint another picture of reality for you. The fact of the matter is that an increasing number of high school graduates choose to attend college, despite all of the good reasons for doing something else instead. There must be some good reasons for going to college.

8   Last summer, 93% of our incoming freshmen said that preparing for a professional career was a very important reason for coming to BGSU. That percentage is higher than the national average, but career preparation is at the top of survey results anywhere you ask the question these days. The truth is that, although there are plenty of jobs for high school graduates, the ones with the highest salaries go to the college grads. If you want to be a dentist, or a CPA, or a school teacher, or a nurse, you need a college degree. Many of those jobs have starting salaries that are better than what you can earn after 20 years with just a high school diploma. If that's your goal, it's worth waiting four years to enter the job market. It's even worth starting with some college debt, so long as you don't go overboard.

9   I would hate to overemphasize money. You can find plenty of businessmen who never went to college and are earning very respectable salaries. And, of course, there are always people like Paul McCartney and Madonna who went straight for the gold. I have had too many miser-

able students who were headed for law school because they were attracted by the money, or because their fathers or mothers were, which is worse. Some of them might have been happier and still made a good income without a college degree. What's truly important is doing something that you believe in and are good at. Still, the point is that many really good careers, with good salaries, are out of reach unless you go to college.

10   What if you don't know what you want to do? That's OK. One of the best reasons to go to college is to find out what you're good at. Most people who become genetic engineers or metallurgists discover their calling after they enter college. Roughly a third of the undergraduate curriculum in most colleges involves General Education, a block of courses meant to encourage students to explore subjects that they might otherwise avoid. Even those who choose a major on the first day can surprise themselves by finding new talents and interests. Plenty of students stumble into their eventual careers this way. I did.

11   In fact, that's what college is all about, in my opinion. Students who come to campus with the single-minded goal of preparing for a career just don't get it. Sitting in class for four years to get a diploma and a job makes about as much sense as riding from here to Los Angeles on a bus with your eyes closed. You'll get there, but you'll miss all the scenery. College is about

discovering who you are and what you can do, sometimes against your will. The challenge is to learn how to think and how to create new solutions to problems that nobody before you has faced, and how to enjoy life along the way.

12   College is hard work and—let's be honest—it's sometimes boring, too. So are a lot of other things that we all do. College is also expensive and it takes a chunk of your life when it may seem more important to get a job, buy a car, and start a family. It is not the right choice for everybody. For a great many people, though, it is a door to career and personal growth opportunities that they cannot gain in any other way. The decision to attend college is an investment in your future—a risk, certainly, but one with a big payoff if it's the right decision for you. Your choice.

Exploring Ideas

1. Based on this essay, what does Richardson think is worthwhile about going to college? What main reason does he ultimately focus on?

2. How is your reason for attending college similar to or different from the one Richardson focuses on in this essay?

3. Survey a variety of people about why someone should or should not attend college. Include both people who have and have not attended. What are the most common responses? What are the least common ones? What responses did you find most interesting and why?

4. Interview several people more in depth about their ideas of why someone should or should not attend college. Try to find the reasoning behind their responses. Why, for example, might one person believe college is about finding out what one wants to do while another person thinks attending college without a clear career goal in mind is a waste of money? The main question you will be asking as you explore further is "Why?"

5. What idea do you think is most important or interesting in Richardson's essay? How might you pursue that idea and contribute something worthwhile to this discussion about college?

Writing Strategies

1. In two or three sentences, describe Richardson's strategy and organization for making his point.

2. How does Richardson establish his credibility?

3. Describe Richardson's voice as a writer. Is it inviting? Alienating? Provide examples to support your claim.

Ideas for Writing

1. What is college all about?

2. What determines what college is about?

> If responding to one of these ideas, go to the **Analysis** section of this chapter to begin developing ideas for your essay.

"Have It Your Way": Consumerism Invades Education

Simon Benlow

Simon Benlow is a writer and composition teacher. This essay, which appeared in a faculty newsletter, came in response to a particular memo within his institution and to a broader trend in higher education. As you read this essay, note how Benlow, whose writing also appears in Chapters 7 and 11, views being a student versus being a consumer. How does Benlow encourage the reader to think differently? In the margin of the text, jot down how Benlow's ideas encourage you to view a concept differently.

1   Two weeks ago, the faculty and staff received a memo regarding "National Customer Service Week." We were urged to take special efforts in serving our customers—presumably, our students. Certainly, I have no objections to extending extra efforts in helping students feel comfortable and situated in the college environment. However, I am deeply troubled (as are many, or most, instructors and professors) by use of the term "customer" to refer to students. I am concerned, in general, about the slow and subtle infiltration of consumerism into education (by companies buying access to students' brains), and I am downright hostile to the way "customer" has suddenly replaced the word (and maybe idea of) "student" in higher education. And because my concerns may seem ungrounded, I'd like to offer a brief analysis—a quick examination of the basic, and not-so-basic, differences between "customer" and "student."

2   "The customer is always right." We hear this hollow phrase resound through (almost) every corridor of our consumerist culture. The motive behind the phrase is painfully clear—to keep customers happy, to keep them from complaining, and most importantly, to keep them coming back. (Of course, the meaninglessness of the phrase is well known too—for those of us who have had the displeasure of talking with Ameritech operators or "customer service" tellers at our banks.) The phrase is meant to maintain a climate in which the substance of anyone's concerns or complaints is obfuscated by friendly and diplomatic cliches—"your business means so much to us"; "we'll do everything we can to address the problem." Ultimately, then, the goal of customer service, in this sense, is to lull customers into a sense of complacency—even though their phones may not be working or their washers throwing sparks.

3   "Have it your way!" Of course, we all know the song and the friendly fried food establishment associated with this slogan. It's a harmless phrase, in and of itself, and one that works particularly well for the franchise. It suggests to customers that their particular appetites can be catered to, that their specific tastes, no matter how eccentric (within the continuum of dip n' serve fried food) can be easily satisfied. It promotes the idea that the institution will shift its entire set of processes to meet the desires of the individual.

4   The meal deal bargain. Recently, in our hyper-drive-thru culture, we've been given a new ticket to ride—a quicker and easier way to get fast food (and a host of other things as well): the combo or meal deal. In the old days, we had to pull up to the drive-thru board, search under "Sandwiches" and THEN go through the labor of exploring "Sides" and "Beverages." It was all too much. Now, we can simply pull up, and say a number. We don't even have to trouble ourselves with uttering all the stuff we want to eat. We just say, "#1 with a diet." The meal deal craze is, of course, not limited to fast food; it is, simply, most explicitly manifested in the fast food industry. That is, in the fast food world, we can clearly see the motives of an increasingly consumerized culture: (1) to limit the interaction between the provider and the customer, (2) to

limit the time the customer has to reflect on his/her wants, and 3) to limit the energy the customer has to exert.

5   Passivity. Customers are encouraged to be passive. We are prompted in a variety of ways not to be agents of our own making. Our needs and desires are met by the work of others. As customers, we pay for someone else's work, for someone else's acts of invention, creation, and production. And we not only hire out our activities (painting our homes, cooking our dinners); we also hire out our imaginations. We don't even have to imagine what is possible. Others have already done the imagining, created a product or service and have told us how we can use it. (They've even taken the extra step of telling us what NOT to do: "Women who are pregnant or who may become pregnant should not take, or even handle, these pills.") In short, *the world of the customer is based on intellectual inactivity*; we merely have to dial the phone, get on-line, say a number. We don't have to reflect, invent, produce, or research (*Consumer's Report* has done it already). Nor do we have to shop: they will deliver. Being a customer means being driven by simple and personal desires . . . and ultimately demanding that those desires be met.

6   Contrary to the passive, personalizing, self-perpetuating, desire-driven customer, students are encouraged to be active. In college, students cannot simply consume knowledge. Even in its most packaged form, the textbook, knowledge must be regenerated, revised, reinterpreted, and remembered in order to be anything beyond an answer on a multiple-choice test. Students who read textbooks, literature, and articles passively will get nothing from them—it is a kind of paralyzing higher education illiteracy. Certainly, they will be able to read something aloud, or even to themselves, and maybe summarize a main point; however, they will not know how to imagine the implications or significance of a textbook chapter. (And this is what academics mean when they say, "our students don't know how to *make meaning*.")

7   Students who come to college with a consumerist attitude are lost. Because they are anticipating their most basic desires will be stimulated (because that's how people are massaged into buying stuff they don't need), consumerist students come to college waiting to be tickled, waiting to see the big boom, waiting for the car chase or the sex scene, waiting for the french fry, waiting for the Cherry Coke. What they encounter, however, are rooms filled with ingredients. They see only black and white words—where they anticipate smashy colors and extravagant tools for getting their attention. In the face of pure ingredients (the stuff for making meaning), they will be confused . . . and ultimately, terribly bored.

8   Consumerist students (or those who have been tricked into thinking like consumers) will also have a difficult time understanding principles. Principles, established doctrines which are to be followed, or evaluated, in the processes of making knowledge, don't really exist in consumer culture (unless you count slogans as doctrines). Because everything is based on the eccentricities of the individual ("hold the pickle, hold the lettuce"), the individual need not ever think outside of his/her own desires and the reality that is created from projecting those desires onto everything and everyone in view. In higher education, principles establish how a discipline works. Physics works on principles of matter and energy. The goal of a physicist is to discover the principles and understand how they can be used. Composition works on principles—conventions of grammar and persuasion. This is not to say that all knowledge is prescribed. On the contrary, students in such classes are encouraged to invent, to break rules, to go beyond. But in order to do so, they need certain ground rules; they need to understand that certain principles exist in the world outside of their own desires. (One cannot do chemistry and simply dismiss algebra because it is distasteful.)

9   When I think back to the best teachers and professors in my education, I recall those who demanded everything contrary to the consumerist

mentality. They insisted on active students; they made us read staggering amounts of material and then actively put that material to use; they prompted us into confusion and disorientation; they made us uncomfortable, and then, sometimes, offered paths to clarity. In short, they made us into critical, reflective agents of our own becoming, rather than passive bags of desire. Everything valuable about my education came from instructors and professors who were free from the ridiculous tyranny of consumerism.

10   There is no way higher education can counter the incredible momentum of consumerist culture. It is far more pervasive than the discourses of physics or composition studies. However, if we continue to allow the term "customer" to replace "student," I fear that students will become increasingly blind to the difference between consumerist culture and college culture. I fear they will become increasingly more confused by the expectations of college, and that in the nightmarish long run, colleges will become simply another extension of the consumerist machine in which everyone is encouraged to pre-package knowledge, to super-size grades, and to "hold" anything even slightly distasteful.

Exploring Ideas

1. What important distinction does Benlow make between "students" and "consumers"?

2. How is the way that you see being a student different from the way Benlow sees it in this essay?

3. What positive consequence could occur from someone reading Benlow's essay? That is, how might someone think or act differently? Did his essay prompt you to think differently?

4. Survey a variety of people (students, nonstudents, people of different ages, and so on), asking them if they think students are "customers." Then identify trends in the data you have collected. For example, do certain groups (students, for example) tend to give the same response, or do their responses vary? What other trends can you look for?

5. Explain Benlow's reasoning to several people who feel strongly that students are the "customers." Record their responses to Benlow's argument. What aspect of Benlow's argument made someone think differently? What were the most convincing, or interesting, responses to what Benlow says?

Writing Strategies

1. Evaluate Benlow's title. Is it effective?

2. How is, or isn't, Benlow's voice appropriate to his subject matter?

3. Benlow alludes throughout his essay to pop culture. Find several allusions that you think are successful and explain why. Which, if any, of his allusions do you think fail?

4. If helping Benlow with his essay, what one suggestion would you make?

5. In your view, what makes Benlow's conclusion effective or ineffective?

Ideas for Writing

1. What term is defined, or thought of, incorrectly?

2. Do members of some other group define themselves incorrectly?

If responding to one of these ideas, go to the **Analysis** section of this chapter to begin developing ideas for your essay.

PLEASE USE
NEXT DOOR
RING BELL FOR ASSISTANCE
→

Why We No Longer Use the "H" Word

Dan Wilkins

Dan Wilkins, whose writing also appears in Chapter 9, is an advocate for people living with disabilities and operates Nth Degree (www.thenthdegree.com), a graphic design company geared toward issues related to the independent living movement, inclusion, diversity, and disability rights. As you read, think about the potential consequences of Wilkins's essay. How does his essay ask the reader to think and act differently?

In the margins of this essay, a reader's comments point to key ideas and writing strategies. As you read the essay, consider how the comments might influence your own reading and writing.

Exploring Ideas

Writing Strategies

What is it about the word "handicap" that so offends many of us living with disabilities? Within our disability culture, progressive thinking has steered us away from using the word "handicapped" as a label or descriptor for someone living with a disability for a couple of reasons. To begin with, contrary to long-time societal thinking, it is not synonymous with the word "disabled." More on this in a moment.

Title indicates main idea; reader must read on to find out why.

The word "handicap" offends for a couple of reasons

Most importantly, it is the very origin of the word that leaves such a bad taste in our mouths. It conjures up imagery that perpetuates archaic misperceptions of the value of people living with disabilities and their potential for contribution to their community and to humanity as a whole.

Introduces concept; suggests why analyzing it is important.

not the same as "disabled"

The word comes from old world England when the only way many with disabilities could survive was to sit on a corner or on the side of the road with a "handy cap" held out for passers-by to fill out of pity. A pretty negative connotation. Not at all an empowering legacy, is it? And, sadly, it is not just a part of our distant past . . .

Compares concept/term to another concept/term.

"handicap" = pity

I do not wish to break from the "handicap vs. disability" issue, but it is important to point out that this basic premise of projecting pity as a mechanism for exacting funds from the masses is still being used today. If I may rant for a paragraph, children and adults with disabilities continue to be exploited every day, most visibly every Labor Day when Jerry Lewis does his annual Smellathon, er, telethon. Twenty-four hours of patting and hugging "poor, helpless cripples" until FINALLY, in the last five minutes, through red blurry eyes, hair mussed, sleeves uncuffed, bow tie loosened and akimbo, sweat dripping and sleep deprived, he tells us, with all the apparent (or is that transparent) sincerity of a really bad lounge singer, that we "will never walk alone." (Hey, Jerry, I'll never walk AGAIN! and,

Explains origin of the term.

Do others agree with Wilkins? Is his opinion popular among disabled people?

To develop analysis, discusses an important, relevant, and popular aspect of the concept.

Exploring Ideas

Is he being too hard on Jerry? Is Jerry helping or causing damage?

Wilkins wants me to think differently, & support organizations that promote independent living, etc.

Does word origin mean there's "little dignity"? Most people don't know the word origin, so does it affect them? How?

"Handicapped" means not being able to reach a goal?

Examples of being "handicapped"? Wilkins wants us to help him and others be self-sufficient.

truth be told, that's OK.) He demands that we, the heart-wrenched public, give, GIVE, until it hurts. GIVE, so that, for another year, we can walk the street unashamed to look someone in the eye; unashamed that we might have fearful, discriminatory thoughts toward "those people," unashamed that our society continues to fight equity and access to all it has to offer. Buy the premise, pay the dues, and it's another year of "no fault insurance."

Jerry isn't the only one, just the most notorious. There are others. Be wary. Kahlil Gibran said "the gifts which derive from Justice are greater than those which spring from Charity." There is power in this statement. If you want to make a difference and, at the same time, help put an end to the pattern of pity and paternalization, find an organization that is promoting self-control and independent living; one whose mission is that of building confidence and ability, awareness and community. Try your local Center for Independent Living. It'll be money or time well spent.

Back to disability vs handicap. Now that we know the origin of the word, we realize that there is little dignity to be found there, except when we look into the souls of those who, over history, wrapped themselves in the label like a banner when there was no other word; who lived, fought, and died defending their right to belong in a world trying so hard to eliminate them or hide them away.

All this is not to say that there is no appropriate context in which to use the word "handicap" or "handicapped." There is. Let me explain.

I have a disability. I broke my neck in an auto accident in 1980. It is an integral part of who I am and, to some degree, it impacts the way I do things in the world. I only become "handicapped" when I cannot reach a goal.

It may be a narrow door, or a set of steps, an inaccessible parking structure or a restaurant with no accessible bathroom. For some it may be no signage or braille menus, no interpreter or service dogs allowed. It may be someone's attitude out there: "Hey! You can't come in here! We didn't vote for the law and we're not making changes" or my own attitude: "I'm just a quad . . . I'll never amount to anything."

Though I'm not big on continuums, let me illustrate it this way. Two lines. One horizontal. One vertical. They form a big plus sign. (See diagram.) The horizontal line represents disability and the (relative, and I stress relative) significance of its involvement and impact on the person, with minimal impact on the left side and significant impact on the right. The vertical line represents the degree

Writing Strategies

Concession/Qualifier: Jerry is not the only one.

Suggests what action the reader can take.

Further develops concept: In the past there was no other word.

Further develops the concept by showing what "handicapped" means.

Provides specific examples of challenges he and others face.

Going beyond common thinking about the concept. Introduces and explains visual.

Uses visual to help illustrate idea.

to which the external or internal (self-concept, confidence, etc.) handicap limits one from reaching a goal. We'll put minimal impact at the bottom and significant impact at the top.

Now let me tell you the story of two friends. "Friend A" (not his real name) has cerebral palsy as his disability. He uses a word board and head stick to communicate with those who do not understand or speak CP. He uses an electric wheelchair and a chin stick to get around. I stressed parenthetically above the issue of relevance with regard to how we perceive the significance of disability. We, not really knowing Friend A but seeing him on the street, might be quick to place him far along the horizontal continuum of disability, considering him to be pretty significantly disabled. And I would tell you that Friend A's self-perception would put him much farther back toward the minimal end. I would also tell you that Friend A is just finishing up his degree in social work at the local university. Here's a guy who most would consider has a significant disability, yet he's out there making a difference in his life and in the lives of others. He's not allowing his disability or society's low expectations to handicap him. He's going to contribute to his community. I would say he sits pretty low on the handicapped scale. Does this make sense?

On the other hand, I have a friend, "Friend B" (not his real name either). He lost a couple of toes in a farm accident. He walks fine. No pain. No limp. Nothing. Pretty minimally disabled, wouldn't you think? But can I get him to go to the beach with me, or swimming? Absolutely not. He'd like to, but he goes nowhere without shoes on. He won't even wear sandals. Pretty minimally disabled but, again, it's relative. He considers himself pretty significantly disabled. So much so that his own attitude, his own self-concept, has him significantly handicapped.

A final difference: if we were to consider these two continuums over a period of time, we would most likely see that the disability continuum, in most people's lives, would remain relatively static when compared to the handicapped continuum, which would fluctuate with every situation and barrier(s) presented.

It is important to understand the context in which to use the words we use. The best way not to offend someone living with a disability, and I often insert the word "living" because we tend to forget that we are all living, breathing, interacting, supporting, pushing, pulling, etc., basically trying to get from Point A to Point B with as little hassle as possible, the best way not to offend someone living with a disability is to refer to them first as just that: as Someone, as a person, as a teacher, a student, an athlete, whatever they happen to be at that moment. That they have a disability is secondary or even tertiary. People are people.

Margin notes (left, "Exploring Ideas"):

Clarifies distinction: friend A is not letting his "disability" "handicap" him.

Friend B is minimally disabled but significantly handicapped.

Disability remains pretty consistent; handicap fluctuates based on situation & barriers.

Margin notes (right, "Writing Strategies"):

Illustrates concept with a specific example of two friends.

"On the other hand," helps reader see relationship between two examples.

"A final difference" functions as a transition to another idea.

Conclusion makes general point about understanding the context of words.

Exploring Ideas

People with disabilities are people. Their disability is secondary or tertiary—only a part of who they are.

People are not diagnoses, or prognoses. They most certainly are not their disabilities. Their disabilities are a part of who they are, perhaps a tenth or twentieth of who they are completely; affording most of all a unique perspective on the world and one's place in it. It is not something of which to be ashamed but something of which to be proud.

Writing Strategies

Makes his main point: that people with disabilities should be viewed as people.

Exploring Ideas

1. While Wilkins's essay is focused on the term "handicapped," how does his essay speak to a larger issue—for example, that of language in general?

2. What words, or terms, have been replaced by others and why? What terms do you think are still in use but shouldn't be?

3. Ask around until you collect five words that people think should be replaced with another word. Write down (1) the word, (2) the word that the person thinks it should be replaced with, (3) the problem with the original word, and (4) how the new word is an improvement. Which word would make for the most interesting essay and why?

4. What old word has been replaced by a new one that is worse? Ask others, collecting as many responses as you can. (You should be able to get quite a few examples.) Remember to ask people *why* they think what they do. What conclusions can you begin to draw about why new words are used to refer to concepts? Do only the words change? Do the concepts also change? What might be the relationship between the two?

5. What new term has been most helpful or most harmful? How has the change in terminology affected the concept? How has the change in the term influenced the way people think or act?

Writing Strategies

1. Describe Wilkins's voice—his persona as a writer. Refer to at least three sentences that illustrate your perception.

2. How important is Wilkins's brief etymology (word history) of "handicap"? Does the etymology strengthen his essay? Would the essay do just as well without it? Explain.

3. What tools, or strategies, does Wilkins use to illustrate his point? What others might he have used?

4. In paragraph 4, Wilkins informs his reader that he is going to "rant." What, if anything, is the effect of this announcement?

5. If workshopping Wilkins's essay, how would you answer the following questions:

   a. The thing I like most about your essay is _____.

   b. I think the main idea of your essay is _____.

   c. The main suggestion I would make about your essay is _____.

Ideas for Writing

1. What two other terms—such as "disability" and "handicap"—require clarification?

2. Have people called you "handicapped," "fat," "skinny," "crazy," "irresponsible," "unapproachable," "beautiful," "lucky"? What word have you had to live with? How has the term been misapplied to you?

If responding to one of these ideas, go to the **Analysis** section of this chapter to begin developing ideas for your essay.

Outside Reading

Find a written text that analyzes a concept and print it out or make a photocopy. You might focus on a concept related to your major or to a major that you are considering. (To explore a specific field or major, examine a related professional journal such as *Nutrition Health Forum, Law Technology,* or *Education Journal.*) To conduct an electronic search of journals and magazines, go to your library's periodical database or to InfoTrac (http://infotrac.galegroup.com/itweb/). For your library database, perform a keyword search, or for InfoTrac, go to the main search box and choose "keywords." Experiment by typing in various concepts, such as *art, society, industry, sportsmanship.* You might limit the search by adding *concept* to the search. (When performing keyword searches, avoid using phrases or articles *(a, an, the)*; instead, use nouns separated by *and.*) The results will yield lists of journal and magazine articles.

You can also search the Internet. Try the search engine Yahoo.com. Like most Internet search engines, Yahoo.com combines words using *and.* In the search box, try various combinations, such as those above.

The purpose of this assignment is to further your understanding of analytical writing. You may discover a text that differs considerably from the essays in this chapter (in tone, rhetorical tools, or organization). As you read through this chapter, keep the text you have discovered close by and notice the elements and strategies the writer uses. Depending on your instructor's suggestions, do one or more of the following:

1. Notice how the writer applies various strategies from this chapter. On the hard copy or photocopy of the text:

   - Highlight the thesis if it is stated. If the thesis is implied, write it in your own words.
   - Identify the major rhetorical strategies (such as narration, description, or figurative language).
   - Identify any passages in which the writer attempts to create public resonance for the topic.

2. Write an essay that discusses the strategies employed by the writer. The following questions may be helpful.

   - How is the writer's voice different from the essays in this chapter?
   - How does the writer support or illustrate his or her thesis?
   - Who is the audience for this text?
   - How does the audience impact the kinds of things said in the text?
   - How does the writer go beyond the obvious? (What new idea does the writer offer?)

3. Write at least three "Exploring Ideas" questions for the text you found.

4. Write at least three "Writing Strategies" questions for the text you found.

5. Write two "Ideas for Writing," such as the ones following the essays in this book, for the text you found.

INVENTION

> "" **W**hat does it mean that success is as danger-
> ous as failure? Whether you go up the ladder
> or down it, your position is shaky. ""
>
> —*Tao Te Ching*

Analyzing concepts involves a good deal of reflection. Valuable analysis goes beyond the first impressions a writer may have about a topic. For the writing in this chapter, you must seek out meaning beyond those initial thoughts about a concept. The following three sections are designed to help you through this process: specifically, to find a particular concept (in **Point of Contact**), develop points about the topic (in **Analysis**), and make it relevant to a community of readers (in **Public Resonance**). The questions in each section are not meant to be answered directly in your final written assignment. They are meant to prompt inventive thinking and lead you toward a topic. After you work through these three sections, the **Delivery** section, which immediately follows, will help you craft your ideas into a written text.

Point of Contact

Finding a Topic in Everyday Life

We carry concepts around with us and, for the most part, do not question them. Our concepts only come into question when they are challenged by something we experience or read. But writers are willing to get underneath concepts that would otherwise go unquestioned. As you consider a possible topic, imagine the concepts that go unnoticed in your everyday life. Use the prompts on the following pages to find a concept:

- **Go** to work, school, church, or even stay home, and take notice of the concepts that lurk in those places. (For instance, many concepts constitute the college experience: success, education, study, discipline, teaching, learning, science, humanities, higher education, evaluation, grade, and so on.)

- **Participate** in some activity such as a sporting event, a concert, an official meeting, a community event. Take notice of the potential concepts: community, entertainment, teamwork, discord, and so on.

- **Examine** key concepts of your major. For instance, someone majoring in education could develop an interesting analysis of a concept such as *learning, success, assessment,* or *high school.* Your major itself might be seen as a concept. For example, *engineering,* one might say, is a concept, and how one works in that field certainly depends upon one's concept of it.

- **Watch** television and look for concepts that lie hidden in particular programs or commercials. The program or commercial may not speak directly about a concept but may suggest or imply a particular understanding of one. For instance, what does a local news program that devotes 60 seconds to world news and several minutes to sports suggest about *news*? Concepts lie hidden in all programs, and the content of the programs suggests a particular meaning. For example:

  What does *The Brady Bunch* suggest about *family*?
  What does *The Real World* suggest about *reality*?
  What does *Sex in the City* suggest about *sex*?
  What does *The Late Show* suggest about *entertainment*?
  What does an automobile commercial suggest about *excitement*?
  What does an insurance commercial suggest about *neighbor*?

As you reflect on the program or commercial, ask yourself if the concept is somehow oversimplified or misrepresented. If so, what is missing or dismissed? Or does the program or commercial fairly represent the concept? Remember that you are not evaluating the television program; rather, you are simply using it to prompt an idea, to discover a concept that may need analysis and explanation.

- **Look** at an advertisement in a magazine or on a billboard. If you consider all the elements of the ad (the pictures, text, images, colors, placement, models, clothing, blank space, audience, and even the surrounding materials such as stories and columns), what concept might the ad suggest? As in television programs, the ad will probably not say anything directly but instead imply a particular concept. For example, the ad on the following page says nothing directly about *fitness*, but uses a particular conception to promote a collection of products.

The ad's images and words help to support a particular way of thinking about fitness. The picture of the woman, for example, suggests that fitness involves a sassy attitude, a youthful appearance, and an attention to fashionable hairstyles and make-up application. The bright colors of the products and posters suggest excitement, and even movement. And the names of the products suggest technological sophistication: Celltech, Nitrotech, Hydroxycut, etc. Such an ad might prompt a close examination of *fitness*. Someone looking at the ad might go beyond the images in the storefront, and discover that fitness involves peace, simplicity, and wisdom—rather than excitement, technology, and youth.

As you consider another ad, consider what it might imply about *youth, sex, love, adventure, power, comfort, class, money, man, woman, teenager, family, success,* and so on. Is the concept somehow oversimplified or misrepresented? Or does the ad suggest an appropriate understanding of the concept? Remember that you are not directly evaluating the ad, but using it as a springboard for your own analysis.

- **Imagine all the concepts that constitute your everyday life:**

responsibility	home	adulthood	soul
college	teacher	Generation X	service
religion	faith	God	education
friendship	pain	America	hope
co-worker	intelligence	American	defeat
employment	courage	dream	cruelty
romance	patriotism	necessity	writing
honesty	freedom	marriage	wisdom
punk	junk	funk	spunk

- **Consider** everyday images, such as the ones below:

Do not limit yourself to familiar concepts. You might, in fact, choose a concept that is somewhat novel or foreign to your experiences. Choose one that you would like to explore or that you would like to understand more deeply.

Invention Activity: Any one of the concepts on the previous page could provide for an interesting and valuable analysis. But do not stop there. Imagine more concepts that define your everyday life. If this can be done in small groups, take turns offering concepts until each participant has chosen a potential topic. If using a class listserv, generate a longer list of possible concepts, with each participant contributing several options. (Each participant should read through previous postings to trigger new ideas.)

Analysis
What Does It Mean?

Analysis involves investigating particular parts, elements, or ideas within the whole. If we were to analyze an object, we might take it apart and look inside. We might, for instance, analyze a computer by opening the case and looking at the internal wires, the cards, and the connections. (Of course, that would only begin the process.) But when examining a concept, we cannot take off the cover and simply look inside—at least, not physically. Instead, we have to depend on intellectual inquiry. Rather than physical tools (screwdrivers or wrenches), we have to develop questions that get inside or underneath the abstraction. We have to ask questions that point to the particular elements of the concept. For example, consider *college*. To analyze the concept, we must break it down and look at particular issues: What does college suggest for people's lives? Is it a time and place for learning specific skills or for exploring boundless ideas? Both? Is it a place for making hard choices or for generating options? Such questions are analytical; that is, they help to shed light on specific issues inside the broader, more abstract idea.

In this chapter, Steven M. Richardson analyzes *college*. As with all the essays in this chapter, he attempts to communicate some of the hidden complexities in the concept. He looks at particular elements (money, majors, degrees) in his analysis. And it is through an investigation of these particulars that we get a sense of the broader concept:

> Students who come to campus with the single-minded goal of preparing for a career just don't get it. Sitting in class for four years to get a diploma and a job makes about as much sense as riding from here to Los Angeles on a bus with your eyes closed. You'll get there, but you'll miss all the scenery. College is about discovering who you are and what you can do, sometimes against your will. The challenge is to learn how to think and how to create new solutions to problems that nobody before you has faced, and how to enjoy life along the way.

In his essay on creativity, S. I. Hayakawa breaks *creativity* into several different traits, such as the ability to endure loneliness:

> The person who would be creative must be able to endure loneliness—even ridicule. If he has a great and original idea that others are not yet ready to accept, there will be long periods of loneliness. There will be times when his friends and relatives think he is crazy, and he'll begin to wonder if they are right. A genuinely creative person, believing in his creation, is able to endure this loneliness—for years if necessary.

Benlow examines two concepts: *customer* and *student*. He devotes four paragraphs to analyzing the various dimensions of *customer*. He does not simply say that customers are always right, hurried, and passive. Instead, he analyzes and gives an illustration of each characteristic, breaking each idea down even further. Notice the analysis in the following paragraph:

> The meal deal bargain. Recently, in our hyper-drive-thru culture, we've been given a new ticket to ride—a quicker and easier way to get fast food (and a host of other things as well): the combo or meal deal. In the old days, we had to pull up to the drive-thru board, search under "Sandwiches" and THEN go through the labor of exploring "Sides" and "Beverages." It was all too much. Now, we can simply pull up, and say a number. We don't even have to trouble ourselves with uttering all the stuff we want to eat. We just say, "#1 with a

diet." The meal deal craze is, of course, not limited to fast food; it is, simply, most explicitly manifested in the fast food industry. That is, in the fast food world, we can clearly see the motives of an increasingly consumerized culture: 1) to limit the interaction between the provider and the customer, 2) to limit the time the customer has to reflect on his/her wants, and 3) to limit the energy the customer has to exert.

In such passages, Benlow explains the fundamental qualities of a customer. Once those qualities are revealed, he compares them to the characteristics of a student:

> Contrary to the passive, personalizing, self-perpetuating, desire-driven customer, students are encouraged to be active. In college, students cannot simply consume knowledge. Even in its most packaged form, the textbook, knowledge must be regenerated, revised, reinterpreted, and remembered in order to be anything beyond an answer on a multiple choice test. Students who read textbooks, literature and articles passively will get nothing from them—it is a kind of paralyzing higher education illiteracy. Certainly, they will be able to read something aloud, or even to themselves, and maybe summarize a main point; however, they will not know how to imagine the implications or significance of a textbook chapter. (And this is what academics mean when they say, "our students don't know how to *make meaning*.")

Because Benlow breaks down *customer* at the beginning of his essay, the passages about students have more impact. In other words, we see the contrast between the two concepts very clearly and specifically. But imagine if Benlow simply told us the difference:

> Customers are different from students. While customers are "always right," hurried, and passive, students are prompted to explore slowly and meticulously. And they are, hopefully, active learners.

Such statements are vague. They do not invite the reader into a close examination of the particulars. Analytical writing attempts to go beneath the broad ideas and reveal specifics. Like Benlow's, Richardson's, and Hayakawa's essays, good analyses dismantle the whole and show us meaning inside the individual elements. By looking at specifics they help us to better understand the concept.

Use the following questions to get inside your concept:

- How does it influence or change people's lives?
- How does it influence people's thoughts?
- What is its primary purpose or function?
- What emotions or thoughts are associated with it?
- What behaviors are associated with it?
- What other issues or concepts does it include?
- What responsibilities come with it?
- What consequences or effects does it have?
- What is necessary to attain it or have it?

As you consider the analysis questions on the previous page, avoid skimming the surface. Go beyond the first answer that comes to mind. Imagine a student, Diana, who has decided to analyze *conspiracy* after watching an episode of *The X Files* on television. In a discussion with other students, she discovers more about the concept than she initially expected:

What behaviors are associated with it?

Diana: In the show, the conspiracy is a big network of people from various national governments who are all trying to deal secretly with aliens. It's a giant plot that involves military agencies, doctors, scientists, politicians, FBI agents, and lots of spies. It's great entertainment, but it seems so far-fetched. A conspiracy doesn't have to be so big and involved. If it were, how could it remain secret?

Linda: I know what you mean. I like that show, but I'm always wondering about the big hidden plot with the aliens. Sometimes it seems like only a small handful of people know about it, like when the conspirators, all men by the way, meet in a dark room. There's a lot of cigarette smoke and hard talk about taking control of the world. Then other episodes suggest that all kinds of people, in all parts of the world, are deeply involved.

Marcus: So the show suggests that a conspiracy is a huge underground plot where a bunch of men secretly plan to take over the world. That IS a conspiracy, right?

Diana: Yes, but can't a conspiracy be smaller than that? Does it have to involve several governments and a plan to help aliens take over the Earth?

Linda: What about these corporate executives that construct plans to grab millions of dollars before the company goes belly-up? There's a conspiracy that, maybe, develops pretty quickly—and is shared by only a few people.

Marcus: But then the accounting firms get involved, too. Then it gets bigger and bigger.

Diana: But the accountants may not be "in," so to speak; they're simply using the numbers to keep their clients afloat so that they, in turn, have jobs.

Linda: So the people don't always have to be knowledgeable about the beginnings of the conspiracy in order to participate in it.

Marcus: But those accountants are doing something suspicious too, right?

Diana: Right! But they're acting for their own self-interests. They weren't necessarily involved in the plan from the ground up.

Linda: So back to the main point: a *conspiracy* doesn't have to involve governments, dark rooms, and huge cover-ups. It can be a bunch of people doing their own thing (for various different reasons) but working, best they can, under the covers so they keep jobs and make money.

The conversation is beginning to open up the concept, to go beyond the idea that Diana first encounters in the television program. This kind of exploration is the key to developing new insights, which lead to engaging writing. It takes writers (and their readers) beyond their opinions—and into a realm of possibilities.

Example: Simon Benlow's Response to Analysis Questions

How does it influence or change people's lives? I'm dealing with two concepts ("student" and "customer"). "Customer" influences people to buy things and ideas, but the concept also makes people believe certain things about themselves—that they are better off only when they have obtained something or some service. It makes people lazy. When people totally buy into the consumer mentality, they feel as though they should be waited on, catered to, and dealt with—no matter what the circumstances. Being a student is the opposite—or at least, being a good student is the opposite. Students have to discover meaning and struggle through their own biases, while customers hope to have their biases fed.

What emotions or thoughts are associated with it? When consumerist students come to college, they get angry and frustrated. Their expectations about institutions have been created, in large part, from their interactions with retail. They've been advertised and sold to for most of their lives. In college, when the tables are turned, when they have to do all the discovering, all the inventing, all the developing, they are often freaked out.

Activity: Conduct a survey of ten people (classmates and/or people outside of college). Ask them the first thing they think of when they hear _____ (your concept). You might go further and ask them how the topic relates to their lives. Record the answers as they respond (either by an audio recording or by note taking). You can conduct this survey via e-mail by sending the question to ten acquaintances. Use the responses to further explore your topic. Your respondents might, for instance, suggest something about your chosen concept that you had not considered. You might incorporate these notions into your understanding of the concept.

Public Resonance
How Does It Matter to Others?

It is up to the writer to make a concept relevant to readers. At some level, your concept already resonates with others; because a concept is, by definition, beyond particulars, it probably relates to others. Whether it is *creativity, college,* or *student,* a concept necessarily involves others. Still, a concept is not always entirely understood—even by those who would, presumably, understand it. Consider *freedom*: As Americans, we often speak of it, sing about it, and even go to war over it, but do most Americans really understand the concept? Even though freedom is part of our collective language, we might not realize its complexities and meaning. The same goes with *college*: millions of people attend colleges every year—and millions of others share in the financial burden. Yet, so many do not have an adequate understanding of the idea. They may walk through certain motions, but not everyone comprehends the meaning of *college.*

Because people often miss or ignore a concept's complexities, writers consider it their business to inform readers, to introduce or even remind readers of those complexities. For instance, Richardson's purpose is to help readers rethink the meaning of college. He sets out to dispel certain misconceptions about college and to introduce important elements of the concept that he feels many people overlook. He even directly explains how students' misconceptions work against them:

> In fact, that's what college is all about, in my opinion. Students who come to campus with the single-minded goal of preparing for a career just don't get it. Sitting in class for four years to get a diploma and a job makes about as much sense as riding from here to Los Angeles on a bus with your eyes closed. You'll get there, but you'll miss all the scenery. College is about discovering who you are and what you can do, sometimes against your will. The challenge is to learn how to think and how to create new solutions to problems that nobody before you has faced, and how to enjoy life along the way.

The concept may seem unrelated to public concerns in some cases. However, a writer's job is to create the bridge between a topic (no matter how minute or esoteric) and the surrounding world. Notice Iyer's strategy. His topic, punctuation, may seem totally divorced from the social world. However, he leads us to the connection:

> Punctuation, then, is a civic prop, a pillar that holds society upright. (A run-on sentence, its phrases piling up without division, is as unsightly as a sink piled high with dirty dishes.) Small wonder, then, that punctuation was one of the first proprieties of the Victorian Age, the age of the corset, that the modernists threw off: the sexual revolution might be said to have begun when Joyce's Molly Bloom spilled out all her private thoughts in thirty-six pages of panting, unperioded, and officially censored prose; and another rebellion was surely marked when e.e. cummings first committed "god" to the lower case.

Here, Iyer forges a connection between something most people probably see as insignificant and a culture's general attitudes. He is making a case for the public resonance of his topic—elevating its significance in readers' minds. (This is an important part of a writer's job: to create new connections.)

As you consider the social significance of your own topic, use the following questions:

- Is the concept generally agreed upon?
- Does the concept raise controversy? Explain why.
- Why is it important that people have an appropriate understanding of this concept?
- Are there complexities to the concept that people might overlook?
- Does the concept need to be rethought? Why?
- In what ways does it contribute to everyday life?
- Is this a popular or high profile concept in society?
- What is the possible connection between the topic and public concerns?

If you choose not to state the public resonance of your concept directly, answering these questions serves another goal: to help you envision the relationship between your audience and your topic. In thinking about the public resonance of your chosen concept, you may come across your *purpose*—the reason you are writing. If you believe that the concept is often misunderstood, then the purpose of your analysis might be to educate your audience. Or if your concept is overlooked, the purpose (as in Iyer's case) may be to elevate the status of the concept in your reader's mind. Your answers to these questions can also be used directly in a text.

Example: Simon Benlow's Response to Public Resonance Questions

Is the concept generally agreed upon? No! That's the whole problem. Many students don't know what it means to be a student.

Why is it important that people have an appropriate understanding of this concept? If college students really understand what it means to be a student (and not a consumerist student), their experience at college will be defined by self-discovery and enlightenment rather than petty frustration and grumbling. If colleges across America continue to confuse "student" with "consumer," education will suffer. Much of the time spent in college will be on customer service (keeping students happy) rather than challenging their beliefs, developing their minds, and broadening their horizons.

Activities

1. Write a memo to your instructor explaining why the main idea of your essay is significant. Your memo should touch on the essay's public resonance and how it might affect a reader's thinking or behavior.
2. In a small group of peers, present the main idea of your essay and explain why it is socially important. After the presentation, the group members might discuss how the topic relates to their lives.

■

DELIVERY

Because you are analyzing an abstraction (an idea, rather than an object or a relationship), you may find it necessary to return to your notes often. The first step is to develop a main idea, and then to begin developing a text that supports it. The following sections (**Rhetorical Tools, Organizational Strategies, Writer's Voice,** and **Revision Strategies**) are designed to help you focus your initial ideas into a sophisticated and engaging text. As you work through the questions, keep your notes and answers to the **Invention** questions close by.

Rhetorical Tools
Developing Your Ideas

Considering Your Thesis: You probably have many different things to say about your topic, but you will still need to develop a thesis statement—a single claim that expresses your particular view on the concept. Look over your notes from the **Analysis** and **Public Resonance** sections. Find a theme or pattern running through those notes and try to articulate that idea in a sentence. Ask yourself: *What is the main point I want to make about this concept?* Regardless of the specific point you make, remember that good writing reveals something beyond or beneath common knowledge, and good writers show the extraordinary in the ordinary.

Remember that a thesis does not materialize out of thin air. It develops over time. It may involve a long process of reflection and discussion. And often, a good thesis emerges only after a writer has thoroughly analyzed the topic. Consider the example from the **Analysis** section, in which Diana's topic, *conspiracy*, is developed through a discussion. Her thesis evolves slowly.

Evolution of a Thesis	
The writer uses television as a point of contact, and thinks of a topic after watching an episode of *The X Files:*	*People think that "conspiracy" means "old men meeting in a smoke-filled room and devising an evil plan," but it is far subtler than that.*
The writer analyzes the topic and discovers some specific elements:	*In a conspiracy, everyone involved does not have to know each other and purposely act in harmony. In fact, people in a conspiracy can simply be protecting their own interests, and in doing so, carrying out an action under society's radar.*
The writer acknowledges the more popular conception, and refines the point:	*Although numbers of people sometimes do conspire together, what some call a conspiracy is, in truth, various people with a similar attitude acting independently in their own self-interests.*

As you consider your own thesis, remember that narrower points yield more interesting writing. At first, you might think, "I can't possibly write more than a paragraph about something so narrow." However, the process of developing the ideas will generate content for your writing. And the more focused thesis will help you to illustrate particular points rather than list many marginally related issues.

Developing Support:

Even though you are dealing with a generalization, an abstract idea that transcends particulars, you can still refer to particular situations or examples to support your take on the concept. In his essay, Richardson explores college, in general, but refers to Bowling Green State University to illustrate points. Iyer offers the reader numerous examples to illustrate a point. Although he explores punctuation as a concept, he supports his understanding of it with specifics:

> Punctuation, in short, gives us the human voice, and all the meanings that lie between the words. "You aren't young, are you?" loses its innocence when it loses the question mark. Every child knows the menace of a dropped apostrophe (the parent's "Don't do that" shifting into a more slowly enunciated "Do not do that") and every believer the ignominy of having his faith reduced to "faith." Add an exclamation point to "To be or not to be . . ." and the gloomy Dane has all the resolve he needs; add a comma, and the noble sobriety of "God save the queen" becomes a cry of desperation bordering on double sacrilege.

Benlow uses a detailed scenario to illustrate his concept of *student*:

> In higher education, principles establish how a discipline works. Physics works on principles of matter and energy. The goal of a physicist is to discover the principles and understand how they can be used. Composition works on principles—conventions of grammar and persuasion. This is not to say that all knowledge is prescribed. On the contrary, students in such classes are encouraged to invent, to break rules, to go beyond. But in order to do so, they need certain ground rules; they need to understand that certain principles exist in the world outside of their own desires. (One cannot do chemistry and simply dismiss algebra because it is distasteful.)

In some cases, a writer may also use details to illustrate how *not* to conceptualize an idea. Notice how Wilkins alludes to a particular television program to detail a misguided understanding of *handicap*:

> Twenty-four hours of patting and hugging "poor, helpless cripples" until FINALLY, in the last five minutes, through red blurry eyes, hair mussed, sleeves uncuffed, bow tie loosened and akimbo, sweat dripping and sleep deprived, he tells us, with all the apparent (or is that transparent) sincerity of a really bad lounge singer, that we "will never walk alone." (Hey, Jerry, I'll never walk AGAIN! and, truth be told, that's OK.) He demands that we, the heartwrenched public, give, GIVE, until it hurts. GIVE, so that, for another year, we can walk the street unashamed to look someone in the eye; unashamed that we might have fearful, discriminatory thoughts toward "those people," unashamed that our society continues to fight equity and access to all it has to offer. Buy the premise, pay the dues, and it's another year of "no fault insurance."

Wilkins uses the "Smellathon" to illustrate the troubling or negative ideas associated with his concept; his allusion helps to support his point. And Benlow goes even further with this strategy by devoting several paragraphs to illustrations of consumerist thinking. (For more on allusions, see pp. 196–197.)

Each of the writers in this chapter puts forth a particular way of seeing a concept. And each must support that way of seeing with scenarios (hypothetical accounts), allusions (references to bits of public knowledge), and examples. Because analyzing concepts requires abstract thinking, writers must be extra careful to illustrate points with concrete examples. To develop support for your topic, ask yourself the following:

- What specific examples in everyday life illustrate my point about the concept?
- What particular features or aspects of the examples illustrate my point?
- Can I construct a hypothetical account that demonstrates the concept?
- What programs, ads, or other examples from everyday life illustrate an inappropriate or oversimplified way of understanding the concept?
- Does anything or anyone from history, current events, popular culture, or literature illustrate my point about the concept?

As you generate a list of possible ideas/allusions/examples to include in your essay, also imagine how you can explain their significance. Often it is not enough to simply mention an example. A more powerful and convincing strategy is to explain in detail how an example or allusion reveals something relevant. For example, Benlow does not simply mention consumerist slogans; he gives detailed explanations of their significance:

> "The customer is always right." We hear this hollow phrase resound through (almost) every corridor of our consumerist culture. The motive behind the phrase is painfully clear—to keep customers happy, to keep them from complaining, and most importantly, to keep them coming back. (Of course, the meaninglessness of the phrase is well known too—for those of us who have had the displeasure of talking with Ameritech operators or "customer service" tellers at our banks.) The phrase is meant to maintain a climate in which the substance of anyone's concerns or complaints is obfuscated by friendly and diplomatic cliches—"your business means so much to us"; "we'll do everything we can to address the problem." Ultimately, then, the goal of customer service, in this sense, is to lull customers into a sense of complacency—even though their phones may not be working or their washers throwing sparks.

As you develop your ideas, write a paragraph that details the relevance for each new example that comes to mind.

Using Definitions: Concepts involve definitions. Sometimes a definition supports a writer's take on a concept; other times a dictionary definition (or *denotation*) is inadequate for exploring a concept's complexities. In all the essays in this chapter, for example, the dictionary definitions associated with the concepts fall short. The writers go far beyond them. Iyer's essay illustrates this point. According to the *American Heritage Dictionary*, punctuation is "[t]he use of standard marks and signs in writing and printing to separate words into sentences, clauses and phrases in order to clarify meaning." But Iyer's analysis does not involve the formal definition. He is more interested in what punctuation means for people, for cultures, for language—a dictionary definition will not yield such ideas. Similarly, Benlow does not bother with dictionary definitions. Instead, he is concerned about the realm of *connotations* (meaning created by the social situations), in which society's habits and behaviors shape the meaning of concepts.

However, sometimes a dictionary definition comes in handy. Some writers, for instance, begin their essays with a simple definition and then explore the connotation. Most often, the goal is not to prove a definition but to prompt readers to rethink connotations. For example, imagine Diana's analysis of *conspiracy* (from the **Analysis** section). She might begin with the dictionary definition, and extend the thinking:

> Most often, a conspiracy is associated with a direct and charted plan: "We'll collect the money and stash it in the laundry baskets in the basement." In fact, the basic definition of conspiracy suggests a prefigured and collective act. According to the *American Heritage Dictionary*, it is "an agreement to perform together an illegal, treacherous, or evil act." However, more recent events in corporate America invite us to rethink how conspiracies work. Even a simple look at corporate fraud reveals a process in which many people, simply acting in their own self-interests, become part of a bigger covert plan that was begun without them and carries on only because they are unwilling to stand in its way.

Here, the dictionary works only as a springboard. Diana uses the dictionary as a way to begin her analysis.

For your own topic, ask yourself the following:

- Is a dictionary definition important to my understanding of my chosen concept?
- If so, how do I go beyond it?
- How is the dictionary definition inadequate?
- What does it help me to illustrate about the concept?

Using Outside Sources: Writers often refer to other writers' ideas to substantiate points. Notice Hayakawa's strategy:

> Finally, the creative person plays hunches. "Pure intellect," says Dr. Hans Selye, the great medical researcher at the University of Montreal, "is largely a quality of the middle-class mind. The lowliest hooligan and the greatest creator in the fields of science are activated mainly by imponderable instincts and emotions, especially faith. Curiously, even scientific research, the most intellectual creative effort of which man is capable, is no exception in this respect."

In this passage, Hayakawa first states a point ("the creative person plays hunches") and then uses Selye's words to extend that point. This is standard practice when using outside sources. While it may be enticing to begin passages with others' words or even to use long passages from other writers, it is most often best to use sources to help develop or illustrate your points. In other words, be careful not to depend on others' words to make your points for you.

To find outside sources that discuss your concept, go to your library's home page and select a periodical database, such as Lexis-Nexis, InfoTrac, or EBSCOHOST, which contains lists of journal and magazine articles. (Ask a librarian if you are uncertain about the perodical databases your library offers.) Try a keyword search, and type in your concept. The search will yield lists of articles on your topic. You might also try an electronic search engine on the Internet. For instance, using Yahoo.com, type your concept in the search box. (However, on the Internet, be cautious of sites that market materials or services. Because the purpose of such sites is to attract customers, the information they offer may be biased. Marketing sites may contain terms and phrases such as "sale," "low prices," and "large selection.") For more guidance in finding and integrating sources, see Chapter 12: Research and Writing.

Organizational Strategies

Addressing Common Concerns

How Should I Begin? Introductions depend on the tone or level of formality of the writing situation. (See more on level of formality on page 567.) An analytical text written for a government agency or a corporate entity would probably begin formally, perhaps with a general discussion about the concept. In less formal situations, introductions vary widely, and the primary goal is *to capture the reader's attention*, to provoke a sense of curiosity. Notice Iyer's powerful opening sentence:

> The gods, they say, give breath, and they take it away. But the same could be said—could it not?—of the humble comma.

The statement seems to be hyperbole (an exaggeration); he compares punctuation to the divine origin of life. However, as we read on, we realize that his statement fits in with his concept of punctuation. The opening, then, does what good introductions should: capture the reader's attention and suggest the point of the text. Other tried and true strategies include asking a question. See Hayakawa's use:

> What distinguishes the creative person? By creative person I don't mean only the great painter or poet or musician. I also want to include the creative housewife, teacher, warehouseman, sales manager. . . .

Hayakawa asks the question, and then qualifies it, directing the reader's attention to a particular line of reasoning. The question, then, serves a very particular purpose. Also, notice that Hayakawa spends the remainder of his essay answering the question. (This is perhaps the most important issue about raising a question: it ultimately needs to be answered.)

Still another way to begin is to re-create the point of contact, that is, to explain how you first encountered the idea. This is often more informal since it requires some personal narration. Notice that Benlow's introduction, for example, begins with the event that provoked his need to write.

If I Started with a Television Program or Advertisement, How Should I Work That into the Essay? Remember that you are not necessarily evaluating the ad or the program; rather, you are using it as a beginning point. You might check with your instructor about the degree to which you should analyze the program or ad, but it need not be a major portion of your text. You might use it to introduce the topic or to illustrate a particular way of seeing the concept. Notice, for example, that Wilkins mentions the Jerry Lewis telethon in the middle of his essay to illustrate a particular problem with the *handicapped* concept.

When Should I Change Paragraphs? Remember that paragraphs are tools to direct your reader's progress. Paragraphs stop the reader and refocus his or her attention on the next point. Hayakawa uses paragraph breaks between each different characteristic of a creative person. Similarly, Iyer begins a new paragraph for each general statement about punctuation: that it provides law and order, that it is a civic prop, that it signifies cultures, that it provides movement for our thoughts, that it initiates the human voice, that it provides aesthetics, that it gives depth, and that it

shows our care for meaning. Each point has its own paragraph, its own space to be developed and illustrated.

Paragraphs can also be used to separate specific support strategies. For instance, a writer using several different allusions might use paragraphs to separate each. Notice Benlow's strategy: each of his first four paragraphs explains a particular element of the consumerist culture. Hayakawa uses paragraphs to separate different elements of creativity, devoting a paragraph to each. These writers use paragraphs to refocus the reader on a new ingredient or element in the discussion.

Where Should My Thesis Go? The thesis is the main point derived from

your analysis. You can state your thesis directly or imply it (that is, suggest it by the content of the essay). The writers in this chapter tend to favor the conclusion as the most valuable place for their thesis statements. Notice Richardson's last paragraph:

> College is hard work and—let's be honest—it's sometimes boring, too. So are a lot of other things that we all do. College is also expensive and it takes a chunk of your life when it may seem more important to get a job, buy a car, and start a family. It is not the right choice for everybody. For a great many people, though, it is a door to career and personal growth opportunities that they cannot gain in any other way. The decision to attend college is an investment in your future—a risk, certainly, but one with a big payoff if it's the right decision for you. Your choice.

Throughout the essay, the information builds up to the thesis: *The decision to attend college is an investment in your future—a risk, certainly, but one with a big payoff if it's the right decision for you.*

How Should I Conclude? As with introductions, the possibilities for con-

clusions are limitless. Short explanatory essays (under 1000 words) usually do not need to summarize main points. Instead, writers often use conclusions to suggest the significance of the ideas expressed in the body of the essay. Consider the strategies used by the authors in this chapter. Iyer concludes by *framing* the essay (returning to the same image or allusion used in the introduction):

> . . . a comma can let us hear a voice break, or a heart. Punctuation, in fact, is a labor of love. Which brings us back, in a way, to gods.

Hayakawa concludes by proclaiming the value of the concept:

> It is first based on communication with oneself, then testing that communication with experience and the realities one has to contend with. The result is the highest, most exciting kind of learning.

Richardson concludes by appealing directly to the reader:

> College is hard work and—let's be honest—it's sometimes boring, too. So are a lot of other things that we all do. College is also expensive and it takes a chunk of your life when it may seem more important to get a job, buy a car, and start a family. It is not the right choice for everybody. For a great many people, though, it is a door to career and personal growth opportunities that they cannot gain in any other way. The decision to attend college is an investment in your future—a risk, certainly, but one with a big payoff if it's the right decision for you. Your choice.

Notice that each strategy is very different and all are effective, yet none of the writers wastes time summarizing or "wrapping up" points that have already been made. Instead, they use their conclusions to extend their points into the reader's world (by scenarios, direct appeals, or examples).

Writer's Voice

Exploring Options

Appropriate voice depends upon the writing situation: the writer's audience, topic, and purpose. An analysis of corporate spending submitted to a board of trustees is likely to be rather formal. The writer would probably not include many metaphors and would exclude many references to him- or herself. The text would also be relatively free of allusions to popular culture and have little or no slang. If the situation allows (if the audience is willing to accept varying degrees of formality), a writer can experiment with voice.

A writer's voice can make the reading experience formal or relaxed, rigorous or casual. But remember that a casual voice does not necessarily mean casual thinking. A very sophisticated analysis can be presented in a casual manner. For example, Wilkins's voice is informal:

> If I may rant for a paragraph, children and adults with disabilities continue to be exploited every day, most visibly every Labor Day when Jerry Lewis does his annual Smellathon, er, telethon. Twenty-four hours of patting and hugging "poor, helpless cripples" until FINALLY, in the last five minutes, through red blurry eyes, hair mussed, sleeves uncuffed, bow tie loosened and akimbo, sweat dripping and sleep deprived, he tells us, with all the apparent (or is that transparent) sincerity of a really bad lounge singer, that we "will never walk alone."

Even though the subject is presented in a casual manner, the analysis is sophisticated. Wilkins makes a complicated point about people's perceptions of disability, but his voice invites the reader to experience the analysis in a comfortable, almost playful, manner.

A writer can also elevate the topic. Consider Iyer's essay:

> Thus all these tiny scratches give us breadth and heft and depth. A world that has only periods is a world without inflections. It is a world without shade. It has a music without sharps and flats. It is a martial music. It has a jackboot rhythm. Words cannot bend and curve. A comma, by comparison, catches the gentle drift of the mind in thought, turning in on itself and back on itself, reversing, redoubling, and returning along the course of its own sweet river music; while the semicolon brings clauses and thoughts together with all the silent discretion of a hostess arranging guests around her dinner table.

Iyer's topic, punctuation, is not often described in such grandiose terms, and most people probably conceptualize it as rather commonplace—if they even consider it at all. But his approach lifts readers' notions about punctuation.

Using Metaphor: A metaphor is a comparison of one thing to another in which one thing is made to share the characteristics of another. While metaphors are support strategies, they also help to create a particular voice. A lighthearted or relaxed voice might depend on simple, everyday metaphors. Notice Iyer's use:

> Punctuation marks are the road signs placed along the highway of our communication—to control speeds, provide directions, and prevent head-on collisions.

Using Allusions: Allusions are references to some public bit of knowledge (such as a historical event, a political situation, or a popular culture figure). An allusion can give a personal essay a more public and broader feeling while also develop-

ing ideas. But allusions can also help create voice. The allusions one chooses contribute to the voice created in the essay. Alluding to Jerry Lewis, for example, is different than alluding to a dark political figure such as Joseph Stalin. Notice how Richardson's allusions add to his voice:

> I would hate to overemphasize money. You can find plenty of businessmen who never went to college and are earning very respectable salaries. And, of course, there are always people like Paul McCartney and Madonna who went straight for the gold. I have had too many miserable students who were headed for law school because they were attracted by the money, or because their fathers or mothers were, which is worse.

Richardson mentions two big pop stars in a discussion about college. These allusions certainly help to characterize Richardson's voice and further develop the knowing-but-informal mood throughout the essay. Had he used two army generals from history, rather than current pop stars, the effect would be different, and his voice would, perhaps, feel more formal.

Promoting Curiosity: One of the primary jobs of a writer is to pique curiosity in readers. Very rarely does a writer (in any situation) seek only to tell readers what they are already thinking. Instead, writers seek to light a small fire in readers' minds, to make them want to consider an issue. Good writers do more than simply tell readers about something; they cast an issue in a way that makes it engaging. One strategy, using metaphor, is illustrated above. Another strategy is to reveal meaning in everyday life. For example, Benlow explains several slogans and behaviors that constitute life in modern America, and then points to their significance. Hordes of people, every day, pull through drive-up windows and utter these phrases, but Benlow brings them to attention, and shows us how to reconsider them.

Perhaps the most important strategy for promoting curiosity is to embody it—that is, to be curious as a writer. In short, curious writers make curious readers. Notice Iyer's own curiosity about the world:

> Punctuation is the notation in the sheet music of our own words, telling us when to rest, or when to raise our voices; it acknowledges that the meaning of our discourse, as of any symphonic composition, lies not in the units but in the pauses, the pacing and the phrasing. Punctuation is the way one bats one's eyes, lowers one's voice, or blushes demurely. Punctuation adjusts color and tone and volume till the feeling comes into perfect focus: not disgust exactly, but but distaste; not lust, or like, but love.

Iyer himself seems curious about—even awed by—language. He connects it to both grand performances (symphonies) and minute moments (batting one's eyes). He seems to be totally unafraid of his own imagination. The person we detect through the language seems full of wonder. And it is not only the content of the passage; notice also the sentence structure. He uses long sentences to keep the reader in his perspective (as though he is holding us underwater without a breath). As you consider your voice, ask yourself the following:

- What uncommon details reveal my point about the concept?
- Can I avoid telling the reader that something is "interesting," "exciting," etc., and instead create images or use examples that show it?
- Can I use metaphors to make the reader see the intensity or scope or depth of the concept?
- Can I show the reader a new way to see an everyday phenomenon?

Revision Strategies

Explaining a concept involves two basic challenges: understanding the concept and expressing it clearly to others—or, put another way, invention and delivery. Writing allows us to do both, and revision allows us to do them better. By stepping back and seeing what we've written from an outsider's point of view, we can both fine-tune our delivery and better understand the concept ourselves. The concept may, in fact, become not simpler or easier for us to understand, but more complicated and more interesting. Revision also gives the writer a last chance to make the concept relevant to others—that is, to show others how a new or better understanding of this concept matters in their lives.

Consider the following revision strategies:

- Review this chapter, keeping your essay in mind. You might (1) explore your Invention notes, looking for helpful ideas and/or respond further in writing to relevant Invention questions; (2) review the **Rhetorical Tools, Organizational Strategies,** and **Writer's Voice** sections with an eye toward making appropriate changes; and (3) review several of the essays, noting the way the writers in this chapter approached this type of essay.

- Set aside at least as much time to revise as you took with invention and delivery.

- Create distance between you and your writing by getting away from it for a few days if possible or a few hours at least.

- Read your paper aloud to hear how it sounds or have someone else read it aloud to you.

- Print out a hard copy of your paper and read it carefully in a different place than where you wrote it.

- Figure out your writing strategy by noticing how the parts of your essay work together to support your main point. Consider making an outline of your essay to help you see this.

- Have someone else read and respond to your essay.

For ideas about **Peer Review,** see page 50.

Global Revision Questions

Invention (Have you thoroughly explored your topic?)

- **Point of Contact:** What other ideas did you consider writing about before selecting this one? Why was this idea more worth pursuing than the others?

- **Analysis:** How has your exploration of this topic gone beyond your initial ideas and questions about it? In what ways have your ideas moved beyond your initial biases and perceptions—and beyond the common beliefs of your reader?

- **Public Resonance:** How might your essay be relevant to, or matter to, your reader? And what might be the consequence(s) of your essay? How might the reader think or act differently?

Delivery (Have you carefully considered your strategy for shaping the reader's consciousness?)

- **Rhetorical Tools:** Re-examine your rhetorical strategy. What tools discussed earlier in this chapter have you used to help get your point across? What other ones might be helpful?

  - Will the main idea be clear to the reader? If the main idea is not stated, should it be? Is the main claim arguable? Do the details (statistics, facts, allusion, anecdotes, scenarios, analogies) support or illustrate the main idea? Would information from outside sources help support the main claim?

  - Should anything be added? Is enough evidence provided to appropriately support the claim? Does the essay need more details or illustrations of the main idea? Does the essay have an engaging title, an introduction that engages the reader and moves steadily toward the heart of the essay, and a conclusion that provides a satisfying ending?

  - Should anything be deleted? Are there places where the reader will lose interest because the information is too obvious? Are any examples, statistics, or other information unnecessary? Are any ideas unnecessarily restated?

- **Organizational Strategies:** Should any information be placed elsewhere? For example, should the main idea of the essay, or main ideas of paragraphs, be stated earlier to help out the reader? Would placing paragraphs in a different order—or information within paragraphs in a different order—help the reader more easily follow along? Are paragraphs coherent (do they address or illustrate a single supporting point)? If used, is information from sources smoothly integrated into the essay? Should transitions be added to make clear the relationship between or among ideas?

- **Writer's Voice:** Is your writer's voice engaging (not hostile), inviting (not alienating), and appropriate to the writing situation (audience, topic, and purpose)? Where in your essay might you make changes in word choice or sentence structure to make your writer's voice more appealing?

■

CONSIDERING CONSEQUENCES

College students are always learning new concepts: some clearly related to a chosen career; others more clearly related to everyday life. While professors and textbooks explain "academic" concepts, the rest of us explain "everyday" concepts. Distinguishing between the two is not always possible. Concepts of marketing, engineering, psychology, art, and so on affect our everyday lives, which is one reason for learning about them— even if our major is something else. The concepts learned in college are sometimes more complex or explained in greater depth. But concepts learned outside college—from childhood to old age—are often just as challenging and just as important. What might be the consequences of your essay for this chapter? That is, what effect might your ideas have on your reader's thoughts and actions? Consider these questions:

- Will the reader better understand the issue about which you wrote?
- Is the reader likely to think or behave differently?
- What might be the benefits to others? How might others be harmed?
- Who besides your instructor might benefit from your ideas?
- How might what you wrote about be affected?
- What might be the effect of these consequences on you, the writer?

Activities

The Consequences of Your Essay

1. List as many individuals as you can imagine whose thinking and/or actions might change if they were to read the essay you wrote for this chapter. For each individual you list, name the possible change in his or her thinking and/or action. (As you consider consequences upon your reader, consider the "ripple effect" of those consequences. If your reader thinks or behaves differently, what is the impact of that thinking or behavior on others?)

2. Write down answers for each of the bulleted questions above. Then interview at least three people who have read your essay, recording their responses to each question. How were your answers similar to or different from your readers' answers? In what ways, if any, did you change your mind about the potential consequences of your essay?

3. Discuss the potential consequences of your essay with several people. Explain what your essay is about and ask the following questions: What impact might this essay have on the reader? How might it make someone think or act differently?

The Consequences of the Chapter Readings

1. How might you think or act differently after having read one of the essays in this chapter? How might you benefit from, or be harmed by, your new way of think-

ing? How might others benefit from, or be harmed by, your new way of thinking and/or acting?

2. How might someone you know benefit from reading one of the essays in this chapter? For example, might a friend who doesn't like to write reconsider the nature of writing after having read "In Praise of the Humble Comma," or might your parents, if they are concerned about you being an undecided major, feel more at ease after having read "College: What's in It for Me?"? Match an essay in this chapter to a particular reader. Then discuss how the essay might influence the reader's ideas.

Considering Images

1. Find an image of someone being creative and explain how it might be viewed differently before and after reading S. I. Hayakawa's "What It Means to Be Creative."

2. Find an image that relates in some way to college, and explain how it might be viewed differently before and after reading Steven M. Richardson's essay "College: What's in It for Me?"

3. Find an image that relates in some way to college, and explain how it might be viewed differently before and after reading Simon Benlow's essay "Have It Your Way: Consumerism Invades Education."

4. Find an image and explain how it might be viewed differently before and after reading Dan Wilkins's "Why We No Longer Use the 'H' Word."

The Consequences of Everyday Writing

1. What written work has helped to define an important concept for you? Name the work and describe how it has influenced your thoughts and behavior.

2. Interview others to find out what written work has been influential in helping them to understand an important concept. To help others respond, it may be helpful to generate a list of concepts such as love, happiness, peace, and so on. It might also be helpful to provide an example of how a written work has helped others, or yourself, to better understand a concept. Record people's responses, and then summarize the results of your interviews in a paragraph or two.

3. What concept should people understand better? What role might the written word play in helping people better understand that concept?

Considering Images

1. Find an image that encourages viewers to think differently about some concept. In a paragraph, explain how the image encourages the viewer to do this and how the viewer *might* think or act differently as a result. Attach a copy of the image to your paragraph.

2. What advertising image has had a significant impact on Americans? What was the consequence of that image?

Writing, Speech, and Action

EVERYDAY RHETORIC

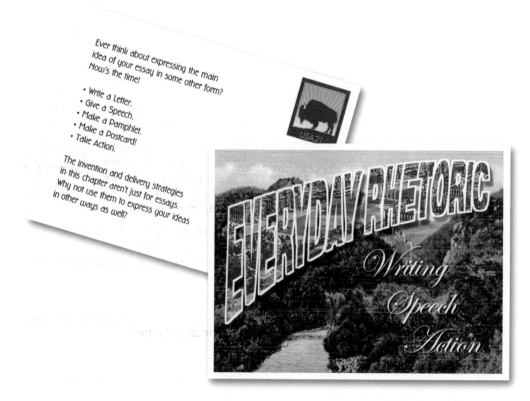

Ever think about expressing the main idea of your essay in some other form? Now's the time!

- Write a Letter.
- Give a Speech.
- Make a Pamphlet.
- Make a Postcard!
- Take Action.

The invention and delivery strategies in this chapter aren't just for essays. Why not use them to express your ideas in other ways as well?

USA 21

EVERYDAY RHETORIC

Writing
Speech
Action

Exploring Visual Rhetoric

I t can be argued that images, too, use rhetoric. And by looking at how images work, we can apply some of the important concepts of rhetoric, not just to writing and speaking, but to images as well. Looking at visual rhetoric can also help us to better understand how rhetoric is used in writing and speech.

Analyzing This Chapter's Opening Image: Analyze this chapter's

opening image using the "Analyzing an Image" questions in Chapter 13 on page 694. What seems to be the main idea of the image? How do the particular elements of the image—content, framing, focus, and so on—help to convey that idea?

1. Explain your analysis in several paragraphs, being certain to show how particular elements of the image help to convey its main idea.

2. Discuss your analysis with several people, exploring through discussion how your understanding of the image is similar to or different from their own. Following the discussion, write down the main similarities and differences in your viewpoints, and explain how your ideas about the image developed or changed through discussion. How did the discussion influence your ideas about the image?

3. Imagine one change in this chapter's opening image. For example, you might add an object (such as a ship on the water or a person on the beach); you might frame the image differently, or take the photo from a different angle. Make one imaginary change in the image and explain how it alters the concept being expressed.

4. How does the context of this chapter's opening image—an "Analyzing Concepts" chapter in a college writing textbook—influence its meaning? Imagine some other context in which you might find this image. How might the image mean something different in that other context?

Find an Image That Relates to Your Essay: What image might

you use in conjunction with the essay you wrote for this chapter?

1. Write a caption for the image.

2. Write an essay explaining the relationship between the image and your text. Consider the following questions:

   • How does the image support or help to explain the text of the essay?

   • What is the theme of the image? What idea does it convey?

   • What specific elements of the image convey the main idea and the support for that idea?

   • How might the reader view the image differently after having read your essay?

   • How might the reader be confused by the relationship of your essay and image?

3. Show the image to several people, and ask each person to read your essay. Then ask them how they view the image differently now.

Find or Create an Image that Defines a Concept

1. Generate a list of major concepts—such as love, hate, peace, freedom, democracy—and then find or create an image that successfully expresses one of those concepts.

   A. Explain how the particular elements of the image convey important aspects of the concept.
   B. Explain how the image fails to convey some important aspect(s) of the concept.
   C. Based on the image you chose, how do you define the concept? For example, if your image suggests *freedom,* how does it relate to your concept of freedom? Use the particulars of the image to explore how you define the concept.

2. Find four different images that express the concept *love.* What kind of love does each image express? What specific elements of each image help to express the concept?

3. Find four different images that express the same concept. How does each image define the concept differently? What elements of each image help to convey the concept, and how do particular images shade the meaning differently?

4. Discuss the images on this page with several friends. What concepts are the images about? Think creatively, explaining various possibilities. What concept do all the images have in common? What do the images say about the concept?

Create a Photo Essay:
Define the concept you wrote about for this chapter, using three to six images and no text. You may take or find photographs, or draw the images yourself. You may arrange them on a single page, present them as a slide show, or display them in some other way. After selecting and arranging the images, explain how they work together to express the concept.

Images in the Media

1. Find an image used in an advertisement. What concept does the image you found convey, and what does the image say about the concept—that is, how does the image define the concept?

2. How can the visual image of an actual person—such as a TV news anchor—be used to help define a concept—such as TV news? For example, watch the news on several channels, using the "Analyzing an Image" questions to study the images on the screen. What does the visual image of network and local news anchors tell you about *the news*? What conclusions can you draw, if any, based on the visual image presented?

3. Study the CD (or old album) covers of a band or solo artist, using the "Analyzing an Image" questions to help you explore the relationship between the cover images and the music.

   A. What concept does one of the covers express? What specific elements of the image help to convey the concept?
   B. Studying several covers from one band or artist, explain how the covers of several CDs convey different concepts, and explain how those concepts relate to the music on the CDs. What remains consistent about the covers and what varies between them? How do the covers represent a change or development, or lack of change, in the music?

4. Go through a friend's CD collection, or go to the library and browse through the CDs, until you find a cover that grabs your attention. Make sure the CD is by an artist you know nothing about. Then use the "Analyzing an Image" questions on page 694 to explore the cover. What concept does it express and how? What does the image suggest about the music? Finally, listen to the CD, noting the relationship between its cover and the music. Was it what you expected?

Images on Campus

1. Find an image on campus that expresses the concept *success*. For example, a brochure or poster promoting your college might argue, "If you attend this school, you will be successful." How does the image you found define *success?* How is the way the image defines *success* similar to or different from the way you define it? How is it similar to or different from the way your classmates define it?

2. Replace the image you found for #1 above, finding three other images that might have been used to say *success*. Explain how each image communicates *success* better than the one that was actually used.

3. Find an image and text (such as a poster, brochure, or sign) on campus that expresses a concept. How do the particular elements of the image convey the important aspects of the concept? What opinion does the image express and how?

4. Continue analyzing the image you found for #3 above. How does the image and text combine to make a point? What does the image and text say about the way the communicator sees the audience? What is the public resonance of the image and accompanying text?

5

Chapter Contents

Making Arguments

What does this image say about argument?
Could argument be visualized differently?
How is the photograph an argument itself?

> **S**omeone who makes an assertion puts forward a claim—a claim on our attention and to our belief.
>
> —*Stephen Toulmin*

Argument is the art of persuading people how to think. This may sound absurd since most people, we hope, already know how to think, or at least *what* to think about particular issues. But with argument, we can change how people view things, even slightly, and so affect how they approach and process ideas. When was the last time *you* argued with someone—or, at least, tried to change someone's mind about something? Why did you do it? What alternative view were you offering?

Arguments come to us in different forms. We hear them given in speeches, debates, and informal discussions. We hear them every day on talk shows, in break rooms, college hallways, and public meeting places like restaurants and pubs. Arguments also get delivered through action. They come explicitly in protests, parades, sit-ins, labor strikes, and voting. They also come in more subtle forms: people donate to charities (thereby expressing their favor of a particular cause); they patronize or boycott a particular store; they choose not to vote or participate in governance (thereby expressing their stance

against the entire political process). Arguments also get made through art—in all media: sculpture, painting, music, etc. And arguments are major elements of literature. For example, it has been said that Aldus Huxley's book *Brave New World* argues against the extremes of materialism and industrialization and that Kate Chopin's *The Awakening* argues for a new vision of women's identity. Even poems offer arguments: Walt Whitman's masterpiece, *Leaves of Grass*, argues for the value of common American workers and their common language.

People in all occupations make or deal with arguments. For example: a human resources manager for a packaging company argues, in a report, that more supervisors should be hired in the coming fiscal year; several department store sales associates collectively write a letter to store and regional managers in which they claim current scheduling practices minimize sales commissions; the public affairs director of a major automobile company argues that a new advertising campaign should not be offensive to a particular minority group; the lawyers for a major computer software company argue, to a district court, that the company's business practices comply with federal anti-trust laws. In academia, argument is everywhere:

- The biology faculty at a state university argue for the need to study cloning and petition the administration for more leeway to do research.
- An historian argues about the number of Native Americans on the continent before European settlers so that people more deeply understand history.
- A psychologist argues that Freudian analysis is overused and that new strategies for exploring patients' psychological make-up should be further developed.
- College administrators argue for more state funds.
- Students in an architecture class argue that a particular structural design is more sound than competing designs.
- Students in a nursing program must convince others that a new staff management technique is valuable for large hospitals.

In any situation, those who can deliver the most sophisticated and engaging arguments tend to have the most influence. Of course, a sophisticated and en-

gaging argument involves a great deal of strategy. For instance, in academic argument, blatant personal attacks, outright aggression, and sugar-coated language are not valued, nor are empty phrases ("don't question what's in my heart") and mean-spiritedness ("your ideas are simply idiotic"). But while academic writers are not out to squash an opponent or cuddle up to audiences, they do more than simply present their opinions. In providing a new way of thinking (about a particular topic), academic writers must also analyze others' ideas and claims and explain how their own claims relate to those of others.

5 This chapter will help you discover an argumentative topic, explore that topic in depth, develop a sophisticated argument, and communicate your argument in writing. The following essays will provide insight to various argumentative strategies. After reading the essays, you can find a topic in one of two ways:

1. Go to the **Point of Contact** section to find a topic from your everyday life.
2. Choose one of the **Ideas for Writing** that follow the essays.

After you find a topic, go to the **Analysis** section to begin developing your argument.

READINGS

In the following essays, notice how each writer offers a particular stance on an issue and develops that stance throughout the entire essay. But each writer also directly engages other positions on the topic under consideration. Whether the essays are longer or shorter (Churchill or Schwind-Pawlak), the writers all manage to put forth their own points while also engaging others' opinions—or positions that compete with their own. Sometimes, the writers bring up other positions only to refute them; that is, they *counterargue*. In other passages the writers grant value to positions other than their own; that is, they *concede* other points.

Crimes Against Humanity

Ward Churchill

Ward Churchill (Keetoowah Band Cherokee) is Professor of American Indian Studies and Chair of the Department of Ethnic Studies at the University of Colorado at Boulder. Among his many books are A Little Matter of Genocide *(1997) and* Struggle for the Land *(1999). "Crimes Against Humanity" was originally written as an official paper of the Colorado chapter of the Confederation of Autonomous chapters of the American Indian Movement (autonomous AIM). Based on this essay, what does Churchill think is wrong with using native names, images, and symbols as sports team mascots? Whether you initially agree or disagree with Churchill's argument, note in the margin of your text any of Churchill's ideas that challenge your current thinking on the topic.*

1   During the past couple of seasons, there has been an increasing wave of controversy regarding the names of professional sports teams like the Atlanta "Braves," Cleveland "Indians," Washington "Redskins," and Kansas City "Chiefs." The issue extends to the names of college teams like Florida State University "Seminoles," University of Illinois "Fighting Illini," and so on, right on down to high school outfits like the Lamar (Colorado) "Savages." Also involved have been team adoption of "mascots," replete with feathers, buckskins, beads, spears and "warpaint" (some fans have opted to adorn themselves in the same fashion), and nifty little "pep" gestures like the "Indian Chant" and "Tomahawk Chop."

2   A substantial number of American Indians have protested that use of native names, images and symbols as sports team mascots and the like is, by definition, a virulently racist practice. Given the historical relationship between Indians and non-Indians during what has been called the "Conquest of America," American Indian Movement leader (and American Indian Anti-Defamation Council founder) Russell Means has compared the practice to contemporary Germans naming their soccer teams the "Jews," "Hebrews," and "Yids," while adorning their uniforms with grotesque caricatures of Jewish faces taken from the Nazis' anti-Semitic propaganda of the 1930s. Numerous demonstrations have occurred in conjunction with games—most notably

during the November 15, 1992 match-up between the Chiefs and Redskins in Kansas City—by angry Indians and their supporters.

3   In response, a number of players—especially African Americans and other minority athletes—have been trotted out by professional team owners like Ted Turner, as well as university and public school officials, to announce that they mean not to insult but to honor native people. They have been joined by the television networks and most major newspapers, all of which have editorialized that Indian discomfort with the situation is "no big deal," insisting that the whole thing is just "good, clean fun." The country needs more such fun, they've argued, and a "few disgruntled Native Americans" have no right to undermine the nation's enjoyment of its leisure time by complaining. This is especially the case, some have argued, "in hard times like these." It has even been contended that Indian outrage at being systematically degraded—rather than the degradation itself—creates "a serious barrier to the sort of intergroup communication so necessary in a multicultural society such as ours."

4   Okay. Let's communicate. We are frankly dubious that those advancing such positions really believe their own rhetoric but, just for the sake of argument, let's accept the premise that they are sincere. If what they say is true, then isn't it time we spread such "inoffensiveness" and "good cheer" around among all the groups so that everybody can participate equally in fostering the national round of laughs they call for? Sure it is—the country can't have too much fun or "intergroup" involvement—so the more, the merrier. Simple consistency demands that anyone who thinks the Tomahawk Chop is a swell pastime must be just as hearty in their endorsement of the following ideas—by the logic used to defend the defamation of American Indians—[to] help us all really start yukking it up.

5   First, as a counterpart to the Redskins, we need an NFL team called "Niggers" to honor Afro-Americans. Half-time festivities for fans might include a simulated stewing of the opposing coach in a large pot while players and cheerleaders dance around it, garbed in leopard skins and wearing fake bones in their noses. This concept obviously goes along with the kind of gaiety attending the Chop, but also with the actions of the Kansas Chiefs, whose team members—prominently including black members—lately appeared on a poster, looking "fierce" and "savage" by way of wearing Indian regalia. Just a bit of harmless "morale boosting," says the Chiefs' front office. You bet.

6   So that the newly-formed Niggers sports club won't end up too out of sync while expressing the "spirit" and "identity" of Afro-Americans in the above fashion, a baseball franchise—let's call this one the "Sambos"—should be formed. How about a basketball team called the "Spearchuckers"? A hockey team called the "Jungle Bunnies"? Maybe the "essence" of these teams could be depicted by images of tiny black faces adorned with huge pairs of lips. The players could appear on TV every week or so gnawing on chicken legs and spitting watermelon seeds at one another. Catchy, eh? Well, there's "nothing to be upset about," according to those who love wearing "war bonnets" to the Super Bowl or having "Chief Illiniwik" dance around the sports arenas of Urbana, Illinois.

7   And why stop there? There are plenty of other groups to include. "Hispanics"? They can be "represented" by the Galveston "Greasers" and the San Diego "Spics," at least until the Wisconsin "Wetbacks" and Baltimore "Beaners" get off the ground. Asian Americans? How about the "Slopes," "Dinks," "Gooks," and "Zipperheads"? Owners of the latter teams might get their logo ideas from editorial page cartoons printed in the nation's newspapers during World War II: slanteyes, buck teeth, big glasses, but nothing racially insulting or derogatory, according to the editors and artists involved at the time. Indeed, this Second World War–vintage stuff can be seen as just another barrel of

laughs at least by what current editors say are their "local standards" concerning American Indians.

8   Let's see. Who's been left out? Teams like the Kansas City "Kikes," Hanover "Honkies," San Leandro "Shylocks," Daytona "Dagos," and Pittsburgh "Polacks" will fill a certain social void among white folk. Have a religious belief? Let's all go for the gusto and gear up the Milwaukee "Mackeral Snappers" and Hollywood "Holy Rollers." The Fighting Irish of Notre Dame can be rechristened the "Drunken Irish" or "Papist Pigs." Issues of gender and sexual preference can be addressed through creation of teams like the St. Louis "Sluts," Boston "Bimbos," Detroit "Dykes," and the Fresno "Fags." How about the Gainsville "Gimps" and the Richmond "Retards," so the physically and mentally impaired won't be excluded from our fun and games?

9   Now, don't go getting "overly sensitive" out there. None of this is demeaning or insulting, at least not when it's being done to Indians. Just ask the folks who are doing it, or their apologists like Andy Rooney in the national media. They'll tell you—as in fact they have been telling you—that there's been no harm done, regardless of what their victims think, feel, or say. The situation is exactly the same as when those with precisely the same mentality used to insist that Step 'n' Fetchit was okay, or Rochester on the Jack Benny show, or Amos and Andy, Charlie Chan, the Frito Bandito, or any other cutesy symbols making up the lexicon of American racism. Have we communicated yet?

10   Let's get just a little bit real here. The notion of "fun" embodied in rituals like the Tomahawk Chop must be understood for what it is. There's not a single non-Indian example used above which can be considered socially acceptable in even the most marginal sense. The reasons are obvious enough. So why is it different where American Indians are concerned? One can only conclude that, in contrast to the other groups at issue, Indians are (falsely) perceived as being too few, and therefore too weak, to defend themselves effectively against racist and otherwise offensive behavior.

11   Fortunately, there are some glimmers of hope. A few teams and their fans have gotten the message and have responded appropriately. Stanford University, which opted to drop the name "Indians" from Stanford, has experienced no resulting drop in attendance. Meanwhile, the local newspaper in Portland, Oregon recently decided its long-standing editorial policy prohibiting use of racial epithets should include derogatory team names. The Redskins, for instance, are now referred to as "the Washington team," and will continue to be described in this way until the franchise adopts an inoffensive moniker (newspaper sales in Portland have suffered no decline as a result). Such examples are to be applauded and encouraged. They stand as figurative beacons in the night, proving beyond all doubt that it is quite possible to indulge in the pleasure of athletics without accepting blatant racism into the bargain.

Nuremberg Precedents

12   On October 16, 1946, a man named Julius Streicher mounted the steps of a gallows. Moments later he was dead, the sentence of an international tribunal composed of representatives of the United States, France, Great Britain, and the Soviet Union having been imposed. Streicher's body was then cremated, and—so horrendous were his crimes thought to have been—his ashes dumped into an unspecified German river so that "no one should ever know a particular place to go for reasons of mourning his memory."

13   Julius Streicher had been convicted at Nuremberg, Germany of what were termed "Crimes Against Humanity." The lead prosecutor in his case—Justice Robert Jackson of the United States Supreme Court—had not argued that the defendant had killed anyone, nor that he had personally committed any especially violent act. Nor was it contended that Streicher had held any particularly important position in

the German government during the period in which the so-called Third Reich had exterminated some 6,000,000 Jews, as well as several million Gypsies, Poles, Slavs, homosexuals, and other *untermenschen* (subhumans).

14   The sole offense for which the accused was ordered put to death was in having served as publisher/editor of a Bavarian tabloid entitled *Der Sturmer* during the early-to-mid 1930s, years before the Nazi genocide actually began. In this capacity, he had penned a long series of virulently anti-Semitic editorials and "news."

15   Stories, usually accompanied by cartoons and other images, graphically depicted Jews in extraordinarily derogatory fashion. This, the prosecution asserted, had done much to "dehumanize" the targets of his distortion in the mind of the German public. In turn, such dehumanization had made it possible—or at least easier—for average Germans to later indulge in the outright liquidation of Jewish "vermin." The tribunal agreed, holding that Streicher was therefore complicit in genocide and deserving of death by hanging.

16   During his remarks to the Nuremberg tribunal, Justice Jackson observed that, in implementing its sentences, the participating powers were morally and legally binding themselves to adhere forever after to the same standards of conduct that were being applied to Streicher and the other Nazi leaders. In the alternative, he said, the victorious allies would have committed "pure murder" at Nuremberg—no different in substance from that carried out by those they presumed to judge—rather than establishing the "permanent benchmark for justice" which was intended.

17   Yet in the United States of Robert Jackson, the indigenous American Indian population had already been reduced, in a process which is on-going to this day, from perhaps 12.5 million in the year 1500 to fewer than 250,000 by the beginning of the 20th century. This was accomplished, according to official sources, "largely through the cruelty of Euro American settlers," and an informal but clear governmental policy which had made it an articulated goal to "exterminate these red vermin" or at least whole segments of them.

18   Bounties had been placed on the scalps of Indians—any Indians—in places as diverse as Georgia, Kentucky, Texas, the Dakotas, Oregon, and California and had been maintained until resident Indian populations were decimated or disappeared altogether. Entire peoples such as the Cherokee had been reduced to half their size through a policy of forced removal from their homelands east of the Mississippi River to what were then considered less preferable areas in the West.

19   Others, such as the Navajo, suffered the same fate while under military guard for years on end. The United States Army had also perpetrated a long series of wholesale massacres of Indians at places like Horseshoe Bend, Bear River, Sand Creek, the Washita River, the Marias River, Camp Robinson and Wounded Knee.

20   Through it all, hundreds of popular novels—each competing with the next to make Indians appear more grotesque, menacing, and inhuman—were sold in the tens of millions of copies in the U.S. Plainly, the Euro American public was being conditioned to see Indians in such a way so as to allow their eradication to continue. And continue it did until the Manifest Destiny of the U.S.—a direct precursor to what Hitler would subsequently call *Lebensraumpolitik* (the politics of living space)—was consummated.

21   By 1900, the national project of "clearing" Native Americans from their land and replacing them with "superior" Anglo American settlers was complete; the indigenous population had been reduced by as much as 98 percent while approximately 97.5 percent of their original territory had "passed" to the invaders. The survivors had been concentrated, out of sight and mind of the public, on scattered "reservations," all of them under the self-assigned "plenary" (full) power of the federal government. There was, of course, no Nuremberg-style tribunal passing judgment on those who had fostered such circumstances in North America. No

U.S. official or private citizen was ever imprisoned—never mind hanged—for implementing or propagandizing what had been done. Nor had the process of genocide afflicting Indians been completed. Instead, it merely changed form.

22   Between the 1880s and the 1980s, nearly half of all Native American children were coercively transferred from their own families, communities, and cultures to those of the conquering society. This was done through compulsory attendance at remote boarding schools, often hundreds of miles from their homes, where native children were kept for years on end while being systematically "deculturated" (indoctrinated to think and act in the manner of Euro Americans rather than as Indians). It was also accomplished through a pervasive foster home and adoption program—including blind adoptions, where children would be permanently denied information as to who they were/are and where they'd come from—placing native youths in non-Indian homes.

23   The express purpose of all this was to facilitate a U.S. governmental policy to bring about the "assimilation" (dissolution) of indigenous societies. In other words, Indian cultures as such were to be caused to disappear. Such policy objectives are directly contrary to the United Nations 1948 Convention on Punishment and Prevention of the Crime of Genocide, an element of international law arising from the Nuremberg proceedings. The forced "transfer of the children" of a targeted "racial, ethnical, or religious group" is explicitly prohibited as a genocidal activity under the Convention's second article.

24   Article II of the Genocide Convention also expressly prohibits involuntary sterilization as a means of "preventing births among" a targeted population. Yet, in 1975, it was conceded by the U.S. government that its Indian Health Service (IHS), then a subpart of the Bureau of Indian Affairs (BIA), was even then conducting a secret program of involuntary sterilization that had affected approximately 40 percent of all Indian women. The program was allegedly discontinued, and the IHS was transferred to the Public Health Service, but no one was punished. In 1990, it came out that the IHS was inoculating Inuit children in Alaska with Hepatitis-B vaccine. The vaccine had already been banned by the World Health Organization as having demonstrated a correlation with the HIV-Syndrome which is itself correlated to AIDS. As this is written [March 1993], a "field test" of Hepatitis-A vaccine, also HIV-correlated, is being conducted on Indian reservations in the northern plains region.

25   The Genocide Convention makes it a crime against "humanity" to create conditions leading to the destruction of an identifiable human group, as such. Yet the BIA has utilized the government's plenary prerogatives to negotiate mineral leases "on behalf of" Indian peoples paying a fraction of standard royalty rates. The result has been "super profits" for a number of preferred U.S. corporations. Meanwhile, Indians, whose reservations ironically turned out to be in some of the most mineral-rich areas of North America, which makes us the nominally wealthiest segment of the continent's population, live in dire poverty.

26   By the government's own data in the mid-1980s, Indians received the lowest annual and lifetime per capita incomes of any aggregate population group in the United States. Concomitantly, we suffer the highest rate of infant mortality, death by exposure and malnutrition, disease, and the like. Under such circumstances, alcoholism and other escapist forms of substance abuse are endemic in the Indian community, a situation which leads both to a general physical debilitation of the population and a catastrophic accident rate. Teen suicide among Indians is several times the national average.

27   The average life expectancy of a reservation-based Native American man is barely 45 years; women can expect to live less than three years longer.

28   Such itemizations could be continued at great length, including matters like the radio-

active contamination of large portions of contemporary Indian Country, the forced relocation of traditional Navajos, and so on. But the point should be made: Genocide, as defined in international law, is a continuing fact of day-to-day life (and death) for North America's native peoples. Yet there has been—and is—only the barest flicker of public concern about or even consciousness of, this reality. Absent any serious expression of public outrage, no one is punished and the process continues.

29   A salient reason for public acquiescence before the ongoing holocaust in Native North America has been a continuation of the popular legacy, often through more effective media. Since 1925, Hollywood has released more than 2,000 films, many of them rerun frequently on television, portraying Indians as strange, perverted, ridiculous, and often dangerous things of the past. Moreover, we are habitually presented to mass audiences one-dimensionally, devoid of recognizable human motivations and emotions: Indians thus serve as props, little more. We have thus been thoroughly and systematically dehumanized.

30   Nor is this the extent of it. Everywhere we are used as logos, as mascots, as jokes: "Big Chief" writing tablets, "Red Man" chewing tobacco, "Winnebago" campers, "Navajo" and "Cherokee" and "Pontiac" and "Cadillac" pickups and automobiles. There are the Cleveland "Indians," the Kansas City "Chiefs," the Atlanta "Braves" and the Washington "Redskins" professional sports teams—not to mention those in thousands of colleges, high schools, and elementary schools across the country, each with their own degrading caricatures and parodies of Indians and/or things Indian. Pop fiction continues in the same vein, including an unending stream of New Age manuals purporting to expose the inner works of indigenous spirituality in everything from pseudo-philosophical to do-it-yourself styles. Blond yuppies from Beverly Hills amble about the country claiming to be reincarnated 17th-century Cheyenne Ushamans ready to perform previously secret ceremonies.

31   In effect, a concerted, sustained, and in some ways accelerating effort has gone into making Indians unreal. It is thus of obvious importance that the American public begin to think about the implications of such things the next time they witness a gaggle of face-painted and war-bonneted buffoons doing the "Tomahawk Chop" at a baseball or football game. It is necessary that they think about the implications of the grade-school teacher adorning their child in turkey feathers to commemorate Thanksgiving. Think about the significance of John Wayne or Charleton Heston killing a dozen "savages" with a single bullet the next time a western comes on TV. Think about why Land-o-Lakes finds it appropriate to market its butter with the stereotyped image of an "Indian princess" on the wrapper. Think about what it means when non-Indian academics profess—as they often do—to "know more about Indians than Indians do themselves." Think about the significance of charlatans like Carlos Castaneda and Jamake Highwater and Mary Summer Rain and Lynn Andrews churning out "Indian" bestsellers one after the other, while Indians typically can't get into print.

32   Think about the real situation of American Indians. Think about Julius Streicher. Remember Justice Jackson's admonition. Understand that the treatment of Indians in American popular culture is not "cute" or "amusing," or just "good, clean fun."

33   Know that it causes real pain and real suffering to real people. Know that it threatens our very survival. And know that this is just as much a crime against humanity as anything the Nazis ever did. It is likely the indigenous people of the United States will never demand that those guilty of such criminal activity be punished for their deeds. But the least we have to expect—indeed to demand—is that such practices finally be brought to a halt.

Exploring Ideas

1. What does Churchill think is wrong with using Native American names, images, and symbols as sports team mascots?

2. How is the way that you see this issue similar to or different from the way Churchill sees it? How is what Churchill thinks different from what you think? How is what he values, feels, or believes different from what you value, feel, or believe?

3. Explain Churchill's argument to a variety of people and record their responses, asking them *why* they respond as they do. How do others think about this issue? Did anyone think differently—change his or her mind—after hearing Churchill's argument?

4. In one clear sentence each, list at least three points Churchill makes that invite you to respond in some way. Write out your response to each point, and then describe the nature of that response. That is, did you expand on what Churchill says, show why you think he is wrong, take his way of thinking and apply it to another situation, or do something else?

5. Return to your notes for question #3 (how others viewed Churchill's argument). How might you argue Churchill's point in order to persuade one of the people who disagreed with him? What was the root of their disagreement, and how can you work with that area of disagreement to encourage better understanding of Churchill's argument? Or, approach it differently: how might you argue someone else's point to help Churchill better understand that point of view?

Writing Strategies

1. Describe Churchill's voice as a writer. Refer specifically to several sentences that support your description. Then explain how Churchill's particular writer's voice might affect his reader. What seems to be Churchill's strategy regarding his writer's voice?

2. Identify places in Churchill's essay where he anticipates his reader's thoughts. How is he able to anticipate them, and how successful is he at responding to them?

3. Describe Churchill's evidence. What type of evidence is it: personal anecdotes, literary allusions, observations, logical reasoning, historical allusions, or something else? What particular evidence did you find most convincing? What evidence did you think fell short?

4. Consider Churchill's opening and closing strategies. How successful are they? How else might he have gotten into and out of his essay?

Ideas for Writing

1. How can you apply some or all of Churchill's way of thinking to another group or situation?

2. How is Churchill's argument played out in your life? That is, in what ways do you encourage and support or discourage and withdraw your support from the use of Native American images and symbols?

> If responding to one of these ideas, go to the Analysis section of this chapter to begin developing ideas for your essay.

Why a Great Books Education Is the Most Practical!

David Crabtree, Ph.D.

David Crabtree, president and one of the founders of Gutenberg College in Eugene, Oregon, teaches at the college's McKenzie Study Center. This essay was posted on the institute's Web site (www. mckenziestudycenter.org). As you read the essay, allow Crabtree's title to focus your attention: Why, according to him, is a great books education the most practical? Make notes in the margin of your text whenever Crabtree offers an idea that you strongly agree with, disagree with, or find puzzling.

1   Gutenberg College is a great books college. The curriculum is designed to develop good learning skills in students; they read and then discuss in small groups the writings produced by the greatest minds of Western culture as they grappled with the most fundamental questions facing human beings of all ages. When I tell people about Gutenberg College, one of the most common responses is: "It's a good idea, but not practical." The thinking seems to be that if one had unlimited time and money, a great books education would be very good to pursue; but in the real world, food has to be put on the table, and a great books education will not do that. I am convinced, however, that a great books education is not only practical, but, in our day and age, the most practical education available.

2   Modern society has adopted the historically recent perspective that the purpose of education is training for the workplace. In this view, college should provide students with skills and knowledge that will prepare them to procure reasonably high-paying, satisfying employment for the rest of their lives. The common wisdom says that the best way to achieve this goal is: first, as an undergraduate, select a promising occupation and major in the appropriate field of study; and second, after graduating, enter directly into the work force or attend a graduate or professional school for more specialized training. The logic seems to be that the sooner one concludes one's education and begins work in one's field, the less will be the cost of education and the better the prospects for advancement into secure, high-paying positions. While this was once a reasonable strategy, it is not suited to the economic environment currently developing.

3   The world is changing at a bewildering pace. Anyone who owns a computer and tries to keep up with the developments in hardware, software, and the accompanying incompatibilities is all too aware of the speed of change. This rapid change, especially technological change, has extremely important implications for the job market. In the past, it was possible to look at the nation's work force, determine which of the existing occupations was most desirable in terms of pay and working conditions, and pick one to prepare for. But the rapid rate of change is clouding the crystal ball. How do we know that a high-paying job today will be high-paying tomorrow?

4   A photographer told me about a talented and highly skilled artisan who touched up photographs. He was the best in our region of the country, and people knew it; because the demand for his skill was so great, he was unable to keep up with the work. A few years ago, however, this artisan suddenly closed his shop; he did not have enough work to stay in business. Due to developments in computer hardware and software, anyone with just a little training can now achieve results previously attainable by only a few highly skilled artisans. Technology had rendered this artisan's skills obsolete. And this is not an isolated case; technology is antiquating many skills.

5   One could try to avoid this fate by finding an occupation unlikely to be automated, but automation is not the only cause of job elimination. Historically, mid-management positions in large corporations provided good incomes and considerable job security. However, AT&T's recent layoffs have drawn attention to the growing trend in American companies to eliminate mid-level managers as the companies restructure to compete better in the world market. As a result, a glut of unemployed executives are having great difficulty finding employment in their field of expertise. Most of them never dreamed they would be standing in unemployment lines.

6   Medicine might be a more promising field. There will always be sick people to treat, and doctors have a reputation for high pay. However, recent news reports have called into question the future of this occupation. There is an excess of doctors in the United States right now, largely due to the number of foreign medical students who decide to remain in this country after they complete their training. And physicians' incomes recently declined for the first time in decades, a change attributed to the proliferation of HMOs and managed health care providers—a trend expected to continue. To further complicate the picture, in the near future a national health care plan may rise from the ashes of President Clinton's ill-fated one. What effect such a program would have on physicians' incomes and working conditions is impossible to predict with certainty, but doctors ought not expect raises under such a plan. In light of such an uncertain future, should a student invest the time and money medical training requires? This is a tough question, but similar uncertainties lie in the future of many professions.

7   One could forego the traditionally desirable occupations and choose a field certain to grow and develop. Clearly the high demand for programmers, electrical engineers, and computer programmers appears to hold great promise for job security in the foreseeable future, even if one must work for several different employers over the years. However, no one in this field will be able to take his job for granted. Due to the rapid rate of technological change in the computer industry, people in this field need to be constantly learning and updating their skills to keep up with the new technology. In areas of state-of-the-art development, some companies do not want software writers or engineers over thirty-five years old because their training is out-of-date and they are too set in their ways to approach problems with fresh thinking. These companies prefer to replace older employees with recent graduates. Thus the longevity of one's career in this fast-changing field could be relatively short.

8   No matter what occupation one chooses, the future is full of question marks. Although this economic dislocation is in its early stages, statistics already indicate a high degree of instability in the job market. According to the United States government, the average American switches careers three times in his or her life, works for ten employers, and stays in each job only 3.6 years. (Note 1)

9   Such unpredictability calls for a different strategy in preparing for the job market. Rather than spending one's undergraduate years receiving specialized training, one ought to learn more general, transferable skills which will provide the flexibility to adjust to whatever changes may occur. A well-educated worker should be able to communicate clearly with co-workers, both verbally and in writing, read with understanding, perform basic mathematical calculations, conduct himself responsibly and ethically, and work well with others. These skills would make a person well-suited to most work environments and capable of learning quickly and easily the requisite skills for a new career, should the need arise. Thus a hard-headed realism, with long-term economic security as the goal, would seem to dictate an undergraduate educational strategy of focusing on sound general learning skills—just what a great books education provides.

Note 1: Sue Brower, "When You Want—or Have—to Make a Career Shift." *Cosmopolitan*, v. 199, no. 2 (Aug 1985), p. 229.

10   Therefore, a great books education makes good sense in terms of dollars spent and dollars gained when calculated over a lifetime, and, therefore, good training for the workplace. This is fortuitous, however, because a great books education is not designed with this as the primary goal. It is designed to achieve the even more practical goal historically assigned to education: to teach students how to live wisely. I say this is practical because that which helps one achieve what needs to be done is practical. Living wisely is the most important thing a person can do in his lifetime. Therefore, education with this focus is quintessentially practical.

11   Wise living means to live as one ought; in other words, to strive to achieve good goals by moral means. This statement immediately evokes an array of fundamental questions: Why are we here? What is valuable or worthwhile? What are the principles of right and wrong? Is there a God? Who is He? What is my relationship to Him? Without having seriously wrestled with these issues, one will be condemned to a life without direction or purpose. Without clearly defined and worthwhile goals, success and fulfillment are impossible. Therefore, one's answers to these questions have very important implications for how one chooses to earn a living.

12   Is such a goal realistic or attainable by education? It is difficult to teach a person how to live wisely. In a sense, such a skill can not be taught; it can only be learned. The student must be challenged to think through these fundamental questions for himself; he must be an extremely active participant in his own education. We all derive our wisdom from careful reflection on our experience, and this reflection can be made more profound by considering the reflections of others who have had similar experiences. That is to say, we can benefit from the wisdom others have attained.

13   A great books education creates an educational environment conducive to the learning of wisdom. Classes are small, personal, and largely discussion-based. The small class size and the discussion format encourage each student to be actively involved in consideration of important issues, and they allow the course of the discussion to be tailored to the concerns of the students. The writings of the most influential thinkers of our cultural tradition are studied, which provides many thought-provoking insights into the fundamental questions. As students work to understand these writings, they develop important learning skills—reading with understanding, thinking clearly, and writing cogently—which equip them to become life-long learners.

14   A great books education is not for everyone. In order to benefit from such an education, a student has to be highly motivated, mature enough to realize the importance of such a focus, and self-disciplined. Whatever reasons one might have for not pursuing a great books education, it cannot be because it is not practical!

Exploring Ideas

1. What does Crabtree mean by "a great books education"?

2. Consider the context of Crabtree's essay. What argument is his essay a response to?

3. In general, what do you think is the purpose of education?

4. Does education serve different purposes? For example, how is the goal of an elementary school education different from that of a college education? Or, how is the goal of a junior high school education different from that of a high school education? List as many different types of "educations" as you can, naming their goals and explaining their relationship to the purpose of education in general.

5. Having read Crabtree's essay, do you agree that a great books education is the most practical? Exploring your thoughts beyond your initial reactions, how might you contribute to Crabtree's great books discussion by explaining a worthwhile point of your own?

Writing Strategies

1. How does Crabtree make his main idea clear to the reader?

2. Crabtree's introduction puts his essay within a context—that is, he lets the reader know why he is writing about a great books education. Why is he writing? To what argument is his essay responding? To whom is he writing?

3. Does Crabtree clearly define a great books education? If so, how? If not, how might he have defined it more clearly?

4. What kinds of evidence (statistics, examples, allusions, personal testimony, reasoning, and so on) does Crabtree provide as support for his main idea?

5. Does Crabtree make concessions or counter-arguments—that is, does he acknowledge weaknesses in his own argument or value in opposing positions (concession), or does he anticipate and respond to likely reactions to his points (counterargument)? If so, how do the concessions and/or counterarguments strengthen his argument? If not, what concessions or counterarguments might he have made that he didn't?

Ideas for Writing

1. Crabtree argues for the practical value of a great books education, but he does not say that a great books education is for *everyone*. What else might you argue has practical value, even though you are not arguing that it is for everyone? (Consider a type of education, a way of doing something, a hobby, and so on.)

2. Why are we here? What is valuable or worthwhile? What are the principles of right and wrong? Is there a God? Who is He? What is my relationship with Him? How might you support or refute Crabtree's claim that "one's answers to these questions have very important implications for how one chooses to earn a living"?

3. Crabtree says that "the writings of the most influential thinkers of our cultural tradition are studied, which provides many thought-provoking insights into the fundamental questions." Can you think of one such insight that has influenced your thinking?

> If responding to one of these ideas, go to the **Analysis** section of this chapter to begin developing ideas for your essay.

Cruelty, Civility, and Other Weighty Matters

Ann Marie Paulin

Ann Marie Paulin teaches English and Gender Studies at Owens Community College in Toledo, Ohio. As you read "Cruelty, Civility, and Other Weighty Matters," ask yourself what Paulin is trying to accomplish. And consider how you might take part in this discussion, whether it be to expand, narrow, or redirect it in some way. While reading, jot down any initial ideas you have to what Paulin says.

In the margins of this essay, a reader's comments point to key ideas and writing strategies. As you read the essay, consider how the comments might influence your own reading and writing.

Exploring Ideas

Writing Strategies

I swear, if I have to sit through one more ad proclaiming that life is not worth living if you aren't thin, I'll slug somebody. So much for the theory that fat people are jolly. But, contrary to what magazines, talk shows, movies, and advertisements proclaim, we aren't all a bunch of sorrowful, empty losers with no friends and no self-esteem, either. As with most complex issues—religion, politics, human relationships—most of what we see in mass media is hugely oversimplified and, therefore, wrong. So, if many of us recognize the media are notorious for getting things less than accurate, you might wonder why I let these images bother me so much. Well, if you were one of the millions of fat Americans living in a culture where you are constantly depicted as some sort of weepy loser, ill-dressed buffoon, or neutered sidekick, your good nature might wear a bit thin as well. But far more important than my ill temper is a creepy sense that these inaccurate images have shifted our vision of what is important in life way out of whack, so far out that people are being hurt. What I'm proposing here is that we need to get some perspective on this issue.

A strong, emphatic (but informal) voice.

"You" makes the voice more informal.

"Our" is a direct strategy to create public resonance.

Pop culture images are simplistic.

Media images have distorted people's perceptions about life.

First of all, let me make it clear that I'm not advocating that everyone in America go out and get fat. According to the news media, we are doing that very handily on our own, in spite of all the messages to the contrary and the shelves of diet food in every supermarket. (One of my colleagues came by today with a newspaper article on the Krispy Kreme Donut chain; evidently, Americans eat three million Krispy Kreme donuts each day. We may talk tofu, but we gobble glazed.) Americans all need to work on eating healthier and getting some exercise. Of course, the thin fanatics claim to advocate a healthy lifestyle as well, but I question

This is a qualification of her argument.

Helps with the public resonance. It shows that Paulin is not alone.

Good support!

Millions of Americans eat poorly . . . are out of sync with the media images.

Counterargument.

Allusion to a related news event.

Using an authority, Pipher, to support point.

how healthy people are when they are living on low-calorie chocolate milk drinks, or taking herbal supplements containing goodness knows what, or loading up on the latest wonder diet pill. Remember Fen-phen? And most diets don't work. Psychologist Mary Pipher, in her book *Hunger Pains: The Modern Woman's Quest for Thinness*, cites a 1994 study which found that "90 percent of dieters regain all the weight they lost within five years" (32). The evidence is beginning to pile up out there that being fat may not be nearly as bad for a person's health as the crazy things people inflict upon their bodies to lose weight.

Fen-phen killed some people?

Diets don't work . . . and inflict bodily damage.

What evidence?

But beyond these physical things, we need to get our minds straightened out. We need to get back to recognizing that a human being is a collection of qualities, good and bad, and that appearance is not the ultimate way to judge a person's character or value to society.

People's understanding of health has been distorted.

Stating an opposing view—or wrong assumption. Setting up the counterargument.

Yet there is definitely a prejudice against fat people in this country. Various articles and news magazine programs have reported that Americans of all sizes make far more than simple aesthetic judgments when they look at a fat person. Fat people are assumed to be lazy, stupid, ugly, lacking in self-esteem and pride, devoid of self-control, and stuffed full of a host of other unpleasant qualities that have nothing to do with the size of a person's belly or thighs. But, as anyone who has ever been the victim of such prejudice can tell you, the impact such foolish notions have on people is real and harmful. For example, Marilyn Wann, in her book *Fat! So?*, reports some alarming statistics: "In a 1977 study, half of the landlords refused to rent an apartment to a fat applicant. All of the landlords were willing to rent the same apartment to a thin applicant" (154). What does dress size have to do with whether or not you pay your rent on time? Or do landlords assume that fat people will not keep the apartments clean? Wann also cites an experiment in which "[r]esearchers placed two fake personal ads, one for a woman described as '50 pounds overweight' and the other for a woman described as a drug addict. The drug addict received 79 percent of the responses" (59). I don't even want to know what the thinking was here. And, finally, Wann points out that the average fat woman earns about $7000 less per year than her thinner sisters (80). In my case, I teach English at a community college. Jobs in academia require an advanced degree, so I happen to have a Ph.D., which has nothing to do with my body size, unless you want to count the weight I gained from thousands of hours sitting reading, sitting at a keyboard, sitting grading papers.

People are more than their body sizes.

Counterargument— she's countering the opposing view.

The study is 25 years old. Has it changed?

Marilyn Wann—fat people are discriminated against.

Real effects of prejudice. Good support.

This weight prejudice hurts real people. When people are denied a place to live or a means of support not because of any bad behavior or lack of character or talent on their part but because

Real effects of prejudice.

Exploring Ideas

Relates the problem to her personal situation. Makes the voice feel personal.

Re-statement of the main idea.

Allusion to popular item.

This addresses a counterargument: that ads are just silly/harmless.

Analysis of the opposing logic.

Transition statement creates coherence between points.

of someone else's wrongheaded notions, then we need to start changing things.

The messages are particularly insidious when they suggest that being thin is more important than a man's or, more often, a woman's relationships with her loved ones or even than her health. The media churn the images out, but the public too often internalizes them. For example, in one commercial for Slim Fast, the woman on the ad is prattling on about how she had gained weight when she was pregnant (seems to me, if you make a person, you ought to be entitled to an extra ten pounds) and how awful she felt. Then there is a shot of this woman months later as a thin person with her toddler in her yard. She joyously proclaims that Slim Fast is "the best thing that ever happened to me!" The best thing that ever happened to her?! I thought I heard wrong. What about that little child romping by her heels? Presumably, there is a daddy somewhere for that little cherub. What about his role in her life? The thought that losing that weight is the most important thing that ever occurred in her life is sad and terrifying. It's even worse for the folks who share that life with her. I kept hoping that was not what she meant. I'm sure her family is really most important. But she didn't say, "Next to my baby, Slim Fast is the best thing that ever happened to me." Advertisers don't spend millions of dollars creating ads that don't say what they intend them to; this message was deliberate. Granted, this is only one ad, but the message is clear: The consumer is the center of the universe, and being thin is the only way to ensure that universe remains a fun place to live. The constant repetition of this message in various forms does the damage to the humans who watch and learn.

While we can shrug off advertisements as silly, when we see these attitudes reflected among real people, the hurt is far less easy to brush away. For instance, in her essay, "Bubbie, Mommy, Weight Watchers and Me," Barbara Noreen Dinnerstein recalls a time in her childhood when her mother took her to Weight Watchers to slim down and the advice the lecturer gave to the women present: "She told us to put a picture of ourselves on the 'fridgerator of us eating and looking really fat and ugly. She said remember what you look like. Remember how ugly you are" (347).

I have a problem with this advice. First, of course, it is too darn common. Fat people are constantly being told they should be ashamed of themselves, of their bodies. And here we see another of those misconceptions I mentioned earlier: the assumption that being fat is the same as being ugly. There are plenty of attractive fat people in the world, as well as a few butt-ugly thin ones, I might add. Honestly, though, the real tragedy is that

Writing Strategies

The real danger of the media images.

Slim Fast ad that directly values thinness over family, life. Good support.

Great support. A real ad illustrating the twisted values/perception.

Thinness ads damage minds/lives.

Keeps returning to the effects on real people—so reader can't dismiss the point.

Ha! The writer is not above judging people . . . this creates an interesting voice.

while few people in this world are truly ugly, many agonize over the belief that they are. Dr. Pipher reported: "I see clients who say they would rather kill themselves than be overweight" (91). I never have figured out how trashing a fellow being's self-esteem is going to help that person be healthier.

Another example of this bullying someone thin comes from Pipher's book *Hunger Pains: The Modern Woman's Tragic Quest for Thinness*. Pipher recounts a conversation she overheard one day in a dress shop:

> I overheard a mother talking to her daughter, who was trying on party dresses. She put on each dress and then asked her mother how she looked. Time after time, her mother responded by saying, "You look just awful in that, Kathy. You're so fat nothing fits you right." The mother's voice dripped with disgust and soon Kathy was crying. (89)

Pipher goes on to suggest that Kathy's mother is a victim of the culture, too, because she realizes how hard the world will be on her fat daughter. Unfortunately, what she doesn't realize is how much better her daughter's quality of life would be if she felt loved by her mother. Any person surrounded by loving family members at home is much better equipped to deal with whatever the cruel world outside throws at her or him.

Dinnerstein was lucky; she had a grandmother who was very loving and supportive. Her grandmother's advice was, "Be proud, be strong, be who you are" (348). Sound advice for any child, and far more likely to produce an all-around healthy human being than a constant barrage of insults.

But the insensitivity doesn't stop when you grow up. In Camryn Manheim's book *Wake Up! I'm Fat*, the actress discusses her battle with her weight. She expected many of the difficulties she encountered from people in the entertainment industry, which is notorious for its inhuman standards of thinness for women. But when she gained some weight after giving up smoking, she was stunned when her father told her she should start smoking again until she lost the weight (78). In *The Invisible Woman: Confronting Weight Prejudice in America*, W. Charisse Goodman cites a 1987 study that concluded: "When good health practices and appearance norms coincide, women benefit; but if current fashion dictated poor health practices, women might then engage in those practices for the sake of attractiveness" (30). Like taking up smoking to stay slim.

Certainly everyone is entitled to his or her own opinion of what is attractive, but no one has the right to damage another

People would rather die than be fat.

Pipher—women are psychologically damaged by the culture of thinness.

Follow-up to the quote makes it more engaging and relevant.

Another authority used for support . . . a public figure.

Camryn Manheim—the insensitivity of the industry.

Goodman—women put health below thinness.

Exploring Ideas

Concession.

Qualifying her main point.

Back to the personal situation and relaxed voice.

Conclusion ties back to the intro.

human being for fun or profit. The media and the diet industry often do just that. While no one can change an entire culture overnight, people, especially parents, need to think about what they really value in the humans they share their lives with and what values they want to pass on to their children. We need to wake up and realize that being thin will not fix all our problems, though advertisements for diets and weight loss aids suggest this. Losing weight may, indeed, give a man or woman more confidence, but it will not make a person smarter, more generous, more loving, or more nurturing. It won't automatically attract the dream job or the ideal lover. On the contrary, people who allow the drive to be thin to control them may find that many other areas of their lives suffer: they may avoid some celebrations or get-togethers because of fear they may be tempted to eat too much or the "wrong" foods. They may cut back on intellectual activities like reading or enjoying concerts or art museums because those activities cut into their exercise time too much. The mania for thinness can cause a person to lose all perspective and balance in life. I know. It happened to me. My moment of revelation came about 12 years ago. I was a size ten, dieting constantly and faithfully keeping lists of every bite I ate, trying to lose 15 more pounds. While I was watching the evening news, a story came on about a young woman who was run over by a bus. I vividly recall that as the station played the footage of the paramedics wheeling the woman away on a stretcher, I said to myself, "Yeah, but at least she's thin." I've been lucky enough to have gained some wisdom (as well as weight) with age: I may be fat, but I'm no longer crazy. There are some things more important than being thin.

Writing Strategies

Being thin is not the answer to life.

The drive for thinness may shrink other parts of life.

Sanity is better than insane thinness.

Works Cited

Dinnerstein, Barbara Noreen. "Bubbie, Mommy, Weight Watchers and Me." *Worlds in Our Words: Contemporary American Women Writers*. Eds. Marilyn Kallet and Patricia Clark. Upper Saddle River, NJ: Prentice Hall, 1997. 347–349.

Goodman, W. Charisse. *The Invisible Woman: Confronting Weight Prejudice in America*. Carlsbad, CA: Gurze, 1995.

Manheim, Camryn. *Wake Up! I'm Fat*. New York: Broadway, 1999.

Pipher, Mary. *Hunger Pains: The Modern Woman's Tragic Quest for Thinness*. New York: Ballantine, 1995.

Wann, Marilyn. *Fat! So? Because You Don't Have to Apologize for Your Size*. Berkeley, CA: Ten Speed, 1998.

Exploring Ideas

1. Make two lists and write down how Paulin's ideas about weight are (1) similar to and (2) different from your own.

2. What is the most interesting similarity or difference between your view and Paulin's? Explore the similarity or difference and explain what is interesting about it.

3. How is weight a public, not just a private, issue? Or, why isn't it a public issue?

4. Return to the initial ideas you wrote down in response to Paulin's essay. Explore the most promising one by responding to the **Point of Contact, Analysis,** and **Public Resonance** sections of this chapter.

Writing Strategies

1. Why do you think Paulin refers to "overweight" people as "fat"? What is the effect of this word on the reader?

2. Paulin helps the reader to understand main ideas by beginning paragraphs with sentences that state or suggest main ideas. Find three paragraphs in this essay that begin with sentences that state or suggest the main idea. Do those sentences also connect the paragraph to the previous paragraph? If so, describe how.

3. Paulin uses written sources to support her argument. In some places she directly quotes the sources; in others she paraphrases or summarizes (that is, she puts what the source says in her own words). Find an example of each (quote; paraphrase; summary). How do you know the information is from a source? Does Paulin make that clear? Notice how Paulin introduces the information and punctuates it.

4. Paulin's conclusion does not merely summarize points she has already made. Reread the conclusion and describe how it goes beyond mere summary. What does it try to do? Is it successful?

Ideas for Writing

1. What point can you help Paulin make by providing different evidence?

2. What idea of Paulin's can you explore further, possibly discovering a different way of seeing it?

If responding to one of these ideas, go to the **Analysis** section of this chapter to begin developing ideas for your essay.

Don't Make Me a Has-Bean!

Jennifer Schwind-Pawlak

Jennifer Schwind-Pawlak, whose writing also appears in Chapter 1, wrote this essay as an assignment for her freshman English class. As you read it, consider the ways in which you and Schwind-Pawlak agree and disagree. What are her strongest and weakest points? Where does she anticipate and respond to her reader's likely reaction?

1 How do college students choose a major? In general, students feed off of their high school experiences. If they were very successful in all of their business classes, they often narrow down their college major to a business field. If science was a strong suit, they tend to major in one of the many fields of science. They generally avoid classes in which they did poorly or in which they have no interest. After all, what is high school for? I think it is meant to be used to gain a strong knowledge base to ready the student for the career of their choice. It is meant to get them started on choosing the college curriculum that will be the means to that end.

2 I started the "college experience" the same way that many other college students do. I went through the admissions process and was directed to talk to an advisor. I was told that an advisor would assist me in determining my class requirements and schedule. I was excited to register for the many business classes that would make up my major. This was not to be the case. Immediate disillusionment set in. I discovered that in addition to the business courses that I longed for, my education would also consist of classes that included biology, geology, Composition I, and Composition II. How do these classes fit into my major? How do these classes prepare me for success as a certified public accountant? These were questions that I asked many people and their answers made me think.

3 I was told of the importance of a "well-rounded" education. I was told that these classes would make me a better citizen. I was told that these classes would enable me to communicate with others better. I was told that

I might not stay in the career of my major so the additional education may be useful to me in the future. I was prepared to give these ideas a second look. After all, there must be some validity to a system that had been in place for so long.

4 I began by asking myself, "How will biology make me a better citizen? Will my ability to label the innards of a bean make me a more knowledgeable and involved citizen?" I can't concede the point. While I would come closer to understanding the damaging effects of pesticides on the legume family, I don't feel that I would be any more compelled to do anything more about it than I do now. I can't concede the point.

5 Then I asked myself, "How would biology make me a better communicator?" My first thought was to immediately dismiss this idea as ludicrous. I mean, how often would I get to exhibit my bean knowledge? At a party? I am pretty sure that if I did it once, I would be eliminated from the short invitation list in the future. But in fairness, I came up with a point that could be used against me. After all, they say that knowledge is power. And they say that power breeds confidence. I have always heard that confident people are better communicators. Thus, you could say that biology, or any education for that matter, would make me a better communicator. While this is a slippery slope that the person arguing against me would be treading, I'll leave it to them to make and I will address it in my "required" Composition I class.

6 The last point that I was given was well-taken. After ten years, the percentage of people

working in the field in which they majored in college is slim. How can I argue that point? Here I was handed a statistic. Finally, a tangible, credible, concrete, "can't argue with the numbers" argument, something that we accountant types can sink our teeth into. After all, our credo is "numbers don't lie." But then it hit me. I almost conceded the point and then my indignant mind reeled me back in. Suppose that I was not working as an accountant some seven years down the line. I am positive that I could tell you what I will not be doing. I WILL NOT be a biologist or a scientist! Even if I had the crazy urge to do so, no law-abiding lab would hire an accountant as a biologist. I would be forced to go back to school for a new degree anyway. I feel confident in my position here. I could not be swayed by this argument.

7   Now that I have told you all that biology would not do for me, let me tell you what it will do for me. It will lower my GPA. I don't enjoy it. I am not good at it and I should spend time on other more enjoyable things like a root canal or watching paint dry. It will hamper my attempts to gain the scholarships that I need to get to be able to remain in school. If I am going against another applicant without the flaw of lower grades, I may not get the financial backing that I need to stay in school. I know several students who dropped out of college due to the required classes that they had no interest in. This is why I think that colleges and universities set students up for failure.

8   Don't get me wrong. I agree that all students should have a well-rounded education, but that it should be done differently. While writing classes are important, essay and re-search papers are not important to everyone. I think that students should be given a choice of writing classes that fit into their overall career objectives. Some examples would be to require six credit hours in writing that could be chosen from business writing, technical writing, essay writing, research writing, and creative writing. The end result would be the same. Communication skills would be gained and students would be able to succeed at it. Most importantly, students could use the knowledge in their careers.

9   In my opinion, government, political science, and humanities classes should all still be required. They are important to being a good citizen and in daily contact. They relate to our everyday lives. I do, however, feel that math, science, and technical classes should be eliminated from the required curriculum unless they relate DIRECTLY to the area of study that the student is majoring in. This means that they must be able to apply the knowledge in their careers on a continuous basis. I was out of school for ten years after high school before I went back to college. I did not use any biology or algebra in the business world. It did not help me one bit to have this information. The goal of each student is to succeed in the career of his or her choice, not line the coffers of the schools by taking classes that will never be used.

10   In conclusion, I must admit that my attempts to get the system changed are probably futile. Little will be gained by my efforts to rationalize the process. So when you see me in the halls, ask me how I'm doing. But don't walk away when I start reciting the benefits of bean life to society as a whole. I've paid a high price for this knowledge and I have to use it somewhere.

Exploring Ideas

1. What does Schwind-Pawlak say about required courses such as biology and composition?

2. What does your response to the reading tell you about the way you view education?

3. List points that Schwind-Pawlak makes in two columns: a column for the points you agree with and a column for the points you disagree with. Explain briefly why you agree or disagree with Schwind-Pawlak.

4. Through written and/or verbal discussion with classmates and others, explore at least one point from each column (#3 above). Record others' views on each point, then examine the ideas of Schwind-Pawlak, others, and yourself. What point seems to require further exploration? What idea might you think more about and then explain to others in an essay?

5. If you have read David Crabtree's essay from this chapter, compare their two points of view. In a paragraph or two, what might Crabtree say to Schwind-Pawlak? What might Schwind-Pawlak say to Crabtree?

Writing Strategies

1. What kinds of evidence does Schwind-Pawlak provide? That is, does she provide examples, statistics, hypothetical situations, and so on? Is her evidence effective? What other evidence might she have used?

2. Introductions and conclusions can be challenging paragraphs to write. Rewrite the introduction to this essay, taking a completely different approach. Then rewrite the conclusion, also taking a completely different approach.

3. Asking questions can be an effective writing technique. Find at least three questions in "Don't Make Me a Has-Bean" and answer the following questions: (1) Does the essay answer the question? (2) If the question is answered, would the question be better off deleted from the essay or incorporated into the answer? (3) If it is not answered, should it have been?

4. In paragraph 3 the author begins the first five sentences with the words "I was." Is this technique effective? Explain its effect.

Ideas for Writing

1. Compare Schwind-Pawlak's and Crabtree's views on education. Then argue for one or the other or for a third and different view.

2. Generate a list of what you consider to be the ten major problems with the U.S. education system. (Your instructor may allow you to generate and refine your list with a group of classmates.) Think carefully over several days about the ten items, seeking an interesting argument about which you can write an essay. (Noticing connections, categories, trends, and exceptions on your list will be helpful.)

If responding to one of these ideas, go to the **Analysis** section of this chapter to begin developing ideas for your essay.

Beware of Drug Sales

Therese Cherry

Therese Cherry wrote this essay about an injustice in her field for a college writing class. At the request of her instructor, she then expressed the same main idea in the form of a letter and a memo that appear in Chapter 13. As you read Cherry's essay, jot down what you think she is trying to accomplish. Also, note in the margin of the text any ideas that made you think differently. Finally, jot down the different ways that her ideas might matter to others.

1 Prescription drug ads are everywhere. You can't turn on the TV or open a magazine these days without finding out if Claritin is "right for you" or being told to ask your doctor about Viagra. Obviously, the makers of prescription drugs want the public to know that there are pills to cure what ails us, and that they don't mind making a little money off our relief. This is how business is run, spending money to make money, marketing the product so that as many consumers as possible are aware of it and will buy it. However, it seems that pharmaceutical companies have taken their role a bit far, marketing their drugs so aggressively that they are actually creating the demand for them. In an industry that sells cars, an ad campaign that sold cars to people who hadn't even realized they wanted to buy one would definitely be a triumph. But to advertise prescription drugs to the extent that people who don't even need them want to buy them is irresponsible and dangerous.

2 According to the United Nations International Narcotics Control Board (INCB), advanced countries are overdosing on quick-fix pills to ease "non-medical" problems like fat and stress ("Rich States Overdosing on Feel-Good Pills"). INCB also stated that mood-altering drugs are often prescribed for social problems, such as unemployment or relationship problems ("Prescription Drugs 'Over-Used'"). Consumers around the globe are taking medication for this disease called life. The fact that people are spending their hard-earned money on medicine they do not need is bad enough, but the harm these unnecessary drugs can do is a much bigger issue. Yet the drug companies keep on telling us, "It's okay, just ask your doctor." The problem is, the doctors don't have all the answers, either.

3 Some statistics cited by the FDA reported that toxic reactions to marketed drugs are estimated to cost more than 30 billion dollars per year and to be among the ten leading causes of death in the United States (Pomper 6). So if these drugs are having these kinds of negative effects on people, why are doctors prescribing them? For one, pharmaceutical companies are advertising more aggressively than they have in the past, in part because of loosened restrictions. In 1997 the FDA caved to heavy pressures from the industry, which made it possible for drug companies to advertise on TV without spending huge chunks of time describing side effects (Pomper 6). Now that drug companies can market directly to consumers, suddenly patients are telling their doctors what drugs they want to use. A recent study published by *Health Affairs* reported that three quarters of the respondents who saw a drug on TV and asked their doctors for it were successful (Pomper 6).

4 Another reason these drugs are being prescribed is because some doctors are influenced to prescribe drugs which are marketed more aggressively, according to the January 2000 *Journal of the American Medical Association*. And since the most heavily advertised drugs tend to be the newest drugs, the long list of possible side effects cannot be known. In fact, six new drugs approved since mid-1996 have been pulled off the market, and 150 deaths were linked to the drugs before they were pulled (Pomper 8).

5   Perhaps the most unjust and appalling fact about this considerably new trend of pharmaceutical peddling is the industry's knowledge of the damage this marketing technique is causing to the health of the public: "Even people in the industry will concede off the record that groups acting as advertising agents for manufacturers should be subject to FDA regulations" (Pomper 10). The INBC stated in its 2000 report that there was a "continuing existence of aggressive sales methods and even some cases of financial support to various advocacy groups to foster sales" and appealed to the pharmaceutical industry to demonstrate social responsibility and voluntary cooperation ("Rich States Overdosing on Feel-Good Pills"). We all need to make this same appeal to the drug companies. A business has every right to turn a profit, but should it really be at the risk of good health? Without your health, money means nothing. So, until the pharmaceutical industry can agree with that, buyer beware.

Works Cited

Pomper, Steven. "Drug Rush." *The Washington Monthly Online.* May 2000. 23 Jan. 2002
    http://www.washingtonmonthly.com/features/2000/0005.pomper.html.

"Prescription Drugs 'Over-Used.'" *BBC News Online.* 21 Feb. 2001. 21 Jan. 2002
    http://news.bbc.com.uk/low/english/heath/newsid_1182000/1182115.stm.

"Rich States Overdosing on Feel-Good Pills." *Dawn the Internet Edition.* 21 Feb. 2001. 21 Jan. 2002
    http://www.dawn.com/2001/02/21/int13.htm.

Exploring Ideas

1. How is the way that Cherry sees prescription drugs similar to or different from the way you see them?

2. How does Cherry encourage the reader to think differently?

3. Summarize Cherry's essay and survey or interview people about their views on prescription drugs. After doing so, summarize in writing the ways in which others agree or disagree with Cherry's argument.

4. With classmates, discuss how Cherry's views on prescription drugs are similar to or different from your own and others'. Then discuss ways in which you might participate in this discussion. That is, how might you respond to Cherry's essay (or contribute to this discussion)?

Writing Strategies

1. What strategy, or strategies, does Cherry use to draw the reader's attention to the point of her essay?

2. What type of evidence does Cherry provide to support her claim? How successful is her evidence? What other evidence might she have provided?

3. Identify any concessions Cherry makes in this essay. That is, where does she acknowledge the validity of a differing viewpoint?

Ideas for Writing

1. Does Cherry's argument about prescription drugs seem like an injustice to you? How is or isn't this an injustice?

If responding to one of these ideas, go to the **Analysis** section of this chapter to begin developing ideas for your essay.

Outside Reading

ind a written argument and print it out or make a photocopy. You might find an argument about a social or political issue in a general readership publication (such as *Time, Newsweek,* or the *New York Times*). For an argument related to your major, explore an academic journal such as *Journal of the American Medical Association, Texas Nursing,* or *Psychology of Women Quarterly.* To conduct an electronic search of journals and magazines, go to your library's periodical database or to InfoTrac http://infotrac.galegroup.com/itweb/. For your library database, perform a keyword search, or go to the main search box for InfoTrac, and select "keywords." Enter word combinations such as *debate and community, opinion and politics, argument and politics, debate and sports, argument and art.* (When performing keyword searches, avoid using phrases or articles [*a, an, the*]; instead, use nouns separated by *and.*) The search results will yield lists of journal and magazine articles.

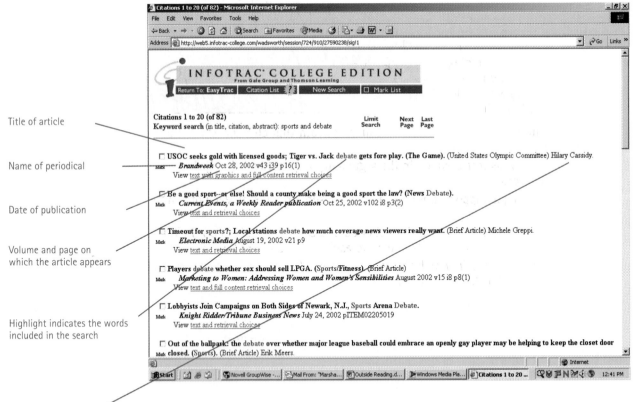

Title of article

Name of periodical

Date of publication

Volume and page on which the article appears

Highlight indicates the words included in the search

Author name

You can also search the Internet. Try the search engine Dogpile.com. Like most Internet search engines, Dogpile combines words using *and*. In the search box, try various combinations, such as those above.

The purpose of this assignment is to further your understanding of argument and to introduce a broad range of argumentative strategies. As you are probably discovering, argument appears in many different places and in many different contexts. Even among the essays in this chapter, arguments range in tone, style, length, and strategy. As you read through this chapter, keep the written argument you have discovered close by and notice the elements and strategies the writer uses. Depending on your instructor's suggestions, do one or more of the following:

Using Boolean Operators. To refine your search, many search engines allow you to use Boolean operators—terms such as AND, OR, NOT, NEAR, and FOLLOWED BY.

AND means that all the terms you specify must appear in your search results. For example, searching "cats and dogs" will produce documents about both cats and dogs, but not just cats.

OR means that at least one of the terms you specify must appear. For example, searching "cats or dogs" may find documents about just cats OR just dogs.

NOT means that at least one of the terms you specify must not appear in the documents. For example, searching "cats not dogs" will find documents about just cats.

NEAR means that the terms you enter should be within a certain number of words of each other.

FOLLOWED BY means that one term must directly follow the other

The best way to learn about how a particular search engine works is to read the help files on the search engine site.

---

1. Notice how the writer applies various strategies from this chapter. On the hard copy or photocopy:
   - Highlight the thesis if it is stated in the argument. If the thesis is implied, write it in your own words.
   - Highlight the major support strategies, and write "support" next to each one in the margin.
   - Highlight any passages in which the writer addresses other opinions on the topic, and write "counterargument" or "ca" next to each one in the margin.
   - Highlight any passages in which the writer grants value to another position, and write "concession" or "c" in the margin.

2. Write an essay that discusses the strategies employed by the writer. The following questions may be helpful.
   - Does this writer seem more or less argumentative than the readings in this chapter? Why?
   - How does the writer support his or her argument?
   - Who is the audience for this argument?
   - How does the audience impact the kinds of things said in the argument?

3. Write at least three "Exploring Ideas" questions for the argument.

4. Write at least three "Writing Strategies" questions for the argument.

5. Write two "Ideas for Writing," such as the ones following the essays in this book, for the argument.

INVENTION

Academic audiences demand more than "three reasons why I believe X" arguments. In other words, they want to experience more in an argument than a writer's personal beliefs; they want to learn a new way of thinking about a topic, so academic writers are often looking for a new stance, a way to make people rethink an issue entirely. In general, a successful argument creates a new position on a familiar topic, offers a position on a fresh topic, responds to a particular situation, or responds critically to a particular argument.

The following three sections are designed to help you develop interesting ideas for your argument: specifically, to discover a topic (in **Point of Contact**), develop particular points about the topic (in **Analysis**), and make it relevant to a community of readers (in **Public Resonance**). The questions in each section are not meant to be answered directly in your final written assignment. However, answering them before you draft your essay will help you discover what you are going to say—and even why you are going to say it. After you work through these three sections, the **Delivery** section, which immediately follows, will help you craft your ideas into a written text.

Point of Contact

Finding a Topic in Everyday Life

Some situations in everyday life are obviously significant—what they mean for our lives, or for the lives of others, is apparent. When our country goes to war or when a new president is elected, for example, most Americans understand the significance. Most situations, however, are far more subtle; their potential meaning is hidden by life's hustle and bustle. This does not mean that more subtle situations or events are less meaningful. But to understand their meaning, we must stop in our tracks and focus on them.

In this **Point of Contact** section, each question focuses on a specific topic. For example, under "Home," the first question invites you to explore student living situations. From that topic, several different arguments could be developed. Someone might argue that living at home while attending college is beneficial while another may argue the opposite—that living in the dorms, surrounded by the academic community, is most advantageous. Use the suggestions and questions to find a topic. If a question seems particularly engaging to you, or if you associate some emotion or idea with the question, stop and write about it (see the example on page 236). Then, you might ask: *"Can I change someone's mind about this situation or issue?"* If you can, you may have a topic. Once you have decided on a topic, proceed to the **Analysis** section to develop the argument. (Also notice the responses that Ann Marie Paulin gives for each section, which eventually lead to the essay in this chapter.)

While the questions on the next two pages will help you generate possible topics, the following images, and ones you encounter in everyday life, will also prompt ideas. In groups or alone, consider the problem(s) these images suggest, and then move to the **Analysis** section to explore them in depth.

Use these images to get you thinking. Remember, you're not looking for the right answer at this point, but, instead, a topic—an idea—about which to write.

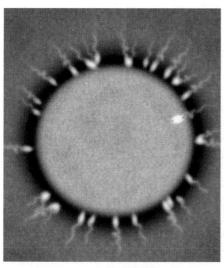

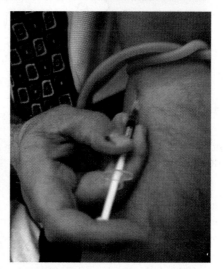

Activity

Find an interesting image of your own and discuss it with some friends. Notice, in the discussion, what claims people make, and which claims might be developed into essays.

- Go to a familiar place (work, school, home, the gym, a park), and examine situations of potential crisis or tension. For example:

Work
Do my co-workers get along OK? Explain why they do or do not.
Do supervisors treat workers fairly? If not, why?
Are the work expectations fair?
Are the working hours suitable? Are they fair to workers?
Do fellow workers do a good job?

School
Does my school address all the students' academic needs? Do my instructors address the students' needs?
Are the work expectations fair?
Do my classes fit the goals of my education (my major)?
Do my peers interfere with my learning? With my goals as a student?
Does the arrangement of the classroom or the campus interfere with my learning?
Is my school green enough? (Does it recycle and promote recycling?)
Was my high school education adequate?

Home
Is my living situation conducive to my goals as a student?
Does living with my family reinforce or oppose my goals as student?
Do my roommates understand and account for one another's needs?
Does my landlord appreciate my needs?

Example: Ann Marie Paulin's Notes for Point of Contact Questions

Does my generation have the right priorities? I often hear women of all ages talking about their diets, what they can't eat, how disgusting they think they look, how they or someone close to them have developed an eating disorder, and so I know this is an issue that has permeated the whole culture, so much so that perhaps most of us don't even think about it any more than we think about the air around us.

"Does my generation have the right priorities?" My response is a resounding NO! When people are indoctrinated into the belief that they cannot be happy if they are not thin, something is wrong. When women who are smart, funny, kind, generous, loving people believe they are worthless because they have plump thighs, wide hips, a round belly, or jiggly upper arms, something is wrong. When people limit their lives—refuse to dance, to swim, to go to parties, to start college, to seek a new job—until they lose some weight, something is wrong. This distortion of our values and diminishing of our spirits because of an obsession with thinness is what I wanted to explore in my essay.

- **Participate in a community event, or drive through your area and consider collective issues:**

  Does my town offer adequate social events for youth?
  Does my town offer adequate support for senior citizens?
  Does my town offer ample mass transit?
  Does my neighborhood feel like a neighborhood?
  Are strangers as kind as they should be?

- **Consider cultural issues:**

  Are people's lives too busy?
  Does my generation have the right priorities?
  What doesn't the older generation understand about kids today?
  What doesn't the younger generation understand about older generation(s)?

- **Examine your major:**

  Are entry-level personnel in my field treated fairly? Paid fairly?
  Is some research in my field or major controversial? Why? (What side are you on?)
  Should my field be regulated more (or less) by the federal government?
  Is my field undervalued by the public?
  Has my field changed any of its practices, for better or worse, in recent years?
  Should my field be more diverse (in gender and/or ethnicity)?

Look through a current journal in your field to find controversial issues. For example, a nursing major might discover, after reading through a nursing journal, that health insurance companies often work against medical professionals' goal of extending the best care possible to patients.

Invention Activity: These questions are not the only possibilities. If they have not prompted a topic for you, develop more invention questions. With a small group of peers, or alone, make a list of other questions that draw attention to situations in the world around you. As you are inventing, question everything. That is, imagine that everything in your life could be different: people around you could act differently; institutions could operate differently; systems could run differently. If you accept the possibilities of *what could be*, then you will more easily find issues to argue.

Do not avoid a topic because you cannot, at this early phase, imagine writing several pages on it. No writer can ever imagine how a topic will develop into the final text. Certainly, a writer who generates a 300-page book does not foresee how the topic will develop before he or she starts writing. The book, like an essay, *emerges out of the process of writing.*

Analysis

What Does It Mean?

This section will help you to analyze your topic, to explore what it means and why it matters to you. As you answer the analysis questions below, avoid answering too quickly. Imagine a student, Jack, who is focusing on his high school education. Notice how the discussion with Marcus develops his thinking on the topic:

What is the particular point of crisis or tension?

> Jack: My high school education was inadequate. I graduated with a B average and I came to college having to take developmental courses before I could even begin taking credit courses.
>
> Marcus: But is that the high school's fault?
>
> Jack: Well, if I couldn't cut the mustard in entry-level college courses, why did I get mostly Bs in high school? It seems like something's out of whack.
>
> Marcus: OK. So the standards are too low in high school?
>
> Jack: Yeah, I think so.
>
> Marcus: Were you ever warned about the standards in college?
>
> Jack: Sure. All the time, teachers would scare us with things like: "wait 'til you get in college; you've got to work constantly to keep your grades up."
>
> Marcus: But did anyone ever share specifics with you? Did you know what kinds of writing, for instance, you would be doing in college?
>
> Jack: Not really. It's all been a big surprise.
>
> Marcus: Maybe that's the issue: high school students (and maybe teachers and administrators) don't really know what kinds of things go on in entry-level college courses.
>
> Jack: Yes—and so there's this huge gap in between, and some students fall right into it.

Here, Jack's thinking on the topic evolves significantly during a brief conversation. As you move through the following questions, allow time and space for your own thinking to develop. Write out answers to the following questions or discuss them with peers:

- What is the particular point of crisis or tension?
- Why do I have an opinion on this topic?
- How has the situation (or condition, behavior, policy) come about?
- Why does the situation (or condition, behavior, policy) continue?
- What are the effects of the situation (or condition, behavior, policy)?
- What caused me to hold my particular beliefs?
- Why is this belief valuable?

Example: Ann Marie Paulin's Notes for Analysis Questions

Why do I have an opinion on this topic? I have been fat since I was a kid. For about two days in my twenties I starved my way down to a size ten, thereby earning this head-turning compliment from the guy I was then dating: "You'd be a real fox if you'd just lose a few more pounds." I've had complete strangers say the most astonishing things to me on the street. For example, on my way through a parking lot to get to my car, I passed a young man who looked over at me and shouted: "I don't !@#$ fat chicks!" Who was asking? While these behaviors have sometimes hurt me, they mostly make me angry. And when I look around at the society in which I live, I don't see any signs that this kind of behavior is discouraged. Indeed, the media seems to suggest that fat people, by their very existence, seem to deserve contempt and abuse.

How has this situation come about? Where it gets tricky is that by the media's definition, damn near everyone is fat. How has this situation come about? I'm not sure, but I've watched it develop. When my mother was young, a size ten or twelve was a respectable dress size. When I was in my twenties, a size eight was a respectable size. Now, you must be a size four, two, or even better, a zero to be considered thin. Now, a six-foot-tall model who wears a size twelve dress is considered plus size. She only gets her photo in Lane Bryant ads and such. It's as if society has completely forgotten the concept of "normal size," and so a person is either thin (if you can count all her bones when she appears in a bathing suit) or she's fat. And that leaves the majority of women believing they are fat and hating themselves for it.

Although the exact language of Paulin's responses may not appear in her essay, her ideas are certainly beginning to develop. Her responses show her making important connections, building a case against media images. She goes on in the essay to analyze the harmful effects of particular advertisements. And like all good writers, Paulin continues to ask how the information she encounters or develops throughout her essay supports her point.

Some of the ideas in Paulin's responses do not appear in her essay. Early on, her analysis extends in various directions and she asks increasingly hard questions:

Who defines beauty? Who cashes in from that definition? Who pays for that definition emotionally and financially?

But the first two questions are not directly answered—and are, in fact, even left behind—in her essay. Paulin's thinking shows how writers work: they often begin with various points, and in the process of analyzing ideas, create various possible writing directions. However, as they begin to develop their projects, writers also become more focused and leave some interesting questions behind.

No matter what your topic may be, continue the analytical process as you write. As many experimenters and theorists have found, the act of writing actually stimulates powerful analytical thinking. So once you turn on the computer and start crafting and shaping ideas, remain open to the possible questions that arise.

Continuing Analysis: As you develop or encounter ideas during the writing process, continue asking: How does this relate to my initial realization or understanding of the topic?

Public Resonance

How Does This Issue Matter to Others?

Writers make things matter to others—and this is the reason for all academic, or all public, writing: to make others think a particular way about a given topic. Writers transform issues or personal concerns into arguable topics, issues that matter in some way to other people. Making a personal concern resonate with a public issue is simply a process of extension. To this end, initial **Point of Contact** questions can be used as springboards from personal concerns to public issues. For example, examine the following question: *Is my living situation conducive to my goals as a student?* You may have answered: "Yes. I live at home with my parents and commute to school." Your situation is not exclusive. Many college students struggle with their living situations—with the decision of living on campus, in a nearby apartment complex, or at home with their parents, away from the campus altogether. This decision involves more than a simple personal choice. It has something to do with college funding, with the success of college students, with the entire college experience. In this sense, your situation resonates with a more public issue. The initial (more personal) question then raises a more public issue—about experiencing or succeeding in college—and so might evolve into a more public question: *Is it beneficial for college students to live at home while going to school?* The personal situation becomes a public issue simply by projecting the issue outward. Use the following questions to help develop public resonance.

- Who might care about this issue? Why?
- What particular community, place, or things does this issue affect?
- How are my readers involved in this issue?
- What group of people might understand or sympathize with my situation?
- To what trends (in living/working/socializing) does my topic point?
- Is this issue an example of some trend?
- Why is it important that others hear my opinion about this issue?

These questions ask you to consider the actual connection between your topic and potential readers. The answers can help you develop your argument. As Paulin's essay shows, the more a topic affects people, the more attention it may deserve.

Example: Ann Marie Paulin's Notes for Public Resonance Questions

Who might care about this issue? Why? This is certainly a very public issue because it is almost impossible to escape the media: magazines, newspaper ads, billboards, radio, TV, movies, ads plastered in public restrooms and on the walls of buses, ads on your e-mail every day. And every one of those images that deals with weight or beauty makes it clear that to be fat is completely unacceptable and completely fixable if only a person tries hard enough and buys the right products.

Now, if this were just an issue of vanity, it might be something that could be shrugged off. But it goes much deeper

than that. If you really pay attention to those ads, their real message is often that if you are fat, no one will love you. Your husband will leave you (if you ever manage to get one to begin with). Your children will be ashamed of you. Your friends will give up on you. You will be alone and unloved because you are fat. That is the message that really hits us where we live. Who wants to be some lonely outcast? We must conform to whatever it takes.

And so, most of us try the diets, the pills, the exercise classes, the wonder machines, and sometimes even more extreme measures like stomach stapling surgery. But in spite of all the time, money, and effort we expend, most of us are still fat. If you look at the studies done, the results are all about the same: anywhere from 90 to 98% of the people who lose weight gain it all back within five years.

Any other group of products with a 90% failure rate would be whisked out of the marketplace by public outrage, but not diet industry products. There, people keep trying and blaming themselves for the failure, and feeling worse and worse about themselves. When you consider the billions of dollars made each year by this industry by selling quack products to people their ad campaigns have helped to depress, you get the idea of how far-reaching the problem is.

Notice that Paulin's responses show her making connections between her own situation and many others. Her response illustrates an intellectual process in which she explores how her own position relates to others. She is developing the public dimensions of her thinking.

As Paulin's essay shows, the answers to the above **Public Resonance** questions can help a writer to make connections to potential readers. But sometimes writers need to go beyond the actual effects or consequences of an issue. Sometimes, they need to *imagine* the possible ways others are involved. For example, consider the following: a writer is arguing about college students living at home. The issue seemingly affects only college students and maybe their parents. But notice how the writer makes the issue resonate with many other potential readers by transforming a personal issue into a public one:

> How college students live is not simply a matter of personal choice and comfort. It is a public issue, a public education issue. At the federal, state, and local levels, Americans are increasingly focused on the out-of-school living conditions of elementary and secondary students. Whenever people talk about the quality of education, invariably they end up discussing the living situation of students—the stability of their homes, the qualities of the neighborhoods. Why? Because people are beginning to realize that education does not occur in a vacuum, that how and where students live impact how they learn. But for some reason, we don't seem to be concerned once students are in college. Consequently, millions of college students swarm off to school every fall, often without deeply considering the implications of where they will live. And when millions of dollars of loans and grants go down the drain when students fail out their first year, we don't seem to ask the same questions we ask about elementary and secondary students.

Here, what might only be a college issue is connected to national concerns about education, and so potential readers can participate in the claims made in the argument. Developing public resonance, then, involves drawing readers' attention to issues that they might otherwise dismiss, and in argumentative writing, it involves drawing readers into a particular perspective—into a way of seeing the topic. Use the following questions to further develop the public resonance of your topic:

- Who SHOULD care about this issue? Why?
- How COULD my reader(s) be involved in this issue?

Activities

1. Write a letter to the editor of either a local or national newspaper, expressing your main idea and support. Since you are sending your letter to a newspaper—to be read by the general public—your letter must have clear public resonance. (See Chapter 13.)
2. Write a fake letter to the editor, but be certain that your letter has no public resonance. Notice how odd such a letter would be. Why would a newspaper not publish such a letter?

DELIVERY

Crafting an essay, or any written text, is a recursive process: writers move back and forth, drafting, re-thinking, re-drafting. It is not a simple step-by-step journey through a chapter. But as they begin drafting, and heading for a final draft, writers benefit from a large collection of strategies, or tools, for building texts and for developing, shaping, and revising passages. The following sections (**Rhetorical Tools, Organizational Strategies, Writer's Voice,** and **Revision Strategies**) are designed to help you build a sophisticated and engaging text—one that emerges from your particular ideas. Each section points to important features or common concerns related to argumentative writing.

Rhetorical Tools

Persuading Your Readers

All writing is, to some degree, persuasive in nature, but in a traditional arguing essay, the arguable point does not lie in the background of a story or an explanation; it is, rather, in the foreground. Remember that academic argument is not necessarily an intellectual battle in which only one side wins. In fact, academic argument need not be seen as a battle at all; the goal of argument does

not necessarily include the destruction of an opponent. On the contrary, the goal of academic argument is simply to show the validity or viability of a particular position.

Academic argument involves four basic ingredients or elements:

- Main Claim/Thesis
- Support
- Counterargument
- Concession

Do not think of these elements as necessary ingredients, but as vital tools for helping you invent—not "stuff I must have in the essay," but rather, "stuff that will help me develop my argument."

Main Claim/Thesis: An argument requires a thesis; or main claim that states the writer's opinion. An argumentative thesis invites debate or suggests that opposing claims exist. For example:

> Although technology has improved society in many ways, we use it indiscriminately, not distinguishing the good uses from the bad.

> But far more important than my ill temper is a creepy sense that these inaccurate images [about body type] have shifted our vision of what is important in life way out of whack, so far out that people are being hurt.

Developing a thesis early on in the process will help to develop focus for the writer as well as the reader. At this early phase in the process, you need not settle into an exact wording, but you should try to generate a sentence or two that expresses your particular stance on the topic. Consider the following criteria for honing in on a thesis statement. An arguable thesis should have three basic qualities:

> **More about Main Claim/Thesis:** For a better understanding of main claim/thesis, you might read about this concept in other chapters: Remembering Who You Were (page 2), Explaining Relationships (page 58), Observing (page 108), Analyzing Concepts (page 160), Responding to Arguments (page 270), Evaluating (page 320), Searching for Causes (page 370), Proposing Solutions (page 418), Exploring the Arts (page 476), Thinking Radically (page 528).

Public Resonance: It should address an issue that resonates with the readers. A good argument addresses a concern that others have *or that a writer thinks they should have*. In other words, a thesis should express something that matters (that has some significance) to readers. It should involve others.

Scope: It should be appropriately narrow. Scope can be addressed by asking narrow enough questions. The questions above are probably sufficiently narrow to at least help you to develop a working thesis. Be careful of broad questions: *Is my town boring?* To answer such a question, one would have to consider all of the town's complexities, all of its goings-on, all of its people, all of its places . . . you get the idea. However, the question *Does my town offer sufficient activities for kids?* is more easily answerable—and ultimately arguable.

Arguability: It should be arguable. That is, an arguable thesis should take a stand on an issue that has two or more possible positions. Perhaps the best way to determine if a claim is arguable is by trying to imagine another way to view the topic. If you can conceive of other possible positions on the topic at hand, you are probably in arguable territory.

> **Before moving on, try to express your point in a sentence and consider the public resonance, scope, and arguability.**

Support:
Support is the material that gives substance and legitimacy to an argumentative claim. Support comes in two general categories: evidence and appeals. You might consider the following as a collection of usable support strategies, a toolbox for persuading readers of your position.

Kinds of Evidence

- **Statistics:** Information (often given numerical value) collected through experimentation, surveys, polls, and research. (See Paulin ¶ 4, Cherry ¶ 3.)
- **Authorities:** References to published (most often written) sources. (See Crabtree ¶ 7, Paulin ¶ 2.)
- **Facts:** Agreed-upon events or truths, or conclusions drawn from investigation. (See Crabtree ¶ 5, Churchill ¶ 19–25.)
- **Examples:** Specific cases or illustrations of a phenomenon. (See Paulin ¶ 6.)
- **Allusion:** References to history, science, nature, news events, films, television shows, or literary texts. (See Crabtree ¶ 5, Churchill ¶ 11.)
- **Personal Testimonies/Anecdotes:** Individual accounts or experiences. (See Paulin ¶ 1–2.)
- **Scenarios:** Hypothetical or fictionalized accounts. (See Crabtree ¶ 6, Churchill ¶ 4–8.)

Kinds of Appeals

- **Appeal to Logic:** Relates the argument to the audience's sense of reason. (See Churchill ¶ 4, Paulin's conclusion.)
- **Appeal to Emotion:** Relates the argument to an emotional state of the audience, or attempts to create a particular emotional state in the audience. (See Churchill ¶ 32.)
- **Appeal of Character:** Relates the argument to a quality of the author/speaker. (See Paulin ¶ 1.)
- **Appeal to Need:** Relates the argument to people's needs (spiritual, economic, physical, sexual, familial, political, etc.). (See Schwind-Pawlak ¶ 8–9, Cherry ¶ 5.)
- **Appeal to Value:** Relates the argument to people's values (judgments about right/wrong, success, discipline, selflessness, moderation, honesty, chastity, modesty, self-expression, etc.). (See Crabtree ¶ 9, Churchill ¶ 32.)

The first three appeals above (to logic, emotion, and character) are often discussed using three ancient Greek terms: *logos* (for logic), *pathos* (for emotion) and *ethos* (for character). *Pathos* and *ethos* have even worked into everyday English usage: e.g., *He has a particularly engaging* ethos. *The newspaper dramatized the* pathos *of the events.*

> When using different kinds of evidence, writers must formally document the use of any information/ideas/expressions taken from sources. When referencing authorities or statistics, for example, writers must follow particular guidelines for documenting the sources of information. For an extended explanation of formal documentation and integration of sources, see Chapter 12: Research and Writing.

Developing Evidence for Your Essay: Writers have the whole world of culture and history within reach. By simply mentioning or pointing to key moments in history or relevant literary texts, a writer can make a point more engaging to readers—or show that his or her point is shared by others. Use the following questions to help construct supporting points for your argument. For example, perhaps you believe that your topic relates to the plot of a book. You can explain the basic plot of the book in a paragraph (or more) and tell why it shows the validity of your ideas. The same thing goes for a movie or a news event.

- Does a historical event or figure illustrate something about my topic?
- Does a historical situation or trend (say, the rise of a particular fashion, organization, or individual) illustrate something about my topic?
- Is my topic an example of something that has occurred in history . . . or recently, in the news?
- Does my topic or situation appear in any movies or television shows? If so, how is it handled?
- Does my topic appear in any works of literature? If so, how is it handled?
- Does my topic relate to anything in nature?
- Has science taught us anything about my topic?
- Do any news events illustrate my point or stance?
- Have I witnessed or experienced someone or something that illustrates my point?
- Can I construct a hypothetical situation that illustrates my point?
- What do other writers or authorities on the matter say about the topic?

> **Activity:** What kind of evidence might you use to support each of the following claims? (Use the list to the left for ideas.)
>
> Although war illustrates how cruel humans can be to each other, it is perhaps the best illustration of how compassionate and loving humans can be.
>
> Most proponents of capital punishment fail to even consider the impact on the executed person's loved ones.
>
> Democracy cannot thrive in a two-party system.
>
> Excessive marketing leads to a lack of civility and respect among the citizens.

(*Go to Chapter 12: Research and Writing for assistance in researching your topic.*)

Using Appeals in Your Essay: While *evidence* involves pointing or referring to something (such as an example or authority), an *appeal* involves engaging the audience. In using appeals, writers must frame ideas in ways that directly engage the opinions, beliefs, and situations of their audience. Use the following questions to develop appeals for your argument:

- How can this topic relate to people's values?
- How can this topic relate to people's basic needs?
- How can this topic relate to people's emotions?
- How can this topic relate to people's sense of reason?
- Does my life (my role in a relationship, on a job, in school, on a team) lend credibility to my position on this topic?

Counterargument: Counterarguments anticipate and refute claims or positions that oppose those being forwarded by the writer. Writers must anticipate and account for positions outside of or opposed to their own claims(s) and include reasoning to offset that potential opposition. For example:

> April, a teenager living with her parents, wants to attend a party, but knows that her parents will protest because the party will go past her curfew. Before asking her parents if she can attend the party, April imagines their concerns and works them into her request—her argument of why she should be able to go.

Notice how Paulin counterargues in her essay:

> While we can shrug off advertisements as silly, when we see these attitudes reflected among real people, the hurt is far less easy to brush away. For instance, in her essay, "Bubbie, Mommy, Weight Watchers and Me," Barbara Noreen Dinnerstein recalls a time in her childhood when her mother took her to Weight Watchers to slim down and the advice the lecturer gave to the women present: "She told us to put a picture of ourselves on the 'fridgerator of us us eating and looking really fat and ugly. She said remember what you look like. Remember how ugly you are" (347).
>
> I have a problem with this advice. First, of course, it is too darn common. Fat people are constantly being told they should be ashamed of themselves, of their bodies. And here we see another of those misconceptions I mentioned earlier: the assumption that being fat is the same as being ugly. There are plenty of attractive fat people in the world, as well as a few butt-ugly thin ones, I might add. Honestly, though, the real tragedy is that while few people in this world are truly ugly, many agonize over the belief that they are. Dr. Pipher reported: "I see clients who say they would rather kill themselves than be overweight" (91). I never have figured out how trashing a fellow being's self-esteem is going to help that person be healthier.

(For more written examples, see Schwind-Pawlak ¶ 5, Crabtree ¶ 2–3.)

Arguments in Everyday Life

Notice the arguments—and the elements of argument—around you. For several days, make a study of argument in everyday life.

Main Claim/Thesis

1. Carefully observe everyday conversations, including the ones you participate in. Notice the claims that people, including you, make. Write down at least ten claims that were made. For example, "Richard said the Steelers would win the Super Bowl"; "Monica claimed that football is boring"; and so on.

2. Watch television, listen to the radio, and read magazines, noticing the claims that are made. Write down at least ten claims.

3. In each of your classes, make a claim, whether to your professor or to a classmate. Write down what you claimed.

4. Claim something at work or at home. Be aware that you are making a claim when you do it.

Support

1. Write down the support for each of the claims that you wrote down under "Main Claim/Thesis" above, then briefly summarize the person's support, naming the particular kind of evidence and appeals. Then explain why you think the support was or was not persuasive.

2. For several of the claims you listed above, explain how the person might have provided more convincing support.

Counterargument

1. For each of the arguments and support you listed above, identify any counterarguments that were made.

2. For each of the arguments and support you listed above, suggest what counterarguments might have been made.

3. Using several counterarguments as examples, explain how counterarguments further discussion, thus helping people to explore an idea and figure something out.

Concession

1. Identify concessions that were made in the arguments you listed above.

2. What concessions might the person have made?

Using Counterargument to Develop Points: Ever hear that phrase, "Keep your friends close and your enemies closer"? In academic argument, your "enemies" (those claims and positions that oppose your own) are extremely beneficial, even vital. Keep them close. In fact, use them to help you develop your own points. An argument paper sets out not only to support a main claim, but also to refute the opposing claims—to show why opposing claims are not as valid or valuable.

In developing your argument, you should try to imagine, write out, and then address those opposing claims. This process will make your argument more complex, more developed, and more persuasive. Apply the following questions:

- Who might disagree with my position? Why?
- What reasons do people have for disagreeing with me?
- What would support an opposing argument?

"What Are You, Nuts?" This activity is designed to generate counterarguments. The process involves an intensive group exchange. Follow these steps:

A.   Assemble writers into small groups (three to four work best).

B.   Each writer should have his or her thesis statement (main argumentative claim) written down.

C.   The first writer should read his or her thesis statement aloud to the group.

D.   Taking turns, each group member then should attempt to refute the position given in the statement (and each member may or may not begin the rebuttal with, "What are you, nuts?"). The idea is to play devil's advocate, to complicate the writer's ideas.

E.   The writer should record each opposing claim that is offered.

F.   After everyone in the group has given an opposing claim to the first writer, the second writer should recite his or her thesis, and the process begins again.

This process also works well if writers have generated some evidence and/or appeals for their arguments. In this case, group members can intervene in a more complicated manner.

Sometimes, counterarguing can even constitute a significant amount of an essay. For example, in "Crimes Against Humanity," Churchill uses opposing claims (even particular phrases and words) to develop his own reasoning. He begins sections with others' claims about team names and then immediately refutes the claims. See Churchill's paragraphs 3–9 on pages 211–212, which begin

> In response, a number of players—especially African Americans and other minority athletes—have been trotted out by professional team owners like Ted Turner, as well as university and public school officials, to announce that they mean not to insult but to honor native people. They have been joined by the television networks and most major newspapers, all of which have editorialized that Indian discomfort with the situation is "no big deal," insisting that the whole thing is just "good, clean fun." The country needs more such fun, they've argued, and a "few disgruntled Native Americans" have no right to undermine the nation's enjoyment of its leisure time by complaining. This is especially the case, some have argued, "in hard times like these." It has even been contended that Indian outrage at being systematically degraded—rather than the degradation itself—creates "a serious barrier to the sort of intergroup communication so necessary in a multicultural society such as ours."

Using Counterargument to Qualify Your Thesis: Thesis statements become narrower and more meaningful when they include an understanding of the broader argument (others' positions on the subject). Let's examine the opposition to our working thesis: *college students benefit from living at home while attending school.* Many college students insist that living away from home during college helps to define "the college experience." They might develop an argument using personal or anecdotal evidence. They might illustrate personal (hence, intellectual) growth that comes from living away from home, away from one's family, away from familiar turf. They might point to stories in literature in which a character leaves her or his homeland to seek knowledge or wisdom in the world and gains insight only because of the new surroundings. They might also point to movies in popular culture that promote that same idea. We would do well to consider these points, and perhaps work against some of them directly. We might even include part of the logic into our own thesis: *Despite the attraction of living away from home and experiencing life in unfamiliar territory, college students benefit from living at home while attending school.*

Rosa Parks Riding the Bus, 1956

Rosa Parks violated a Montgomery, Alabama, city law in 1955 when she refused to give up her bus seat to a white man. Her action made her a celebrated figure in the American civil rights movement.

Evolution of a Thesis

Writer responds to a Point of Contact question: "Is my living situation conducive to my goals as a student?"	*Yes. I live at home with my parents and commute to school.*
Writer broadens personal issue to a more public issue:	*Is it beneficial for college students to live at home while going to school?*
Writer transforms this from a question into a statement:	*College students benefit from living at home while attending school.*
Writer considers other arguments and develops the thesis accordingly:	*Despite the attraction of living away from home and experiencing life in unfamiliar territory, college students do benefit from living at home while attending school.*

Concession: While counterarguments refute objections, concessions acknowledge the value of positions or claims other than those being forwarded by the writer. Or, put another way, a writer should always anticipate objections. If the writer says that the objection or alternative is wrong, the response is a counterargument; but if he or she says that the objection or alternative is right, that response is a concession. Notice the difference between counterargument and concession in the following example:

> Imagine you and a friend are driving and the car breaks down in the middle of nowhere. You make a claim: "Let's get a ride." Saying that hitchhiking is too dangerous, your friend objects. But you counterargue: "But we are safe with two people." On the other hand, if you acknowledge the danger involved, you concede the point; however, you could still argue your case—that hitchhiking would be better than remaining in the middle of nowhere, vulnerable to the elements. In short, if you disagree with an objection, what you say (your response) is a counterargument; if you agree, what you say (your response) is a concession.

Concession is a vital aspect of academic argument. Notice how Crabtree concedes a point in the conclusion of his essay. Although he argues for the value of a great books education throughout his essay, he does concede that it demands a particular kind of commitment:

> A great books education is not for everyone. In order to benefit from such an education, a student has to be highly motivated, mature enough to realize the importance of such a focus, and self-disciplined. Whatever reasons one might have for not pursuing a great books education, it cannot be because it is not practical! (Also, see Schwind-Pawlak ¶ 6.)

Concessions might also acknowledge the limitations of, or make clear boundaries for, the writer's own argument. In this case, they are sometimes called *qualifiers:* When giving a speech on the evils of corporate tax evasion, a senator qualifies her statements: "Granted, most companies in America pay taxes responsibly, but we must focus on those few rogue, and politically powerful, companies." When arguing for a salary increase, a union leader acknowledges a point made by the opposition: "We understand that economic times ahead could be perilous and that a salary increase could make the company more financially vulnerable to outside forces, but the future of the company certainly depends upon the well-being of its loyal employees."

Notice Paulin's qualifier:

> First of all, let me make it clear that I'm not advocating that everyone in America go out and get fat. According to the news media, we are doing that very handily on our own, in spite of all the messages to the contrary and the shelves of diet food in every supermarket.

In qualifying her points at the beginning of her essay, she makes clear that her argument is more complicated than an outright defense of obesity.

Making Concessions: Conceding in academic argument does not make an argument wishy-washy. In fact, a good concession shows that a writer has a broad sense of his or her claims—that they fit into a larger context. A good argument might discuss the logic of another argument, and show, *to some degree,* how that argument has validity. This does not mean that the original argument is shaky; on the contrary, it means that the original argument is *so* strong and valid that it can even acknowledge the soundness of other arguments. (See more on this in the **Writer's Voice** section.)

Consider the following questions for your argument:

- Are there other valid positions that one could take on my topic?
- Are there legitimate reasons for taking another position on this topic?
- Does my argument make any large, but necessary, leaps?
- Do I ask my audience to imagine a situation that is fictional?
- Do I ask my audience to accept generalizations?

The idea in conceding and qualifying is to acknowledge any legitimate concerns that the reader might have so that he or she does not become too suspicious about your argument. For instance, if a writer were making a generalization about college students, he or she might note an opposing fact but still move on with the argument:

Younger college students are often overwhelmed by the amount of new experiences in their lives. *Of course, not all younger students are consumed by the novelty of social freedom;* however, many find themselves swimming in a sea of lifestyle options that work against their abilities to focus on schoolwork.

In this example, the writer qualifies the generalized statement about college students, understanding that readers may not accept the idea that all college students are affected the same way. This reveals the writer's depth and understanding of the topic and the writing situation.

Activities

1. Discuss what rhetorical tools might be effective in communicating your idea for this essay. Share your writing idea with a few classmates (groups of three to five), and discuss specific examples of the various rhetorical tools you are using. Then, for your own benefit, summarize the main points of the discussion about your essay.

2. Write a brief summary of your essay and exchange it with a classmate. Then, write a memo, in response to your classmate's summary, suggesting at least seven counterarguments a reader is likely to have while reading his or her essay. (See Chapter 13.)

Caution: Logical Fallacies Ahead: Logical fallacies are flaws in the structure of an argument that make the claims invalid. You might think of fallacies as logical bumps that stop or derail the forward movement of the argument. Fallacies are often subtle—hidden beneath appealing language—but if detected, they may prompt the reader to dismiss an argument entirely. The ability to detect (and avoid) logical fallacies is tremendously important. Recognizing flawed arguments (by politicians, advertisements, political organizations, and corporations) can keep the average citizen aware of others' agendas. In academia, recognizing logical fallacies is part of being a critical thinker in all disciplines (and there is no quicker way to make readers of your own work suspicious than committing logical fallacies). Be careful not to commit any of the following when making an argument:

Ad Hominem (Latin for *to the person*): Attacks a person directly rather than examining the logic of the argument.

- We cannot possibly consider Ms. Smith's proposal because she is a Catholic.
- Mr. Mann's argument is suspicious because he is a socialist.

Strawperson: Exaggerates a characteristic of a person or group of people and then uses the exaggeration to dismiss an argument.

- Islamic fundamentalists are crazy. They only want to destroy Americans. We cannot accept their claims about imperialism.
- Environmentalists are radical. They want to end everyone's fun by taking cars and boats away.

Faulty Cause/Effect: Confuses a sequential relationship with a causal one. Assumes that event A caused event B because A occurred first.

- Since the construction of the new baseball stadium, homelessness in the downtown area is decreasing.
- The tax cut made energy rates decrease.

Either/Or Reasoning: Offers only two choices when more exist.

- Either we destroy Russia or it will destroy us.
- The American people will choose to control their own lives or give away their wills to socialist candidates.

Hasty Generalization: Draws a conclusion about a group of people/events/things based on insufficient examples (often, the logical flaw behind racist, sexist, or bigoted statements).

- Men are too possessive. My ex-boyfriend would never let me go out alone.
- French people are rude. When I went to France, the civilians grunted French statements when I asked for help.

Non Sequitur (Latin for *it does not follow*): Skips several logical steps in drawing a conclusion.

- If we do not trash the entire tax code, the downtown area will slowly deteriorate.
- A new baseball stadium downtown will help with the homelessness problem.

Oversimplification: Does not acknowledge the true complexity of a situation or offers easy solutions to complicated problems.

- If we could give kids something to do, they wouldn't get depressed.
- This credit card will end all of my financial problems.

Slippery Slope: Assumes that a certain way of thinking or acting will necessarily continue or extend in that direction (like a domino effect). Such an argument suggests that once we begin down a path, we will inevitably slip all the way down, and so the effects of a particular action or idea are exaggerated.

- If the college makes students take more mathematics, the next thing we know, advanced calculus and quantum physics will be requirements for all graduates.
- If North Vietnam succeeds in making South Vietnam communist, it will eventually threaten the shores of the United States of America.

False Analogy: Makes a comparison between two things that are ultimately more unlike than alike. The differences between the things make the comparison ineffective or unfair, or the comparison misrepresents one or both of the things involved.

- Writing is like breathing: you just do what comes naturally.
- Like Galileo, Bill Clinton was setting new ground, but no one understood him.

Begging the Question: Attempts to prove a claim by using (an alternative wording of) the claim itself.

- Girls should not be allowed into the Boys' Military Academy because it is for boys only.
- All cigarette smoking should be banned from public places because I believe it in my heart.

Consider the Image on page 252.

A. What logical fallacies might you overhear in an argument between a baseball coach and an umpire? Imagine such an argument and write down any logical fallacies you might hear. Or actually hold a mock argument between two people (one playing the coach and one playing the umpire) and write down any fallacies you overhear.

B. What logical fallacies might you overhear in other everyday situations? Consider the following scenarios: a customer trying to return _____; a store clerk trying to sell an extended warranty; a teacher explaining why a student cannot receive credit for a late assignment; a student arguing that he or she should receive a better grade; two politicians debating a tax cut; a husband explaining why he should go fishing with his cousin all weekend.

C. In groups, create several other scenarios (such as the ones in B), then act them out. The scenarios might involve two or more actors, or one person might perform a monologue. Others, the audience, should listen for and write down any logical fallacies, then discuss them afterward.

Practice: Explain the problem with the logic in the bumper stickers below, and name the fallacy.

Chocolate fixes everything

YOU DESERVE
WHAT YOU ACCEPT

Don't vote.
Things are perfect just the way they are.

DON'T BLAME ME.
I voted.

One who knows HOW will always have a job
working for one who knows WHY

Giving money and power to government is like giving whiskey and car keys to teenage boys
—P.J. O'ROURKE

POLITICAL CORRECTNESS IS A DISEASE

STRIP MINING PREVENTS FOREST FIRES

You can observe a lot by watching.
—Yogi Berra

Exploring Further

- In groups, write an example for each of the fallacies listed in the chapter.
- In groups, write short argumentative essays loaded with logical blunders. Someone in each group should read the completed essay aloud and the class should attempt to point out and name the fallacies.
- Look for logical fallacies in the world around you. Listen to commercials. Look at magazine advertisements. Read the opinion pages in the local newspaper. Watch nighttime talk shows or morning news programs.

Organizational Strategies

Arranging Your Argument

How Should I Begin? As with all essays, the sky is the limit. Remember some of the basic introductory tools (anecdote, provocative question, shocking statement). You might also begin with a broader statement about the nature of the debate. Or you might begin by teaching the reader a bit about the topic. Remember, too, that introductions not only create focus for the topic, but also establish the tone of the essay.

> Check the essays in this chapter. Notice the difference among introduction strategies. Do the introductions help to establish the tone in each essay?

How Should I Include Evidence? Do not simply throw evidence at a reader. You have to integrate evidence into your points and provide an explanation of the evidence. In other words, you need to explain why the evidence (the anecdote, the allusion, the scenario, the reference, or the statistics) is important. You need to make the connection between the evidence and your argument. Here is a standard paragraph strategy for giving evidence:

    Main idea or topic sentence
    Evidence
    Evidence
    Explanation

See Paulin's essay in this chapter. She patterns many of her paragraphs in this way. Of course, as with all organizational strategies, this can be manipulated. But however evidence is organized, information should never be left dangling, without explanation.

Where Should I Put Counterarguments? Counterarguments can be tricky, but they need not be. First, they can be placed anywhere in a paper: at the beginning, throughout the body, and even at the conclusion. The best thing to do is to let them work for you—let them set up your reasoning. For instance, you might explain an opposing point and then counter, explain another opposing point and then counter. (Depending on the amount of detail given to each counter, each point might be an entire paragraph, or more, with supporting evidence.)

    Opposing Point A
    Your counterargument
    Opposing Point B
    Your counterargument
    Opposing Point C
    Your counterargument

Schwind-Pawlak's essay in this chapter proceeds in this fashion. She uses counterargument to organize her claims.

Some writers use the turnabout paragraph for counterarguments. A turnabout paragraph begins with one point, and then changes directions at some point—always giving the reader a clear indication of that change. For example, you might begin a paragraph explaining an opposing position, and then counterargue in that same paragraph, perhaps explaining why that opposing position is short-sighted:

> Some people argue that global warming is not a problem at all. They suggest that all the discussion about the ozone layer is merely fear-mongering by left-wing political activists. This argument, however, ignores the volumes of evidence compiled by scientists (many of whom are Nobel Prize winners) from around the world—scientists from different cultures, from different religious contexts, from different political systems, and with different political agendas. The amount of data they have collected and the sheer din of their collective voices ought to be enough to convince people that global warming is much more than the delusions of a few environmental groups.

In this example, the opposing claim (that global warming is not a real problem) is addressed within the paragraph. The paragraph also includes the change of direction ("This argument, however . . .").

You might decide that the opposing viewpoint(s) require significant explanation, and that it would be best to keep them grouped together. Therefore, you might devote a chunk of space at the beginning of your paper before even countering:

Opposing Point A
Opposing Point B
Opposing Point C
Your counterargument to A
Your counterargument to B
Your counterargument to C

You also might decide that your argument only needs a single main counterargument. That counter might come after you have given your supporting evidence and appeals, or it might even begin the argument. Or several opposing claims might be discussed, and addressed, in one paragraph. (See Paulin ¶ 2.)

> Examine the essays in this chapter for counterarguments. Notice the different ways they are addressed.

How Should I Make Transitions?

Regardless of your general organization strategy, make certain to cue the reader when giving a counterargument. It is important that the reader understand when the focus is shifting from counter to main argument. You might begin a paragraph with an opposing viewpoint: "Some opponents might argue that . . ." If so, you will need to shift the reader back to your logic: "But they do not understand that . . ." Here is a list of some strategic transitions when doing counterargument:

- On the other hand,
- Contrary to this idea
- Although many people take this stance,
- However, (; however,)
- Despite the evidence for this position,
- But

Writer's Voice
Finding an Appropriate Strategy

Argument need not be cast as an act of aggression or belligerence. While arguments are sometimes heated and intense, they need not attempt to belittle their opponents. In fact, the fastest way to alienate, or turn off, a reader is to sound narrow-minded, mean, arrogant, or intimidating. A good argument attracts readers and engages those who might oppose the claims being made; a bad or unsuccessful argument loses readers. Here are some strategies for maintaining a cool tone—one that invites readers rather than alienates them.

Making Concessions: Conceding or qualifying a point can make an argument seem more controlled and more inviting; therefore, even when writers have a very strong conviction, they will often acknowledge the value of some other point or the limits of their own argument. Imagine the following argument:

> First-year college students are not mature enough to live on their own, without the guidance of parents and the familiarity of home turf. Dorm life, for students, is a celebration of self-destruction and disorientation. The social distractions draw students away from the real purpose of college and defeat even the most focused and determined students. Colleges should re-think the requirements for first-year students to live on campus.

While these claims unfairly generalize college students (see *logical fallacies*) and threaten the logical soundness of the argument, they also project a hasty or pushy voice. Such unqualified claims create a certain character in readers' minds—someone who is overly anxious and forceful. But notice how the same argument can be cast with a different voice (which uses concession):

> Dorm life does hold some value for young students. It can create a climate of inquiry and academic engagement. However, many young college students are overcome by the utter freedom, lack of genuine guidance, and constant social distractions. And too many students, who would otherwise succeed in their first years at college are suffering or failing because they are forced to live on campus. Colleges should, at least, begin to reevaluate requirements for on campus living.

Notice how this paragraph acknowledges the value of dorm life and does not simply cast away all of its value. The voice seems fairer and less alienating.

While conceding can create a more engaging voice, conceding unnecessarily, or too often, can have negative results. Imagine the same argument:

> Living in dorms can be the best thing possible for a college student; however, dorm life can also defeat many students. Sometimes, even the brightest and most determined students can be overcome by the social distractions. It all depends on the individual student's personality and upbringing, but college dorm life can actually work against the whole purpose of going to college. Certainly, each college should consider the characteristics of its own student body, but policies that require students to live on campus should be reevaluated.

This degree of concession is distracting. All the concessions undermine the importance of the argument. The voice behind the text seems concerned, primarily, about offending potential readers. But, ironically, such writing makes readers feel distant or detached from the ideas. Because the writer seems uncommitted, readers have no reason to engage the ideas. (Be cautious not to concede away your argument—and your level of commitment.)

Avoiding Harsh Description: It is often easy to use the most emotionally loaded terms to describe something or someone, to proclaim an opposing view as "dumb" or "evil." Such description, however, is most often exaggerated, and suggests that the writer has not fully investigated the subject. Notice Paulin's strategy:

> Certainly everyone is entitled to his or her own opinions of what is attractive, but no one has the right to damage another human being for fun or profit. The media and the diet industry often do just that. While no one can change an entire culture overnight, people, especially parents, need to think about what they really value in the humans they share their lives with and what values they want to pass on to their children.

Here, Paulin does not attack the media and the diet industry with aggressive adjectives, but argues that they damage people's lives. This is a far more sophisticated and useful strategy than merely dismissing them with a simple negative word or phrase.

Avoiding Character Slams and Preaching Problems: It is often easy to attack the character of opponents, but it is more engaging, and more persuasive, to direct the argument at behaviors, policies, or attitudes rather than people. Notice Churchill's strategy:

> Okay. Let's communicate. We are frankly dubious that those advancing such positions really believe their own rhetoric but, just for the sake of argument, let's accept the premise that they are sincere. If what they say is true, then isn't it time we spread such "inoffensiveness" and "good cheer" around among all the groups so that everybody can participate equally in fostering the national round of laughs they call for? Sure it is—the country can't have too much fun or "intergroup" involvement—so the more, the merrier. Simple consistency demands that anyone who thinks the Tomahawk Chop is a swell pastime must be just as hearty in their endorsement of the following ideas—by the logic used to defend the defamation of American Indians—[to] help us all really start yukking it up.

Churchill refrains from attacking those who advocate using American Indian symbols in sports media. Rather than attack his opponents, Churchill uses their logic in his own argument. That is, his opponents argue that the American Indian images are actually inoffensive, that they are used for a simple game, and that American Indians should be honored by their use. Churchill, then, borrows their logic and applies it to other ethnic and religious groups.

> First, as a counterpart to the Redskins, we need an NFL team called "Niggers" to honor Afro-Americans. Half-time festivities for fans might include a simulated stewing of the opposing coach in a large pot while players and cheerleaders dance around it, garbed in leopard skins and wearing fake bones in their noses. This concept obviously goes along with the kind of gaiety attending the Chop, but also with the actions of the Kansas Chiefs, whose team members—prominently including black members—lately appeared on a poster, looking "fierce" and "savage" by way of wearing Indian regalia. Just a bit of harmless "morale boosting," says the Chiefs' front office. You bet.

When Churchill applies the logic of his opponents, the result is a surprising list of offensive names and characterizations. His strategy, then, reveals the sloppy argument of his opponents. But imagine a less sophisticated approach:

> These people need to realize they are wrong. No matter how much fun they might be having with their Tomahawk Chop and other silly pastimes, they are offending thousands of people. They need to realize that defaming any group of people in America is wrong, and that other groups would not tolerate it.

This approach is fundamentally different from Churchill's. While Churchill points to the logic of his opponents, the latter approach preaches about "these people." While Churchill invites the reader into an analysis of ideas, the latter approach calls on the reader to condemn people. It does not invite reflection; it merely states that certain people "are wrong." While Churchill invites the reader to see flawed logic, the latter approach shuts down reflection and makes a simplistic statement. Another, more serious problem with such an approach is that it could be used by any position. Imagine the following:

> These people need to realize that they are wrong. No matter how much they complain about the Tomahawk Chop and other great pastimes, they are keeping thousands of people from having fun. They need to realize that people are not trying to be harmful.

This passage is also preachy. It does not invite reflection or analysis; it merely spouts a flatly worded opinion. And besides the logical problems, it serves to alienate any reader who might have a different opinion. However, writers such as Churchill avoid preaching or condemning people. They bring readers into an intensive analysis—even if that analysis reveals troubling logic.

Talking with, Not Arguing at, Readers: An academic argument is not an argument with readers. It is a *conversation with readers about an argumentative position.* And, if that conversation is compelling, the reader may find that position valuable. In other words, argumentative writing speaks with the reader about a particular position or set of positions and attempts to make one position more logical and/or valuable than others.

To help visualize the role of the writer and reader, imagine the following: The writer sits beside the reader pointing at, and directing attention to, a set of claims. The writer does not sit in front of and point his or her finger at the reader. This may seem like a subtle difference, but notice how it may change a passage. Notice Crabtree's passage from his essay in this chapter:

> No matter what occupation one chooses, the future is full of question marks. Although this economic dislocation is in its early stages, statistics already indicate a high degree of instability in the job market. According to the United States government, the average American switches careers three times in his or her life, works for ten employers, and stays in each job only 3.6 years. (Note 1)
>
> Such unpredictability calls for a different strategy in preparing for the job market. Rather than spending one's undergraduate years receiving specialized training, one ought to learn more general, transferable skills which will provide the flexibility to adjust to whatever changes may occur. A well-educated worker should be able to communicate clearly with co-workers, both verbally and in writing, read with understanding, perform

basic mathematical calculations, conduct himself responsibly and ethically, and work well with others. These skills would make a person well-suited to most work environments and capable of learning quickly and easily the requisite skills for a new career, should the need arise.

Here, he speaks to the reader about the need for workers in America to be intellectually capable of changing work environments. He does not command the reader. But imagine a different approach:

> Such unpredictability should make you realize the need to be ready for a shifting job market. Rather than spending undergraduate years receiving specialized training, you ought to learn more general, transferable skills which will provide the flexibility to adjust to whatever changes may occur.

This writer does not offer an argument to the reader, but assumes that the reader is directly involved in the topic (undergraduate education). The second-person pronoun, *you*, refers directly to the reader—the person holding the paper or looking at the computer screen. And because academic writing (or public writing) most often assumes an audience of many different readers, *you* is usually avoided.

Activity: How would you describe the voice of these images? In groups or alone, look carefully at each image on this page, considering its content, colors, composition, and so on (For help in analyzing an image, see page 694.). Then describe, in a word or two, the voice of the image; and explain, in a few sentences, what specific elements of that image help to create its voice.

Revision Strategies

R evision means "re-seeing" your entire essay: your purpose for writing, your reader, your main idea, what you say to support that idea and the way you say it, your voice (the way you sound to the reader), and so on. You re-see it all, and this takes time. For this assignment, you were to make an argument. So you should ask yourself, "Does my essay meet the requirements of the assignment?" or, to phrase it another way, "What prevents my essay from meeting the requirements of the assignment, and how can I fix it?" If, for example, you reread your draft and find that you have merely told a story or stated some observations, you have not made an argument. Or if you find that you have made an argument but that you have not dealt with counterarguments or that your essay has no public resonance, you will need to revise to improve your argument.

Consider the following revision strategies:

- Review this chapter, keeping your essay in mind. You might (1) explore your **Invention** notes, looking for helpful ideas and/or respond further in writing to relevant Invention questions; (2) review the **Rhetorical Tools, Organizational Strategies,** and **Writer's Voice** sections with an eye toward making appropriate changes; and (3) review several of the essays, noting the way the writers in this chapter approached this type of essay.

- Set aside at least as much time to revise as you took with invention and delivery.

- Create distance between you and your writing by getting away from it for a few days if possible or a few hours at least.

- Read your paper aloud to hear how it sounds or have someone else read it aloud to you.

- Print out a hard copy of your paper and read it carefully in a different place than where you wrote it.

- Figure out your writing strategy by noticing how the parts of your essay work together to support your main point. Consider making an outline of your essay to help you see this.

- Have someone else read and respond to your essay.

For ideas about **Peer Review,** see p. 50.

Global Revision Questions

Invention (What have you learned by exploring your topic?)

- **Point of Contact:** What other ideas did you consider writing about before selecting this one? Why was this idea more worth pursuing than the others?

- **Analysis:** How has your exploration of this topic gone beyond your initial ideas and questions about it? In what ways have your ideas moved beyond your initial biases and perceptions—and beyond the common beliefs of your reader?

- **Public Resonance:** How might your essay be relevant to, or matter to, your reader? And what might be the consequence(s) of your essay? How might the reader think or act differently after reading it?

Delivery (What writing decisions have you made as part of your writing strategy?)

- **Rhetorical Tools:** What rhetorical tools discussed earlier in this chapter have you used to help get your point across? What other tools might you consider using?

  - What is the main claim of your argument, and how have you conveyed that claim to the reader? What, besides your intended main idea, might the reader imagine your main idea to be? How might you help the reader focus on your main points?

  - Where might you provide more evidence for your claims? Or where might a different type of evidence help the reader to better understand you? What might be the reader's likely responses to your claims and their support, and have you anticipated these responses and responded accordingly? How might your title, introduction, and conclusion provide more helpful information regarding the main point of your essay?

  - What information can you weed out of your essay to make it more focused? Where might the reader lose interest or get bogged down because you have over-explained or restated an idea? While drafting your essay, what information crept in but can now be eliminated? What information might you delete to allow space for more relevant information?

- **Organizational Strategies:** You might begin by describing, or outlining, the structure of your essay to get a better sense of your overall organizational strategy. How have you arranged these elements for ease of reading? How might you rearrange the elements (claims; evidence; concessions; counterarguments) to allow the reader to better understand your ideas? How might you rearrange ideas within paragraphs? What ideas might be more helpful to the reader if placed earlier, or later, or near some other idea? How might connections and relationships between ideas be made more clear to the reader?

- **Writer's Voice:** Describe your writer's voice. Is it appropriate in this essay? How might a reader perceive you, the writer, in this essay? What about your writer's voice is inviting to the reader? What about your writer's voice might alienate the reader? What changes might make your writer's voice more inviting?

■

CONSIDERING CONSEQUENCES

While writers consider consequences throughout the writing process, this text draws attention to them here as a post-writing activity, to remind you that after an idea is communicated, consequences follow. The act of writing does not end with turning in an essay or writing a letter. Instead, that is just the beginning.

Well-made arguments engage readers, causing them to think and perhaps act differently. For example, because of an essay, readers might change their opinions and think that a certain belief, behavior, or thing is acceptable, or unacceptable—or at least undesirable. What might be the consequences of your essay for this chapter? That is, what effect might your ideas have on your reader's thoughts and actions? Consider these questions:

- Will the reader better understand the topic?
- Is the reader likely to think or behave differently?
- What might be the benefits to others? How might others be harmed?
- Who besides your instructor might benefit from your ideas?
- How might what you wrote about be affected?
- What might be the effect of these consequences on you, the writer?

Activities

The Consequences of Your Essay

1. List as many individuals as you can imagine whose thinking and/or actions might change if they were to read the essay you wrote for this chapter. For each individual you list, name the possible change in his or her thinking and/or action. (As you consider consequences upon your reader, consider the "ripple effect" of those consequences. If your reader thinks or behaves differently, what is the impact of that thinking or behavior on others?)

2. Ask someone to read your essay and to then write down what he or she thinks its consequences might be on various readers. Then discuss, in person or in writing, how the potential consequences of your ideas contribute to the overall quality of the essay.

3. List three other forms of delivery that you might have used to express your idea (report, letter, poster, screenplay, Web site, speech, song, poem, action). How might the consequences of your message have been different if delivered by way of these other forms?

The Consequences of the Chapter Readings

1. How might *you* think and/or behave differently because of one of the readings? And, how might *others* benefit, or be harmed, by your new way of thinking and/or acting?

2. How might one of these readings change the world? That is, Churchill's subject matter is Native American mascots and images; Crabtree's is a great books education; Paulin's is, among other things, the diet industry; and so on. How might these subjects (mascots, college education, and so on) change as a result of the arguments?

3. How might *the writers* in this chapter be influenced by what they write? How might they think or act differently? How might they be treated differently by others?

Considering Images

1. Explain how someone might view one of the following images differently after reading the related essay. Be specific when you describe how someone might view the image before reading the essay, and how it might be viewed differently after the reading.

   A. The woman weighing herself (page 246), after reading Ann Marie Paulin's "Cruelty, Civility, and Other Weighty Matters."
   B. The sperm fertilizing an ovum (page 235), after reading Jennifer Schwind-Pawlak's "Don't Make Me a Has-Bean!"

2. Find an image and explain how someone might view it differently after reading one of the essays in this chapter.

3. After reading one of the essays in this chapter, how might someone view a person, place, or thing differently? Take a snapshot of life, either with a camera or describing it in a paragraph or two, and then write an essay explaining how a person might view that snapshot differently after reading either one of the essays in this chapter or your own argument essay.

The Consequences of Everyday Arguments

1. Write down the consequences that a specific written argument has had on people who have never read it. What was the argument? What were its consequences?

2. Make a list of written arguments and their consequences, and then divide your list into two categories: (1) famous or (2) everyday consequences. What was the main claim of each written argument you listed? Which particular argument do you think has had the greatest consequence? Write an essay supporting your choice.

Considering Images

1. Find an image and write an essay that attempts to change the way someone views that image.

2. Find an image, creating one of your own if you like, that speaks to the idea of consequences. That is, the image should show a consequence or show something likely to produce, or lead to, a consequence. Explain how the image does this. How do the specific elements of the image (what is shown, arrangement of the items, colors, shadows, texture, and so on) interact to encourage the reader to think about the consequence?

EVERYDAY RHETORIC

Writing, Speech, and Action

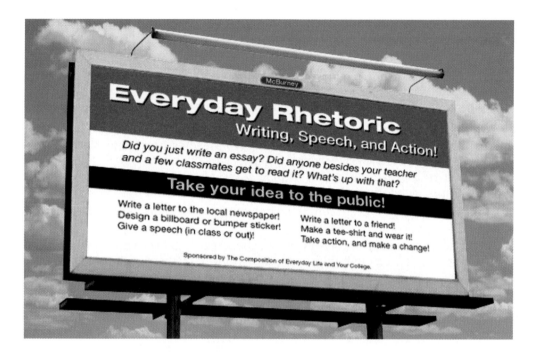

The invention and delivery strategies discussed earlier in this chapter apply to other forms of communication as well. For example, one might argue not just in an essay, but in a letter or a memo, in a speech or as part of a discussion, or through more visual means such as a poster, a photograph, or a painting. Of course, one might make an argument by taking action—such as participating in a protest or volunteering at a soup kitchen. For practice at applying this chapter's rhetorical tools and strategies to other forms, you might do one of the following activities. (For a more detailed explanation of these forms, see Chapter 13.)

Exploring Visual Rhetoric

I t can be argued that images, too, use rhetoric. And by looking at how images "work," we can apply some of the important concepts of rhetoric, not just to writing and speaking, but to images as well. Looking at visual rhetoric can also help us to better understand how rhetoric is used in writing and speech.

Consider This Chapter's Opening Image: Describe the rhetoric of this chapter's opening image—boxing gloves and a stool in the corner of a ring. Use the "Analyzing an Image" questions (on page 694) to help you figure out how the image conveys an idea.

A. Discuss your analysis of the chapter's opening image with several classmates. Explore through discussion how your understanding of the image is similar to or different from theirs. Following the discussion, write down the main similarities and differences in your viewpoints, and explain how your ideas about the image developed or changed through discussion. What did you learn, or how because of the discussion did you come to think differently about the image?

B. Consider the public resonance of the opening image. What public concern does it speak to? To whom might this concern matter? How might people benefit by exploring the photograph's possible meanings?

Find or Take an Image That Relates to Your Essay: What image might you use in conjunction with the essay you wrote for this chapter?

A. Write a caption for the image.

B. Write an essay explaining the relationship between the image and your text. Consider the following questions:

- How does the image support or help to explain the text of the essay?
- What does the image argue? What claim does the image make?
- What specific elements of the image convey the main idea and the support for that idea?
- How might the reader view the image differently after having read your essay?
- How might the reader be confused by the relationship of your essay and image?

C. Show the image to several people, and ask each person to read your essay. Then ask them how they view the image differently now.

D. Describe the rhetoric of your own photograph or image, using "Analyzing an Image" questions on page 694.

Consider Other Images in This Chapter: Explore the relationship, or interaction, between the images in this chapter and a corresponding essay.

"Crimes Against Humanity" (page 210)

A. Find at least two images that could be used with Churchill's essay. Write a caption for each image.

B. In an essay, explain how at least two of the images you found for question A above could be used along with Churchill's text to develop his main idea. Discuss the impact each image might have on the reader. How, for example, might one image work better, worse, or just differently than the other(s)? How might the different images encourage the reader to see Churchill's argument in different ways?

Woman Weighing Herself (page 246)

A. Does the photograph of the woman on a scale make an argument? If so, what might that argument be? Consider the following questions: What argument does the image make? What specific elements of the image express that argument?

B. Imagine changes in certain details of this photograph (such as the woman's facial expression, her weight, her age, the type of scale, the background, the number of people in the image, the colors, what else is included or not included in the image, and so on). How would these changes affect the argument being made?

Sperm Fertilizing an Ovum (page 235)

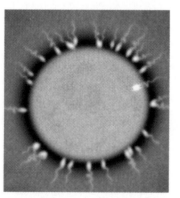

A. Does the image of a sperm fertilizing an ovum make an argument? If so, what might that argument be? What specific elements of the image express that argument?

B. What is the relationship between the image and Jennifer Schwind-Pawlak's argument in "Don't Make Me a Has-Bean!"? How does the image speak to what Schwind-Pawlak is talking about?

C. How might someone view the image of a sperm fertilizing an ovum differently after reading "Don't Make Me a Has-Bean!" Or, how might someone view the essay differently after viewing the image?

D. Find some other image that goes with "Don't Make Me a Has-Bean!" Explain how the image complements the essay. What meaning does the image take on when it is connected to the essay? Or, how does the image encourage the reader to think about the words of the text?

Consider Five Photographs of One Statue:

Use the "Analyzing an Image" questions on page 694 to explore visual rhetoric. Might each of the photographs of General George Armstrong Custer have a different theme or dominating idea? What argument might each image be making?

1. What seems to be the main idea of each image? What argument might each image be making? How do content, framing, composition, focus, lighting, texture, angle, and vantage point help to convey the idea or argument?

2. Using the five images of the General Custer statue, write an essay explaining how content, framing, and so on can be used to make an argument.
3. Consider the rhetoric of the monument itself. What argument does the monument make? And how do specific characteristics of the monument help it to make that argument?
4. Identify three specific characteristics of the monument and explain how each makes an argument.

6

Chapter Contents

Responding to Arguments

In what ways do people respond to arguments?

Arguments are all around us. They lurk in nearly every behavior and event of our lives, and we often respond to arguments that hover around us but are not stated directly in a text. Imagine an American citizen protesting nuclear energy; she carries a sign that says, "Nuclear energy ≠ clean energy!" Her sign is a response to the argument that nuclear energy is cleaner than energy from oil and coal. The protester is not necessarily responding to a particular text or person, but to an argument made by many people (such as politicians) in many different contexts. The sign actually evokes (or brings to mind) this argument and directly refutes it.

People also respond critically to arguments that are made indirectly: in movies, advertisements, billboards, and so on. For instance, someone might respond to the argument suggested by an advertisement that cigarettes promote social and physical pleasures. Such an ad argues that a certain kind of cigarette provides pleasure beyond inhaling the smoke and feeling the nicotine, and a writer might (quite easily) argue the opposite.

In academia, writers most often respond to arguments that are formally delivered (such as an essay or editorial). They can respond to a particular text or person and to particular statements or claims:

- A psychologist responds to Freud's theory of ego development. She explains that such a theory is not valuable in treating women patients.

- A political science student supports a revised historical account of U.S. foreign policy that holds Henry Kissinger partly responsible for atrocities in Chile during the 1970s.

- Law students respond to a Supreme Court ruling that upholds the rights of law enforcement officers to detain citizens for traffic violations. They argue that the ruling erodes "unreasonable search and seizure."
- An English professor reviews a controversial new book and defends its claims against rampant consumerism.

As these examples suggest, responding to an argument does not necessarily mean disagreement. The initial argument (whether a court ruling, a book, an essay, or a historical account) provides the position on a topic. A writer, then, has many options beyond agreement or disagreement. For instance, he or she might agree with the initial argument and extend the ideas with additional points, disagree with a particular point, redefine the issue, or point out some logical flaws.

As you can imagine, this is a somewhat more sophisticated task than what we examined in Chapter 5: Making Arguments. However, responding to arguments is an engaging activity, one that is not only vital to and valued in academia, but also necessary for maintaining a democracy.

6 Although a writer can respond to many different kinds of argument, this chapter primarily focuses on arguments that are formally delivered. The chapter will help you discover and analyze an argument, develop a sophisticated argumentative response, and communicate your position in writing. Read the following essays, which illustrate a variety of arguing strategies. After reading the essays, you can find an argument in one of several ways:

1. Go to the **Point of Contact** section to find an argument from everyday life.
2. Choose one of the **Ideas for Writing** that follow the essays.
3. Respond to any argumentative essay from another chapter in this book.

After you find a topic, go to the **Analysis** section to begin developing your response.

READINGS ■

Most of the essays in this chapter respond to written arguments. For instance, Betsy Taylor's response to Juliet Schor's essay (which appears in Chapter 8: Searching for Causes) points to specific claims in the original argument and explains why those claims are either sound or unsound. (You may also notice that Taylor's response points to some of Schor's assumptions.) All of the essays in this chapter develop their own arguments, using their own logic and support from outside the original arguments. Daniel Bruno, for example, spends the majority of his essay developing an idea beyond the original. Alice Walker's and Ann Causey's essays differ from the others in the chapter: they respond to arguments that are not written, but that hover around the issues of smoking and hunting.

Response to Juliet Schor

Betsy Taylor

Betsy Taylor is executive director of the Center for a New American Dream (www.newdream.org) and author of What Kids Want That Money Can't Buy (2003). This essay is a response to Juliet Schor's essay, "The Politics of Consumption," which appears in Chapter 8: Searching for Causes. Schor's essay was originally published in the Boston Review's "New Democracy Forum," which includes a major piece (such as Schor's) and various responses (such as Taylor's). These pieces can be found on the Internet at www.bostonreview.mit.edu. As you read Taylor's essay, notice how it is a response to an argument. Highlight or underline Schor's major points and Taylor's responses to those points. After reading, write down what you think Taylor is trying to accomplish.

1   Americans are consuming like there may be no tomorrow. The dominance of consumerism is arguably more pervasive now than at any time in human history. Our most popular national pastime is watching television, followed closely by recreational shopping. The United States has the highest per capita consumption rate in the industrial world. While our material gains have improved the quality of life in some notable ways, there are many hidden costs to our "more is better" definition of the American dream. Juliet Schor is one of the few intellectuals to rigorously examine these costs. Her call for a new politics of consumption warrants serious debate.

2   Schor does an excellent job of exposing the underbelly of our consumerist culture. Her analytic work, including her recent book, *The Overspent American,* focuses primarily on how our work-and-spend lifestyles undermine the quality of our lives. In the chase for more, Americans are working longer hours, racking up more debt, while finding fewer hours to enjoy their material acquisitions. Schor's research also reveals a troubling new trend: our collective tendency to always want much more than we have. In a culture that reveres Bill Gates, the rising stock market, and status goods, people are no longer comparing themselves to the textbook Joneses, but rather to the wealthy celebrities they see on television. For many, this never-ending expansion of wants leads to conspicuous consumption, psychological stress,

and a preoccupation with meeting non-material needs materially.

3   In her essay, Schor points to the other hidden costs of excessive consumerism. Perhaps most troubling, though—and something Schor might have addressed in greater detail—is the environmental damage wreaked by American consumption. With less than 5 percent of the world's population, the United States consumes nearly 30 percent of global resources. Since 1940, Americans alone have used up as large a share of the Earth's mineral resources as all previous humans put together. We use twice as much energy and generate more than twice as much garbage as the average European. The typical American discards nearly a ton of trash per year. We consume 40 percent of the world's gasoline and own 32 percent of the world's cars. The average new house built in the United States has doubled in size since 1970. Two-thirds of those homes have two-car garages. To offer some perspective, scientists recently issued a study for the Earth Council indicating that if everyone on Earth consumed as the average North American does, we would need four extra planets to supply the resources and absorb the waste.

4   What does this mean for the environment? Every product comes from the earth and returns to it. To produce our cars, houses, hamburgers, televisions, sneakers, newspapers, and thousands upon thousands of other consumer items, we rely on chains of production that stretch around the globe. The unintended consequences of these chains include global warming, rapid deforestation, the depletion of over 25 percent of the world's fish stocks, and the permanent loss of hundreds of plant and animal species—including the very real possibility of losing all large mammals in the wild within the next 50 years.

5   Along with taking a heavy toll on our quality of life and the planet, consumerism is also placing tremendous pressure on low-income families. The American preoccupation with acquisition afflicts the rich and poor alike. But our collective fixation on keeping up with commercial consumerist norms often wreaks havoc for those in low-income communities and exacerbates the growing gap between the rich and poor. Few would dispute that those living on the economic margins need more material goods. But the culture of consumerism weighs heavily on the 35 million Americans living below the poverty line. The relentless marketing of status footwear, high-cost fashion, tobacco, and alcohol to low-income neighborhoods is one of the most pernicious aspects of consumer culture. The politics that Schor describes would challenge a culture that encourages people to define themselves through their stuff and would especially support and empower young Americans who feel enormous pressure to acquire things as the only avenue for gaining love, respect, and a sense of belonging.

6   Schor describes seven basic elements to a new "politics of consumption." Her elements—or guiding principles for an emerging movement—invite a fusion of those working for justice with those working for environmental sustainability. Her first principle, the right to a decent standard of living, requires affluent environmentalists and progressives to look anew at what structures must be put in place to ensure a level of safety and security for all Americans. If people don't feel safer—about the future and about their kids—they can't entertain the deeper moral and environmental question, "how much is enough?" Schor does not specify the components necessary to give people greater security, but the litany of real needs is well known: affordable housing, quality healthcare, living wage jobs, medical care in old age, funds for retirement, and affordable college education for children. People feel alone. It's hard to stop the chase for money, if not stuff, when you feel no support structures. Unless progressives re-embrace these concerns, those in poor and middle class families will have difficulty connecting with Schor's politics. Too many progressives have become seduced by the culture of desire: we, too, look up instead of down. We spend too much time in isolation from those living in poverty. With some exceptions, we have lost our edge. Perhaps we are just too comfortable. Perhaps this is unavoidable in a noisy culture that bombards us with 3,000 commercial messages a day.

7   Schor's other principles ring true. Millions of Americans obviously share her call for more fun, less stuff. Millions are opting to downshift, choosing to make less money in search of more time. A growing number of people also affirm her call for responsible consumption—a call for a much higher consciousness about the environmental and human costs of each consumer decision we make. Her call to democratize consumer markets seems a bit naïve, since humans have probably always sought to define themselves in part through their stuff. But in an age of excessive materialism, the times may be ripe to challenge the dominant ethos. Perhaps we can make it cool to shun fashion and footgear with corporate logos and redefine hip as simple, real, and non-commercial.

8   Her fifth principle taps into growing opposition to globalization and a dismaying recognition that Bangkok and New York look the same. After two decades of mega-mergers and five years of intense globalization, the homogenization of retail environments is destroying local businesses and cultures. A recommitment to local economies, independent small businesses, and consumer products that are locally designed and produced could be good for jobs, the environment, and cultural diversity.

9   The only principle that seems missing to me is one that goes to the heart of our values. Progressives tend to squirm when encouraged to examine values at a personal level. We want to change the system yet we remain uncomfortable with "soft" discussions of individual transformation. But there is a huge churning underway about values, purpose, and spirit. Progressives can dogmatically dismiss these forces as elements of religious dogmatism or New Age narcissism, or they can connect with this churning. I would argue that a politics of consumption—and we need a better name for this—should include guiding principles of humility and compassion. Humility and awe in surrendering to the "not knowing" about the cosmology of things, coupled with an affirmation of all those who hunger to experience the Light, however one defines that. We need a politics that embraces compassion for the Earth, for each other as individuals of equal human value, and especially for children who will inherit the future. Can we not come together with new energy, passion, and vision—combining forces for justice and sustainability with the hunger for rekindled spirits? Does a critique of consumer culture open up this discussion in new and encouraging ways? Schor argues that it does. I am persuaded that she is on to something.

Exploring Ideas

1. Taylor says that "while our material gains have improved the quality of life in some notable ways, there are many hidden costs to our 'more is better' definition of the American dream." Generate a list of as many "hidden costs" as you can by interviewing others to help you generate ideas. Organize your list into categories. Then explain what you think is the most dangerous one.

2. According to Taylor, "Few would dispute that those living on the economic margins need more material goods." Interview others and observe your community to define what you and others mean by "economic margins." How is your understanding of "economic margins" similar to or different from others' understanding of the term?

3. Explore the "chase for money" that Taylor refers to. Is it, as Taylor says, "hard to stop the chase for money"? Why? What makes it so hard? In what ways is this chase harmful? How is it beneficial?

4. Taylor says that we need a better name than the "politics of consumption." In groups or alone, come up with a better name. Then present to the class your new name and your reasons for why it is better.

Writing Strategies

1. Describe the nature of Taylor's response. Would you say she disagrees completely, agrees, disagrees on a few minor points, or something else? What is her primary reason for responding to Schor?

2. Describe the tone of Taylor's essay. Is it hostile, friendly, patient, praising, distant, cold, etc.? Provide examples to support your claim.

3. What kind of evidence does Taylor provide to support her argument? Does she use statistics, personal experience, written sources, hypotheticals, or other kinds?

4. In Schor's response to Taylor, she says,

> I appreciate Taylor's pointing out that I gave short shrift to the environmental effects of consumption, and that those must play a central role in any political discourse of consumption. Coming to terms with our current destruction of the planetary ecology will be an important part of coming to a new set of values.

Has Taylor, in your opinion, communicated her main idea successfully and has Schor understood it? In two sentences, summarize Taylor's conclusion, and compare your summary to that of several classmates.

Ideas for Writing

1. Why do or don't we "need a politics that embraces compassion for the Earth"?

2. How does consumerism affect your chosen field? For example, if you are a nursing major, how does consumerism affect the nursing profession or the medical profession in general?

If responding to one of these ideas, go to the Analysis section of this chapter to begin developing ideas for your essay.

My Daughter Smokes

Alice Walker

Alice Walker is a writer of short stories, novels, and poetry. Her works include The Color Purple *(1982), a novel for which she won the Pulitzer Prize, and* In Love and Trouble *(1973), a collection of short stories. As you read "My Daugher Smokes" (1987), think about what Walker is arguing. Write down what you think is the main claim of her essay, and what her main claim is a response to.*

1   My daughter smokes. While she is doing her homework, her feet on the bench in front of her and her calculator clicking out answers to her algebra problems. I am looking at the half-empty package of Camels tossed carelessly close at hand. Camels. I pick them up, take them into the kitchen, where the light is better, and study them—they're filtered, for which I am grateful. My heart feels terrible. I want to weep. In fact, I do weep a little, standing there by the stove holding one of the instruments so white, so percisely rolled, that could cause my daughter's death. When she smoked Marlboros and Players I hardened myself against feeling so bad; nobody I knew ever smoked these brands.

2   She doesn't know this, but it was Camels that my father, her grandfather, smoked. But before he smoked "ready-mades"—when he was very young and very poor, with eyes like lanterns—he smoked Prince Albert tobacco in cigarettes he rolled himself. I remember the bright-red tobacco tin, with a picture of Queen Victoria's consort, Prince Albert, dressed in a black frock coat and carrying a cane.

3   The tobacco was dark brown, pungent, slightly bitter. I tasted it more than once as a child, and the discarded tins could be used for a number of things: to keep buttons and shoelaces in, to store seeds, and best of all, to hold worms for the rare times my father took us fishing.

4   By the late forties and early fifties no one rolled his own anymore (and few women smoked) in my hometown, Eatonton, Georgia. The tobacco industry, coupled with Hollywood movies in which both hero and heroine smoked like chimneys, won over completely people like my father, who were hopelessly addicted to cigarettes. He never looked as dapper as Prince Albert, though; he continued to look like a poor, overweight, overworked colored man with too large a family; black, with a very white cigarette stuck in his mouth.

5   I do not remember when he started to cough. Perhaps it was unnoticeable at first. A little hacking in the morning as he lit his first cigarette upon getting out of bed. By the time I was my daughter's age, his breath was a wheeze, embarrassing to hear; he could not climb stairs without resting every third or fourth step. It was not unusual for him to cough for an hour.

6   It is hard to believe there was a time when people did not understand that cigarette smoking is an addiction. I wondered aloud once to my sister—who is perennially trying to quit—whether our father realized this. I wondered how she, a smoker since high school, viewed her own habit.

7   It was our father who gave her her first cigarette, one day when she had taken water to him in the fields.

8   "I always wondered why he did that," she said, puzzled, and with some bitterness.

9   "What did he say?" I asked.

10   "That he didn't want me to go to anyone else for them," she said. "which never really crossed my mind."

11   So he was aware it was addictive, I thought, though as annoyed as she that he assumed she would be interested.

12   I began smoking in eleventh grade, also the year I drank numerous bottles of terrible sweet,

very cheap wine. My friends and I, all boys for this venture, bought our supplies from a man who ran a segregated bar and liquor store on the outskirts of town. Over the entrance there was a large sign that said COL- ORED. We were not permitted to drink there, only to buy. I smoked Kools, because my sister did. By then I thought her toxic darkened lips and gums glamorous. However, my body simply would not tolerate smoke. After six months I had chronic sore throat. I gave up smoking, gladly. Because it was a ritual with my buddies—Murl, Leon, and "Dog" Farley—I continued to drink wine.

13   My father died from "the poor man's friend," pneumonia, one hard winter when his bronchitis and emphysema had left him low. I doubt he had much lung left at all, after coughing for so many years. He had so little breath that, during his last years, he was always leaning on something. I remember once, at a family reunion, when my daughter was two, that my father picked her up for a minute—long enough for me to photgraph them—but the effort was obvious. Near the very end of his life, and largely because he had no more lungs, he quit smoking. He gained a couple of pounds, but by then he was so emaciated no one noticed.

14   When I travel to Third World countries I see many people like my father and daughter. There are large billboards directed at them both: the tough, "take-charge," or dapper older man, the glamorous, "worldly" young woman, both puffing away. In these poor countries, as in American ghettos and on reservations, money that should be spent for food goes instead to the tobacco companies; over time, people starve themselves of both food and air, effectively weakening and addicting their children, eventually eradicating themselves. I read in the newspaper and in my gardening magazine that cigarette butts are so toxic that if a baby swallows one, it is likely to die, and that the boiled water from a bunch of them makes an effective insecticide.

15   My daughter would like to quit, she says. We both know the statistics are against her; most people who try to quit smoking do not succeed.

16   There is a deep hurt that I feel as a mother. Some days it is a feeling of futility. I remember how carefully I ate when I was pregnant, how patiently I taught my daughter how to cross a street safely. For what, I sometimes wonder; so that she can wheeze through most of her life feeling half her strength, and then die of self-poisoning, as her grandfather did?

17   But, finally, one must feel empathy for the tobacco plant itself. For thousands of years, it has been venerated by Native Americans as a sacred medicine. They have used it extensively—its juice, its leaves, its roots, its (holy) smoke—to heal wounds and cure diseases, and in ceremonies of prayer and peace. And though the plant as most of us know it has been poisoned by chemicals and denatured by intensive mono-cropping and is therefore hardly the plant it was, still, to some modern Indians it remains a plant of positive power. I learned this when my Native American friends, Bill Wahpepah and his family, visited with me for a few days and the first thing he did was sow a few tobacco seeds in my garden.

18   Perhaps we can liberate tobacco from those who have captured and abused it, enslaving the plant on large plantations, keeping it from freedom and its kin, and forcing it to enslave the world. Its true nature suppressed, no wonder it has become deadly. Maybe by sowing a few seeds of tobacco in our gardens and treating the plant with the reverence it deserves, we can redeem tobacco's soul and restore its self-respect.

19   Besides, how grim, if one is a smoker, to realize one is smoking a slave.

20   There is a slogan from a battered women's shelter that I especially like: "Peace on earth begins at home." I believe everything does. I think of a slogan for people trying to stop smoking: "Every home a smoke-free zone." Smoking is a form of self-battering that also batters those who must sit by, occasionally cajole or complain, and helplessly watch. I realize now that as a child I sat by, through the years, and literally watched my father kill himself: surely one such victory in my family, for the rich white men who own the tobacco companies, is enough.

Exploring Ideas

1. What is Walker arguing? What argument do you think she is responding to? How does the argument to which Walker is responding help to shape her response?

2. In a sentence or two, write down your view on smoking.

3. Pass a hat around the room and have each student put his or her view (#2 above) in it. Each student draws another student's view. Respond in a paragraph to the view you drew.

4. Share responses (#3 above) with the class, discussing what makes each response convincing and how the response might be made more convincing.

5. Explore what shaped your view on smoking. Is it that you smoke or don't smoke? Did your view determine whether or not you became a smoker or quit smoking? Is your view on smoking consistent with your view on other issues? (For example, if you believe people have a right to smoke if they want to, do you feel the same way about seat belts, guns, abortion, and so on?)

6. Someone once said that one person's right to swing his arms ends when he hits another person. Do you agree? Explain how the same reasoning does or does not apply to a person's right to smoke.

Writing Strategies

1. Select one paragraph that stands out as being especially effective and list several reasons why you think so. Be specific.

2. What type of evidence does Walker use to support her main idea—her claim?

3. Evaluate Walker's conclusion. Is it successful? What seems to be her closing strategy?

4. Look carefully at Walker's sentence structure and word choice. How would you describe her style? Is it effective?

5. Reread Walker's essay, then very carefully reread a few select paragraphs. Then, without looking at her text, write several paragraphs of your own, attempting to copy her style.

Ideas for Writing

1. How might you respond to Walker's closing sentence?

2. What argument can you respond to that is not written, but that hovers around an issue?

> If responding to one of these ideas, go to the **Analysis section of this chapter to begin developing ideas for your essay.**

Entitlement Education

Daniel Bruno

Daniel Bruno wrote this essay for his college writing class after reading Peter Sacks's Generation X Goes to College. *As you read "Entitlement Education," identify (1) the argument to which Bruno is responding, (2) the main claim he is making in response, and (3) any responses to his own argument that he anticipates and deals with in his essay. Also, in the margins, write down any initial responses you have to his essay.*

In the margins of this essay, a reader's comments point to key ideas and writing strategies. As you read the essay, consider how the comments might influence your own reading and writing.

Exploring Ideas

Writing Strategies

In his book *Generation X Goes to College,* Peter Sacks describes, among other things, the sense of entitlement that some students in today's consumerist culture have toward a college education. One entire chapter explores this issue alone, providing examples of this "sense" and looking into its "humble beginnings." Sacks shows how consumerism has invaded education, leading some students to expect good grades for little effort. But he fails, it seems, to emphasize enough a most harmful effect of this sense of entitlement.

Overall summary of original argument.

Entitlement: expecting to get good grades for little effort.

The biggest problem as I see it is that although students are able to graduate from high school (and even some colleges) with minimal effort, those students may find themselves cheated in the long run. For example, one might argue that students find themselves cheated because upon graduation they will not be prepared to do their jobs: engineers will build defective bridges; doctors will botch their operations; and marketers will have no clue how to market. Yet I doubt that any of this is the case. There will always be competent, and even excellent, workers to do any job. We all know, for example, that engineering schools are full of Asian students happy to remain in the United States and build our bridges for us.

Cheated out of adequate job preparation.

Main response to the original argument.

(Attention to "I") Bruno's thesis, and distinction between his argument and the original.

Generalization?

One might also claim that students will be cheated because their lives will somehow *be less*. This argument claims that a person's intelligence contributes to her quality of life. Here we must remember that "intelligence" is not just "knowledge." Instead, it is being able to use knowledge, to make connections and figure things out, to see causes and solve problems. A person may have much knowledge—that is, she may have accumulated a

Cheated out of quality of life.

Turnabout paragraph.

lot of facts—but not have much intelligence . . . or so the argument goes. As one goes from first grade to twelfth, from twelfth grade to college, and from college freshman to senior, education shifts focus from mere accumulation of information (knowledge) to application of information (intelligence). And while we may accumulate more knowledge as a senior in college than we did as a senior in high school, the focus in college has (or should have) shifted from mere knowledge to intelligence—that is, to the ability to make good use of one's knowledge.

> Intelligence = being able to use knowledge.

> Analysis of several possible arguments about the results of student entitlement.

Other standard arguments claim other ways students might be cheated. For example, we might feel sorry for someone who doesn't get a joke or a reference. Allusions to literature, history, philosophy and so on allow us to say much in few words. But does the listener understand? If a person is unaware of common references—the Battle of the Bulge, Normandy, Existentialism, T. S. Eliot, World War I, Rasputin, John the Baptist, Gandhi, apartheid, Jonas Salk, Johnny Appleseed, Lewis and Clark, The Trail of Tears, slavery, the Donner Party, and so on—she misses out on conversations, on meaning, on *connecting with her fellow humans*. Of course, here one might counter that you don't need to know all of these things. And, I agree, you don't. People tend to hang out with people who have similar interests and tastes.

> Transition

> Uses historical and other allusions to prove his point about allusions.

> Cheated out of standard cultural knowledge.

> Concession.

One more argument claims that because we live in a democracy, we must be well-educated. Since all the citizens are responsible for the government, our forefathers promoted public education so that all citizens—not just the wealthy and elite—would know how to read and write. Suffice it to say that citizens with poor thinking skills can easily be tricked by expert communicators. And here is where basic seventh- or eighth-grade reading skills aren't enough. One can read with either more intelligence or less intelligence—noticing or missing the logical fallacies that others use to sell laundry soap, SUVs, political leaders, and a general way of living.

> This gives the topic extra public resonance (since the democratic process is at stake).

> Cheating the whole democracy.

True enough, these are all ways that students who are allowed to just slide by end up getting cheated. But another way (and one less talked about) strikes me as being far more offensive. This reason hinges on the fact that many students are not just sliding by.

> Transition paragraph that leads us to Bruno's particular stance.

In *Generation X Goes to College,* Peter Sacks illustrates that all of today's college students cannot just be thrown in the same big barrel. In describing the modern/postmodern clash in education, he spends the majority of his time talking about those students who are underprepared, who lack the basic study skills required in academic work, and who demonstrate little real commitment to their own education. Yet, he does not discuss this problem in isolation. He also mentions another type of student. For example, he introduces the reader to Marissa and Carol: "As

> Modern = marked by distinctions between lowbrow and highbrow thought. Postmodern = marked by chaos and blurring of boundaries.

> Return to the original argument.

Exploring Ideas

¼ students feel
entitled.

¾ students do not.

Diversity in skill
and attitude.

Motivated students
are cheated.

Under-motivated
students are cheated.

Gap between students
grows bigger.

very good students, [their views] were virtually excluded by The College in order to accommodate the whiners and complainers" (61). And he says they "suffered not only educationally" (63). In addition to discussing specific good students, an entire chapter presents survey results about students' attitudes toward education. While he makes claims such as "nearly a quarter of the students . . . harbored a disproportionate sense of entitlement," this very statement tells the reader that a full three quarters (that is, three out of four) students *do not* "harbor a disproportionate sense of entitlement" (54–59). He wraps up the book by focusing on another student, Andie, who he describes as "a good student, constantly picking [his] brain for information and feedback on her work" (186-7). His final paragraph before the epilogue says, "Let's create a system that encourages people like Andie at least as much as the ones who don't give a damn" (187). Thus, Sacks shows that today's students are a more diverse group—in skill level, background, and attitude toward education—than has ever before been gathered together in the college classroom.

Now when we connect two things—the present grade-inflated, entitlement-driven education system that has got a foothold in most of America's high schools and colleges AND the diversity in skill and attitude toward education of today's college students—two problems appear.

One problem is that the motivated students are not being as challenged as they could be. Although their situation is not ideal, it is far from hopeless. They have at least three options: (1) take advantage of the easy system and learn a little along the way; (2) motivate themselves, working harder (and learning more) than the system requires them to; and (3) attend a more academically rigorous school (of course such schools still exist, though they are likely to cost more to attend).

While motivated students suffer in our too-lax system, so do the un- (or under-) motivated ones. And these students, who need our help the most, are the ones most cheated. As Sacks says, "I now believe the students are the real victims of this systematic failure of the entitlement mindset" (189). The students who are allowed to slide by, who are content to slide by, who perhaps don't even realize that they are sliding by because sliding by is all they know—those students find themselves arriving at college less prepared and less motivated than the "better students." And what happens next? Sadly, the gap between these two groups grows even wider.

The motivated student with good study skills (the one who has had at least an adequate high school education) attends class, takes notes, understands reading assignments, follows instructions, develops even better habits of mind, gains even more

Quotations illustrate
particular points
of the original.

More summary of the
original argument.

Transition paragraph.

Sacks's quotation
supports Bruno's
argument.

Exploring Ideas

Writing Strategies

knowledge, and learns ways of making that knowledge work for her and her fellow humans. But in a system where B's are average and C's might indicate that although a student "tried" she did not demonstrate understanding or skill, the poorer students continue to advance through the system while remaining trapped at the bottom. Their level of thinking does not change much, while that of their better-prepared peers does.

Scenarios are the main support tool.

The injustice, then, has been done to the students (as Sacks says, the students are the victims). While the student has happily skipped (or unhappily slogged) along through sixteen years of formal education, she is allowed, if she wants, to come away with very little in terms of education. She is allowed, unfortunately, to escape practically unscathed by learning. The problem, of course, is that the two students have entered college on different academic levels and the one on the higher level has graduated on an *even higher* level while the one on the lower level has remained pretty much the same.

Sacks and Bruno argue the same point.

They do not even realize they are being cheated.

Students would do well to look around them, at the room full of fellow classmates. They should imagine that many of those students will be graduating one day. And they should imagine the students in the classroom next door and across the hall and in all the other buildings on campus. They will be graduating, too. They should also imagine all those students at the more than 4,000 other colleges throughout the country: Ohio State, Michigan, Michigan State, Findlay College, Iowa State, Oklahoma A&M, The University of Utah, California This or That. (*The Chronicle of Higher Education* 2000–2001 Almanac lists 4,096 colleges in the United States.) Many of those students are well-prepared, working hard, and developing even better habits and thinking skills.

The statistic creates some alarm for student readers.

Competition for jobs and status.

In our competitive world, the sad truth is that even some of the very good students, though their college dreams were to be doctors and lawyers and pharmacists and engineers, will be waiting tables. Don't get me wrong: there is no shame in that. The point is, that's not why they went to college. The truth is that for some students, college will be a tough uphill climb (a climb that could have been avoided with a more adequate high school education). A sadder truth, I am afraid, is that because of skills and attitudes developed in high school, for some students the reality of genuine learning (as opposed to just getting by) might already be too late.

Qualifier.

The "I" draws attention to Bruno's personal concern.

It's too late for many!

Works Cited

"Almanac." *The Chronicle of Higher Education.* 18 Oct. 2000
    http://chronicle.com/free/almanac/2000/almanac.htm.
Sacks, Peter. *Generation X Goes to College.* Chicago and LaSalle, IL: Open Court, 1996.

Exploring Ideas

1. What do you think is Bruno's purpose in writing? That is, what is he trying to accomplish?

2. Which of Bruno's points do you think is most important or interesting and worth pursuing further? Why is it worth pursuing?

3. Consider the nature of your initial responses to Bruno's argument. If you agreed or disagreed, explore why. If you were unclear about what he meant, explore that. Explore at least one of your initial responses by thinking through your ideas in several long paragraphs.

4. Share your strongest or most interesting response with others, asking them to tell you why you might be wrong or what you might be missing. Then jot down the ideas that helped you most in exploring the issue.

5. How might you respond to Bruno's essay with an essay of your own? Write down your main claim in one clear and concise sentence, and then jot down your ideas for support.

Writing Strategies

1. Are you able to understand Bruno's response to Peter Sacks, even if you have not read *Generation X Goes to College*? What helpful background information does Bruno provide? What other information might have been helpful?

2. Bruno defines "intelligence" in his essay. How is this definition important? Might he have deleted this definition without damaging his essay?

3. What is Bruno's main idea? Does he state it explicitly or imply it? Why is or isn't his strategy successful?

4. Explain how Bruno's essay has public resonance. That is, how is what he says important to others besides himself?

5. What evidence does Bruno provide to support his claim? Does he refer to statistics, outside sources, experience, logical reasoning, etc? What other kind of evidence might he have provided?

Ideas for Writing

1. What is the relationship between "knowledge" and "intelligence" in your field of study? Either use Bruno's definitions of those terms or revise his definitions as you see fit. Which is more important in your field: "intelligence" or "knowledge"?

2. Should students in the United States be required to attend high school? Should first-year writing courses be required?

If responding to one of these ideas, go to the **Analysis** section of this chapter to begin developing ideas for your essay.

Is Hunting Ethical?

Ann F. Causey

Ann Causey originally wrote "Is Hunting Ethical?" as a speech she delivered to the first annual Governor's Symposium on North America's Hunting Heritage in 1992. Before you read, write a paragraph exploring your views on hunting. As you read this essay, take notes on how Causey sees hunting. Underline or highlight key statements that shed light on her point of view, and jot down your initial reactions to them.

1   The struggling fawn suddenly went limp in my arms. Panicked, I told my husband to pull the feeding tube out of her stomach. Though Sandy had quit breathing and her death was clearly imminent, I held her head down and slapped her back in an attempt to clear her trachea. Warm, soured milk ran from her mouth and nose, soaking my clothes and gagging us with its vile smell. I turned Sandy over in my arms, and my husband placed his mouth over her muzzle. While he blew air into her lungs, I squeezed her chest as a CPR course had taught me to do for human infants in cardiac arrest.

2   After a minute or so I felt her chest for a pulse. Nothing at first, then four weak beats in rapid succession. "She's alive! Keep breathing for her."

3   My husband gagged, then spit to avoid swallowing more of the soured milk, and continued his efforts to revive Sandy. I kept working her chest, hoping that through some miracle of will she would recover. Come on, Sandy, wake up. Please wake up!

4   Sandy never woke up. My husband, a wildlife biologist, and I had nursed over two dozen white-tailed deer fawns that summer for use in a deer nutrition and growth study he was conducting. Most of the animals were in poor shape when we got them. People around the state found them—some actually orphaned, others mistakenly thought to be abandoned. After a few days of round-the-clock feedings, the fun gave way to drudgery and frustration. That's when they would call their county conservation officer, who in turn called us.

5   All the animals we raised required and got from us loving care, attention, and patience, no matter how sick or recalcitrant they may have been. All were named, and we came to know each one as an individual with unique personality traits and behavior patterns. Though most lived to become healthy adults, each fatality was a tragic loss for us, and we mourned each and every death.

6   The afternoon Sandy died, however, was not convenient for mourning. We were going to a group dinner that evening and had to prepare a dish. Through tears I made a marinade for the roast. While the meat smoked over charcoal and hickory, we brooded over Sandy's death.

7   When the roast was done, we wiped away our tears, cleaned up, and went to the dinner. Our moods brightened as our roast was quickly gobbled up, and the evening's high point came when several guests declared that our roast was the best venison they'd ever eaten. The best deer meat. Part of an animal my husband, an avid hunter, had willfully killed and I had gratefully butchered, wrapped, and frozen—a deer that once was a cute and innocent little fawn . . . just like Sandy.

8   If any one word characterizes most people's feelings when they reflect on the morality of killing an animal for sport, it is "ambivalence." With antihunters insisting that hunting is a demonstration of extreme irreverence for non-human life, thoughtful hunters must concede, albeit uncomfortably, the apparent contradiction of killing for sport while maintaining a reverence for life. Yet I know of few hunters who do not claim to have a deep reverence for

nature and life, including especially the lives of the animals they seek to kill. It seems that this contradiction, inherent in hunting and increasingly the focus of debate, lies at the core of the moral conundrum of hunting. How can anyone both revere life and seek to extinguish it in pursuit of recreation? The opponents of hunting believe they have backed its proponents into a logical corner on this point, yet the proponents have far from given up the battle for logical supremacy. Is either side a clear winner?

9   None who know me or my lifestyle would label me "antihunting." Most of the meat in my diet is game. And many is the time I've defended hunting from the attacks of those who see all hunters as bloodthirsty, knuckle-dragging rednecks.

10   Yet I have on occasion found myself allied with antihunters. But it's an uneasy and selective alliance, my antihunting sentiments limited to diatribes against such blatantly unethical behavior as Big Buck contests, canned Coon Hunt for Christ rallies, and bumper stickers proclaiming "Happiness Is a Warm Gutpile."

11   There is also a subtler reason for my concerns about hunting, stemming, I believe, from my disappointment with the responses of many hunters and wildlife managers to questions concerning the morality of hunting. In the interest of enlivening and, I hope, elevating the growing debate, it is these moral questions, and their answers, I wish to address here.

12   To begin, I should point out some errors, common to ethical reasoning and to the current debate, that we should do our best to avoid. The first is confusing prudence with morality. Prudence is acting with one's overall best interests in mind, while morality sometimes requires that one sacrifice self-interest in the service of a greater good.

13   While thorough knowledge is all that's required to make prudent decisions, the making of a moral decision involves something more: conscience. Obligations have no moral meaning without conscience. Ethical hunters do not mindlessly follow rules and lobby for regulations that serve their interests; rather, they follow their consciences, sometimes setting their own interests aside. In short, ethics are guided by conscience.

14   Another important distinction is between legality and morality. While many immoral activities are prohibited by law, not all behavior that is within the law can be considered ethical. The politician caught in a conflict of interest who claims moral innocence because he has broken no laws rarely convinces us. Nor should hunters assume that whatever the game laws allow or tradition supports is morally acceptable. The ethical hunter is obligated to evaluate laws and traditions in light of his or her own moral sense. Conscience is not created by decree or consensus, nor is morality determined by legality or tradition.

15   Finally, it's all too tempting to dismiss the concerns of our opponents by questioning their motives and credentials instead of giving serious consideration to the questions they raise. Hunters do hunting no favors by hurling taunts and slander at their opponents. The questions raised about hunting deserve a fair hearing on their own merits. Consideration of antihunting messages must not be biased by personal opinions of the messengers, nor should hunters' efforts remain focused on discrediting their accusers. Rather, ethical hunters must undertake the uncomfortable and sometimes painful processes of moral deliberation and personal and collective soul-searching that these questions call for.

16   The first difficulty we encounter in addressing the morality of hunting is identifying and understanding the relevant questions and answers. To me, the most striking feature of the current debate is the two sides' vastly different understanding of the meaning of the question, Is hunting a morally acceptable activity?

17   Those who support hunting usually respond by citing data. They enumerate the acres of habitat protected by hunting-generated funds; how many game species have experienced

population increases due to modern game management; how much the economy is stimulated by hunting-related expenditures; how effectively modern game laws satisfy the consumptive and recreational interests of the hunting community today while assuring continued surpluses of game for future hunters; and how hunters, more than most citizens, care deeply about ecosystem integrity and balance and the global environment.

18   While these statements may be perfectly true, they're almost totally irrelevant to the question. Antihunters are not asking whether hunting is an effective management tool, whether it's economically advisable, or whether hunters love and appreciate nature. Rather, they're asking, Is it ethical to kill animals for sport? Are any forms of hunting morally right?

19   The hunter says yes; the antihunter says no, yet they are answering entirely different questions. The hunter answers, with data, what he or she perceives as a question about utility and prudence; the antihunter, though, has intended to ask a question about morality, about human responsibilities and values. It's as if one asked what day it is and the other responded by giving the time. While the answer may be correct, it's meaningless in the context of the question asked.

20   The point is that moral debates, including this one, are not about facts but about values. Moral controversy cannot be resolved by examination of data or by appeal to scientific studies.

21   An obsession with "sound, objective science" in addressing their opponents has led many hunters not only to avoid the crucial issues but to actually fuel the fires of the antihunting movement. Animal welfare proponents and the general public are primarily concerned about the pain, suffering, and loss of life inflicted on hunted animals, and the motives and attitudes of those who hunt. They're offended by references to wild animals as "resources." They're angered by the sterile language and, by implication, the emotionally sterile attitudes of those who speak of "culling," "controlling," "harvesting," and "managing" animals for "maximum sustained yield." And they're outraged by those who cite habitat protection and human satisfaction data while totally disregarding the interests of the sentient beings who occupy that habitat and who, primarily through their deaths, serve to satisfy human interests.

22   Antihunters insist that nontrivial reasons be given for intentional human-inflicted injuries and deaths—or that these injuries and deaths be stopped. An eminently reasonable request.

23   Even when hunters acknowledge the significance of the pain and suffering inflicted through hunting, they too often offer in defense that they feel an obligation to give back more than they take, and that hunters and wildlife professionals successfully have met this obligation. Granted, it may be that the overall benefits to humans and other species that accrue from hunting outweigh the costs to the hunted. Nevertheless, this utilitarian calculation fails to provide moral justification for hunting. Is it just, hunting's detractors ask, that wild animals should die to feed us? To clothe us? To decorate our bodies and den walls? To provide us with entertainment and sport?

24   *These* are the questions hunters are being asked. *These* are the questions they must carefully consider and thoughtfully address. It will not suffice to charge their opponents with biological naïveté, as theirs are not questions of science. Nor will charges of emotionalism quiet their accusers, since emotion plays an integral and valid part in value judgments and moral development. Both sides have members who are guided by their hearts, their minds, or both. Neither side has a monopoly on hypocrisy, zealotry, narrow-mindedness, or irrationalism. Opposition to hunting is based in largest part on legitimate philosophical differences.

25   It has been said that hunting is the most uncivilized and primitive activity in which a modern person can legally engage. Therein lies ammunition for the biggest guns in the anti-

hunters' arsenal; paradoxically, therein also lies its appeal to hunters and the source of its approval by many sympathetic nonhunters.

26 Hunting is one of few activities that allows an individual to participate directly in the life and death cycles on which all natural systems depend. The skilled hunter's ecological knowledge is holistic and realistic; his or her awareness involves all the senses. Whereas ecologists study systems from without, examining and analyzing from a perspective necessarily distanced from their subjects, dedicated hunters live and learn from within, knowing parts of nature as only a parent or child can know his or her own family. One thing necessary for a truly ethical relationship with wildlife is an appreciation of ecosystems, of natural processes. Such an appreciation may best be gained through familiarity, through investment of time and effort, through curiosity, and through an attitude of humility and respect. These are the lessons that hunting teaches its best students.

27 Not only have ethical hunters resisted the creeping alienation between humans and the natural out-of-doors, they have fought to resist the growing alienation between humans and the "nature" each person carries within. Hunters celebrate their evolutionary heritage and stubbornly refuse to be stripped of their atavistic urges—they refuse to be sterilized by modern culture and thus finally separated from nature. The ethical hunter transcends the mundane, the ordinary, the predictable, the structured, the artificial. As Aldo Leopold argues in his seminal work *A Sand County Almanac,* hunting in most forms maintains a valuable element in the cultural heritage of all peoples.

28 Notice, though, that Leopold does not give a blanket stamp of moral approval to hunting; nor should we. In fact, Leopold recognized that some forms of hunting may be morally depleting. If we offer an ecological and evolutionary defense for hunting, as Leopold did and as many of hunting's supporters do today, we must still ask ourselves, For which forms of hunting is our defense valid?

29 The open-minded hunter should carefully consider the following questions: To what extent is shooting an animal over bait or out of a tree at close range after it was chased up there by a dog a morally enriching act? Can shooting an actually or functionally captive animal enhance one's understanding of natural processes? Does a safari to foreign lands to step out of a Land Rover and shoot exotic animals located for you by a guide honor your cultural heritage? Does killing an animal you profess to honor and respect, primarily in order to obtain a trophy, demonstrate reverence for the animal as a sentient creature? Is it morally enriching to use animals as mere objects, as game pieces in macho contests where the only goal is to outcompete other hunters? Is an animal properly honored in death by being reduced to points, inches, and pounds, or to a decoration on a wall? Which forms of hunting can consistently and coherently be defended as nontrivial, meaningful, ecologically sound, and morally enriching?

30 Likewise, we who hunt or support hunting must ask ourselves: Does ignoring, downplaying, and in some cases denying the wounding rate in hunting, rather than taking all available effective measures to lower it, demonstrate reverence for life? Does lobbying for continued hunting of species whose populations are threatened or of uncertain status exemplify ecological awareness and concern? Is the continued hunting of some declining waterfowl populations, the aerial killing of wolves in Alaska, or the setting of hunting seasons that in some areas may sentence to slow death the orphaned offspring of their legally killed lactating mothers, consistent with management *by* hunters—or do these things verify the antihunters' charges of management primarily *for* hunters?

31 These questions and others have aroused hunters' fears, indignation, defensive responses, and collective denial. Yet no proponent of ethical hunting has anything to fear from such questions. These are questions we should have

been asking ourselves, and defensibly answering, all along. The real threat comes not from outside criticism but from our own complacency and uncritical acceptance of hunting's status quo, and from our mistaken belief that to protect *any* form of hunting, we must defend and protect *all* forms. In fact, to protect the privilege of morally responsible hunting, we must attack and abolish the unacceptable acts, policies, and attitudes within our ranks that threaten all hunting, as a gangrenous limb threatens the entire body.

32   The battle cry "Reverence for Life" has been used by both sides, at times with disturbing irony. Cleveland Amory, founder of the Fund for Animals, described in the June 1992 issue of *Sierra* magazine the perfect world he would create if he were appointed its ruler: "All animals will not only be not shot, they will be protected—not only from people but as much as possible from each other. Prey will be separated from predator, and there will be no overpopulation or starvation because all will be controlled by sterilization or implant."

33   A reverence for life? Only if you accept the atomistic and utterly unecological concept of life as a characteristic of individuals rather than systems.

34   But neither can all who hunt legitimately claim to hold a reverence for life. In a hunting video titled "Down to Earth," a contemporary rock star and self-proclaimed "whack master" and "gutpile addict" exhorts his protégés to "whack 'em, stack 'em, and pack 'em." After showing a rapid sequence of various animals being hit by his arrows, the "master whacker" kneels and sarcastically asks for "a moment of silence" while the viewer is treated to close-up, slow-motion replays of the hits, including sickening footage of some animals that clearly are gut shot or otherwise sloppily wounded. A reverence for life? Such behavior would seem to demonstrate shocking *irreverence*, arrogance, and hubris. As hunters, we toe a fine line between profundity and profanity and must accept the responsibility of condemning those practices and attitudes that trivialize, shame, and desecrate all hunting. To inflict death without meaningful and significant purpose, to kill carelessly or casually, or to take a life without solemn gratitude is inconsistent with genuine reverence for life.

35   To be ethical, we must do two things: we must *act* ethically, and we must *think* ethically. The hunting community has responded to its critics by trying to clean up its visible act: we don't hear many public proclamations of gutpile addictions anymore; we less frequently see dead animals used as hood ornaments while the meat, not to be utilized anyway, rapidly spoils; those who wound more animals than they kill are less likely nowadays to brag about it; and, since studies show that the public opposes sport hunting as trivial, hunters are coached to avoid the term "sport" when they address the public or their critics.

36   What's needed, though, for truly ethical hunting to flourish is not just a change of appearance or vocabulary but a change of mindset, a deepening of values. Hunters may be able to "beat" antihunters through a change of tactics, but to win the wrong war is no victory at all. Some morally repugnant forms of hunting are *rightfully* under attack, and we can defend them only by sacrificing our intellectual and moral integrity. We should do all we can to avoid such "victories." Hunters must reexamine and, when appropriate, give up some of what they now hold dear—not just because doing so is expedient but because it's *right*. As T. S. Eliot, quoted by Martin Luther King, Jr., in his "Letter from a Birmingham Jail," reminds us, "The last temptation is the greatest treason: To do the right deed for the wrong reason."

37   Can anyone give us a final answer to the question, Is hunting ethical?

38   No.

39   For one thing, the question and its answer depend heavily on how one defines "hunting." There are innumerable activities that go by this term, yet many are so different from one another that they scarcely qualify for the same appellation. Moreover, there is no one factor

that motivates one hunter on each hunt; nor is there such a thing as the hunter's mind-set.

40   Second, and even more important, is the recognition that in most cases one cannot answer moral questions for others. Two morally mature people may ponder the same ethical dilemma and come to opposite, and equally valid, conclusions. The concept of ethical hunting is pluralistic, as hard to pin down as the definition of a virtuous person. Unlike our opponents, we who are hunting proponents do not seek to impose a particular lifestyle, morality, or spirituality on all citizens; we merely wish to preserve a variety of options and individualities in all our choices concerning responsible human recreation, engagement with nature, and our place in the food web. It's doubtful that any one system, whether it be "boutique" hunting, vegetarianism, or modern factory farming, is an adequate way to meet the ethical challenges of food procurement and human/nonhuman relationships in our diverse culture and burgeoning population.

41   Like education of any sort, moral learning cannot be passively acquired. In fact, the importance of answering the question of whether hunting is ethical is often exaggerated, for the value of ethics lies not so much in the product, the answers, as in the process of deep and serious deliberation of moral issues. To ponder the value of an animal's life versus a hunter's material and spiritual needs and to consider an animal's pain, suffering, and dignity in death is to acknowledge deeper values and to demonstrate more moral maturity than one who casually, defensively dismisses such ideas.

42   No matter the result, the process of moral deliberation is necessarily enriching. Neither side can offer one answer for all; we can only answer this question each for ourself, and even then we must be prepared to offer valid, consistent moral arguments in support of our conclusions. This calls for a level of soul-searching and critical thinking largely lacking on both sides of the current debate.

43   Today's ethical hunter must abandon the concept of hunting as fact and replace it with the more appropriate concept of hunting as challenge—the challenge of identifying and promoting those attitudes toward wildlife that exemplify the values on which morally responsible hunting behavior is based. Heel-digging and saber-rattling must give way to cooperation, to increased awareness and sensitivity, to reason and critical analysis, and to honest self-evaluation and assessment.

44   The Chinese have a wonderful term, *wei chi,* that combines two concepts: crisis . . . and opportunity. The term conveys the belief that every crisis present an opportunity. I submit that the hunting community today faces its greatest crisis ever and, therein, its greatest opportunity—the opportunity for change, for moral growth, for progress.

Exploring Ideas

1. What is Causey trying to accomplish with this essay?

2. What points do you find most interesting in this essay and why? Which of Causey's ideas make you think differently?

3. Interview various people to find out their views on hunting. Record their responses, and then write several paragraphs explaining how others' views are similar to or different from Causey's.

4. What issues, in addition to hunting, can Causey's ethical approach be applied to? That is, what issue do others discuss in terms of data or legality when you feel the issue should be ethics?

Writing Strategies

1. Do you consider Causey's opening narrative (paragraphs 1–7) to be effective? Explain how her opening is or is not a strength of her essay.

2. How does Causey make the purpose of her essay clear to the reader?

3. Examine Causey's essay for coherence. Provide several examples of how she connects ideas for the reader. What different strategies does she employ?

4. What writing decisions does Causey make to avoid alienating hunters? What decisions does she make to avoid alienating nonhunters?

5. What, if anything, about Causey's essay alienated you as a reader?

Ideas for Writing

1. What point that Causey makes can you respond to? What point might you expand on or refute?

2. How can hunting be made more ethical?

If responding to one of these ideas, go to the **Analysis** section of this chapter to begin developing ideas for your essay.

Outside Reading

E very academic discipline (such as sociology, chemistry, history, etc.) rests on, and puts forth, arguments. Even disciplines that seem objective (beyond opinion) are highly argumentative. Claims that seem uncontested are often debated, so that disciplines are always changing and evolving. Notice the following statements taken from various books used in college classes. What arguable claims are offered?

> Indeed, it is an important fact that we can think about combinations of pictures and words, abstract ideas and concrete ones, and so forth. Therefore, there must be somewhere in the mind that all these contents can be brought together "under one roof"; how else could we think about these combinations?
>
> *Cognition: Exploring the Science of the Mind*

> Constituted as they are of people with their inbuilt frailties, institutions are built of vices as well as virtues. When the vices—in-group versus out-group loyalties, for example—get compounded by numbers, the results can be horrifying to the point of suggesting (as some wag has) that the biggest mistake religion ever made was to get mixed up with people.
>
> *The World's Religions*

> Only one fear was greater than the fear of black rebellion in the new American colonies. That was the fear that discontented whites would join black slaves to overthrow the existing order. In the early years of slavery, especially, before racism as a way of thinking was firmly ingrained, while white indentured servants were often treated as badly as black slaves, there was a possibility of cooperation.
>
> *A People's History of the United States*

> An anxiety disorder, as the term suggests, has an unrealistic, irrational fear or anxiety of disabling intensity at its core and also as its principal and most obvious manifestation.
>
> *Abnormal Psychology and Modern Life*

Find an argument in another textbook, and use the following questions to analyze the claims:

1. How is the passage you found an argument?

2. What evidence or reasoning does the passage offer?

3. Does the passage make any attempt to convince the reader that the argument is sound (or is it assumed that the reader will accept the claims)?

4. What view of people or behavior or physical reality does it take?

5. Who might challenge the view put forward by the book? Why?

6. Does the passage use a metaphor to illustrate a concept? (How is the metaphor an argument?)

INVENTION

Responding to an argument involves some sophisticated thinking and planning, much of which depends on the nature and quality of the original argument. Therefore, the invention steps, which include finding an argument and developing a position, are vital. The following three sections are designed to help you through the invention process: specifically, to find an argument (in **Point of Contact**), develop a stance in relation to it (in **Analysis**), and make your argument relevant to a community of readers (in **Public Resonance**). After you work through these three sections, the **Delivery** section, which immediately follows, will help you craft your ideas into a written text.

Point of Contact

Finding an Argument

In Chapter 5: Making Arguments, the point of contact is a situation, behavior, or policy. But in this chapter, the point of contact is an actual argument. That is, you will be responding to an explicit argument that someone else has formulated or an argument that is expressed by many people. Remember that an argument need not be an essay; arguments are also made in advertisements, posters, and billboards. For example, notice the following political argument.

While this billboard is an advertisement for a radio station, it also argues that the Republican and Democratic presidential candidates for 2000 were, to say the least, unqualified, and that a third choice, Ralph Nader, was the best. At the time, many voters were unhappy with the two main candidates and with the process that keeps only two parties in control of presidential elections. The billboard was a response to those two candidates and their political parties.

To find an argument that may relate directly to the goings-on of your life and community, examine the following options:

- Local/city/campus newspapers
  Search the editorial pages and letters to the editor for arguments.

- National newspapers
  Newspapers (such as the *New York Times, USA Today, The Wall Street Journal*) also have editorial pages and columnists who offer arguments on various political and social issues.

- Magazines
  Magazines (such as *Newsweek,* the *Nation, Time, US News and World Report*) and monthly or quarterly magazines (such as *Utne Reader* or *The New Republic*) are filled with argumentative articles and personal columns on social and political issues.

- A publication from your major (such as *Education Journal, Nursing, Applied Science and Engineering*)
  Examine not only main articles, but also reviews and personal columns.
- Disciplinary databases (databases that focus on specific disciplines).
  Go to your library and check the electronic databases for your major or a closely related one.
- Web sites: You might explore argumentative Web sites. Go to your favorite search engine (such as Yahoo.com, Dogpile.com, Google.com) and enter topical keywords (*dogs, skateboards, economy*, etc.). You might find argumentative sites or pages more quickly if you combine potential topics with words such as *law, policy, argument, crisis,* or *debate.* (Remember to avoid prepositions (*in, of, on,* etc.) and verbs, and to join words with *and.*) For example:

> Search the Web: | **dogs and law and debate** | **Search**

You can also explore Web sites devoted to college, community, cultural, or political issues. For links, go to this textbook's Web site: http://english.heinle.com/maukmetz.

Choose an argument that interests you and that you can address with some authority. Once you have found a potentially interesting argument, answer the following questions:

- Why does the argument interest me?

  Because something or someone has been omitted?
  Because something or someone has been misrepresented?
  Because I disagree or agree with it?
  Because it raises an important issue that should be further discussed?
  Because it changed my mind on a topic?
  Because it is potentially important (helpful or dangerous)?

- What have I seen, experienced, or read that gives me some insight to the topic?

  Remember that you need not strongly disagree or agree with a particular argument. You can write a powerful response even if you are only in partial agreement/disagreement with a text.

Example: Daniel Bruno's Notes for Point of Contact Questions

Why does the argument interest me? Because something or someone has been omitted?
Peter Sacks talks about the sense of entitlement that many of today's students have. He talks about the negative aspects of this sense of entitlement, but not all students have this sense of entitlement. I know of many students who work hard and think that they are graded fairly. Some even think their grades are better than they deserve and classes aren't as challenging as they should be. Many students have the old-fashioned attitude of hard work.

Analysis

How Does the Argument Work?

When responding to an argument, you are not simply agreeing or disagreeing. You are evaluating claims and analyzing an issue—one that has already been defined by someone else. It is not enough to simply say, "I don't agree with this argument." Instead, it is important to discover *why* you agree or disagree with *particular points* in an argument. But even beyond your personal agreement or disagreement, you will also need to analyze the argument in front of you. That is, you will need to evaluate the soundness of the argument—and to do this, you will need some particular analytical tools.

Toulmin's Analytical Tools: Responding to arguments is such an important activity that theorists have actually developed tools designed specifically for the job. Stephen Toulmin has developed a powerful analytical system for arguments. In his perspective, every argument has a structure with interrelated parts. Using this, we can see how those parts relate, and how well they function. Here are the three basic elements:

Claim: The main argumentative position (or thesis) being put forward.

Grounds: The support for the position (evidence, examples, illustrations, etc.).

Warranting Assumption: The idea, often unstated, that connects the claim and the grounds— or that justifies the use of the grounds for the claim.

The warranting assumption lies (often hidden) between the claim and the grounds. See how the elements work in the following example:

Claim: Sports utility vehicles (SUVs) are dangerous.

Grounds: Many different models roll over easily.

Warranting Assumption: Vehicles that roll over easily are dangerous.

In this example, the rollover frequency of SUVs supports the claim that they are dangerous. The warranting assumption (vehicles that roll over easily are dangerous) lies between the claim and the grounds. The assumption is entirely acceptable; few people would challenge it. In many arguments, warranting assumptions go unstated because they are so obviously acceptable. But consider a different argument:

Claim: Sport utility vehicles are valuable to the average American driver.

Grounds: The extra-large carrying capacity and four-wheel drive capability meet traveling needs.

Warranting Assumption: Extra-large carrying capacity and four-wheel drive are valuable for the average American driver's traveling needs.

The assumption here is less acceptable. Someone might argue against the warranting assumption on the grounds that the average American driver does not need extra-large carrying capacity and four-wheel drive, and that these aspects are actually unnecessary for most drivers. Stating the assumption, thus, reveals a particular weakness in the argument and provides an opportunity to respond.

Dissecting arguments in this fashion allows for various critical opportunities. Writers can focus attention on (take exception or agree with) two different layers of an argument: grounds and/or assumptions. Consider, for example, the first claim: *Sport utility vehicles are dangerous.* Although the assumption *vehicles that roll over easily are dangerous* is acceptable, the grounds for the claim, that *many models roll over easily,* can be challenged. Someone might agree with the assumption but cite statistics showing that only a few models are prone to rollover accidents.

Claim:	Sport utility vehicles are dangerous.	
Grounds:	Many different models roll over easily.	(Arguable)
Warranting Assumption:	Vehicles that roll over easily are dangerous.	(Acceptable)

Responding with such statistics could help a writer challenge the original argument. In this case, the responding writer would be challenging the grounds. For other arguments, both the grounds and assumption might be arguable:

Claim:	The environment is not in danger from human influence.	
Grounds:	The environment is supporting the Earth's population today.	(Questionable)
Warranting Assumption:	The present human population directly illustrates the health of the environment.	(Arguable)

Here, both the grounds and the warranting assumption are questionable. While the grounds could be refuted on their own terms (by illustrating the vast numbers of people starving throughout the world), the more interesting response might point to the warranting assumption. The mere presence of people, of course, does *not* indicate the health of the environment. Someone, for instance, might easily point to dramatic increases in skin and other cancers to illustrate the effects of greenhouse gases and environmental contamination. In this case, discovering the warranting assumption would allow a responding writer to point out a flaw in the logic.

Activity: In groups, decide on the warranting assumption for the following claims and explain why each assumption is acceptable or questionable.

Claim: Consumerism is out of control in American life.
Grounds: Many people are going into debt to pay for luxury items.

Claim: America is losing a sense of community and social connectedness.
Grounds: The number of bowling teams has steadily decreased in the past 20 years.

Claim: People rely too much on technology that puts us out of touch with our neighbors and our own bodies.
Grounds: Leaf blowers are increasingly popular.

Claim: College students should not have to take required classes outside of their majors.
Grounds: Courses outside a chosen major are academically irrelevant.

Now go to the argument you have chosen to examine (from the **Point of Contact** section), and answer the following questions. They will help you to develop a response.

- What is the main claim/thesis?
- What are the grounds (means of support) for the main claim?
- Do the grounds support the claim sufficiently?
- What is the warranting assumption?
- Is the assumption acceptable or arguable?
- Can I prove that the assumption is incorrect?
- What else does the author of the argument assume (about life, identity, society, people's behavior, time, politics, human nature, etc.)?
- Is the issue defined correctly? (Is the focus too narrow? Too broad?)

One Step Further: Backing Up the Warranting Assumption: Occasionally, an assumption is stated and even defended in an argument. In these cases, the writers will attempt to support their assumptions with the same strategies they use to support their main claims (with evidence and appeals). If you are examining an argument that states and defends its assumptions, ask yourself if the support is sufficient and appropriate. Consider, for example, the following argument:

Claim: College classes should be shorter.

Grounds: Most students get bored in long classes.

Warranting Assumption: Class length should be determined by students' attention spans.

The assumption here might seem rather absurd, but it might seem less absurd if the writer dealt with it explicitly in an essay. Someone making such an argument might explain why college courses should work harder to appeal to students' inclinations since they are, after all, the clients. (Others might argue with the assumption by suggesting that students should expect their attitudes to change in college.)

Despite the content of the ideas, you can see that backing up a warranting assumption creates another layer to an argument. But remember that writers can argue for or against ideas directly or indirectly—they need not openly say, "The assumption is wrong and here's why." In fact, writers are often not so direct and instead offer claims that *suggest* the problems in the original argument.

Considering Purpose: Although Toulminian analysis is a valuable tool for examining arguments, it does not provide insight to every conceivable argument. If Toulminian analysis is not particularly helpful, you might use the evaluation strategies (explained in more detail in Chapter 7) to critically engage the original argument. Evaluating something, especially an argument, is more than simply celebrating or condemning it. You must develop criteria—principles that establish a means of judgment. Use the following questions to help develop criteria for judging the original argument:

- What is the purpose of the original argument?
- To what degree does the argument achieve that purpose?
- What elements help or hinder the purpose?

  The use or accuracy of evidence
  The structure of the argument
  The relevance of the issue to the audience
  The complexity of the stance
  The use of appeals

- If the argument is proposing a solution, is the solution realistic? Manageable?

Example: Daniel Bruno's Response to Analysis Questions

Is the issue correctly defined? Sacks defines the issue correctly as far as he defines it. Entitlement education has the negative effect that he says it does, but he fails, it seems, to discuss or focus on an important aspect of the issue, which is that some students, who don't have an entitlement mentality, learn a great deal in school while others, who do, don't learn a great deal, or very much at all. The students who have the entitlement mentality slide by while their classmates are learning more and more. The gap between the two groups widens. So, what does this mean to those students who feel entitled to good grades because they showed up (high school) or paid the tuition (college)? They get grades, but did they learn anything? Did they get an education?

Activity: In groups, examine the essays in this chapter. Each group should examine one essay and ask the following questions:

1. Does the author challenge (or support) an assumption from the original argument?
2. Does the author challenge (or support) the grounds used in the original argument?
3. How does the author support his or her own claims?
4. Does the author refer explicitly to his or her own assumptions?

The groups should then report their findings to the class.

Public Resonance

How Does the Topic Matter to Others?

Public resonance refers to the way in which a topic (or argument) involves a community. In most cases, an argument that you find will already have public resonance, especially if the argument comes from a newspaper, magazine, or journal. Your job, however, is not complete. A writer should always attempt to project the significance of the argument outward to the public.

Notice how Walker extends her topic outward:

> Perhaps we can liberate tobacco from those who have captured and abused it, enslaving the plant on large plantations, keeping it from freedom and its kin, and forcing it to enslave the world. Its true nature suppressed, no wonder it has become deadly. Maybe by sowing a few seeds of tobacco in our gardens and treating the plant with the reverence it deserves, we can redeem tobacco's soul and restore its self-respect.

Here, Walker expands a personal argument (one between her and her daughter) to a broader public—everyone participating in a smoking society.

As a responding writer, you can also draw attention to the effects (good or bad) of the original argument on its readers and on the community at large. To develop public resonance, examine the argument to which you will respond and answer the following questions:

- Did the argument have an impact on readers? Any person or people?
- How could the argument affect people (negatively or positively)?
- What other issues or situations does the argument relate to or address?
- How can I relate the argument to the needs/wants of my audience (or anyone who is involved in the topic)?

The above questions can be used to extend your thinking and develop your argument. Imagine a writer, Diana, who is responding to Ward Churchill's essay in Chapter 5: Making Arguments. In a discussion with peers, her topic argument takes on several layers:

How could the argument affect people (negatively or positively)?

Diana: Churchill's argument made me mad, and I think it may do the same to a lot of people. It basically suggests that everyone who supports certain professional sports teams is somehow tied to genocide.

Jack: I think that's his point, isn't it?

Diana: Yes, and I don't buy it, and I don't think most people would.

Jack: Does that mean that most people are right, or that most people don't see their own racism? Like Churchill says, during World War II most Americans were okay with the racist stereotypes of Japanese people. So, does that make such stereotyping okay?

Diana: Of course not. But making such an extreme point as Churchill seems counterproductive. When he comes out and says that wearing a Cleveland Indians baseball hat is like committing genocide, I think he's setting himself up for a certain amount of disagreement.

Marcus: But is he really making the connection that clearly?

Diana: Well, maybe not, but I think most people would see it that way . . . and they wouldn't like it.

Jack: Maybe that's an important point. Churchill's argument is probably more involved than what people want to hear.

Diana: And that's usually the case with arguments about race. But, still, calling mainstream America racist and making a connection between a national pastime and the Holocaust is going too far.

Jack: Why? Are you afraid of offending mainstream Americans who like sports?

Diana: No. I just wonder how valuable it is.

Jack: But isn't that what mainstream America said to the civil rights activists of the '60s? They didn't want activists to be offensive or confrontational, but most people are not going to change their thinking unless they are moved deeply—and sometimes that means they have to be offended.

Diana: So you're saying that mainstream America needs to be pushed before it will accept new ideas? Maybe.

Jack: Yeah, I think that's been shown throughout history. People don't just change their minds and suddenly become more enlightened.

Notice how Diana's thinking begins to extend beyond her initial reaction, and the discussion focuses on how Churchill's argument may, or may not, resonate with popular opinion. In Diana's case, the public resonance is the point of contention. She is not necessarily focused on the logic of Churchill's argument; she is concerned about the public acceptance of Churchill's points. And this can be an interesting place to begin her own argument.

Example: Daniel Bruno's Response to Public Resonance Questions

How can I relate the argument to the needs/wants of my audience (or anyone who is involved in the topic)? Some students feel entitled, which means expecting a good grade automatically, without working or learning anything. Some don't. The wants of the entitlement students are different than their needs. They want a grade or degree but need to learn and work. Interestingly, the students who feel entitled are the ones missing out, while the ones who don't feel entitled benefit. Maybe the students who believe they are entitled would benefit from thinking about the students who think differently, the ones who they will be competing against in the future, the ones who will be better prepared and have a better work ethic, perhaps. The entitlement-minded students may find out too late that others are working hard and developing good skills and attitudes.

Activities

1. Make a rough poster of your main idea and support. Try to represent your ideas in both images and text. Because you are developing a poster, which depends on big, attention-grabbing phrases, try to compact your ideas into intense phrases or short sentences.

2. With a classmate, discuss the main idea of your response. Explain the argument to which you are responding, and the issues you address in your response. (See Chapter 13: Everyday Rhetoric.)

DELIVERY

Obviously, responding to arguments is complicated because another set of claims must be engaged. But do not let those other claims confuse you. Resist chasing ideas throughout the original argument, and instead focus on a particular issue and then springboard into your own reasoning. The following sections (**Rhetorical Tools**, **Organizational Strategies**, **Writer's Voice**, and **Revision Strategies**) are designed to help you build a sophisticated and engaging text—one that emerges from your particular ideas. Each section points to important features or common concerns related to argumentative writing.

Rhetorical Tools

Developing Your Own Argument

Even though you are responding to someone else's argument, you are still creating your own argument—which will be stronger if the four elements (thesis, support, counterargument, concession) are appropriately used. Depending on your emphasis (which elements of the original argument you agree or disagree with), your argument might do one or more of the following:

- Redefine the issue according to your understanding.
- Argue for the value of a particular point or assumption in the original text.
- Argue against a particular point or assumption in the original text.
- Disprove the conclusions of the original argument.
- Prove the conclusions of the original argument by using different strategies (of evidence and/or appeal).
- Extend the original argument to include a broader set of ideas.
- Narrow the argument and suggest an important emphasis.

Considering Your Thesis: You will have an argument of your own to develop—one that relates to the specifics of the argument in front of you. It is not enough to say, "I disagree" or "I agree." A responding writer must develop an entire set of claims and grounds that refer back to a specific point or issue raised in the original argument. Use all of your analytical tools (such as Toulmin's strategies) to closely examine what is being said, and then develop a particular stance based on that examination. Make certain that you have a single main point rather than simply responding to each point made in the original argument. Decide what main point you want to address. Or, make a general statement that encapsulates your understanding of the original argument. In the example in the **Public Resonance** section, Diana might develop a working thesis that focuses on how people might respond to Churchill's argument: *Churchill's "Crimes against Humanity" reminds us that mainstream opinions often do not change unless they encounter shocking, even offensive, claims.*

Evolution of a Thesis	
The writer chooses an argument and explains the main idea:	*In "Crimes against Humanity," Ward Churchill argues that the use of Native American symbols for sports teams is racist.*
The writer focuses on the public resonance of the original argument:	*Churchill's argument made me mad, and I think it may do the same to a lot of people. It basically suggests that everyone who supports certain professional sports teams is somehow tied to genocide.*
The writer reconsiders the problem in light of a discussion:	*Mainstream America might need to be pushed before it will accept new ideas.*
The writer focuses the idea into a working thesis:	*Churchill's "Crimes against Humanity" reminds us that mainstream opinions often do not change unless they encounter shocking, even offensive, claims.*

Your thesis might also emerge from one particular point about the original argument. Notice Daniel Bruno's thesis—which emerges from his reaction to Peter Sacks's book, *Generation X Goes to College*:

> Sacks shows how consumerism has invaded education, leading some students to expect good grades for little effort. But he fails, it seems, to emphasize enough a most harmful effect of this sense of entitlement.

Bruno's essay then goes on to argue about the effects of this "sense of entitlement." While Sacks's book provides a topic, Bruno's understanding of the topic generates an interesting position outside of the original argument.

Use the following questions to help generate the thesis of your argumentative response:

- With what points do I agree or disagree?

  The nature of the issue
  The relevance or meaning of examples
  The use of certain key terms
  The use of certain names/people
  The scope of the issue (how the writer defines or explains it)

- What unstated assumptions (about life, identity, government, truth, right, wrong, education, comedy, art, community, sports, war, family, gender, commitment, love, sex, etc.) does the writer have?
- How are my assumptions different from or similar to those of the writer?
- How is the original argument too narrow or too exclusive?
- How can I extend or broaden the original argument?

Using Support: Consider using the same support strategies you would use for any argument essay. Remember that you have the whole world beyond the original argument to support your points. You can use various forms of evidence (such as personal testimony, examples, facts, as well as allusions to history, popular culture and news events) and appeals. (See p. 247 for help in developing evidence and appeals for your argument.)

Counterarguing: As you address opposing claims in the original text, you are counterarguing. In other words, since you are directly addressing someone else's perspective, you are making a counterargument. But be sure that you specifically express which points you want to counter. Notice, for example, Ann Causey, who responds to a set of claims rather than to one particular text but still addresses those claims individually as she develops her argument:

> Those who support hunting usually respond by citing data. They enumerate the acres of habitat protected by hunting-generated funds; how many game species have experienced population increases due to modern game management; how much the economy is stimulated by hunting-related expenditures; how effectively modern game laws satisfy the consumptive and recreational interests of the hunting community today while assuring continued surpluses of game for future hunters; and how hunters, more than most citizens, care deeply about ecosystem integrity and balance and the global environment.
>
> While these statements may be perfectly true, they're almost totally irrelevant to the question. . . .

As you develop your own argument, examine the particular points of the original argument with which you disagree or find fault. You may find yourself agreeing or confirming much of the original argument. If so, you should still consider opposing claims. Consider the following questions:

- Beyond the author of the original argument, who might disagree with my position? Why?
- What reasons do people have for disagreeing with me?
- What evidence would support an opposing argument?

Conceding and Qualifying Points: When responding to argument, a writer should be especially mindful of giving credit to others' points. For example, in Bruno's response to Peter Sacks's book, he acknowledges several important elements of Sacks's argument:

> His final paragraph before the epilogue says, "Let's create a system that encourages people like Andie at least as much as the ones who don't give a damn" (187). Thus, Sacks shows that today's students are a more diverse group—in skill level, background, and attitude toward education—than has ever before been gathered together in the college classroom.

Although Bruno argues that Sacks's argument falls short in some ways, he acknowledges the value of several points. This shows that Bruno is not one-sided and that his perspective is larger than his own argument.

Answering the following questions will help you to see possible concessions for your own argument:

- Does the original argument make any valid points?

- Does my argument make any large, but necessary, leaps? (Should I acknowledge them?)

- Do I ask my audience to imagine a situation that is fictional? (Should I acknowledge the potential shortcomings of a fictional or hypothetical situation?)

- Do I ask my audience to accept generalizations? (Should I acknowledge those generalizations?)

How is this bumper sticker an example of making a concession?

Remembering Logical Fallacies: As we suggest in Chapter 5: Making Arguments, logical fallacies are logical stumbles—gaps or shortcomings in reasoning. Examine the original argument closely to determine if it is free of fallacies. Finding logical fallacies in an argument can help you to generate a response. For example, in the following passage, the writer points to a logical shortcoming in the original argument:

> Smith argues that incoming college students cannot handle the intellectual rigors of academia. He characterizes an entire generation as "undisciplined and whimsical." But like all arguments about entire generations, Smith's depends upon a hasty generalization. The truth about today's college students is far more complex than Smith's assertions, and any statement that seeks to characterize them as a whole should be looked upon with suspicion.

See a list and examples of logical fallacies on pages 252–253.

Activity: Explain why the statements below are logical fallacies, and give the name of the fallacy.

1. We cannot say what is right because everyone is entitled to his or her own opinion.
2. If we don't teach Shakespeare in high schools, our cultural values will certainly erode.
3. On the road of life, there are drivers and there are passengers.
4. With its harsh sounds and lyrics, heavy metal music has caused many teenagers to take their own lives.
5. Because Ronald Reagan was an actor before he became president, Keanu Reeves would probably also make a good president.

Organizational Strategies
Addressing Common Concerns

Should I Quote the Original Argument? Quoting is like putting a spotlight on a key passage. Responding writers sometimes want to draw attention not only to a point, but also to the particular way the author delivered it. A quote can flag the shortcoming in the original text:

> In her argument, Ross claims banks "only share customers' personal information with affiliated companies" (43). However, an "affiliated company" in the present economic environment can be any company with which a bank does business. Because most financial institutions are parts of huge conglomerates, they can be justified in "sharing" information with a practically unlimited number of companies seeking to exploit people and invade their personal lives. In other words, Ross's argument only further conceals the exploitive policies of many financial institutions.

Sometimes writers quote the original argument to illustrate the importance or value of a particular point, or to extend an idea. Notice Bruno's quotation of Peter Sacks:

> While motivated students suffer in our too-lax system, so do the un- (or under-) motivated ones. And these students, who need our help the most, are the ones most cheated. As Sacks says, "I now believe the students are the real victims of this systematic failure of the entitlement mindset" (189). The students who are allowed to slide by, who are content to slide by, who perhaps don't even realize that they are sliding by because sliding by is all they know—those students find themselves arriving at college less prepared and less motivated than the "better students." And what happens next? Sadly, the gap between these two groups grows even wider.

Here, Bruno builds his argument from Sacks's point. That is, he begins with Sacks's idea, and then goes further to show the greater extent of the problem.

Using quotation can be a powerful strategy in drawing attention to key passages. However, be careful not to quote too often. (Notice how seldom the writers in this chapter use direct quotation.) Rather than quote the original argument (or any outside source), you have two other tools available: summary and paraphrase.

Integrating Summary: A summary is a restated and abbreviated version of the original passage. Writers can abbreviate (shorten) any length passage (from a paragraph to an entire chapter). For instance, in the introduction to his essay, Daniel Bruno summarizes Peter Sacks's book in a few sentences. Also notice how Betsy Taylor briefly summarizes Schor's essay (see ¶ 2).

Integrating Paraphrase: A paraphrase is a restatement in your own words of an original passage. Occasionally (but not in this chapter), writers restate ideas in their own words without abbreviating, or shrinking, the original passage. This is done when writers want to discuss particular points in great detail.

> For more information on quoting, summary, and paraphrase, see Chapter 12: Research and Writing.

How Should I Structure My Response? The structure of your essay largely depends on what you intend to address from the original argument. You can use some standard organization strategies for argument essays, such as:

Point A (from original argument)
Your evaluation and response

Point B (from original argument)
Your evaluation and response

Point C (from the original argument)
Your evaluation and response

Etc.

Of course, you might have points D, E, F, and so forth. And each of your evaluations and responses can vary in length, from a sentence to several paragraphs, depending on the main point of your essay.

You might decide that the opposing viewpoint requires significant explanation, and that it would be best to keep all your points grouped together rather than separating them with passages from the original:

Point A (from original argument)
Point B (from original argument)
Point C (from original argument)
Your evaluation and response to A
Your evaluation and response to B
Your evaluation and response to C

> Remember that the turnabout paragraph (see also p. 257) is a good strategy for counterargument. A turnabout paragraph begins with one point, and then changes directions at some point—always giving the reader a clear indication of that change.

How Can I Integrate Toulminian Analysis, Argument, and Counterargument?

Responding to arguments might involve various elements and rhetorical tools. But it need not be confusing. You might consider all the elements as ingredients of the bigger argumentative project. Notice how Ann Causey analyzes (or inspects particular points within) the hunting debate and then evaluates those points.

> Antihunters insist that nontrivial reasons be given for intentional human-inflicted injuries and deaths—or that these injuries and deaths be stopped. An eminently reasonable request.
>
> Even when hunters acknowledge the significance of the pain and suffering inflicted through hunting, they too often offer in defense that they feel an obligation to give back more than they take, and that hunters and wildlife professionals successfully have met this obligation. Granted, it may be that the overall benefits to humans and other species that accrue from hunting outweigh the costs to the hunted. Nevertheless, this utilitarian calculation fails to provide moral justification for hunting.

This passage works to support a broader point about the hunting debate. Causey is analyzing others' claims about hunting, and at the same time building her own argument about the debate. In short, the analysis helps to support her argument. Similarly, Walker uses analysis to support her argument:

> When I travel to Third World countries I see many people like my father and daughter. There are large billboards directed at them both: the tough, "take-charge," or dapper old man, the glamorous, "worldly" young woman, both puffing away. In these poor countries, as in American ghettos and on reservations, money that should be spent for food goes instead to the tobacco companies; over time, people starve themselves of both food and air, effectively weakening and addicting their children, eventually eradicating themselves.

In pointing to the power of billboards and to the damaging effects of cigarettes (an analytical move), Walker builds momentum for her argument.

> Notice that Walker also uses narrative and personal memory as support for her argument—a viable and engaging strategy.

Writer's Voice

Exploring Options

Remember that argument need not be aggressive; in fact, argument does not have to be confrontational at all. A good argument attracts readers and engages those who might oppose the claims being made; a bad or unsuccessful argument alienates its readers. In responding to argument, you should be especially cautious not to dismiss the original argument entirely; after all, if you decided to address the argument in the first place, it must have some value—or some potential impact.

Because argument can potentially create hostility and turn people away from each other, Carl Rogers developed an argumentative perspective that emphasizes building connections between different positions. People who do Rogerian argument look for similarities, rather than differences, between arguments. Such a strategy creates an engaging voice—one that invites exploration of ideas rather than harsh dismissals. Notice, for example, Betsy Taylor's Rogerian strategy:

> Schor's other principles ring true. Millions of Americans obviously share her call for more fun, less stuff. Millions are opting to downshift, choosing to make less money in search of more time. A growing number of people also affirm her call for responsible consumption—a call for a much higher consciousness about the environmental and human costs of each consumer decision we make. Her call to democratize consumer markets seems a bit naïve, since humans have probably always sought to define themselves in part through their stuff. But in an age of excessive materialism, the times may be ripe to challenge the dominant ethos. Perhaps we can make it cool to shun fashion and footgear with corporate logos and redefine hip as simple, real, and non-commercial.

Although she finds one of Schor's ideas "a bit naïve," Taylor focuses much of her essay on the value of Schor's argument. Similarly, as you examine argument, see if you can find claims and/or assumptions that resonate with your own. (But also be cautious to avoid excessive enthusiasm and simply celebrate the argument without offering an analysis of the ideas.)

Avoiding Character Slams:
Be careful not to belittle the author(s) of the original argument—or anyone who might ascribe to it. Name-calling and coarse language, after all, work against a writer and suggest an unsophisticated and hostile state of mind. Causey's argument is especially interesting because it walks in the middle of two antagonistic sides of the hunting debate. And while she points to some logical problems on both sides, she also manages to stay focused on the logic of the claims rather than the character of hunters and anti-hunters. Notice the following passage, in which she examines the argument of a particular hunter:

> In a hunting video titled "Down to Earth," a contemporary rock star and self-proclaimed "whack master" and "gutpile addict" exhorts his protégés to "whack 'em, stack 'em, and pack 'em." After showing a rapid sequence of various animals being hit by his arrows, the "whack master" kneels and sarcastically asks for "a moment of silence" while the viewer is treated to close-up, slow-motion replays of the hits, including sickening footage of some animals that clearly are gut shot or otherwise sloppily wounded. A reverence for life? Such behavior would seem to demonstrate shocking *irreverence*, arrogance, and hubris.

Notice how Causey carefully manages to step around the "whack-master's" character, and instead focuses on what the "behavior would seem to demonstrate."

The Invisible/Present "I":

Often writers wonder if they should include the first-person pronoun *I* in their writing. It may be especially tempting to include *I* in argumentative writing. However, many academic disciplines favor writing that does not draw attention to the writer (to the *I*). And writing for English courses, which often focuses on personal insights and reflection, avoids unnecessary attention to *I*. This is because argumentative writing implies or assumes the presence of the writer. In other words, every claim or position in a paper that is not attributed to some other source belongs to the writer; therefore, phrases such as "I think that," "In my opinion," or "I believe," are often unnecessary.

However, occasionally the first-person pronoun can be used to make a distinction between an outside argument and the writer's own opinion. If the writer is dealing with several ideas or outside opinions, he or she might decide that using the first-person pronoun refocuses attention on the main argument. Notice Taylor's strategy:

> Progressives can dogmatically dismiss these forces as elements of religious dogmatism or New Age narcissism, or they can connect with this churning. I would argue that a politics of consumption—and we need a better name for this—should include guiding principles of humility and compassion.

Here, Taylor uses the phrase "I would argue" to draw attention to "the only principle" she wants to raise, the only idea that is excluded from Schor's argument. Although this strategy is helpful, it is still unnecessary; that is, Taylor could still make the distinction without attention to *I*. And so it often becomes a choice about formality and style: inserting *I* can help create a less formal or more intimate style.

Activity: If you are enrolled in multiple courses, ask each instructor about his or her stance on first-person pronouns in writing. You might also ask about the standard practice of your major, or examine a professional journal in your field of study to see how (and how much) first-person pronouns are used.

Consider Tone: If you are responding to a specific argument, you are encountering a tone (the color or mood of a writer's voice). Sometimes writers who are responding to an argument choose to mimic the tone of the original argument. In other words, if you are responding to a very sober and formal argument, you might do well to respond in kind. On the other hand, changing the tone of a discussion is often a powerful rhetorical tool. When writers want to challenge an argument, they may not only argue against the ideas but also shift the tone to their own particular liking. For example, imagine a politician arguing against the comedic rants of Howard Stern. The politician might put forth a very sober argument against Stern—thereby arguing on her own ground rather than on Stern's comedic turf. The opposite is often done: many writers (and public figures) argue informally to challenge a seemingly formal argument. Consider programs such as *Mad TV* and *Saturday Night Live* or Michael Moore's film *Roger & Me.* They respond to "serious" political arguments by spoofing them—by revealing their flaws and deliberately changing their tone.

Changing the tone of an argument can even be very subtle. For instance, the debate about smoking is often public, since it involves issues such as healthcare policies, laws, and cigarette advertising. But Alice Walker reorients the argument. Her tone, her attention to the personal, to the intimate, to the familial, casts the argument in a particular way:

> There is a deep hurt that I feel as a mother. Some days it is a feeling of futility. I remember how carefully I ate when I was pregnant, how patiently I taught my daughter how to cross a street safely. For what, I sometimes wonder; so that she can wheeze through most of her life feeling half her strength, and then die of self-poisoning, as her grandfather did?

And such an intimate and personal tone is certainly the opposite of political arguments that defend cigarette smoking and tobacco companies. In other words, Walker's tone, in itself, is a stance against smoking.

As you examine your chosen argument (the one to which you are responding) and your own position, consider tone. Ask yourself the following:

- Has the tone been established by someone else's argument?
- Do I want to change the tone slightly, or dramatically?
- What effect would a change in tone have on the argument?

Activities

1. Write a memo to your instructor in which you briefly explain your rhetorical strategy for this essay: which tools you used, and why; what major rhetorical decisions you made about this essay; which ones you had trouble deciding about.
2. Write a brief summary of your essay and exchange it with a classmate. Then write a memo in response to your classmate's summary, suggesting at least seven counterarguments a reader is likely to have while reading his or her essay. (See Chapter 13: Everyday Rhetoric.)

Revision Strategies

evising an essay in which you respond to an argument is much like revising any other essay. You must step back, allowing space between you and your essay, and re-see the entire piece. An additional concern with this type of essay is to make sure you have accurately represented the argument to which you are responding. Are you dealing with it seriously? Are you being fair? Are you being persuasive—making counterarguments and concessions where necessary? Have you controlled your tone and avoided insulting or offending your reader?

Consider the following revision strategies:

- Review this chapter, keeping your essay in mind. You might (1) explore your **Invention** notes, looking for helpful ideas and/or respond further in writing to relevant Invention questions; (2) review the **Rhetorical Tools, Organizational Strategies,** and **Writer's Voice** sections with an eye toward making appropriate changes; and (3) review several of the essays, noting the way the writers in this chapter approached this type of essay.

- Set aside at least as much time to revise as you took with invention and delivery.

- Create distance between you and your writing by getting away from it for a few days if possible or a few hours at least.

- Read your paper aloud to hear how it sounds, or have someone else read it aloud to you.

- Print out a hard copy of your paper and read it carefully in a different place than where you wrote it.

- Figure out your writing strategy by noticing how the parts of your essay work together to support your main point. Consider making an outline of your essay to help you see this.

- Have someone else read and respond to your essay.

For ideas about **Peer Review,** see page 50.

Global Revision Questions

Invention (What have you learned by exploring your topic?)

- **Point of Contact:** What other ideas did you consider writing about before selecting this one? Why was this idea more worth pursuing than the others?

- **Analysis:** How has your exploration of this topic gone beyond your initial ideas and questions about it? In what ways have your ideas moved beyond your initial biases and perceptions—and beyond the common beliefs of your reader?

- **Public Resonance:** How might your essay be relevant to, or matter to, your reader? And what might be the consequence(s) of your essay? How might the reader think or act differently after reading it?

Delivery (What writing decisions have you made as part of your writing strategy?)

■ **Rhetorical Tools:** What writing decisions have you made to ensure the reader a better chance of understanding what you mean? Reexamine your rhetorical strategy for this essay. What rhetorical tools discussed earlier in this chapter have you used to help get your point across? What other tools might you consider using?

   • What is the main claim of your response, and how have you conveyed that claim to the reader? What, besides your *intended* main idea, might the reader imagine your main idea to be? How might you help the reader hear what you are trying to say?

   • How will the reader know what argument you are responding to and why you are responding to it? Where might you provide more evidence for your response? Or where might a different type of evidence help the reader to better understand your response? What might be the reader's likely responses to your claims and their support? How have you anticipated these responses and responded accordingly, making appropriate counterarguments and concessions? How might your title, introduction, and conclusion provide more helpful information regarding the main point of your essay?

   • What information can you weed out of your essay to make it more focused? What information about the original argument (the one to which you are responding) could be deleted? Where might the reader lose interest or get bogged down because you have over-explained or restated an idea? While drafting your essay, what information crept in but can now be eliminated? What information might you delete to allow space for more relevant information?

■ **Organizational Strategies:** You might begin by describing, or outlining, the structure of your essay to get a better sense of your overall organizational strategy. How have you arranged these elements for ease of reading? How might you rearrange the elements (claims; evidence; concessions; counterarguments) to allow the reader to better understand your ideas? How might you rearrange ideas within paragraphs? What ideas might be more helpful to the reader if placed earlier, or later, or near some other idea? How might connections and relationships between ideas be made more clear to the reader?

■ **Writer's Voice:** Describe your writer's voice. Is it appropriate in this essay? When drafting a response, writers may sometimes slip into a harsh or aggressive tone or resort to character slams. How might a reader perceive you, the writer, in this essay? What about your writer's voice is inviting to the reader? What about your writer's voice might alienate the reader? What changes might make your writer's voice more inviting?

■

CONSIDERING CONSEQUENCES

While writers consider consequences throughout the writing process, this text draws attention to them here as a post-writing activity, to remind you that after an idea is communicated, consequences follow. The act of writing does not end with turning in an essay or writing a letter. Instead, that is just the beginning.

Responding to an argument is an everyday activity. We respond to arguments, hoping that what we say will have a positive consequence—that it will affect the way another person thinks or acts. What might be the consequences of your essay for this chapter? That is, what effect might your ideas have on your reader's thoughts and actions? Consider these questions:

- Will the reader better understand the issue about which you wrote?
- Is the reader likely to think or behave differently?
- What might be the benefits to others? How might others be harmed?
- Who besides your instructor might benefit from your ideas?
- How might what you wrote about be affected?
- What might be the effect of these consequences on you, the writer?

Activities

The Consequences of Your Essay

1. List as many individuals as you can imagine whose thinking and/or actions might change if they were to read the essay you wrote for this chapter. For each individual you list, name the possible change in his or her thinking and/or action. (As you consider consequences upon your reader, consider the "ripple effect" of those consequences. If your reader thinks or behaves differently, what is the impact of that thinking or behavior on others?)

2. Ask someone to read your essay and write down what he or she thinks its consequences might be on various readers. Then discuss with that person how the potential consequences of your ideas contribute to the overall quality of the essay.

3. How might the consequences of your argument be different if you express your ideas in one of the following ways?

- A letter to the editor in your local paper
- A poster in a local coffee house
- A painting or photograph in an art gallery
- A speech on campus
- A play performed in a local theatre
- A Hollywood movie
- A letter to a friend
- A music CD
- A Web site
- A grassroots movement

The Consequences of the Chapter Readings

1. How might you think or act differently after having read one of the essays in this chapter? How might you benefit from, or be harmed by, your new way of thinking? How might *others* benefit from, or be harmed by, your new way of thinking and/or acting?

2. How might someone famous benefit from reading one of the essays in this chapter? Match an essay in this chapter to a particular famous person. Then discuss how the essay might influence that person's ideas.

3. How might one of the writers of this chapter be influenced by his or her own writing? For example, what might *the writer* have learned, or discovered, as a result of writing and how might he or she now think or act differently?

The Consequences of Everyday Responses

1. In groups, create a list of arguments that have been made in writing. To generate your list, think in categories: for example, arguments about food, arguments about shelter, arguments about clothing; or arguments about local concerns, arguments about national concerns, arguments about international concerns. The categories will help you to generate ideas. Come up with about 20 arguments, and then determine what each argument is a response to.

2. Select one of the arguments you listed for #1 above that might be a response to different arguments. That is, as you tried to determine what argument it was a response to, you thought of several possibilities. Explain in writing what different arguments it might be a response to, and how it responds to each.

3. What argument, written or otherwise, do you think requires a strong response? For example, is someone or some group arguing for or against a certain behavior or attitude that you think is extremely harmful to certain individuals or to society overall? Write down the argument, how it is being made, and what response you think is called for.

Considering Images

1. Find a popular visual image that makes an argument you think is harmful to certain individuals or to society overall. In writing, explain the negative consequences of the image.

2. Continue to explore the image you found for #1 above. What argument is the image a response to? That is, how is the image itself a response to some other argument? Might the image have any positive consequences? What other popular images are a response to the image you found for #1 above?

Writing, Speech, and Action

EVERYDAY RHETORIC

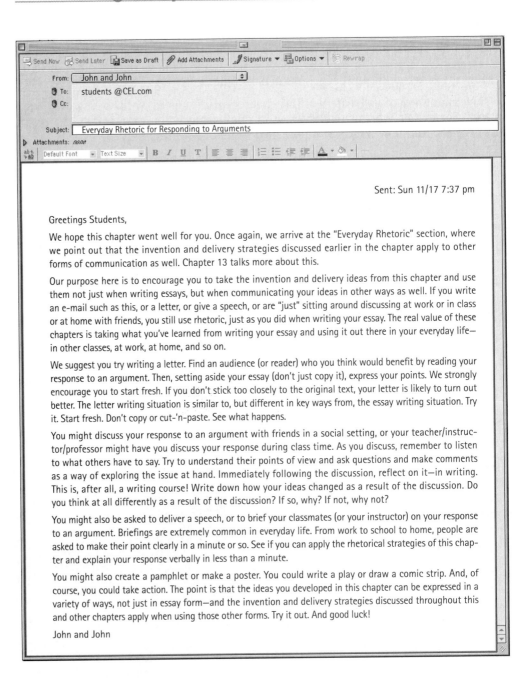

Sent: Sun 11/17 7:37 pm

Greetings Students,

We hope this chapter went well for you. Once again, we arrive at the "Everyday Rhetoric" section, where we point out that the invention and delivery strategies discussed earlier in the chapter apply to other forms of communication as well. Chapter 13 talks more about this.

Our purpose here is to encourage you to take the invention and delivery ideas from this chapter and use them not just when writing essays, but when communicating your ideas in other ways as well. If you write an e-mail such as this, or a letter, or give a speech, or are "just" sitting around discussing at work or in class or at home with friends, you still use rhetoric, just as you did when writing your essay. The real value of these chapters is taking what you've learned from writing your essay and using it out there in your everyday life—in other classes, at work, at home, and so on.

We suggest you try writing a letter. Find an audience (or reader) who you think would benefit by reading your response to an argument. Then, setting aside your essay (don't just copy it), express your points. We strongly encourage you to start fresh. If you don't stick too closely to the original text, your letter is likely to turn out better. The letter writing situation is similar to, but different in key ways from, the essay writing situation. Try it. Start fresh. Don't copy or cut-'n-paste. See what happens.

You might discuss your response to an argument with friends in a social setting, or your teacher/instructor/professor might have you discuss your response during class time. As you discuss, remember to listen to what others have to say. Try to understand their points of view and ask questions and make comments as a way of exploring the issue at hand. Immediately following the discussion, reflect on it—in writing. This is, after all, a writing course! Write down how your ideas changed as a result of the discussion. Do you think at all differently as a result of the discussion? If so, why? If not, why not?

You might also be asked to deliver a speech, or to brief your classmates (or your instructor) on your response to an argument. Briefings are extremely common in everyday life. From work to school to home, people are asked to make their point clearly in a minute or so. See if you can apply the rhetorical strategies of this chapter and explain your response verbally in less than a minute.

You might also create a pamphlet or make a poster. You could write a play or draw a comic strip. And, of course, you could take action. The point is that the ideas you developed in this chapter can be expressed in a variety of ways, not just in essay form—and the invention and delivery strategies discussed throughout this and other chapters apply when using those other forms. Try it out. And good luck!

John and John

Exploring Visual Rhetoric

I t can be argued that images, too, use rhetoric. And by looking at how images work, we can apply some of the important concepts of rhetoric, not just to writing and speaking, but to images as well. Looking at visual rhetoric can also help us to better understand how rhetoric is used in writing and speech.

Analyze This Chapter's Opening Image: Analyze this chapter's opening image using the "Analyzing an Image" questions in Chapter 13 on page 694. What seems to be the main idea of the image? How do the particular elements of the image—content, framing, focus, and so on—help to convey that idea?

1. Explain your analysis in several paragraphs, being certain to show how particular elements of the image help to convey a main idea.

2. Discuss your analysis with several people, exploring through discussion how your understanding of the image is similar to or different from theirs. Following the discussion, write down the main similarities and differences in your viewpoints, and explain how your ideas about the image developed or changed through discussion. How did the discussion influence your ideas about the image?

3. Imagine one change in this chapter's opening image. For example, you might add an object, frame the image differently, or take the photo from a different angle. Make one imaginary change in the image and explain how that change might alter the image's message.

Find an Image That Relates to Your Essay: What image might you use in conjunction with the essay you wrote for this chapter?

1. Write a caption for the image.

2. Write an essay explaining the relationship between the image and your text. Consider the following ideas:

   - How does the image support or help to explain the text of the essay?
   - What is the theme of the image? What idea does it convey?
   - What specific elements of the image convey the main idea and the support for that idea?
   - How might the reader view the image differently after having read your essay?
   - How might the reader be confused by the relationship of your essay and image?

3. Show the image to several people, and ask each person to read your essay. Then ask them how they now view the image differently.

Create a Photo Essay: Respond to some argument by creating a visual essay, consisting of at least four separate images. You may take or find photographs, or draw the images yourself. You may arrange them on a single page, present them as a slide show, or display them in some other way. After selecting and arranging the images, explain in a brief essay how your photo essay is a response to an argument. Use the "Analyzing an Image" questions on page 694 and the **Invention** and **Delivery** sections of this chapter for help.

Considering Other Images in This Chapter

1. Explain how one of the images in this chapter is a response to an argument. What argument is it responding to? And what argument does the image make in response? To help you explain specifically how the image makes an argument, use the "Analyzing an Image" questions in Chapter 13 as well any information in the **Invention** and **Delivery** sections of this chapter.

    A. Present your ideas from #1 above to your classmates in the form of a one-minute briefing.
    B. Send an e-mail to your instructor presenting your ideas from #1 above.
    C. Write a memo to your instructor presenting your ideas from #1 above.

2. Discuss your idea from #1 above with several classmates, asking them to help you develop support for your claim—that the image makes the particular argument that you say it does. Then write a memo to your instructor explaining how the discussion was or was not helpful in developing your ideas about the image. Be specific in explaining what new ideas you discovered.

3. Select one image from this chapter and explain what response it invites. What argument does the image make and how does the image encourage the reader to think?

Considering Images from Everyday Life

1. Take a picture of, or describe in writing, a billboard. Explain how the billboard responds to some argument. If the billboard has an image, analyze it using the "Analyzing an Image" questions on page 694 and explain how the image helps to respond to an argument.

2. Find an image in a grocery store or deli that is a response to an argument. What argument does the image respond to, and what argument does it make in response? Analyze the image and explain how its elements (content, framing, and so on) help it to make an argument.

3. Watch television for at least 30 minutes, looking for images that make arguments. Take notes, writing down what images you see and what arguments they might be making. Then consider how each argument might be a response to some other argument. Choose the most interesting example and explain how the image from television makes an argument in response to some other argument.

4. Do clothes make an argument? What about hair? Visit the mall or look through current magazines, recording your observations. What argument does a particular fashion or style make? What might that argument be a response to?

5. Look through other chapters in this book until you find several images that may be responding to an argument. In writing, explain how each image functions as a responding argument. Use the "Analyzing an Image" questions to help you explain how the images express ideas.

Responding to the ROTC Sign

1. Create your own sign encouraging students to join ROTC, and then give it to a classmate to write responses on.

2. Create a sign encouraging people to do _____, and then give it to a classmate to write a response.

3. Revise the sign you made for #1 or #2 above so that you make your argument clearly and it is more difficult for others to respond to what it says. Then compare the text of the original sign to the revised sign. What changes did you make and why?

4. Write an essay arguing the point of the original ROTC sign.

5. Write an essay arguing the point made by the responses written on the ROTC sign.

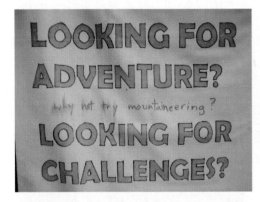

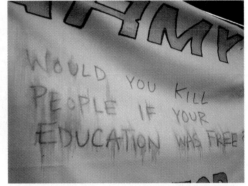

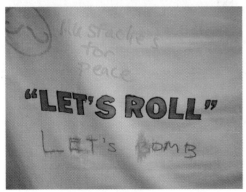

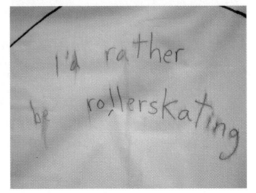

7

Chapter Contents

■ **Readings**

Evaluating

Can we evaluate and be entertained at the same time? What is the relationship between evaluation and entertainment?

> **"** The trouble with normal is
> it always gets worse. **"**
>
> —*Bruce Cockburn*

Evaluating is the act of judging the value or worth of a given subject. We make informal judgments constantly throughout our daily lives. For example, we decide that we like a particular car more than another, or that one song on the radio is better than another. Such evaluations are informal because they involve little analysis; that is, we do not usually take the time to thoroughly analyze each song we hear on the radio as we are sweeping through stations. We also take part in formal evaluation, a process that goes beyond an expression of likes and dislikes: teachers must evaluate student performance; jury members must evaluate events, people, and testimony; voters must evaluate political candidates; members of unions must evaluate contracts; managers must evaluate employees; executives must evaluate business proposals; citizens must evaluate laws and lawmakers. In such situations, mere personal tastes cannot dictate evaluative decisions. Instead, a formal process—sometimes entirely intellectual, sometimes organized in visible steps—is necessary for sound evaluation.

The ability to make formal evaluations is essential to academic thinking and writing:

- Biologists at a national conference evaluate the success of a particular molecular research process.
- Law enforcement students are assigned to evaluate a new highway safety program.
- Crime lab scientists must evaluate a particular procedure for gathering evidence.
- University civil engineers evaluate a downtown rezoning plan.
- English professors evaluate a new textbook for the department literature courses.
- Education faculty members and graduate students evaluate the state's controversial new standardized tests.
- Art students must evaluate a set of paintings from the early Modernist era.

Much literary work is also evaluative. William Copeland's book *Generation X*, for example, may be viewed as an evaluation of the culture created by the baby boomer generation. Toni Morrison's *Jazz* may be seen as an evaluation of 1920s culture. And Jonathan Swift's *Gulliver's Travels*, perhaps one of the most famous examples of evaluative literature, critiques (or *satirizes*) political and economic institutions of eighteenth-century England.

Whether one is an author, jury member, civil engineer, or voting citizen, the person who can evaluate well and make judgments outside of his or her personal tastes is able to make valuable decisions, to help distinguish the best course of action, to clarify options when many seem available. And in a culture that is increasingly filled with choices (among political candidates, retirement plans, religious paths, and lifestyles, to name just a few), it is increasingly important for the literate citizen to evaluate well.

7 This chapter will help you develop a formal evaluation of a particular subject and communicate your evaluation in writing. The following essays will provide valuable insight to various evaluation strategies. After reading the essays, you can find a subject in one of two ways:

1. Go to the **Point of Contact** section to find a topic from your everyday life.
2. Choose one of the **Ideas for Writing** that follow the essays.

After finding a subject, go to the **Analysis** section to begin developing the evaluation.

READINGS

The essays in this chapter all make judgments, and in doing so, present the subjects to the reader in a particular light. In other words, each writer gives an opinion about the subject (be it a theme park, television show, etc.) and then supports that opinion by showing selected details of the subject. While the writers give some form of overview (some general summary about the subject), they also focus the reader's attention on the details that support their judgments. This is fair play. In drawing attention to certain details (and ignoring others), they are simply creating argumentative positions—the positions they want the reader to accept. Notice, also, that the writers tend to draw on support outside their subjects; that is, they refer to other like subjects to show particular points (to give credibility to their judgments). Both Ebert and Benlow, for instance, point to other movies, Stayer refers to another theme park, and Bell reminds the reader of other television shows. This strategy helps the reader to share in the writer's perspective.

Star Wars

Roger Ebert

Roger Ebert, one of America's best-known film critics, appears on television and writes for the Chicago Sun-Times. *He has written many books and articles as well as the screenplay for* Beyond the Valley of the Dolls *(1970). As you read this evaluation, which originally appeared in* Sunday Showcase *in 1997, identify Ebert's overall judgment of the film (good, bad, important, harmful, etc.) as well as the standards upon which he bases that judgment.*

1   To see *Star Wars* again after 20 years is to revisit a place in the mind. George Lucas's space epic has colonized our imaginations, and it is hard to stand back and see it simply as a motion picture because it has so completely become part of our memories. It's as goofy as a children's tale, as shallow as an old Saturday afternoon serial, as corny as Kansas in August—and a masterpiece. Those who analyze its philosophy do so, I imagine, with a smile in their minds. May the Force be with them.

2   Like *Birth of a Nation* and *Citizen Kane*, *Star Wars* was a technical watershed that influenced many movies that came after. These films have little in common, except that they came along at crucial moments in cinema history, when new methods were ripe for synthesis. *Birth of a Nation* brought together the developing language of shots and editing. *Citizen Kane* married special effects, advanced sound, a new photographic style, and a freedom from linear storytelling. *Star Wars* melded a new generation of special effects with the high-energy action picture; it linked space opera and soap opera, fairy tales and legend, and packaged them as a wild visual ride.

3   *Star Wars* effectively brought to an end the golden era of early-1970s personal filmmaking

and focused the industry on big-budget special-effects blockbusters, blasting off a trend we are still living through. But you can't blame it for what it did, you can only observe how well it did it. In one way or another all the big studios have been trying to make another *Star Wars* ever since (pictures like *Raiders of the Lost Ark, Jurassic Park,* and *Independence Day* are its heirs). It located Hollywood's center of gravity at the intellectual and emotional level of a bright teenager.

4   It's possible, however, that as we grow older, we retain the tastes of our earlier selves. How else to explain how much fun *Star Wars* is, even for those who think they don't care for science fiction? It's a good-hearted film in every frame, and shining through is the gift of a man who knew how to link state-of-the-art technology with a deceptively simple, very powerful story. It was not by accident that George Lucas worked with Joseph Campbell, an expert on the world's basic myths, in fashioning a screenplay that owes much to man's oldest stories.

5   By now the ritual of classic film revival is well established: An older classic is brought out from the studio vaults, restored frame by frame, re-released in the best theaters, and relaunched on home video. With this "special edition" of the

Star Wars trilogy (which includes new versions of *Return of the Jedi* and *The Empire Strikes Back*), Lucas has gone one step beyond. His special effects were so advanced in 1977 that they spun off an industry, including his own Industrial Light & Magic Co., the computer wizards who do many of today's best special effects.

6   Now Lucas has put ILM to work touching up the effects, including some that his limited 1977 budget left him unsatisfied with. Most of the changes are subtle; you'd need a side-by-side comparison to see that a new shot is a little better. There are about five minutes of new material, including a meeting between Han Solo and Jabba the Hutt that was shot for the first version but not used. (We learn that Jabba is not immobile, but sloshes along in a spongy undulation.) There's also an improved look to the city of Mos Eisley ("a wretched hive of scum and villainy," says Obi-Wan Kenobi). And the climactic battle scene against the Death Star has been rehabbed.

7   The improvements are well done, but they point up how well the effects were done to begin with: If the changes are not obvious, that's because *Star Wars* got the look so right in the first place. The obvious comparison is with Stanley Kubrick's *2001: A Space Odyssey,* made in 1968, which also holds up perfectly well today. (One difference is that Kubrick went for realism, trying to imagine how his future world would really look, while Lucas cheerfully plundered the past; Han Solo's Millennium Falcon has a gun turret with a hand-operated weapon that would be at home on a World War II bomber, but too slow to hit anything at space velocities.)

8   Two Lucas inspirations started the story with a tease: He set the action not in the future but "long ago," and jumped into the middle of it with "Chapter 4: A New Hope." These seemingly innocent touches were actually rather powerful; they gave the saga the aura of an ancient tale, and an ongoing one.

9   As if those two shocks were not enough for the movie's first moments, I learn from a review by Mark R. Leeper that this was the first film to

pan the camera across a star field: "Space scenes had always been done with a fixed camera, and for a very good reason. It was more economical not to create a background of stars large enough to pan through." As the camera tilts up, a vast spaceship appears from the top of the screen and moves overhead, an effect reinforced by the surround sound. It is such a dramatic opening that Lucas paid a fine and resigned from the Directors Guild rather than obey its demand that he begin with conventional opening credits.

10   The film has simple, well-defined characters, beginning with the robots C-3PO (fastidious, a little effete) and R2-D2 (childlike, easily hurt). The evil Empire has all but triumphed in the galaxy, but rebel forces are preparing an assault on the Death Star. Princess Leia (pert, sassy Carrie Fisher) has information pinpointing the Death Star's vulnerable point and feeds it into R2-D2's computer; when her ship is captured, the robots escape from the Death Star and find themselves on Luke Skywalker's planet, where soon Luke (Mark Hamill as an idealistic youngster) meets the wise, old, mysterious Kenobi (Alec Guinness) and they hire the free-lance space jockey Han Solo (Harrison Ford, already laconic) to carry them to Leia's rescue.

11   The story is advanced with spectacularly effective art design, set decoration and effects. Although the scene in the intergalactic bar is famous for its menagerie of alien drunks, there is another scene—when the two robots are thrown into a hold with other used droids—that equally fills the screen with fascinating details. And a scene in the Death Star's garbage bin (inhabited by a snake with a head shaped like E.T.'s) also is well done.

12   Many of the planetscapes are startlingly beautiful, and owe something to fantasy artist Chesley Bonestell's imaginary drawings of other worlds. The final assault on the Death Star, when the fighter rockets speed between parallel walls, is a nod in the direction of *2001*, with its light

trip into another dimension: Kubrick showed, and Lucas learned, how to make the audience feel it is hurtling headlong through space.

13   Lucas fills his screen with loving touches. There are little alien rats hopping around the desert and a chess game played with living creatures. Luke's weather-worn "Speeder" vehicle, which hovers over the sand, reminds me of a 1965 Mustang. And consider the details creating the presence, look and sound of Darth Vader, whose fanged face mask, black cape and hollow breathing are the setting for James Earl Jones's cold voice of doom.

14   Seeing the film the first time, I was swept away, and have remained swept ever since. Seeing this restored version, I tried to be more objective and noted that the gun battles on board the spaceships go on a bit too long; it is remarkable that the Empire marksmen never hit anyone important; and the fighter raid on the enemy ship now plays like the computer games it predicted. I wonder, too, if Lucas could have come up with a more challenging philosophy behind the Force. As Kenobi explains it, it's basically just going with the flow. What if Lucas had pushed a little further, to include elements of non-violence or ideas about intergalactic conservation? (It's a waste of resources to blow up star systems.)

15   The film philosophies that will live forever are the simplest-seeming ones. They may have profound depths, but their surfaces are as clear to an audience as a beloved old story. I know this because the stories that seem immortal— *The Odyssey, Don Quixote, David Copperfield, Huckleberry Finn*—are all the same: a brave but flawed hero, a quest, colorful people and places, sidekicks, the discovery of life's underlying truths. If I were asked to say with certainty which movies will still be widely known a century or two from now, I would list *2001, The Wizard of Oz*, Keaton and Chaplin, Astaire and Rogers, and probably *Casablanca* . . . and *Star Wars*, for sure.

Exploring Ideas

1. First, ask several people to review or evaluate *Star Wars*—even if based solely on their memory of the film. Then identify their main judgment about the film and their reasons for judging it that way. For example, someone might say it was good because it was fun. "Good" would be the overall judgment and "fun" or "entertaining" would be the standard upon which they based their judgment. Make a chart of people's evaluations, listing the overall judgments and the reasons for those judgments.

2. How is the way that Ebert sees *Star Wars* similar to or different from the way others (#1) see it? What did they say (or imply by their responses) was the film's purpose? What did they say (or imply) was its value?

3. What standards of judgment besides "entertaining" might be used to evaluate a film? That is, what might be the purpose or value of a film beyond or in addition to mere entertainment? List at least three films that have value beyond mere entertainment.

4. Select a film that you think is especially good. Explain why you like the film, and then do research, through reading and discussion with others, to find out what similar films came before it. Attempt through your research to learn the history of that type of film. Explain how earlier films "influenced" the film that you like.

Writing Strategies

1. In your own words, write down the main point Ebert makes about *Star Wars*.

2. What criteria—or standards of judgment—does Ebert rely on when evaluating *Star Wars*? What other standards might he have used?

3. Ebert uses support outside the subject—such as other movies—to develop his evaluation. How does this outside support help to develop his evaluation?

4. Reread Ebert's introduction and conclusion. How do those two paragraphs "frame" his essay? What do they tell you, without reading anything else, that the rest of the essay is about?

5. Does Ebert seem credible? If you were looking for sources for a paper you were writing, would you decide that Ebert's information is reliable or not? Upon what would you base your decision?

Ideas for Writing

1. What film set a trend that other films have followed, or what film do you believe is likely to set a trend that other films will follow, although they have not followed it yet?

2. What CD, music video, television show, or work from some other form of media has been influential?

> If responding to one of these ideas, go to the **Analysis** section of this chapter to begin developing ideas for your essay.

Whales R Us

Jayme Stayer

Jayme Stayer teaches at Texas A&M University—Commerce and is a member of the Board of Directors of the T. S. Eliot Society. "Whales R Us," provoked by a visit to Sea World with his family, questions what Sea World is "saying" in its skits and programs and what Stayer feels the park communicates to its audience. Based on this essay, how does Stayer see entertainment parks such as Sea World? Stop several times as you read, and write down your initial reactions to Stayer's ideas. Also, underline or highlight any ideas you find to be striking or confusing.

1   Mickey Mouse scares the bejesus out of me. Shamu, on the other hand, simply makes me queasy. I'm not the first to express loathing for Mickey & Co.: a giggling rodent as mascot for a nasty, litigious, multi-media *Über*-corporation. But you don't hear too many people railing against Sea World, though Shamu has a dark side too.

2   One of the first things to irk me at a Sea World park happened during a bird show. A perky blonde was displaying a few parrots, and she kept up a stream of banter about their feeding habits and origins. "When our ancestors came to this continent," she breezily explained to an audience chock full of non-Europeans, "they brought with them this breed of parrot from Africa." Since I'm almost certain that slaves brutally shipped to the Americas were not allowed bird cages as carry-on luggage, what she should have said was that European—not "our"—ancestors stopped off in Africa and loaded up with parrots and slaves. One needn't be a fanatical multiculturalist to be ruffled by inaccurate history and specious assumptions about an audience's makeup.

3   In America, unexamined notions of history and the coercive politics of majority identity go hand in hand with boorish nationalism. (See, for example, the debate over the Confederate flag and its supposed status as symbol of a unitary "Southern" culture.) Oddly, the bird show at Sea World confirmed this. Her parrots now retired, the perky woman waltzed around the stage with this magnificent creature while the audience was subjected to a chummy patriotic tune. So the eagle was presented not as the largest or most impressive of birds, or as indigenous to Canada, or even as another instance of the marvels of creation, but as the Bird of American Democracy—this, in spite of the fact that eagles' politics tend to the monarchist side and that their feeding habits indicate a predisposition for brutal dictatorship. The bird becomes valued, in other words, for the cultural associations "we" Americans slapped onto it, not for any of its intrinsic properties. The eagle, in Sea World's monistic version of the world, becomes just another happy commodity—like parrots, slaves, designer clothes sweatshops—that makes America the Great Nation It Has Always Been.

4   But not all employees were as chipper as the bird show people. There are two types of teenagers who work at Sea World: the aggressively happy and the sullenly aggrieved. These two opposed mentalities are as old as the summer job itself: namely, the optimism of youths who want to change the world vs. the cynicism of kids who despise their jobs, resent their pay, and wouldn't give a hooey if they were fired because some enraged Yuppie did not get good service with a grovelling smile when he bought his Sno-Cone. I personally sided with the disaffected and wished I had brought copies of *The Communist Manifesto* to slip into their pockets.

5   The most important job at Sea World—and teenagers are particularly good at it—is making lots of noise. Since most Americans are terrified of being alone in a store without Muzak, Sea World willingly obliges its customers with rock-concert levels of decibels. All of the shows keep

up a noxious patter complete with ear-splitting sound effects; the walkways have abrasively loud music piped over them; and even the exhibits have teenagers chained there with microphones in hand, droning their mantra of dull facts.

6   It is ironic that a park putatively designed to extol the wonders of nature is obsessed with high-tech wizardry and mega-voltage noise, noise, noise—even when it is extolling the wonders of nature's silence. Another talking point of the bird show featured how silently an owl could fly. The bird's flight began in blissful silence, but halfway through its flight the soundtrack faded back in with a shimmer of violins, followed by a cymbal crash when the owl landed. Even the absence of noise is packaged with noise: the owl's silence is first framed with amplified yakking (noise), then underlined as it happens (quiet noise), then punctuated (big noise) so the audience knows when to clap (make more noise).

7   One of the most ludicrous moments of the Shamu show was an assertion by another relentlessly cheerful teenager: "We here at Sea World believe we have the greatest jobs in the world." With its overtones of Orwellian party-speak, it was only slightly risible until she added: "We get to work with nature's most wonderful animals and contribute to the world's knowledge about them." Her jejune assumption that "world knowledge" exists as some kind of huge, accumulative spittoon—rather than a set of competing claims and shifting paradigms—was hilarious enough, particularly coming from a kid who is probably still struggling with basic algebra and who wouldn't recognize "world knowledge" if it landed on her in a heap. I imagined her logging on to a marine biology chat group and making an announcement—in all caps, no doubt—followed by an emoticon: "SHAMU DID A BACK FLIP TODAY!!! :)" Thus does the world's cup of knowledge runneth over.

8   And that insistent refrain of "We here at Sea World believe" was another thing that rankled me, because it was usually followed by patronizing flimflam. Some prime examples: "We here at Sea World believe that animals should not be taken from their natural habitat." Or: "We here at Sea World believe only in the use of positive reinforcement in the training of animals." The audience is supposed to believe that these are lovely sentiments. How noble that they try to find injured or orphaned animals to "befriend." How comforting to know Shamu isn't being shocked with electricity or poked in the eye when he's tired or just damned fed up with giving piggyback rides. Most disturbing was that these credos came mostly out of the mouths of the teenage staff, whose inexperience made their We-Believe proclamations ring even more hollowly.

9   Taken individually, some of these moments were only mildly unnerving, but there was one occurrence that stood out as gratuitous. Situated on a lake, the Sea World I visited featured a water show with ski jumps and corny skits. The theme of that year's show was *Baywatch*, which involved—predictably enough—nubile bodies in poorly choreographed dance routines, the bold rescue of someone in the water, and the odd appearances of two buffoons (fat old man with hysterical wife), all of which was irritatingly narrated by an emcee's we-havin'-fun-yet? voice-over. At one point, the old man and his wife were "accidentally" pulled into view: the man (vertical) on skis, the woman (horizontal) with her legs wrapped around his torso. They were in the unmistakable position of sex, the two actors in a

flurry of feigned embarrassment at having been "caught." (Whut in tarnation cud be more funny than ol' fat folks havin' sex? Har dee har har.) The emcee and other characters on stage slyly absolved themselves of complicity in this vulgarity by shrugging their shoulders, as if to say: "Golly, what was that all about?" Sea World, by the way, bills itself as a place for the whole family.

10 You might think that a park that sponsors PG-13 shows would divest itself of prudishness. Alas, there was more self-righteousness there than at a revival. Case in point: the shark exhibit. Before we could enter, we were forced to watch a short film about sharks; the doors to the exhibit were pointedly barred until after the film was over. The film gave us a hellfire-and-damnation scolding: you thought that sharks were human predators? WRONG. You thought sharks were abundant in the ocean? WRONG AGAIN. After airing its grievances with us—the ill-informed public—it asserted that much damage had been inflicted on these misunderstood fishies. Because we've all been shark-haters at heart, fishermen have felt free to kill them. Quivering with virtue, the film called "intolerable" the fishermen who "senselessly" destroyed the sharks, either because the sharks got caught in the nets or because the sharks fed on prized fish. With vast self-contentment Sea World then relayed how they had successfully worked to stop this great evil.

11 While I'm pleased to have my horror-film notions of sharks corrected, the film's smugness was unbearable. And in spite of Sea World's professed vigilance, I'm not convinced that sharks aren't still being arbitrarily killed somewhere in the world. Even so, I wonder if sharks, given the choice, would prefer to stay in a Sea World bathtub for the rest of their lives or take a chance with those fishnets.

12 Of the many inanities hurled at me, my favorite was an emcee's sign-off: "And remember," she intoned from a precipitously high moral ground, "before we can have peace *on* the earth, we have to make peace *with* the earth." Indeed. As if, in the interest of world peace, the United Nations agenda should be scuttled in favor of dotting the globe with Sea Worlds to promote feel-good vibes between humans and dolphins. Here's more glib reasoning: to make peace *with* the earth implies the earth was a peaceful place before we humans mucked things up. Yet the last time I looked, the earth was full of viruses, earthquakes, predatory animals, and a survival-of-the-fittest mentality that Sea World has apparently never heard of.

13 And maybe it was petty of me to be irked when the woman narrating Shamu's activities insisted that whales scratch their backs on the pebbled shores when they're contented. There was captive Shamu scratching his back on the simulated shore. The audience oohed and aahed. Nevermind that Shamu had been explicitly directed to scratch his back, and that to have disobeyed would have resulted not in a whack on the head (lucky for him) but in the withholding of food (not so lucky). Is that contentment then? With the help of an extraordinarily costly visual aid, the audience was expected to "learn" a fact of whale behavior that could be shown only at the cost of candor.

14 Sea World, I realized after an afternoon of learning very little, was a place that was desperately trying to present itself as a place where education occurs. And for twenty-some bucks, your educational experience goes roughly like this: you can give up an afternoon of watching vapid TV shows and take your whole family to watch a skit based on a vapid TV show. You get to ogle busty women and hirsute men. You get to have constant noise crowd out any independent thoughts that might be percolating to the surface of your brain. You get to harbor the illusion that America is a happy, white, European family, as well as a leading maker of world knowledge, and that Sea World is largely responsible for such happiness and abundance. You get to imagine you hold the key to world peace (remember to give the dog a kiss when you get home). You get to indulge in patriotic goosebumps ("the *American* eagle!"), have your heart-strings jolted ("Ah—Shamu's happy to be here!"), get your sluggish sense of morality

jump-started ("*baaaad* fishermen, *gooood* sharkie"). And if you're willing to invest another three bucks, you can fling a sardine at dolphins that have been petted to within an inch of their lives. Best of all, at the end of the day you get to go home with the vaguely self-congratulatory feeling that you've *learned* something, by God.

15   I'm an educator, and I pay close attention when someone is trying to teach me something. So on my way out of Sea World, I asked myself what I had learned. Like a student who has crammed for an exam, I was able to recall lots of idiocies, but could only say I had truly learned two things. (1) Thanks to the film, I learned that sharks attack humans only when provoked, and, (2) thanks to their anthropomorphizing skits, I learned that sea otters are *cute* little buggers. Even if these elements were judicious pedagogical objectives (which they are not), they still don't add up to anything resembling education. In fact, the entire experience of Sea World is suspiciously similar to the exact opposite of education: mind-control.

16   It was only in retrospect that I realized that these annoyances were related: the high-pitched entertainment and trivial sexual jokes, the shut-up-and-listen attitude, the constant noise and verbal presence, the Big Brotherly refrains of exactly what "We here at Sea World believe." These are all rhetorical strategies of a government diverting its citizens, masking something it doesn't want the public to know. And what is it that Sea World doesn't want its customers to think about?

17   In a review lambasting Disney World, an author hilariously describes the ideology of the place as "benign fascism": the streets are immaculately clean; the workerbees wear impossibly happy smiles; the rides and trains run on time; and every day, the gloved hero appears on parade, where the hordes worship him and his lickspittles with songs and fireworks. The author's comparison of Mickey to Mussolini is more than just amusing: he ties it into his critique of how history is portrayed at the Epcott center. Because Disney does not want to offend any of its ethnically and racially diverse customers (Sea World: take note), their film on American history carefully controls the emotional barometer of its vacationers. The Disney film of American history is whitewashed to the point of banality, and such central topics as the atomic bomb, racial conflict, and imperialist genocide are entirely avoided. The point is that fascists, benign or not, always have political and economic reasons for telling history the way they do. And like Disney World and other fascist operations, Sea World likes to keep a tight grip on what and how its visitors think.

18   Take, for example, the "we-believe-animals-should-be-treated-in-this-way" gestures that continually crop up. These assertions pose as facts the audience ought to memorize in preparation for an exit quiz. Yet the nervous tic of emphasizing the politically correct means of treating animals in captivity belies Sea World's uneasiness with the larger, unasked question: should we even have animals in captivity for our bourgeois amusement? Nowhere in their literature, exhibit signs, or rehearsed prattle of their miked minions is this basic question broached or answered.

19   Part of the way Sea World can get away with ignoring the obvious fact that these animals are there for our entertainment is that it nervously insists that it is a place of science and research, and disingenuously implies that entertainment easily meshes with education and research. While I scoff at the idea that important research gets done at Sea World, the problem isn't really with what kinds of knowledge Sea World makes, or how much, or how important it is. Rather, the problem is Sea World's communication of that knowledge, or to be more explicit, their refusal to level with its visitors about its real cultural role and worth. If they would fess up to the fact that Sea World is essentially a playground and not a classroom, that might be a start towards a real educational experience.

20   Sea World keeps up its image of itself as a classroom by propagating signs with facts and statistics on them. These factoids—and their Post-It Note ubiquity—are a peculiar manifestation of "textbook knowledge": boring chunks of data unconnected to any larger, compelling theme. There were a plethora of facts swimming around at Sea World and a dearth of ideas, which is why I couldn't remember anything at the end of my day. Like the eager student who has a bad teacher, I was given no complex or interesting framework inside of which ideas jostled about; so I was reduced to cramming lists of unconnected information in preparation for a never-to-be-taken exam.

21   I'm not suggesting that Sea World become a place that sponsors round-table discussions of animal rights and lets biology students present their theses during Shamu intermissions. But I do think that instead of slavishly subscribing to popular notions of science, Sea World might call them into question. This is what real education does.

22   As it stands, none of our deeply rooted cultural beliefs are explored or challenged at Sea World. After a trip there the visitor is likely to keep thinking that facts are equivalent to knowledge; that America is synonymous with Europe; that science and technology are the greatest goods imaginable; that education means being fed a list of facts in a condescending manner; and that sated, docile fish—who decorously eat buckets of non-cute sardines—are practically vegetarians.

23   A skit in which a lovably frisky sea otter has its head chomped off by a hungry predator is not the kind of bloody epiphany Sea World is likely to promote. Imagine the screams of the unsuspecting children. Imagine the lawsuits of offended suburbanites who like their nature sanitized and safe. But imagine, too, how such a moment would educate an audience about the dangers of humanizing certain animals at the expense of others. Such a skit might end with a question to the audience about why its government enacts laws to protect the habitat of owls but not of insects or low-income humans.

24   The only cultural assumption that was seriously challenged at Sea World was the premise of *Jaws*—and that was much too heavy-handed, not to mention incorrect, as events in Florida have shown. It turns out that sharks *will* attack idle swimmers. It should come as no surprise that a capitalist venture like Sea World can't even get its basic facts straight. Neither can the tobacco industry seem to grasp what everyone else knows about nicotine addiction. Nor is Disney equipped to navigate the treacherous waters of American history.

25   Surely the most real moments at Sea World occurred when the fascists lost control, for example, when the staff had trouble getting the animals to obey their directions. Such glitches in the program put their slapstick routines and canned jokes on hold, and forced them to talk to the audience about fixing this problem. It also gave the teenage apparatchiks an opportunity for some inspired ad-libbing, disburdening them from their less endearing lecture notes.

26   If the ideology of Disney is benign fascism, then the ideology of Sea World is exploitative spectacle masquerading as education. Too occupied with obscuring the real moral, environmental, and scientific issues at stake, Sea World is constitutionally incapable of teaching respect for nature. Love of nature is spiritually informed and politically assertive. It is not the kind of passive, sentimental quackery Sea World prefers, and it cannot be taught with the crude tools in Sea World's lesson plans: glib moralizing, base pandering, and clichés masquerading as insights.

27   But in the last analysis, Sea World—to paraphrase Auden—makes nothing happen. Sea World is a reflection of American culture: a consequence, not a cause; a mirror of consumerist desires, not a promoter of political change via education. The American traits Sea World reflects most clearly are its gullibility and irrationality. It's a consolation, albeit a small one, to consider that Americans are likewise gullible to the very real beauty of nature. It's that kind of openness—and not Sea World's preaching—that makes the connection between humans and dolphins seem

worth investigating. It's less of a comfort to consider another analogy between Americans and marine life that Sea World leaves unexplored: America's exorbitant arms race, its rape of the environment, its valorization of guns and violence, its giddy, media-fueled acclamation of the death sentence that disproportionately murders minorities: are these not strikingly similar to the fierce logic of the food chain? Screw the little guy; I'm hungry and more powerful.

28 So my advice is to go to Sea World anyway. Even inside the ideological frame where they are forced, the creatures there—including the teenagers—are amazing, hilarious, and terrifying. Who can remain unimpressed when a mammal the size of a Mack truck lifts itself out of the water? As for Sea World itself: if aided by earplugs and skepticism you can ignore what they're trying to teach you, you just might learn something.

Work Cited

Alexander, Maxwell. "Promise Redeemed: At Long Last Mickey." *Johns Hopkins Magazine* April 1995: 5.

Exploring Ideas

1. Based on this essay, how is the way that Stayer sees entertainment parks similar to or different from the way you see them?

2. Based on this essay, how is what Stayer thinks, values, believes, or feels similar to or different from you?

3. In several paragraphs, write an evaluation of an entertainment park or other entertainment activity you remember well. Then compare your approach to Stayer's. What is your overall judgment? What is his? What criteria—or standards upon which you based your judgment—did you use? What criteria does Stayer use? What did you assume the purpose of the park or activity to be? What is the purpose of the park to Stayer?

4. How does Stayer's thinking go beyond one's initial ideas about entertainment parks?

5. How might you evaluate some entertainment activity (theme park, concert, movie theater, race track, etc.), going beyond one's initial thinking about that activity?

Writing Strategies

1. Evaluate Stayer's introduction and conclusion. First consider the goal of an introduction and conclusion, and then consider Stayer's particular goal. How well does he achieve it and why?

2. What word would you use to describe the tone of this essay—humorous, serious, urgent, angry, light, etc.? Identify several passages to support your description.

3. In evaluation, understanding the purpose of the subject—Sea World, in this case—is essential. According to Stayer, what is, or should be, the purpose of Sea World? Are the criteria he uses responsive to the purpose of the subject?

4. If workshopping Stayer's essay, what three suggestions would you make?

Ideas for Writing

1. What public place—such as Sea World—does not achieve the purpose that it should or that it claims to?

2. What public place does achieve its purpose?

If responding to one of these ideas, go to the **Analysis** section of this chapter to begin developing ideas for your essay.

The Andy Griffith Show: Return to Normal

Ed Bell

Ed Bell's writing also appears in Chapter 9. "The Andy Griffith Show: Return to Normal" evaluates one of his favorite television shows. As you read, consider how Bell explores the TV sitcom beyond it being just entertainment. Highlight or underline ideas that go beyond one's initial thoughts about entertainment television. And in the margin, write down how Bell's essay attempts to connect The Andy Griffith Show *to the viewer's quality of life.*

In the margins of this essay, a reader's comments point to key ideas and writing strategies. As you read the essay, consider how the comments might influence your own reading and writing.

Exploring Ideas

Connects to life of viewer: do sitcoms instruct? how?

they entertain

do they comfort? probably.

Okay, but there must be "other" shows like Andy—such as *Leave It to Beaver.*

Writing Strategies

Introduction discusses what sitcoms do (their purpose): instruct, entertain, comfort. Evaluation of show can be based on how well the shows do this.

Main claim: "More than any other sitcom . . ."

Criteria for evaluation. How *Andy Griffith* differs from other shows—it's more comforting because things return to normal.

Develops argument by discussing what happens in other shows: things work out okay, but don't return to normal.

From those early days of Lucy and Ricky to our own Dharma and Greg, situation comedies have been part of American culture. And for all the advancements, it still seems like the plots of most of them are something cooked up by Lucy who dragged along Ethel and got caught (and ultimately forgiven) by Fred and Barney . . . uh . . . Fred and Ricky, I mean. Whether or not these shows instruct is, I suppose, debatable. But what is not debatable is that over the past 50 years they have entertained millions. And, I would suggest, through that very act of entertaining us, they have comforted us—the most comforting of them all being *The Andy Griffith Show.*

More than any other sitcom, *The Andy Griffith Show* leaves its viewers with a sense that everything is alright. While *Three's Company* or *Dharma and Greg* or *MASH* may also wind things up happily after 30 minutes, there is—even though the complication of that particular week's crisis has been worked out—always a sense on those shows that things are not quite right. Yet *The Andy Griffith Show* leaves us with the feeling that, even though our friends sometimes get big-headed ideas or strangers from Raleigh come driving or dancing or swindling their mixed-up way into our peacefulness, life will eventually *return to normal*, all warm and wonderful.

On *Three's Company* or *Seinfeld* or *Friends,* things work out in the end. The friends are getting along just fine, but we can see that they are bound for another conflict in a week or so. Though this week's crisis has worked itself out, the pace of their lives or their natural temperaments or their complicated living conditions are still spinning wildly and we know next week they're in for trouble again. On *Dharma and Greg* or *Green Acres* or *I Love Lucy* (even on *The Dick Van Dyke Show*), the family has once again survived, but as with the shows about friends, on the shows about families

Exploring Ideas

This seems to go beyond initial thinking. (I've never thought about it.)

Goes beyond initial thinking here. Gets specific. Show provides comfort 'cause someone's wise. Madness because of:
1) intruders,
2) natural growing up,
3) ego, ambition, pride

This seems to go beyond initial thinking: things are normal and get wacky, instead of things generally just being wacky.

Is this true? Doesn't it have to ensue becaue of Barney, etc.?

there seems to be only temporary comfort in the happy ending. Dharma and Greg are still bound for a divorce. Lisa, on *Green Acres,* is only putting up with the farm life a little while longer and Oliver loves it so much that he is never going back to the city. Though she is ironically more suited to the place than he is, she longs always to live elsewhere. No one could possibly put up with all Lucy's scheming. And as for Richard and Laura Petrie, the most stable of our sample couples, to the average American they seem only a step away from falling into the New York swinger crowd. On *MASH* or *Hogan's Heroes* or *Gomer Pyle,* they are either at war or could be. There's little real and lasting comfort in these folks who are gathered together out of necessity so far from home. Yes, they're buddies and that's nice, but it's all so temporary.

This doesn't exhaust all the sitcoms or all the types, but it does set up the reasons that *The Andy Griffith Show* comforts us more than the others. The show's main character, Andy, is full of southern wisdom. He is quiet and listens and makes better decisions in the midst of all the madness than we could have. That is comfort number one: Someone—the general, the man in charge, *the sheriff*—has things under control. All the madness results from one of three things: either intruders, but Andy gets rid of them after they have caused only a little trouble; or just boys (Opie and sometimes his friends) going through what is natural to go through growing up, but Andy deals with this expertly, too; or ego, ambition, and pride—usually Barney is having the trouble here, though it could be Aunt Bea or one of the others. Andy understands all of this, though not so well or right away that the show isn't a little bit interesting. The plot is better than most sitcoms: there is always a solution that takes a little while to get to, and we believe it when we finally do.

What's most comforting about this show, however, is that things *return to normal.* That is, *The Andy Griffith Show* offers us a normal that can be returned to. With *Andy Griffith* we get a sense that the complication has blown through like a summer thunderstorm, instead of us getting the sense that a little blue sky has blown through a place where it is otherwise always thunderstorming. The characters are at home. They're not strangers thrown together, and they haven't been transplanted in some strange land (such as Hooterville, New York City, or Postmodern America). They are familiar with their surroundings and like (both "similar to" and "fond of") each other. The zaniness on *Andy Griffith* could just as well not ensue . . . but it does. On all those other shows, it must ensue. How couldn't it?

The situation itself—small-town people in a small town—is comforting. The show develops this sense with Andy's quiet wisdom, but also with the integrity of the wacky supporting characters. All of them to some degree are like Barney—a liability and an asset all at once. They are, like us, good people flawed. We are

Writing Strategies

Author concedes that there are other sitcoms and other types of sitcoms.

Develops argument through specific analysis of *The Andy Griffith Show.* Shows specifically why/how AG comforts us.

Main idea: Says what is most comforting about the show (relates to title of essay).

Connects to reader (public resonance): They are, like US, good people flawed. The use of "we" (though not required) helps make this connection.

The situation itself (small-town life) contributes to comforting.

The show captures something. What is it?

Connects to viewers because it is comforting. Assures viewer that blue skies, not storms, are normal (even if this is not true? Is it?).

all familiar with the show's gentle theme song, whistled as Andy and Opie walk along with fishing poles. And the black and white camera shots are always perfectly composed, like a photo we'd see in *Life Magazine*. The dialog is quiet, engaging, funny, real. For 30 minutes we are practically back in the womb of Mayberry—a place that doesn't exist, but does. It is a place that, whether we ever felt it as a child or not, as adults we feel that we once knew. We can feel it now, and *The Andy Griffith Show* captures what we all now think that we once felt back then.

Not all sitcoms set out to comfort, though all do set out to entertain. Some, such as *All in the Family* or *Soap* or *Will and Grace*, might even set out to challenge us, to make us think. But *The Andy Griffith Show*, I believe, sets out to entertain and comfort and it succeeds as no other show ever has . . . or ever will. *The Cosby Show* could only circle in *Andy's* orbit. The reason is, I suppose, because the times have changed. Today an attempt to create the comfort of Mayberry (an attempt to say your small-town life is idylic) would somehow fail. It would seem a lie without any of the twenty-first-century issues (drugs, pregnancy, homosexual kissing), without any of the edgy technology, the music, the rapid-fire slick wit, the self-aware writing and directing. Mayberry exists, cliché as it sounds, in our hearts. The show, like no other, captured what we want to remember, whether it happened or not. It tells us that blue skies are normal.

Concession/Qualifier: Not all sitcoms set out to comfort. Some may even do the opposite.

Concludes by providing a possible reason why *The Andy Griffith Show* is more comforting than today's shows.

Exploring Ideas

1. How does Bell's essay encourage the reader to think differently about *The Andy Griffith Show*?

2. How does Bell's essay encourage the reader to think differently about TV sitcoms in general, or about entertainment in general?

3. Interview others until you discover at least three entertainment shows that people think impact the quality of the viewer's life. Explain how each show might influence the way that people think or act.

Writing Strategies

1. What criteria (standards of judgment) does Bell use to evaluate *The Andy Griffith Show*? List several other criteria he might have used but didn't.

2. Highlight or underline any background (summary/presentation) information necessary to understand evaluation. Where does such information appear? Why is it helpful? Where might more or less background information have been presented?

Ideas for Writing

1. What TV show can you evaluate, stating more than "it is entertaining" or "funny"?

2. What person, place, or thing can you evaluate, focusing your evaluation on a less usual (less obvious) purpose of that thing?

If responding to one of these ideas, go to the **Analysis** section of this chapter to begin developing ideas for your essay.

Pulp Fiction: Valuable Critique or Useless Titillation?

Simon Benlow

Simon Benlow, whose writing also appears in Chapters 4 and 11, is a writer and composition teacher. As you read, ask yourself how Benlow encourages the reader to think about Pulp Fiction. *What question(s) does his essay raise about this film and others like it? Highlight or underline the passages that prompt you to think in new ways.*

1   *Pulp Fiction,* Quentin Tarantino's first big box office film, hit the movie scene like a silver bullet—it shot right through the forehead of good taste and subtlety. In some ways, it is another shoot-'em-up, snort-'em-up, get-laid thriller in a long, tiresome list of American gangster movies. In many ways, it is downright silly, filled with junior high level slapstick humor and petty revenge. Many scenes take the easy way out—opting for quick laughs and shock-for-shock-sake images. But, in other ways, *Pulp Fiction* manages to make a point or two about the very genre it barely escapes. That is, it points out, reveals, and even turns upside down American moviegoers' fascination with violent characters.

2   *Pulp Fiction* exists alongside of, or maybe because of, a movie tradition that features violent protagonists. Movies such as *Terminator, First Blood, Dirty Harry,* and the droves of their carbon copies follow a lead male character through an uncomplicated narrative in which he must shoot his way through legions of nameless (and faceless) men. As he penetrates through some murky landscape or urban jungle, he blows away body after body, building after building, and ultimately comes out the victor. By the end of the journey, he has killed off hundreds of people, and yet manages to walk humbly off into the sunset with gentle (happy) music washing over the credits. And because the audience is "on his side," we gladly forget the bloodbath left behind. In fact, in these movies, the nature of the action prompts, even urges, the audience to view the protagonist's enemies (or victims?) as inconsequential—as faceless targets who fall lifelessly over balconies, down cliffs, or through windows. Like the protagonist, we walk happily out of the theater without even a drop of blood on our collective conscience.

3   Contrary to this tradition, this bloodless bloodbath in which the consequences of violent shooting sprees are absent, *Pulp Fiction* steeps the lead male characters (and the audience) in victims' blood. As the lead characters (two veteran henchmen for a crime boss) are traveling down the highway, one of them (played by John Travolta) accidentally shoots one of their acquaintances in the head. The victim's brains are, quite literally, scattered throughout the inside of the car and onto the lead characters. The following scenes show the two men cleaning the car, hosing themselves down, and eventually (but only after a painfully ironic night of quibbling) getting rid of the shattered body. This sequence of events, unlike the tradition of Schwarzenegger-esque movies, keeps the protagonists and the audience swimming in the bloody goo of violence. It is, in fact, ridiculous, but no more ridiculous, and maybe even significantly less, than those countless movie plots that keep the effects of violence in the background like some simpleton teenage arcade game.

4   *Pulp Fiction* also manages to reveal another troubling tradition of American movie making—the glorification of gangsters. For many decades, American audiences have warmed up to movie villains, and more recently have taken

a liking to mob crime bosses. There's no other figure in contemporary American culture that embodies violence, power, grim determinism, and petty desire—all the things that seem to make the most base systems of our society turn—like the mobster. Throughout the 1980s and '90s, a load of movies featured, indeed glamorized, crime bosses and their henchmen: *Goodfellas, The Godfather* and *The Godfather Part II, Billy Bathgate, Hoffa, Donnie Brasco, The Untouchables, Capone,* etc. These movies characterize gangsters as strong-willed, proud, and charismatic. They may be homicidal, but they dress nice and have loyal followers.

5   *Pulp Fiction* pokes an important hole in the gangster image. The gangsters in Tarantino's world are petty, clumsy, and are even victims of violent will. In one horrifying scene, the most powerful crime boss and one of his lesser thugs are captured by two backwards freaks. In a disturbing set of events, the two men are tied and gagged. The crime boss is sodomized before the two of them manage a violent escape. What's particularly disorienting about this scene is that the two offenders are nobodies—that is, they are not fated enemies seeking revenge for a lost brother, nor are they defending family turf; they are, quite simply, nameless sodomizing creeps. The point? Crime bosses are not above the cesspool of crime. Unlike the Hollywood image of smooth-talking, invincible patriarchs, these

gangsters get the bad end of the stick. Perhaps the most fitting example of this point comes at the end of the movie when Travolta's character is offed while sitting on the toilet—or, specifically, getting up from the toilet only to meet an intruder who shoots him with his own gun. His demise is not the result of a romantic gunfight or a dramatic shoot out between feuding archrivals. It is the opposite: empty and purposeless.

6   Certainly, *Pulp Fiction* is not a perfect critique of violence in movies. Perhaps the best reason for this is that these gestures of critique are probably lost on a large population of moviegoers. Proof of this abounds. For example, I heard a few young teenage men praise the gore—"Man, that was soooooo cool when that guy's head got blown off!" Such statements reveal the sheer passivity of many movie audiences—men and women alike who are willing only to swallow the surface images of a movie, and not to chew on their meaning. However, *Pulp Fiction* comes as a result of a tradition in which audiences are cajoled into applauding, even sympathizing with, murderous petty thugs. And after hundreds upon hundreds of these uncomplicated plots, self-righteous murderers, and bloodless shooting sprees that ask nothing of audiences except to participate in the glorification, and ultimate comfortable forgetting, of violence, it seems fitting to get at least one movie that prompts a little discomfort.

Exploring Ideas

1. How does Benlow encourage the reader to think differently about *Pulp Fiction*?

2. How does Benlow encourage the reader to think differently about films in general?

3. How might you benefit by thinking differently about films after having read Benlow's essay?

4. Read several movie reviews (in magazines, newspapers, and on-line), looking for reviews that talk about how the films are significant. They may be significant in the way they impact the viewer's thinking or actions, or in the way they influence (or speak back to) other films. List films that others consider to be significant and explain their significance.

5. Interview others until you discover three films that people think are influential in some way. Then view one of the films and evaluate it objectively.

Writing Strategies

1. What is the main idea of Benlow's evaluation?

2. Identify at least five transitions throughout Benlow's essay. How does he lead the reader from one idea to another? Or, put another way, how does he show the relationships between ideas?

3. Identify one concession—if possible, the one that you think is the most important. What point is Benlow conceding and why? Should he concede it earlier, later, or where he does?

4. What standards of judgment (criteria) does Benlow use to evaluate *Pulp Fiction*? What others might he have used? What one might you have used to develop his thesis (main idea)?

5. Explain how Benlow's evaluation is also an argument. What is he arguing?

Ideas for Writing

1. What important film can you evaluate, focusing on its role in movie history? Consider how is it responding to earlier movies, and how might it influence subsequent ones.

2. Evaluate this textbook and send the evaluation to its authors.

If responding to one of these ideas, go to the Analysis section of this chapter to begin developing ideas for your essay.

Rethinking Divorce

Barbara Dafoe Whitehead

Barbara Dafoe Whitehead, whose writing also appears in Chapter 10, is a sociologist and author of the book Divorce Culture: How Divorce Became an Entitlement and How It Is Blighting the Lives of Our Children *(1997). "Rethinking Divorce" was originally published in the* Boston Globe *(1997). As you read, highlight or underline any ideas that you think are especially convincing, important, or new to you. When you finish reading, write down what you think Whitehead is trying to accomplish in this essay.*

1   During the past 30 years, divorce has moved from the margin of society into the mainstream. It is now an American way of life and a commonplace childhood event. Close to half of all children in the United States will experience divorce before they reach age 18. Half of those are also likely to go through a second divorce. This alone is cause for concern, since a mounting body of evidence shows that divorce creates hardship, loss, and disadvantage for many of the roughly 1 million children each year who experience it firsthand.

2   But the harmful impact of divorce goes far beyond just those lives. Widespread divorce has also given rise to a set of ideas and values that are antithetical to the interests of all the nation's children and destructive of the social commitments that promote their well-being. It is no coincidence that the cruel loss of the welfare entitlement for children has come on the heels of the divorce revolution. For the current rationale for divorce also undermines the case for public support for the next generation as a whole.

3   This rationale has emerged as the result of a historic change in the way Americans think about divorce and its consequences.

4   Divorce has been a feature of Western social life for 300 years, and, until recently, most Americans believed that divorce caused such severe and sometimes lasting damage to children that it should be avoided, except in cases where marriages were torn apart by violence or other severe abuse. Consequently, parents were enjoined to work out their marital problems (or at least conceal them), so that they could pre-serve the marriage, as the popular saying had it, "for the sake of the children."

5   This social injunction was not designed to ruin the lives of parents. Rather, its main purpose was to acknowledge that children are stakeholders in the parents' marriage, and so deserve to have their interests represented. According to this way of thinking, marriage was children's most basic form of social insurance. It tied both parents to the child's household and also brought together two families whose help and support might be turned to the child's advantage. Marriage also attached fathers to their biological children and promoted steady, ongoing parental support and sponsorship. The legal dissolution of a marriage weakened the child's claim on these resources and thus was not to be entered into lightly.

6   Underlying this injunction against parental divorce was a child-centered ethic. It assumed that parents, as independent adults, had an obligation to represent and serve the interests of their dependent children. It viewed parents as emotionally resilient and able to withstand adversity, whereas children were emotionally vulnerable and should be protected from it.

7   After the mid-1960s, this injunction lost support and credibility, both as a statement about the sources of security for children and as a statement about the obligations of parents to their children. In 1972, advice columnist Ann Landers announced that she also no longer believed in staying together for the children. Academics, therapists, even clergy counseled against it. Women increasingly rejected the idea that parents should remain in unhappy marriages. In

1962, women were evenly divided over this question. Fifteen years later, 80 percent of women said parents should not stay together.

8   A new rationale emerged that justified divorce. It argued that a child's happiness depended on the happiness of the individual parent, especially the mother, rather than on the marriage itself. Thus, parents should look out for their own well-being first, and the children would benefit as well—a view one scholar has called "psychological trickledown."

9   This reversed the ethic. It was no longer child-centered. Now it was adults who were the emotionally fragile ones and thus had to be protected against adversity while children were the resilient ones and could take it. Not surprisingly, as this new ethic gained broad acceptance in the culture, the percentage of divorces involving children increased. Today 6 out of every 10 divorces occur in families with children.

10   As a consequence of this cultural shift, middle-class Americans today see divorce as an individual entitlement that must be protected against challenge, criticism or infringement. They reject the idea that children have an independent stake in the marriage partnership, and thus reject any social norm that affirms the child's stake. Indeed, so thoroughly does this sense of individual entitlement shape public thinking that any expression of concern for the children of divorce is interpreted as an unfeeling attack on the divorced themselves.

11   For this reason, politicians of every stripe duck the issue of middle-class divorce. Democrats avoid it, too, because they do not want to anger their large constituency of women who see divorce as a hard-won freedom and prerogative, nor do they want to seem unsympathetic to divorced mothers. Republicans do not want to antagonize their wealthy constituents or the party's libertarian wing, both of whom favor easy divorce. Nor does either party wish to call attention to divorce among its own leadership.

12   This bipartisan consensus has been politically expedient, but it has taken an enormous toll on our public commitment to children.

13   For one thing, it allows the middle class to define family breakup as a "them" problem—concentrated among the poor and underclass—rather than a problem that also implicates "us": the divorcing middle class. Mainstream America clings to the comfortable illusion that the declining well-being of children has to do almost solely with the behavior of unwed teenage mothers or poor women on welfare rather than with the instability of marriage and the fragility of parental commitment within its own ranks.

14   This isolates poor children and weakens our sense of shared obligation to improve their lot. It leads to the scapegoating of the nation's most vulnerable families. Policymakers focus on the eclipse of marriage among the most economically stressed members of the society as the root cause of family decline in the nation today. Welfare legislation urges poor parents to get married and stay married. But no one is sending this marriage to the country club crowd.

15   Moreover, and even more troublingly, today's divorce ethic undermines the social foundation for our public commitment to children. A society cannot sustain a public ethic of obligation to children if it also embraces a private ethic that devalues and disenfranchises children. If parents are entitled to put their needs and interests before those of their own children, why should they or any other adults feel an obligation to help somebody else's children?

16   Despite marches on Washington, D.C., and media campaigns, children's advocates are having trouble gaining support for their cause. Their struggles remind us that altruism cannot be generated by exhortation alone. For the foundation of altruism lies chiefly in family life, where it must be cultivated and practiced. A sense of obligation to others grows out of a sense of binding obligation to kith and kin. Durable social bonds depend heavily on the existence of lasting and dependable family bonds.

17   Yet today's children are coming of age at a time when bonds are increasingly fragile and commitments notably weak. According to survey research, high school students say that they aspire

to long-lasting, mutually satisfying relationships, but despair that they will be able to achieve them. Theirs is not the angst of adolescence but realistic expectation based on life experience. Children whose parents are divorced are two to three times more likely to get divorced themselves. So the breaking of the bonds is gaining cultural and generational momentum.

18   Unfortunately, the weakening of commitment to children could not have come at a worse time. Today's children need higher levels of both public and parental investment if they are to succeed in a demanding global economy. The characteristics that are most essential to making one's way in a dynamic world—initiative, re-

sourcefulness, independence, risk-taking—are the very characteristics that children are less likely to acquire if they lose permanence and security in their primary family bonds. At the very time the world is asking more of today's children, we are giving them less and less.

19   Consequently, there is an urgent need to begin a conversation about divorce. Its purpose should not be to second-guess or criticize divorced adults. Divorce is a necessary institution. Instead, the conversation should help us reconsider our current philosophy of divorce. What's at stake is the ability of children and young adults to fulfill their desires for durable bonds and lasting commitments.

Exploring Ideas

1. What does Whitehead say about divorce? What does she think is valuable?

2. How is the way that you see divorce similar to or different from the way Whitehead sees it?

3. Ask various people about the effects of divorce in their own lives. Be sure to accurately record their responses. Then compare what they say to Whitehead's ideas. Which responses support what Whitehead says? Which refute what she says?

4. How might you participate in this discussion about divorce? Consider expanding on a point, clarifying a point, redirecting the discussion, and so on.

Writing Strategies

1. What is Whitehead claiming about divorce? That is, what is her overall judgment? And what criteria—or standards of judgment—does Whitehead use to evaluate divorce?

2. What type of evidence does Whitehead use to support her claims (anecdotes, allusions, statistics, etc.)? What evidence do you think is most convincing?

3. How does Whitehead help the reader go from one idea to another? Provide several examples of strategies she uses to make her writing flow.

Ideas for Writing

1. Whitehead says, "There is an urgent need to begin a conversation about divorce." What other issue needs to be discussed? How might you begin that conversation?

2. What during the past 30 years has moved from the margin of society into the mainstream, and what has been its effect?

> If responding to one of these ideas, go to the **Analysis** section of this chapter to begin developing ideas for your essay.

Outside Reading

Find a written evaluation and make a photocopy or print it out. You might find an evaluation of a government policy or politician in a news magazine (such as the *National Review, Slate,* or *Pundit*). General readership magazines such as *Spin* and *Rolling Stone* regularly feature reviews of movies, music CDs, and performances. Your local city or campus newspaper may also feature reviews of movies, music, and restaurants. And you can always find book reviews in the *New York Times.*

To conduct an electronic search of journals and magazines, go to your library's periodical database or to InfoTrac (http://infotrac.galegroup.com/itweb/). For your library database, perform a keyword search, or for InfoTrac, go to the main search box and click on "keywords." Type in subjects that interest you (such as *books, political policy, music, restaurant*) and combine that keyword with an evaluative term *(critique, review, evaluation),* such as *book and review, political and policy and critique, restaurants and reviews, punk and music and review.* (When performing keyword searches, avoid using phrases or articles such as *a, an, the*; instead, use nouns separated by *and.*) The search results will yield lists of journal and magazine articles. This same strategy can be used with a newspaper database.

You can also search the Internet. Try the search engine Altavista.com. Like most Internet search engines, Altavista.com combines words using *and.* In the search box, try various combinations, such as those above.

The purpose of this assignment is to further your understanding of evaluation and to introduce a broad range of evaluation strategies. As you are probably discovering, evaluation appears in many different places and in many different contexts. But despite the subject or the audience, some elements of evaluation are consistent. As you read through this chapter, keep the written evaluation you have discovered close by and notice the elements and strategies the writer uses. Depending on your instructor's suggestions, do one or more of the following:

1. Notice how the writer applies various strategies from this chapter. On the hard copy or photocopy:

   - Highlight the thesis if it is stated. If the thesis is implied, write it in your own words.
   - Identify (or write in the margins) the *criteria*, or standards of judgment, the writer uses to judge the subject.
   - Identify any counterarguments or concessions (elements of argument from Chapter 5).

2. Write an essay that discusses the strategies employed by the writer. The following questions may be helpful.

   - Do you believe the writer uses appropriate criteria? Why?
   - How does the writer support his or her judgment about the subject?
   - Who is the audience for this evaluation?
   - How does the audience impact the kinds of things said in the evaluation?

3. Write at least three "Exploring Ideas" questions for the evaluation.

4. Write at least three "Writing Strategies" questions for the evaluation.

5. Write two "Ideas for Writing," such as the ones following the essays in this book.

INVENTION

Remember that invention is the primary strategy for producing writing that goes beyond common assumptions. As you work through the following three sections, imagine possibilities beyond your initial thoughts. The **Point of Contact** section will help you to find a subject for the evaluation; **Analysis** will help you to develop particular points about the subject; and **Public Resonance** will help make it relevant to a community of readers. As in the other chapters, the questions in each section are not meant to be answered directly in your final written assignment. They are meant to prompt reflection and discovery; however, your answers may evolve and find their way directly into your drafts. After you work through these three sections, the **Delivery** section, which immediately follows, will help you focus on a particular point and shape your ideas into a written text.

Point of Contact

Finding a Subject in Everyday Life

An evaluator needs to have particular insight into his or her subject, so choose something that you can examine carefully. (Your instructor may provide particular subjects.) Use the suggestions and questions below to seek out and focus on a particular subject. The questions will help you focus on details that can be used to develop your evaluation.

- **Go** to a place (such as a restaurant, movie theater, night club, amusement park, college classroom or campus, shopping mall, grocery store, etc.) and record information. Use notes, audio or video recorders, and/or photographs to gather details about the place. The following questions will help you focus on details. (Ignore the questions that are not relevant to your subject.)

What does the outside of the building(s) look like?
How is the inside of the building(s) organized?
How does the interior design influence the mood of the place?
What is the furniture like? (Observe the color, style, and condition.)
How is the lighting? (What kind of mood does it create?)
What is on the walls? How does this influence the mood of the place?
Besides buildings, what kinds of structures are there? How are they arranged?
How much open space is available?
What other areas constitute the place (yards, fields, paths, walks, roads, etc.)?
Are they maintained or decorated a particular way?
Who comes to this place? (Observe the demographics.)
How are people dressed? How do they act?
How do people communicate? (Do they talk loudly? Intimately?)
What sounds occur here?
How do things taste and smell?

- Go to or observe an event (such as a carnival, circus, beauty pageant, dance, tractor pull, art show, concert, poetry reading, company meeting, college class, etc.). Make certain to record information about the event in some way, using notes and/or recording. Also, see observation techniques in Chapter 12: Research and Writing (p. 576). Some of these questions will be more relevant to your subject than others.

  Who is involved? How are they acting and interacting?
  What are the demographics of the participants? Of the audience or class?
  How are participants dressed? (How is the audience or class dressed?)
  Do the participants seem engaged by the event? (How?)
  What sounds occur at the event?
  What happens before the event? What is the mood?
  How are the participants treated during the event?
  What kinds of interaction occur during the event?
  Where does the event take place?

- Focus on a person (such as a government official, doctor, minister, talk show host, roommate, professional athlete, work supervisor or manager, work associate, parent, grandparent, etc.). Evaluating a person can be tricky because it is easy to fall into an explanation of one's likes and dislikes. But instead of developing your personal likes or dislikes, focus on the qualities or actions of the person as one who holds a particular position or title. Use the following questions to help focus on the particular qualities or actions that are relevant to a person's position or title.

  > People are often put in the position of evaluating other people—and so they must put aside their personal likes or dislikes and evaluate objectively. For example, a manager of a store must evaluate the employees. She must put aside the fact that she enjoys spending time with some employees outside of working hours, and depend upon criteria beyond her personal affiliations.

  How does the person dress?
  Does he or she talk loudly or quietly?
  What level of formality does he or she use?
  Does he or she use formal or informal language?
  What kinds of gestures does he or she use?
  What kinds of facial expressions does this person have?
  Does he or she look at people when conversing with them?
  Does he or she ask questions?
  Does he or she make requests or give orders?
  Is he or she willing to listen to people? For how long?
  What does he or she do while listening to someone?
  How do people respond or react to this person?
  Are people comfortable around this person?
  Is this person entertaining, enlightening, engaging, comforting, informative, energizing (or the opposite of any of these)?

- **See** a movie or show (such as a motion picture, sitcom, documentary, television drama, music video). Popular media can also be tricky to evaluate. If you choose one of the above, avoid giving personal likes and dislikes. The following questions will aid you in developing a perspective that goes beyond simple likes and dislikes and leads to a sophisticated analysis of the subject.

Who are the primary figures (people or characters)?
What is the role of the primary figures in the action or plot?
Are the primary figures simple, predictable, or complex?
Are the primary figures likeable or detestable or both? Why?
What action occurs? (What's the plot?) Is the resolution predictable or surprising?
Does music accompany the action? What kind? At what points?
Does dialogue fill the movie/show, or are there long periods of silence? What's the effect of that silence?
Does the dialogue reveal something about the characters that their actions do not?
What kinds of graphic or sexually explicit images are in the movie/show?
Is the movie/show humorous or frightening in some way? How?
What message(s) does the movie/show offer?
Does the movie/show have stereotypes (of rich people, poor people, women, men, racial groups, children, elderly)?

- **Read** a text (such as a book, article, poster, letter, Web site, etc.). You might consider texts from your major. In this case, go to one of the journals for your major, or to a database in your library. In some ways, evaluating a text is easy because it can be examined closely—without rewinding or traveling somewhere. However, a written text can be a complicated mass of elements. Use the following questions to focus on the particular elements of a written text:

What is the main idea or main argument of the text?
What kind of evidence or support is used? How are the ideas developed?
How is information organized (in paragraphs, bullets, etc.)?
How formal is the language?
What is the tone of the text?
If the text is an argument, does it address counterarguments? Does it use concession?
What strategies are used to draw the reader into the ideas of the text?
How does the text use illustrations, photos, charts, or diagrams?

Invention Activity: The categories on the preceding pages are only a starting point; many other categories are possible. Consider, for example, evaluating a policy, a behavior, or even a philosophy. Once you have settled on a subject, try to generate more questions for recording details. Think of the questions as tools of exploration, as strategies for revealing everything that's occurring, as flashlights for lighting up different aspects of your subject. If groups are available, each person within a small group (three to four people) should take turns informing the group of his or her chosen subject. Then the other members should take turns offering a question about the subject while the writer records each question.

Evaluate a Behavior:

What behavior of mine has caused me the most problems in life?
What behavior of someone else has caused problems?
    Others the most problems?
What behavior of others, in general, has caused me the most problems?
    Others the most problems?
What is the cause of THAT behavior? How common is it?
    Why does it create a problem?
What other behavior causes similar problems, worse problems, no problems?

Example: Simon Benlow's Responses to Point of Contact Questions

Are the primary figures simple, predictable, or complex? In some ways, these are typical gangsters and thugs, but they are also different than most movie gangsters. One of the two lead characters (played by Samuel L. Jackson) wants to leave the business—and testifies about God throughout. Also, they go through situations that are atypical—e.g., the capture of mob boss and the death of henchman (Travolta).

How is the plot or action resolved at the end? It's not really—we just see how all the events relate to one another—and ultimately what happens to Travolta's henchman character.

Is the resolution predictable or surprising? It's different than most gangster movies. It doesn't end typically.

What message does the movie/show offer? This is tough . . . on the surface level, the movie suggests, easily enough, that this life (organized crime) is excessive, rough—downright terrible. But it also plays with stereotypes—with typical gangster images. In fact, if we look at this movie as a "gangster movie," it suggests some interesting things about movie making. It is saying something about violence: in one way, this is one of the most horribly violent movies, but it also spoofs the violence—the two henchmen are joking about cleaning up the brains of their unfortunate, and accidental, shooting victim.

Analysis

Discovering and Applying Criteria

Imagine taking your car to a mechanic because you heard a strange knocking sound when you accelerate. As you pull into the garage, the mechanic smiles and exclaims, "Hey, nice car! I love Ford Mustangs! There's nothing wrong with *that* car." Obviously, you'd be a bit disoriented—and maybe a little grumpy. You would probably complain, too: "Hey, I want you to tell me what's wrong with the car—tell me why it's making that sound!"

The problem with this scenario is that the mechanic does no analysis, and uses no *criteria* (the standards on which judgments are based). The evaluation of the car is not based on analysis, but only on the mechanic's own particular likes and dislikes.

Or imagine reading a review of a fine Italian restaurant. While ignoring the wine list, entrees, and presentation of the food, the reviewer gives the restaurant a very low rating because of a limited number of ice cream flavors. In this scenario, the reviewer uses the *wrong* criteria. The reviewer evaluates a fine dining establishment with criteria for judging an ice-cream shop. This would be similar to judging a historical drama negatively because it is not funny: historical dramas are not necessarily supposed to be funny; nor are fine Italian restaurants supposed to have wide varieties of ice cream.

Analyzing the Subject to Discover Appropriate Criteria

The first analytical step is to discover the subject's purpose or goal—to understand, in other words, what the subject is attempting to achieve. We can only develop criteria and then evaluate a subject if we know the subject's purpose and audience. For example, we can evaluate a movie only if we understand what the movie is attempting to do: to succeed as a comedy for teens, to maintain high action adventure for adults, or to retell a classic fairy tale for children. Evaluating something means understanding what that subject is attempting to do. For example, when Stayer examines Sea World, he concludes that the park is attempting to educate: Stayer argues that Sea World falls short of its intended purpose—or even confuses its own purpose. His essay, then, gives specific illustrations of the park's educational shortcomings.

While the specifics you recorded from the **Point of Contact** section tell you what your subject *does*, the **Analysis** questions (below) ask you what the subject is trying to achieve or *should* try to achieve. The following questions will help you discover the purpose of your subject, and criteria for the evaluation:

- What does this subject try to achieve? (Be specific. For example, an Italian restaurant may be attempting to provide an elegant dining experience with a particular ethnic cuisine. This is different from the goal of a general chain restaurant such as Denny's, which attempts to provide economically priced food from a general menu.)

- What do other like subjects try to achieve? (Developing criteria for a subject also involves looking at other like subjects. For example, to evaluate an Italian restaurant, one must first develop criteria, or standards, based on restaurants, and then, more specifically, Italian restaurants. Think about subjects similar to yours—other teachers, other comedic movies, other restaurants, and so on.)

- What is the subject's audience? (Whom does your subject attempt to engage or attract?) If you have not already considered the audience, imagine who might use, benefit from, and interact with the subject.

- What goals *should* this subject, or all subjects like it, have? (It might be argued, for instance, that a restaurant should attempt to elevate the dining experience, to transform the mundane act of eating into a cultural and social event. Once this criterion is established, someone might then use it to judge a particular restaurant.)

The answer to the above question can be used directly in an evaluation. In other words, an evaluation might include a discussion about the particular criteria, or argue for the application of some criteria. For example:

> Some people have argued that teachers need not worry about their ability to entertain. Teachers, it is often said, need not consider how boring their presentations are. Such a claim, however, ignores the needs of the student. No matter how old or literate, students benefit from engaging presentations, from intensive interaction, and good old-fashioned excitement. Teachers should, in fact, be judged on their skill at arousing attention in their students.

In this example, the writer explains, even argues for, the application of a particular criterion in evaluating teachers.

Applying Criteria to the Subject: Now that you have standards (criteria), you can begin making specific evaluative points about your subject. Answering the following questions will provide you with the raw material for your evaluation. In answering them, refer to your notes from the **Point of Contact** section:

- In what particular ways does the subject achieve its goal? What specific parts, tools, or strategies help the subject to achieve its goal? (For example, a restaurant depends upon such things as servers, atmosphere, and interior design, in addition to the actual food.)

- In what particular ways does the subject fall short of achieving its goal?

- What goals does the subject ignore?

- How does the subject compare and contrast to other similar subjects?

- What is unique about your subject's approach or strategy to achieving its goal?

Example: Simon Benlow's Responses to Analysis Questions

What does this subject try to achieve? It's obviously not out to uphold the gangster movie tradition. It's playing around with the typical gangster images and the typical way violence is dealt with in such movies.

In what particular ways does the subject achieve its goal? Maybe the goal of PF is to point to, play with, reveal (or something) the tradition of violence—the way violence works in popular culture movies—esp. gangster movies. The violence is almost THE central issue or feature of many scenes. The characters are actually caught up in their own violence—as opposed to the "standard" violent mobster movie in which the characters participate in extremely violent acts but then move on to the next scene or situation.

Notice that Benlow has not yet developed a concrete stance. He is exploring the possible ways the movie *Pulp Fiction* works—and, particularly, what the violence means. His overall evaluation seems to be both good and bad. He sees something potentially interesting about the movie, but also thinks it falls short in some ways. Many writers try to avoid this uncertainty; however, it serves Benlow well because it allows him to make a sophisticated point about the movie.

Public Resonance

How Does This Subject Involve Others?

A meaningful evaluation considers how the subject affects or influences people—how it resonates with people's lives and concerns. For example, a movie critic might argue that children's movies carry the responsibility of developing notions of right and wrong. The subject, a children's movie, would then concern the general public—especially if there is disagreement about right and wrong. Or someone might suggest that a restaurant affects the health and well-being of a community and influences the image of a neighborhood. Some topics, such as divorce, seem to automatically include public concern. In Whitehead's essay, for example, she does not have to convince the reader that her topic involves a broader public. However, she goes beyond saying that divorce affects people; she explores further. In fact, she spends much of her essay showing the extent to which divorce influences public life, and public policy and attitude influence divorce:

> Moreover, and even more troublingly, today's divorce ethic undermines the social foundation for our public commitment to children. A society cannot sustain a public ethic of obligation to children if it also embraces a private ethic that devalues and disenfranchises children. If parents are entitled to put their needs and interests before those of their own children, why should they or any other adults feel an obligation to help somebody else's children?

As Whitehead's essay suggests, an evaluation often depends on making the reader see how much the subject relates to the deep layers of public life. Likewise, Stayer makes a deep connection between the values of a theme park and American culture, and Ebert shows the relationship between *Star Wars* and contemporary American life.

The idea in discovering public resonance is to understand how a topic fits into or influences its surrounding community or larger society. Use the following questions to develop a sense of public resonance for your evaluation:

- How does the subject influence people's lives (their health, attitudes, living conditions, etc.)?
- Why is this subject important in people's lives?
- What do people expect from the subject?
- What are the effects and consequences of these expectations not being met?
- Why is it important that the subject meets people's expectations?

Be careful not to move too quickly through the questions above. Interesting ideas often emerge only after considering many possible answers. Imagine a student, Linda, who is evaluating a new restaurant in her town, and in a discussion with peers, develops her initial thoughts:

Why is this subject important in people's lives?

Linda: That's easy . . . a restaurant serves people food. And people need food.
Marcus: But do restaurants just provide food?
Jack: No, they also provide service—someone bringing you the food. And they also make eating a social event.

Linda: But that isn't the important part.

Marcus: Well, it isn't the main part, but I'd say people need that social aspect in their lives, and eating is naturally a social activity. That's what's so enjoyable about eating out—you get to feel social.

Linda: But eating is also a personal thing, right? It's about the home and family, too.

Jack: I would say that restaurants are important because they provide a place where people can feel slightly special—like they're somewhere besides their living room with a bowl of cereal. They make eating feel elevated.

Linda: If that's the case, what's the deal with all these restaurants saying they're "just like home"?

Marcus: Well, that's the goal of those chain restaurants, which really aren't like home at all. They're trying to make people feel close to home.

Linda: So these restaurants provide something psychologically to people. I guess that's why restaurants spend so much on atmosphere and advertising.

Marcus: So what about the particular restaurant, Chunky's? Does it make people feel "at home"?

Linda: Not really. It feels like a chain restaurant that's attempting to not feel like a chain restaurant.

Marcus: That's interesting. What things make it feel that way?

Linda's initial, quick response was to see restaurants as having only one (obvious) purpose. But her discussion leads to a more complicated understanding of the subject and its relationship to people's lives. She understands a deeper connection between her subject and the public, and this understanding could impact how she evaluates the particular restaurant. In fact, for Linda, the public resonance may be the primary issue in evaluating the restaurant.

Example: Simon Benlow's Notes to Public Resonance Questions

Why is this subject important in people's lives? Americans are drowned in violent images—in movies, shows, commercials, songs, etc. *Pulp Fiction* might be important because it points to (reminds us of the sheer amount and degree of) the violence that seeps throughout pop culture. At first, the movie is probably shocking and offensive, but what is more shocking and offensive, to me, is that millions of people adore violent heroes—or are just outright oblivious to the amount of violence around them.

What do people expect from the subject? What they expect from a box-office thriller is violence—but a certain kind. Many people expect to feel good after a movie, even if (or maybe because) a bunch of people get blown away. Violent (shoot-'em-up type) movies are expected to contain a few grizzly deaths, but people also anticipate that those deaths will only be part of a scene—and the gore will conveniently go away within a few seconds. But PF doesn't make it that easy . . . and maybe people need to be shocked back to their senses.

Crafting an essay, or any written text, is a recursive process: writers move back and forth, drafting, re-thinking, re-drafting. It is not a simple step-by-step journey through a chapter. But as they begin drafting, and heading for a final draft, writers benefit from a large collection of strategies, or tools, for building texts: for developing, shaping, and revising passages. The following sections (**Rhetorical Tools, Organizational Strategies, Writer's Voice**, and **Revision Strategies**) are designed to help you build a sophisticated and engaging text—one that emerges from your particular ideas. Each section points to important features or common concerns related to evaluative writing.

Rhetorical Tools

Developing the Evaluative Argument

Writers developing evaluations should carefully consider the most persuasive strategies available to them. While the main goal is to show the worth of a given subject, it is good to remember that evaluative writing is argumentative. That is, the reader must be persuaded to accept a particular way of seeing the subject.

Considering Your Thesis: An evaluation makes a judgment about a subject: "This is the best ice cream in town"; "Joe is an excellent shortstop." An evaluative thesis need not be completely positive or negative about the subject. It need not, for example, claim that a particular movie is absolutely great or downright rotten. Many evaluative thesis statements are a mixture of judgments. A critic may claim: "While the movie's cinematography is engaging, the plot is unnecessarily confusing."

The thesis should provide focus for the evaluation. That is, it should cue the reader on the primary issues under consideration. For example, the statement above *(While the movie's cinematography is engaging, the plot is unnecessarily confusing)* tells the reader that the evaluation focuses primarily on cinematography and plot—and not on, say, character development and costumes. Or consider Linda's focus on restaurants (in the **Public Resonance** section). Notice how her thesis gains focus:

Evolution of a Thesis	
The writer discovers the subject's purpose: What does this subject try to achieve?	*Chunky's attempts to give people a variety of good food and friendly service.*
In exploring the public resonance, the writer discovers another, less obvious, layer: Why is this subject important in people's lives?	*People like to feel attached to their surroundings, to the places they shop and eat. Restaurants such as Chunky's try to create the illusion that diners are patronizing a friendly neighborhood grill.*
The writer refines the idea into an evaluative claim:	*Although Chunky's attempts to make people feel comfortable in a small neighborhood grill, the atmosphere and food still seem prepared by a distant corporate chef.*

To focus your evaluation and generate a thesis, answer the following question: *What are the main criteria of my evaluation? (About which particular point(s) do I want to speak the most?)*

Using the Elements of Evaluation: Like argument, evaluation has

some basic ingredients. Also like argument, these evaluative elements can work together in an unlimited number of ways. Read about the following elements and then develop them according to your own subject.

Presentation/Summary: A reader expects to know something about the subject in an evaluation. Therefore, a writer should present the subject as part of the evaluation. The presentation or summary of the subject should *not* constitute the majority of an evaluation but should offer only the relevant details about the subject. For example, an evaluation using the thesis *While the movie's cinematography is engaging, the plot is unnecessarily confusing* would not devote long passages to the dress or appearance of the characters. Such information would be unnecessary and irrelevant to the evaluation.

Analysis: Analysis involves developing and applying criteria. The analytical element of the essay provides the close examination of the subject. Notice Stayer's analytical strategy:

> It was only in retrospect that I realized that these annoyances were related: the high-pitched entertainment and trivial sexual jokes, the shut-up-and-listen attitude, the constant noise and verbal presence, the Big Brotherly refrains of exactly what "We here at Sea World believe." These are all rhetorical strategies of a government diverting its citizens, masking something it doesn't want the public to know. And what is it that Sea World doesn't want its customers to think about?

Here, Stayer reveals his analytical process. He shows us the connection between events and tells us the significance of that connection. As readers, we can see the particular way that he makes sense of the smaller, and otherwise unrelated, details about Sea World. (This is the same thought process suggested by the questions in the **Analysis** section above.)

Argument/Support: In many ways, an evaluation is an argument—and some evaluations are even explicitly argumentative. In other words, an evaluation puts forth a particular, and potentially debatable, opinion about a subject. And when any debatable opinion is put forth, it should be supported. For example, if a writer were to claim that a movie's plot is unnecessarily complicated, she would have to support that claim with specific details, probably in a brief explanation of the plot. Ultimately, then, another writer could claim the opposite—arguing that the plot is *appropriately* complicated. Of course, this writer would have to show the appropriate twists and turns of the plot.

Evaluations can also involve other ingredients of argument: counterarguments, concessions, evidence, and appeals (see Chapter 5, p. 206). For example, a writer who makes a positive evaluation about a government leader might anticipate opposing claims that condemn the leader. Those people who supported President Clinton throughout the Lewinsky affair, for example, had to address constant accusations against him. That is, they could not simply ignore the negative evaluations; rather, they had to deal with them directly.

> It has been said that Clinton's transgression with Monica Lewinsky has compromised his ability to lead the country. But such a claim ignores the important distinction between public and private life. Public leaders throughout history have, in fact, maintained this distinction, serving the country in profound ways while enduring complicated personal lives. Certainly, Franklin Roosevelt is an important example. While his private life was filled with a troubled marriage and physical hardship, his public role was vital to a nation pulling itself out of the Depression. Like the people of Roosevelt's era, American citizens need to understand the function of the private/public distinction and to allow Bill Clinton the opportunity to do what many other leaders have done—carry on, and even endure the hardship of, a personal life beyond the duties of public office.

In this passage, the writer directly addresses an argument that opposes his positive evaluation of President Clinton. In this way, counterargument (one of the elements of argument) can help develop an evaluation.

The Elements of Evaluation	
Presentation/Summary **Analysis** • Defining Criteria • Applying Criteria **The Elements of Argument and Support** • Support (evidence and appeals) • Counterargument • Concession	As shown here, the elements of evaluation involve other elements (as in the four elements of argument—main idea, support, counterargument, and concession). Counterargument and concession, two elements of argument, may not be as important in an evaluation. They can, however, help to develop and enrich evaluative arguments.

Using Support about the Subject:
As in all argumentative writing, support is vital in evaluation. Each evaluative claim about the subject must be supported with details. Most of the claims made in evaluations are supported with specific information about the subject itself. That is, writers support general claims by pointing to particular details. Notice the use of particulars that Roger Ebert uses in this paragraph:

> Lucas fills his screen with loving touches. There are little alien rats hopping around the desert and a chess game played with living creatures. Luke's weather-worn "Speeder" vehicle, which hovers over the sand, reminds me of a 1965 Mustang. And consider the details creating the presence, look and sound of Darth Vader, whose fanged face mask, black cape and hollow breathing are the setting for James Earl Jones's cold voice of doom.

For your evaluative claims, be sure to use details about your subject. As you develop support, ask the following: *Which details best show my point about the subject's worth or shortcomings?*

Using Support outside the Subject:
As we explain in Chapter 5, writers have the world of history and culture at their disposal. This idea applies not only to argument, but to evaluation as well. While the primary mode of support in evaluation is focusing on details about the subject at hand, writers may also refer to outside issues/ideas/subjects to substantiate their claims. This might involve reference to other related subjects—such as the above example about President Clinton. To prove a point about the public/private distinction, the writer goes outside the subject (outside Clinton's life) and borrows from the life of Franklin Roosevelt. Notice Ebert's use of other like subjects for his evaluation:

> Like *Birth of a Nation* and *Citizen Kane*, *Star Wars* was a technical watershed that influenced many movies that came after. These films have little in common, except that they came along at crucial moments in cinema history, when new methods were ripe for synthesis. *Birth of a Nation* brought together the developing language of shots and editing. *Citizen Kane* married special effects, advanced sound, a new photographic style and a freedom from linear storytelling. *Star Wars* melded a new generation of special effects with the high-energy action picture; it linked space opera and soap opera, fairy tales and legend, and packaged them as a wild visual ride.

Also, see Bell's comparisons to other television sitcoms (¶ 3), Benlow's reference to other gangster movies (¶ 4), and Stayer's reference to Disney (¶ 1).

To develop claims using outside support, consider the following questions:

- Does a historical event or figure illustrate something about my topic?
- Does a historical situation or trend (say, the rise of a particular fashion, organization, or individual) illustrate something about my topic?
- Is my topic an example of something that has occurred in history . . . or recently, in the news?
- Does my topic or situation appear in any movies or television shows? If so, how is it handled?
- Does my topic appear in any works of literature? If so, how is it handled?
- Does my topic relate to anything in nature?
- Has science taught us anything about my topic?
- Do any news events illustrate my point or stance?
- Have I witnessed or experienced someone or something that illustrates my point?
- Can I construct a hypothetical situation that illustrates my point?

Organizational Strategies
Addressing Common Concerns

How Should I Arrange the Elements of Evaluation? Of

course, this largely depends on the subject and the writer's particular treatment, but arrangement generally depends upon how the different elements (presentation, analysis, argument) are developed. The elements may be mixed together or developed separately. You might simply begin the evaluation with a presentation or summary of the subject, followed by an analysis, and then an argument (showing support and dealing with counterarguments). In other words, these three sections, in this order, could easily serve as appropriate organization.

However, such a basic design limits possibilities. Often writers need to make several argumentative points as they present and analyze their subjects. Rather than separate the presentation, analysis, and argument, writers introduce the subject throughout the analysis, and develop their arguments as they proceed.

In Bell's essay, the presentation, analysis, and argument all work together throughout. Notice how Bell's main argument is given, and it is then supported with presentation and analysis:

> What's most comforting about this show, however, is that things *return to normal.* That is, *The Andy Griffith Show* offers us a normal that can be returned to. With *Andy Griffith* we get a sense that the complication has blown through like a summer thunderstorm, instead of us getting the sense that a little blue sky has blown through a place where it is otherwise always thunderstorming. The characters are at home. They're not strangers thrown together, and they haven't been transplanted in some strange land (such as Hooterville, New York City or Postmodern America). They are familiar with their surroundings and like (both "similar to" and "fond of") each other. The zaniness on *Andy Griffith* could just as well not ensue . . . but it does. On all those other shows, it must ensue. How couldn't it?

(For more examples, see Stayer ¶ 6–12, Benlow ¶ 3–5.)

Some writers find it valuable to give an overview of the subject early in the evaluation, and then to offer specifics throughout as part of analysis. Others, such as Roger Ebert, present small portions of the subject only when making a particular point. In his evaluation of *Star Wars*, he does not begin with a plot summary, but presents small bits of plot only when an element from the plot supports his claim:

> The story is advanced with spectacularly effective art design, set decoration and effects. Although the scene in the intergalactic bar is famous for its menagerie of alien drunks, there is another scene—when the two robots are thrown into a hold with other used droids—that equally fills the screen with fascinating details. And a scene in the Death Star's garbage bin (inhabited by a snake with a head shaped like E.T.'s) also is well done.
>
> Many of the planetscapes are startlingly beautiful, and owe something to fantasy artist Chesley Bonestell's imaginary drawings of other worlds. The final assault on the Death Star, when the fighter rockets speed between parallel walls, is a nod in the direction of *2001,* with its light trip into another dimension: Kubrick showed, and Lucas learned, how to make the audience feel it is hurtling headlong through space.

How Should I Include Support outside of the Subject? Like

any support tool, the possibilities are limitless. You might reference another similar subject briefly to help describe something—as Ebert does:

> And a scene in the Death Star's garbage bin (inhabited by a snake with a head shaped like E.T.'s) also is well done.

The reference to E.T. is quick. It serves only to describe the scene, and so the attention on the original subject, *Star Wars,* is only briefly interrupted or broken. However, sometimes writers want to put more attention on something other than the original subject, and so develop a new paragraph entirely.

When Should I Change Paragraphs? It may be helpful to think of a

television documentary of the Civil War. The camera may pan across an old battlefield while the host's voice narrates events. Then the scene breaks, and the camera focuses on a city that housed the soldiers; then the scene breaks again to focus on plantations that encircled a key battlefield. And occasionally, the camera shifts to a studio where the host sits talking with us about the deeper significance of the scenes. That is, when an in-depth analysis is in order, the camera focuses on the speaker, so that she or he can expound on one issue.

Paragraphs in an evaluation can work similarly: they can break when the writer wants the reader to focus on a new aspect of the subject. And they can even shift whenever the writer wants to give an extended analysis of a particular point. For example, notice the beginning sentences of several of Stayer's paragraphs:

> One of the first things to irk me at a Sea World park happened during a bird show. A perky blonde was displaying a few parrots, and she kept up a stream of banter about their feeding habits and origins.

> In America, unexamined notions of history and the coercive politics of majority identity go hand in hand with boorish nationalism.

> But not all employees were as chipper as the bird show people. There are two types of teenagers who work at Sea World: the aggressively happy and the sullenly aggrieved.

> The most important job at Sea World—and teenagers are particularly good at it—is making lots of noise.

Not only does Stayer use paragraphs to examine a new part of the subject, Sea World, but he also begins a new paragraph whenever he explores the deeper significance of one point. The second paragraph break above, for example, shows that Stayer is continuing his analysis of the bird show, but he launches into a brief analysis of history ("In America, unexamined notions of history . . ."), developing his thoughts in an entirely separate paragraph. You might imagine the camera shifting to a studio and focusing on Stayer rather than on some particular aspect of Sea World. However, for the next paragraph break, the camera is again focused on another aspect of Sea World: teenagers.

Activity: On a separate sheet of paper, write out the purpose of each paragraph in Benlow's essay.

How Should I Deal with Counterargument?

As in any argument, counterargument can be addressed in an unlimited number of ways. It may depend on the nature of your subject and on your position. If you are taking a relatively controversial stance (or one that is not often taken), you should be prepared to counterargue. For example, imagine a writer giving a negative evaluation of *Good Morning, America*, a popular and seemingly harmless television program:

> *Good Morning, America* confuses news with feel-good entertainment. Like an evening sitcom, its primary goal seems to be making the viewer feel that all is right with the world—or, specifically, all is right with the shiny happy upper-middle-class world in America. Certainly, many would argue that feel-good shows are a plus and that a morning show devoted to gloom and doom would be a great disservice. But the problem is not with the feel-good mood. It is that *Good Morning, America* postures itself as a quasi-news program, so any "news" that is given is ultimately framed by dimwitted celebrities making gratuitous appearances and exercise tips for the on-the-go lifestyle. The show smears news of the world across the same screen as the movie of the week. It's newstainment.

Notice here, in this turnabout paragraph, that the writer briefly addresses an opposing view: "Certainly, many would argue that feel-good shows are a plus and that a morning show devoted to gloom and doom would be a great disservice." Then the writer counters that idea for the remainder of the paragraph. But the writer could also further develop the opposing position in a separate paragraph, and then respond in yet another paragraph:

opposing position ¶
your counterargument ¶

And if the topic would require attention to more opposing points, the pattern can be repeated, to illustrate the repeating structure:

opposing position ¶
your counterargument ¶

opposing position ¶
your counterargument ¶

Make a Plan: Now that you have the basic elements of your evaluation, plan how you might organize the parts: Will you integrate the presentation of the subject and the analysis? Will you state your main judgment in the introduction and illustrate it throughout while presenting the subject? Do you want to separate or integrate the elements? After you organize your ideas, present them to a small group of classmates.

Writer's Voice

Exploring Options

Evaluations can sometimes sound too lofty—or what is sometimes called *stilted*. That is, writers can be in danger of sounding above the issue and above the audience. However, a good evaluation can be strongly worded without being stilted. A productive evaluation, like a good argument, attracts readers and engages those who might oppose the claims being made; a bad or unsuccessful evaluation loses readers. Here are some strategies for maintaining a cool but engaging tone.

Avoiding the Harsh Description:
It is often easy to use the most emotionally loaded terms to describe something or someone, to proclaim a subject "ridiculous" or "dumb." Such description, however, is most often exaggerated, and suggests that the writer has not fully investigated the subject. Be cautious of dismissing a subject by using especially harsh words. Imagine the following passage in which a writer evaluates a government official:

> Mayor G. is out of his mind. He has no understanding of the political spectrum and no concept of city governance. He is just some crazy power-hungry man looking for a soapbox to stand on. If the city really understood the depth of his insanity, it would kick him out of office immediately.

Such language is not only full of logical fallacies, but it also reveals the writer's unfocused aggression more than revealing an interesting and important point about the mayor. Such language also distracts readers from the subject (and a successful writerly voice should prompt the reader to investigate the subject closely).

Avoiding the Enthusiasm Crisis:
Also be careful not to overwhelm your reader with enthusiasm. If a writer comes off too amused or enthralled with a subject, readers may react with suspicion. Imagine a glowing evaluation of a political candidate:

> Zelda Brown is the best politician the country has seen. She has a perfect record as a community leader. Her insights into state politics are responsible for the American dream we are all living.

Certainly, any conscious and critical reader would recognize such claims as overblown and ungrounded. Too much enthusiasm alienates a reader in the same way as excessive negativity does. It is better to invite the reader into a close examination of the subject by drawing attention to particular details.

Exploring the Boundaries: Some writers perform. The language suggests, "Look at what I'm saying, and how I'm saying it!" Some writers lay low. Their language says, "I'm here, but only to give you some information." Some writers hide. Their language says, "I hope no one sees me in this essay." Every writer has a comfort zone, the place where he or she feels most at ease. The problem is that our most comfortable voices are not always the most appropriate for every situation, and only using our most comfortable voices does not allow us to explore how we can use language. The intensely performative writer may need, in some situations, to be invisible and understated. The writer hiding behind sentences may occasionally need to step forward and be noticed. The writers in this chapter display a wide range of voices. While Whitehead seems to be laying low in her work, Stayer seems as though he is standing on top of his own essay.

Activity: Examine Stayer's and Whitehead's essays. In a paragraph, describe their voices and point to particular passages that best illustrate your description. With peers, discuss the value and liability of both strategies.

The best writers, in all disciplines, occupations, and walks of life, are not locked into a voice. They can work with various voices, depending on the writing situation. As you consider your own voice and your own habits, imagine breaking from your comfort zone. Explore the following:

Asides: Writers often use parentheses or dashes to make an aside comment or ask a rhetorical question. The material separated by parentheses or dashes is often a more intimate or personal note (something one might share only with the person sitting closest at the table). These often help create a particular voice because they reveal insights that are less public than other information:

> The theme of that year's show was *Baywatch*, which involved—predictably enough—nubile bodies in poorly choreographed dance routines, the bold rescue of someone in the water, and the odd appearances of two buffoons (fat old man with hysterical wife) . . .

In both asides Stayer seems to be less public. He is sharing his personal reactions and assumptions. Although the first aside—"predictably enough"—seems insignificant, it reveals Stayer's predisposition: that is, we see that he cynically expects Sea World to mimic the television show *Baywatch*. And when we read the aside, we get a little nudge from the writer, as though he is saying in our ear: "We both knew that would happen, eh?"

Intensive Description: When writers stay abstract and general, when they do not commit to particulars, their voices may remain less visible. That is, voices often hide behind abstraction. But when writers characterize their subjects in particular and focused words, their voices become recognizable. For instance, notice the evaluative passage about Sea World:

> Sea World does not deal with real moral, environmental and scientific issues, and is unable to teach a true respect for nature. True respect for nature involves the spiritual and political, two directions that Sea World avoids in favor of less important and shallow entertainment.

And notice Stayer's more descriptive passage:

> Too occupied with obscuring the real moral, environmental, and scientific issues at stake, Sea World is constitutionally incapable of teaching respect for nature. Love of nature is spiritually informed and politically assertive. It is not the kind of passive, sentimental quackery Sea World prefers, and it cannot be taught with the crude tools in Sea World's lesson plans: glib moralizing, base pandering, and clichés masquerading as insights.

Stayer commits to specific characterizations, such as "sentimental quackery," that actually do more than describe. They also create a presence in the writing. A voice that calls something "sentimental quackery" is radically different from one that calls the same thing "shallow entertainment."

As you consider your own writing, explore by giving details and characterizing your subject with particular descriptors. Experiment by revising abstract passages and committing to particulars.

Allusions: When writers refer to something in popular culture or history or literature, they add to the nature of their voices. As in any social situation (a business meeting or a party) someone who alludes to Shakespeare consistently probably seems different than someone who always quotes Garth Brooks. The same goes for writers. Notice Ebert's use of the popular phrase from *Star Wars*:

> Those who analyze its philosophy do so, I imagine, with a smile in their minds. May the Force be with them.

Such a small gesture creates a somewhat playful voice, one enamored with the movie and at ease with celebrating it. Or notice how Bell's allusions add to the informality of his voice:

> On *MASH* or *Hogan's Heroes* or *Gomer Pyle*, they are either at war or could be. There's little real and lasting comfort in these folks who are gathered out of necessity so far from home. Yes, they're buddies and that's nice, but it's all so temporary.

While allusions do not automatically stamp a voice as either sophisticated or lowbrow, they do add to the overall quality of the voice. As you consider your own writing, explore allusions that help characterize your presence.

Revision Strategies

Now it is time to revise—to re-see your entire essay. Even though people evaluate informally throughout the day, writing a formal evaluation requires special attention to specific elements. While one purpose of this chapter is to give you practice at writing formal evaluations, such practice can also make you a better everyday evaluator. Careful revision will help you get a better grasp of the complexities of thinking through and writing an evaluation. Is your entire essay based on a claim, whether stated or implied, that makes an evaluative judgment about your topic? Do you provide the reader with the appropriate amount of summary/presentation, analysis, and argument? Are your criteria appropriate and made clear to the reader?

Consider the following revision strategies:

- Review this chapter, keeping your essay in mind. You might (1) explore your **Invention** notes, looking for helpful ideas and/or respond further in writing to relevant Invention questions; (2) review the **Rhetorical Tools, Organizational Strategies,** and **Writer's Voice** sections with an eye toward making appropriate changes; and (3) review several of the essays, noting the way the writers in this chapter approached this type of essay.

- Set aside at least as much time to revise as you took with invention and delivery.

- Create distance between you and your writing by getting away from it for a few days if possible or a few hours at least.

- Read your paper aloud to hear how it sounds, or have someone else read it aloud to you.

- Print out a hard copy of your paper and read it carefully in a different place than where you wrote it.

- Figure out your writing strategy by noticing how the parts of your essay work together to support your main point. Consider making an outline of your essay to help you see this.

- Have someone else read and respond to your essay.

For **Peer Review** see page 50.

Global Revision Questions

Invention (What have you learned by exploring your topic?)

- **Point of Contact:** What other ideas did you consider writing about before selecting this one? Why was this idea more worth pursuing than the others?

- **Analysis:** How has your exploration of this topic gone beyond your initial ideas and questions about it? In what ways have your ideas moved beyond your initial biases and perceptions—and beyond the common beliefs of your reader?

- **Public Resonance:** How might your essay be relevant to, or matter to, your reader? And what might be the consequence(s) of your essay? How might the reader think or act differently after reading it?

Delivery (What writing decisions have you made as part of your writing strategy?)

- **Rhetorical Tools:** Writers use strategies to allow the reader a better chance of hearing what they have to say. What rhetorical tools have you used to help get your point across? What ones didn't you use that might be helpful?

  - What is the main idea of your evaluation, and how have you conveyed that idea to the reader? What, besides your *intended* main idea, might the reader imagine your main idea to be? How might you help the reader hear what you are trying to say?

  - Revising involves filling in gaps—from adding a transitional expression to adding an entire section. In an evaluation, what criteria might the reader be expecting you to use? Have you failed to use a key criterion? And what criteria might the reader be surprised that you used? Have you explained your reason for selecting, or not selecting, any criteria your reader might wonder about? Where might you provide more evidence? Where might a different type of evidence help the reader understand? How might your title, introduction, and conclusion provide more helpful information regarding the main point of your essay?

  - Drafts can be wordy, repetitious, and contain unnecessary or irrelevant information. The extra information can be a distraction, often slowing the pace of the essay to a crawl. What summary/presentation information might you eliminate without hurting the reader's chance of understanding you? Where might the reader lose interest or get bogged down because you have over-explained or restated an idea?

- **Organizational Strategies:** You might begin by describing, or outlining, the structure of your essay to get a better sense of your overall organizational strategy. Essays can benefit from a writer's careful analysis of the arrangement of ideas—the overall structure of the piece. How might you rearrange elements (summary/presentation; claims; evidence; concessions; counterarguments) to allow the reader to better understand your ideas? How might you rearrange ideas within paragraphs? What ideas might be more helpful to the reader if placed earlier, or later, or near some other idea? How might connections and relationships between ideas be made more clear to the reader?

- **Writer's Voice:** Describe your writer's voice. Two essays might evaluate the same subject using the same criteria and providing the same support, but be received differently by the reader. One reason could be the writer's voice. Might your draft come across as sounding stilted or wishy-washy, for example? While writers consider their voice as they compose, revising allows them to re-see (or re-hear) the way they sound. What about your writer's voice is inviting to the reader? What about your writer's voice might alienate the reader? What changes might make your writer's voice more inviting?

CONSIDERING CONSEQUENCES

Evaluations are serious business. Like other types of writing, they can have important consequences. An employee who has been evaluated negatively may not receive a raise or a promotion. Worse yet, she may lose her job. On the other hand, if a flawed policy receives a positive evaluation, it will probably not be revised as it should be. This may lead to disastrous results later on. It is important that evaluations be fair—whether they are positive or negative. What might be the consequences of your essay for this chapter? That is, what effect might your ideas have on your reader's thoughts and actions? Consider these questions:

- Will the reader better understand the issue about which you wrote?
- Is the reader likely to think or behave differently?
- What might be the benefits to others? How might others be harmed?
- Who besides your instructor might benefit from your ideas?
- How might what you wrote about be affected?
- What might be the effect of these consequences on you, the writer?

Activities

The Consequences of Your Essay

1. List as many individuals as you can imagine whose thinking and/or actions might change if they were to read the essay you wrote for this chapter. For each individual you list, name the possible change in his or her thinking and/or action. (As you consider consequences upon your reader, consider the "ripple effect" of those consequences. If your reader thinks or behaves differently, what is the impact of that thinking or behavior on others?)

2. Summarize your essay for several people, and then ask them to help you consider its potential consequences. Write down any consequences they suggest that you did not already consider.

3. List three other forms of delivery that you might have used to express your idea (report, letter, poster, and so on). How might the consequences of your message have been different if delivered by way of these other forms?

The Consequences of the Chapter Readings

1. How might you think or act differently after having read one of the essays in this chapter? How might *you* benefit from, or be harmed by, your new way of thinking? How might *others* benefit from, or be harmed by, your new way of thinking and/or acting?

2. How might someone you know benefit from reading one of the essays in this chapter? Match an essay in this chapter to a particular person. Then explain in writing how the essay might influence that person's thoughts or actions. If possible, have the person read the essay, or summarize it for him or her, and then find out if the essay influenced the person as you imagined it might.

3. How might one of the *writers* of this chapter be influenced by his or her own writing? For example, what might the writer have learned, or discovered, as a result of writing, and how might he or she now think or act differently?

Considering Images

1. Find an image that you think goes with one of the essays in this chapter. Then explain in writing what you think the relationship is between the image and the essay. For example, how might the image help to illustrate a point being made in the essay? Or how might it encourage the reader to think about a certain point?

2. Explain how someone might view the image you found for #1 above differently after having read the appropriate essay. Be specific in explaining how the person might view the image before reading the essay and then after reading the essay.

3. Show the image you found for #1 above to several people, and ask them to read the corresponding essay. Then find out how they view the image differently after having read the essay. Did the written text affect the way they viewed the image?

4. After reading one of the essays for this chapter, how might someone view a person, place, or thing differently? Describe the person, place, or thing in writing or create a visual image of it (by taking a photograph, drawing or painting it, and so on). Explain in writing how the particular essay might influence the person's thinking.

The Consequences of Everyday Evaluations

1. Make a list of recent evaluations you have made, along with their consequences. You have, for example, probably evaluated your clothes, your meals, your classes, your friends, and so on. Make two columns, listing in one column what you have evaluated and in the other the consequence(s) of your evaluation.

2. Select an important item from your list for #1 above and explore the consequences of your evaluation more thoroughly. In writing, explain how you made your evaluation and how its consequences affected you and others. You might consider the ripple effect of your evaluation. For example, if you evaluated your college before attending it, how did that evaluation affect not just you, but your friends, your parents, your teachers, strangers, and so on?

3. Think of an evaluation someone you know made that affected you. What did the person evaluate, and how did it affect you and others?

4. Think of an evaluation, expressed in writing or otherwise, that has influenced many people. For example, people—such as government officials, college administrators, drivers of motor vehicles, and so on—often make evaluations that impact others. Whom did the evaluation affect and how?

5. Make a list of evaluations that have been made throughout history, and then explain which evaluation has affected people's lives the most.

Considering Images

1. Find an image that makes an evaluative claim and, in writing, discuss its consequences. What claim does the image make, and how? You might look for images in popular magazines, the newspaper, on the Internet, on campus, or elsewhere.

2. Find an image in this textbook that makes an evaluative claim. What claim does the image make, and how?

Writing, Speech, and Action

EVERYDAY RHETORIC

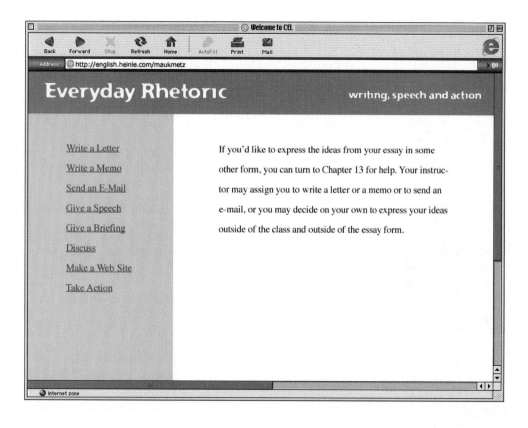

Everyday Rhetoric writing, speech and action

Write a Letter

Write a Memo

Send an E-Mail

Give a Speech

Give a Briefing

Discuss

Make a Web Site

Take Action

If you'd like to express the ideas from your essay in some other form, you can turn to Chapter 13 for help. Your instructor may assign you to write a letter or a memo or to send an e-mail, or you may decide on your own to express your ideas outside of the class and outside of the essay form.

Exploring Visual Rhetoric

I t can be argued that images, too, use rhetoric. And by looking at how images work, we can apply some of the important concepts of rhetoric not just to writing and speaking, but to images. Looking at visual rhetoric can also help us to better understand how rhetoric is used in writing and speech.

Analyzing This Chapter's Opening Image:
Analyze this chapter's opening image using the "Analyzing an Image" questions in Chapter 13, on page 694. What seems to be the main idea of the image? How do the particular elements of the image—content, framing, focus, and so on—help to convey that idea?

1. Explain your analysis in several paragraphs, being certain to show how particular elements of the image help to convey a main idea.

2. Discuss your analysis with several people, exploring through discussion how your understanding of the image is similar to or different from their own. Following the discussion, write down the main similarities and differences in your viewpoints, and explain how your ideas about the image developed or changed through discussion. How did the discussion influence your ideas about the image?

3. Imagine one change in this chapter's opening image. For example, you might add an object, frame the image differently, or take the photo from a different angle. Make one imaginary change in the image and explain how that change might alter the image's message.

Find an Image That Relates to Your Essay:
What image might you use in conjunction with the essay you wrote for this chapter?

1. Write a caption for the image.

2. Write an essay explaining the relationship between the image and your text. Consider the following ideas:

   - How does the image support or help to explain the text of the essay?
   - What is the theme of the image? What idea does it convey?
   - What specific elements of the image convey the main idea and the support for that idea?
   - How might the reader view the image differently after having read your essay?
   - How might the reader be confused by the relationship of your essay and image?

3. Show the image to several people, and ask each person to read your essay. Then ask them how they now view the image differently.

Considering Other Images in This Text

1. Explain how one of the images in this textbook makes an evaluative claim.

    A. Present your ideas from #1 above to your classmates in the form of a one-minute briefing.
    B. Send an e-mail to your instructor, presenting your ideas from #1 above.
    C. Write a memo to your instructor, presenting your ideas from #1 above.

2. Discuss your idea from #1 above with several classmates, asking them to help you develop support for your claim. Then write a memo to your instructor explaining how the discussion was or was not helpful in developing your ideas about the image. Be specific in explaining what new ideas you discovered.

3. Select one image from this text and explain what response it invites. What argument does the image make and how does the image encourage the reader to think?

Considering Images from Everyday Life

1. Refer to the "Analyzing an Image" questions on page 694 and the **Invention** and **Delivery** strategies in this chapter to help you evaluate an image. What is the image's purpose, and how successfully does it achieve that purpose? You might consider posters, advertisements, and so on.

    A. Evaluate an image from the popular media.
    B. Evaluate an image on campus.
    C. Evaluate an image created by a government official or agency.
    D. Evaluate an image created by fashion.

2. Create a flag, either for the United States, for your state, your local community, or your school. Then write an essay evaluating the flag's design.

3. Evaluate a classmate's flag after reading his or her evaluation of it. Use the **Invention** and **Delivery** sections of this chapter along with the "Analyzing an Image" questions on page 694 for help.

Find an Image That Relates to a Classmate's Essay

1. Read a classmate's essay and then find an image that you think goes well with it. Write a caption for the image, and explain briefly in writing how the image relates to the written text.

2. Find at least four images that you think go well with a classmate's essay. Then use those four images to create a photo (or image) essay. Arrange the images in an appropriate order and explain how they work together to convey your classmate's idea.

3. Evaluate a classmate's photo (or image) essay from #2 above. For help, use the **Invention** and **Delivery** strategies from earlier in this chapter as well as the "Analyzing an Image" questions on page 694.

8

Chapter Contents

Searching
for Causes

*What are all the causes of automobile
accidents? (Consider attitudes, policies,
circumstances, and behaviors beyond
the obvious.)*

> **"A**ll human beings should try to learn before they die what they are running from, and to, and why. **"**
>
> *—James Thurber*

When something happens in a community, everyone wants to know why. Why did the apartment building catch on fire? Why did the incumbent mayor's campaign lose momentum? Why are so many kids absent from school? What causes the traffic jam on I-95 every day? Why did the stock market suddenly drop? Why did the terrorists attack? Of course, everybody has guesses, but it takes a close analysis (usually by professionals in a given field) to discover the possible causes of such phenomena. Fire officials inspect the ashes of a burned apartment building; political scientists examine candidates' speeches and poll results; civil engineers look closely at travel patterns and highway capacity; economists deliberate over consumption trends and overseas markets. In all these cases, the people searching for causes are detectives attempting to find answers amidst a dizzying array of possibilities.

The search for causes constitutes much of the workload in many occupations. Doctors, of course, diagnose patients (looking for the cause of particular symptoms). Psychologists try to understand the causes of personality disorders or behavioral problems in children. Business executives hold weekly meetings and discuss the causes of production failures. Education specialists work with children to find the cause of scholastic problems. And, as you can imagine (or as you may have witnessed), the search for such causes is not easy. Any number of factors can contribute to an effect. Take, for example, low proficiency test scores in public schools: School administrators might argue that poor teaching is the cause; teachers may point to poor parenting and discipline problems in the classroom; parents may point to bullying on school grounds or drug abuse; others might point to the tests themselves as the cause. The search for this cause, as it turns out, is a heated debate.

In academia, students spend much of their time studying causes:

- In an engineering class, students try to discover what causes one generator to produce more energy than another.
- Educational psychology students discuss why a particular student has lost all motivation.
- In history and economics seminars, students study economic conditions of the nineteenth century and debate the causes of the American Civil War.
- A class of physics students tries to determine the cause of black holes.

It might even be said that academia prepares people to understand causes in different fields. That is, the study of a particular discipline gives students the critical perspectives necessary for asking the right questions (to find the right answers) within their fields. But despite the particular field or discipline, the process of discovery (of focusing and analyzing) is much the same, and the act of communicating one's discoveries is key in every situation.

8 This chapter will help you focus on a particular topic (a behavior, event, trend), discover a possible cause, and then develop an argument in favor of that particular cause. The following essays will provide valuable insight to necessary writing strategies. After reading the essays, you can find a topic in one of two ways:

1. Read the following essays and choose one of the **Writing Topics** that follow each.
2. Go to the **Point of Contact** section to find a problem from your everyday life.

After finding a subject, go to the **Analysis** section to begin developing the evaluation.

READINGS

In the following essays, notice how each writer offers a particular stance on an issue and develops that stance throughout the entire essay. In many ways the texts in this chapter are arguments: they put forward a particular belief (about the cause of a phenomenon) and attempt to prove its validity. Some of the essays also make explicit use of counterargument: they refute opposing claims, or more specifically, they refute other interpretations of cause. For example, Schor refutes others' interpretation of the cause of overconsumption. Some of the writers argue about the cause of a phenomenon because they hope for a change in behavior or policy. Jacoby, for instance, explains the cultural causes for girls' deficiency in science and math so that it may be avoided. And Schor hopes to point out the cause of the "consumption problem" in order to redirect Americans' economic habits. As you read, consider how these essays embody the writing strategies discussed in earlier chapters: observation, concept analysis, the elements of argument, and the elements of evaluation.

The New Politics of Consumption: Why Americans Want So Much More Than They Need

Juliet Schor

Juliet Schor is an economist and the Director of Women's Studies at Harvard University. "The New Politics of Consumption" as reprinted here is the first part of an article that originally appeared in the Boston Review *in 1999. As you read her essay, consider how it relates to your own spending habits. Also, highlight or underline passages that ask you to think differently, and in the margin jot down each "new idea" Schor raises.*

1   In contemporary American culture, consuming is as authentic as it gets. Advertisements, getting a bargain, garage sales, and credit cards are firmly entrenched pillars of our way of life. We shop on our lunch hours, patronize outlet malls on vacation, and satisfy our latest desires with a late-night click of the mouse.[1]

[1] Sources for much of the data cited in this article can be found in the notes to *The Overspent American: Why We Want What We Don't Need* (New York: HarperPerennial, 1999) or by contacting the author.

2   Yet for all its popularity, the shopping mania provokes considerable dis-ease: many Americans worry about our preoccupation with getting and spending. They fear we are losing touch with more worthwhile values and ways of living. But the discomfort rarely goes much further than that; it never coheres into a persuasive, well-articulated critique of consumerism. By contrast, in the 1960s and early '70s, a far-reaching critique of consumer culture was a part of our political discourse. Elements of the

New Left, influenced by the Frankfurt School, as well as by John Kenneth Galbraith and others, put forward a scathing indictment. They argued that Americans had been manipulated into participating in a dumbed-down, artificial consumer culture, which yielded few true human satisfactions.

3   For reasons that are not hard to imagine, this particular approach was short-lived, even among critics of American society and culture. It seemed too patronizing to talk about manipulation or the "true needs" of average Americans. In its stead, critics adopted a more liberal point of view, and deferred to individuals on consumer issues. Social critics again emphasized the distribution of resources, with the

more economistic goal of maximizing the incomes of working people. The good life, they suggested, could be achieved by attaining a comfortable, middle-class standard of living. This outlook was particularly prevalent in economics, where even radical economists have long believed that income is the key to well-being. While radical political economy, as it came to be called, retained a powerful critique of alienation in production and the distribution of property, it abandoned the nascent intellectual project of analyzing the consumer sphere. Few economists now think about how we consume,

and whether it reproduces class inequality, alienation, or power. "Stuff" is the part of the equation that the system is thought to have gotten nearly right.

4   Of course, many Americans retained a critical stance toward our consumer culture. They embody that stance in their daily lives—in the ways they live and raise their kids. But the rejection of consumerism, if you will, has taken place principally at an individual level. It is not associated with a widely accepted intellectual analysis, and an associated *critical politics of consumption*.

5   But such a politics has become an urgent need. The average American now finds it harder to achieve a satisfying standard of living than 25 years ago. Work requires longer hours, jobs are less secure, and pressures to spend more intense. Consumption-induced environmental damage remains pervasive, and we are in the midst of widespread failures of public provision. While the current economic boom has allayed consumers' fears for the moment, many Americans have long-term worries about their ability to meet basic needs, ensure a decent standard of living for their children, and keep up with an ever-escalating consumption norm.

6   In response to these developments, social critics continue to focus on income. In his impressive analysis of the problems of contemporary American capitalism, *Fat and Mean*, economist David Gordon emphasized income *adequacy*. The "vast majority of US households," he argues, "can barely make ends meet. . . . Meager livelihoods are a *typical* condition, an *average* circumstance." Meanwhile, the Economic Policy Institute focuses on the distribution of income and wealth, arguing that the gains of the top 20 percent have jeopardized the well-being of the bottom 80 percent. Incomes have stagnated and the robust 3 percent growth rates of the 1950s and '60s are long gone. If we have a consumption problem, this view implicitly states, we can solve it by getting more income into more people's hands. The goals are redistribution and growth.

7   It is difficult to take exception to this view. It combines a deep respect for individual choice (the liberal part) with a commitment to justice and equality (the egalitarian part). I held it myself for many years. But I now believe that by failing to look deeper—to examine the very nature of consumption—it has become too limiting. In short, I do not think that the "income solution" addresses some of the most profound failures of the current consumption regime.

8   Why not? First, consuming is part of the problem. Income (the solution) leads to consumption practices that exacerbate and reproduce class and social inequalities, resulting in—and perhaps even worsening—an unequal distribution of income. Second, the system is structured such that an *adequate* income is an elusive goal. That is because adequacy is relative—defined by reference to the incomes of others. Without an analysis of consumer desire and need, and a different framework for understanding what is adequate, we are likely to find ourselves, twenty years from now, arguing that a median income of $100,000—rather than half that—is adequate. These arguments underscore the social context of consumption: the ways in which our sense of social standing and belonging comes from what we consume. If true, they suggest that attempts to achieve equality or adequacy of individual incomes without changing consumption patterns will be self-defeating.

9   Finally, it is difficult to make an ethical argument that people in the world's richest country need more when the global income gap is so wide, the disparity in world resource use so enormous, and the possibility that we are already consuming beyond the earth's ecological carrying capacity so likely. This third critique will get less attention in this essay—because it is more familiar, not because it is less important—but I will return to it in the conclusion.

10   I agree that justice requires a vastly more equal society, in terms of income and wealth. The question is whether we should also aim for a society in which our relationship to consuming changes, a society in which we consume *differ-ently*. I argue here for such a perspective: for a critique of consumer culture and practices. Somebody needs to be for quality of life, not just quantity of stuff. And to do so requires an approach that does not trivialize consumption, but accords it the respect and centrality it deserves.

The New Consumerism

11   A new politics of consumption should begin with daily life, and recent developments in the sphere of consumption. I describe these developments as "the new consumerism," by which I mean an upscaling of lifestyle norms; the pervasiveness of conspicuous, status goods and of competition for acquiring them; and the growing disconnect between consumer desires and incomes.

12   Social comparison and its dynamic manifestation—the need to "keep up"—have long been part of American culture. My term is "competitive consumption," the idea that spending is in large part driven by a comparative or competitive process in which individuals try to keep up with the norms of the social group with which they identify—a "reference group." Although the term is new, the idea is not. Thorstein Veblen, James Duesenberry, Fred Hirsch, and Robert Frank have all written about the importance of relative position as a dominant spending motive. What's new is the redefinition of reference groups: today's comparisons are less likely to take place between or among households of similar means. Instead, the lifestyles of the upper middle class and the rich have become a more salient point of reference for people throughout the income distribution. Luxury, rather than mere comfort, is a widespread aspiration.

13   One reason for this shift to "upscale emulation" is the decline of the neighborhood as a focus of comparison. Economically speaking, neighborhoods are relatively homogeneous groupings. In the 1950s and '60s, when Americans were keeping up with the Joneses down the street, they typically compared themselves to other households of similar incomes. Because

of this focus on neighbors, the gap between aspirations and means tended to be moderate.

14   But as married women entered the workforce in larger numbers—particularly in white collar jobs—they were exposed to a more economically diverse group of people, and became more likely to gaze upward. Neighborhood contacts correspondingly declined, and the workplace became a more prominent point of reference. Moreover, as people spent less time with neighbors and friends, and more time on the family-room couch, television became more important as a source of consumer cues and information. Because television shows are so heavily skewed to the "lifestyles of the rich and upper middle class," they inflate the viewer's perceptions of what others have, and by extension what is worth acquiring—what one must have in order to avoid being "out of it."

15   Trends in inequality also helped to create the new consumerism. Since the 1970s, the distribution of income and wealth have shifted decisively in the direction of the top 20 percent. The share of after-tax family income going to the top 20 percent rose from 41.4 percent in 1979 to 46.8 percent in 1996. The share of wealth controlled by the top 20 percent rose from 81.3 percent in 1983 to 84.3 percent in 1997. This windfall resulted in a surge in conspicuous spending at the top. Remember the 1980s—the decade of greed and excess? Beginning with the super-rich, whose gains have been disproportionately higher, and trickling down to the merely affluent, visible status spending was the order of the day. Slowed down temporarily by the recession during the early 1990s, conspicuous luxury consumption has intensified during the current boom. Trophy homes, diamonds of a carat or more, granite countertops, and sport utility vehicles are the primary consumer symbols of the late-1990s. Television, as well as films, magazines, and newspapers ensure that the remaining 80 percent of the nation is aware of the status purchasing that has swept the upper echelons.

16   In the meantime, upscale emulation had become well-established. Researchers Susan Fournier and Michael Guiry found that 35 percent of their sample aspired to reach the top 6 percent of the income distribution, and another 49 percent aspired to the next 12 percent. Only 15 percent reported that they would be satisfied with "living a comfortable life"—that is, being middle class. But 85 percent of the population cannot earn the six-figure incomes necessary to support upper-middle-class lifestyles. The result is a growing aspirational gap: with desires persistently outrunning incomes, many consumers find themselves frustrated. One survey of US households found that the level of income needed to fulfill one's dreams doubled between 1986 and 1994, and is currently more than twice the median household income.

17   The rapid escalation of desire and need, relative to income, also may help to explain the precipitous decline in the savings rate—from roughly 8 percent in 1980, to 4 percent in the early 1990s, to the current level of zero. (The stock market boom may also be inducing households not to save; but financial assets are still highly concentrated, with half of all households at net worths of $10,000 or less, including the value of their homes.) About two-thirds of American households do not save in a typical year. Credit card debt has skyrocketed, with unpaid balances now averaging about $7,000 and the typical household paying $1,000 each year in interest and penalties. These are not just low-income households. Bankruptcy rates continue to set new records, rising from 200,000 a year in 1980 to 1.4 million in 1998.

18   THE NEW CONSUMERISM, with its growing aspirational gap, has begun to jeopardize the quality of American life. Within the middle class—and even the upper middle class—many families experience an almost threatening pressure to keep up, both for themselves and their children. They are deeply concerned about the rigors of the global economy, and the need to have their children attend "good" schools. This means living in a community with relatively high housing costs. For some households this also means providing their children with advantages

purchased on the private market (computers, lessons, extra-curriculars, private schooling). Keeping two adults in the labor market—as so many families do, to earn the incomes to stay middle class—is expensive, not only because of the second car, child-care costs, and career wardrobe. It also creates the need for time-saving, but costly, commodities and services, such as take-out food and dry cleaning, as well as stress-relieving experiences. Finally, the financial tightrope that so many households walk—high expenses, low savings—is a constant source of stress and worry. While precise estimates are difficult to come by, one can argue that somewhere between a quarter and half of all households live paycheck-to-paycheck.

19   These problems are magnified for low-income households. Their sources of income have become increasingly erratic and inadequate, on account of employment instability, the proliferation of part-time jobs, and restrictions on welfare payments. Yet most low-income households remain firmly integrated within consumerism. They are targets for credit card companies, who find them an easy mark. They watch more television, and are more exposed to its desire-creating properties. Low-income children are more likely to be exposed to commercials at school, as well as home. The growing prominence of the values of the market, materialism, and economic success make financial failure more consequential and painful.

20   These are the effects at the household level. The new consumerism has also set in motion another dynamic: it siphons off resources that could be used for alternatives to private consumption. We use our income in four basic ways: private consumption, public consumption, private savings, and leisure. When consumption standards can be met easily out of current income, there is greater willingness to support public goods, save privately, and cut back on time spent at work (in other words, to "buy leisure"). Conversely, when lifestyle norms are upscaled more rapidly than income, private consumption "crowds out" alternative uses of in-come. That is arguably what happened in the 1980s and 1990s: resources shifting into private consumption, and away from free time, the public sector, and saving. Hours of work have risen dramatically, saving rates have plummeted, public funds for education, recreation, and the arts have fallen in the wake of a grass-roots tax revolt. The timing suggests a strong coincidence between these developments and the intensification of competitive consumption—though I would have to do more systematic research before arguing causality. Indeed, this scenario makes good sense of an otherwise surprising finding: that indicators of "social health" or "genuine progress" (i.e., basic quality-of-life measures) began to diverge from GDP in the mid-1970s, after moving in tandem for decades. Can it be that consuming and prospering are no longer compatible states?

21   To be sure, other social critics have noted some of these trends. But they often draw radically different conclusions. For example, there is now a conservative jeremiad that points to the recent tremendous increases in consumption and concludes that Americans just don't realize how good they have it, that they have become overly entitled and spoiled. Reduced expectations, they say, will cure our discontents. A second, related perspective suggests that the solution lies in an act of psychological independence—individuals can just ignore the upward shift in consumption norms, remaining perfectly content to descend in the social hierarchy.

22   These perspectives miss the essence of consumption dynamics. Americans did not suddenly become greedy. The aspirational gap has been created by structural changes—such as the decline of community and social connection, the intensification of inequality, the growing role of mass media, and heightened penalties for failing in the labor market. Upscaling is mainly defensive, and has both psychological and practical dimensions.

23   Similarly, the profoundly social nature of consumption ensures that these issues cannot be resolved by pure acts of will. Our notions of

what is adequate, necessary, or luxurious are shaped by the larger social context. Most of us are deeply tied into our particular class and other group identities, and our spending patterns help reproduce them.

24   Thus, a collective, not just an individual, response is necessary. Someone needs to address the larger question of the consumer culture itself. But doing so risks complaints about being intrusive, patronizing, or elitist. We need to understand better the ideas that fuel those complaints.

Exploring Ideas

1. In a paragraph or so, explain what you think Schor is trying to accomplish in this essay.

2. How does Schor encourage the reader to think about consumerism?

3. How is the way that Schor sees consumerism, or consumption, similar to or different from the way you see it? Write down your major areas of agreement and disagreement. Then explain the reason you agree or disagree.

4. Keeping in mind Schor's ideas, explore your own spending habits and the habits of those around you. What evidence can you find for Schor's argument? What evidence can you find to refute what Schor says?

5. Discuss Schor's main ideas and how they are or are not played out in your life and the lives of your classmates and others. Then, through discussion, writing, and further research, attempt to discover the causes of the way you consume, and its consequences.

Writing Strategies

1. Schor's essay is longer than the type of essay often written in college writing classes. What strategies does she employ that help the reader to follow her lengthy discussion/argument?

2. Find one paragraph in Schor's essay that you think is especially well-written. What is the main idea of that paragraph? And how (in what way or ways—example, allusion, statistics, and so on) does she support that main idea?

3. How does Schor let the reader know the main idea of her essay? Does she state it or imply it? If implied, is it clear without a statement of the main idea?

4. Schor introduces the reader to new terms (or concepts) such as "the new consumerism." What strategy does she use to make this term clear to the reader? What other new terms (or concepts) does she use? How does she make them clear to the reader?

5. Describe Schor's overall organizational strategy. How are her ideas arranged and connected for the benefit of the reader?

Ideas for Writing

1. What is the cause of some negative trend in behavior?

2. What is the cause of some problem on your campus or in the field you are studying?

> If responding to one of these ideas, go to the **Analysis** section of this chapter to begin developing ideas for your essay.

Throwing Up Childhood

Leonard Kress

Leonard Kress, whose writing also appears in Chapter 1, teaches humanities and writing courses at Owens Community College and has published three collections of poetry. His fourth, Orphics, was published in 2003 by Kent State University Press. As you read "Throwing Up Childhood," think about Kress's purpose in writing. How might his essay be of value to others? That is, what might be a positive consequence of someone else listening to what Kress has to say?

In the margins of this essay, a reader's comments point to key ideas and writing strategies. As you read the essay, consider how the comments might influence your own reading and writing.

Exploring Ideas

Writing Strategies

I remember standing breathless and exhilarated in the hotel lobby, the rest of my family still in the dining room finishing their evening meal. I'm not sure whether or not they can see what I see—the thin gray broken line on the carpet, leading all the way to the back entrance. This time I don't make it out to the patio, the swimming pool, down to the beach, inundated this summer with jellyfish and jelly lichen, Portuguese Man O'War. If only they would leave their table, they could easily find me by following the half-digested dinner rolls and the masticated but intact sirloin morsels, the bitter tomato-broth they soak in. Hansel, whom I imagine to be about my age (seven and a half), couldn't have left a better trail for him and his sister to follow back to their woodland cottage. Even if the birds had pecked it clean, that bile-stain would still remain, like a stripe dividing a country highway. We are here in Miami Beach to visit my grandparents, Ada and Max, and since they live in a tiny apartment, we are staying in this beachfront hotel, more luxurious than we are used to. It occurs to me that only the desk clerk has been following my whole grand performance with any interest. Whatever others there might be carefully and kindly turn away their gaze. But the desk clerk glances over to me and across the lobby, as if surveying both the damage and the cause of it. I recognize that smirk and wonder, was he a vomiter too? I don't have a clue and don't really care; he assiduously computes the cleaning bill.

Begins with personal narrative.

Very detailed description.

Allusion to Hansel and Gretel.

He is a type of child—a "vomiter."

This isn't the first time. As far back as I can remember, meals out with my parents were capped with similar grand gestures. It didn't matter whether it was a Howard Johnson's, a deli, a steakhouse—sometimes I'd conveniently make it to the bathroom sink or toilet, other times I'd leave a pile on the floor, splatter the

New paragraph pulls the reader out of the details.

Exploring Ideas

No obvious reason for his vomiting.

He was not an overeater.

He was not obese or unhealthy.

Active & energetic— otherwise "normal"?

Anorexia and bulimia are the same type of disease? (The disease of '90s.)

Eating disorders associated with psychological problems.

door, the parking lot, the car. I don't know how it happened; I can't make sense of the progression that leads up to it. I ordered from the menu like my brother and sister—appetizer, entrée, dessert. I didn't steal from anyone's plate, stabbing a slab of beef or spearing a soggy fry while they tied a shoe or fidgeted over a response to some parental inquiry. I didn't pick their dregs, dumping half-gnawed bones onto my own fully gnawed pile, I didn't reach across plates and setting to grab a soppy crust of bread or buttered roll. We were all healthy eaters in my family, and we were all well within the recommended weight guidelines. Granted, I was a fast eater; my father and brother were also fast eaters—we lacked the patience to chew, always anxious to move on to something new. I certainly didn't deliberate over the plate like my younger sister did, who always ate like a bird. She'd barely be attending to her main course while the rest of us scraped up the last of our desserts. Compared to her, I wolfed my food, scarfed it, inhaled it, terms I heard over and over again much later. I was a healthy, active second grader; dinner meant disjuncture, interruption, tactic of delay constructed by mothers to keep their sons from the real work of childhood—hide and seek, wiffle ball, bikes, backyard Olympiad.

I often wonder now what led me to such disgusting behavior— what might lead any child to such disgusting behavior. Like any good 21st-century questioner/researcher, I go to the Internet, hopeful that a search of current medical literature will provide answers and understanding. So I begin my search, seated in front of my computer. I find a gopher (its name is OVID—aptly named for the ancient Roman writer of *Metamorphoses* or *Transformations*), and it's as versatile as a left-handed shortstop, a triple-threat, able to simultaneously search pediatric, psychology, anthropology, and other allied health databases. I'm confident that with the right *keyword search*, the exact *cross-referencing* or *Boolean limitation*, I will be able to call up some insight. This should be a breeze, I think, *childhood bulimia,* thousands of hits, hundreds of studies from millions of research dollars. After all, anorexia/bulimia was, arguably, *the disease* of the 1990s. I do find something. In *The International Journal of Eating Disorders* (1995) there's an article titled, "Premorbid Onset of Psychopathology in Long-term Recovered Anorexia Patients." And the abstract tells me that 58% of anorexics reported "childhood anxiety disorders at age ten (plus or minus five years)." The most common is childhood depression beginning well before the eating disorder. I also locate "Determinants of Adolescent Obesity: A Comparison with Anorexia Nervosa," *Adolescence* (1988), which claims that "both anorexics and the obese are characterized by overprotectedness and enmeshment, resulting from a poor sense of identity and effectiveness."

Writing Strategies

Intensive details.

Paragraph shift indicates the new focus: from describing the behavior to searching for causes.

An allusion to the writer. Are the titles significant?

Narrating the actual searching process.

Outside source.

Exploring Ideas

Exploring Ideas

The literature does not describe his case.

Details to show he was healthy and energetic.

Why is this the most vivid detail for him? Is there a connection?

Here's the first connection between the search and his experience: it's pleasurable.

After a whole week of research, this seems to be the extent of my findings. I can find nothing to urge me to go beyond the abstracts, nothing at all, though I type in "eating disorder," "vomiting," "obesity," "abnormal psychology," "gluttony," "disgusting and destructive behavior"—always cross-referenced with "childhood."

I was a happy child. I really was. And not only in my parents' estimation. I see it now in old snapshots and projected slides. When I was two, the neighbors nicknamed me "Smiley." It stuck. Nothing fazed me—not even the most traumatic incident of my early life, driving my trike over the sides of that same neighbor's screened-in porch, the screens removed for spring cleaning. The tumble left a pus-filled bruise, two weeks in draining. My parents said that I never flinched or lost that smile, even as that neighbor dug and poked and pressed and guiltily reapplied her expert pity dressings, the whole time boasting incessantly about her favorite nephew, a fighter pilot almost blasted out of the Korean sky a few years back. "Praise God," I remember her saying, "that he wasn't tortured or starved." Thank God he returned, intact, and (my parents informed me years later) in time to be chosen as one of the original Mercury 7 astronauts. Somehow it seems that this might have been right about the time that I began my career as a public barfer.

Only once do I remember doing it in secret. It was at my grandparents' golden wedding anniversary celebration, a feast my grandmother herself with the help of her Kovno and Litwak sisters, Bronx nieces, and Jersey City daughters prepared. I am not one, however, to gorge on a sumptuous catalogued recitation of the feast (more scrumptious than the feast itself?). For the food itself never seemed to matter. For the most part, I ate whatever was cast in front of me. The party took place at my aunt's apartment in Stuyvesant Town on the East Side, where the shouts of roller skaters and stickball players rose up from the playground, mixing with the shrill stab of ambulance, police car, fire truck, and the play-by-play of the Yankees . . . and it is this final detail that I most vividly recall—not the carp swimming all night in the bathtub, walloped against the porcelain rim in the morning, then beheaded and sopped in a bucket of brine. Not the pickled tongue or brisket or pot roast, and kasha, knishes, blintzes served up beneath gobs of sour cream, like Checkhov's "crisp bleenies, lacy and plump as the shoulder of a merchant's daughter." There was a full week of food preparation that I gobbled down and then disposed of with great ease and easing. I didn't even have to stick my finger down my throat; I could simply will the partially chewed hearty chunks of meat and potato up from their sour churning stock. It felt so good! The *Encyclopedia of Pediatric Psychology* (1979) reports that children who

Writing Strategies

Paragraph shifts from the search back to describing the past.

Could this be a connection?

The details show the culinary tradition of his family.

The outside source integrated (colliding with?) his experiences.

Exploring Ideas

Writing Strategies

vomit, farfetched as it sounds, even "those who have learned society's aversions . . . can overcome such scruples and experience vomiting as cathartic, even orgasmic."

Counterargument?

I still find it odd that my parents never questioned why I did it. They never seemed to mind, though I'm sure they did, privately. They must have been embarrassed, if not mortified by my behavior. In spite of that, we went out to dinner often, several times a month. Not once did they ask me to modify my order, limit my portion. They never motioned the waitress aside, and with the promise of a bigger tip, asked her to go easy on the fries. My brother and sister were silent, too, as though my barfing were a perfectly acceptable alternative to an after-dinner mint, a toothpick, a wet-wipe wrapped like a condom. Perhaps they were too busy stashing away the details of the affront, safekeeping for a time of need—like Aesop's despicable, self-righteous ant. I can only imagine the hay they might have later made by simple melodramatic evocations of the sounds of my gagging, as it echoed in tiny bathrooms. The deep, throaty sound of plosively expelling vomit. "Well, whatever I did can't be as gross and disgusting as THAT," I can hear them repeating over and over till they got what they wanted. Or did they have their own equally disgusting but self-customized techniques of catharsis and orgasm back then— I wondered. Does everyone, I still wonder? And how could a "D" in French or a detention or a missed meal or a dent in the car compare with what I did, over and over and over?

New paragraph: focus on others around him

Catharsis = relief/ release of tension.

Allusion to the ant and grasshopper story.

Public resonance: does everyone have a technique for releasing tension?

The main cause is need for catharsis?

It couldn't, of course, it would pale in comparison to that cathartic act of throwing up (knowing that others could hear my retching) that left my face bloodless and pale, my extremities tingling, my chest heaving with giddiness. Perhaps earlier generations of parents and child psychologists had a better understanding of its power and attraction. And that's why older writings on the subject, rare but not unheard of, prescribe such drastic, almost Draconian treatment to stop the behavior. *The Encyclopedia of Pediatric Psychology* (1970) lacks entries for either anorexia or bulimia and refers to it as "psychogenic vomiting." It predates the public and medical concern over the condition, and takes a stern, almost Victorian approach to treatment:

Draconian = code of extreme severity or rigor.

More public resonance: the behavior is not new or even that unusual.

> Karo syrup, Phenobarbital, anticonvulsants, chlorpromazine, antihistamines, chin straps, esophageal blocks, thickened feedings, removal of normal appendix, electric shock therapy, and even intensive prayer are all reported to have been used successfully to resolve the problem.

His situation, again, seems slightly different than the literature suggests.

In some cases, and in my case, I suppose, the patient simply outgrows it.

Exploring Ideas

1. What is Kress trying to accomplish in his essay?

2. Who might benefit from reading Kress's essay? What might be the benefit?

3. What questions—besides what caused him to vomit—does Kress's essay raise? How might readers use these questions as points of contact (or springboards) for participating in this discussion?

4. Explore a past behavior of your own, searching for what caused it. Research the behavior by reading about it and/or talking to others. Your goal is to arrive not at *the* cause, but at several possible causes. List the possible causes.

5. Evaluate each of the possible causes you discovered for #4. Which ones seem most likely to be the cause of your behavior? Provide convincing evidence to support your conclusion.

Writing Strategies

1. Evaluate Kress's introduction. Does it grab the reader's interest? Does it lead purposefully into the body of the essay? Does it establish a tone? What else does it do? What does it fail to do?

2. Identify several sentences that bring Kress's essay to life. Explain why you identified those particular sentences.

3. How does Kress use secondary (written) sources in his essay? Are they helpful? In what way or ways do they help him to make his point?

4. Identify at least two allusions in Kress's essay, and then use these allusions to explain not merely what an allusion is, but how an allusion conveys meaning.

5. Imagine you are workshopping Kress's essay with him. Identify what you consider to be the essay's main strength and offer one suggestion for improvement.

Ideas for Writing

1. Reflect as an adult on a puzzling childhood experience. What might be the cause of a certain behavior that you to this point have not understood?

2. Kress considers his family's reaction to his throwing up. What is the cause of someone else's puzzling reaction to you?

> If responding to one of these ideas, go to the **Analysis** section of this chapter to begin developing ideas for your essay.

Sex, Lies, and Conversation: Why Is It So Hard for Men and Women to Talk to Each Other?

Deborah Tannen

Deborah Tannen, a linguist, has published numerous books and articles on language and linguistics. As you read this essay, highlight or underline ideas that help you to figure out the point of her essay. Then review those ideas and write a brief summary of Tannen's essay.

1   I was addressing a small gathering in a suburban Virginia living room—a women's group that had invited men to join them. Throughout the evening, one man had been particularly talkative, frequently offering ideas and anecdotes, while his wife sat silently beside him on the couch. Toward the end of the evening, I commented that women frequently complain that their husbands don't talk to them. This man quickly concurred. He gestured toward his wife and said, "She's the talker in our family." The room burst into laughter; the man looked puzzled and hurt. "It's true," he explained. "When I come home from work I have nothing to say. If she didn't keep the conversation going, we'd spend the whole evening in silence."

2   The episode crystallizes the irony that although American men tend to talk more than women in public situations, they often talk less at home. And this pattern is wreaking havoc with marriage.

3   The pattern was observed by political scientist Andrew Hacker in the late '70s. Sociologist Catherine Kohler Riessman reports in her new book *Divorce Talk* that most of the women she interviewed—but only a few of the men—gave lack of communication as the reason for their divorces. Given the current divorce rate of nearly 50 percent, that amounts to millions of cases in the United States every year—a virtual epidemic of failed conversation.

4   In my own research, complaints from women about their husbands most often focused not on tangible inequities such as having given up the chance for a career to accompany a husband to his, or doing far more than their share of daily life-support work like cleaning, cooking, social arrangements and errands. Instead, they focused on communication: "He doesn't listen to me," "He doesn't talk to me." I found, as Hacker observed years before, that most wives want their husbands to be, first and foremost, conversational partners, but few husbands share this expectation of their wives.

5   In short, the image that best represents the current crisis is the stereotypical cartoon scene of a man sitting at the breakfast table with a newspaper held up in front of his face, while a woman glares at the back of it, wanting to talk.

Linguistic Battle of the Sexes

6   How can women and men have such different impressions of communication in marriage? Why the widespread imbalance in their interests and expectations?

7   In the April [1990] issue of *American Psychologist*, Stanford University's Eleanor Maccoby reports the results of her own and others' research showing that children's development is most influenced by the social structure of peer interactions. Boys and girls tend to play with children of their own gender, and their sex-separate groups have different organizational structures and interactive norms.

8 I believe these systematic differences in childhood socialization make talk between women and men like cross-cultural communication, heir to all the attraction and pitfalls of that enticing but difficult enterprise. My research on men's and women's conversations uncovered patterns similar to those described for children's groups.

9 For women, as for girls, intimacy is the fabric of relationships, and talk is the thread from which it is woven. Little girls create and maintain friendships by exchanging secrets; similarly, women regard conversation as the cornerstone of friendship. So a woman expects her husband to be a new and improved version of a best friend. What is important is not the individual subjects that are discussed but the sense of closeness, of a life shared, that emerges when people tell their thoughts, feelings, and impressions.

10 Bonds between boys can be as intense as girls', but they are based less on talking, more on doing things together. Since they don't assume talk is the cement that binds a relationship, men don't know what kind of talk women want, and they don't miss it when it isn't there.

11 Boys' groups are larger, more inclusive, and more hierarchical, so boys must struggle to avoid the subordinate position in the group. This may play a role in women's complaints that men don't listen to them. Some men really don't like to listen, because being a listener makes them feel one-down, like a child listening to adults or an employee to a boss.

12 But often when women tell men, "You aren't listening," and the men protest, "I am," the men are right. The impression of not listening results from misalignments in the mechanics of conversation. The misalignment begins as soon as a man and a woman take physical positions. This became clear when I studied videotapes made by psychologist Bruce Dorval of children and adults talking to their same-sex best friends. I found that at every age, the girls and women faced each other directly, their eyes anchored on each other's faces. At every age, the boys and men sat at angles to each other and looked elsewhere in the room, periodically glancing at each other. They were obviously attuned to each other, often mirroring each other's movements. But the tendency of men to face away can give women the impression they aren't listening even when they are. A young woman in college was frustrated: Whenever she told her boyfriend she wanted to talk to him, he would lie down on the floor, close his eyes, and put his arm over his face. This signaled to her, "He's taking a nap." But he insisted he was listening extra hard. Normally, he looks around the room, so he is easily distracted. Lying down and covering his eyes helped him concentrate on what she was saying.

13 Analogous to the physical alignment that women and men take in conversation is their topical alignment. The girls in my study tended to talk at length about one topic, but the boys tended to jump from topic to topic. The second-grade girls exchanged stories about people they knew. The second-grade boys teased, told jokes, noticed things in the room and talked about finding games to play. The sixth-grade girls talked about problems with a mutual friend. The sixth-grade boys talked about 55 different topics, none of which extended over more than a few turns.

Listening to Body Language

14 Switching topics is another habit that gives women the impression men aren't listening, especially if they switch to a topic about themselves. But the evidence of the 10th-grade boys in my study indicates otherwise. The 10th-grade boys sprawled across their chairs with bodies parallel and eyes straight ahead, rarely looking at each other. They looked as if they were riding in a car, staring out the windshield. But they were talking about their feelings. One boy was upset because a girl had told him he had a drinking problem, and the other was feeling alienated from all his friends.

15 Now, when a girl told a friend about a problem, the friend responded by asking probing questions and expressing agreement and

understanding. But the boys dismissed each other's problems. Todd assured Richard that his drinking was "no big problem" because "sometimes you're funny when you're off your butt." And when Todd said he felt left out, Richard responded, "Why should you? You know more people than me."

16 Women perceived such responses as belittling and unsupportive. But the boys seemed satisfied with them. Whereas women reassure each other by implying, "You shouldn't feel bad because I've had similar experiences," men do so by implying, "You shouldn't feel bad because your problems aren't so bad."

17 There are even simpler reasons for women's impression that men don't listen. Linguist Lynette Hirschman found that women make more listener-noise, such as "mhm," "uhuh," and "yeah," to show "I'm with you." Men, she found, more often give silent attention. Women who expect a stream of listener-noise interpret silent attention as no attention at all.

18 Women's conversational habits are as frustrating to men as men's are to women. Men who expect silent attention interpret a stream of listener-noise as overreaction or impatience. Also, when women talk to each other in a close, comfortable setting, they often overlap, finish each other's sentences and anticipate what the other is about to say. This practice, which I call "participatory listenership," is often preceived by men as interruption, intrusion and lack of attention.

19 A parallel difference caused a man to complain about his wife, "She just wants to talk about her own point of view. If I show her another view, she gets mad at me." When most women talk to each other, they assume a conversationalist's job is to express agreement and support. But many men see their conversational duty as pointing out the other side of the argument. This is heard as disloyalty by women, and refusal to offer the requisite support. It is not that women don't want to see other points of view, but that they prefer them phrased as suggestions and inquiries rather than as direct challenges.

20 In this book, *Fighting for Life,* Walter Ong points out that men use "agonistic" or warlike, oppositional formats to do almost anything; thus discussion becomes debate, and conversation a competitive sport. In contrast, women see conversation as a ritual means of establishing rapport. If Jane tells a problem and June says she has a similar one, they walk away feeling closer to each other. But this attempt at establishing rapport can backfire when used with men. Men take too literally women's ritual "troubles talk," just as women mistake men's ritual challenges for real attack.

The Sounds of Silence

21 These differences begin to clarify why women and men have such different expectations about communication in marriage. For women, talk creates intimacy. Marriage is an orgy of closeness: you can tell your feelings and thoughts, and still be loved. Their greatest fear is being pushed away. But men live in a hierarchical world, where talk maintains independence and status. They are on guard to protect themselves from being put down and pushed around.

22 This explains the paradox of the talkative man who said of his silent wife, "She's the talker." In the public setting of a guest lecture, he felt challenged to show his intelligence and display his understanding of the lecture. But at home, where he has nothing to prove and no one to defend against, he is free to remain silent. For his wife, being home means she is free from the worry that something she says might offend someone, or spark disagreement, or appear to be showing off; at home she is free to talk.

23 The communication problems that endanger marriage can't be fixed by mechanical engineering. They require a new conceptual framework about the role of talk in human relationships. Many of the psychological explanations that have become second nature may not be helpful, because they tend to blame either women (for not being assertive enough) or men (for not

being in touch with their feelings). A sociolinguistic approach by which male-female conversation is seen as cross-cultural communication allows us to understand the problem and forge solutions without blaming either party.

24   Once the problem is understood, improvement comes naturally, as it did to the young woman and her boyfriend who seemed to go to sleep when she wanted to talk. Previously, she had accused him of not listening, and he had refused to change his behavior, since that would be admitting fault. But then she learned about and explained to him the differences in women's and men's habitual ways of aligning themselves in conversation. The next time she told him she wanted to talk, he began, as usual, by lying down and covering his eyes. When the familiar negative reaction bubbled up, she reassured herself that he really was listening. But then he sat up and looked at her. Thrilled she asked why. He said, "You like me to look at you when we talk,

so I'll try to do it." Once he saw their differences as cross-cultural rather than right and wrong, he independently altered his behavior.

25   Women who feel abandoned and deprived when their husbands won't listen to or report daily news may be happy to discover their husbands trying to adapt once they understand the place of small talk in women's relationships. But if their husbands don't adapt, the women may still be comforted that for men, this is not a failure of intimacy. Accepting the difference, the wives may look to their friends or family for that kind of talk. And husbands who can't provide it shouldn't feel their wives have made unreasonable demands. Some couples will still decide to divorce, but at least their decisions will be based on realistic expectations.

26   In these times of resurgent ethnic conflicts, the world desperately needs cross-cultural understanding. Like charity, successful cross-cultural communication should begin at home.

Exploring Ideas

1. How does Tannen's essay invite others to think about communication?

2. Reflect on the way that you talk with others. You might first jot down any initial ideas you have, and then recall comments others have made about the way you communicate. In several paragraphs, describe your own conversational behavior.

3. Interview various people about the way they think men and women communicate. Carefully formulate several interview questions to discover whether or not others agree with Tannen's ideas.

4. Over the course of several days make your own observations about the way men and women communicate. How are your observations similar to or different from Tannen's?

5. Is it acceptable to generalize, as Tannen does, about men and women? What makes her generalizations valid? Or, why aren't they valid? What other generalizations can you make about men and women or about other groups of people? Spend a few days interviewing others and making observations, and then write down several generalizations others or you make, explaining why each generalization is or is not fair and valid.

Writing Strategies

1. Describe Tannen's voice as a writer and refer to several passages to support your description.

2. Read several paragraphs from Susan Jacoby's "When Bright Girls Decide That Math Is a 'Waste of Time,'" which follows this essay, and compare Tannen's voice to Jacoby's. How would you say they are similar or different?

3. In your own words, write down Tannen's main idea.

4. Discuss with several classmates what you wrote down for #3. How is your understanding of Tannen's idea similar to or different from your classmates'? After discussing, write one statement of Tannen's main idea that you and your group members agree on.

5. What support, or evidence, does Tannen provide to explain a cause? That is, does she tell stories, provide statistics, or something else?

Ideas for Writing

1. What is the cause of some other difference in the way men and women think or act?

2. What is the cause of some difference in the way two groups of people think or act?

> If responding to one of these ideas, go to the **Analysis** section of this chapter to begin developing ideas for your essay.

When Bright Girls Decide That Math Is a "Waste of Time"

Susan Jacoby

Susan Jacoby has worked as a journalist for the Washington Post *and written several books including* The Possible She *(1979) and* Wild Justice: The Evolution of Revenge *(1983). This essay appeared in the* New York Times. *As you read, identify passages that explain why bright girls decide math is a "waste of time" and jot down any responses you have to such passages.*

1   Susannah, a 16-year-old who has always been an A student in every subject from algebra to English, recently informed her parents that she intended to drop physics and calculus in her senior year of high school and replace them with a drama seminar and a work-study program. She expects a major in art or history in college, she explained, and "any more science or math will just be a waste of my time."

2   Her parents were neither concerned by nor opposed to her decision. "Fine, dear," they said. Their daughter is, after all, an outstanding student. What does it matter if, at age 16, she has taken a step that may limit her understanding of both machines and the natural world for the rest of her life?

3   This kind of decision, in which girls turn away from studies that would give them a sure footing in the world of science and technology, is a self-inflicted female disability that is, regrettably, almost as common today as it was when I was in high school. If Susannah had announced that she had decided to stop taking English in her senior year, her mother and father would have been horrified. I also think they would have been a good deal less sanguine about her decision if she were a boy.

4   In saying that scientific and mathematical ignorance is a self-inflicted female wound, I do not, obviously, mean that cultural expectations play no role in the process. But the world does not conspire to deprive modern women of access to science as it did in the 1930s, when Rosalyn S. Yalow, the Nobel Prize-winning physicist, graduated from Hunter College and was advised to go to work as a secretary because no graduate school would admit her to its physics department. The current generation of adolescent girls—and their parents, bred on old expectations about women's interests—are active conspirators in limiting their own intellectual development.

5   It is true that the proportion of young women in science-related graduate and professional schools, most notably medical schools, has increased significantly in the past decade. It is also true that so few women were studying advanced science and mathematics before the early 1970s that the percentage increase in female enrollment does not yet translate into large numbers of women actually working in science.

6   The real problem is that so many girls eliminate themselves from any serious possibility of studying science as a result of decisions made during the vulnerable period of midadolescence, when they are most likely to be influenced—on both conscious and subconscious levels—by the traditional belief that math and science are "masculine" subjects.

7   During the teen-age years the well-documented phenomenon of "math anxiety" strikes girls who never had any problem handling numbers during earlier schooling. Some men, too, experience this syndrome—a form of panic, akin to a phobia, at any task involving numbers—but women constitute the overwhelming majority of sufferers. The onset of acute math anxiety during the teen-age years is, as Stalin was fond of saying, "not by accident."

8   In adolescence girls begin to fear that they will be unattractive to boys if they are typed as "brains." Science and math epitomize unfeminine braininess in a way that, say, foreign languages do not. High-school girls who pursue an advanced interest in science and math (unless they are students at special institutions like the Bronx High School of Science where everyone is a brain) usually find that they are greatly outnumbered by boys in their classes. They are, therefore, intruding on male turf at a time when their sexual confidence, as well as that of the boys, is most fragile.

9   A 1981 assessment of female achievement in mathematics, based on research conducted under a National Institute for Education grant, found significant differences in the mathematical achievements of 9th and 12th graders. At age 13 girls were equal to or slightly better than boys in tests involving algebra, problem solving and spatial ability; four years later the boys had outstripped the girls.

10   It is not mysterious that some very bright high-school girls suddenly decide that math is "too hard" and "a waste of time." In my experience, self-sabotage of mathematical and scientific ability is often a conscious process. I remember deliberately pretending to be puzzled by geometry problems in my sophomore year in high school. A male teacher called me in after class and said, in a baffled tone, "I don't see how you can be having so much trouble when you got straight A's last year in my algebra class."

11   The decision to avoid advanced biology, chemistry, physics and calculus in high school automatically restricts academic and professional choices that ought to be wide open to anyone beginning college. At all coeducational universities women are overwhelmingly concentrated in the fine arts, social sciences and traditionally female departments like education. Courses leading to degrees in science- and technology-related fields are filled mainly by men.

12   In my generation, the practical consequences of mathematical and scientific illiteracy are visible in the large number of special programs to help professional women overcome the anxiety they feel when they are promoted into jobs that require them to handle statistics.

13   The consequences of this syndrome should not, however, be viewed in narrowly professional terms. Competence in science and math does not mean one is going to become a scientist or mathematician any more than competence in writing English means one is going to become a professional writer. Scientific and mathematical illiteracy—which has been cited in several recent critiques by panels studying American education from kindergarten through college—produces an incalculably impoverished vision of human experience.

14   Scientific illiteracy is not, of course, the exclusive province of women. In certain intellectual circles it has become fashionable to proclaim a willed, aggressive ignorance about science and technology. Some female writers specialize in ominous, uninformed diatribes against genetic research as a plot to remove control of childbearing from women, while some well-known men of letters proudly announce that they understand absolutely nothing about computers, or, for that matter, about electricity. This lack of understanding is nothing in which women or men ought to take pride.

15   Failure to comprehend either computers or chromosomes leads to a terrible sense of helplessness, because the profound impact of science on everyday life is evident even to those who insist they don't, won't, can't understand why the changes are taking place. At this stage of history women are more prone to such feelings of helplessness than men because the culture judges their ignorance less harshly and because women themselves acquiesce in that indulgence.

16   Since there is ample evidence of such feelings in adolescence, it is up to parents to see that their daughters do not accede to the old stereotypes about "masculine" and "feminine" knowledge. Unless we want our daughters to share our intellectual handicaps, we had better tell them no, they can't stop taking mathematics and science at the ripe old age of 16.

Exploring Ideas

1. According to Jacoby, why do bright girls decide math is "too hard" or a "waste of time"?

2. What decisions, if any, can you recall having made that already have, or might in the future, limit your academic or professional choices? Why did you make those choices? Were they influenced by any stereotypes, social pressures, or perceived social pressures?

3. How might you respond to Jacoby? Consider expanding, narrowing, or refocusing her discussion.

4. How might you reconsider your take on math, English, or some other subject after having read Jacoby's essay? How might you reconsider your take, or approach, to some other area of life, such as sports, socializing, and so on?

5. Interview others to find out what they take pride in not knowing. What is their reason for not knowing it? Why do they take pride in not knowing? How are the reasons similar to or different from the ones Jacoby describes?

Writing Strategies

1. Describe Jacoby's voice as a writer and provide several passages to support your description.

2. What type of evidence does Jacoby provide in explaining a cause? What evidence is most convincing? What other type of evidence might she have provided?

3. In your own words, write down Jacoby's reasoning for bright girls deciding that math is a waste of time.

4. Discuss what you wrote down for #3 with a group of classmates. How are their ideas similar to or different from your own?

5. How does Jacoby conclude her essay?

Ideas for Writing

1. What thing do some people take pride in not knowing, and why? That is, what is the cause of their (a) not knowing and (b) taking pride in not knowing?

2. What causes many students to think school is a "waste of time"?

If responding to one of these ideas, go to the **Analysis** section of this chapter to begin developing your ideas.

Outside Reading

ind an essay or report that explores causes and print it out or make a photocopy. To explore a specific field or major, search a related professional journal, such as *Nutrition Health Forum, Law Technology,* or *Education Journal.* Keep an eye out for titles of articles that begin with *why.* You might also find articles about causes in local and national newspapers. To search a library database, go to your library's home page, and then choose from its magazine or periodical databases. (It may also say "full text" in the title.) Using a keyword search, enter *cause and* plus any noun that interests you, such as *cause and flu, cause and recession, cause and global warming, cause and traffic jams.*

You can also search the Internet. Try a Google search, but go to Google's special search for government studies and reports: www.Google.com/unclesam. At the site, you will notice that "Google" is red, white, and blue. At the search box, type any topic of interest, and *cause.* (In Google, Boolean operators such as *and* are unnecessary.) The search results will yield only government-sponsored studies and reports.

The purpose of this assignment is to explore the range of possibilities for writing. You may discover a writing that differs considerably from the essays in this chapter (in tone, rhetorical strategies, or organization). As you read through this chapter, keep the text you have discovered close by and notice the elements and strategies the writer uses. Depending on your instructor's suggestions, do one or more of the following:

1. Notice how the writer applies various strategies from this chapter. On the hard copy or photocopy:

   - Highlight the thesis if it is stated. If the thesis is implied, write it in your own words.

   - Identify the major rhetorical strategies (appeals, evidence, counterargument, concession, etc.).

   - Identify any passages in which the writer attempts to create public resonance for the topic.

2. Write an essay that discusses the strategies employed by the writer. The following questions may be helpful.

   - How is the writer's voice different from the essays in this chapter?
   - How does the writer support or illustrate his or her thesis?
   - Who is the audience for this text?
   - How does the audience impact the kinds of things said in the text?
   - How does the writer go beyond the obvious? (What new idea does the writer offer?)

3. Write at least three "Exploring Ideas" questions for the text you found.

4. Write at least three "Writing Strategies" questions for the text you found.

5. Write two "Ideas for Writing," such as the ones following the essays in this book, for the text you found.

INVENTION

Invention is an act of discovery. It involves opening all the intellectual cases we have closed in everyday life. It involves asking questions where we had assumed we knew the answers. For this chapter, invention involves asking why something occurs (or has occurred) and going beyond the first (and second) guess. In **Point of Contact,** ask adventurous questions to find a topic. In **Analysis,** imagine unseen causes, and in **Public Resonance,** consider the ways your topic extends outward and affects the public. The questions in each section are not meant to be answered directly in your final written assignment. In fact, as you work through the sections, avoid simply answering them and then moving on. Instead, use them to explore and to develop more questions. After you work through these three sections, the **Delivery** section, which immediately follows, will help you craft your ideas into a written text.

Point of Contact

Finding a Topic in Everyday Life

The authors of the essays in this chapter have a deep understanding of their topics. Certainly, Schor has an expert perspective (as a professor of economics). While you need not have years of training and study about your topic, you will benefit from some degree of personal experience. Consider Kress's personal experiences, which give him some valuable insight, perhaps even more than many experts in child psychology and physiology! That is, his particular experiences shed light on a possible cause of bulimic behavior in children, a cause that may go overlooked by traditional perspectives.

Use the following suggestions to find a topic. Remember to focus on a topic that you can speak of with some authority (having witnessed, experienced, or studied it in your life). The following questions will help you begin your search. For some topics, you may need to do research; discuss the process with your instructor and see Chapter 12: Research and Writing. After you have decided on a particular topic, go to the **Analysis** section to continue your search for causes.

- **Observe your co-workers or ask them about situations or policies at the workplace:**

  Why are some sections/groups/teams more successful than others?
  Why is workplace efficiency up or down?
  Why are profits for the company or organization up or down?
  Why are some workers more content or fulfilled than others?

- **Read a local newspaper and consider local events or situations:**

  What behaviors, policies, or perspectives caused a recent accident in your
    community?
  Why is urban sprawl taking place in your community?
  Why is a local sports team winning or losing?
  What events or behaviors led to a recent political crisis?
  Why are some areas of town more policed than others?

- **Discuss social trends with a classmate or non-classmate peer:**

  What causes road rage? Child abuse?
  Why do teenagers rebel against their parents? Conform to fashion trends?
  Why are the elderly isolated?
  Why is depression on the rise in the United States?
  Why are violent video games so popular?
  Why do women's magazines focus so much attention on weight loss?
  Why do Americans love sport utility vehicles?
  Why does the condition of streets change throughout a city?
  Why do people support (or oppose) military actions?

- **Discuss academic or campus issues with several college students, or consider the behaviors of the students on your campus:**

  Why do college students binge drink?
  Why do some students cheat? Procrastinate?
  Why are some classes more difficult for large numbers of students?
  Why do some students abstain from sexual activity?
  Why have test scores in schools risen or fallen?

- **Read** a national newspaper or news magazine and consider national political affairs:

  Why did a particular presidential candidate win (or lose) an election?
  Why do younger generations tend not to vote?
  Why does a certain community consistently vote Democratic or Republican?
  Why do minority voters tend toward Democratic candidates?

- **Consider** your personal life:

  Why has your education gone the way it has?
  Why are you in a particular kind of relationship?
  What caused your behavior as a child?
  Why did/do you have a certain kind of friend?

- **Explore** your major:

  What has caused the field to thrive (or deteriorate) in recent years?
  What has fueled a recent debate in the field? Why has the debate continued?

  Find the cause of a subject in your field. For example:

  History: a revolution, a military victory or loss
  Art: a style (such as impressionism), an artistic revolution
  Geology: mudslides, a volcanic eruption
  Biology: an organism's short life span
  Criminal Justice: a jury decision, a Supreme Court decision to hear a case
  Business Marketing: the success or failure of a specific marketing campaign
  Architecture: the appeal of a recent building design, the change in mid-twentieth-century buildings

Invention Activity: Although the chapter readings tend to focus on problems (such as bulimia or overconsumption), you might focus on any phenomenon, good or bad. In a group (in class, on a listserv, or in a chatroom), generate more options for seeking out a topic. Share your ideas with the class.

Example: Leonard Kress's Response to Point of Contact Question

What caused your behavior as a child? I have seen some discussion about high school wrestlers—I even recall a friend who subsisted on popsicles for two days to "make weight," and who occasionally vomited in the boys room—all with the coach's approval. But children? Young boys? This didn't seem to fit the mold. I have these vivid images of places where I vomited, of scenes I caused, of my parents' quiet exasperation.

Analysis
What's the Cause?

Now that you have a topic (any phenomenon from the above or your own set of questions), the next step is to begin searching for possible causes. (We use the term "phenomenon" here to refer to anything you are exploring—any behavior, event, situation, attitude, issue, idea, and so on.) You may already have some guesses about the cause. But keep an open mind. Any single phenomenon can be a consequence of many factors, both physical and abstract. For example, consider Schor's analysis of consumption. She points to many different causes for the new kind of consumerism:

> Americans did not suddenly become greedy. The aspirational gap has been created by structural changes—such as the decline of community and social connection, the intensification of inequality, the growing role of mass media, and heightened penalties for failing in the labor market. Upscaling is mainly defensive, and has both psychological and practical dimensions.

Schor shows that a phenomenon can be caused by complex, and sometimes very abstract, factors—everything from economic trends to prevailing social attitudes.

As you probe for causes, go beyond the first assumption. Explore how broader, unseen factors may factor in to your topic. Respond to the following questions and refer back to your notes as you continue the process.

- What events or behaviors led to the phenomenon?
- What social conditions or prevailing attitudes led (or could lead) to the phenomenon?
- What economic conditions led to the phenomenon?
- What state of mind or psychological need may have led to the phenomenon?
- What are all the possible reasons someone would carry out this behavior?

Even though some questions might seem irrelevant, do not be quick to dismiss them. Explore the impact of each question on your topic. Imagine a student, Jack, who is using the analysis questions in a discussion with peers. Notice how the conversation develops Jack's initial thoughts about his topic: why people join cults.

What state of mind or psychological need may have led to the phenomenon?

    Jack: These people are obviously sick—mentally ill.

    Diana: What kind of mental illness?

    Jack: I don't know . . . probably some kind of schizophrenia or something.

    Diana: But a lot of the people who join cults are otherwise productive members of society—with jobs, families, homes, social responsibilities. I've even heard that some cults attract people who are smarter than average. It doesn't seem like these people are downright mentally ill—at least in the way most people talk about mental illness.

    Jack: So if they aren't sick in some way, why would they possibly leave behind their families and friends, give all their money to a group of strangers, and lose their identities?

    Marcus: Well, I've heard that a lot of those people don't have friends—they're lonely.

    Jack: How can people be lonely if they have families and jobs?

    Diana: Working a job and supporting a family doesn't necessarily make someone truly connected to others. Think about mid-life crises—where people run out and have wild flings or buy ridiculously expensive sports cars. They're obviously unfulfilled.

    Jack: But wouldn't you say that joining a cult is a little more extreme than buying a car or having an affair?

    Diana: Sure, but remember that a lot of people long for something more than sex and fast cars. They wonder what's out there, what their purpose is, what's beyond this life.

    Jack: And religious cults have all those answers—well, at least that's the argument.

    Diana: Yeah, so the whole issue may be related to loneliness and longing rather than sickness.

    Jack: Well, I'd say a really deep and extreme type of loneliness and longing.

Example: Leonard Kress's Response to Analysis Questions

What state of mind or psychological need may have led you to the phenomenon? I'm just beginning to learn how to do computer searches, which makes the research easy, immediate, and private. Somehow it seems appropriate to combine highly personal, idiosyncratic memories and hard research—sort of setting them side-by-side and figuring out if the experience matched the theories.

Notice how Kress's ideas show up in his essay, which puts his own experiences in direct relationship with the outside research. In this case, the writer is conducting two layers of analysis: (1) to see what causes childhood bulimia and (2) to see the differences in explanations.

Using Outside Sources: Find an outside source (a Web site, article, or book) about your concept. (Consult Chapter 12: Research and Writing to help you explore.) The author(s) of the source may have a different understanding of the causes. Summarize the main points of the source, then answer the following questions:

- Does the source suggest a cause for the phenomenon?
- If not, does the source imply or assume a cause?
- Does the source account for the most direct cause?
- Does the source account for indirect or multiple causes? Hidden causes?

You can use this information as part of your analysis. Your answers to these questions can help develop your insights into the cause. For instance, the source may provide you with some interesting notions that you had not considered in your own analysis. As you develop your ideas, outside sources can help substantiate your points. For instance, notice how Deborah Tannen uses the claims of other researchers:

> The pattern was observed by political scientist Andrew Hacker in the late '70s. Sociologist Catherine Kohler Riessman reports in her new book *Divorce Talk* that most of the women she interviewed—but only a few of the men—gave lack of communication as the reason for their divorces.

But immediately after referring to other sources, she mentions her own research:

> In my own research, complaints from women about their husbands most often focused not on tangible inequities such as having given up the chance for a career to accompany a husband to his, or doing far more than their share of daily life-support work like cleaning, cooking, social arrangements and errands. Instead, they focused on communication . . .

Tannen's own observations resonate with the conclusions of others. Her claims, then, do not rest exclusively on outside sources. Like all good writers, she does not depend on the sources, but uses them to show how her own ideas fit into a broader discussion on the topic. (See Chapter 12: Research and Writing, p. 576 for further guidance in evaluating, integrating, and documenting sources.)

Using Surveys: Exploratory surveys often reveal a range of new insights about a topic. Use the following to develop and conduct a survey on your topic:

1. Develop a short list of questions about your topic. You might ask people's opinions on the cause. For instance, for Jack's analysis of cults, he might ask: *Why do you think people join cults? What makes them leave behind their families, friends, and jobs?* Or he might try to probe for causes: *Have you ever considered, even for an instant, leaving your present life? Why?* Such questions may reveal something about the cause that you may not have considered.

2. After you have a short list of questions (no more than five), type and print them.

3. Depending on the time you have, distribute the questions to a variety of people (at work, at school, at home, at a shopping center, etc.). If you ask the questions verbally, make certain to record the answers in writing or with an audio recorder. (See Chapter 12: Research and Writing, p. 576 for more hints on conducting surveys.)

Public Resonance

How Does This Matter to Others?

ome topics automatically resonate with public concerns or interests. Schor's topic, obviously, involves public interest and even includes the reader, as a consumer, in its analysis. Susan Jacoby's topic certainly involves the public; after all, she is discussing a trend in education. But she emphasizes the scope and significance of the trend:

> The consequences of this syndrome should not, however, be viewed in narrowly professional terms. Competence in science and math does not mean one is going to become a scientist or mathematician any more than competence in writing English means one is going to become a professional writer. Scientific and mathematical illiteracy—which has been cited in several recent critiques by panels studying American education from kindergarten through college—produces an incalculably impoverished vision of human experience.

And Jacoby goes even further to show how the trend affects life beyond the boundaries of formal education:

> Failure to comprehend either computers or chromosomes leads to a terrible sense of helplessness, because the profound impact of science on everyday life is evident even to those who insist they don't, won't, can't understand why the changes are taking place.

What about topics that do not have immediate relevance to a broader community and potential readers? Every topic is potentially engaging to a reader. Who would think that childhood vomiting could be an interesting topic or make for a valuable essay? Kress makes his own vomiting experience resonate (in more than one way) with readers:

> My brother and sister were silent, too, as though my barfing were a perfectly acceptable alternative to an after-dinner mint, a toothpick, a wet-wipe wrapped like a condom. Perhaps they were too busy stashing away the details of the affront, safekeeping for a time of need—like Aesop's despicable, self-righteous ant. I can only imagine the hay they might have later made by simple melodramatic evocations of the sounds of my gagging, as it echoed in tiny bathrooms. The deep, throaty sound of plosively expelling vomit. "Well, whatever I did can't be as gross and disgusting as THAT," I can hear them repeating over and over till they got what they wanted. Or did they have their own equally disgusting but self-customized techniques of catharsis and orgasm back then—I wondered. Does everyone, I still wonder? And how could a "D" in French or a detention or a missed meal or a dent in the car compare with what I did, over and over and over?

In this paragraph, Kress broadens the scope, including his siblings and "everyone." The broad scope does not mean that Kress is losing focus but that he is bringing others into the issue. Later in the essay, Kress also manages to invite the reader (even readers who did not vomit throughout childhood) into the search.

When writers like Kress and Jacoby emphasize the public nature of a topic, the reader becomes engaged directly in the claims. Use the following questions to help generate a sense of public resonance for your topic:

- What are the effects of this phenomenon?
- Whom does it affect? How does it affect them?
- How does it affect people indirectly?

- If the cause does not affect people, why might someone be interested in it?
- How can I make the topic interesting to a general reader (someone not steeped in the discipline or issue)?
- How does my position or understanding relate to popular perspectives on the topic?

Imagine how your topic involves others who are not associated with it directly. For instance, Jack's topic, cults, might seem to only affect cult members, their families, maybe the communities surrounding the cult. But Jack may go further than that.

How does it affect people indirectly?

If people are drawn to cults through deep loneliness, then cults potentially relate to everyone—that is, anyone who cares about family, friends, the quiet neighbor, etc. Our days are filled with constant inattention to others. Most people choose their narrow paths (their jobs and their small circle of friends) and leave everyone else. Many of us will go weeks without truly acknowledging anyone outside of our little circles. Rarely do we invite the quiet guy from work out with us; rarely do we call our cousin to see how she's doing. We leave lonely people behind us every day.

Here, Jack is imagining the broader and subtler factors. He might even explore the messages that popular culture sends to people: that we must have intense social engagement to achieve happiness and fulfillment, that solitude should be avoided, that excitement and purpose should define every minute of our lives. Jack would then be exploring the culture surrounding cults. He would be thinking like a sociologist, and assuming that any one behavior is linked to a broad system of attitudes, messages, and group behaviors.

Example: Leonard Kress's Response to Public Resonance Questions

How does your position or understanding relate to popular perspectives on the topic? In writing this, I guess I am caught in the popular mania of confession. I consider myself to be a fairly private person, but all around I see people (in books, articles, TV, etc.) revealing the most personal and embarrassing details about their lives. And doing so with relish. The fact that this piece deals with childhood makes it somewhat easier, of course. This is as close as I came to a taboo subject—and it intrigues me that my experience was so different from the media and pop-psychology take on eating disorders and adolescent girls.

Activities

1. Make a poster of your ideas thus far. Graphically display the elements: the event, behavior, trend, the most direct cause, other possible causes, and even the public resonance. (See pp. 662–667 for more suggestions about making posters.) Or make a poster that sends a message about the cause of a phenomenon to the public.
2. Present your ideas to a small group of peers. Explain specifically how the phenomenon is caused. Also, explain the public resonance: that is, how this phenomenon relates to the concerns and lives of others. Call for a follow-up discussion about the phenomenon by asking the group members to consider how it affects their lives.

■

DELIVERY

This writing project can take many possible directions. It is both an argument and an analysis. Some writers emphasize the range of possible causes; others focus on a particular cause and its direct impact on the topic at hand. As you consider your topic, decide on your emphases: will it be important to thoroughly describe several causes or to focus on one? The following sections (**Rhetorical Tools, Organizational Strategies, Writer's Voice,** and **Revision Strategies**) are designed to help you focus your ideas into a sophisticated and engaging text. As you work through them, keep your notes and answers to the **Invention** questions close by.

Rhetorical Tools

Developing the Argument

Remember that you are not simply explaining a cause—you are arguing that a particular cause (or set of causes) could be responsible for a phenomenon. You are arguing that your understanding of the cause/effect relationship is worth considering. Therefore, let us consider the four elements of argument (from Chapter 5: Making Arguments):

Considering Your Thesis: The kind of writing done in this chapter is both analytical and argumentative. Each author of the chapter readings offers an analysis of the topic and also an argument for his or her understanding of the cause. Despite the various rhetorical tools used, each author still has a thesis that focuses on the causes or set of causes most responsible for the phenomenon. Notice how Jack's thesis evolves from his initial thoughts into a sophisticated point.

Evolution of a Thesis	
The writer focuses on a particular phenomenon:	*What makes people leave everything and everyone behind and join cults?*
The writer uses Analysis questions to probe for causes:	*What state of mind or psychological need may have led to the phenomenon? Some form of mental disease makes people join cults.*
The writer works through his initial thoughts and discovers a less obvious cause:	*Deep loneliness and lack of purpose in life cause people to leave their families and join cults.*
The writer struggles to integrate public resonance into his understanding of the cause:	*The deep loneliness and loss created in our society cause people to crave belonging and purpose in their lives, and cults can meet those needs.* *The deep loneliness and loss fostered by our hurried society create desperate searches for belonging and purpose, and cults sometimes fulfill those needs.*

As you consider your own topic, let your ideas evolve. Your main idea may not come into focus immediately. You may even begin writing and drafting before your ideas take shape. Your thesis might:

- Argue for a particular cause.
- Argue that several factors equally cause the phenomenon.
- Argue against an apparent cause (or widely held belief) and for a less obvious or more complicated cause.

Developing Support: As with any argumentative writing, you can support your claims with a number of tools. Remember the following types of evidence: statistics, authorities, facts, examples, allusions, personal anecdotes, scenarios, and analogies. (See Chapter 5, p. 206, for a detailed look at types of evidence.)

In the essays for this chapter, the writers use a broad range of support strategies. Kress, for instance, depends on information collected in his personal everyday life (personal testimony and anecdotes) to support his argument. Personal experience (in the form of narration) is his primary support. Jacoby strategically uses an example to open her argument, but also refers to statistics.

> Examine the essays in this chapter. Decide, first, on the thesis of the essay and then on the different supporting strategies being used in each.

Use the following questions to develop support for your thesis:

- What specific physical or natural facts support my point?
- Does a historical event or figure help to show the cause?
- Can I allude to a similar phenomenon (with a similar cause) to support my point?
- Does a popular culture medium (a movie, television show, etc.) help to support my point?
- Does a literary work (a novel, poem, drama) support my point?
- Do other writers discuss this cause? Do they support my point?
- Does something in nature (in animal or plant life) support my point?
- Has anyone done scientific study on this phenomenon? Does it support my point?
- Have I witnessed or experienced someone or something that illustrates my point?
- Can I construct a hypothetical situation that illustrates my point?

Counterarguing: Counterarguments defend against opposing claims. Writers must anticipate and account for positions outside of or opposed to their own claims(s) and include reasoning to offset that potential opposition. In many cases, writers must contend directly with arguments that forward another cause. Kress, for example, argues against prevailing views of the behavior and explains the way his position differs from others. Here, Kress points to authorities who seem to miss the mark:

> I also locate "Determinants of Adolescent Obesity: A Comparison with Anorexia Nervosa," *Adolescence* (1988), which claims that "both anorexics and the obese are characterized by overprotectedness and enmeshment, resulting from a poor sense of identity and effectiveness." After a whole week of research, this seems to be the extent of my findings. I can find nothing to urge me to go beyond the abstracts, nothing at all, though I type in "eating disorder," "vomiting," "obesity," "abnormal psychology," "gluttony," "disgusting and destructive behavior"—always cross-referenced with "childhood."

Because Kress mentions these other causes (or other takes on the phenomenon), we get the sense that he has a broad understanding of the topic—that he is not simply guessing at a cause, but has explored other possibilities. Juliet Schor also addresses positions outside of her own—and even explains her previous acceptance of another take on the phenomenon of consumption.

> In response to these developments, social critics continue to focus on income. In his impressive analysis of the problems of contemporary American capitalism, *Fat and Mean*, economist David Gordon emphasized income *adequacy*. The "vast majority of US households," he argues, "can barely make ends meet. . . . Meager livelihoods are a *typical* condition, an *average* circumstance." Meanwhile, the Economic Policy Institute focuses on the distribution of income and wealth, arguing that the gains of the top 20 percent have jeopardized the well-being of the bottom 80 percent. Incomes have stagnated and the robust 3 percent growth rates of the 1950s and '60s are long gone. If we have a consumption problem, this view implicitly states, we can solve it by getting more income into more people's hands. The goals are redistribution and growth.
>
> It is difficult to take exception to this view. It combines a deep respect for individual choice (the liberal part) with a commitment to justice and equality (the egalitarian part). I held it myself for many years. But I now believe that by failing to look deeper—to examine the very nature of consumption—it has become too limiting. In short, I do not think that the "income solution" addresses some of the most profound failures of the current consumption regime.

As you have already found, every phenomenon has many possible causes—and every possible cause comes with an argument (which you must, in some way, consider). Use the following questions to develop counterarguments:

- What other causes could be attributed to this phenomenon? (Why are these other causes less acceptable or less valid?)
- What other reasons do people have for disagreeing with me?
- What would support an opposing argument?

Activity: To help generate counterarguments for your topic, use "What Are You, Nuts?" exercise in Chapter 5, p. 248.

Conceding: Concessions acknowledge the value of positions or claims other than those being forwarded by the writer. Remember that a good writer (with a broad understanding of the topic) is able to concede the value of some points or qualify his or her own points well. Notice, for example, that Schor does not simply mention other points to knock them down, but genuinely acknowledges the value of another position:

> In response to these developments, social critics continue to focus on income. In his impressive analysis of the problems of contemporary American capitalism, *Fat and Mean*, economist David Gordon emphasized income *adequacy*.

Although she ultimately disagrees with David Gordon, Schor still acknowledges his "impressive analysis" and clearly understands the value of other arguments.

Jacoby makes a slightly different move. Rather than acknowledge the value of someone else's claims, she *qualifies* her own; that is, she explains that men also have low estimations of their own mathematical abilities:

> Scientific illiteracy is not, of course, the exclusive province of women. In certain intellectual circles it has become fashionable to proclaim a willed, aggressive ignorance about science and technology. Some female writers specialize in ominous, uninformed diatribes against genetic research as a plot to remove control of childbearing from women, while some well-known men of letters proudly announce that they understand absolutely nothing about computers, or, for that matter, about electricity.

Although Jacoby's essay focuses on women and girls' self-limiting perspectives, she qualifies or opens up her point in the above paragraph. This move puts her argument in a bigger context—and shows that she understands that other arguments exist parallel to her own.

As you consider your own argument, use the following questions to develop concessions and qualifiers:

- Are there other valid positions that one could take on my topic?
- Are there legitimate reasons for taking another position on this topic?
- Does my argument make any large, but necessary, leaps?
- Do I ask my audience to imagine a situation that is fictional?
- Do I ask my audience to accept generalizations?

Activity: Discuss your topic with a non-classmate (a family member, friend, co-worker, or even a stranger). You might e-mail an acquaintance for this discussion. Ask him or her about the cause of your chosen topic, and why the topic is important. Write a brief summary of the discussion, or if you have the discussion recorded in e-mail, write a brief response that articulates the differences and similarities between your perspectives on the topic. You might use the ideas that emerge from this discussion as part of your own delivery.

Organizational Strategies
Addressing Common Concerns

Where Should I Explain the Phenomenon?
Like any argument, the elements of your project can be arranged in many ways. Perhaps one tendency among writers is to explain the phenomenon before getting into possible causes. Whether using narrative, examples, or illustrations, writers tend to detail the phenomenon (the behavior, event, trend, and so on) before getting into a discussion of causes. Notice Jacoby's introduction. She gives a brief illustration of the phenomenon (girls dropping math and science from their priorities):

> Susannah, a 16-year-old who has always been an A student in every subject from algebra to English, recently informed her parents that she intended to drop physics and calculus in her senior year of high school and replace them with a drama seminar and a work-study program. She expects a major in art or history in college, she explained, and "any more science or math will just be a waste of my time."

Now that Jacoby has given a snapshot of the phenomenon, she can go on to discuss its significance and its public resonance, and to explore possible causes. However, like the other authors in this chapter, Jacoby continues to illustrate the phenomenon throughout her essay to develop its complexity and to show how certain causes are linked to it.

How Should I Deal with Other Causes?
Other causes, those that seem less significant, can help develop counterarguments. That is, you can argue against other causes in favor of the cause you put forth. For example:

> Some may argue that people join cults because they are mentally ill, nuts, freaked out. It is easy to write off cult members as lunatics. They willingly cast away their families and friends, give all of their life belongings to a bunch of strangers, wear uniform-like apparel, and sometimes even cut their hair to match the group. In short, they throw away their identities, something next to insanity in a culture that honors individualism as the greatest good. However, insanity may not be the main reason people join cults. In fact, many cult members are highly intelligent, entirely reasonable, and healthy individuals. But they long for something, something that everyone longs for—belonging and purpose.

Here, the writer points to a possible cause of cult membership, but refutes the idea in favor of another: loneliness. In this case, the argument that mental illness causes people to join cults is an opposing position—one that the writer counters.

If you have potential counterarguments, remember some standard strategies from Chapter 5. Counterarguments might come directly after opposing points in counterpoint, point, counterpoint, point manner. Depending on the amount of detail given to each counter, each point might be an entire paragraph—or more—with supporting evidence:

Opposing Point A
Your counterargument
Opposing Point B
Your counterargument

How Should I Include Outside Sources? For any argument and any

topic, an academic writer can (and sometimes should) refer to outside sources (print and electronic sources or even conclusions from field research). If you have used outside sources, see Chapter 12: Research and Writing (and make sure that your instructor is aware of your choice to consult outside sources). But if you have already gathered some information and know how you want to use it, keep in mind that any information from your research should only be included as part of your purpose for the paper. In other words, *be careful not to include information just for the sake of including it.* You might include information from outside sources to explain other perspectives on the cause, support your argument about the cause, or help to explain the phenomenon.

Schor and Kress both use outside sources to illustrate what others think about the cause; Schor also uses them to support her argument for the causes of consumption. Her use of outside research (when she points to other studies and other economic theories) is always part of her purpose. We always know where she stands, and how the information being presented relates to her stance:

> In the meantime, upscale emulation had become well-established. Researchers Susan Fournier and Michael Guiry found that 35 percent of their sample aspired to reach the top 6 percent of the income distribution, and another 49 percent aspired to the next 12 percent. Only 15 percent reported that they would be satisfied with "living a comfortable life"–that is, being middle class. But 85 percent of the population cannot earn the six-figure incomes necessary to support upper-middle-class lifestyles.

Here, Schor uses statistics and others' research to explain the phenomenon–the behavior of increased consumption. Notice that Schor's use of the statistics and outside research fits into her larger plan: first, as part of a paragraph and then as part of her general argument.

How Should I Use Paragraphs? As in all academic prose (the language

that scholars use to communicate ideas), paragraphs are used to clump information. But we should also think of paragraphs as rhetorical tools–strategies for focusing and refocusing readers' attention. In this sense, paragraphs focus readers on a single idea, point, or example. For an argument about causes, a single paragraph might focus readers on a single illustration of a cause, an outside source that argues for a particular cause, a personal narrative that coincides or counters the outside source, or a concession to an outside perspective.

Remember that the turnabout paragraph is a good tool for addressing opposing views. It often begins by expressing an opposing position (one different than the writer's) and then it turns to counter that position. In the following passage, Schor explains a perspective, or "view," outside of her own. She then begins a new paragraph that initially grants value to the perspective but then turns to show its failing.

> If we have a consumption problem, this view implicitly states, we can solve it by getting more income into more people's hands. The goals are redistribution and growth.
>
> It is difficult to take exception to this view. It combines a deep respect for individual choice (the liberal part) with a commitment to justice and equality (the egalitarian part). I held it myself for many years. But I now believe that by failing to look deeper–to examine the very nature of consumption–it has become too limiting. In short, I do not think that the "income solution" addresses some of the most profound failures of the current consumption regime.

Writer's Voice

Exploring Options

Creating Credibility: At this point, you are familiar with many different tools for creating an engaging voice. As earlier chapters discuss, good writers are inviting and curious; they avoid preachiness and hostility. Writers also need to create a sense of credibility, the quality that makes points believable. In argumentative writing, and especially in more complicated types such as in this chapter, it is important to be credible to readers so they consider your claims.

A credible voice is not necessarily commanding or domineering. It might simply be very logical or insightful. Juliet Schor seems credible by virtue of her intensive analysis and extensive research. Tannen's own research makes her credible:

> Switching topics is another habit that gives women the impression that men aren't listening, especially if they switch to a topic about themselves. But the evidence of the 10th-grade boys in my study indicates otherwise. The 10th-grade boys sprawled across their chairs with bodies parallel and eyes straight ahead, rarely looking at each other.

She offers a particular slice of her own research to ground her claims and create credibility.

But this does not mean that all claims need to be supported with years of scientific research. Tannen, or any of the writers in this chapter, could appear unbelievable if her claims were disconnected from her research. Imagine if Tannen had gone on in her essay to claim that "women are better talkers than men." Nothing in her research, at least as it is reported to us, would suggest such a conclusion. So, despite years of research, Tannen would lose credibility. However, Tannen's claims are appropriately focused and illustrated by the observations she shares with her readers. In other words, readers accept ideas when the support seems proportional and related to the claims.

Some writers, such as Leonard Kress, use personal experience to build credibility. In his essay, we get the sense that he may know more about the behavior than many of the supposed experts because of his experiences. It is not necessarily *The Encyclopedia of Pediatric Psychology* that gives credibility to Kress's voice; it is, rather, the manner in which he uses the information to highlight his own understanding. By the time Kress discovers the important passage in the encyclopedia, he seems to have established his own credibility:

> . . . I could simply will the partially chewed hearty chunks of meat and potato up from their sour churning stock. It felt so good! *The Encyclopedia of Pediatric Psychology* (1979) reports that children who vomit, farfetched as it sounds, even "those who have learned society's aversions . . . can overcome such scruples and experience vomiting as cathartic, even orgasmic."

Remember, then, that you can be credible by examining personal experiences as well as others' research. In considering your own writing, ask yourself the following:

- How will my own experiences or insights create credibility?
- How might outside sources add to my credibility?

Projecting Wonder: Some people assume that a sense of credibility means that the writer is unquestionable and unquestioning. However, credibility does not have to diminish a sense of curiosity. Even though the writers in this chapter have justification for speaking authoritatively about their topics (from research and observation), they also create a sense of curiosity and even wonder. Sometimes, the most authoritative voice is also the most curious. Notice Kress's voice. Even though he has reason to be certain about his claims, he is also curious:

> I often wonder now what led me to such disgusting behavior—what might lead any child to such disgusting behavior. Like any good 21st-century questioner/researcher, I go to the Internet, hopeful that a search of current medical literature will provide answers and understanding. So I begin my search, seated in front of my computer.

Now think of your own topic and your stance on it. Ask yourself the following:

- What about my topic is mysterious or unknown?
- How does my topic extend beyond usual perception or thinking?
- How is my topic unordinary?
- What details or ideas associated with my topic might make the reader curious?

Avoiding Preachiness: Because this essay is argumentative in nature, it could potentially involve accusatory language. Remember that most readers do not accept language that demeans people or tells people what they need. Imagine if Jacoby had become accusatory toward adolescent girls and their parents:

> Girls should know better than to dump math and science classes. They need to realize that math and science are important for their intellectual development, and that dropping these courses means they will remain behind their male counterparts in many occupations. Their decision to replace math and science courses with drama and art shows their lack of responsibility.

Such language does nothing to help a reader understand the phenomenon or accept a particular cause. Instead, it merely spouts opinions about behavior. This passage also moves away from an argument about why something occurs to an argument against certain people. Most often, academic writing avoids telling readers what people should do and instead shows readers the value or liability of certain behavior. Notice Jacoby's actual argument:

> In saying that scientific and mathematical ignorance is a self-inflicted female wound, I do not, obviously, mean that cultural expectations play no role in the process. But the world does not conspire to deprive modern women of access to science as it did in the 1930s. . . . The current generation of adolescent girls—and their parents, bred on old expectations about women's interest—are active conspirators in limiting their own intellectual development.

Jacoby does not attack adolescent girls and their parents. Instead, she explains the complicated cultural process by which they accept their own low expectations in scientific and mathematical proficiency. Jacoby's analysis is not a blame game, but an examination of cause and effect.

As you consider your own voice, avoid condemning people or behaviors. Instead, try to explain *why* situations occur or *why* people act in a particular way. Try to reveal the complexities behind behaviors or events. This strategy will help create a voice that is reflective and analytical.

Revision Strategies

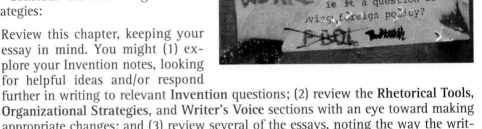

Writing about a cause goes far beyond one's initial thinking on the topic. What appears to be a cause might not be, or it might be a factor but not the only factor. If the cause you write about is too obvious, readers might wonder why they are reading about it. And if other possible causes exist—even if only in people's minds—readers will expect your essay to show how these possible causes fit into your argument. Revising, or re-seeing, from a reader's point of view should make your essay a more effective and more persuasive piece of writing.

Consider the following revision strategies:

- Review this chapter, keeping your essay in mind. You might (1) explore your Invention notes, looking for helpful ideas and/or respond further in writing to relevant **Invention** questions; (2) review the **Rhetorical Tools, Organizational Strategies,** and **Writer's Voice** sections with an eye toward making appropriate changes; and (3) review several of the essays, noting the way the writers in this chapter approached this type of essay.

- Set aside at least as much time to revise as you took with invention and delivery.

- Create distance between you and your writing by getting away from it for a few days if possible or a few hours at least.

- Read your paper aloud to hear how it sounds, or have someone else read it aloud to you.

- Print out a hard copy of your paper and read it carefully in a different place than where you wrote it.

- Figure out your writing strategy by noticing how the parts of your essay work together to support your main point. Consider making an outline of your essay to help you see this.

- Have someone else read and respond to your essay.

For ideas about **Peer Review,** see page 50.

Global Revision Questions

Invention (What have you learned by exploring your topic?)

- **Point of Contact:** What other ideas did you consider writing about before selecting this one? Why was this idea more worth pursuing than the others?

- **Analysis:** How has your exploration of this topic gone beyond your initial ideas and questions about it? In what ways have your ideas moved beyond your initial biases and perceptions—and beyond the common beliefs of your reader?

- **Public Resonance:** How might your essay be relevant to, or matter to, your reader? What might be the consequence(s) of your essay? How might the reader think or act differently after reading it?

Delivery (What writing decisions have you made as part of your writing strategy?)

- **Rhetorical Tools:** Re-examine your rhetorical strategy for discussing a problem. What rhetorical tools have you used? What other tools might be helpful?

  - What is the main idea of your essay, and how have you conveyed that idea to the reader? What, besides your *intended* main idea, might the reader imagine your main idea to be? How might you help the reader hear what you are trying to say?

  - How might you explain the cause more clearly? What additional information might you provide to better help your reader understand it? Where might you provide more evidence to persuade the reader? How might information from outside sources help support your main idea? What counterarguments and concessions might be helpful? How might your title, introduction, and conclusion provide more helpful information regarding the main point of your essay?

  - What information might be deleted? Where might a reader lose interest? What examples, statistics or other information might be unnecessary? What words, sentences, or entire paragraphs slow the pace of your writing without adding helpful information?

- **Organizational Strategies:** How might you re-arrange paragraphs to help the reader see your main ideas more clearly? How might you re-arrange ideas within paragraphs? What ideas might be more helpful to the reader if placed earlier, or later, or near some other idea? If used, how might information from outside sources be more smoothly integrated into your essay? How might connections/relationships between ideas be made more clear?

- **Writer's Voice:** Describe your writer's voice. How might you sound to the reader? How might the reader perceive you, the writer, in this essay? What about your writer's voice is inviting to the reader? What about your writer's voice might alienate the reader? What changes might make your writer's voice more inviting?

■

CONSIDERING CONSEQUENCES

This chapter begins: "When something happens in a community, everyone wants to know why. . . ." People want to know why because they are naturally curious. Beyond that, knowing why allows people to understand a situation better and to go about making appropriate changes. In academia, at work, and at home, understanding causes is not just curiosity, but can have serious consequences. Exploring and writing about such issues is likely to have consequences for the reader, the writer, and their community as a whole. What might be the consequences of your essay for this chapter? That is, what effect might your ideas have on your reader's thoughts and actions? Consider these questions:

- Will the reader better understand the issue about which you wrote?
- Is the reader likely to think or behave differently?
- What might be the benefits to others? How might others be harmed?
- Who besides your instructor might benefit from your ideas?
- How might what you wrote about be affected?
- What might be the effect of these consequences on you, the writer?

Activities

The Consequences of Your Essay

1. List as many individuals as you can imagine whose thinking and/or actions might change if they were to read the essay you wrote for this chapter. For each individual you list, name the possible change in his or her thinking and/or action. (As you consider consequences upon your reader, consider the "ripple effect" of those consequences. If your reader thinks or behaves differently, what is the impact of that thinking or behavior on others?)

2. Discuss the possible consequences of your essay with others. Explain what your essay is about, and then ask for feedback. You might ask the following questions: What impact might this essay have on the reader? How might this essay change the way someone thinks or acts? How did it make you think differently? How might it make you act differently?

3. List three other forms of delivery that you might have used to express your idea (report, letter, poster, screenplay, Web site, speech, song, poem, action). How might the consequences of your message have been different if delivered by way of these other forms?

The Consequences of the Chapter Readings

1. How did one of the chapter readings help you to better understand a cause? How did you look at the issue before the reading, and how did you look at it differently after reading the essay? What part of the essay influenced you the most, and why?

2. How might *you* think and/or behave differently because of one of the readings? And, how might *others* benefit, or be harmed, by your new way of thinking and/or acting?

3. How might someone you know think or act differently after reading one of the essays in this chapter?

4. How might *the writers* in this chapter be influenced by what they write? How might they think or act differently? How might they be treated differently by others?

Considering Images

1. Explain how someone might view one of the images in this chapter differently after having read one of the essays in this chapter. What particular part of the written text might be most influential in changing the person's viewpoint?

2. Find an image not in this text and explain how someone might view it differently after having read one of the essays in this chapter.

3. Take a snapshot of a cause, either with a camera or by describing it in a paragraph or two, and write an essay explaining how a person might view that "snapshot" differently after reading one of the essays in this chapter or your own essay.

Causes in Everyday Life

1. How has some written text that explains a cause been influential in your life? You may consider novels, articles, advertisements, and so on. Briefly summarize the text and explain its effect on you. What was your life like before you read it? How did your life change after you read it?

2. How has some written text that explains a cause been influential in the lives of Americans?

3. How does some written text inaccurately explain a cause? What does the text claim is the cause, and what is the actual cause? Why does the text get the cause wrong?

Considering Images

1. Find an image that identifies or suggests a cause. What effect might the image have on the people who view it? How might the viewer think or act differently after having seen the image?

2. Share the image you found for #1 above with several people, asking them how they think it might affect those who view it. Then write an essay explaining the potential consequences of the image. Might it help or harm others? Would its effects be intended or accidental?

Writing, Speech, and Action

EVERYDAY RHETORIC

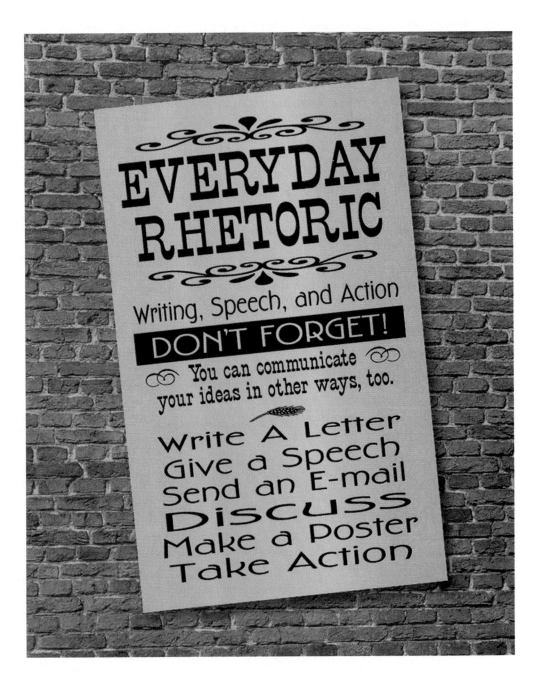

Exploring Visual Rhetoric

I t can be argued that images, too, use rhetoric. And by looking at how images "work," we can apply some of the important concepts of rhetoric, not just to writing and speaking, but to images as well. Looking at visual rhetoric can also help us to better understand how rhetoric is used in writing and speech.

Consider This Chapter's Opening Image: Describe the rhetoric of this chapter's opening image—cars stacked on top of each other. Use the "Analyzing an Image" questions in Chapter 13 on page 694 to help you figure out how the image conveys an idea.

A. Discuss your analysis of the chapter's opening image with several classmates. Explore through discussion how your understanding of the image is similar to or different from theirs. Following the discussion, write down the main similarities and differences in your viewpoints, and explain how your ideas about the image developed or changed through discussion. What did you learn, or how because of the discussion did you come to think differently about the image?

B. Consider the public resonance of the opening image. What public concern does it speak to? To whom might this concern matter? How might people benefit by exploring the photograph's possible meanings?

Find an Image That Relates to Your Essay: What image might you use in conjunction with the essay you wrote for this chapter?

A. Write a caption for the image.

B. Write an essay explaining the relationship between the image and your text. Consider the following questions as you develop your ideas:

- How does the image support or help to explain the text of the essay?
- What does the image argue? What claim does the image make?
- What specific elements of the image convey the main idea and the support for that idea?
- How might the reader view the image differently after having read your essay?
- How might the reader be confused by the relationship of your essay and image?

C. Write an essay in which you explain how your essay influenced the way others viewed the image. To do research for your essay, (1) show the image to several people, and (2) ask them how they view it. (Record their responses.) Then (3) ask them to read your essay and (4) explain how they now view the image differently.

D. Describe the rhetoric of your own photograph or image, using the "Analyzing an Image" questions on page 694.

Consider Other Images in This Chapter: Consider how the images in this chapter encourage people to search for causes.

1. Explore the relationship, or interaction, between an image in this chapter and an essay in this chapter. Select one image and one essay and explain the relationship between the written text and the visual image. How does the image encourage the reader to think about the text, and how does the text encourage the reader to think about the image?

2. Use one of the images in this text as a point of contact for a "Searching for Causes" essay. Instead of writing the essay, write down the essay ideas that the image invites you to consider.

   A. Share your ideas from #2 above with several people, asking them what "Searching for Causes" ideas the image brings to mind. Add their ideas to your list, and then explain which ideas would be most worth pursuing in an essay.

   B. Using the "Analyzing an Image" questions on page 694, explain how the particular elements of the image you selected for #2 above work together to make an argument about a cause.

Find an Everyday Image That Suggests a Cause: Notice images throughout the course of the day—as you work, attend classes, travel, and so on. Write down each image you find that you think identifies or suggests a cause and consider the following questions about each image: What cause does the image encourage the viewer to think about? How does the image encourage people to think and/or act differently?

A. Share one of the images you found with several other people, asking them what the image says to them. Record their responses.

B. Analyze people's reactions to the image you showed them. Consider the following questions:

   • What reaction was most common?

   • What reaction was most unusual?

   • Why did others have the reaction they did? How did the particular elements of the image influence them? What attitudes and beliefs of each individual played an important role in his or her understanding of the image?

   • What reaction did you find to be most interesting and why?

C. Having thought about others' reactions, how have your ideas about the image developed or changed?

D. Using the "Analyzing an Image" questions on page 694 for help, describe the rhetoric of the image you found.

Create a Photo (or Image) Essay:
Use at least four images to encourage people to think about a cause. Select and arrange the images carefully, then in writing explain how the images work together to make your point. Use the "Analyzing an Image" questions on page 694, as well as the **Invention** and **Delivery** sections in this chapter, to help you explain the rhetoric of your photo (or image) essay.

Explore a Photo Essay:
How does the photo essay "Road Salt" encourage people to think about a cause? How do the four images work together to make some point? (Consider the content, and other elements, of the individual images and the relationships of the images to each other.) What other images might the writer have used and why? What other order might the images have been placed in?

9

Chapter Contents

Proposing Solutions

What problem does this image point out?
What is the solution, and how is it ironic?
Does the absurdity of the image suggest
something about the problem?

In everyday life, crisis is a constant. Problems emerge in every facet of our existence: In occupations, problems arise in working conditions, policy implementation, co-worker relations, labor/management relations, and governmental standards. In our communities, problems such as homelessness, pollution, school violence, terrorism, and urban sprawl must be encountered daily. At home, of course, the list of possible problems is endless. While many of us have the privilege of ignoring such problems, someone, in some capacity, has to address them. Whether elected official, shift supervisor, environmental scientist, department chair, or scout leader, someone ultimately has to engage daily crises and propose solutions.

In academia, people in all disciplines have to propose solutions:

- In an engineering class, students propose solutions to structural problems in a building designed before earthquake construction codes.
- In a business class, students must convince their peers that a particular strategy for solving a company's financial problems is the most strategic.
- In a calculus class, students explore several different ways to solve a problem, and then convince their peers and instructor that one particular way is the best.
- For a national conference on employment trends, graduate students and faculty members propose strategies to meet the increasing demand for low-salary instructors.

When writers propose solutions to problems, they are involved in many layers of analysis. They must analyze the problem to discover its causes—some of which may lie hidden in abstraction. They must also consider all the possible ways for addressing the problem and then come to some conclusion about the most appropriate. Proposing solutions also involves argument: writers have to convince readers that the problem must be addressed, that action is necessary. Also, writers must argue for the value of their particular solution. This is what politicians do for a living; members of Congress, after all, spend much of their time arguing, first, that particular problems deserve allocated funds and, second, that those funds should be used in particular ways. Therefore, you might think of proposing a solution as a double-layered argument: first, you must argue that a problem exists (one worthy of attention or action) and, second, that a particular solution will best solve it. Proposing a solution, then, involves all the elements of an argument (thesis, support, counterargument, and concession).

9 This chapter will help you discover a problem, develop a solution, and develop a written argument for the solution. The following essays will provide valuable insight to necessary strategies for proposing solutions. After reading the essays, you can find a problem in one of two ways:

1. Go to the **Point of Contact** section to find a problem from your everyday life.
2. Choose one of the **Ideas for Writing** that follow each essay.

After finding a subject, go to the **Analysis** section to begin developing ideas for your essay.

READINGS

In the following essays, each writer addresses a specific problem and gives many illustrations or examples for that problem. Some writers go to great lengths to express the degree of the problem being discussed. As you may notice, the more abstract or hidden the problem, the more the writer has to work to illustrate it. (The effect of pesticides on human life, for instance, is a fairly difficult problem to illustrate, and so Carson goes to considerable lengths to make it apparent.) For some problems, the solution is equally complex. Writers who acknowledge the true complexities of their problems and solutions will better engage their readers and will meet with less opposition. (For example, consider politicians who encounter opposition because they dance around the hard truths of social problems.) Some solutions, as Didion's essay illustrates, are not necessarily complicated physical solutions, but simple reconsiderations—that is, new ways of thinking about an inescapable problem.

The Obligation to Endure

Rachel Carson

Rachel Carson, a marine biologist, taught zoology at the University of Maryland (1931–1936) and was an aquatic biologist at the U.S. Bureau of Fisheries and the Fish and Wildlife Service (1936–1952). Her books include The Sea Around Us *(1951) and* Silent Spring *(1962), in which "The Obligation to Endure" originally appeared. As you read, think about whether or not Carson's ideas are relevant today. In the margins of your text, write down whether or not you find certain ideas to still be important, and why.*

1 The history of life on earth has been a history of interaction between living things and their surroundings. To a large extent, the physical form and the habits of the earth's vegetation and its animal life have been molded by the environment. Considering the whole span of earthly time, the opposite effect, in which life actually modifies its surroundings, has been relatively slight. Only within the moment of time represented by the present century has one species—man—acquired significant power to alter the nature of his world.

2 During the past quarter century this power has not only increased to one of disturbing magnitude but it has changed in character. The most alarming of all man's assaults upon the environment is the contamination of air, earth, rivers, and sea with dangerous and even lethal materials. This pollution is for the most part irrecoverable; the chain of evil it initiates not only in the world that must support life but in living tissues is for the most part irreversible. In this now universal contamination of the environment, chemicals are the sinister and little-

recognized partners of radiation in changing the very nature of the world—the very nature of its life. Strontium 90, released through nuclear explosions into the air, comes to earth in rain or drifts down as fallout, lodges in soil, enters into the grass or corn or wheat grown there, and in time takes up its abode in the bones of a human being, there to remain until his death. Similarly, chemicals sprayed on croplands or forests or gardens lie long in soil, entering into living organisms, passing from one to another in a chain of poisoning and death. Or they pass mysteriously by underground streams until they emerge and, through the alchemy of air and sunlight, combine into new forms that kill vegetation, sicken cattle, and work unknown harm on those who drink from once pure wells. As Albert Schweitzer has said, "Man can hardly even recognize the devils of his own creation."

3   It took hundreds of millions of years to produce the life that now inhabits the earth—eons of time in which that developing and evolving and diversifying life reached a state of adjustment and balance with its surroundings. The environment, rigorously shaping and directing the life it supported, contained elements that were hostile as well as supporting. Certain rocks gave out dangerous radiation; even within the light of the sun, from which all life draws its energy, there were short-wave radiations with power to injure. Given time—time not in years but in millennia—life adjusts, and a balance has been reached. For time is the essential ingredient; but in the modern world there is no time.

4   The rapidity of change and the speed with which new situations are created follow the impetuous and heedless pace of man rather than the deliberate pace of nature. Radiation is no longer merely the background radiation of rocks, the bombardment of cosmic rays, the ultraviolet of the sun that have existed before there was any life on earth; radiation is now the unnatural creation of man's tampering with the atom. The chemicals to which life is asked to make its adjustment are no longer merely the calcium and silica and copper and all the rest of the minerals washed out of the rocks and carried in rivers to the sea; they are the synthetic creations of man's inventive mind, brewed in his laboratories, and having no counterparts in nature.

5   To adjust to these chemicals would require time on the scale that is nature's; it would require not merely the years of a man's life but the life of generations. And even this, were it by some miracle possible, would be futile, for the new chemicals come from our laboratories in an endless stream; almost five hundred annually find their way into actual use in the United States alone. The figure is staggering and its implications are not easily grasped—500 new chemicals to which the bodies of men and animals are required somehow to adapt each year, chemicals totally outside the limits of biologic experience.

6   Among them are many that are used in man's war against nature. Since the mid-1940's over 200 basic chemicals have been created for use in killing insects, weeds, rodents, and other organisms described in the modern vernacular as "pests"; and they are sold under several thousand different brand names.

7   These sprays, dusts, and aerosols are now applied almost universally to farms, gardens, forests, and homes—nonselective chemicals that have the power to kill every insect, the "good" and the "bad," to still the song of birds and the leaping of fish in the streams, to coat the leaves with a deadly film, and to linger on in soil—all this though the intended target may be only a few weeds or insects. Can anyone believe it is possible to lay down such a barrage of poisons on the surface of the earth without making it unfit for all life? They should not be called "insecticides," but "biocides."

8   The whole process of spraying seems caught up in an endless spiral. Since DDT was released for civilian use, a process of escalation has been going on in which ever more toxic materials must be found. This has happened because insects, in a triumphant vindication of Darwin's principle of the survival of the fittest, have evolved super races immune to the particular

insecticide used, hence a deadlier one has always to be developed—and then a deadlier one than that. It has happened also because, for reasons to be described later, destructive insects often undergo a "flareback," or resurgence, after spraying, in numbers greater than before. Thus the chemical war is never won, and all life is caught in its violent crossfire.

9   Along with the possibility of the extinction of mankind by nuclear war, the central problem of our age has therefore become the contamination of man's total environment with such substances of incredible potential for harm—substances that accumulate in the tissues of plants and animals and even penetrate the germ cells to shatter or alter the very material of heredity upon which the shape of the future depends.

10   Some would-be architects of our future look toward a time when it will be possible to alter the human germ plasm by design. But we may easily be doing so now by inadvertence, for many chemicals, like radiation, bring about gene mutations. It is ironic to think that man might determine his own future by something so seemingly trivial as the choice of an insect spray.

11   All this has been risked—for what? Future historians may well be amazed by our distorted sense of proportion. How could intelligent beings seek to control a few unwanted species by a method that contaminated the entire environment and brought the threat of disease and death even to their own kind? Yet this is precisely what we have done. We have done it, moreover, for reasons that collapse the moment we examine them. We are told that the enormous and expanding use of pesticides is necessary to maintain farm production. Yet is our real problem not one of *overproduction*? Our farms, despite measures to remove acreages from production and to pay farmers *not* to produce, have yielded such a staggering excess of crops that the American taxpayer in 1962 is paying out more than one billion dollars a year as the total carrying cost of the surplus-food storage program. And is the situation helped when one branch of the Agriculture Department tries to reduce production while another states, as it did in 1958, "It is believed generally that reduction of crop acreages under provisions of the Soil Bank will stimulate interest in use of chemicals to obtain maximum production on the land retained in crops."

12   All this is not to say there is no insect problem and no need of control. I am saying, rather, that control must be geared to realities, not to mythical situations, and that the methods employed must be such that they do not destroy us along with the insects.

13   The problem whose attempted solution has brought such a train of disaster in its wake is an accompaniment of our modern way of life. Long before the age of man, insects inhabited the earth—a group of extraordinarily varied and adaptable beings. Over the course of time since man's advent, a small percentage of the more than half a million species of insects have come into conflict with human welfare in two principal ways: as competitors for the food supply and as carriers of human disease.

14   Disease-carrying insects become important where human beings are crowded together, especially under conditions where sanitation is poor, as in time of natural disaster or war or in situations of extreme poverty and deprivation. Then control of some sort becomes necessary. It is a sobering fact, however, as we shall presently see, that the method of massive chemical control has had only limited success, and also threatens to worsen the very conditions it is intended to curb.

15   Under primitive agricultural conditions the farmer had few insect problems. These arose with the intensification of agriculture—the devotion of immense acreages to a single crop. Such a system set the stage for explosive increases in specific insect populations. Single-crop farming does not take advantage of the principles by which nature works; it is agriculture as an engineer might conceive it to be. Nature has introduced great variety into the landscape, but man

has displayed a passion for simplifying it. Thus he undoes the built-in checks and balances by which nature holds the species within bounds. One important natural check is a limit on the amount of suitable habitat for each species. Obviously then, an insect that lives on wheat can build up its population to much higher levels on a farm devoted to wheat than on one in which wheat is intermingled with other crops to which the insect is not adapted.

16   The same thing happens in other situations. A generation or more ago, the towns of large areas of the United States lined their streets with the noble elm tree. Now the beauty they hopefully created is threatened with complete destruction as disease sweeps through the elms, carried by a beetle that would have only limited chance to build up large populations and to spread from tree to tree if the elms were only occasional trees in a richly diversified planting.

17   Another factor in the modern insect problem is one that must be viewed against a background of geologic and human history: the spreading of thousands of different kinds of organisms from their native homes to invade new territories. This worldwide migration has been studied and graphically described by the British ecologist Charles Elton in his recent book *The Ecology of Invasions*. During the Cretaceous Period, some hundred million years ago, flooding seas cut many land bridges between continents and living things found themselves confined in what Elton calls "colossal separate nature reserves." There, isolated from others of their kind, they developed many new species. When some of the land masses were joined again, about 15 million years ago, these species began to move out into new territories—a movement that is not only still in progress but is now receiving considerable assistance from man.

18   The importation of plants is the primary agent in the modern spread of species, for animals have almost invariably gone along with the plants, quarantine being a comparatively recent and not completely effective innovation. The United States Office of Plant Introduction alone has introduced almost 200,000 species and varieties of plants from all over the world. Nearly half of the 180 or so major insect enemies of plants in the United States are accidental imports from abroad, and most of them have come as hitchhikers on plants.

19   In new territory, out of reach of the restraining hand of the natural enemies that kept down its numbers in its native land, an invading plant or animal is able to become enormously abundant. Thus it is no accident that our most troublesome insects are introduced species.

20   These invasions, both the naturally occurring and those dependent on human assistance, are likely to continue indefinitely. Quarantine and massive chemical campaigns are only extremely expensive ways of buying time. We are faced, according to Dr. Elton, "with a life-and-death need not just to find new technological means of suppressing this plant or that animal"; instead we need the basic knowledge of animal populations and their relations to their surroundings that will "promote an even balance and damp down the explosive power of outbreaks and new invasions."

21   Much of the necessary knowledge is now available but we do not use it. We train ecologists in our universities and even employ them in our governmental agencies but we seldom take their advice. We allow the chemical death rain to fall as though there were no alternative, whereas in fact there are many, and our ingenuity could soon discover many more if given opportunity.

22   Have we fallen into a mesmerized state that makes us accept as inevitable that which is inferior or detrimental, as though having lost the will or the vision to demand that which is good? Such thinking, in the words of the ecologist Paul Shepard, "idealizes life with only its head out of water, inches above the limits of toleration of the corruption of its own environment . . . Why should we tolerate a diet of weak poisons, a home in insipid surroundings, a circle of acquaintances who are not quite our enemies, the noise of motors with just enough

relief to prevent insanity? Who would want to live in a world which is just not quite fatal?"

23   Yet such a world is pressed upon us. The crusade to create a chemically sterile, insect-free world seems to have engendered a fanatic zeal on the part of many specialists and most of the so-called control agencies. On every hand there is evidence that those engaged in spraying operations exercise a ruthless power. "The regulatory entomologists . . . function as prosecutor, judge and jury, tax assessor and collector and sheriff to enforce their own orders," said Connecticut entomologist Neely Turner. The most flagrant abuses go unchecked in both state and federal agencies.

24   It is not my contention that chemical insecticides must never be used. I do contend that we have put poisonous and biologically potent chemicals indiscriminately into the hands of persons largely or wholly ignorant of their potentials for harm. We have subjected enormous numbers of people to contact with these poisons, without their consent and often without their knowledge. If the Bill of Rights contains no guarantee that a citizen shall be secure against lethal poisons distributed either by private individuals or by public officials, it is surely only because our forefathers, despite their considerable wisdom and foresight, could conceive of no such problem.

25   I contend, furthermore, that we have allowed these chemicals to be used with little or no advance investigation of their effect on soil, water, wildlife, and man himself. Future generations are unlikely to condone our lack of prudent concern for the integrity of the natural world that supports all life.

26   There is still very limited awareness of the nature of the threat. This is an era of specialists, each of whom sees his own problem and is unaware of or intolerant of the larger frame into which it fits. It is also an era dominated by industry, in which the right to make a dollar at whatever cost is seldom challenged. When the public protests, confronted with some obvious evidence of damaging results of pesticide applications, it is fed little tranquilizing pills of half truth. We urgently need an end to these false assurances, to the sugar coating of unpalatable facts. It is the public that is being asked to assume the risks that the insect controllers calculate. The public must decide whether it wishes to continue on the present road, and it can do so only when in full possession of the facts. In the words of Jean Rostand, "The obligation to endure gives us the right to know."

Exploring Ideas

1. What is Carson trying to accomplish with this essay?

2. What change does Carson want the reader to consider?

3. What ideas of Carson's are still relevant today? What ideas are no longer relevant?

4. Spend several days observing your environment, looking for evidence from your everyday life to support or refute any of Carson's ideas. Write down each piece of evidence you discover and the way it relates to what Carson says.

5. How might you participate in this discussion about the environment? Consider various ways of expanding, narrowing, redirecting, or updating the discussion.

Writing Strategies

1. Evaluate Carson's introduction and conclusion. Why is, or isn't, each effective? How else might she have begun and concluded her essay?

2. Write a new introduction and conclusion for Carson's essay. Then discuss with classmates the advantages and disadvantages of the introduction and conclusion you wrote.

3. What strategies (historical allusion, hypothetical situation, personal experience, observation of a trend, statistics/data, and so on) does Carson use to support her main idea? (Refer to the **Delivery** section of this chapter for more help.)

4. A convincing argument is likely to include both concessions and counterarguments. Identify one of each in Carson's essay. Then explain how each strengthens her argument.

5. Identify at least three transitional words or expressions used to help the reader more easily go from one idea to another.

Ideas for Writing

1. Carson questions commonly accepted practices, such as a farmer devoting "immense acreages to a single crop." What problem (environmental or other) can you think of that is the result of a commonly accepted practice? What is the problem, what caused it, and how might it be solved?

2. For what problem on campus can you propose a solution?

If responding to one of these ideas, go to the **Analysis** section of this chapter to begin developing ideas for your essay.

In Bed

Joan Didion

Joan Didion has written articles, novels, screenplays, and nonfiction pieces such as "In Bed," which appeared in her book The White Album *(1979). Her other works include collections of essays such as* Slouching Towards Bethlehem *(1968), and* After Henry *(1992); novels, including* Run River *(1963),* Play It as It Lays *(1970),* A Book of Common Prayer *(1973),* Democracy *(1984), and* The Last Thing He Wanted *(1996); and screenplays such as* A Star Is Born *(1976) and* True Confessions *(1981). As you read this essay, consider how Didion invites the reader to think about her problem. How might her solution—or way of thinking—be applied to your own or someone else's problem?*

1   Three, four, sometimes five times a month, I spend the day in bed with a migraine headache, insensible to the world around me. Almost every day of every month, between these attacks, I feel the sudden irrational irritation and the flush of blood into the cerebral arteries which tell me that migraine is on its way, and I take certain drugs to avert its arrival. If I did not take the drugs, I would be able to function perhaps one day in four. The physiological error called migraine is, in brief, central to the given of my life. When I was 15, 16, even 25, I used to think that I could rid myself of this error by simply denying it, character over chemistry. "Do you have headaches *sometimes? frequently? never?*" the application forms would demand. "Check one." Wary of the trap, wanting whatever it was that the successful circumnavigation of that particular form could bring (a job, a scholarship, the respect of mankind and the grace of God), I would check one. "*Sometimes*," I would lie. That in fact I spent one or two days a week almost unconscious with pain seemed a shameful secret, evidence not merely of some chemical inferiority but of all my bad attitudes, unpleasant tempers, wrongthink.

2   For I had no brain tumor, no eyestrain, no high blood pressure, nothing wrong with me at all: I simply had migraine headaches, and migraine headaches were, as everyone who did not have them knew, imaginary. I fought migraine then, ignored the warnings it sent, went to school and later to work in spite of it, sat through lectures in Middle English and presentations to advertisers with involuntary tears running down the right side of my face, threw up in washrooms, stumbled home by instinct, emptied ice trays onto my bed and tried to freeze the pain in my right temple, wished only for a neurosurgeon who would do a lobotomy on house call, and cursed my imagination.

3   It was a long time before I began thinking mechanistically enough to accept migraine for what it was: something with which I would be living, the way some people live with diabetes. Migraine is something more than the fancy of a neurotic imagination. It is an essentially hereditary complex of symptoms, the most frequently noted but by no means the most unpleasant of which is a vascular headache of blinding severity, suffered by a surprising number of women, a fair number of men (Thomas Jefferson had migraine, and so did Ulysses S. Grant, the day he accepted Lee's surrender), and by some unfortunate children as young as two years old. (I had my first when I was eight. It came on during a fire drill at the Columbia School in Colorado Springs, Colorado. I was taken first home and then to the infirmary at Peterson Field, where my father was stationed. The Air Corps doctor prescribed an enema.) Almost anything can trigger a specific attack of migraine: stress, allergy, fatigue, an abrupt change in barometric pressure, a contretemps over a parking ticket. A flashing light. A fire drill. One inherits, of course, only the predisposition. In other words I spent yesterday in bed with a headache not merely because of my bad

attitudes, unpleasant tempers and wrongthink, but because both my grandmothers had migraine, my father has migraine and my mother has migraine.

4   No one knows precisely what it is that is inherited. The chemistry of migraine, however, seems to have some connection with the nerve hormone named serotonin, which is naturally present in the brain. The amount of serotonin in the blood falls sharply at the onset of migraine, and one migraine drug, methysergide, or Sansert, seems to have some effect on serotonin. Methysergide is a derivative of lysergic acid (in fact Sandoz Pharmaceuticals first synthesized LSD-25 while looking for a migraine cure), and its use is hemmed about with so many contraindications and side effects that most doctors prescribe it only in the most incapacitating cases. Methysergide, when it is prescribed, is taken daily, as a preventive; another preventive which works for some people is old-fashioned ergotamine tartrate, which helps to constrict the swelling blood vessels during the "aura," the period which in most cases precedes the actual headache.

5   Once an attack is under way, however, no drug touches it. Migraine gives some people mild hallucinations, temporarily blinds others, shows up not only as a headache but as a gastrointestinal disturbance, a painful sensitivity to all sensory stimuli, an abrupt overpowering fatigue, a strokelike aphasia, and a crippling inability to make even the most routine connections. When I am in a migraine aura (for some people the aura lasts fifteen minutes, for others several hours), I will drive through red lights, lose the house keys, spill whatever I am holding, lose the ability to focus my eyes or frame coherent sentences, and generally give the appearance of being on drugs, or drunk. The actual headache, when it comes, brings with it chills, sweating, nausea, a debility that seems to stretch the very limits of endurance. That no one dies of migraine seems, to someone deep into an attack, an ambiguous blessing.

6   My husband also has migraine, which is unfortunate for him but fortunate for me: perhaps nothing so tends to prolong an attack as the accusing eye of someone who has never had a headache. "Why not take a couple of aspirin," the unafflicted will say from the doorway, or "I'd have a headache, too, spending a beautiful day like this inside with all the shades drawn." All of us who have migraine suffer not only from the attacks themselves but from this common conviction that we are perversely refusing to cure ourselves by taking a couple of aspirin, that we are making ourselves sick, that we "bring it on ourselves." And in the most immediate sense, the sense of why we have a headache this Tuesday and not last Thursday, of course we often do. There certainly is what doctors call a "migraine personality," and that personality tends to be ambitious, inward, intolerant of error, rather rigidly organized, perfectionist. "You don't look like a migraine personality," a doctor once said to me. "Your hair's messy. But I suppose you're a compulsive housekeeper." Actually my house is kept even more negligently than my hair, but the doctor was right nonetheless: perfectionism can also take the form of spending most of a week writing and rewriting and not writing a single paragraph.

7   But not all perfectionists have migraine, and not all migrainous people have migraine personalities. We do not escape heredity. I have tried in most of the available ways to escape my own migrainous heredity (at one point I learned to give myself two daily injections of histamine with a hypodermic needle, even though the needle so frightened me that I had to close my eyes when I did it), but I still have migraine. And I have learned now to live with it, learned when to expect it, how to outwit it, even how to regard it, when it does come, as more friend than lodger. We have reached a certain understanding, my migraine and I. It never comes when I am in real trouble. Tell me that my house is burned down, my husband has left me, that there is gunfighting in the streets and panic in the banks, and I will not respond by getting a headache. It comes instead when I am fighting not an open but a guerrilla war with

my own life, during weeks of small household confusions, lost laundry, unhappy help, canceled appointments, on days when the telephone rings too much and I get no work done and the wind is coming up. On days like that my friend comes uninvited.

8   And once it comes, now that I am wise in its ways, I no longer fight it. I lie down and let it happen. At first every small apprehension is magnified, every anxiety a pounding terror. Then the pain comes, and I concentrate only on that. Right there is the usefulness of migraine, there in that imposed yoga, the concentration on the pain. For when the pain recedes, ten or twelve hours later, everything goes with it, all the hidden resentments, all the vain anxieties. The migraine has acted as a circuit breaker, and the fuses have emerged intact. There is a pleasant convalescent euphoria. I open the windows and feel the air, eat gratefully, sleep well. I notice the particular nature of a flower in a glass on the stair landing. I count my blessings.

Exploring Ideas

1. How does Didion see migraine?

2. What is Didion's solution?

3. How might others benefit by reading Didion's essay?

4. Summarize Didion's essay and ask several migraine sufferers for their response. How is the way others see migraine similar to or different from the way Didion sees it?

5. How might you participate in Didion's discussion? What interesting point might you add to her discussion of migraine, or how might you apply her way of thinking to some other problem? Might you apply a completely different way of thinking to some problem?

Writing Strategies

1. Study several of Didion's paragraphs. How are they organized? Does she state or imply main ideas? How does her organization help or hinder the reader?

2. Does Didion's essay resonate with the public—that is, do her points relate to others beyond herself? How does her essay convey this public resonance?

3. Compare Didion's conclusion to one you might have written. How does she begin her conclusion? How does she end it? Why is, or isn't, her conclusion effective?

4. How does Didion help the reader understand the problem? What did you learn about migraine from this essay?

Ideas for Writing

1. What problem is central to the "given" of your life, and how might one deal with such a problem?

2. What physical condition have you come to terms with?

If responding to one of these ideas, go to the Analysis section of this chapter to begin developing ideas for your essay.

How to Say Nothing in 500 Words

Paul Roberts

Paul Roberts, who taught English at San Jose State College and Cornell University, wrote a number of books including Understanding Grammar *(1954) and* Patterns of English *(1956). "How to Say Nothing in 500 Words" was first published in* Understanding English *(1958) and has been reprinted in many college writing texts. As you read, write down what problem you think Roberts is addressing and what solution, or solutions, he is proposing. Highlight or underline any points you find striking or memorable and in the margin jot down why.*

1   t's Friday afternoon and you have almost survived another week of classes. You are just looking forward dreamily to the weekend when the English instructor says: "For Monday you will turn in a five-hundred-word composition on college football."

2   Well, that puts a good hole in the weekend. You don't have any strong views on college football one way or the other. You get rather excited during the season and go to all the home games and find it rather more fun than not. On the other hand, the class has been reading Robert Hutchins in the anthology and perhaps Shaw's "Eighty-Yard Run," and from the class discussion you have got the idea that the instructor thinks college football is for the birds. You are no fool. You can figure out what side to take.

3   After dinner you get out the portable typewriter that you got for high school graduation. You might as well get it over with and enjoy Saturday and Sunday. Five hundred words is about two double-spaced pages with normal margins. You put in a sheet of paper, think up a title, and you're off:

Why College Football Should Be Abolished

> College football should be abolished because it's bad for the school and also for the players. The players are so busy practicing that they don't have any time for their studies.

4   This, you feel, is a mighty good start. The only trouble is that it's only thirty-two words. You still have four hundred and sixty-eight to go, and you've pretty well exhausted the subject. It comes to you that you do your best thinking in the morning, so you put away the typewriter and go to the movies. But the next morning you have to do your washing and some math problems, and in the afternoon you go to the game. The English instructor turns up too, and you wonder if you've taken the right side after all. Saturday night you have a date, and Sunday morning you have to go to church. (You can't let English assignments interfere with your religion.) What with one thing and another, it's ten o'clock Sunday night before you get out the typewriter again. You make a pot of coffee and start to fill out your views on college football. Put a little meat on the bones.

Why College Football Should Be Abolished

> In my opinion, it seems to me that college football should be abolished. The reason why I think this to be true is because I feel that football is bad for the colleges in nearly every respect. As Robert Hutchins says in his article in our anthology in which he discusses college football, it would be better if the colleges had race horses and had races with one another, because then the horses would not have to attend classes.

I firmly agree with Mr. Hutchins on this point, and I am sure that many other students would agree too.

One reason why it seems to me that college football is bad is that it has become too commercial. In the olden times when people played football just for the fun of it, maybe college football was all right, but they do not play college football just for the fun of it now as they used to in the old days. Nowadays college football is what you might call a big business. Maybe this is not true at all schools, and I don't think it is especially true here at State, but certainly this is the case at most colleges and universities in America nowadays, as Mr. Hutchins points out in his very interesting article. Actually the coaches and alumni go around to the high schools and offer the high school stars large salaries to come to their colleges and play football for them. There was one case where a high school star was offered a convertible if he would play football for a certain college.

Another reason for abolishing college football is that it is bad for the players. They do not have time to get a college education, because they are so busy playing football. A football player has to practice every afternoon from three to six and then he is so tired that he can't concentrate on his studies. He just feels like dropping off to sleep after dinner, and then the next day he goes to his classes without having studied and maybe he fails the test.

(Good ripe stuff so far, but you're still a hundred and fifty-one words from home. One more push.)

Also I think college football is bad for the colleges and the universities because not very many students get to participate in it. Out of a college of ten thousand students only seventy-five or a hundred play football, if that many. Football is what you might call a spectator sport. That means that most people go to watch it but do not play it themselves.

(Four hundred and fifteen. Well, you still have the conclusion, and when you retype it, you can make the margins a little wider.)

These are the reasons why I agree with Mr. Hutchins that college football should be abolished in American colleges and universities.

5   On Monday you turn it in, moderately hopeful, and on Friday it comes back marked "weak in content" and sporting a big "D."

6   This essay is exaggerated a little, not much. The English instructor will recognize it as reasonably typical of what an assignment on college football will bring in. He knows that nearly half of the class will contrive in five hundred words to say that college football is too commercial and bad for the players. Most of the other half will inform him that college football builds character and prepares one for life and brings prestige to the school. As he reads paper after paper all saying the same thing in almost the same words, all bloodless, five hundred words dripping out of nothing, he wonders how he allowed himself to get trapped into teaching English when he might have had a happy and interesting life as an electrician or a confidence man.

7   Well, you may ask, what can you do about it? The subject is one on which you have few convictions and little information. Can you be expected to make a dull subject interesting? As a matter of fact, this is precisely what you are expected to do. This is the writer's essential task. All subjects, except sex, are dull until somebody makes them interesting. The writer's job is to find the argument, the approach, the angle, the wording that will take the reader with him. This is seldom easy, and it is particularly hard in subjects that have been much discussed: College Football, Fraternities, Popular Music, Is Chivalry Dead?, and the like. You will feel that there is

nothing you can do with such subjects except repeat the old bromides. But there are some things you can do which will make your papers, if not throbbingly alive, at least less insufferably tedious than they might otherwise be.

Avoid the Obvious Content

8   Say the assignment is college football. Say that you've decided to be against it. Begin by putting down the arguments that come to your mind: it is too commercial, it takes the students' minds off their studies, it is hard on the players, it makes the university a kind of circus instead of an intellectual center, for most schools it is financially ruinous. Can you think of any more arguments, just off hand? All right. Now when you write your paper, make sure that you don't use any of the material on this list. If these are the points that leap to your mind, they will leap to everyone else's too, and whether you get a "C" or a "D" may depend on whether the instructor reads your paper early when he is fresh and tolerant or late, when the sentence "In my opinion, college football has become too commercial," inexorably repeated, has brought him to the brink of lunacy.

9   Be against college football for some reason or reasons of your own. If they are keen and perceptive ones, that's splendid. But even if they are trivial or foolish or indefensible, you are still ahead so long as they are not everybody else's reasons too. Be against it because the colleges don't spend enough money on it to make it worthwhile, because it is bad for the characters of the spectators, because the players are forced to attend classes, because the football stars hog all the beautiful women, because it competes with baseball and is therefore un-American and possibly Communist-inspired. There are lots of more or less unused reasons for being against college football.

10   Sometimes it is a good idea to sum up and dispose of the trite and conventional points before going on to your own. This has the advantage of indicating to the reader that you are going to be neither trite nor conventional. Something like this:

> We are often told that college football should be abolished because it has become too commercial or because it is bad for the players. These arguments are no doubt very cogent, but they don't really go to the heart of the matter.

Then you go to the heart of the matter.

Take the Less Usual Side

11   One rather simple way of getting into your paper is to take the side of the argument that most of the citizens will want to avoid. If the assignment is an essay on dogs, you can, if you choose, explain that dogs are faithful and lovable companions, intelligent, useful as guardians of the house and protectors of children, indispensable in police work—in short, when all is said and done, man's best friends. Or you can suggest that those big brown eyes

conceal, more often than not, a vacuity of mind and an inconstancy of purpose; that the dogs you have known most intimately have been mangy, ill-tempered brutes, incapable of instruction; and that only your nobility of mind and fear of arrest prevent you from kicking the flea-ridden animals when you pass them on the street.

12   Naturally personal convictions will sometimes dictate your approach. If the assigned subject is "Is Methodism Rewarding to the Individual?" and you are a pious Methodist, you have really no choice. But few assigned subjects, if any, will fall in this category. Most of them will lie in broad areas of discussion with much to be said on both sides. They are intellectual exercises, and it is legitimate to argue now one way and now another, as debaters do in similar circumstances. Always take the side that looks to you hardest, least defensible. It will almost always turn out to be easier to write interestingly on that side. This general advice applies where you have a choice of subjects. If you are to choose among "The Value of Fraternities" and "My Favorite High School Teacher" and "What I Think About Beetles," by all means plump for the beetles. By the time the instructor gets to your paper, he will be up to his ears in tedious tales about a French teacher at Bloombury High and assertions about how fraternities build character and prepare one for life. Your views on beetles, whatever they are, are bound to be a refreshing change.

13   Don't worry too much about figuring out what the instructor thinks about the subject so that you can cuddle up with him. Chances are his views are no stronger than yours. If he does have convictions and you oppose him, his problem is to keep from grading you higher than you deserve in order to show he is not biased. This doesn't mean that you should always cantankerously dissent from what the instructor says; that gets tiresome too. And if the subject assigned is "My Pet Peeve," do not begin, "My pet peeve is the English instructor who assigns papers on 'my pet peeve.'" This was still funny during the War of 1812, but it has sort of lost its edge since then. It is in general good manners to avoid personalities.

Slip out of Abstraction

14   If you will study the essay on college football [near the beginning of this essay], you will perceive that one reason for its appalling dullness is that it never gets down to particulars. It is just a series of not very glittering generalities: "football is bad for the colleges," "it has become too commercial," "football is big business," "it is bad for the players," and so on. Such round phrases thudding against the reader's brain are unlikely to convince him, though they may well render him unconscious.

15   If you want the reader to believe that college football is bad for the players, you have to do more than say so. You have to display the evil. Take your roommate, Alfred Simkins, the second-string center. Picture poor old Alfy coming home from football practice every evening, bruised and aching, agonizingly tired, scarcely able to shovel the mashed potatoes into his mouth. Let us see him staggering up to the room, getting out his econ textbook, peering desperately at it with his good eye, falling asleep and failing the test in the morning. Let us share his unbearable tension as Saturday draws near. Will he fail, be demoted, lose his monthly allowance, be forced to return to the coal mines? And if he succeeds, what will be his reward? Perhaps a slight ripple of applause when the third-string center replaces him, a moment of elation in the locker room if the team wins, of despair if it loses. What will he look back on when he graduates from college? Toil and torn ligaments. And what will be his future? He is not good enough for pro football, and he is too obscure and weak in econ to succeed in stocks and bonds. College football is tearing the heart from Alfy Simkins and, when it finishes with him, will callously toss aside the shattered hulk.

16   This is no doubt a weak enough argument for the abolition of college football, but it is a

sight better than saying, in three or four variations, that college football (in your opinion) is bad for the players.

17   Look at the work of any professional writer and notice how constantly he is moving from the generality, the abstract statement, to the concrete example, the facts and figures, the illustrations. If he is writing on juvenile delinquency, he does not just tell you that juveniles are (it seems to him) delinquent and that (in his opinion) something should be done about it. He shows you juveniles being delinquent, tearing up movie theatres in Buffalo, stabbing high school principals in Dallas, smoking marijuana in Palo Alto. And more than likely he is moving toward some specific remedy, not just a general wringing of the hands.

18   It is no doubt possible to be too concrete, too illustrative or anecdotal, but few inexperienced writers err this way. For most the soundest advice is to be seeking always for the picture, to be always turning general remarks into seeable examples. Don't say, "Sororities teach girls the social graces." Say, "Sorority life teaches a girl how to carry on a conversation while pouring tea, without sloshing the tea into the saucer." Don't say, "I like certain kinds of popular music very much." Say, "Whenever I hear Gerber Sprinklittle play 'Mississippi Man' on the trombone, my socks creep up my ankles."

Get Rid of Obvious Padding

19   The student toiling away at his weekly English theme is too often tormented by a figure: five hundred words. How, he asks himself, is he to achieve this staggering total? Obviously by never using one word when he can somehow work in ten.

20   He is therefore seldom content with a plain statement like "Fast driving is dangerous." This has only four words in it. He takes thought, and the sentence becomes:

> In my opinion, fast driving is dangerous.

Better, but he can do better still:

> In my opinion, fast driving would seem to be rather dangerous.

If he is really adept, it may come out:

> In my humble opinion though I do not claim to be an expert on this complicated subject, fast driving, in most circumstances, would seem to be rather dangerous in many respects, or at least so it would seem to me.

Thus four words have been turned into forty, and not an iota of content has been added.

21   Now this is a way to go about reaching five hundred words, and if you are content with a "D" grade, it is as good a way as any. But if you aim higher, you must work differently. Instead of stuffing your sentences with straw, you must try steadily to get rid of the padding, to make your sentences lean and tough. If you are really working at it, your first draft will greatly exceed the required total, and then you will work it down, thus:

> It is thought in some quarters that fraternities do not contribute as much as might be expected to campus life.
>
> Some people think that fraternities contribute little to campus life.
>
> The average doctor who practices in small towns or in the country must toil night and day to heal the sick.
>
> Most country doctors work long hours.
>
> When I was a little girl, I suffered from shyness and embarrassment in the presence of others.
>
> I was a shy little girl.
>
> It is absolutely necessary for the person employed as a marine fireman to give the matter of steam pressure his undivided attention at all times.
>
> The fireman has to keep his eye on the steam gauge.

22   You may ask how you can arrive at five hundred words at this rate. Simple. You dig up

more real content. Instead of taking a couple of obvious points off the surface of the topic and then circling warily around them for six paragraphs, you work in and explore, figure out the details. You illustrate. You say that fast driving is dangerous, and then you prove it. How long does it take to stop a car at forty and at eighty? How far can you see at night? What happens when a tire blows? What happens in a head-on collision at fifty miles an hour? Pretty soon your paper will be full of broken glass and blood and headless torsos, and reaching five hundred words will not really be a problem.

Call a Fool a Fool

23   Some of the padding in freshman themes is to be blamed not on anxiety about the word minimum but on excessive timidity. The student writes, "In my opinion, the principal of my high school acted in ways that I believe every unbiased person would have to call foolish." This isn't exactly what he means. What he means is, "My high school principal was a fool." If he was a fool, call him a fool. Hedging the thing about with "in-my-opinion's" and "it-seems-to-me's" and "as-I-see-it's" and "at-least-from-my-point-of-view's" gains you nothing. Delete these phrases whenever they creep into your paper.

24   The student's tendency to hedge stems from a modesty that in other circumstances would be commendable. He is, he realizes, young and inexperienced, and he half suspects that he is dopey and fuzzyminded beyond the average. Probably only too true. But it doesn't help to announce your incompetence six times in every paragraph. Decide what you want to say and say it as vigorously as possible, without apology and in plain words.

25   Linguistic diffidence can take various forms. One is what we call euphemism. This is the tendency to call a spade "a certain garden implement" or women's underwear "unmentionables."

It is stronger in some eras than others and in some people than others but it always operates more or less in subjects that are touchy or taboo: death, sex, madness, and so on. Thus we shrink from saying "He died last night" but say instead "passed away," "left us," "joined his Maker," "went to his reward." Or we try to take off the tension with a lighter cliché: "kicked the bucket," "cashed in his chips," "handed in his dinner pail." We have found all sorts of ways to avoid saying "mad": "mentally ill," "touched," "not quite right upstairs," "feebleminded," "innocent," "simple," "off his trolley," "not in his right mind." Even such a now plain word as "insane" began as a euphemism with the meaning "not healthy."

26   Modern science, particularly psychology, contributes many polysyllables in which we can wrap our thoughts and blunt their force. To many writers there is no such thing as a bad schoolboy. Schoolboys are maladjusted or unoriented or misunderstood or in the need of guidance or lacking in continued success toward satisfactory integration of the personality as a social unit, but they are never bad. Psychology no doubt makes us better men and women, more sympathetic and tolerant, but it doesn't make writing any easier. Had Shakespeare been confronted with psychology, "To be or not to be" might have come out, "To continue as a social unit or not to do so. That is the personality problem. Whether 'tis a better sign of integration at the conscious level to display a psychic tolerance toward the maladjustments and repressions induced by one's lack of orientation in one's environment or—" But Hamlet would never have finished the soliloquy.

27   Writing in the modern world, you cannot altogether avoid modern jargon. Nor, in an effort to get away from euphemism, should you salt your paper with four-letter words. But you can do much if you will mount guard against those roundabout phrases, those echoing polysyllables that tend to slip into your writing to rob it of its crispness and force.

Exploring Ideas

1. What is the purpose of Roberts's essay?

2. Have you experienced the problem that Roberts describes? Discuss with several classmates or others outside of class any difficulties you have had coming up with ideas for an essay. Take notes on what people say as you explore this problem. Then draw conclusions: what seem to be the reasons that some people have a hard time coming up with good ideas for their essays?

3. How does writing an essay help students to develop worthwhile thinking skills?

4. How might Roberts's ideas be important beyond merely writing an essay? That is, how might they be of value in schoolwork that does not involve essay writing; how might they be of value in the workplace; and how might they be of value in everyday life?

5. Why is Roberts's essay, first published in 1958, still relevant today?

Writing Strategies

1. Is Roberts's essay engaging (or inviting)? That is, does it make you want to read on? Why or why not?

2. What strategy does Roberts use to make the problem clear to the reader? Must he convince his reader of a problem before offering a solution? Explain.

3. Roberts supports his points by giving specific examples. Did any stand out to you? Without rereading, recall several examples, and then connect them to the main points they illustrate. Why might those examples have stood out to you?

4. Are Roberts's headings helpful? Should, or might, he have used more? When might *you* use headings (love letters, business reports, college essays, shopping lists, etc.)? What drawbacks do headings have?

5. Roberts uses lively language. Identify at least five lively words or expressions that struck you as you read. What makes these expressions lively? What is the value of such lively language?

Ideas for Writing

1. Avoiding a simple step-by-step instructional approach and instead making worthwhile points that could benefit your reader, what can you tell someone how to do?

2. How can a student succeed either (a) at college, (b) at his or her freshman year of college, or (c) at the first two weeks of college? Narrow your focus to suit your comfort level. For example, if you have been in college only a few months, you may not feel comfortable telling others how to succeed for all four years.

If responding to one of these ideas, go to the Analysis section of this chapter to begin developing ideas for your essay.

Technology, Movement, and Sound

Ed Bell

Ed Bell, whose writing also appears in Chapter 6, wrote "Technology, Movement, and Sound" after having been awakened by a neighborhood leaf blower. Based on this essay, what does Bell care about? How does his essay speak to community (and not just individual) issues?

In the margins of this essay, a reader's comments point to key ideas and writing strategies. As you read the essay, consider how the comments might influence your own reading and writing.

Exploring Ideas

Technology used "indiscriminately"

Leaf blowers, for ex.

Leaf blowers can be okay (when?)

Benefits of Raking:
1) Does as good a job
2) Time well spent
3) Provides needed exercise
4) Sounds nice?
   Must mean more—is natural, pleasant, maybe, good for the soul?

True

Good point

Like rowing machine, stair climber, spinning, etc. Machines at student rec center are based on natural activities people avoid.

Point: no time to rake; must pay for leaf blower + stuff like it.

Although technology has improved society in many ways, we use it indiscriminately, not distinguishing the good uses from the bad. We could talk about cell phones, oversized SUVs, fast food, or a variety of other advancements. But the cool air and falling leaves of autumn bring to mind the leaf blower—a monster whose decibel level far exceeds her practical value.

While I'm willing to admit that under certain circumstances the leaf blower can be useful, I think most people are missing out on the natural benefits of using a rake:

1) Raking does just as good a job as blowing.

2) If it actually does take longer to rake (a fact of which I'm not certain), the time "saved" and used otherwise would in many ways have been better spent raking.

3) Raking provides more exercise—the necessary physical movement our twenty-first-century bodies are lacking.

4) Raking makes <u>only</u> the most wonderful sound as it scratches across the leafy ground.

As for point one, beautifully raked yards existed long before noisy leaf blowers—there's no denying that it is, at the very least, possible to rake leaves and not have to blow them. As for point two, how many Americans who argue they don't have time to rake all those leaves will stand there blowing them, then rush off to the health club to use a rowing machine or a stair-climber? How long will it be until the most popular workout machine is the one that simulates leaf raking? But if you don't rush off to a health club (no doubt because you don't have the time), you're probably too busy working. After all, you have bills to pay: the new leaf blower, the new cell phone, the new computer, the new car, and that badly needed vacation to get away from it all.

But even if it does take longer to rake than to blow, the extra time spent raking provides the exercise that we need. One look at the human body will tell you it is built for raking—it *wants* to rake! According to Pete Egoscue, renowned anatomical

Writing Strategies

Begins with concession and main point. Narrows focus to leaf blowers—a specific example of the larger issue (technology).

Makes a concession. Shows public resonance—how ideas matter to others.

Lists and numbers main supporting ideas for the reader's benefit.

Develops points 1 and 2.

Provides common sense/observational support for first point.

Provides reasoning to support the second point.

Develops third point by providing evidence from an outside source.

Exploring Ideas

Bell cares about exercise, movement, health. He's arguing that people aren't exercising in natural ways. He's saying they work to pay for things so they don't have to move their bodies, then claim they don't have time to move their bodies.

Interesting point: Why is so much protection required? Maybe not because leaf blowers are dangerous, but because of lawsuits. Still, leaf blowers probably are more dangerous than rakes.

Rakes are simple, convenient. Leaf blowers, etc., break down.

Main point: leaf blowers bug the neighbors. Bell cares about this, too. And this deals with community.

Tech will solve problems + create new ones.

Main point: Use technology more discriminately. Why not (1) exercise, (2) be considerate of others?

functionalist and author of *The Egoscue Method of Health Through Motion*, "movement is as much a biological imperative as food and water." Many people today, he says, don't "move enough to beat the overwhelming odds that one day this motionless lifestyle will catch up with them." Do we sit at computers and cash registers doing repetitive movements, then relax with a little TV? Should we add standing and holding a noisy leaf blower to our routine? Just think about all the various body movements required by leaf raking.

The human body is built to move, yet we treat our physical human movement as an inconvenience. Egoscue says that "what all of us must do is deliberately and systematically get our bodies back in motion despite a modern lifestyle that discourages movement, and even encourages us to believe that we can survive and prosper as sedentary beings who treat motion as an inconvenience that can be minimized with the help of technology." A few sore muscles (and blisters) from a little leaf raking is, I would say, just what we need.

The man who blows the leaves on my campus wears special equipment—big spaceman goggles for his eyes and headphone-like muffs to protect his ears. His get-up alone indicates a problem to me: if you can't gather up leaves without protecting your own eyes and ears, perhaps there's a better way of doing it. Stop and compare the man with the rake to the one with the leaf blower. Which one is better off? The rake is simple; it stores easily; it doesn't cost much; it is quiet and doesn't bother the neighbors; it encourages necessary body movement; it's not very dangerous; and so on. But the leaf blower is bound to break down; it takes up more space and combined with its cousins (the weed-whacker, the electric hedge trimmers, and so on), it will eventually convince you to build a bigger garage; it (and machines like it) costs more money, which is why you are working too much to rake leaves; it is loud, which is unpleasant, if not for you, for the neighbors; it is apparently dangerous—I'm assuming this because of the equipment the man on campus wears.

Technology is likely to come along and solve all of these problems. It's not hard to imagine a quieter leaf blower someday. Of course, the old-fashioned leaf-blowing folk will long for the good old days when a leaf blower could be heard for blocks away. But soon enough they'll all have the newer, lighter, more ergonomically correct models too. And then, of course, we'll have another problem to deal with—a problem that we can't even imagine until it occurs. Through all of that, however, two things will remain true: (1) we should not make too much noise around other people and (2) we should get our bodies moving. We should, I suggest, use our technology more discriminately—instead of using it just because we can.

Writing Strategies

Introduces source and quotes sparingly (only the information that is most helpful in making the point).

Makes point through asking the reader questions and to think about leaf raking.

Continues to develop third point.

Provides support from a source.

Concludes paragraph by commenting.

Through description and reasoning argues that rakes are better than leaf blowers.

Provides specific evidence to compare rakes and leaf blowers.

Conclusion leaves the reader with something to think about: technology will solve current problems and create new ones. So, we should be considerate of others and keep moving our bodies as they were built to move.

Makes closing point—general, main idea.

Exploring Ideas

1. Explain the relationship Bell sees between three things: technology, movement, and sound.

2. Explain how Bell moves from an individual concern (point of contact) to a community concern (public resonance).

3. In your own words, describe the problem Bell writes about and the solution he proposes.

4. Share your description (#3) with several classmates and discuss the similarities and differences in the way you and your classmates understood Bell's essay.

5. Share Bell's ideas with several people outside of class and get their responses. (You may have them read the essay, or you may summarize it for them.) How is the way others think about technology and movement different from the way Bell thinks about it? What difference might be worth further exploration?

6. With others, generate a list of concepts such as "technology," "movement," "noise," "cars," "school," "work," "family," "food," "fast food," "homelessness," "money," and so on. As you generate your list, think in categories (food, shelter, clothing; local, national, international; work, play; etc.) and make connections (for example, "food" might lead you to think of "fast food," which might lead you to think of "hamburgers," which might lead you to think of "feed lots"). Then discover a relationship among three of the ideas, as Bell does among "technology," "movement," and "sound." (Admittedly, this exercise is artificial, but it can be fun and helps to develop thinking skills.)

Writing Strategies

1. What types of evidence (statistics, facts, allusions, anecdotes, scenarios, analogies) does Bell use to support his claims (opinions)?

2. Does Bell make any concessions (acknowledging possible weaknesses in his argument or value in opposing positions) or counterarguments (anticipating and responding to his reader's possible questions and concerns)? Write down at least one concession and one counterargument that he might have made, but didn't.

3. Bell uses one secondary source, Pete Egoscue. Specifically, how does he let the reader know when he is referring to Egoscue and when he is not? After reviewing the entire essay, can you distinguish between when Bell is expressing Egoscue's ideas and when Bell is expressing his own?

4. Bell uses concrete words such as "cell phones," "stair climber," "goggles," and "blisters." These words create images (you see them in your mind when you hear the word). Refer to previous essays you have written or one you are writing now to see what concrete words you have used. Are there places where you have been abstract ("communication device") and could have been concrete ("cell phone")?

5. Bell uses nearly every form of punctuation. Did you notice his punctuation throughout the essay? Or was it "invisible" to you? Where might he have punctuated differently in order to help you more readily understand his points?

Ideas for Writing

1. What common practice, some generally accepted way of doing something, can you point out a problem with?

2. What technology (cell phone, portable stereo, air conditioning, lawn sprinkler, recliner chair, etc.) possesses some lesser-known danger?

> If responding to one of these ideas, go to the Analysis section of this chapter to begin developing ideas for your essay.

Thoughts on the International Access Symbol

Dan Wilkins

Dan Wilkins, whose writing also appears in Chapter 4, is an advocate for people living with disabilities and operates Nth Degree (www.thenthdegree.com), a graphic design company geared toward issues related to the independent living movement, inclusion, diversity, and disability rights. What problem does Wilkins see with the current international access symbol, and what solution does he propose? As you read, consider how Wilkins's essay looks beyond himself and deals with the circumstances of others.

1   As I was getting out of my van in the parking lot of an area store this older woman with white hair pulled into the accessible parking space next to mine. I sat on the lift waiting for her to get out of her car and lock the door. She had a placard on the dash. Suddenly, as she was making sure she had her keys, a man walking by stopped, took one look at me, and addressed her somewhat demonstratively, saying, "You can't park there!!!" He pointed at the sign and then at me. "That space is for people who use wheelchairs...you can't park there." This guy, it seemed, was trying to advocate for ME!

2   I looked at the woman. She was turning toward him. She was also turning red. I felt I needed to do something. I felt a need to advocate for her; to help this wanna-be good samaritan to understand that not all people with disabilities use chairs. I wanted to tell him how important it is to first look for the placard or plate. I never got the chance.

3   The woman put her keys in her purse, slammed the car door, took one step toward the gentleman and advocated for herself (loudly), "LISTEN, BUCKO!" she said, "I've had two heart attacks and five bypass surgeries in the last three years. I CAN PARK HERE!" I thought to myself, "Geez, lady, don't have another one." With a look that dared him to rebut, she walked briskly by the dumbstruck pedestrian and into the store.

4   I spent about five minutes practically counseling the poor guy. He'd only come to buy

nails. He thought he was doing the right thing. I told him about hidden disabilities, of being denied legitimacy as one who's "really disabled" by an exclusionary symbol that does more to perpetuate misconceptions than to empower and unite a culture. He walked away somewhat enlightened but mumbling something to the effect of "Never again...."

5   Yeah, even though I'm a chair user, I have a problem with the access symbol. It disenfranchises many of my friends who live with disabilities but who do not use chairs. It is a major cause of grief. To an uninformed public, the access symbol by its very design equates disability with wheelchairs and relegates folks like the

woman above, those with less obvious disabilities, to always having to prove themselves as worthy of accommodation. The symbol also implies to those who do not know us that those of us who do use chairs tend to stay in our chairs, confined or bound to them.

6   We, as advocates and activists, rally around the symbol because it has been around for a long time, because it is recognized, because it is all that we have. With so few members of our disability culture using wheelchairs—10%, maybe less—why do we keep it around? Let's see . . . 90% of 55 million Americans (let alone 11% of the rest of the world) . . . we're talking about 49.5 million people for whom the design is not really representative. So what can we do about it? How do we find a symbol that truly represents the expanse of disability culture? How do we incorporate into a design chair users, cane users, dog users, sign language users, people with hidden disabilities, brain injuries, cognitive and developmental disabilities? How about folks with mental illnesses? The list is long and as individual as there are people living with a disability.

7   It seems to me the only way to not alienate anyone is to get away from a design that speaks to a certain disability or body type, like the current access symbol does. We may have to abandon any type of representation of a human form. This is not to be misconstrued as eliminating the "person" or the humanity from disability. I only wish to refocus attention.

8   Every time I have ever been involved in an access or accommodation dispute the focus has always been on me, or the person with the disability in question. We, folks with disabilities, are always seen as the troublemakers, as "the problem." All we want is an equal shot at what our community has to offer: access, accommodation, equity, respect, a chance to contribute; to feel and know that we belong. Nothing more. Nothing less. A new symbol, one to be placed on signs in parking lots, on or beside doors to public buildings, restrooms, paths of travel, next to mission statements and on telephones, should

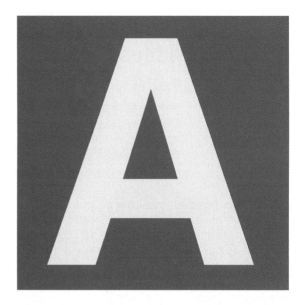

focus attention on the real barrier to full inclusion: on the attitudes of those controlling the spaces; on those providing the access.

9   So let's trash the wheelchair symbol, keep the same blue field, and throw a big bold capital "A" in the middle. Keep it white for continuity. Why an "A"? A for Accessible. A for Accommodating. A for All. A for Aw heck, you too. The "A" doesn't just focus on architectural access but on attitudinal access. If you, as a store owner, as a city park, as an airline or hotel have it on your door, you've earned it. You've also earned our respect and our business. No small potatoes when you consider the respect and buying power of not only 55 million folks with existing disabilities but the 70 million baby boomers hitting fifty.

10   That's a lot of latent disability. Face it, we get older and, when we do, disability often happens. And let's not forget the 37 million or so AARP members. Laws aside, providing real access and accommodation is the right thing to do, but if that's not enough, for no other reason, it makes good business sense.

11   No confusion. No misrepresentation. No explanation or proof necessary. A symbol we ALL can rally around.

Exploring Ideas

1. What does Wilkins say about the current international access symbol?

2. How do you see the current international access symbol? How is the way that you see it similar to or different from the way Wilkins sees it?

3. How might Wilkins's essay be helpful to others?

4. Interview others to find out what symbols they think should be changed. Be certain to provide them enough background to understand what you are asking. For example, you might briefly summarize Wilkins's argument as a way of contextualizing your question, then ask the person if he or she thinks any other symbols create a problem. Be sure to follow up by asking the person *why* he or she thinks the symbol should be changed.

5. Collect at least five symbols (from home, work, school, etc.) and evaluate each one. Answer the following questions: What is the purpose of a symbol? What does each particular symbol represent? Are the symbols accurate and easy to understand for the intended audiences? What problems might be caused by the symbol? What other symbol might work better?

Writing Strategies

1. Wilkins starts his essay with a narrative. Does his opening engage the reader? How else might he have begun his essay? Why do you suppose he began it this way?

2. In paragraph 4, Wilkins says of the man, "He'd only come to buy nails." What is the impact of this sentence on the reader? Why should, or shouldn't, Wilkins share it with us?

3. What strategy does Wilkins use to convince you that the current international access symbol is a problem? How successful is he? What else might he have done?

4. In Wilkins's conclusion, he broadens his point: "Laws aside, providing real access and accommodations is the right thing to do, but if that's not enough, for no other reason, it makes good business sense." Is his conclusion appropriate, or does he bring up extraneous information (such as "it makes good business sense")? Evaluate his conclusion.

5. Describe Wilkins's voice as a writer—that is, the way he comes across sounding to the reader—and explain how it might affect the reader.

Ideas for Writing

1. What cause (such as world peace) or concept (such as *environmentally friendly*, *ecumenical*, *childproof*, or your major) can you design an acceptable symbol for?

2. What other symbols do people rally around? Are any of these symbols flawed? Do people rally together without having a symbol to rally around? Do symbols ever become sacred? Do they ever become too important—more than a symbol?

> **If responding to one of these ideas, go to the Analysis section of this chapter to begin developing ideas for your essay.**

Television: Destroying Childhood

Rose Bachtel

Rose Bachtel wrote this essay for a College Composition I class in her first semester of college. Based on this essay, what does Bachtel think is valuable? As you read, jot down your initial ideas about how you might participate in this discussion, including how you might expand on what Bachtel says or might offer an alternate way of seeing the problem.

1   When my grandparents were little, they spent their free time riding bicycles outside, playing dolls or dress-up, or curling up with a good book. Nowadays, my younger siblings consume every free moment they have in front of a television. "Times have changed. It is just another form of entertainment," some say. Should this obsession be handled so lightly? Is there nothing wrong with sitting in front of a television set all day? Of course this poses a problem, especially where children are concerned! They are at a vital growing period in their lives and how they are raised will play a strong role in who they will become. Watching television will not work any muscle groups, so a child will not get the proper amount of exercise he or she needs. This will lead to future health problems, whether it be in the near future or years down the road. Also, because TV does not demand effort or interaction of the person watching it, children who watch television frequently often become lazy and expect that everything should come to them instantaneously and without work. This lowers a child's patience because he or she wants instant gratification and will not engage in activities or events that require time or complicated components. These same children will also experience a decline in creativity because the television is creative for them. This is not healthy because childhood is the most vital time for stimulating a young person's mind and forcing him or her to develop it.

2   How can parents stop their children's bodies and minds from eroding? My solution is quite simple. Parents should not keep a television in the home. It may sound a bit drastic at first, but when analyzed, it makes sense. Without the convenience of a television, children are forced to think of other forms of keeping themselves entertained. This would lead them to exercise more since most activities involve using more muscle groups than are involved in stagnantly watching television. Also, since children would be forced to seek out other forms of entertainment, they would be, in turn, forced to use their brains more and think creatively in order to come up with something to do. They would have to use their minds to search for information about their world instead of having it handed to them by TV. Also, since a child is no longer confined to inside of the house, he or she can venture outside and explore nature while getting fresh air and vitamin D from the sun's rays. Another problem with TV is that many television show producers feel that sex and violence sell, so consequently, many of today's programs contain these elements. Since people at a young age are very impressionable, they pick up on these messages and are influenced by them. Without a television set in the home, children will be less exposed to sex and violence. Another benefit of my proposal is the fact that parents do not have to worry about monitoring the content of the television shows their children watch if there is no TV set in the home to begin with. Their kids will not be able to watch unapproved shows when the parents are not home to supervise.

3   Still, many people may feel apprehensive towards this proposal because they have lived with televisions for so long that they cannot imagine

functioning without them. "How will we know what's going on in the world or what the weather is going to be like?" they might ask. Sure, television stations provide very useful information, but so do other forms of communication such as newspapers and magazines. These sources of information can be just as convenient as television. Of course, a news program can give more up-to-date information, but written periodicals are not far behind. There is also the Internet, which is perhaps more current than television. "What about all of the shows on TV that the adults want to watch?" Television does offer a great deal of American entertainment, but it is not the only way to be entertained. People could try reading a good book, going out on the town, or enjoying the outdoors. Adults will find that if there is not TV in the house to distract them, they will have a lot more free time on their hands to really enjoy life. A good argument brought up by television supporters is the point that there are a lot of educational programs that teach children. These programs keep the attention of children and help them grow mentally. Yes, these stations are helpful, but what would be better and more effective to children is if someone taught them about the world in a "hands on" fashion instead of through a television set. Another protest against my proposal is that TV acts as a sort of babysitter for children. It keeps them quiet and entertained so that the parents can get all of their tasks accomplished. My response to that argument is that raising the children should be a parent's number one priority. The best way to raise a child is to constantly interact with him or her, spending many hours of quality time, because it shows the child that he or she is important and loved. This aspect of raising a young one will be lost if he or she is constantly sat in front of the TV.

4   Granted, many television shows are not moral and should be kept away from children. That is not the problem. The real problem with TV is the fact that it consumes so much of an American's time that could be invested into a more productive activity. Sure, television use could just be minimized, but I think that it would be better to get rid of televisions in the home altogether. The problem with owning one but not watching it as often is that it is easier said than done. When the temptation is there, it is hard to resist. Paul Klein, who worked for NBC in the 1950s, believed that people would watch TV just to watch TV, meaning that even if nothing interesting is on, people will still sit in front of a television set. For example, when I first moved into my apartment, I did not have a TV for a few days. During those few days, I was very efficient, using every minute of my time to study, clean, or perform any other needed task. I accomplished a lot of things in those first few days. However, when my television finally arrived, I found myself turning on the set and watching shows that I did not necessarily have any interest in. I was also not keeping up on my studies as well as I had before or cleaning as much. This scenario is true for many Americans. The television does not have one single essential use. People functioned perfectly fine before this invention. Sure, it is entertaining, informative, and convenient, but it also has many hidden side effects that are hurting the younger generations. By getting rid of televisions in the home, children will spend their childhood as they should, not watching television, but playing, creating, and learning about their world through their own eyes.

Exploring Ideas

1. Describe how, based on this essay, Bachtel is concerned about community and others.

2. How is the way that you see television similar to or different from the way Bachtel sees it?

3. Briefly summarize Bachtel's main idea, then ask others to respond to it. Write down the three responses that interest you the most and explore what you find to be interesting about them. How are each of the responses similar to or different from what Bachtel says?

4. How might you respond to Bachtel's ideas? Write down at least three ways you might contribute something worthwhile to this discussion.

5. One way you might respond to #4 above is to expand on Bachtel's solution by suggesting various benefits of giving up television. Some will be obvious, but think of some less obvious ones, too. Then explore these benefits further through discussion. Finally, write down the benefits you discovered through your exploration—ones that you did not think of right away.

Writing Strategies

1. What evidence does Bachtel provide to explain the problem? What evidence does she provide to support her solution?

2. Describe Bachtel's voice as a writer and refer to several passages as evidence.

3. Write a new introduction and conclusion for Bachtel's essay, taking a very different approach for each.

4. In small groups, discuss the introductions and conclusions (#3) that you and your classmates wrote. What are the advantages and disadvantages of each introduction and conclusion? Which introduction and conclusion do you prefer?

5. Provide several examples of how Bachtel helps the reader go from one idea to another.

Ideas for Writing

1. What else is destroying childhood?

2. How might television be used better, instead of not at all?

> If responding to one of these ideas, go to the Analysis section of this chapter to begin developing ideas for your essay.

Outside Reading

F ind a text that proposes a solution and make a photocopy or print it out. Solutions for social problems are often published in general readership publications (*Time, Newsweek*), and in national or local newspapers (on opinion pages). More in-depth solutions might appear in monthly or quarterly journals (*Utne Reader* or the *New Republic*). You also might find an interesting solution related to your major. In that case, explore academic journals such as *Criminal Law, Engineering,* or *Elementary Education.* To conduct an electronic search of journals and magazines, go to your library's periodical database or to InfoTrac (http://infotrac.galegroup.com/itweb/). For your library database, perform a keyword search, or go to the main search box for InfoTrac and choose "keywords." Enter word combinations such as *problems and schools, problems and flying, problems and food, solutions and sewage, solutions and farms,* etc. (When performing keyword searches, avoid using phrases or articles such as *a, an, the.* The search results will yield lists of journal and magazine articles.

You can also search the Internet. Try the search engine Yahoo.com. Like most Internet search engines, Yahoo combines words using *and.* In the search box, try various combinations, such as those above; however, if using *solutions* in your search, be cautious of the many business and corporate sites in the search results.

The purpose of this assignment is to further your understanding of writing that proposes solutions. As you are probably discovering, such writing is sometimes very argumentative, and other times appears to be neutral; however, even the most neutral-sounding text offers a position—a stance that requires support. As you read through this chapter, keep the text you have discovered close by and notice the elements and strategies the writer uses. Depending on your instructor's suggestions, do one or more of the following:

1. Notice how the writer applies various strategies from this chapter. On the photocopy or hard copy:
   - Identify the passage that most clearly states the problem, and write "problem" in the margin.
   - Identify the passage that most clearly states the solution and write "solution" in the margin.
   - Identify the passages in which the author offers support for the solution and write "support" next to each one in the margin.
   - Find any passages in which the writer addresses other opinions on the topic and write "counterargument" or "ca" next to each one in the margin.
   - Find any passages in which the writer grants value to another position (or alternative solution) and write "concession" or "c" in the margin.

2. Write an essay that discusses the strategies employed by the writer. The following questions may be helpful.
   - Does this writer seem more or less argumentative than the readings in this chapter? Why?
   - How does the writer support his or her proposed solution?
   - Who is the audience for this argument?
   - How does the audience affect the kinds of things said in the argument?

3. Write at least three "Exploring Ideas" questions for the text you found.

4. Write at least three "Writing Strategies" questions for the text you found.

5. Write two "Ideas for Writing," such as the ones following the essays in this chapter.

INVENTION

> ❝ You know, the courts might not work any more, but as long as everyone is videotaping everyone else, justice will be done. ❞
>
> —*Marge Simpson*

The following three sections are designed to help you through the invention process: specifically, to discover a problem (in **Point of Contact**), develop an understanding of its causes and develop a possible solution (in **Analysis**), and make it relevant to a community of readers (in **Public Resonance**). The questions in each section are not meant to be answered directly in your final written assignment. However, answering them here, before drafting, will help you develop what you are going to say—and even why you are going to say it. After you work through these three sections, the **Delivery** section, which immediately follows, will help you craft your ideas into a written text.

Point of Contact

Finding a Topic in Everyday Life

For this chapter, your topic will be a particular problem—some situation that needs to be changed or idea that needs to be rethought. Be cautious of global problems like hunger, poverty, or racism. This does not mean such problems are unapproachable or unsolvable, but such big problems usually have local or particular expressions; and it is the local or particular that is often the most appropriate place to start. Focusing on a particular problem also sets the ground for a manageable solution. For example, solving financial difficulty for single-parent students is more manageable than solving poverty in general.

Social problems are not necessarily physical or material; they can be intellectual, spiritual, and psychological. Consider problems related to bad policies (all first-year students must live on campus), narrow thinking (a governmental administration that assumes energy must come from fossil fuels), or troubled systems (a bureaucracy in which all decisions must be made at the executive level before action can be taken).

Using Images as a Point of Contact

While the questions on the next two pages will help you generate possible topics, the following images, or ones you encounter in everyday life, may also prompt ideas. In groups or alone, consider the problem(s) raised in these images, and then move to the **Analysis** section to explore them in depth.

Use these images to get you thinking. Remember, you're not looking for the right answer at this point, but, instead, a topic—an idea—about which to write.

Activity: Find an image of your own that suggests a problem or a solution. Or, find any image and show it to a friend, then discuss what problems or solutions come to mind.

Writers often do best with topics with which they are familiar—or with which they can become familiar. To discover particular problems, consider the different circles of your life. Use the following suggestions and questions to help dig up a problem that you, as a writer, witness or experience, and attempt to see problems that others might disregard. See the problems that lurk behind the obvious. If one of the suggestions prompts you to see a problem, begin by recording details—that is, try to explain the particulars of the problem.

- **Go to your school or any educational institution and focus on potential problems:**

  Are students missing too many classes?

  Are students in this class (or any class) tardy?

  Do my instructors communicate poorly with students?

  Are my peers lazy?

  Are my instructors' methods for communicating course materials appropriate?

  Are enough courses offered to students?

  Are courses offered at appropriate times?

  Do instructors give enough or too many exams?

  Do instructors provide enough feedback?

  Is writing too much or not enough of a contributing factor in my education?

  Did my high school education adequately prepare me for work and/or college?

  Is the curricular gap between high school and college too wide?

  Is course work too difficult or too easy?

- **Walk, drive, or take a bus through your community and look for signs of social problems:**

  Are kids violent, abusive, disrespectful, lazy, or overworked?

  Are the elderly people in my family or community isolated?

  Do people in my neighborhood ignore one another?

  Does traffic in my community interfere with daily life?

  Do people in my community disobey the laws?

  Do the police in my community lack respect for the civilians?

  Are drivers too aggressive?

  Are billboards tasteless or offensive?

  Are there abandoned buildings?

  Are there too many chain stores and restaurants?

  Are there too many strip malls?

- Read a local newspaper or community magazine and consider your civic or state government:

  Does the city government do enough for children?
  Does the city government do enough for senior citizens?
  Is Congress doing enough to move bills forward?
  Does state government overlook the needs of my community?
  Are citizens sufficiently involved in local government?
  Are my local or state politicians honest?
  Are my tax dollars spent honestly?
  Do average citizens know how tax dollars are spent?
  Are there enough women and minorities in public office?
  Do politicians represent the concerns of their constituents?

- Watch television or browse several popular magazines and consider these questions:

  Is prime time television too violent or too sexy . . . or negative in some other way?
  Are sports televised too much?
  Is there something wrong with the way sports are televised?
  Are talk shows tasteful?
  Has art been abandoned by popular culture?
  Are women or men portrayed poorly in magazines or on television?

- Explore your major by browsing several journals in your field and watch for crisis situations or professional problems:

  What are the problems related to employment in the field I am considering?
  What about job security? Safety for the workers? Safety for the public?
  Are there problems with government regulations?

Invention Activity: Now go beyond these suggestions. In groups or alone, develop more strategies for encountering and exploring social problems. Imagine what might be wrong, or what can be better than it is.

Example: Ed Bell's Notes to Point of Contact Questions

Do people in my neighborhood ignore one another? I think people do ignore each other. Not always, or in all ways. Once there was a traffic accident outside and by the time I got to the phone and dialed 911, the accident had already been reported and people were on the street lending a hand. But a couple of times a week someone honks their horn about 8 o'clock in the morning, picking up someone in their driveway and waking up anyone (me) who is sleeping. And just this morning a leaf blower was going for what seemed like hours. So, people come to the rescue of others (which is good) but they also seem oblivious to others in some pretty basic ways.

Analysis
Looking at Problems and Solutions

Problems: Any solution must address the causes of a problem. Therefore, analyzing a problem to discover all possible causes is essential to developing a good solution. But often the causes of a problem are not clear. A problem may originate from an abstract source, such as a long tradition, a widely held attitude, or a flawed assumption. And writers must search through such abstractions to find the possible causes. For instance, Bell's problem is, seemingly, a simple item: a leaf blower. However, the cause of rampant leaf blower use is a bit more vague. But Bell traces the source of the problem to a cultural trend:

> As for point two, how many Americans who argue they don't have time to rake all those leaves will stand there blowing them, then rush off to the health club to use a rowing machine or a stair-climber? How long will it be until the most popular workout machine is the one that simulates leaf raking? But if you don't rush off to a health club (no doubt because you don't have the time), you're probably too busy working. After all, you have bills to pay: the new leaf blower, the new cell phone, the new computer, the new car, and that badly needed vacation to get away from it all.

Here, Bell implies (with his rhetorical questions) that leaf blowers are part of a broader issue—an unhealthy lifestyle brought on by indiscriminate use of technology.

The causes of some problems can be evasive or misunderstood, and so writers must sometimes analyze various possibilities. For example, Didion's problem, migraine headaches, is commonly misunderstood, and many people even assume the wrong thing about their cause. Didion, therefore, spends a good deal of her essay dismissing some causes while explaining the true complexities of the problem. As in the following paragraph, Didion helps the reader to see new dimensions of the problem:

> No one knows precisely what it is that is inherited. The chemistry of migraine, however, seems to have some connection with the nerve hormone named serotonin, which is naturally present in the brain. The amount of serotonin in the blood falls sharply at the onset of migraine, and one migraine drug, methysergide, or Sansert, seems to have some effect on serotonin.

Every problem has many potential consequences or effects—which may go far beyond the problem at hand. When writers can envision these effects (far into the future), they can better understand the nature of the problem, and convince others that it must be taken seriously. Sometimes, writers must include a discussion of the effects (long- and short-term) for readers to understand the full extent of the issue. For example, notice Carson's discussion of long-term consequences:

To adjust to these chemicals would require time on the scale that is nature's; it would require not merely the years of a man's life but the life of generations. And even this, were it by some miracle possible, would be futile, for the new chemicals come from our laboratories in an endless stream; almost five hundred annually find their way into actual use in the United States alone. The figure is staggering and its implications are not easily grasped—500 new chemicals to which the bodies of men and animals are required somehow to adapt each year, chemicals totally outside the limits of biologic experience.

To understand the full complexities of your problem, respond to the following questions. Answers to these questions may be useful not only in helping the writer understand the problem but also in illustrating the nature or degree of the problem to readers.

- What are the causes of the problem?
- What are some illustrations or examples of the problem?
- What are the most troubling or alarming images associated with the problem?
- What are the short-term effects? Long-term effects?
- How does this problem affect attitudes or other behaviors?
- How might this problem snowball?
- What other situation (event, attitude) does this problem resemble?

In answering these questions, the goal is to see different layers of the problem, to explore the nature of the problem and all its possible effects. The questions, then, are opportunities for probing meaning. Avoid moving too quickly as you imagine answers. Consider the hidden effects, the invisible consequences. Notice Dan Wilkins's deep understanding of the access symbol. Wilkins explains the subtle effects of the access symbol—how it influences people's perceptions:

> Yeah, even though I'm a chair user, I have a problem with the access symbol. It disenfranchises many of my friends who live with disabilities but who do not use chairs. It is a major cause of grief. To an uninformed public, the access symbol by its very design equates disability with wheelchairs and relegates folks like the woman above, those with less obvious disabilities, to always having to prove themselves as worthy of accommodation. The symbol also implies, to those who do not know us that those of us who do use chairs, tend to stay in our chairs, confined or bound to them.

As Wilkins's essay suggests, sometimes the invisible effects (on attitude and perspective) are greater, and more difficult to address, than the visible effects. And the job of the writer may be to seek out and reveal those hidden aspects of the problem.

Activity: After you have answered the questions on your own, conduct an informal survey. Ask several others (classmates, family members, friends, or co-workers) to help you analyze the problem. Ask each person two or three questions about the problem. You can use any of the questions from this section or develop more general questions, for example: *Do you believe _____ is a problem? Why? What causes it? Have you had experience with _____?* Record the answers in writing. You might include the answers and opinions in your explanation of the problem. If one of the respondents has had a unique or significant experience, you can include it to illustrate the nature of the problem. Make certain that you do NOT use names or personal information of the respondents. (See Chapter 12, p. 576 for more information on surveys.)

Solutions: Offering a solution involves far more than simply suggesting an idea. You must consider how the solution will work, how it will address the causes of the problem, and how it might fail. The solution must also address the causes of the problem. That is, the writer must show how the solution will head off the causes and change the outcome of events or behaviors. For Didion, the solution is somewhat complicated. It is not a particular drug or behavior, or policy change. It is merely an intellectual shift—from resistance to acceptance. Because the cause of migraine is so evasive, she (like many others) cannot discover a perfect solution. Instead, she develops a new awareness about the problem:

> I have tried in most of the available ways to escape my own migrainous heredity . . . but I still have migraine. And I have learned now to live with it, learned when to expect it, how to outwit it, even how to regard it, when it does come, as more friend than lodger.

Didion shows us the broad range of possible maneuvers a writer can make in addressing a problem. She does not oversimplify the problem, or conjure a fake solution, or even dodge the issue altogether. Instead, she offers a subtle solution to migraines, and then goes on to explain how that solution works:

> And once [the migraine] comes, now that I am wise in its ways, I no longer fight it. I lie down and let it happen. At first every small apprehension is magnified, every anxiety a pounding terror. Then the pain comes, and I concentrate only on that. Right there is the usefulness of migraine, there in that imposed yoga, the concentration on the pain. For when the pain recedes, ten or twelve hours later, everything goes with it, all the hidden resentments, all the vain anxieties. The migraine has acted as a circuit breaker, and the fuses have emerged intact.

As Didion's essay shows, solutions need not involve specific physical steps or policy changes. They might simply involve a new way of thinking.

Rachel Carson's proposal may seem modest given the nature of the problem. After all, she describes the constant introduction of toxic chemicals into the environment, but her solution simply involves making the public aware:

> We urgently need an end to these false assurances, to the sugar coating of unpalatable facts. It is the public that is being asked to assume the risks that the insect controllers calculate. The public must decide whether it wishes to continue on the present road, and it can do so only when in full possession of the facts. In the words of Jean Rostand, "The obligation to endure gives us the right to know."

As Carson's argument shows, a solution need not entirely wipe the problem clean away. Solutions to complicated problems, in fact, might simply begin the process of change. A solution might change the intellectual environment so that physical changes can take place later; a solution might alter conditions so that significant changes can *begin* to occur, or a solution might merely propose a way of talking about a complicated problem. Of course, many solutions involve physical steps and implementation, but as Didion and Carson show, genuine solutions do not require physical or structural changes.

As you consider your own solution, remember to acknowledge the complexity. Be careful not to shut out subtle strategies for addressing the problem. Respond to the following questions to develop your solution.

- What action will best address the causes of the problem?
- How can that action (or set of actions) be implemented?
- What might stand in the way of this action?
- How could those involved overcome impediments?
- How will the action change the situation?
- Has this kind of solution been tried before (in other situations)? How did it go?
- Does this solution have potential shortcomings or limitations?
- Could this solution fall short? (Under what circumstances?)

Answers to the above questions will be vital to developing your solution and to making it persuasive to readers. While you will benefit from understanding all of the above issues, your readers may need some points emphasized over others. Ask yourself what points seem least obvious, or most debatable, to your audience. These will be the best points to develop more thoroughly in your text. For instance, if your solution is something that involves an intellectual change (if you call for people to think differently), then a lengthy discussion about implementation will not be necessary. However, if your solution involves several physical steps (or institutional changes), then implementation may be far more important.

Example: Ed Bell's Notes to Analysis Questions

What are the short-term effects? Long-term effects? The short-term effects: hmmm. People get woken up. People might get angry and get in fights. I don't see that happening, to be honest. But maybe people are just grouchy. Maybe one inconsideration leads to another, which may be more of a long-term effect. It's just noisy, which may create tension in individual lives and in interaction among people. Another effect is that standing there holding a leaf blower for an hour might be easy, but it's loud and annoying and the person doing it isn't getting much exercise. Raking would be better for the person. It'd take more time, maybe, but in the "long-term"! it would be more peaceful, because it'd be quieter and the person would get their body moving, get some exercise, work up a sweat, and not impose on everyone else in the neighborhood.

What action will best address the causes of the problem? Raking instead of leaf blowing. Why? Because the raker gets exercise, burns calories, feels better, and doesn't make so much noise. This improves the quality of everyone's life. People will say they're too busy to rake, but busy doing what? What are they busy doing? It seems important, running around, but what if they didn't do it? What if they raked leaves instead? What would happen?

Public Resonance

How Does This Issue Matter to Others?

Writers must express the particular ways that a problem extends outward and involves people—including potential readers. The problem you have chosen may obviously affect (or potentially affect) a community or society at large. However, no matter how much your problem involves or affects people, you still must make it known, and emphasizing the social impact of the problem is an important part of developing your initial thoughts. For example, examine the following question: *Is the Ottowa River healthy?* Of course, the condition of a single river in one town may, in fact, be a sign of a greater phenomenon. An unhealthy river system in one area may be evidence of a bigger pollution problem throughout the country. In this sense, a particular situation brings up a highly public issue. The initial, more local, question resonates with people beyond the banks of the Ottowa River and involves many potential communities.

As you consider your own topic, respond to the following questions to help develop public resonance:

- Who might care about this issue? Why?
- Who should care about this issue? Why?
- What particular community, place, or thing does this issue affect?
- How might my reader(s) be involved in this issue?
- How could my reader(s) be involved in this issue?
- What group of people might understand or sympathize with this situation?
- To what trends (in living/working/socializing) does my topic point?
- Is this issue an example of some trend?
- Why is it important that others hear my opinion about this issue?

Avoid moving too quickly through these questions. At first, the public resonance may not be clear. But working through all the possibilities can help a writer's topic to expand in interesting ways.

Imagine a student, Marcus, who has discovered a problem in his community: that elderly people in nursing homes and senior living centers are isolated from others. In a discussion with peers, Marcus develops his initial thinking:

What group of people might understand or sympathize with this situation?

Marcus: Primarily the elderly. Senior citizens are primarily concerned about this issue, and as medical advances allow people to live longer, it seems like we all should be worried—because we'll all be old someday.

Linda: But shouldn't the younger generations be concerned about the isolation of the elderly, too—I mean beyond just caring about themselves as they age?

Diana: Yeah . . . even if they don't care, it seems like stuffing the elderly away from mainstream society can't be a good thing, for anybody.

Marcus: It's like we are ignoring a huge group of people—the group that probably has the most insight and experience about big social problems.

Linda: And I would even say personal and family problems. I know in my family, it was always my grandmother who understood everyone's problems and could talk through them without getting angry or mean. She was the one that gave everyone a sense of direction.

Marcus: So when society shuts away its elderly, maybe the biggest victims are the younger generations. Of course, it's bad for the elderly, but in a more indirect and long-term way, maybe their absence from mainstream society is an even bigger wrong. Maybe the younger generations feel the effects in the long term without their patience, insights, and experience.

Marcus could then develop this thinking, and perhaps explain how younger generations suffer from the absence of older generations. These ideas could be used as part of his argument. Like Marcus, any writer can use public resonance by pointing out the effects of a problem on a community, or on a society at large.

Notice, for example, Rachel Carson's approach:

> We have subjected enormous numbers of people to contact with these poisons, without their consent and often without their knowledge. If the Bill of Rights contains no guarantee that a citizen shall be secure against lethal poisons distributed either by private individuals or by public officials, it is surely only because our forefathers, despite their considerable wisdom and foresight, could conceive of no such problem.
>
> I contend, furthermore, that we have allowed these chemicals to be used with little or no advance investigation of their effect on soil, water, wildlife, and man himself. Future generations are unlikely to condone our lack of prudent concern for the integrity of the natural world that supports all life.

Here, Carson makes the issue relevant to American citizens and even suggests the impact of the problem on future generations. Although the topic itself naturally involves public well-being, Carson pushes the reader to see how it relates to public doctrines—and even a fundamental aspect of American culture, the Bill of Rights. Carson, then, is writing about more than pesticides; she extends the idea so it bleeds out into other areas of life: basic human rights. Like all good writers, Carson discusses a particular and focused topic, but she also shows how that particular topic involves many people in profound ways.

Some topics may seem more difficult to connect to a broad public concern. That is, you might imagine that some topics are only the concern of a few. However, good writers bring seemingly marginal topics into the center of public consciousness. Notice Dan Wilkins's strategies for bringing attention to the problem of disability access:

> So let's trash the wheelchair symbol, keep the same blue field, and throw a big bold capital "A" in the middle. Keep it white for continuity. Why an "A"? A for Accessible. A for Accommodating. A for All. A for Aw heck, you too. The "A" doesn't just focus on architectural access but on attitudinal access. If you, as a store owner, as a city park, as an airline or hotel have it on your door, you've earned it. You've also earned our respect and our business. No small potatoes when you consider the respect and buying power of not only 55 million folks with existing disabilities but the 70 million baby boomers hitting fifty.
>
> That's a lot of latent disability. Face it, we get older and, when we do, disability often happens. And let's not forget the 37 million or so AARP members. Laws aside, providing real access and accommodation is the right thing to do, but if that's not enough, for no other reason, it makes good business sense.

Here, Wilkins shows the degree of public resonance for disability access: he involves people in business and government and he explains the large numbers of disabled, presently and potentially. In only a few sentences, he makes clear that access and accommodation are "no small potatoes," and should be primary public concerns.

Finally, notice Bell's strategy for making a seemingly small concern one of public well-being:

> But even if it does take longer to rake than to blow, the extra time spent raking provides the exercise that we need. One look at the human body will tell you it is built for raking—it *wants* to rake! According to Pete Egoscue, renowned anatomical functionalist and author of *The Egoscue Method of Health Through Motion*, "movement is as much a biological imperative as food and water." Many people today, he says, don't "move enough to beat the overwhelming odds that one day this motionless lifestyle will catch up with them." Do we sit at computers and cash registers doing repetitive movements, then relax with a little TV? Should we add standing and holding a noisy leaf blower to our routine? Just think about all the various body movements required by leaf raking.
>
> The human body is built to move, yet we treat our physical human movement as an inconvenience.

Bell makes an important connection for the reader between a simple act, leaf blowing, and the design of the human body. Suddenly, Bell's essay is not simply about leaf blowing; it is an argument about the relationship between the human body and the tendencies of mainstream culture.

Example: Bell's Notes to Public Resonance Questions

To what trends (in living/working/socializing) does my topic point? This has to do with the trend of people using technology because they can. Talking about nothing on cell phones while not paying attention to their driving. That sounds pretty cranky, but I think it's true. It's about people going to a gym to work out and not wanting to walk a few hundred yards in their daily lives. Raking leaves would be good for people in lots of ways, but they'd rather stand there blowing them with a noisy machine. So, machines, not all of them but a lot of them, are noisy and annoying and make people "lazy" or make them not move their bodies as much as people used to. They don't get exercise. People should get more exercise and wonder if the noise they are making might be bothering OTHERS.

Activities

1. E-mail two acquaintances about your subject. (You don't need to tell them you are writing a paper on it.) Ask them if they have ever thought of it, and how they feel about it. If they raise ideas you have not yet considered, you might include them in your perspective. If they dismiss the idea as uninteresting, you might consider part of your work in **Delivery** to be attracting the interest of such readers.
2. Write a letter proposing your solution to someone who can take action on it. (See Chapter 13: Everyday Rhetoric.)

DELIVERY

Remember that proposing a solution is a form of arguing. In fact, depending on the problem and solution, the process may involve two layers of argument: (1) persuading the reader about the nature or degree of the problem and (2) showing the value of a particular solution. As you work through the following sections (**Rhetorical Tools, Organizational Strategies, Writer's Voice,** and **Revision Strategies**), you may see many argumentative features. Consider all of these features as you craft your ideas into a written argument.

Rhetorical Tools

Persuading Your Readers

Like any argument, one that proposes a solution should guide readers to a new understanding of the topic, and make them see the value of the writer's position. The goal is not necessarily to convince readers that only one solution is possible, but that a particular solution, to an important problem, has merit.

Articulating Your Thesis: The thesis statement in a proposing argument should, of course, include some idea of the problem and solution. The actual thesis can be implied—it need not be stated explicitly in the essay—but a thesis statement will guide you into the process of writing. Notice how a thesis might evolve out of the invention process, and then try to express your own problem and your solution in a sentence before moving on.

Evolution of a Thesis	
Writer responds to a Point of Contact question: Is prime-time television too violent or too sexy . . . or negative in some other way?	*Television promotes sex. It's just sex, sex, sex.*
Writer thinks analytically about her topic: What action will best address the causes of the problem?	*The individual cannot realistically influence TV programming. Others have tried and failed. People can influence their own habits by turning off the TV and finding something better to do.*
Writer broadens her thinking to deal with public concerns: How might my readers be involved in this issue?	*By participating in and organizing activities in their community, people can provide community members—friends, family, neighbors, and so on—with more interesting entertainment than watching television.*

Although the act of proposing solutions can vary greatly, good proposal essays have certain key elements (which you have already begun to develop):

- **Problem:** Includes illustrations or examples, an explanation of causes, and a picture of short- and long-term effects.

- **Solution:** Includes an explanation of how that solution will address, confront, or stop the causes of the problem.

- **Counterargument:** Addresses concerns about or opposing claims to the solution or the articulation of the problem.

- **Alternative Solutions:** Include any other potential strategies for addressing the problem. Articulating alternative solutions requires an explanation of why these are less desirable than the main solution being offered.

- **Concessions/Qualifiers:** Acknowledges any possible shortcomings of the solution or concedes value to some opposing claim or alternative solution.

The development of these elements depends upon your particular problem and solution. Some problems, for instance, require significant explanation. That is, you might need to work hard just to make the reader aware of the complexities of the problem (as do Carson and Didion) or perhaps you have a problem that is rather apparent (such as abandoned buildings plaguing an entire section of town). Consider how your audience may view the problem, and make certain to convince your readers to see the problem as you do.

Also, remember the strategies from Chapter 5: Making Arguments. Writers have the whole world of culture, history, and science within reach. By simply mentioning or pointing to key historical moments, relevant literary texts, news events, or popular culture figures, a writer can make claims more persuasive to readers—or show that his or her position is shared by others. Use these questions to help construct supporting points for your argument (and see the examples in the chapter readings):

- Does a historical event or figure illustrate something about my topic? (See Didion ¶ 3.)

- Does a historical situation or trend (say the rise of a particular fashion, organization, or individual) illustrate something about my topic? (See Carson ¶ 8, 17–18 and Bell.)

- Does my topic relate to anything in nature? (See Carson.)

- Has science taught us anything about my topic? (See Carson and Bell.)

- Do any news events illustrate my point or stance? (See Bell ¶ 1.)

- Have I witnessed or experienced someone or something that illustrates my point? (See Bell ¶ 6 and Didion.)

- Can I construct a hypothetical situation that illustrates my point? (See Roberts ¶ 1–10.)

Remember that proposing a solution involves two layers: persuading the readers that the problem is worthy of addressing and persuading them that the solution is appropriate and valuable.

Discovering Counterarguments:

In proposing a solution, you are giving an argument: arguing that a problem exists and that a particular solution will address it. But someone might argue with you about several different points: that the problem is no problem at all, that your solution will not work, that your solution is inappropriate—too costly, inhumane, unmanageable, etc., and a sophisticated argument addresses those possible objections. For example, notice how Dan Wilkins briefly points to opposing arguments, and then counters:

> Every time I have ever been involved in an access or accommodation dispute the focus has always been on me, or the person with the disability in question. We, folks with disabilities, are always seen as the troublemakers, as "the problem." All we want is an equal shot at what our community has to offer: access, accommodation, equity, respect, a chance to contribute; to feel and know that we belong. Nothing more. Nothing less.

While Wilkins sees the access symbol as a problem, the opposing perspective sees disabled "folks" as a problem, and Wilkins responds by explaining the basic goal of the disabled: to gain equal access.

Use the following questions to help anticipate counters to your argument:

- Who might not see this as a problem? Why?
- Why might the solution not work?
- Who might be offended by or resistant to my solution? Why?

Considering Alternative Solutions:

Every problem has many possible solutions, and a good writer acknowledges other possibilities. But acknowledging other solutions (those other than your own) also involves explaining their shortcomings. That is, as you mention other solutions, you must also make it clear that they are, for some reason, not as valuable as yours. Other solutions, for instance, might be less efficient, more dangerous, less ethical, less manageable, or simply inadequate. Apply the following questions to your own proposal:

- What other solutions could be (or have been) attempted?
- Why did (or how could) these solutions fail or fall short?
- Why is the solution I am proposing better?

Considering other solutions can also help you understand the strengths and shortcomings of your own solution (the one you are promoting). For instance, imagine Marcus's problem (from the **Public Resonance** section): isolation of the elderly. His solution might involve refiguring the concept of the nuclear family to include grandparents, uncles, aunts, and cousins. Only in reconceptualizing the basic family unit, he might argue, will elderly members of society find more genuine social engagement. But he might also address other solutions, such as programs that bring together school children and nursing home residents. According to his argument, such solutions might fall short of creating deep and lasting relationships for the elderly.

Considering Logical Fallacies: Review the logical fallacies from Chapter 5.

Ad Hominem (Latin for *to the person*): Attacks a person directly rather than examining the logic of the argument.

Strawperson: Exaggerates a characteristic of a person or group of people and then uses the exaggeration to dismiss an argument.

Faulty Cause/Effect: Confuses a sequential relationship with a causal one. Assumes that event A caused event B because A occurred first.

Either/Or Reasoning: Offers only two choices when more exist.

Hasty Generalization: Draws a conclusion about a group of people/events/things based on insufficient examples. (Often, the logical flaw behind racist, sexist, or bigoted statements.)

Non Sequitur (Latin for *it does not follow*): Skips several logical steps in drawing a conclusion.

Oversimplification: Does not acknowledge the true complexity of a situation or offers easy solutions to complicated problems.

Slippery Slope: Assumes that a certain way of thinking or acting will necessarily continue or extend in that direction (like a domino effect). Such an argument suggests that once we begin down a path, we will inevitably slip all the way down, and so the effects of a particular action or idea are exaggerated.

False Analogy: Makes a comparison between two things that are ultimately more unlike than alike. The differences between the things make the comparison ineffective or unfair, or the comparison misrepresents one or both of the things involved.

Begging the Question: Attempts to prove a claim by using (an alternative wording of) the claim itself.

In proposing solutions be especially cautious of **faulty cause/effect, non sequitur,** and **slippery slope.** When considering the possible long-term effects, writers may fall into the trap of unfairly extending present circumstances to their most dramatic conclusion. For instance, consider Marcus's topic (explained in **Public Resonance**): *mainstream society isolates the elderly*. It might be valuable for Marcus to project the long-term effects of this problem. For instance, he might argue that without the insight of older generations, mainstream society may continuously forget the social crises of the past, and have to relive many burdens. However, Marcus should be careful of more extreme claims: that society will eventually keep everyone over 50 years old locked away, that America will have to go through another two world wars because it has completely forgotten the past, or that everyone will eventually think like children without the elderly in everyday life. Such claims are slippery slope fallacies.

Activity: Take one classmate's thesis and debate it. Split the class so that some people argue for the solution and others against it.

Organizational Strategies
Arranging Your Argument

How Should I Separate Problem and Solution?
Many components go into a proposing solutions text: the problem, illustrations or support for the problem, the solution and support for the solution, the alternative solutions, shortcomings of those solutions, counterarguments and concessions. Ultimately, these can be arranged in any imaginable order. Here are two standard strategies:

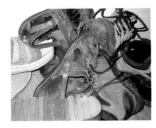

- Problem
  Examples/Illustrations
- Solution
  Examples/Illustrations
- Alternative Solution
  Explanation
  Shortcoming
- Alternative Solution
  Explanation
  Shortcoming

OR

- Problem
- Alternative Solution A/Shortcoming
- My Solution
- Alternative Solution B/Shortcoming
- My Solution
- Alternative Solution C/Shortcoming
- My Solution

Of course, all of these strategies depend upon the amount of detail and illustration the writer develops. A problem can be developed in great detail, and in cases such as the Carson essay, the problem actually requires significant explanation and illustration. Generally, the more a writer vividly portrays the problem, the more the reader will see a need for solving it.

If the causes of the problem are explained well enough, a brief articulation of the solution may suffice. Notice Didion's strategy: her solution comes at the very end of her essay, in one paragraph:

> And once it comes, now that I am wise in its ways, I no longer fight it. I lie down and let it happen. At first every small apprehension is magnified, every anxiety a pounding terror. Then the pain comes, and I concentrate only on that. Right there is the usefulness of migraine, there in that imposed yoga, the concentration on the pain. For when the pain recedes, ten or twelve hours later, everything goes with it, all the hidden resentments, all the vain anxieties. The migraine has acted as a circuit breaker, and the fuses have emerged intact. There is a pleasant convalescent euphoria.

But in some cases, when the solution involves many meticulous steps, it needs significant explanation. In the Roberts essay, for example, the problem, the task of writing a 500-word essay, is presented quickly. The solution is developed with specific details—specific how-to strategies.

How Should I Include Counterarguments?
Often counterarguments (responses to those opposing your claims) are arranged in separate paragraphs. You might develop a counter in an entire paragraph—explaining why, for example, some people are opposed to your understanding of the problem. Then, in a new para-

graph, explain why your understanding is most appropriate or correct or valuable. Some writers use the turnabout paragraph for counterarguments. A turnabout paragraph begins with one point, and then changes directions at some point, always giving the reader a clear indication of that change. For example, you might begin a paragraph with an opposing claim, and then counterargue in that same paragraph:

> Some people may argue that television is too important to average Americans, that people would rather spend time with familiar sitcom characters than develop a sense of community among their neighbors. However, the average American also seems to know that too much television is bad. After all, we implicitly denounce it by calling it the "boob tube" or the "idiot box" but continue watching because more meaningful, local activities are rarely offered in its place.

In this example, the opposing claim (that television is too important to average Americans) is countered within the paragraph.

Counterarguments can also be addressed in a subtler manner. Notice Didion's strategy:

> For I had no brain tumor, no eyestrain, no high blood pressure, nothing wrong with me at all: I simply had migraine headaches, and migraine headaches were, as everyone who did not have them knew, imaginary. I fought migraine then, ignored the warnings it sent, went to school and later to work in spite of it, sat through lectures in Middle English and presentations to advertisers with involuntary tears running down the right side of my face, threw up in washrooms, stumbled home by instinct, emptied ice trays onto my bed and tried to freeze the pain in my right temple, wished only for a neurosurgeon who would do a lobotomy on house call, and cursed my imagination.

Notice how Didion refers to the notion that migraines are merely imaginary (not real physical afflictions), and then lists real physical consequences of migraines. She acknowledges an opposing point and then makes it irrelevant by showing the opposite to be true.

Where Should I Put Alternative Solutions? Alternative solutions, those strategies other than the one forwarded by the writer, can come early or late in an essay. Some writers acknowledge other possibilities soon after their introductions. Notice Roberts's strategy: in his scenario, a student hands in an essay using typical get-it-done strategies, and receives a "D." The hypothetical writing process of the student is the alternative solution, which, as Roberts argues, is not a very good one, and he explains this after showing us the hypothetical paper on college football:

> On Monday you turn it in, moderately hopeful, and on Friday it comes back marked "weak in content" and sporting a big "D."

In this case, the solution most often employed by students faced with a writing assignment is to write papers that are "weak in content." Once Roberts shows the negative side of such a strategy (primarily the grade), he then goes on to give a detailed solution to writing assignments.

Didion's strategy is much the same: she offers some alternative, and rather ineffective, methods for dealing with migraine (such as "taking a couple of aspirin") before giving her new way of coping in the conclusion. Other writers wait to mention alternative methods until they have fully explained (what they deem) the best.

Writer's Voice
Finding an Appropriate Strategy

ecause proposing a solution is an argumentative process, the **Writer's Voice** strategies from Chapter 5: Making Arguments apply here as well (see p. 206). But proposing solutions brings with it some particular concerns and strategies. The following strategies will help you develop and maintain an engaging writer's voice.

Creating Reasonable Tone: It might be said that

tone is the way a writer treats readers. In argumentative writing, as you know, tone is vital to maintaining readers' interest. One that is too emotional can overwhelm readers; one that is condescending is apt to alienate readers. When proposing solutions, writers must be careful not to force problems *at* readers. Instead, it is the writer's job to present a problem and illustrate its significance *for* readers. For example, notice Carson's strategy for making the reader understand the significance of a problem:

> In this now universal contamination of the environment, chemicals are the sinister and little-recognized partners of radiation in changing the very nature of the world—the very nature of its life. Strontium 90, released through nuclear explosions into the air, comes to earth in rain or drifts down as fallout, lodges in soil, enters into the grass or corn or wheat grown there, and in time takes up its abode in the bones of a human being, there to remain until his death.

It would be easy, or at least tempting, for Carson to scream at her readers—to shout about the state of the environment. Imagine the following:

> With evil chemicals, humankind has completely and utterly ruined the environment and is in the process of transforming nature, indeed the world itself. Through nuclear explosions, we release terrible chemicals such as Strontium 90 into the air, which then fall to the ground and contaminate the plants that human beings eventually eat. And then, in an insanely nightmarish process, the unsuspecting humans ingest this horrific chemical until it eventually kills them.

The latter passage is over the top. It forces the problem at the reader—and demands that readers feel a particular emotion. Carson's passage is less confrontational, while still intense. That is, it does not make emotional demands on the reader; instead, it presents the rather grizzly details of environmental contamination and leaves the reader to reflect on them. Carson's approach allows the reader's emotions to build up, while the latter passage forces certain emotions onto the reader. It is a small, but significant, difference.

Inviting the Reader: Remember writerly invitations—phrases that promote

curiosity in a reader, that entice him or her to examine a particular subject.

Question: Asking the right question can make a reader concerned about the subject: *Why are the computer labs at University Hall a problem? How safe is the drinking water in our community?* Notice Wilkins's strategy for inviting the reader with questions:

> So what can we do about it? How do we find a symbol that truly represents the expanse of disability culture? How do we incorporate into a design chair users, cane users, dog users, sign language users, people with hidden disabilities, brain injuries, cognitive and developmental disabilities? How about folks with mental illnesses? The list is long and as individual as there are people living with a disability.

Group Inclusion: A writer can include potential readers in a relevant group (small or large) that is affected by the subject: *All college students and faculty should be deeply concerned about the school reform bill.* Didion creates an "us" for those who have migraine:

> All of us who have migraine suffer not only from the attacks themselves but from this common conviction that we are perversely refusing to cure ourselves by taking a couple of aspirin . . .

Statement: A simple claim that calls the reader's attention to the matter is often the most effective: Notice Carson's strong statement at the beginning of her essay:

> The most alarming of all man's assaults upon the environment is the contamination of air, earth, rivers, and sea with dangerous and even lethal materials.

Considering Verb Mood: There are three moods in English: *indicative* (used for stating facts or statements about the world, *subjunctive* (used to express conditions that are not facts, such as a recommendation, a wish, a requirement, or a statement contrary to fact), and *imperative* (used for issuing commands or suggestions, such as: "Before leaving in the morning, turn off the lights." "Remember the Alamo!" "Workers of the world, unite!" "Ssh!"). Many passages in this very text are in the imperative mood. (Find one right now.) Rather than informing the reader about possible ways to act (as in the subjunctive), imperative mood orders the reader to act.

Imperative mood is not often used in academic essays or formal proposals because it puts the reader in the position of action. Of course, there are exceptions. Roberts's essay is written, almost entirely, in the imperative mood. Because his strategy is to give his audience the particular steps to solving a problem, the imperative mood is appropriate. It is also appropriate because his audience is very specific—college writers. He assumes that the audience has (or will have) a personal encounter with the problem.

Many writers shift to imperative mood in their conclusions—in order to create an explicit call to action. However, this can be tricky. A sudden shift to imperative can sometimes result in a bossy or demanding tone. Imagine Carson's conclusion if it shifted to the imperative mood:

> . . . When the public protests, confronted with some obvious evidence of damaging results of pesticide applications, it is fed little tranquilizing pills of half truth. Stop giving false assurances and sugar coating the unpalatable facts because the public must take the risks that insect controllers calculate. The public must decide whether it wishes to continue on the present road, and it can do so only when in full possession of the facts . . .

Revision Strategies

Proposing a solution can be tricky. You must adequately explain the problem, which may take as little as a sentence or as much as several pages; and you must adequately explain your proposed solution, which, again, may take as little as a sentence or as much as several pages. You must also anticipate your reader's concerns (making appropriate counterarguments or concessions), use qualifiers, cultivate an appealing writer's voice, and organize all this information to make reading and understanding it as pleasant as you can. Revision, as you can see, is essential.

Consider the following revision strategies:

- Review this chapter, keeping your essay in mind. You might (1) explore your **Invention** notes, looking for helpful ideas and/or respond further in writing to relevant Invention questions; (2) review the **Rhetorical Tools, Organizational Strategies,** and **Writer's Voice** sections with an eye toward making appropriate changes; and (3) review several of the essays, noting the way the writers in this chapter approached this type of essay.

- Set aside at least as much time to revise as you took with invention and delivery.

- Create distance between you and your writing by getting away from it for a few days if possible or a few hours at least.

- Read your paper aloud to hear how it sounds or have someone else read it aloud to you.

- Print out a hard copy of your paper and read it carefully in a different place than where you wrote it.

- Figure out your writing strategy by noticing how the parts of your essay work together to support your main point. Consider making an outline of your essay to help you see this.

- Have someone else read and respond to your essay.

For help with **Peer Review,** see page 50.

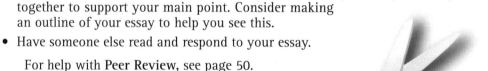

Global Revision Questions

Invention (What have you learned by exploring your topic?)

■ **Point of Contact:** What other ideas did you consider writing about before selecting this one? Why was this idea more worth pursuing than the others?

■ **Analysis:** How has your exploration of this topic gone beyond your initial ideas and questions about it? In what ways have your ideas moved beyond your initial biases and perceptions—and beyond the common beliefs of your reader?

■ **Public Resonance:** How might your essay be relevant to, or matter to, your reader? And what might be the consequence(s) of your essay? How might the reader think or act differently after reading it?

Delivery (What writing decisions have you made as part of your writing strategy?)

■ **Rhetorical Tools:** Reexamine your rhetorical strategy for proposing a solution. What rhetorical tools have you used? What other tools might be helpful?

 • What is the main idea of your essay, and how have you conveyed that idea to the reader? What, besides your *intended* main idea, might the reader imagine your main idea to be? How might you help the reader hear what you are trying to say?

 • Revising involves filling in gaps—from adding a transitional expression to adding an entire section. What information might you provide to better help your reader understand your proposed solution? How might you explain the problem more clearly? Where might you provide more evidence to persuade the reader of your solution? What competing solutions is the reader likely to wonder about? And how might dealing with these solutions help to make the one you're proposing more acceptable to the reader? How might your title, introduction, and conclusion provide more helpful information regarding the main point of your essay?

 • What information might be deleted? How might you focus the reader more on your proposed solution? If you've discussed competing solutions, how might you place more emphasis on the one you are proposing? What words, sentences, or entire paragraphs slow the pace of your writing without adding helpful information?

■ **Organizational Strategies:** You might begin by describing, or outlining, the structure of your essay to get a better sense of your overall organizational strategy. How might you rearrange elements to help the reader see your main ideas more clearly? How might you rearrange ideas within paragraphs? What ideas might be more helpful to the reader if placed earlier, or later, or near some other idea? If you've discussed other possible solutions, how have you explained their relationship to the solution you are proposing? Will the relationship be clear to the reader? How might connections and relationships between ideas be made more clear?

■ **Writer's Voice:** Describe your writer's voice. Have you carefully considered the way you might sound to the reader? How might the reader perceive you, the writer, in this essay? What about your writer's voice is inviting to the reader? What about your writer's voice might alienate the reader? What changes might make your writer's voice more inviting?

■

CONSIDERING CONSEQUENCES

When proposing a solution, one naturally hopes that others act upon, or at least think about, the proposed solution. Because the essay you just wrote was for a class, the consequences will involve your grade and your improved ability to think and write about problems. But time spent considering other potential consequences of your essay can help you to better see the importance of this type of thinking and writing. What might be the consequences of your essay for this chapter? That is, what effect might your ideas have on your reader's thoughts and actions? Consider these questions:

- Will the reader better understand that a problem exists?
- Is the reader likely to consider a new approach to solving that problem?
- What might be the benefits to others? What might be the harm to others?
- Might the reader act differently, possibly even putting the proposed solution into action?
- How might your essay affect the problem you wrote about?
- What might be the effect of these consequences on you, the writer?

Activities

The Consequences of Your Essay

1. List as many individuals as you can imagine whose thinking and/or actions might change if they were to read the essay you wrote for this chapter. For each individual you list, name the possible change in his or her thinking and/or action. (As you consider consequences upon your reader, consider the "ripple effect" of those consequences. If your reader thinks or behaves differently, what is the impact of that thinking or behavior on others?)

2. Discuss the possible consequences of your essay with others. Explain what your essay is about and then ask for feedback. You might ask the following questions: What impact might this essay have on the reader? Might he or she better understand the problem or even put your proposed solution into action? How might this essay change the way someone thinks or acts? How did it make you think differently? How might it make you act differently?

3. List three other forms of delivery that you might have used to express your idea (report, letter, poster, screenplay, Web site, speech, song, poem, action). How might the consequences of your message have been different if delivered by way of these other forms?

The Consequences of the Chapter Readings

Which reading in this chapter helped you to better understand a problem? Respond to the following questions:

- How did you look at the problem before the reading, and how did you look at it differently after reading the essay?
- What specific part of the essay influenced you the most and why? Try to pinpoint an element of the reading that helped to change your mind, or pinpoint how certain elements worked together to help change your mind.

Considering Images

1. Explain how someone might view one of the following images differently after reading the related essay. Be specific when you describe the way in which someone might view the image before reading the essay, and how it might be viewed differently after the reading.

    A. The strawberry (page 422), after reading Rachel Carson's "The Obligation to Endure."
    B. The rake (page 438), after reading Ed Bell's "Technology, Movement, and Sound."
    C. The current international access symbol (page 441), after reading Dan Wilkins's "Thoughts on the International Access Symbol."

2. Find an image and explain how someone might view it differently after having read one of the essays in this chapter.

3. Take a snapshot of a problem, either with a camera or by describing it in a paragraph or two, and write an essay explaining how a person might view that snapshot differently after reading one of the essays in this chapter or your own essay.

The Consequences of Everyday Arguments

1. Find a proposed solution that has influenced many people throughout the course of history. What problem does it address and what solution does it propose?

2. Find a proposed solution, written in the last ten years, that affects many people's lives today. What problem does it address and what solution does it propose? What are some competing proposals? What solution might you propose for solving the problem?

    (Thinking in categories will help you come up with ideas. For example, you might think first of problems related to your major, then move on to problems related to other majors. Or you might think of local, national, or international problems; or problems related to work, and then problems related to play. Make connections among ideas. If you come up with the problem "world hunger," for example, you might try connecting that problem to another category, such as "local," thus coming up with other problems: "wasted food in your community," "what to do with leftovers," "health effects of large fast-food portions," and so on.)

Considering Images

Find an image that shows a problem and write an essay that proposes a solution to the problem. You may return to the **Analysis** and **Public Resonance** sections of this chapter to develop your ideas.

Writing, Speech, and Action

EVERYDAY RHETORIC

Exploring Visual Rhetoric

It can be argued that images, too, use rhetoric. And by looking at how images "work," we can apply some of the important concepts of rhetoric, not just to writing and speaking, but to images. Looking at visual rhetoric can also help us to better understand how rhetoric is used in writing and speech.

Consider This Chapter's Opening Image: Describe the rhetoric of this chapter's opening image—a fish wearing a gas mask. Use the following questions and come up with more of your own to help figure out how the image conveys an idea.

A. Discuss your analysis of the chapter's opening image with several classmates. Explore through discussion how your understanding of the image is similar to or different from theirs. Following the discussion, write down the main similarities and differences in your viewpoints, and explain how your ideas about the image developed or changed through discussion. What did you learn, or how did you come to think differently about the image because of the discussion?

B. Consider the public resonance of the opening image. What public concern does it speak to? To whom might this concern matter? How might people benefit by exploring the photograph's possible meanings?

Find an Image That Relates to Your Essay: What image might you use in conjunction with the essay you wrote for this chapter?

A. Write a caption for the image.

B. Write an essay explaining the relationship between the image and your text. Consider the following questions as you develop your ideas:

- How does the image support or help to explain the text of the essay?
- What does the image argue? What claim does the image make?
- What specific elements of the image convey the main idea and the support for that idea?
- How might the reader view the image differently after having read your essay?
- How might the reader be confused by the relationship of your essay to the image?

C. Write an essay in which you explain how your problem-solving essay influenced the way others viewed the image. To do research for this essay, (1) show the image to several people, and (2) ask them how they view it. (Record their responses.) Then (3) ask them to read your essay and (4) explain how they now view the image differently.

D. Describe the rhetoric of your own photograph or image, using the questions in the previous section on this page.

Consider Other Images in This Chapter: Explore the relationship, or interaction, between the images in this chapter and their corresponding essay.

Rake (page 438). How does the image of a rake relate to Ed Bell's main idea in "Technology, Movement, and Sound"?

- What specific elements of the image support Bell's text? (In this case, consider what is absent from the image as well as what is present.)
- How might the reader view this image differently after reading Bell's essay?
- What other images might work well with this essay?

A. Find another image that would work well with Bell's essay and write a caption for the image.

B. In an essay, explain the relationship between the image you found and "Technology, Movement, and Sound."

Nothing (page 433). How does the image of this stack of essays relate to Paul Roberts's essay "How to Say Nothing in 500 Words"?

- What specific elements of the image illustrate Roberts's ideas?
- What elements help to bring out some idea in Roberts's text?
- What elements, if any, might be counterproductive to Roberts's main idea?
- What other images might work well with this essay?

A. In an essay, suggest how this image might be less than effective in illustrating Roberts's essay and propose a better image, although one that still includes a copy of an essay called "Nothing."

B. In an essay, suggest how this image might be less than effective in illustrating Roberts's essay, and propose a better image—something completely different than this one.

Critique Any Chapter Image. Imagine you are a textbook reviewer and the publisher has asked you to critique the images in this chapter. Write a memo to the publisher addressing a problem with one of the images and proposing a solution.

Design or Redesign Your State's Quarter

A. Design or redesign your state's quarter, and then write a problem-solving essay showing how your design solved the problem of designing an appropriate state quarter. To help support your solution, discuss the content, framing, composition, and so on of your design. Include a visual of your design with your essay.

B. Get feedback from several people about your design. What did they feel should have been included but wasn't? What did you include that others thought you shouldn't have? Write an essay responding to the major objections about your design.

C. Write a letter to the editor arguing for your design. Instead of merely describing the design, explain how it solves the problems of accurately representing your state, not alienating certain groups, and so on.

Find an Image That Speaks to a Problem and/or Proposes

a Solution: This chapter's opening image addresses a problem by proposing a solution of sorts. Look through your personal photographs as well as photographs (or images) on-line or in books or magazines for an image that addresses a problem and/or proposes a solution. Explore the image by responding to the following prompts:

- What problem does the image address? What solution does it propose?

- How does it encourage people to think and/or act differently?

A. Share your image with several other people and ask what the image says to them. Record their responses.

B. Analyze people's reactions to the image you showed them. Consider the following questions:

- What reaction was most common?

- What reaction was most unusual?

- Why did others have the reaction they did? How did the particular elements of the image influence them? What attitudes and beliefs of each individual played an important role in his or her understanding of the image?

- What reaction did you find to be most interesting and why?

C. How have your ideas about the image developed or changed based on your analysis of others' reactions?

D. Describe the rhetoric of your own photograph, or image, using the questions in the "Consider This Chapter's Opening Image" section on page 473 .

E. In writing, explain how the image you found suggests at least five problems and/or solutions; then explain how at least three could be developed into an essay.

Problems This Image Might Suggest:

1. Not enough people ride bikes

2. Must park bicycles outside

3. Crime: must lock bikes to prevent theft

4. Inadequate bike racks

5. ???

10

Chapter Contents

- **Readings**

Artistic Works

Essays Responding to the Arts

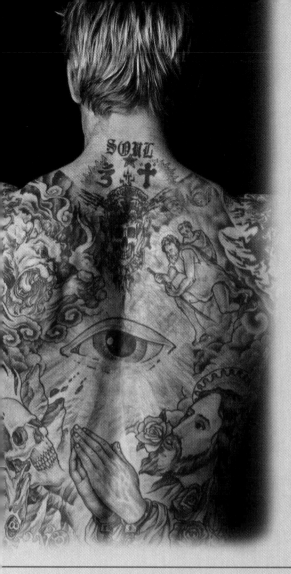

Exploring the Arts

Would you call this art? Why or why not?

If reading literature is an act of discovery, then the same thing might be said about listening to music and taking in the visual arts. Art is more than entertainment. It calls on readers, listeners, or viewers to participate in the creation of ideas. Whether they are involved in novels, Shakespeare plays, folk songs, or Picasso paintings, people engaging in art are inventing as they take it in: they are developing thoughts, envisioning situations, seeing connections, and imagining worlds that they had not previously encountered. While the arts help us imagine other worlds, they also help us to make sense of our own. Art, in whatever form, offers something to everyday experience—maybe answers to the gnawing uncertainties of daily existence, maybe mystery and intensity in a world that seems too plain, maybe a framework for exploring people's behavior, or maybe a deeper understanding of our place in society. Exploring and responding to the arts, then, is the process of developing and communicating ideas, not simply about a story, poem, song, or painting, but about life.

Of course, not all works that could be considered art promote valuable insight; more sophisticated pieces of art tend to promote more sophisticated ideas, which, perhaps, is why college courses focus on art that is more complex than popular romance novels or teen dance music. Although art varies in complexity and form, we will assume art is *any creative work that intends to provoke new ideas or insights in its audience.* Such a definition does create some boundaries, excluding, for example, a piece of work produced to make pre-adolescents thoughtlessly excited, but any definition creates boundaries.

The definition of art has been contested for thousands of years, and it continues to be today. If our definition does not suit you, create another one. Ask five people for their definitions of art (either in class or by surveying non-classmate peers). Considering those ideas, write out a definition that you can use in your exploration for this chapter.

The formal study of the arts can become a highly specialized practice, dependent on particular theories and terms. Such advanced study is often relegated to particular disciplines: English departments study literature, drama, and poetry; art schools study painting and sculpture; music majors examine the formalities of composition. However, the arts transcend any one discipline or academic field:

- In addition to government publications, military records, and personal memoirs, historians also read the literature and study the art of a given era to understand its culture.
- Sociologists, anthropologists, and political scientists study the literature and art of a culture to understand its perspectives, moral crises, and attitudes.
- Psychologists study the arts to further their understanding of the human experience.
- Lawyers and law officials study the arts to explore the relationship between individual action and civic duty—or to understand the workings of the criminal mind.

All of these disciplinary approaches emphasize an important point: art is deeply connected to how and what people think. Exploring art is not simply an examination of one person's expressions; it is an investigation into human thought and imagination as well as culture and society.

Key Terms and Concepts: The following terms are helpful in reading and writing about art.

Genre: A category of artistic work based on form, style, and subject matter
Setting: The place and time in which events occur
Theme: The controlling idea or primary message
Style: An author's particular characteristics that distinguish him or her from others
Plot: The arrangement or course of events
Narrator: The voice speaking to the audience, which may also be a character
Stanza: A unit of verse in poetry
Ensemble: The collection and placement of instruments or voices in a performance
Arrangement: The structure of a song

10 This chapter will help you examine and analyze a subject (a work or works of art), develop a specific point about it, and communicate your ideas to an audience. The chapter readings include works of art and analytical essays. Reading and discussing the works of art (a story, poems, and a song) will help focus your attention on various artistic features. The essays will provide valuable insight to necessary writing strategies. You can find a topic in one of two ways:

1. Go to the **Point of Contact** section for help finding an artistic work outside of this chapter.
2. Choose one of the **Ideas for Writing** that follow each work of art or essay.

After finding a subject, go to the **Analysis** section to begin developing your ideas.

READINGS

The readings for this chapter include both artistic works (a short story, two poems, and a song) and analytical essays about artistic works. Even though the artistic works are of different genres (or categories), they have some similarities: they use language to create a vivid reality for the reader; they promote a sense of wonder; and they bring a particular idea or situation into sharp focus so the reader can experience it in a new way. Like all artistic works, the ones in this chapter intend to show the reader a new or particularly intensive way of imagining something—thereby changing the reader's perspective.

Encountering an artistic work calls for a certain degree of intellectual adventure. We must be willing to follow the artist into a way of thinking and seeing. And while it is impossible to leave behind all of our biases and opinions, we benefit by approaching art and literature willing to explore the subtleties of language and thought.

The essays in the chapter attempt to show what various artistic works do for people—how they promote ideas and influence thinking. Of course, to discuss what art does, writers must understand how it works; that is, they must *analyze* the artistic work. Notice how the writers use analysis and how they draw attention to particular lines, images, or characters. Notice also that each writer offers a focused point about an artistic work, group of works, or genre.

You will also notice that some essays (Whitehead and Bennett) focus on works by several artists. Although the subjects may be broad, their main points are very specific. McCovey's essay, however, focuses on only one work. Although the subjects are different (an art form, a specific genre, or one particular work), the authors use many similar strategies for supporting their claims.

A Very Old Man with Enormous Wings

Gabriel García Márquez

Gabriel García Márquez, born in 1928 in Colombia, has published many novels and short story collections. His novel One Hundred Years of Solitude *(1967) has been hailed as one of the greatest novels ever written. He was awarded the Nobel Prize for literature in 1982.*

1   On the third day of rain they had killed so many crabs inside the house that Pelayo had to cross his drenched courtyard and throw them into the sea, because the newborn child had a temperature all night and they thought it was due to the stench. The world had been sad since Tuesday. Sea and sky were a single ash-gray thing and the sands of the beach, which on March nights glimmered like powdered light, had become a stew of mud and rotten shellfish. The light was so weak at noon that when Pelayo was coming back to the house after throwing away the crabs, it was hard for him to see what it was that was moving and groaning in the rear of the courtyard. He had to go very close to see that it was an old man, a very old man, lying face down in the mud, who, in spite of his tremendous efforts, couldn't get up, impeded by his enormous wings.

2   Frightened by that nightmare, Pelayo ran to get Elisenda, his wife, who was putting compresses on the sick child, and he took her to the rear of the courtyard. They both looked at the fallen body with mute stupor. He was dressed like a ragpicker. There were only a few faded hairs left on his bald skull and very few teeth in his mouth, and his pitiful condition of a drenched great-grandfather had taken away any sense of grandeur he might have had. His huge buzzard wings, dirty and half-plucked, were forever entangled in the mud. They looked at him so long and so closely that Pelayo and Elisenda very soon overcame their surprise and in the end found him familiar. Then they dared speak to him, and he answered in an incomprehensible dialect with a strong sailor's voice. That was how they skipped over the inconvenience of the wings and quite intelligently concluded that he was a lonely castaway from some foreign ship wrecked by the storm. And yet, they called in a neighbor woman who knew everything about life and death to see him, and all she needed was one look to show them their mistake.

3   "He's an angel," she told them. "He must have been coming for the child, but the poor fellow is so old that the rain knocked him down."

4   On the following day everyone knew that a flesh-and-blood angel was held captive in Pelayo's house. Against the judgment of the wise neighbor woman, for whom angels in those times were the fugitive survivors of a celestial conspiracy, they did not have the heart to club him to death. Pelayo watched over him all afternoon from the kitchen, armed with his bailiff's club, and before going to bed he dragged him out of the mud and locked him up with the hens in the wire chicken coop. In the middle of the night, when the rain stopped, Pelayo and Elisenda were still killing crabs. A short time afterward the child woke up without a fever and with a desire to eat. Then they felt magnanimous and decided to put the angel on a raft with fresh water and provisions for three days and leave him to his fate on the high seas. But when they went out into the courtyard with the first light of dawn, they found the whole neighborhood in front of the chicken coop having fun with the angel, without the slightest reverence, tossing him things to eat through the openings in the wire as if he weren't a supernatural creature but a circus animal.

5   Father Gonzaga arrived before seven o'clock, alarmed at the strange news. By that time onlookers less frivolous than those at dawn had already arrived and they were making all kinds of conjectures concerning the captive's future. The simplest among them thought that he should be named mayor of the

world. Others of sterner mind felt that he should be promoted to the rank of five-star general in order to win all wars. Some visionaries hoped that he could be put to stud in order to implant on earth a race of winged wise men who could take charge of the universe. But Father Gonzaga, before becoming a priest, had been a robust woodcutter. Standing by the wire, he reviewed his catechism in an instant and asked them to open the door so that he could take a close look at that pitiful man who looked more like a huge decrepit hen among the fascinated chickens. He was lying in a corner drying his open wings in the sunlight among the fruit peels and breakfast leftovers that the early risers had thrown him. Alien to the impertinences of the world, he only lifted his antiquarian eyes and murmured something in his dialect when Father Gonzaga went into the chicken coop and said good morning to him in Latin. The parish priest had his first suspicion of an imposter when he saw that he did not understand the language of God or know how to greet His ministers. Then he noticed that seen close up he was much too human: he had an unbearable smell of the outdoors, the back side of his wings was strewn with parasites and his main feathers had been mistreated by terrestrial winds, and nothing about him measured up to the proud dignity of angels. Then he came out of the chicken coop and in a brief sermon warned the curious against the risks of being ingenuous. He reminded them that the devil had the bad habit of making use of carnival tricks in order to confuse the unwary. He argued that if wings were not the essential element in determining the difference between a hawk and an airplane, they were even less so in the recognition of angels. Nevertheless, he promised to write a letter to his bishop so that the latter would write to his primate so that the latter would write to the Supreme Pontiff in order to get the final verdict from the highest courts.

6   His prudence fell on sterile hearts. The news of the captive angel spread with such rapidity that after a few hours the courtyard had the bustle of a marketplace and they had to call in troops with fixed bayonets to disperse the mob that was about to knock the house down. Elisenda, her spine all twisted from sweeping up so much marketplace trash, then got the idea of fencing in the yard and charging five cents admission to see the angel.

7   The curious came from far away. A traveling carnival arrived with a flying acrobat who buzzed over the crowd several times, but no one paid any attention to him because his wings were not those of an angel but, rather, those of a sidereal bat. The most unfortunate invalids on earth came in search of health: a poor woman who since childhood had been counting her heartbeats and had run out of numbers; a Portuguese man who couldn't sleep because the noise of the stars disturbed him; a sleepwalker who got up at night to undo the things he had done while awake; and many others with less serious ailments. In the midst of that shipwreck disorder that made the earth tremble, Pelayo and Elisenda were happy with fatigue, for in less than a week they had crammed their rooms with money and the line of pilgrims waiting their turn to enter still reached beyond the horizon.

8   The angel was the only one who took no part in his own act. He spent his time trying to get comfortable in his borrowed nest, befuddled by the hellish heat of the oil lamps and sacramental candles that had been placed along the wire. At first they tried to make him eat some mothballs, which, according to the wisdom of the wise neighbor woman, were the food prescribed for angels. But he turned them down, just as he turned down the papal lunches that the penitents brought him, and they never found out whether it was because he was an angel or because he was an old man that in the end he ate nothing but eggplant mush. His only supernatural virtue seemed to be patience. Especially during the first days, when the hens pecked at him, searching for the stellar parasites that proliferated in his wings, and the cripples pulled out feathers to touch their defective parts with, and even the most merciful threw stones at him, trying to get him

to rise so they could see him standing. The only time they succeeded in arousing him was when they burned his side with an iron for branding steers, for he had been motionless for so many hours that they thought he was dead. He awoke with a start, ranting in his hermetic language and with tears in his eyes, and he flapped his wings a couple of times, which brought on a whirlwind of chicken dung and lunar dust and a gale of panic that did not seem to be of this world. Although many thought that his reaction had been one not of rage but of pain, from then on they were careful not to annoy him, because the majority understood that his passivity was not that of a hero taking his ease but that of a cataclysm in repose.

9   Father Gonzaga held back the crowd's frivolity with formulas of maid-servant inspiration while awaiting the arrival of a final judgment on the nature of the captive. But the mail from Rome showed no sense of urgency. They spent their time finding out if the prisoner had a navel, if his dialect had any connection with Aramaic, how many times he could fit on the head of a pin, or whether he wasn't just a Norwegian with wings. Those meager letters might have come and gone until the end of time if a providential event had not put an end to the priest's tribulations.

10   It so happened that during those days, among so many other carnival attractions, there arrived in town the traveling show of the woman who had been changed into a spider for having disobeyed her parents. The admission to see her was not only less than the admission to see the angel, but people were permitted to ask her all manner of questions about her absurd state and to examine her up and down so that no one would ever doubt the truth of her horror. She was a frightful tarantula the size of a ram and with the head of a sad maiden. What was most heart-rending, however, was not her outlandish shape but the sincere affliction with which she recounted the details of her misfortune. While still practically a child she had sneaked out of her parents' house to go to a dance, and while she was coming back through the woods after having danced all night without permission, a fearful thunderclap rent the sky in two and through the crack came the lightning bolt of brimstone that changed her into a spider. Her only nourishment came from the meatballs that charitable souls chose to toss into her mouth. A spectacle like that, full of so much human truth and with such a fearful lesson, was bound to defeat without even trying that of a haughty angel who scarcely deigned to look at mortals. Besides, the few miracles attributed to the angel showed a certain mental disorder, like the blind man who didn't recover his sight but grew three new teeth, or the paralytic who didn't get to walk but almost won the lottery, and the leper whose sores sprouted sunflowers. Those consolation miracles, which were more like mocking fun, had already ruined the angel's reputation when the woman who had been changed into a spider finally crushed him completely. That was how Father Gonzaga was cured forever of his insomnia and Pelayo's courtyard went back to being as empty as during the time it had rained for three days and crabs walked through the bedrooms.

11   The owners of the house had no reason to lament. With the money they saved they built a two-story mansion with balconies and gardens and high netting so that crabs wouldn't get in during the winter, and with iron bars on the windows so that angels couldn't get in. Pelayo also set up a rabbit warren close to town and gave up his job as bailiff for good, and Elisenda bought some satin pumps with high heels and many dresses of iridescent silk, the kind worn on Sunday by the most desirable women in those times. The chicken coop was the only thing that didn't receive any attention. If they washed it down with creolin and burned tears of myrrh inside it every so often, it was not in homage to the angel but to drive away the dungheap stench that still hung everywhere like a ghost and was turning the new house into an old one. At first, when the child learned to walk, they were careful that he not get too close to the chicken coop. But then they began to lose their fears and got used to the smell,

and before the child got his second teeth he'd gone inside the chicken coop to play, where the wires were falling apart. The angel was no less standoffish with him than with other mortals, but he tolerated the most ingenious infamies with the patience of a dog who had no illusions. They both came down with chicken pox at the same time. The doctor who took care of the child couldn't resist the temptation to listen to the angel's heart, and he found so much whistling in the heart and so many sounds in his kidneys that it seemed impossible for him to be alive. What surprised him most, however, was the logic of his wings. They seemed so natural on that completely human organism that he couldn't understand why other men didn't have them too.

12   When the child began school it had been some time since the sun and rain had caused the collapse of the chicken coop. The angel went dragging himself about here and there like a stray dying man. They would drive him out of the bedroom with a broom and a moment later find him in the kitchen. He seemed to be in so many places at the same time that they grew to think that he'd been duplicated, that he was reproducing himself all through the house, and the exasperated and unhinged Elisenda shouted that it was awful living in that hell full of angels. He could scarcely eat and his antiquarian eyes had also become so foggy that he went about bumping into posts. All he had left were the bare cannulae of his last feathers. Pelayo threw a blanket over him and extended him the charity of letting him sleep in the shed, and only then did they notice that he had a temperature at night, and was delirious with the tongue twisters of an old Norwegian. That was one of the few times they became alarmed, for they thought he was going to die and not even the wise neighbor woman had been able to tell them what to do with dead angels.

13   And yet he not only survived his worst winter, but seemed improved with the first sunny days. He remained motionless for several days in the farthest corner of the courtyard, where no one would see him, and at the beginning of December some large, stiff feathers began to grow on his wings, the feathers of a scarecrow, which looked more like another misfortune of decrepitude. But he must have known the reason for those changes, for he was quite careful that no one should notice them, that no one should hear the sea chanteys that he sometimes sang under the stars. One morning Elisenda was cutting some bunches of onions for lunch when a wind that seemed to come from the high seas blew into the kitchen. Then she went to the window and caught the angel in his first attempts at flight. They were so clumsy that his fingernails opened a furrow in the vegetable patch and he was on the point of knocking the shed down with the ungainly flapping that slipped on the light and couldn't get a grip on the air. But he did manage to gain altitude. Elisenda let out a sigh of relief, for herself and for him, when she saw him pass over the last houses, holding himself up in some way with the risky flapping of a senile vulture. She kept watching him even when she was through cutting the onions and she kept on watching until it was no longer possible for her to see him, because then he was no longer an annoyance in her life but an imaginary dot on the horizon of the sea.

Exploring Ideas

1. According to the events and descriptions of this story, do angels exist? If so, what are they? What is their relationship to humanity? (Or, what is humanity's relationship to angels?)

2. The people's reaction in the story is perhaps as important as the winged old man's presence. What does their reaction say about people? Their fears? Their treatment of strangers?

3. With the events in this story as your basis, explain our fear of the unknown and how it influences behavior.

Fire

Joy Harjo

Joy Harjo, born in 1951 in Tulsa, Oklahoma, has published several books of award-winning poetry. "Fire" appears in How We Became Human, New and Selected Poems *(2003), and first appeared in* What Moon Drove Me to This? *Her poetry often focuses on Native American life and identity.*

1   a woman can't survive
    by her own breath
    alone
    she must know
5   the voices of mountains
    she must recognize
    the foreverness of blue sky
    she must flow
    with the elusive
10 bodies
    of night winds
    who will take her
    into herself

    look at me
15 i am not a separate woman
    i am the continuance
    of blue sky
    i am the throat
    of the mountains
20 a night wind
    who burns
    with every breath
    she takes

Exploring Ideas

1. What does this poem do for women? How is the message of this poem important for women living at the dawn of the twenty-first century?

2. Does this poem speak only to women? Does it offer anything to men? Explain what this poem may or may not offer to men.

Dover Beach

Matthew Arnold

Matthew Arnold (1822–1888) was an English poet and essayist. While he produced poetry in his early years, he devoted much of his later life to essays on literature and culture. His most famous, Culture and Anarchy, is often quoted in discussions about the role of morality in societies. "Dover Beach," which is set on the coast of England, was published in 1867 in his second book of poetry.

1 The sea is calm to-night.
The tide is full, the moon lies fair
Upon the straits;—on the French coast the light
Gleams and is gone; the cliffs of England stand,
5 Glimmering and vast, out in the tranquil bay.
Come to the window, sweet is the night-air!

Only, from the long line of spray
Where the sea meets the moon-blanch'd land,
Listen! you hear the grating roar
10 Of pebbles which the waves draw back, and fling,
At their return, up the high strand,
Begin, and cease, and then again begin,
With tremulous cadence slow, and bring
The eternal note of sadness in.

15 Sophocles long ago
Heard it on the Aegean, and it brought
Into his mind the turbid ebb and flow
Of human misery; we
Find also in the sound a thought,
20 Hearing it by this distant northern sea.

The Sea of Faith
Was once, too, at the full, and round the earth's
    shore
Lay like the folds of a bright girdle furl'd.
But now I only hear
25 Its melancholy, long, withdrawing roar,
Retreating, to the breath
Of the night-wind, down the vast edges of drear
And naked shingles of the world.

Ah, love, let us be true
30 To one another! for the world, which seems
To lie before us like a land of dreams,
So various, so beautiful, so new,
Hath really neither joy, nor love, nor light,
Nor certitude, nor peace, nor help for pain;
35 And we are here as on a darkling plain
Swept with confused alarms of struggle and
    flight,
Where ignorant armies clash by night.

Exploring Ideas

1. What is the Sea of Faith (in the fourth stanza)? How is the idea similar to or different from religious or philosophical metaphors that you have used or heard?

2. Sophocles was a playwright in ancient Greece who wrote the tragic story of Oedipus. How does the allusion to Sophocles support the main idea of the poem?

3. How does Arnold make you rethink your connection to other people and societies, both in the present and long ago?

Running to Stand Still

U2

From Dublin, Ireland, U2 has been on popular music charts around the world since 1980. Emerging from the punk scene of the early 1980s, U2 developed worldwide attention as a band with highly charged political and social messages. The band's lead singer, Bono, has rallied political and religious leaders to help poor and oppressed people throughout the world. "Running to Stand Still" appears on The Joshua Tree *(Island Records, 1987).*

1 And so she woke up
Woke up from where she was
Lying still
Said I gotta do something
5 About where we're going
Step on a steam train
Step out of the driving rain, maybe
Run from the darkness in the night
Singing ha, ah la la la de day
10 Ah da da da de day
Ah la la de day
Sweet the sin
Bitter taste in my mouth
I see seven towers
15 But I only see one way out
You got to cry without weeping
Talk without speaking
Scream without raising your voice

You know I took the poison
20 From the poison stream
Then I floated out of here
Singing . . . ha la la la de day
Ha la la la de day
Ha la la de day
25 She runs through the streets
With her eyes painted red
Under black belly of cloud in the rain
In through a doorway she brings me
White gold and pearls stolen from the sea
30 She is raging
She is raging
And the storm blows up in her eyes
She will . . .
Suffer the needle chill
35 She's running to stand . . .
Still.

Exploring Ideas

1. Explain how the images in this song help us to see a life of addiction.

2. What does "Running to Stand Still" suggest about art's relationship to life?

3. Listen to "Heroin" by the Velvet Underground (off the album *Velvet Underground & Nico)*. What qualities do "Heroin" and "Running to Stand Still" share? Explain how U2's song plays off of "Heroin" and what this might suggest about influence and art.

The Plight of High-Status Women

Barbara Dafoe Whitehead

Barbara Dafoe Whitehead, a sociologist whose writing also appears in Chapter 7 of this text, is author of the book Divorce Culture: How Divorce Became an Entitlement and How It Is Blighting the Lives of Our Children *(1997). "The Plight of High-Status Women" originally appeared in* The Atlantic Monthly *(1999). As you read, jot down what you think Whitehead is saying about "dump literature." What point is she trying to make?*

1 Women's tastes in popular reading have long favored two kinds of romances. One is the romance of falling in love and making a brilliant marriage. This centuries-old staple traces the progress of true love from wooing to wedding, through all the confusions and complications along the way. The other is more contemporary and appears prominently in women's magazines, especially those aimed at educated women in the Baby Boom generation. It is the romance of finding a job and making a brilliant career. Here the progress is from first job to first six-figure salary. Complications arise in this narrative as well, but it ends happily with the acquisition of an executive title, a great wardrobe, and a bicoastal social life. What the two romances have in common is the optimistic and essentially liberal faith that a young woman can get what she wants through the shrewd exercise of her own intelligence, talents, and discerning judgment.

2 Now, however, a vastly different kind of popular literature is emerging. It is written for and about the privileged members of a new generation. These young women, the highly educated daughters of educated Baby Boomers, are in their twenties and thirties, living and working on their own. Compared with earlier generations, they spend a long time in the mating market, and thus face prolonged exposure to the vicissitudes of love, including multiple breakups, fears of sexually transmitted disease, and infertility anxieties. They must also go through a prolonged period of higher education and career apprenticeship in order to establish themselves in a demanding job market. During these years they may be laid off, downsized, or fired at least once or twice. Neither their love life nor their work life is settled or secure.

3 The new literature reflects these dual realities. Like traditional women's stories, it deals with themes of love and work, often interweaving the two, but it breaks sharply with the romantic view of both. The defining theme in this literature isn't finding the dream guy or landing the great job but precisely the opposite. It's getting dumped—by a boyfriend or a boss or both. What's more, these books challenge the idea that a young woman blessed with talent and education, and filled with desire and ambition, can get what she wants.

4 The purest statement of the signature theme in this literature can be found in a batch of self-help books published over the past few years, with titles such as *Dumped!; He Loved Me, He Loves Me Not; The Heartbreak Handbook; Getting Over Him; Exorcising Your Ex; How to Heal the Hurt by Hating;* and *The Woman's Book of Revenge.* There is also a *Complete Idiot's Guide to Handling a Breakup.* But this theme is not limited to self-help literature. It crosses over into other genres. Suzanne Yalof's *Getting Over John Doe* is a mini-memoir. Candace Bushnell's *Sex and the City* is a collection of her columns in the *New York Observer.* Perhaps the most thorough treatment of the theme is found in recent coming-of-age fiction such as Melissa Bank's critically acclaimed *The Girls' Guide to Hunting and Fishing,* Amy Sohn's *Run Catch Kiss,* Kate Christensen's *In the Drink,* and Laura Zigman's *Animal Husbandry.*

5 Like Jane Austen's Emma, the young women in these four books are handsome, clever, and rich in educational advantage (a good education is the contemporary equivalent of propertied wealth). After graduating from elite colleges they move to Manhattan, find minuscule apartments,

and seek their fortunes. Eventually they land jobs in the glamorous media or entertainment industry. But their jobs are low-level and short-term; they are temps, part-timers, and free-lancers. What's more, their employment prospects don't improve as time goes on: instead of moving up the career ladder, they get stuck at the level of the temp job. Far from making brilliant careers, they forever remain Girl Fridays.

6   Their love lives aren't much more successful. They go out with attractive, high-profile men, but these men are not looking for a lifelong mate—they're already encumbered by a wife or a live-in girlfriend, or they have weird habits (wearing mouse slippers to bed) or "multiple substance issues." Far from making brilliant marriages, these smart, funny, talented women forever remain girlfriends or ex-girlfriends.

7   Consider Claudia Steiner, the twenty-nine-year-old protagonist of *In the Drink*. A Swarthmore graduate, she has spent nine post-college years in New York City in low-level jobs (receptionist, dog walker, phone-sex scriptwriter, temp, waitress, housecleaner, and temp again) when she lands an $18-an-hour position as a personal assistant to and ghostwriter for a celebrity author of mystery romances. Her boss, Jackie del Castellano, turns out to be egotistical and tyrannical; she insists on pretending that Claudia, who is turning Jackie's literary straw

into best-selling gold, is merely providing a fresh insight or two. What's more, Jackie routinely yells at, humiliates, and mistreats Claudia, and finally dumps her.

8   Claudia's home life isn't much better. She lives alone in a "rathole on an airshaft," eats takeout, and drinks too much. She says, "I was like a tiny version of the city itself: all my systems were a welter of corruption and neglect." And her love life is a mess. Although she is desperately in love with William, her childhood friend, she can't find the "bridge between friendship and romance." Instead she falls into and out of relationships that follow a predictable course: "bantering dive-bar pickup, drunken sex, a rushed exchange of phone numbers afterwards on a subway platform, then other nights with more dive-bar bantering and drunken sex."

9   Bosses and boyfriends behave a lot alike in the novels. They make nice to you (ever so briefly). Then they dump you. The bosses are invariably vain, capricious, self-centered, and hard-shelled women, not mentors but tormentors. In *The Girls' Guide to Hunting and Fishing,* Jane Rosenal is a rising star in her publishing company until Mimi Howlett, her new boss, arrives. Mimi demotes Jane from the promising position of associate book editor to de facto personal assistant. She also relentlessly criticizes Jane's professional work while generously offering her tips on how to improve her appearance.

10   Jobs go from bad to worse following a firing. After Ariel Steiner, the protagonist in *Run Catch Kiss*, is dumped from her freelance job as a sex columnist and from her temp job in a Manhattan publishing company, she slides from a temp job in a bank in Queens to a part-time job in Brooklyn before hitting bottom with a waitressing job at a twelve-table restaurant in the Village. (Her salary plummets from a high of $18 an hour to a low of $5.50 an hour plus tips.) Jane Rosenal languishes as a temp worker in a bank.

11   Boyfriends look good on paper—they're a mostly upscale crowd of writers, publishers, artists, fund managers, and investment bankers—

but they turn out to be cruel, careless, self-absorbed, socially clueless, and sexually inept. What's more, as prospective mates they're virtually indistinguishable.

12 In the traditional romance there was one special guy for every special girl. The special girl found her special guy by administering a set of means and morals tests and then using her powers of discernment to pick him out of the pack. Dump literature rejects this premise. It takes the opposing view—that men are all the same. "I've gone out with the short, fat, and ugly," says a woman journalist in *Sex and the City,* "and it doesn't make any difference. They're just as unappreciative and self-centered as the good-looking ones." In short, the existence of many men doesn't guarantee the existence of many choices. There's just One Guy. Take him or leave him. More precisely, take him and he'll leave you.

Part II

13 When it comes to ending a relationship, male behavior is entirely predictable. According to dump literature, it's over when he says (pick one): (a) "I think maybe we should cool things for a while," (b) "I've been doing a lot of thinking," (c) "God, this week is going to be terrible . . . I'm completely swamped," or (d) "It's not you, it's me."

14 Once dumped, however, the ex-girlfriends and ex-Girl Fridays don't get downhearted. They get even. In these books the functional equivalent of romantic passion is revenge, served up fast and hot. The self-help books reject the therapeutic approach of grieving over a loss, which was popular in an earlier generation of books aimed mainly at divorcing couples. The best therapy, many of them advise, is to work through your grief on his property. Since many contemporary breakups involve a household as well as a relationship, the revenge schemes focus on destroying or defacing his stuff, including his car and clothing. Some of this is intended as mere fantasy, or played for laughs. But some scenarios recur so frequently—obsessively calling

his answering machine and driving past his place, shredding his pictures or clothes, getting mutual friends to spy on him—that it is hard not to assume that they have been battle-tested.

15 For the characters in the novels, writing is the best revenge. As one observes, "It's the ultimate revenge fantasy. You get rich and famous writing about something you're already obsessed with." In *Run Catch Kiss,* Ariel Steiner takes revenge on the disgusting men she goes out with by lampooning them in her popular sex column. After her boyfriend dumps her, Jane Goodall, the protagonist in *Animal Husbandry,* turns to animal research for evidence on why men flee. She invents a theory based on the observation that a bull will ditch an old cow as soon as a new cow appears, and then gets a job writing about her "Old-Cow-New-Cow" theory as a pseudonymous science columnist for a men's magazine. Bosses are likewise targets for revenge. In a twist on the writing-as-revenge tactic, Claudia Steiner strikes back by unwriting: she erases the disk containing the text of her boss's nearly completed book.

16 Revenge is psychologically expedient, but it does not accomplish lasting personal transformation, much less social change. What is striking is how little this literature protests the cycle of temping and dumping and how little hope it holds out for an end to it. This is all the more surprising because these books are about young women blessed by all the advantages that education, fond parents, and a good therapist can provide. Nevertheless, the challenge for these women is not to avoid, let alone alter, the bleak disjunctions of life but merely to survive them—to get over them and move on.

17 In a world so blindly indifferent to individual merit and mettle a woman's chief psychological resource is humor, and her only form of activism is to laugh it off and get back in the game. Despite its resignation, this literature is hardly weary or despondent. It is full of riffs, spoofs, quips, and mordant observations about men, women, and their mating and relating problems. The most appealing element of this

humor is not its acidulous portrait of men and bosses but its unsparing view of women's weaknesses and self-deceptions. "I couldn't get enough of the most unsuitable men," one character says. Another explains why she and her female boss were attracted to each other: "She was desperate, and I was available."

18 However, an undercurrent of anxiety runs through the hilarity. After all, what is funny at twenty-five might be less so at thirty-five. Some of the characters are haunted by a vision of themselves in the future, living alone in a dark studio apartment, eating out of an open refrigerator, and earning a meager wage stuffing envelopes at home. And although the fiction resorts to the expedient of the happy ending, the girl-gets-guy resolutions that some employ are thoroughly unconvincing and entirely at odds with everything that has come before.

19 Of course, no one believes that dump literature offers a documentary portrait of today's educated young women. In its depiction of work it draws heavily on the experience of the authors (themselves young), who, like aspiring actors, may have taken part-time or temp jobs in order to devote themselves more fully to their craft. Theirs is a very narrow slice of work life, hardly representative of the experience of the many post-college single women who enjoy far greater success in their careers than these fictional characters. Nor can the sex lives of these women be taken as typical. Few young women spend every night at clubs or have sex, drunken or otherwise, with a string of partners. What does ring true, however, is the depiction of what might be called the plight of the high-status woman.

20 Given the high divorce rate, today's young women cannot rely on marriage for economic security. Even if they aspire to marriage (and according to survey research, most do), they have to be ready and able to support themselves with their own earnings. This has meant ever-increasing education beyond high school. For women pursuing high-status professions the schooling can extend several years beyond college, well into their twenties. Then, for as much as another decade, such women must invest heavily in developing their careers. Indeed, women on the make adopt the same priorities as men on the make. Work is in the foreground, love in the middle distance or the background. Neither men nor women have the time or a pressing desire for marriage, especially when they can get some marriagelike benefits without it. So they put it off and enter into relationships that offer some combination of sex, companionship, convenience, and economies of scale.

21 By the time high-status single men and women reach their early thirties, however, their marriage prospects begin to diverge. Men's educational and career achievements enhance their marriageability and increase the pool of prospective mates, because men tend to marry women of similar or lesser education, and the supply at or below their achievement level is large. For women of the same age and education the opposite is the case: high-status women tend to seek husbands of higher levels of education and achievement, and their lofty status decreases the pool of eligible mates. For men, age is no barrier to attracting women. A few gray hairs can be sexy. For women, age is no asset. A few gray hairs can send a woman racing to the colorist.

22 Moreover, intragender competition can be fierce. High-status women find themselves in competition not only with other high-status women but also with younger women of lesser education, in lower occupations. The classic example is thirtyish female physicians who, having finished their rigorous training, are ready for marriage. They find themselves up against slightly younger residents and interns along with a large pool of twentysomething nurses and other health professionals. Since the nurses and the physical therapists are in careers that can be disrupted and then picked up again, they may be more willing than the female physicians to stay home and raise children while their husbands pursue careers. This, too, can be a source of competitive disadvantage for the female physicians.

23 By this stage in life single women of talent and accomplishment begin to grasp the principle

that life is unfair in at least one key domain. Men may be able to pursue their careers singlemindedly during their twenties and postpone marriage until their thirties without compromising their fertility or opportunities to find a suitable mate, but women cannot. Just at the moment when they are ready to slow down and share the pleasures of life with similarly successful mates, they look around and find that many of the most desirable men are already taken. What is left is an odd assortment: married men who want a girlfriend on the side; divorced men with serious financial, child-custody, or ex-wife problems; and single men who invite suspicion simply because they're still single. These mating patterns lead to a plaint familiar among upscale single women in their thirties: "There are no good men left."

24   Thus the career strategy now favored by well-educated young women, in part to establish their own economic viability as a cushion against the likelihood of an eventual divorce, exacts a maddening cost of its own: it makes it less likely that they will marry in the first place. This is a classic case of what is known as goods in conflict.

25   Taken separately, most of the dump books can be read as entertainments; taken together, however, they suggest that an important and recent change is occurring in the lives of educated young women. The romance of love and marriage took its inspiration from a long-standing mating system, but the defining institutions of the old system are breaking down. Courtship is dead. Marriage is in decline. A new mating system is emerging, with its own complications and confusions, including the conflict that faces high-status women. These books are field reports on the new rules of engagement—and disengagement.

Exploring Ideas

1. How does Whitehead view "dump literature"? What point does she think it is making, and how does it make it?

2. How is the way that you view the plight of high-status women similar to or different from the way Whitehead views it?

3. Interview a variety of people to discover their views on the present courtship, marriage, and mating system. Attempt to interview people of different backgrounds, ages, and gender. How are their views similar to or different from Whitehead's?

4. You may not read "dump literature," but instead might watch a certain type of movie or television show or read a certain type of magazine. Taken together, what do these movies, shows, or magazines suggest about the status of a certain group?

Writing Strategies

1. In your own words, write down Whitehead's main idea.

2. Identify one concession Whitehead makes and explain why it is worth making.

3. Describe Whitehead's introduction and conclusion. How does each function—that is, what does Whitehead seem to be trying to achieve with her introduction and conclusion?

4. Find one colon and semicolon in Whitehead's essay and explain how they function.

Ideas for Writing

1. What type of literature, film, music, and so on suggests something interesting about a certain group?

2. What form of art suggests a new trend?

If responding to one of these ideas, go to the **Point of Contact** section of this chapter to begin developing ideas for your essay.

The Parting Breath of the Now Perfect Woman

Chester McCovey

Chester McCovey wrote this essay for a college writing class. As you read, highlight passages in which McCovey states his own ideas and underline passages in which he refers to Nathaniel Hawthorne's "The Birthmark." Read with an eye toward identifying the main idea of McCovey's essay. As you read or after you finishing reading this essay, write down what you think McCovey is trying to accomplish.

In the margins of this essay, a reader's comments point to key ideas and writing strategies. As you read the essay, consider how the comments might influence your own reading and writing.

Exploring Ideas

Writing Strategies

A masterpiece of literature offers its readers unlimited opportunities for thought, analysis, discovery, insight, interpretation. Though an old story's language may be difficult for some, if that old story is a masterpiece, its characters and plot develop a timeless theme as relevant today as it was yesterday. Nathaniel Hawthorne's "The Birthmark" is such a story.

Claim: old story still relevant— timeless theme

Introduces main idea: "The Birthmark is relevant today." It has public resonance.

Hawthorne's theme is clear. In the story's opening paragraph we read:

> The higher intellect, the imagination, the spirit, and even the heart might all find their congenial ailment in pursuits which, as some of their ardent votaries believed, would ascend from one step of powerful intelligence to another, until the philosopher should lay his hand on the secret of creative force and perhaps make new worlds for himself. We know not whether Aylmer possessed this degree of faith in man's ultimate control over Nature.

man believes he can control nature

Uses direct quote to convey story's theme. Indents long quote and does not use quotation marks.

See what I mean about the language? But the point here is that even though we now speak—and write—differently, Aylmer *did* apparently possess this degree of faith in man's ultimate control over nature. And in attempting to remove his young wife's only blemish—a small, hand-shaped birthmark on her left cheek—he "removes" her very life. The story's climax comes when after much science, Aylmer is successful—the birthmark is gone:

don't mess with nature?

States a main idea and supports it with a quote from the story.

> "By Heaven! It is well-nigh gone!" said Aylmer to himself, in almost irrepressible ecstasy. "I can scarcely trace it now. Success! success! And now it is like the faintest rose color. The lightest flush of the blood across her cheek would overcome it. But she is so pale!"

Quotation marks are used because a character from the story is speaking, not because the source is quoted.

Exploring Ideas

And while Georgiana is now "perfect" and Aylmer's science has been "successful," Georgiana is, of course, not just "pale." She is dying . . . then dead. And the young beauty—who because she had been told so often that her birthmark was a charm was in her own words, "simple enough to imagine that it might be so"— now speaks her dying words:

thinks he had success, but she is dying

> "My poor Aylmer," she repeated, with a more than human tenderness, "you have aimed loftily; you have done nobly. Do not repent that with so high and pure a feeling, you have rejected the best the earth could offer. Aylmer, dearest Aylmer, I am dying."

The quotation shows the tension between the natural world and human arrogance.

He rejects the best "the earth" could offer

Reading "The Birthmark" for a second time, one plainly sees that the author laid everything out in the first paragraph. It could, of course, turn out no other way. And today's reader, raised on *Frankenstein* and stories like it, is probably not surprised by the ending. After the bombing of Hiroshima and Nagasaki, Americans spent their 1950s watching (Birthmark-like) movies in which havoc-wreaking mutants warned us about the dangers of man's faith in his ultimate control over Nature. Yet Hawthorne's masterpiece is so perfectly crafted, one eagerly reads on to find out what is about to happen.

Develops idea with historical and literary references.

We are used to such stories now: since A-bomb, technological advances

As a masterpiece of literature, "The Birthmark" deserves much attention: attention to Hawthorne's plot, which contains perfect foreshadowing throughout; attention to his characters— poor Aylmer, and simple Georgiana who one cannot help but fall in love with; attention to word choice and sentence structure, though these are not so easy to be attracted to because of our modern tastes in writing. And also deserving attention, the theme of the story—a story written in the early nineteenth century—is not only *worth* pondering today—at the dawn of a twenty-first century—but it would be, in fact, difficult to imagine how someone could *not* ponder it.

Discusses literary elements of the story: plot, style, theme.

Why it's a masterpiece of literature: plot, style (word choice, sentence structure), theme (timeless, still relevant)

The attentive reader is already a step ahead of me: cloning, stem cell research, genetic engineering. The incidents of humans "perfecting" nature—or fiddling with nature in attempts to perfect it—are forever in today's headlines. But cloned sheep and the possibility of cloned people is not the only science "The Birthmark" asks today's reader to think about.

How it's relevant (public resonance): cloning, stem cell research, genetic engineering

While Georgiana's birthmark represents abstract imperfection, and Aylmer's faith in man represents humankind's efforts to perfect nature in general, the birthmark obviously reminds us of today's little "imperfections": (too small) breasts, a (too large) nose, (no) chin, (fat) thighs, and so on. The reader should not miss the point. No one is saying that cleft palates or clubbed feet should not be corrected—at least no one is saying that in this essay. But

Relates "The Birthmark" to today's world. Shows how it's relevant.

Concession

Exploring Ideas

What is beauty?
What is perfection?
How does "society"
determine this?

Aylmer went too far.
We, today, are going
too far (McC claims).
Are we?

Can we improve
on nature? Have we
gone too far in trying?
Are we outa control?

Have we gone too far
in trying to improve
what is natural? And
what is the cost?

Georgiana's birthmark was "of the smallest pygmy size" and her lovers were "wont to say that some fairy at her birth hour had laid her tiny hand upon the infant's cheek, and left this impress there in token of the magic endowments that were to give her such sway over all hearts. Many a desperate swain would have risked life for the privilege of pressing his lips to the mysterious hand." The "mad scientist" is us—eager to erase these "imperfections" of Nature.

Perhaps the story's most important warning—indeed! it *is* the story's most important warning—comes so subtly that one might overlook it. When Georgiana, for the first time, goes into her husband's off-limits laboratory where he is working on one last concoction, she is scolded for her lack of faith in him. But she *has* faith and tells him so, and then she fails to tell him her reason for coming. She has felt a "sensation in the fatal birthmark, not painful, but which induced a restlessness throughout her system." One can hardly imagine the sensation was nothing at all, that it was just an excuse for a master storyteller to prolong his story. It is also unlikely that this sensation was a *negative* reaction to Aylmer's first treatment—after all, it was a "sensation" and it was not "painful." We thus imagine that Aylmer's first treatment was on its way to working, then he went too far.

Earlier in the story Aylmer shows Georgiana a powerful drug, and says, "With a few drops of [it] in a vase of water, freckles may be washed away as easily as the hands are cleansed." When asked, "Is it with this lotion that you intend to bathe my cheek?" Aylmer replies, "Oh, no . . . this is merely superficial. Your case demands a remedy that shall go deeper." And so, Aylmer's remedy ends up going too far. To him, the birthmark is not "superficial," but something that "has clutched its grasp into [her] being." His cure *does* work. The birthmark is removed. And his young wife is perfect, just as he planned . . . but only for a moment.

Great literature survives—it survives time, and multiple readings, and critical analysis, and skeptical hearts and minds. And it not only survives, but it thrives. Read "The Birthmark" twice and you will know what I mean. Hawthorne's theme is just as relevant today. And Georgiana's dying words express the real complexity of the issue.

As for physical imperfection in the twenty-first century, it seems odd that on one level we promote respect for all sorts of human "imperfections," yet on another level, we strive as we do to eliminate them whenever we can. It seems odd because so many times they are not imperfections at all.

Alas! It was too true! The fatal hand had grappled with the mystery of life, and was the bond by which an angelic

Writing Strategies

Discusses further
public resonance:
We attempt to perfect
nature today as
Aylmer did in
the story.

Summary of the
story with a few
small quotes.

Quotes are used
sparingly—worked
into a summary
of the story.

McCovey restating
his main idea.

Pointing out the complexity of this issue.

Concludes with relevant
quote from the story.

spirit kept itself in union with a mortal frame. As the last crimson tint of the birthmark—that sole token of human imperfection—faded from her cheek, the parting breath of the now perfect woman passed into the atmosphere, and her soul, lingering a moment near her husband, took its heavenward flight.

Exploring Ideas

1. Based on this essay, what does McCovey seem to care about?

2. How does McCovey encourage the reader to think differently?

3. In a paragraph, explain how McCovey connects Hawthorne's story to twenty-first-century life in America.

4. State McCovey's main idea in no more than a few sentences, and then compare your statement with those of several classmates. Discuss the similarities and differences in the way you and your classmates understand McCovey's essay. Then revise your statement of his main idea, and explain how your understanding changed, if it did, through discussion.

5. Explain McCovey's main idea to several friends, co-workers, and family members, asking for their input. How do others agree or disagree with McCovey's ideas?

Writing Strategies

1. Describe McCovey's voice and identify several specific passages to support your description.

2. Identify at least one counterargument McCovey makes. What other counterargument might he have made to strengthen his argument?

3. Study the ways in which McCovey refers to the story "The Birthmark" in his essay. Look for quotes and paraphrases. When he quotes, look for (a) long passages set off by themselves, (b) shorter passages quoted within McCovey's sentences, and (c) individual words from the story worked into McCovey's sentences. Based on McCovey's essay (and at least two others in this text) write a one- or two-page essay explaining various ways in which writers can refer to sources (in this case a story) in their text.

4. How does McCovey convey the point of "The Birthmark" to the reader? How does he convey the point of his own essay to the reader?

Ideas for Writing

1. How is the theme of some short story written before 1950 still relevant—better yet, *more* relevant—today?

2. What work of art relates to a contemporary issue that concerns you?

If responding to one of these ideas, go to the **Point of Contact** section of this chapter to begin developing ideas for your essay.

Hip-Hop: A Roadblock or Pathway to Black Empowerment?

Geoffrey Bennett

Geoffrey Bennett was editor-in-chief of the Maroon Tiger *college newspaper at Morehouse College in Atlanta. This essay appeared in the* Black Collegian On-Line *(www.black-collegian.com). As you read, write down in the margin your initial responses to Bennett's ideas. Which points do you agree with, disagree with, find interesting, or find new to you? Based on this essay, how does Bennett encourage the reader to see the relationship between art and life?*

1   In the early 1980s, a highly percussive, cadenced, and repetitive musical form seeped from the inner city streets of the South Bronx to a virtually exclusive African-American audience. Harbingered by originators such as Run DMC, the Sugar Hill Gang, Public Enemy, Afrika Bambaata and others, the medium was a simple reflection of the daily lives of its creators with topics ranging from the trivial, such as the style of one's new Adidas sneakers, to the significant, like the infuriation spurred by police harassment.

2   Rap music, as it came to be known, lacked major commercial support in its early stages, and, as a result, it was authentic and unaffected; it was truly "CNN for the streets," as Chuck D once commented. Twenty years later, however, hip-hop culture has since flooded mainstream culture, and rap music is as prevalent in suburban homes as it once was in its native environment, moving from American subculture to the forefront of American attention. "Hip-hop is more powerful than any American cultural movement we've ever had," said rap music impresario Russell Simmons.

3   Hip-hop is one of the fastest-growing music genres in the United States, accounting for $1.84 billion in sales last year out of a $14.3 billion total for the U.S. recording industry, according to industry statistics. Interestingly, nearly 70 percent of those sales are to white suburban youth, a striking transformation considering rap music's beginnings. Most importantly, perhaps, rap music and its associated hip-hop culture have become a new component of the Black cultural aesthetic. With its rhythmical roots firmly planted in African tradition, hip-hop music is more than just musical expression. For some, it is a way of life, affecting their speech, style of dress, hairstyle, and overall disposition.

4   Like any other expressive art form, rappers have tested the boundaries of social responsibility, legality, free speech, and old fashioned "good taste." Labeled as misogynistic, reckless, and even criminal, rappers endured years of public scrutiny with African Americans among some of their most relentless critics. After years of incessant scrutiny, hip-hop mogul Russell Simmons organized a three-day hip-hop music summit for 200 rappers, industry executives and African-American politicians, the first event of its kind. Sean Combs, LL Cool J, Queen Latifah, Wyclef Jean, Wu-Tang Clan, Chuck D, Jermaine Dupri, KRS-1, Luther Campbell, Ja Rule and Talib Kweli were just a few of the influential hip-hop artists in attendance at the conference held last June in New York City.

5   Stars joined forces with some of Black America's intellectual and political elite, including NAACP President Kweisi Mfume; Urban League President Hugh Price; Nation of Islam Minister Louis Farrakhan; Martin Luther King, Jr., III, leader of the Southern Christian Leadership Council; Georgia Democratic Congressional Representative Cynthia McKinney; and authors Cornel West and Michael Eric Dyson. The summit ended with musicians and industry executives agreeing to follow voluntary guidelines to advise parents of music's lyrical content while vowing to protect rap artists' freedom of speech

by fighting Congressional efforts to censor the music. Minister Louis Farrakhan of the Nation of Islam, one of the political activists who attended the summit, told rappers, "You've now got to accept the responsibility you've never accepted. You are the leaders of the youth of the world."

6   Today's African-American college students, many of whom as youth were the original fans during rap music's formative years, still remain avid rap music connoisseurs. Rap music, however, has taken a decidedly different direction in recent years. Since rap music is clearly a profitable commercial commodity, rappers consequently perpetuate images and stereotypes that will sell their products, ranging from the excessively violent to the extravagantly wealthy. "Many rappers do not live the type of lives they claim. Those that claim to be affluent often are not, and those that claim to be poor gang-bangers are often millionaires. Fortunately, most college students have the ability to decipher between rap's glamorous image and the realities of life. A problem arises for the younger, impressionable audience, many of whom buy into rap's surface image," said Morehouse College Student Government Association President Christopher J. Graves.

7   As role models, acceptance of the designation or not, rappers have a unique responsibility to be cognizant of their message and their intended audience. Since American pop culture reveres stardom, rappers often garner more attention and respect than they deserve. Consequently, rap music and hip-hop culture have the power to either adversely or positively affect African Americans in specific, and the larger

culture in general. While a summit on rap music cannot adequately address all of its dilemmas, a dialogue between interested parties must continue in order to preserve the distinctive art form, while protecting the rich heritage of the African-American cultural aesthetic.

Exploring Ideas

1. How does Bennett encourage the reader to look at hip-hop?

2. How does Bennett's idea fit into a larger discussion? That is, how can what he says be applied not just to hip-hop but to other art forms?

3. Observe the relationship between different art forms (hip-hop, country music, film, painting, etc.) and people in your community. How does art seem to influence their thoughts and actions (or behavior)? How do the people seem to influence the art form?

4. In addition to art, what influences people? Go out and observe the way people in your community choose to live—how they drive around, shop, eat, work, play. What are the major influences on what they wear, what they eat, how they get around, what they do for a living, what they do in their spare time?

5. How might you respond to Bennett's ideas? For example, how might you take his conclusion and be more specific, or what earlier point in his essay might you develop further or take exception to?

Writing Strategies

1. Describe how Bennett's introduction functions. What is he attempting to do? How does it assist the reader in understanding the rest of the essay? What, if anything, else do you think it does?

2. Describe Bennett's voice and evaluate its appropriateness for this subject matter. Provide several passages to support your evaluation.

3. How does Bennett get his main idea across to the reader? Does he state his main idea or imply it? What type of background information and evidence does he provide?

4. Evaluate the effectiveness of Bennett's sources. How do they help the reader to understand his argument or to accept his claims?

Ideas for Writing

1. What responsibility do you think rappers have? Or, what responsibility do artists in some other art form have?

2. What problems arise when people buy into the surface images of some particular art form?

> If responding to one of these ideas, go to the **Point of Contact** section of this chapter to begin developing ideas for your essay.

Outside Reading

Find an article that discusses a particular piece or type of art and print it out or make a photocopy. It might examine the art's significance, worth, or general relationship to society. To conduct an electronic search of journals and magazines, go to your library's periodical database or to InfoTrac (http://infotrac.galegroup.com/itweb/). For your library database, perform a keyword search, or go to the main search box and click on "keywords" for InfoTrac. In the search box, you might enter a genre or form of art (such as *modern painting, poetry, contemporary fiction*), or a particular artist or work of art (such as *Hillman* or *The Sound and the Fury*). Focus your search by entering other keywords, such as *art, society, culture, value.* You might even explore specific topics; for example: *women and Hispanic and poetry* or *rap and art and society.* (When performing keyword searches, avoid using phrases or articles such as *a, an, the*; instead, use nouns separated by *and*.) The search results will yield lists of journal and magazine articles. This same strategy can be used with a newspaper database.

You can also search the Internet. Try the search engine Google.com. Like most Internet search engines, Google combines keywords (nouns and proper nouns), but Google requires no joining words (Boolean operators) such as *and*. In the search box, try various word combinations, such as those above.

The purpose of this assignment is to explore the range of options in writing about art. As you read through this chapter, keep the text you have discovered close by and notice the elements and strategies the writer uses. Depending on your instructor's suggestions, do one or more of the following:

1. Notice how the writer applies various strategies from this chapter. On the hard copy or photocopy:

   - Highlight the thesis if it is stated. If the thesis is implied, write it in your own words.
   - Identify (or write in the margins) passages that are argumentative, evaluative, descriptive, narrative.
   - Identify any counterarguments or concessions (elements of argument from Chapter 5).

2. Write an essay that discusses the strategies employed by the writer. The following questions may be helpful.

   - Do you believe the writer shows the public resonance of the art? How?
   - How does the writer support his or her point about the art?
   - Who is the audience for this text?
   - How does the audience influence the ideas or language used?

3. Write at least three "Exploring Ideas" questions for the article you found.

4. Write at least three "Writing Strategies" questions for the article.

5. Write two "Ideas for Writing" questions, such as the ones following the essays in this book.

In addition to text, consider the artistic dimension of images. Examine the images above (a CD cover, a wall, a vase, and a concert poster), and with a classmate, discuss how they work artistically—how they might stimulate a new way of looking at or thinking about their subjects. Then find several other images on your own and, in writing, explain how each image might prompt someone to think dfferently.

■

INVENTION

The following three sections are designed to help you develop ideas for your essay. The **Point of Contact** questions will help you choose a subject (an artistic work or form of art) and collect some basic information on it. The **Analysis** section will help you closely examine different elements of the work, and the **Public Resonance** section will help you consider the relevance of the work to your readers. The questions in each section are not meant to be answered directly in your final written assignment. However, answering them will help you explore the subject and develop points. After you work through these three sections, the **Delivery** section, which immediately follows, will help you craft your ideas into a written text.

Point of Contact
Finding Art in Everyday Life

Choosing a subject for your writing might be a simple process of choosing your favorite literary text, musical piece, or visual work. However, your favorite work of art may not be the best subject to examine. Remember that you are not simply explaining how much you like a particular work; rather, you are exploring what the work, or a particular form of art, means for people, what it offers an audience. To that end, look for a work or set of works that might have some value beyond your likes and dislikes.

As in all the previous chapters of this book, the **Point of Contact** section here is designed not only to help you find a subject, but also to create focus: to draw your attention to details about the subject that might otherwise go unnoticed. First, choose a literary text, a musical work, or a visual piece.

- Browse through a literary anthology (a large collection of various works by many authors) or go to a library and search for a collection of short stories or poems by a writer you have never read.

- Visit a museum or browse through an art book (such as Gardner's *Art Through the Ages*).

- Search a library database or the Internet for an artist or writer of particular ethnicity or from a particular time period. For example, you might try a search using words such as: *African American writers, Hispanic writers, Women writers, contemporary painters, Renaissance painters, Impressionists, Baroque composers, modern composers.*

- Watch an artistic film. For ideas, check out the following sites: *The Berkeley Art Museum and Pacific Film Archive* (http://www.bampfa.berkeley.edu), *The British Academy of Film and Television Arts* (http://www.bafta.org), *Independent Movie Database* (http://indie.imdb.com), the *UCLA Film and Television Archive* (http://www.cinema.ucla.edu), or the *Online Film Critic Society* (http://ofcs.rottentomatoes.com).

Recording the Basics:
After you have found your subject (a work of art), use the questions below that correspond to your chosen work.

Literary Works: Literature comes in many categories or *genres*: drama, poem, novel, short story, and an unlimited combination of all these. Within each genre, individual pieces can vary widely. In fact, many of the most successful and widely read authors consistently transcend whatever rules or conventions a genre may have. And the purpose for each piece of literature can vary: a poem may celebrate love; a drama may explore the issue of revenge; a short story may chronicle the lifestyle of a particular region and a particular people; a novel may reveal the complexities of human madness.

> What is the *plot* (the arrangement or course of events)?
> What is the *setting* (the time and place in which events occur)?
> Who is the *narrator* (the main voice speaking to the audience)?
> What are the primary images given to the audience?
> Who are the characters?

Musical Works: Musical arts include everything from Mozart to hip-hop. Like other works of art, musical pieces often transcend conventions and go beyond the audience's expectations. While the lyrics of a song may point to themes, create characters, or even develop a story, the music itself influences the listener's understanding of the lyrics.

> If the piece contains lyrics, what events, ideas, or feelings do they communicate?
> If the piece does not have lyrics, through what moods does it take the listener?
> What is the *ensemble* (the collection and placement of instruments or voices in the performance)?
> What is the *arrangement* (the structure of the song)?

Visual Arts: Painting, sculpture, and architecture all fit into visual arts. And the visual arts include a vast array of mediums such as weaving or embroidery. All of these can communicate complex ideas to an audience; of course, the communicative tools are vastly different than in literary and musical art. Visual artists must rely on images, color, and placement to convey meaning, although titles help establish a concept.

> What is the title?
> What is the medium (the materials used in creation of the work)?
> What is the form (the shape and structure)?
> What is the composition (the placement or arrangement of images)?
> What colors are emphasized?
> Are the colors strong and contrasting or soft and blended?

Film: Many people do not consider movies to be art (because they often depend on celebrity actors to live out oversimplified, predictable, and formulaic plots). However, many movies, or films, attempt to do more. Like a good painting, short story, or ballad, they attempt to provoke new ideas and insights, and some even attempt to redefine audiences' expectations.

> What is the title?
> What is the plot?
> Who are the main characters?
> What is the setting?

Analysis

How Do the Elements Work?

Analyzing an artistic work is much like analyzing a written text: both involve exploring how the individual elements function. While knowing the basic features of a work is important, we have to go further: we have to know how those basic features function in the work. Either with a small group of peers or alone, ask questions to examine each feature of your subject and discover how it functions. For instance, when considering the title, you might ask:

Why is the title important?
What does the title make people think?
Why should a work of art have a title?

The important thing about analytical thinking is to maintain a constant state of curiosity. It is easy to trick oneself into seeing an answer where another question is waiting. And often the easy answer is the least valuable and least interesting. As you explore the features of your subject, use the categories and questions below. Ask what each feature means, what it does for the work, and how it might affect its audience. Go beyond quick answers. If someone offers a quick answer, write it down, but then explore further.

Themes: In the same way that essays have thesis statements, artistic works have themes, which are issues or controlling ideas. A theme in one piece of art usually appears in many pieces—and throughout different art forms and genres. For example, consider the theme *governments produce and conceal corruption*, which appears in novels, in dramas, and in countless songs and poems. Consider the following themes and how they have appeared in different works: *love overcomes selfishness; nature provides freedom; racism destroys lives; technology can control humans; the grace of God redeems human life; war is not a romantic adventure*. Of course, each artist treats and presents a theme differently; themes may be made obvious (as they tend to be in songs) or they can lurk with more subtlety.

- What themes emerge in the images or plot of the text?
- What point, idea, or issue does the artist explicitly bring out?
- What hidden idea or issue lurks in the piece?

Conflict: When you think of conflict or struggle or crisis, you might imagine overt kinds of struggle: antagonism between people, wars between countries, people against time. (These are the kinds of conflicts that typically propel Hollywood movies.) However, artistic works often go beyond these and deal with more abstract conflicts such as moral, psychological, or spiritual dilemmas. Sometimes, the conflict is not obvious; it can be subtle or implied by the placement of details.

- What conflicts or tensions occur in the work?
- How are conflicts dealt with or resolved?
- How does conflict or tension help develop the theme?
- How does the conflict prompt the audience to think differently?

Character Development: Art, especially fiction and drama, often shows the development or evolution of a character or characters. The particular way a character develops can be important. That is, how a character changes throughout a story can illustrate a point to readers.

- How do the characters evolve or transform throughout the text?
- Who or what might the characters represent?
- What human quality (weakness or strength) do the characters illustrate?
- What do the characters show the audience about human life—or life in general?

Conventions: All art forms have conventions, or commonly accepted strategies, for conveying ideas. Some conventions are so common that we do not even consider them: novels depend on a series of chapters that help create the story; contemporary pop songs have repeating choruses. Sometimes artists work to transcend the conventions, or break the rules, of a given genre, which may result in a piece that seems weird or totally bizarre at first glance or listen. However, breaking the rules is often the most vital aspect of art. For instance, the Beatles broke conventions of ensemble and production when they integrated instruments and sounds of Eastern cultures into Western popular music.

- How is the piece a typical example of its genre? (For example, how is it a typical pop song or short story)?
- How does the piece challenge or transcend the conventions of the genre?
- What value does the piece have? What does it offer to people?
- Why is this work especially valuable?

Style: Artists have particular characteristics, or styles, that distinguish them from others. Style may be associated with a consistent artistic device or way of representing ideas. The novelist William Faulkner, for instance, is known for lengthy and involved sentences, and the poet Emily Dickinson is known for short lines of verse separated with dashes. Style affects how ideas are communicated and impressions are made, or put another way, artists communicate through style.

- What is the author's style?
- How does it affect the ideas being communicated?

Context: It is often said that great art transcends time, that its meaning and value are communicated to people who are alive long after the piece was created. The assumption behind this statement is that the social climate surrounding the creation of the artwork does not necessarily give the work its value. Of course, this is a safe assumption for many artistic pieces. One need not explore cultural attitudes about beauty to appreciate the complexity of the Mona Lisa. However, every piece of art does emerge out of a context (a setting that helps give it meaning) and understanding that context can deepen the analytical process. For instance, knowing that the Beatles' "Revolution" was written during a time of significant social and political unrest helps give it meaning. Some artistic works explicitly function to recall or memorialize a past era. In these cases, the context is important, because it may reveal the values of the age in which the art was produced.

- What is the context of the work? (When and where was the work created?)
- What was the social and political climate? (Was it a time of war, oppression, class tension, national expansion, technological advancement, economic boon, or industrial revolution?)
- Does the context somehow show up or manifest itself in the work?
- Is the work a response to a particular social or political condition?
- How does understanding the context help the audience understand the work or an important idea related to the work?

Example: Chester McCovey's Responses to Analysis Questions

What themes emerge in the images or plot of the text? The old sci-fi theme: some guy starts messing with chemicals trying to improve on nature and it backfires. Frankenstein, etc. Once again, man tries to control nature, instead of accepting nature. Man tries imposing his will. So, Hawthorne says man can improve on life (or perfect it) only by destroying it? When the blemish goes, Georgiana dies. But Hawthorne pre-dates Frankenstein, etc. He seems ahead of his time in that sense. The theme is still relevant today, though the story was written in the 1800s.

Activity: Consider the following works of art. In groups, discuss how each work may have been influenced by its context (its political, cultural, aesthetic climate). You may have to research the work by doing a quick Internet search. Try Google.com.

The Empire State Building
Titanic, the movie
"Respect," Aretha franklin
The Last Supper, by Leonardo di Vinci
"This Land is Your Land" by Woodie Guthrie
The Taj Majal

Explore the role context plays in the images on
this page. What context does the work emerge from?
And how might understanding that context help to
deepen the analytical process?

Public Resonance

How Does the Subject Relate to Others?

All art has a certain degree of public resonance because it attempts to address people; it deals with issues that go beyond the artist. For example, the poem "Fire" by Joy Harjo is not necessarily about one woman (the speaker of the poem). It resonates, or seeks to resonate, with all women. Márquez's "A Very Old Man with Enormous Wings" tells the story of a particular village, but the ideas about supernatural beings and people's treatment of others are available to many (maybe all) societies.

When writing about the arts, you should attempt to emphasize or highlight issues of public value, pointing to the important or significant issues in the art, thereby making it resonate even more with readers. You might say that the goal of the writing in this chapter is to connect readers and art—to emphasize important issues that lurk within an artistic work. For example, notice Bennett's rather direct explanation of hip-hop's public resonance:

> Since American pop culture reveres stardom, rappers often garner more attention and respect than they deserve. Consequently, rap music and hip-hop culture have the power to either adversely or positively affect African Americans in specific, and the larger culture in general.

His main idea is tied to hip-hop's role in popular culture, so the public resonance is an especially important part of his essay. Whitehead's essay also focuses on the relationship between art (books) and popular culture. Notice how she makes the connection in her conclusion:

> Taken separately, most of the dump books can be read as entertainments; taken together, however, they suggest that an important and recent change is occurring in the lives of educated young women. The romance of love and marriage took its inspiration from a long-standing mating system, but the defining institutions of the old system are breaking down. Courtship is dead. Marriage is in decline. A new mating system is emerging, with its own complications and confusions, including the conflict that faces high-status women. These books are field reports on the new rules of engagement—and disengagement.

However, public resonance is also important when the main idea is related to other features of the work, even if the main idea involves conflict, character, theme, or any element. For example, notice how McCovey explains the public resonance of "The Birthmark" in his introduction:

> A masterpiece of literature offers its readers unlimited opportunities for thought, analysis, discovery, insight, interpretation. Though an old story's language may be difficult for some, if that old story is a masterpiece, its characters and plot develop a timeless theme as relevant today as it was yesterday. Nathaniel Hawthorne's "The Birthmark" is such a story.

As you consider your chosen subject, use the following questions to develop public resonance for your own writing:

- What value does the work have?
- Why should people understand the message or theme of the work?

- Why should people understand the characters?
- Why should people understand the conflict? Does the particular conflict have any bearing on people's lives today?
- How does the work help us to understand society? Individual life?
- How does the work challenge our assumptions about beauty or art?
- How is the context of the work similar to or different from present times or your particular culture?

Example: Chester McCovey's Responses to Public Resonance Questions

What value does the work have? It is a well-written story in various ways. It is beautifully pieced together. Reading it a second time, you see that Hawthorne lays it all out in the opening paragraph. Also, we do more of Aylmer's sort of thing now than ever before. Our society wants to fix life (animal and plant). We want to genetically engineer rhubarb. We want to get rid of our hideous birthmarks. So, what's wrong with that? Is anything wrong with that? Can that be taken too far? It's not that all these attempts at improvement lead to death. What do they lead to? More and more attempts at improving more and more things, perhaps. Just like Aylmer who may have been onto something. But came up with something stronger. Perhaps engineering bigger tomatoes or insect resistant apples is not a problem. (Or is it?) But where does it stop? (Be careful of a lame slippery slope argument here.) Are we fixing things that are fine? Are we fixing things that are beautiful, and calling them hideous? By fixing these things that can be seen as either beautiful or hideous are we heading down a path where we can't see natural beauty . . . or beauty? The 19th-century work says to the 21st-century reader: be careful about trying to perfect nature; instead of improving it (or as you improve it), you may be destroying it.

McCovey's response illustrates a reflective thought process. Here, he is not simply answering the question, but exploring intellectual directions. He is making a connection between particular issues in the work and the world around him (or "the 21st-century reader"), going far beyond the original question *(What value does the work have?).*

Activity: Share the work of art with someone outside of your class. Tell this person why you like the work and see how he or she responds. If you have a short poem or song, you can send it as an e-mail attachment. Or if you have a longer work or visual art, you might find the text on the Internet, and forward the Web address. For literary or visual works, go to a search engine and type the author's name and the title in quotation marks: *Gwendolyn Brooks and "We Real Cool."* For song lyrics, you can type the artist's name and "lyrics" in a search engine: *U2 and lyrics.* You will then find several websites devoted, specifically, to song lyrics.

DELIVERY

Remember that writing about art is like building a bridge between your readers and the work of art. For this reason, it is important to have a copy of the artwork close by so that you can return to it often and discover (or rediscover) details. Also, it is important to consider your readers, who are not experiencing the art along with you. As you begin drafting your ideas, remember to keep your readers involved in the art and not leave them behind as you develop ideas. During the drafting process, you may discover new ideas or details about the work. In that case, do not hesitate to rethink your main ideas. Remember that crafting an essay, or any written text, is a recursive process: writers move back and forth, drafting, rethinking, re-drafting. It is not a simple step-by-step journey through a chapter. The following sections (**Rhetorical Tools, Organizational Strategies, Writer's Voice,** and **Revision Strategies**) are designed to help you build a sophisticated and engaging text—one that emerges from your particular ideas. Each section points to important features or common concerns related to argumentative writing.

Rhetorical Tools

Developing Your Ideas

Writing for this chapter might involve any number of rhetorical tools, such as the elements of argument and evaluation or the focus on detail from observation. In many ways, the writing for this chapter is argumentative—writing that puts forth a potentially arguable claim about a subject. But the exploration of the artwork also involves analyzing concepts and conventions of art.

Discovering Your Thesis: Your thesis depends primarily on your project's goal. Your project might do any of the following:

Argue for or against the value of a given work of art or a particular art form.

Argue that an element (characters, theme, conflict, setting, etc.) in a work of art influences people in a particular way.

Explain how a particular work of art or art form influences society or conventional thinking.

Explain what a work of art offers to people in a given time and place.

Explain how the conflict in a work or works of art relates to people in a given time and place.

Explain how any feature of a given work influences the audience's imagination or challenges conventional thinking.

Evolution of a Thesis

The writer discovers something valuable about her subject:	*"Running to Stand Still" is more than a pop song: it raises a social issue.*
The writer discovers a particular issue in the work:	*U2's "Running to Stand Still" reveals the contradictory world of a drug addict.*
The writer considers how public resonance develops the idea:	*To a society that treats addiction as criminal behavior, U2's "Running to Stand Still" offers a much-needed glimpse into the complexities of drug addiction.*

While a thesis statement is apt to evolve during the writing process and may not even be stated directly in an essay, writers benefit from having a sense of their main ideas. As you begin writing, state your main idea.

A Little Help from Your Friends: After exploring ideas further by considering your rhetorical tools options, prepare a briefing for a small group of classmates. (See Chapter 13, p. 642.) In the briefing, summarize the artistic work you plan to write about, and write down your thesis about it. Then ask classmates to help you answer some of the bulleted questions on the following three pages. If your class is set up to communicate electronically, send the briefing (no longer than two paragraphs) along with your questions and elicit electronic responses.

Developing Support

Using Support about the Subject: Regardless of any particular stance or thesis, claims about the work of art need to be supported with specific details. For example, a writer making a claim about the relevance of a particular theme would have to support the idea in at least two different ways. First, the writer would have to show the theme being played out in the work. This would involve highlighting elements of the work (part of the plot, some of the lyrics, part of an image) featuring that theme. For example, in Whitehead's essay, she refers to the characters in several different novels to illustrate her points:

> Bosses and boyfriends behave a lot alike in the novels. They make nice to you (ever so briefly). Then they dump you. The bosses are invariably vain, capricious, self-centered, and hard-shelled women, not mentors but tormentors. In *The Girl's Guide to Hunting and Fishing*, Jane Rosenal is a rising star in her publishing company until Mimi Howlett, her new boss, arrives. Mimi demotes Jane from the promising position of associate book editor to de facto personal assistant. She also relentlessly criticizes Jane's professional work while generously offering her tips on how to improve her appearance.

Notice that she refers only to specific scenes and situations that prove her thesis. As you consider your ideas, ask the following question: *What particular features or details of the work illustrate my point?*

Using Support outside the Subject: Pointing to details within the work is not enough if the writer is claiming something about its relevance or importance or value. The writer would also have to use support outside the subject. Beyond the particular work of art, writers have the world of everyday life, history, popular culture, and other art to support ideas. Notice Whitehead's use of trends in everyday life:

> Given the high divorce rate, today's young women cannot rely on marriage for economic security. Even if they aspire to marriage (and according to survey research, most do), they have to be ready and able to support themselves with their own earnings. This has meant ever-increasing education beyond high school. For women pursuing high-status professions the schooling can extend several years beyond college, well into their twenties. Then, for as much as another decade, such women must invest heavily in developing their careers. Indeed, women on the make adopt the same priorities as men on the make.

Imagine a writer is arguing that Márquez's story challenges readers to rethink popular notions of angels. She would not only discuss particular passages from the story; she would also point to the treatment of angels in popular culture. Only then could she support her claim. In other words, the writer would use details from the work of art and details from everyday life to make her claims. Use the following questions to find support outside the subject.

- Does anything in everyday life help illustrate my point about the work of art?
- Does anything in nature or science help illustrate my point about the work of art?
- Do any other works of art exemplify my point?

Considering Counterargument: In arguing about a work of art (or putting forth a potentially arguable claim), writers may need to consider using counter-arguments, passages that anticipate and refute claims that oppose those being forwarded by the writer. This is especially true in writing about art, which can be taken so many different ways.

Imagine a writer arguing for the value of punk rock music:

> Critics of punk rock argue that it merely panders to the most basic and simplistic desires of its listeners. But in societies that tend toward artificiality and hyper-materialism, punk rock is a necessary art form. Its simplicity reminds people that absurd amounts of luxury and thoughtless reverence of money can be overcome—or drowned out with primal noise.

The writer takes on a position that counters her own and defends punk music from critics. She might, then, go on to cite particular examples of punk music that support her point.

As you consider your own point and your own argument about the worth of the art, consider ways that other perspectives might help to clarify your points. Ask yourself the following questions:

- Who might disagree with my claims about the artistic work, and what would they say?
- What claims about the artistic work might oppose my own?

Considering Concession: An argument may also benefit from concessions, passages that acknowledge the value of positions or claims other than those being forwarded by the writer. Or a writer might also *qualify* statements by acknowledging limitations or exceptions. Notice McCovey's strategy:

> No one is saying that cleft palates or clubbed feet should not be corrected—at least no one is saying that in this essay. But Georgiana's birthmark was "of the smallest pygmy size" and her lovers were "wont to say that some fairy at her birth hour had laid her tiny hand upon the infant's cheek, and left this impress there in token of the magic endowments that were to give her such sway over all hearts. Many a desperate swain would have risked life for the privilege of pressing his lips to the mysterious hand." The "mad scientist" is us—eager to erase these "imperfections" of Nature.

McCovey is arguing that the scientist in "The Birthmark" resembles present desires to erase human imperfection. He suggests that this desire is perilous and uncontrolled (as it is in the short story), but he also acknowledges the good that can come from medical reconstruction. That is, he does not argue that all science is bad. (Such a claim could be dismissed too easily.)

As you consider your own points, consider the following questions:

- Are there other valid claims one could make about the artistic work?
- Do my claims make any large, but necessary, leaps?
- Do I ask my audience to accept generalizations?

Using the Elements of Evaluation: Your project may involve evaluation. That is, you may need to convince your readers that your chosen subject (work of art) is good, bad, superior, and so on. If assessing the value of the work is important to your overall project, use the elements of evaluation. The first step in evaluation is to develop criteria, which involves finding the subject's purpose and audience.

- What does this subject try to achieve?
- What do other like subjects try to achieve?
- Who is the audience for the subject?
- What goals *should* this subject, or all subjects like it, have?

After you have established criteria (the standards by which that particular kind of art can be judged) apply them to your subject:

- In what particular ways does the subject achieve its goal? What specific parts, tools, or strategies help the subject to achieve its goal? (For example, a restaurant depends upon such things as servers, atmosphere, interior design, in addition to the actual food.)
- In what particular ways does the subject fall short of achieving its goal?
- What goals does the subject ignore? (All possible criteria are not always figured into the subject; they can be left out or ignored.)
- What is unique about your subject's approach or strategy to achieving its goal?

Evaluation need not constitute a major part of your essay. In fact, it might simply help show the value of your chosen work of art. Notice below how evaluation might serve as a particular part of an essay. Imagine a writer arguing about the qualities of U2's "Running to Stand Still."

> A good pop song should do more than titillate its listeners. In fact, as we learned with the protest songs of the late 1960s and early 1970s, popular music can be an agent of political and social change. Artists such as Bob Dylan and Neil Young helped create political awareness, which led to significant social action and civic dialogue. Although politically aware artists went out of style through the disco era, and stayed on the fringes of the '80s metal scene, some artists continued to use popular music as a medium for exploring social issues. Perhaps the most successful, and most committed to this goal, was U2.
>
> On U2's acclaimed album, *The Joshua Tree*, "Running to Stand Still" depicts the life of addiction, particularly its inherent contradiction and tension. The voice in the song seems to speak back to a culture that too easily dismisses addiction as a simple problem of will.

Here, the writer uses the elements of evaluation in the introduction to establish the idea of a "good pop song," and then alludes to other artists (Dylan and Young) to illustrate the point. Once the idea is established, the writer introduces the particular song and begins the analysis.

In the following CD review, which appeared in *The Glass Eye* (a regional entertainment magazine out of Toledo, Ohio), notice how the author uses specific criteria to inform his evaluation. Harrington also puts the CD in context to help explain its appeal and value.

Artist: Aimee Mann
Title: *Lost in Space*
Company: Superego Records/United Musicians
Rating: 3.5 (out of 4.0) Eyes
Reviewer: Jay Harrington

Lost in Space is the latest collection of brilliant songs from music industry survivor Aimee Mann. Her decade-plus solo career began after the disbanding of her 1980s new wave/pop group 'Til Tuesday and saw her struggle on with major labels and their heavy-handed, butterfingers approach through her first two critically acclaimed solo albums, *Whatever* and *I'm with Stupid*. After running into more problems with her next effort, *Bachelor No. 2,* and its perceived "lack of commercial appeal," Aimee had finally had enough. She used the proceeds from her Grammy-nominated soundtrack to *Magnolia* to buy back her master tapes from Interscope who, after Geffen got swallowed up by Universal, became her label by default and had no idea what to do with her. She then started her own label, Superego, put the thing out herself and sold an unheard of 200,000+ copies. Now she's back with this CD, which stands out as a testament to what can be achieved when a talented, hard-working artist is left alone to create on her own terms.

The packaging alone is exquisite and contains a 30-page lyric/picture booklet designed by graphic novelist Seth, something that a major label would never have allowed or wanted to pay for. But Aimee wanted the CD to be as good as it could be, so there it is. The album is unified in its themes of alienation, love gone wrong, and loss as evidenced by the title. But it's also buoyed by pretty, ambient-pop melodies and her incredibly supple voice, not to mention sharp, concise lyrics and sparse but cleverly layered production. Several of the songs on the record ("High on Sunday 51," "Pavlov's Bell," "This Is How It Goes," "Humpty Dumpty") are, from a songwriting perspective, simply as good as it gets, and there isn't a clinker to be found anywhere on the album. It manages to be very introspective without making the all too common mistake of self-indulgence. All in all, it's a great release and deserves a hundred times the attention it will, in all likelihood, get. But 42-year-old Aimee is through with trying to please the masses and the industry. She now makes music for herself and her devoted core of fans and *Lost in Space* is a triumph indeed for them.

Organizational Strategies

Addressing Common Concerns

Where Should I Summarize or Detail the Work? Imagine you
are about to go on a bus tour of New York City. After you take your seat on the bus,
the tour guide, standing in the front talking over the intercom, begins to explain the
tour itinerary. She explains the de-
tails of every single block you will
see on the tour. After twenty minutes of hearing the minute details,
you think: "OK, already! Let's go!"
The problem is that the tour guide
is giving too much introductory
summary. She could more easily,
and more appropriately, give a
more general description: "The bus
will take us through midtown
Manhattan where we will see
Times Square, and then we will
head toward the Village."

Similarly, writers can create a
problem by spending too much time introducing their subject. A brief introductory
summary, however, may be an appropriate strategy for settling the reader into the
work of art. You may decide to give a brief general summary of the subject (especially for longer literary works) at the beginning of your own text, and then mention
only pertinent specifics as they relate to each point. A general summary need not
take several paragraphs; in fact, a lengthy retelling of events or details, with no guiding point, should be avoided in shorter papers (under 1,000 words). An introductory
summary can even be a few sentences:

> In Gabriel García Márquez's story, "An Old Man with Enormous Wings," an angelic figure
> falls to earth in a storm. The figure, an old man, is taken into town and kept in a barn
> where people come to stare, taunt, gawk, and wonder at him. Eventually, the old man's
> wings recover from his stormy fall, and he flies off into the sky again.

From here, the writer could go on to develop a particular point, and then refer to more
particular events or details from the story as they are needed to support claims. Such
a general statement gives readers the gist of the work without putting off analysis.

How Should I Begin? One strategy is to begin with a brief overall summary
of the work. For instance, McCovey explains the timelessness of his subject, "The Birthmark," and Bennett gives a historical account of his subject, hip-hop music.

However, the main idea need not be completely introduced in the first paragraph. For instance, Whitehead's essay takes three paragraphs to set up the main idea. Her opening paragraph simply begins an explanation of romance novel themes. It is not until the third paragraph that Whitehead focuses the reader on her specific point, which she then illustrates throughout her essay:

> The new literature reflects these dual realities. Like traditional women's stories, it deals with themes of love and work, often interweaving the two, but it breaks sharply with the romantic view of both. The defining theme in this literature isn't finding the dream guy or landing the great job but precisely the opposite. It's getting dumped—by a boyfriend or a boss or both. What's more, these books challenge the idea that a young woman blessed with talent and education, and filled with desire and ambition, can get what she wants.

As in all essays, you have many options available for introducing your ideas. Focusing on a work of art does not erase the possible introductory strategies from other chapters, such as personal anecdote, scenario, question, statement, and so on.

How Should I Integrate Lines of Songs, Poems, or Stories?

Integrating others' words into your own writing can be tricky business. While there are many strategies for doing so, the rule of thumb is to avoid free-standing quotations (quotations that are not introduced by your own words). In other words, a reader should not encounter an artist's words without first understanding why they are referenced. The words of an artistic piece should be included only to illustrate a point that is already expressed, so the reader understands how to process the words.

When essay writers integrate the language of other writers into their own texts, they can often work the lines in directly:

> As the philosopher Diana Raffman has pointed out, "our ability to discriminate or compare values considerably exceeds our ability to identify or recognize them."

They can do this because the language is from the same genre (an essay). However, integrating poetry or song lyrics into an essay or letter is different, and most often the artist's lines need to be clearly separated. A colon is a standard strategy for introducing a literary passage or poetic line:

> The story's climax comes when after much science, Aylmer is successful—the birthmark is gone:
>
> > "By Heaven! It is well-nigh gone!" said Aylmer to himself, in almost irrepressible ecstasy. "I can scarcely trace it now. Success! success! And now it is like the faintest rose color. The lightest flush of the blood across her cheek would overcome it. But she is so pale!"

Quoting poetry involves yet another step. A slanted line (/) represents a line break in the poem:

> Emily Dickinson also broke convention by speaking directly to the reader: "I'm nobody. Who are you? / Are you nobody too?"

And use of a double slant (//) shows a stanza break.

Writer's Voice

Exploring Options

Avoiding the Enthusiasm Crisis: Imagine going to a movie theater, and in the lobby an usher begins jumping up and down and screaming, "That is the best movie ever! I love it! I love it!" Besides drawing attention away from the movie and onto his own giddiness, the usher may even make you apprehensive and think, "How could a movie be *that* good?" This is the enthusiasm crisis. It is easy to appear over-enthusiastic about artistic work or an artist. If a writer is moved enough by art to write about it, it makes sense that he or she would be enthusiastic; however, bald enthusiasm can have the opposite effect on a reader. Imagine the following passage about a popular song, the Indigo Girls' "Galileo":

> The Indigo Girls are a great folk duo who write songs about all kinds of issues. Their outstanding vocal harmonies and angelic voices create an amazing listening experience, but more interestingly, their lyrics create a powerful intellectual experience. The lyrics to "Galileo" are a perfect example of their stellar abilities to consume a listener's thoughts.

Ironically, such glowing praise does not invite a reader into reflection about the art. In fact, such dramatic and puffy language excludes the reader. Although this writer clearly enjoys the Indigo Girls, his overly positive language overwhelms the reader. To avoid bald enthusiasm, be cautious of the following:

1. Overly positive adjectives. Vague descriptive words such as *great, outstanding, superior, excellent, perfect* leave little room for reflection.

2. Unsupported judgments. Readers would prefer not to have judgments forced upon them; instead, they want to experience a new idea about the subject.

3. Overly broad claims about the art or artists. Often baldly enthusiastic claims have little focus. They generalize about the art or artist's worth, so perhaps the best defense against alienating your reader with enthusiasm is to develop a focused thesis.

Activities

1. Write a paragraph that illustrates the enthusiasm crisis. Using your chosen subject, write a paragraph that alienates your readers with overly positive adjectives, unsupported judgments, and overly broad claims. Share the paragraph with others in your class.

2. Choose a paragraph from any one of the chapter readings and rewrite it. Make the paragraph overly enthusiastic about the subject, and then discuss with peers how your paragraph differs, in particular ways, from the original.

Avoiding Harsh Description: Imagine going to a movie and in the lobby someone angrily announces her disgust of the movie you're about to see: "That's the worst movie ever made!" Such language usually draws more attention to the speaker than to the actual subject. Like the enthusiasm crisis, excessively harsh description draws attention to the emotions of the speaker rather than inviting reflection. For example, imagine a writer arguing about the value of a museum exhibit:

> "Art of the World" offers nothing artistic to viewers. It is entirely devoid of worth, and it should be avoided at all costs.

Like most harsh description, such language overshadows any particular elements of the subject and draws attention to itself. A better strategy is to steer toward subtlety:

> "Art of the World" does not invite the reader into various cultures of the world. Instead, it displays paintings that represent only dominant countries in the world: China, France, Russia, United States, Brazil, India. Moreover, the paintings themselves offer stereotypical representations of their homelands, for example, a Chinese painting of rice fields.

This passage, while still negative, gives a more specific examination of the subject, so the reader can share in the point being made.

Promoting Wonder: While writers do not want to alienate readers with their enthusiasm, they also do not want to dull the reader's senses. Writing about art should create a certain degree of intensity. It should make both writer and reader feel a sense of wonder. Wonder is probably best achieved by showing the reader powerful aspects of the artistic work. But beyond that, writers can also embody the kind of wonder they want to bestow in readers. They can use language and sentence structure that dramatizes the thoughts and feelings associated with the artistic work.

Considering the Tone of the Art: A writer's voice certainly depends on the subject. Even the most strategic writer would have some difficulty maintaining a comedic voice when discussing a very sober tale such as *Heart of Darkness*. However, writers need not fall entirely in line with their subjects. Notice, for example, that Geoffrey Bennett maintains a formal voice even though he is discussing hip-hop—an art form characterized by slang or "street" language. And Chester McCovey does not echo the highly formal language in "The Birthmark":

> Hawthorne's theme is clear. In the story's opening paragraph we read:
>
> > The higher intellect, the imagination, the spirit, and even the heart might all find their congenial ailment in pursuits which, as some of their ardent votaries believed, would ascend from one step of powerful intelligence to another, until the philosopher should lay his hand on the secret of creative force and perhaps make new worlds for himself. We know not whether Aylmer possessed this degree of faith in man's ultimate control over Nature.
>
> See what I mean about the language? But the point here is that even though we now speak—and write—differently, Aylmer *did* apparently possess this degree of faith in man's ultimate control over nature.

Although he draws attention to the formality of the story, McCovey's voice is informal. McCovey, like Bennett and Whitehead, has a voice that is distinct from the art he discusses.

Revision Strategies

ommunicating an insightful idea about the arts requires revision, or stepping back and questioning what one is saying and how it is being said. Once you have a completed draft, you must again look critically at the work of art, further exploring ideas and finding meaning, then narrowing your focus and presenting main points with convincing support. This requires time, patience, a sense of curiosity, and should produce a more engaging essay.

Writers find the following revision strategies helpful with this stage of the writing process.

- Review this chapter, keeping your essay in mind. You might (1) explore your **Invention** notes, looking for helpful ideas and/or respond further in writing to relevant Invention questions; (2) review the **Rhetorical Tools, Organizational Strategies,** and **Writer's Voice** sections with an eye toward making appropriate changes; and (3) review several of the essays, noting the way the writers in this chapter approached this type of essay.

- Set aside at least as much time to revise as you took with invention and delivery.

- Create distance between you and your writing by getting away from it for a few days if possible or a few hours at least.

- Read your paper aloud to hear how it sounds or have someone else read it aloud to you.

- Print out a hard copy of your paper and read it carefully in a different place than where you wrote it.

- Figure out your writing strategy by noticing how the parts of your essay work together to support your main point. Consider making an outline of your essay to help you see this.

- Have someone else read and respond to your essay.

For ideas about **Peer Review,** see page 50.

Global Revision Questions

Invention (What have you learned by exploring your topic?)

■ **Point of Contact:** What other ideas did you consider writing about before selecting this one? Why was this idea more worth pursuing than the others?

■ **Analysis:** How has your exploration of this topic gone beyond your initial ideas and questions about it? In what ways have your ideas moved beyond your initial biases and perceptions—and beyond the common beliefs of your reader?

■ **Public Resonance:** How might your essay be relevant to, or matter to, your reader? And what might be the consequence(s) of your essay? How might the reader think or act differently?

Delivery (What writing decisions have you made as part of your writing strategy?)

■ **Rhetorical Tools:** Reexamine your rhetorical strategy for writing about a work of art. What rhetorical tools discussed earlier in this chapter have you used to help get your point across? What other ones might be helpful?

  • What is the main idea of your essay, and how have you conveyed that idea to the reader? What, besides your *intended* main idea, might the reader imagine your main idea to be? How might you make your main idea more clear to the reader?

  • Where might you provide more evidence? Or, where might a different type of evidence help the reader to better understand you? Have you used support *about* the work? And have you used support *outside* the subject—from the world of everyday life, history, pop culture, and so on? What might be the reader's likely responses to your claims and their support? How have you anticipated these responses and responded accordingly? If evaluating the work, have you used the elements of evaluation, developing criteria based on the subject's purpose and audience?

  • What information can you weed out of your essay to make it more focused? Where might the reader lose interest or get bogged down because you have retold the plot or overdescribed the work at the expense of analyzing it? What information might you delete to allow space for more relevant information?

■ **Organizational Strategies:** You might begin by looking at how much you summarize or describe the work of art compared to how much you analyze it. For example, highlight the parts of your essay that merely report: that is, where you summarize plot, describe a painting, and so on. Then identify what parts *analyze* the work by explaining how its elements function to create an artistic piece that deals with a public concern. What summary information can be deleted to make way for more of your own analysis? What summary information can be placed elsewhere to avoid giving the reader too much summary-without-purpose?

■ **Writer's Voice:** What about your writer's voice might alienate the reader? For example, have you praised the work without providing sound evidence for your claims about it? What about your writer's voice is inviting to the reader? For example, have you projected a sense of wonder? What changes might make your writer's voice more inviting?

CONSIDERING CONSEQUENCES

What you say about an individual work of art or a body of work can change how people think and how they live. Helping people to better understand a particular work of art, a body of work, or art in general can provide them with a valuable new way of thinking. Written works about art can also influence the field of art itself. Consider these questions:

- Will the reader better understand the issue about which you wrote?
- Is the reader likely to think or behave differently?
- What might be the benefits to others? How might others be harmed?
- Who besides your instructor might benefit from your ideas?
- How might what you wrote about be affected?
- What might be the effect of these consequences on you, the writer?

Activities

The Consequences of Your Essay

1. List as many individuals as you can imagine whose thinking and/or actions might change if they were to read the essay you wrote for this chapter. For each individual you list, name the possible change in his or her thinking and/or action. (As you consider consequences upon your reader, consider the "ripple effect" of those consequences. If your reader thinks or behaves differently, what is the impact of that thinking or behavior on others?)

2. Write down answers for each of the bulleted questions above. Then ask several people to read your essay and answer the bulleted questions. How were your answers similar to or different from theirs? In what ways, if any, did their answers make you think differently about the consequences of your essay?

3. List three other forms of delivery that you might have used to express your idea (report, letter, poster, screenplay, Web site, speech, song, poem, action). How might the consequences of your message have been different if delivered by way of these other forms?

4. Using your ideas from 1–3 above, write an essay about the potential consequences of your essay.

The Consequences of the Chapter Readings

1. Which of the chapter readings did you find to be most interesting and why? How did the reading encourage you to think differently? What specific part(s) of the reading affected you the most?

2. How might *you* think and/or behave differently because of one of the readings? And, how might *others* benefit, or be harmed, by your new way of thinking and/or acting?

3. How might someone you know think or act differently after reading one of the essays in this chapter?

4. How might *the writers* in this chapter be influenced by what they write? How might they think or act differently? How might they be treated differently by others?

The Consequences of Exploring Art in Everyday Life

1. How has some written or spoken exploration or discussion of art or the arts influenced you? How do you think and/or act differently as a result?

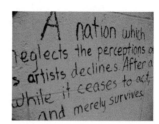

2. How has some artistic expression—whether a painting, book, CD, performance, or something else—made you think differently? How has some artistic expression made you behave differently?

3. Regarding #2 above, what has been the consequence for others of your different way of thinking or acting? How might others benefit or be harmed?

4. How might some particular artistic expression—painting, poster, novel, CD—be harmful or helpful to others? How might it appear harmful but actually be helpful? Or, how might it appear to be helpful but actually be harmful?

Considering Images

1. Find an image that comments on the value of the arts. What effect might the image have on those who view it? How might the viewer consider the arts differently after having seen the image?

2. Share the image you found for #1 above with several people, asking them how they think it might affect those who view it. Then write an essay explaining the potential consequences of the image. Might it help or harm others? Would its effects be intended or accidental?

3. What one work of art has been influential in many people's lives? Interview a variety of people, asking them to name works of art that have been important to them. Record their responses, and then in writing, explain how one such work has been influential in making many people think or act differently.

Writing, Speech, and Action

EVERYDAY RHETORIC

writing, speech, and action

write a letter
give a speech

discuss

create
a work
of art!

take action

(see chapter 13)

Exploring Visual Rhetoric

It can be argued that images, too, use rhetoric. And by looking at how images "work," we can apply some of the important concepts of rhetoric, not just to writing and speaking, but to images as well. Looking at visual rhetoric can also help us to better understand how rhetoric is used in writing and speech.

Consider This Chapter's Opening Image: Describe the rhetoric of this chapter's opening image—a man with tattoos. Use the "Analyzing an Image" questions in Chapter 13, on page 694 to help you figure out how the image conveys an idea.

A. Discuss your analysis of this chapter's opening image with several people, exploring how your understanding of the image is similar to or different from theirs. Following the discussion, write down the main similarities and differences in your viewpoints, and then explain how your ideas about the image developed or changed because of the discussion. What did you learn, or how did you come to think differently about the image because of the discussion?

B. Consider the public resonance of the opening image as it relates to art. What public concern does it speak to? To whom might this concern matter? How might people benefit by exploring the photograph's possible meanings?

Find an Image That Relates to Your Essay: What image might you use in conjunction with the essay you wrote for this chapter?

A. Write a caption for the image.

B. Write an essay explaining the relationship between the image and your text. Consider the following questions as you develop your ideas:

- How does the image support or help to explain the text of the essay?
- What does the image argue? What claim does the image make?
- What specific elements of the image convey the main idea and the support for that idea?
- How might the reader view the image differently after having read your essay?
- How might the reader be confused by the relationship of your essay and image?

C. Write an essay in which you explain how your essay might influence the way others view the image. To do research for your essay, (1) show the image to several people, and (2) ask them how they view it. (Record their responses.) Then (3) ask them to read your essay and (4) explain how they now view the image differently.

D. Describe the rhetoric of your image using the "Analyzing an Image" questions in Chapter 13, on page 694.

Consider Other Images in This Chapter: Consider how the images in this chapter encourage people to think about the arts in general, or about one art form in particular.

1. Explore the relationship, or interaction, between an image in this chapter and an essay in this chapter. Select one image and one essay and explain the relationship between the written text and the visual image. How does the image encourage the reader to think about the text, and how does the text encourage the reader to think about the image?

2. Use one of the images in this text as a point of contact for an "Exploring the Arts" essay. Instead of writing the essay, write down the essay ideas that the image invites you to consider.

   A. Share your ideas from #2 above with several people, asking them what "Exploring the Arts" ideas the image brings to mind. Add their ideas to your list, and then explain which ideas would be most worth pursuing in an essay.

   B. Using the "Analyzing an Image" questions on page 694, explain how the particular elements of the image you selected for #2 encourage the viewer to participate in the creation of ideas.

Exploring Visual Art in Your World: Notice images throughout the course of the day, looking for ones that encourage people to participate in the creation of ideas. Select a few of the images that interest you the most and answer the following questions for each: How does the image encourage people to participate in the creation of ideas? How does the image encourage people to think and/or act differently?

Art Exhibits: Visit an art museum, gallery, or exhibit, and pay careful attention to which works engage you the most. Which work of art do you spend the most time looking at and why? Which work do you spend the most time thinking about and why? Which work do you return to, or do you find yourself thinking about later in the day? In writing, explain why you find one particular work of art to be engaging.

Art in the Media: Find four images in the popular media—newspaper, magazines, television, and so on—that you consider to be art. In writing, explain how each image encourages you to think. That is, how do the work of art and your mind interact to create ideas?

Art in the Street: Find two works of art in the street (or at the mall, on campus, and so on). One of the works should be a work that was intended to be art, and the other work should not have been intended as art. (We might call the second work "found art.") In writing, explain how each work (intended and found) helps people to either imagine other worlds or make sense of their own.

Art on Doors: Make a study of professors' doors. Are some of them works of art created by various smaller works of art? How does the context (a professor's door) affect the meaning of the works on the door? In writing, explore one particular professor's door, or explore the genre of professors' doors.

Create a Work of Art: Create your own work of art out of everyday materials. Then in writing, explain how the work encourages the viewer to participate in the creation of ideas. Among other things, you might explain how the nature of the "found" materials affects the relationship between the work of art and the person viewing it. You might also consider how what you did with the found materials changes their relationship to the public (the viewer). And you might explain how you, the artist, experienced new ideas as a result of this creative process.

Words are everyday materials. The ones below are from the introduction to this chapter. Below the original paragraph, these words have been re-arranged to create a poem.

If reading literature is an act of discovery, then the same thing might be said about listening to music and taking in the visual arts. Art is more than entertainment. It calls on readers, listeners, or viewers to participate in the creation of ideas. Whether they are involved in novels, Shakespeare plays, folk songs, or Picasso paintings, people engaging art are inventing as they take it in: that is, they are developing thoughts, envisioning situations, seeing connections, and imagining worlds that they had not previously encountered. While the arts help us imagine other worlds, they also help us to make sense of our own. Art, in whatever form, offers something to everyday experience: maybe answers to the gnawing uncertainties of daily existence, maybe mystery and intensity in a world that seems too plain, maybe a framework for exploring people's behavior, or maybe a deeper understanding of one's place in society. Exploring and responding to the arts, then, is the process of developing and communicating ideas not simply about a story, poem, song, or painting, but about life.

a poem about art

an act of discovery
listening to music
taking in the visual arts

Shakespeare, Picasso
folk songs, paintings

imagining other worlds
to make sense of your own

gnawing uncertainties, daily existence
mystery and intensity in a world that seems plain
—too plain

Art is more than entertainment.
It calls on us to participate
          in the creation
          of ideas.

1. How can text (words on a page) be viewed visually? How can text be presented artistically?
2. Write your own poem by rearranging text from some written piece.
3. How does the poem above encourage the reader to participate in the creation of ideas?

11

Contents

- **Readings**

Thinking Radically: Re-Seeing the World

What is radical about this image? How does it change your thinking about cows, farms, people, or food?

> **"** We must therefore look in the most obscurest corners and summon up courage to shock the prejudices of our age if we want to broaden the basis of our understanding of nature. **"**

L iving in a society demands a certain degree of conformity. As individuals in a society, we conform to laws, clothing styles, hairstyles, and even culinary tastes (most Americans like french fries but not raw oysters). We also conform to ways of thinking; that is, we learn to follow intellectual conventions. This is not to say that we all think alike—not by a long shot—but we do buy into conventional modes or patterns of thought that, on the one hand, allow us to participate in shared knowledge but, on the other hand, limit intellectual possibilities.

Mainstream thought invites us to accept a particular view of reality, and with it, certain assumptions. Consider the following:

- Progress involves technological advancement.
- The past is behind us.
- People who make lots of money are successful.
- Poor people are worse off than rich people.
- We make individual choices.
- Time is constant.

Such ideas are what we might call *common sense*, in that they represent widely held, and largely unexamined, beliefs. But some people have examined and even challenged such common ideas. For example, agrarians such as Wendell Berry challenge the idea that human progress necessarily involves increased dependence on technology; several important religious figures (Jesus, Buddha, Mohammed) overturned the inherent value of monetary riches; and Albert Einstein showed the world that time is not constant but relative. We might say that such figures transcend and challenge common-sense thinking. They call into question those beliefs that rest beneath layers of intellectual practice and everyday life. They show us questions where we may have assumed solid answers.

People who transcend conventional thinking are not *radical* in the sense that they want to destroy mainstream life. (We are not talking here about anarchists, religious zealots, or political positions.) Rather, they are radical *thinkers*: they escape conventional thought patterns. While convention calls on us to think within the lines, radical thinkers work to see beyond those lines, and then communicate what ideas are possible. Their writing, then, seeks to reform conventional thinking.

Radical thinking is not necessarily a matter of topic choice; in fact, topics are not, in themselves, radical. Radical thinking involves an adventurous *approach* to a topic and offers a new way to think. For example, in 1784, Ben Franklin first put forth the idea of daylight savings time. After waking at an unusually early hour in the morning and discovering that the sun had risen, he imagined that people could change their clocks to coincide with the sunrise throughout the seasons.

History is filled with such intellectual adventurers, those who transcended norms to see relationships beyond the obvious, to find meaning outside of cultural norms, and to imagine perspectives beyond the present. For example, in 1543, Nicolaus Copernicus challenged the conventional theory that the Earth is the center of the universe. He defied church law and common sense and claimed that the Earth rotates around the sun. In the twentieth century:

- W. E. B. Dubois argued against mainstream thinking about African Americans' place in society. While most politicians, educators, and civic leaders walked a moderate line, assuming that black people in America could thrive in subservient positions, Dubois imagined that African Americans should act as leaders for national and global change.

- Psychologist Carl Jung broke away from his colleague, Sigmund Freud (and the conventional wisdom of the psychological community), to argue that human unconscious is, in part, a collective rather than an individual phenomenon.

- Georgia O'Keeffe transcended artistic conventions by focusing on the organic. While art and popular culture were increasingly transfixed on the abstract, O'Keeffe sought out the most pure and basic forms of identity in images such as flowers and landscapes.

Throughout history, many radical thinkers also changed how laws, government, and institutional policy work. People such as Thomas Jefferson, Mahatma Gandhi, Eleanor Roosevelt, Martin Luther King, Jr., and Martin Luther articulated ideas and policies that were beyond conventional thinking of their times.

In academic study and everyday life, methods often evolve because real people transcend the common sense of their fields; that is, they imagine the possibilities beyond what is assumed. The people who are able to think beyond *what is* and to conjure images of *what could be* are those who most often provide direction for improvement in the quality of daily work and daily life. As you explore this chapter, remember that all those people who have helped bring about change are those who first had to imagine a reality beyond the status quo.

11 This chapter will help you transcend conventional thought, focus on a particular topic, develop a focused thesis, and communicate your ideas in writing. The following essays will provide valuable insight to various strategies. After reading the essays, you can find a topic in one of two ways:

1. Go to the **Point of Contact** section to find a topic from your everyday life.
2. Choose one of the **Ideas for Writing** following the essays.

After finding a subject, go to the **Analysis** section to begin developing your thoughts.

READINGS

The writing in this chapter exemplifies thinking that transcends convention. The authors go beyond standard, comfortable notions about farming, corporations, the female body, and everyday life. The authors understand, and even point to, conventional thought and attempt to take the reader to a new intellectual place. At first their claims may seem shocking or even offensive. Writers such as Michael Moore, for example, may be attempting to ask questions that seem, initially, absurd. However, being shocked or offended can be a valuable intellectual experience—if the reader is ready. It is easy to dismiss claims when they collide with our prejudices, but it is often more enriching (and valuable) to transform shock into curiosity. As you read, be prepared to accept, or at least consider, a new way of thinking.

Farming and the Global Economy

Wendell Berry

Wendell Berry is a poet, essayist, novelist, and farmer. He has taught at New York University and the University of Kentucky and has published many books, including The Unsettling of America: Culture and Agriculture *(1977),* Sex, Economy, Freedom, & Community *(1993), and* Life Is a Miracle: An Essay against Modern Superstition *(2000). As you read this essay, make notes on any of Berry's ideas that are new to you and jot down your initial reactions to what he says.*

1 We have been repeatedly warned that we cannot know where we wish to go if we do not know where we have been. And so let us start by remembering a little history.

2 As late as World War II, our farms were predominantly solar powered. That is, the work was accomplished principally by human beings and horses and mules. These creatures were empowered by solar energy, which was collected, for the most part, on the farms where they worked and so was pretty cheaply available to the farmer.

3 However, American farms had not become as self-sufficient in fertility as they should have been—or many of them had not. They were still drawing, without sufficient repayment, against an account of natural fertility accumulated over thousands of years beneath the native forest trees and prairie grasses.

4 The agriculture we had at the time of World War II was nevertheless often pretty good, and it was promising. In many parts of our country we had begun to have established agricultural communities, each with its own local knowledge, memory, and tradition. Some of our farming practices had become well adapted to local conditions. The best traditional practices of the Midwest, for example, are still used by the Amish with considerable success in terms of both economy and ecology.

5 Now that the issue of sustainability has arisen so urgently, and in fact so transformingly,

we can see that the correct agricultural agenda following World War II would have been to continue and refine the already established connection between our farms and the sun and to correct, where necessary, the fertility deficit. There can be no question, now, that that is what we should have done.

6   It was, notoriously, not what we did. Instead, the adopted agenda called for a shift from the cheap, clean, and, for all practical purposes, limitless energy of the sun to the expensive, filthy, and limited energy of the fossil fuels. It called for the massive use of chemical fertilizers to offset the destruction of topsoil and the depletion of natural fertility. It called also for the displacement of nearly the entire farming population and the replacement of their labor and good farming practices by machines and toxic chemicals. This agenda has succeeded in its aims, but to the benefit of no one and nothing except the corporations that have supplied the necessary machines, fuels, and chemicals—and the corporations that have bought cheap and sold high the products that, as a result of this agenda, have been increasingly expensive for farmers to produce.

7   The farmers have not benefited—not, at least, as a class—for as a result of this agenda they have become one of the smallest and most threatened of all our minorities. Many farmers, sad to say, have subscribed to this agenda and its economic assumptions, believing that they would not be its victims. But millions, in fact, have been its victims—not farmers alone but also their supporters and dependents in our rural communities.

8   The people who benefit from this state of affairs have been at pains to convince us that the agricultural practices and policies that have almost annihilated the farming population have greatly benefited the population of food consumers. But more and more consumers are now becoming aware that our supposed abundance of cheap and healthful food is to a considerable extent illusory. They are beginning to see that the social, ecological, and even the economic costs of such "cheap food" are, in fact, great. They are beginning to see that a system of food production that is dependent on massive applications of drugs and chemicals cannot, by definition, produce "pure food." And they are beginning to see that a kind of agriculture that involves unprecedented erosion and depletion of soil, unprecedented waste of water, and unprecedented destruction of the farm population cannot by any accommodation of sense or fantasy be called "sustainable."

9   From the point of view, then, of the farmer, the ecologist, and the consumer, the need to reform our ways of farming is now both obvious and imperative. We need to adapt our farming much more sensitively to the nature of the places where the farming is done. We need to make our farming practices and our food economy subject to standards set not by the industrial system but by the health of ecosystems and of human communities.

10   The immediate difficulty in even thinking about agricultural reform is that we are rapidly running out of farmers. The tragedy of this decline is not just in its numbers; it is also in the fact that these farming people, assuming we will ever recognize our need to replace them, cannot be replaced anything like as quickly or easily as they have been dispensed with. Contrary to popular assumption, good farmers are not in any simple way part of the "labor force." Good farmers, like good musicians, must be raised to the trade.

11   The severe reduction of our farming population may signify nothing to our national government, but the members of country communities feel the significance of it—and the threat of it—every day. Eventually urban consumers will feel these things, too. Every day farmers feel the oppression of their long-standing problems: overproduction, low prices, and high costs. Farmers sell on a market that because of overproduction is characteristically depressed, and they buy their supplies on a market that is characteristically inflated—which is necessarily a recipe for failure, because farmers do

not control either market. If they will not control production and if they will not reduce their dependence on purchased supplies, then they will keep on failing.

12   The survival of farmers, then, requires two complementary efforts. The first is entirely up to the farmers, who must learn—or learn again—to farm in ways that minimize their dependence on industrial supplies. They must diversify, using both plants and animals. They must produce, on their farms, as much of the required fertility and energy as they can. So far as they can, they must replace purchased goods and services with natural health and diversity and with their own intelligence. To increase production by increasing costs, as farmers have been doing for the last half century, is not only unintelligent; it is crazy. If farmers do not wish to cooperate any longer in their own destruction, then they will have to reduce their dependence on those global economic forces that intend and approve and profit from the destruction of farmers, and they will have to increase their dependence on local nature and local intelligence.

13   The second effort involves cooperation between local farmers and local consumers. If farmers hope to exercise any control over their markets, in a time when a global economy and global transportation make it possible for the products of any region to be undersold by the products of any other region, then they will have to look to local markets. The long-broken connections between towns and cities and their surrounding landscapes will have to be restored. There is much promise and much hope in such a restoration. But farmers must understand that this requires an economics of cooperation rather than competition. They must understand also that such an economy sooner or later will require some rational means of production control.

14   If communities of farmers and consumers wish to promote a sustainable, safe, reasonably inexpensive supply of good food, then they must see that the best, the safest, and most dependable source of food for a city is not the global economy, with its extreme vulnerabilities and extravagant transportation costs, but its own surrounding countryside. It is, in every way, in the best interest of urban consumers to be surrounded by productive land, well farmed and well maintained by thriving farm families in thriving farm communities.

15   If a safe, sustainable local food economy appeals to some of us as a goal that we would like to work for, then we must be careful to recognize not only the great power of the interests arrayed against us but also our own weakness. The hope for such a food economy as we desire is represented by no political party and is spoken for by no national public officials of any consequence. Our national political leaders do not know what we are talking about, and they are without the local affections and allegiances that would permit them to learn what we are talking about.

16   But we should also understand that our predicament is not without precedent; it is approximately the same as that of the proponents of American independence at the time of the Stamp Act—and with one difference in our favor: in order to do the work that we must do, we do not need a national organization. What we must do is simple: we must shorten the distance that our food is transported so that we are eating more and more from local supplies, more and more to the benefit of local farmers, and more and more to the satisfaction of local consumers. This can be done by cooperation among small organizations: conservation groups, churches, neighborhood associations, consumer co-ops, local merchants, local independent banks, and organizations of small farmers. It also can be done by cooperation between individual producers and consumers. We should not be discouraged to find that local food economies can grow only gradually; it is better that they should grow gradually. But as they grow they will bring about a significant return of power, wealth, and health to the people.

17   One last thing at least should be obvious to us all: the whole human population of the

world cannot live on imported food. Some people somewhere are going to have to grow the food. And wherever food is grown the growing of it will raise the same two questions: How do you preserve the land in use? And how do you preserve the people who use the land?

18   The farther the food is transported, the harder it will be to answer those questions correctly. The correct answers will not come as the inevitable by-products of the aims, policies, and procedures of international trade, free or unfree. They cannot be legislated or imposed by international or national or state agencies. They can only be supplied locally, by skilled and highly motivated local farmers meeting as directly as possible the needs of informed local consumers.

Exploring Ideas

1. Based on this essay, what is Berry concerned about?

2. How is the way that you see farming different from the way that Berry sees it?

3. What does your response to the reading tell you about the way that you view the world?

4. How might you benefit by reconsidering your views of farming?

5. Based on interviews and observations, how do you think others view farming? What do they think is important, and how are their views similar to or different from Berry's and your own?

6. Explain why you think Berry's ideas are or are not a good example of thinking radically.

Writing Strategies

1. Describe Berry's opening strategy. How does his introduction lead the reader into the body of his essay?

2. Make an outline of Berry's essay, dividing it into several major sections. Describe Berry's organizational strategy.

3. Describe Berry's voice as a writer and identify several passages to support your description.

4. How does Berry express the public resonance of his ideas? That is, how does he relate his ideas to the reader?

Ideas for Writing

1. What other idea is "represented by no political party and is spoken for by no national public officials of any consequence"?

2. What major problem has a simple solution?

> If responding to one of these ideas, go to the **Analysis** section of this chapter to begin developing ideas for your essay.

Why Doesn't GM Sell Crack?

Michael Moore

Michael Moore is a filmmaker (Bowling for Columbine; Roger & Me; Pets or Meat: The Return to Flint; Canadian Bacon; The Big One) *and author. His books include* Downsize This! *(1996) and* Stupid White Men: And Other Sorry Excuses for the State of the Nation *(2002). Based on this essay, what does Moore think is valuable? What is he trying to accomplish with this essay?*

1   People in the business world like to say, "Profit is supreme." They like chanting that. "Profit is king." That's another one they like to repeat. They don't like to say, "I'll pick up the check." That means less profit. Profit is what it's all about. When they say "the bottom line," they mean their *profit*. They like that bottom line to contain a number followed by a lot of zeroes.

2   If I had a nickel for every time I heard some guy in a suit tell me that "a company must do whatever is necessary to create the biggest profit possible," I would have a very big bottom line right now. Here's another popular mantra: "The responsibility of the CEO is to make his shareholders as much money as he can."

3   Are you enjoying this lesson in capitalism? I get it every time I fly on a plane. The bottom-line feeders have all seen *Roger & Me*, yet they often mistake the fuselage of a DC-9 for the Oxford Debating Society. So I have to sit through lectures ad nauseam about the beauties of our free market system. Today the guy in the seat next to me is the owner of an American company that makes office supplies—in Taiwan. I ask the executive, "How much is 'enough'?"

4   "Enough what?" he replies.

5   "How much is 'enough' profit?"

6   He laughs and says, "There's no such thing as 'enough'!"

7   "So, General Motors made nearly $7 billion in profit last year—but they could make $7.*1* billion by closing a factory in Parma, Ohio, and moving it to Mexico—that would be okay?"

8   "Not only okay," he responds, "it is their duty to close that plant and make the extra $.1 billion."

9   "Even if it destroys Parma, Ohio? Why can't $7 billion be enough and spare the community? Why ruin thousands of families for the sake of $.*1* billion? Do you think this is *moral*?"

10   "Moral?" he asks, as if this is the first time he's heard that word since First Communion class. "This is not an issue of morality. It is purely a matter of economics. A company must be able to do whatever it wants to make a profit." Then he leans over as if to make a revelation I've never heard before.

11   "Profit, you know, is supreme."

12   So here's what I don't understand: if profit is supreme, why doesn't a company like General Motors sell crack? Crack is a *very* profitable commodity. For every pound of cocaine that is transformed into crack, a dealer stands to make a profit of $45,000. The dealer profit on a two-thousand-pound car is less than $2,000. Crack is also safer to use than automobiles. Each year, 40,000 people die in car accidents. Crack, on the other hand, kills only a few hundred people a year. And it doesn't pollute.

13   So why doesn't GM sell crack? If profit is supreme, why not sell crack?

14   GM doesn't sell crack because it is illegal. Why is it illegal? Because we, as a society, have determined that crack destroys people's lives. It ruins entire communities. It tears apart the very backbone of our country. That's why we wouldn't let a company like GM sell it, no matter what kind of profit they could make.

15   If we wouldn't let GM sell crack because it destroys our communities, then why do we let them close factories? *That, too*, destroys our communities.

16   As my frequent-flier friend would say, "We can't prevent them from closing factories be-

cause they have a right to do whatever they want to in order to make a profit."

17   No, they don't. They don't have a "right" to do a lot of things: sell child pornography, manufacture chemical weapons, or create hazardous products that could conceivably make them a profit. We can enact laws to prevent companies from doing anything to hurt us.

18   And downsizing is one of those things that is hurting us. I'm not talking about legitimate layoffs, when a company is losing money and simply doesn't have the cash reserves to pay its workers. I'm talking about companies like GM, AT&T, and GE, which fire people at a time when the company is making record profits in the billions of dollars. Executives who do this are not scorned, picketed, or arrested—they are hailed as heroes! They make the covers of *Fortune* and *Forbes*. They lecture at the Harvard Business School about their success. They throw big campaign fund-raisers and sit next to the President of the United States. They are the Masters of the Universe simply because they make huge profits regardless of the consequences to our society.

19   Are we insane or what? Why do we allow this to happen? It is *wrong* to make money off people's labor and then fire them after you've made it. It is *immoral* for a CEO to make millions of dollars when he has just destroyed the livelihood of 40,000 families. And it's just plain *nuts* to allow American companies to move factories overseas at the expense of our own people.

20   When a company fires thousands of people, what happens to the community? Crime goes up, suicide goes up, drug abuse, alcoholism, spousal abuse, divorce—everything bad spirals dangerously upward. The same thing happens with crack. Only crack is illegal, and downsizing is not. If there was a crack house in your neighborhood, what would you do? You would try to get rid of it!

21   I think it's time we applied the same attitudes we have about crack to corporate downsizing. It's simple: if it hurts our citizens, it should be illegal. We live in a democracy. We enact laws based on what we believe is right and wrong. Murder? Wrong, so we pass a law making it illegal. Burglary? Wrong, and we attempt to prosecute those who commit it. Two really big hairy guys from Gingrich's office pummel me after they read this book? Five to ten in Sing Sing.

22   As a society, we have a right to protect ourselves from harm. As a democracy, we have a responsibility to legislate measures to protect us from harm.

23   Here's what I think we should do to protect ourselves:

1. Prohibit corporations from closing a profitable factory or business and moving it overseas. If they close a business and move it within the U.S., they must pay reparations to the community they are leaving behind. We've passed divorce laws that say that if a woman works hard to put her husband through school, and he later decides to leave her after he has become successful, he has a responsibility to compensate her for her sacrifices that allowed him to go on to acquire his wealth. The "marriage" between a company and a community should be no different. If a corporation packs up and leaves, it should have some serious alimony to pay.

2. Prohibit companies from pitting one state or city against another. We are all Americans. It is no victory for our society when one town wins at another's expense. Texas should not be able to raid Massachusetts for jobs. It is debilitating and, frankly, legal extortion.

3. Institute a 100 percent tax on any profits gained by shareholders when the company's stock goes up due to an announcement of firings. No one should be allowed to profit from such bad news.

4. Prohibit executives' salaries from being more than thirty times greater than an average employee's pay. When workers have to take a wage cut because of hard times, so, too, should the CEO. If a CEO fires a large number of employees, it should be illegal for him to collect a bonus that year.

5. Require boards of directors of publicly owned corporations to have representation from both workers and consumers. A company will run better if it has to listen to the people who have to build and/or use the products the company makes.

24   For those of you free-marketers who disagree with these modest suggestions and may end up on a plane sitting next to me, screaming, "You can't tell a business how it can operate!"—I have this to say: Oh, yes, we can! We legally require companies to build safe products, to ensure safe workplaces, to pay employees a minimum wage, to contribute to their Social Security, and to follow a host of other rules that we, as a society, have deemed necessary for our well-being. And we can legally require each of the steps I've outlined above.

25   GM can't sell crack. Soon, I predict, they and other companies will not be able to sell us out. Just keep firing more workers, my friends, and see what happens.

Exploring Ideas

1. What change does Moore call for?

2. How does Moore encourage the reader to think about capitalism?

3. Summarize Moore's essay in a paragraph or two, and then discuss your understanding of his essay with several classmates. How is your understanding of his essay similar to or different from your classmates'?

4. Interview a variety of people of different ages and professions to find out what they think about Moore's ideas. How are their views similar to or different from Moore's? Write down the differing viewpoints that you think are most interesting or most convincing.

5. With classmates, discuss the differing viewpoints you discovered for #4. Select two or three of the strongest arguments against what Moore says and develop a response strategy. What evidence, for example, can you provide to help support Moore's argument?

Writing Strategies

1. Describe Moore's voice and how it is or is not effective in this essay.

2. Summarize Moore's argument. Show how he gets from closing factories to selling crack, and how he makes his point in doing so.

3. Whether you agree or disagree with Moore, look for gaps in his argument. That is, how would someone who disagrees with him argue against his reasoning? Where might his argument be most vulnerable?

4. Identify what you consider to be several of Moore's most interesting points. How does he support them? Why do you think these points are interesting?

5. Evaluate Moore's introduction and conclusion. Are they effective? Why or why not?

Ideas for Writing

1. Write an editorial for your college paper titled "Why Doesn't [Your College's Name Here] Sell Crack?" Use Moore's reasoning, or reasoning similar to Moore's, to make your point. (Change the title of your editorial as you see fit.)

2. What generally accepted practice is clearly inappropriate?

If responding to one of these ideas, go to the Analysis section of this chapter to begin developing ideas for your essay.

The Menstrual Cycle

Christiane Northrup, M.D.

Christiane Northrup is a physician, surgeon, speaker, and writer. She writes a monthly newsletter (Health Wisdom for Women) *and maintains a Web site (www.drnorthrup.com) that provides information and support regarding women's health issues. "The Menstrual Cycle" appears as the first part of one chapter in her book* Women's Bodies, Women's Wisdom *(1998). As you read, take notes on how Northrup views the menstrual cycle. Identify any sentences or larger passages that encourage you to think differently.*

How might it have been different for you if, on your first menstrual day, your mother had given you a bouquet of flowers and taken you to lunch, and then the two of you had gone to meet your father at the jeweler, where your ears were pierced, and your father bought you your first pair of earrings, and then you went with a few of your friends and your mother's friends to get your first lip coloring; and then you went,

> for the very first time,
> to the Women's lodge,
> to learn
> the wisdom of women?

How might your life be different?

Judith Duerk, *Circle of Stones*

1   We can reclaim the wisdom of the menstrual cycle by tuning in to our cyclic nature and celebrating it as a source of our female power. The ebb and flow of dreams, creativity, and hormones associated with different parts of the cycle offer us a profound opportunity to deepen our connection with our inner knowing. This is a gradual process for most women, one that involves unearthing our personal history and then, day by day, thinking differently about our cycles and living with them in a new way.

Our Cyclical Nature

2   The menstrual cycle is the most basic, earthy cycle we have. Our blood is our connection to the archetypal feminine. The macrocosmic cycles of nature, such as the ebb and flow of the tides and the changes of the seasons, are reflected on a smaller scale in the menstrual cycle of the individual female body. The monthly ripening of an egg and subsequent pregnancy or release of menstrual blood mirrors the process of creation as it occurs not only in nature, unconsciously, but in human endeavor. In many cultures, the menstrual cycle has been viewed as sacred.

3   Even in modern society, where we are cut off from the rhythms of nature, the cycle of ovulation is influenced by the moon. Studies have shown that peak rates of conception and probably ovulation appear to occur at the full moon or the day before. During the new moon, ovulation and conception rates are decreased overall, and an increased number of women start their menstrual bleeding. Scientific research has documented that the moon rules the flow of fluids (ocean tides as well as individual body fluids) and affects the unconscious mind and dreams.[1] The timing of the menstrual cycle, the fertility cycle, and labor also follows the moon-dominated tides of the ocean. Environmental cues such as light, the moon, and the tides play a documented role in regulating women's menstrual cycles and fertility. In one study of nearly two thousand women with irregular menstrual cycles, more than half of the subjects achieved regular menstrual cycles of twenty-nine days' length by sleeping with a light on near their beds during the three days around ovulation.[2]

4   The menstrual cycle governs the flow not only of fluids but of information and creativity. We receive and process information differently at different times in our cycles. I like to describe

menstrual cycle wisdom this way: From the onset of menstruation until ovulation, we're ripening an egg and—symbolically, at least—preparing to give birth to someone else, a role that society honors. Many women find that they are at their peak of expression in the outer world from the onset of their menstrual cycle until ovulation. Their energy is outgoing and upbeat. They are filled with enthusiasm and new ideas. At midcycle, we are naturally more receptive to others and to new ideas—more "fertile." Sexual desire also peaks for many women at midcycle, and our bodies secrete into the air hormones that have been associated with sexual attractiveness to others.[3] (Our male-dominated society values this very highly, and we internalize it as a "good" stage of our cycle.) One patient, a waitress who works in a diner where many truckers stop to eat, has reported to me that her tips are highest at midcycle, around ovulation. Another man described his wife as "very vital and electric" during this time of her cycle.

The Follicular and Luteal Phases

5   The menstrual cycle itself mirrors how consciousness becomes matter and how thought creates reality. On the strictly physical level, during the time between menses and ovulation (known as the follicular phase) an egg grows and develops, while deep within the wall of the uterus circular collections of immune system cells, known as lymphoid aggregates, also begin to develop.[4] On the expanded level of ideas and creativity, this first half of the cycle is a very good time to initiate new projects. A researcher friend of mine tells me that she has the most energy to act on ideas for new experiments during this part of her cycle. Ovulation, which occurs at midcycle, is accompanied by an abrupt rise in the neuropeptides FSH (follicle-stimulating hormone) and LH (luteinizing hormone). The rise in estrogen levels that accompanies this has been associated with a rise in left-hemisphere activity (verbal fluency) and a decline in right-hemisphere activity (visual-spatial ability, such as the ability to draw a cube or read a map).[5] Ovulation repre-

sents mental and emotional creativity at its peak; the FSH-LH surge that accompanies ovulation may be the biological basis for this. The weeks following ovulation lead up to the menses; this is evaluative and reflective time, looking back upon what is created and on the negative or difficult aspects of our lives that need to be changed or adjusted. My researcher friend notes that during this part of her cycle, she prefers to do routine tasks that do not require much input from others or expansive thought on her part.

6   Our creative biological and psychological cycle parallels the phases of the moon; recent research has found that the immune system of the reproductive tract is cyclic as well, reaching its peak at ovulation, and then beginning to wane. From ancient times, some cultures have referred to women having their menstrual periods as being "on their moon." When women live together in natural settings, their ovulations tend to occur at the time of the full moon, with menses and self-reflection at the dark of the moon. Scientific evidence suggests that biological cycles as well as dreams and emotional rhythms are keyed into the moon and tides as well as the planets. Specifically, the moon and tides interact with the electro-magnetic fields of our bodies, subsequently affecting our internal physiological processes. The moon itself has a period when it is covered with darkness, and then slowly, beginning at the time of the new moon, it becomes visible to us again, gradually waxing to fullness. Women, too, go through a period of darkness each month, when the life-force may seem to disappear for a while (premenstrual and menstrual phases).[6] We need not be afraid or think we are sick if our energies and moods naturally ebb for a few days each month. In many parts of India, it's perfectly acceptable for women to slow down during their periods and rest more. I have come to see that all kinds of stress-related disease, ranging from PMS to osteoporosis, could be lessened a great deal if we simply followed our body's wisdom once per month. Demetra George writes that it is here, at the dark of the moon, that "life

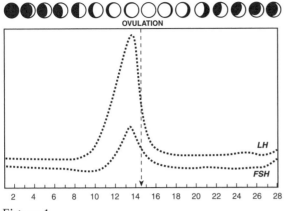

Figure 1

cleanses, revitalizes, and transforms itself in its evolutionary development, spiraling toward attunement with its essential nature."[7] Studies have shown that most women begin their menstrual periods during the dark of the moon (new moon) and begin bleeding between four and six A.M.—the darkest part of the day.[8] Many women, including me, have noticed that on the first day or two of our periods, we feel an urge to organize our homes or work spaces, cleaning out our closets—and our lives. Our natural biological cleansing is accompanied by a psychological cleansing as well.

7   If we do not become biologically pregnant at ovulation, we move into the second half of the cycle, the luteal phase—ovulation through the onset of menstruation. During this phase, we quite naturally retreat from outward activity to a more reflective mode. During the luteal phase we turn more inward, preparing *to develop or give birth to something that comes from deep within ourselves.* Society is not nearly as keen on this as it is on the follicular phase. Thus we judge our premenstrual energy, emotions, and inward mood as "bad" and "unproductive." (See Figures 1 and 2.)

8   Since our culture generally appreciates only what we can understand rationally, many women tend to block at every opportunity the flow of unconscious "lunar" information that comes to them premenstrually or during their menstrual cycle. Lunar information is reflective and intuitive. It comes to us in our dreams, our emotions, and our hungers. It comes under cover of darkness. When we routinely block the information that is coming to us in the second half of our menstrual cycles, it has no choice but to come back as PMS or menopausal madness, in the same way that our other feelings and bodily symptoms, if ignored, often result in illness.[9]

9   The luteal phase, from ovulation until the onset of menstruation, is when women are *most in tune with their inner knowing and with what isn't working in their lives.* Studies have shown that women's dreams are more frequent and often more vivid during the premenstrual and menstrual phases of their cycles.[10] Premenstrually, the "veil" between the worlds of the seen and unseen, the conscious and the unconscious, is much thinner. We have access to parts of our often unconscious selves that are less available to us at all other times of the month. In fact, it has been shown experimentally that the right hemisphere of the brain—the part associated with intuitive knowing—becomes more active premenstrually, while the left hemisphere becomes less active. Interestingly enough, communication between the two hemispheres may be increased as well.[11] The premenstrual phase is therefore a time when we have greater access to our magic—our ability to recognize and transform the more difficult and painful areas of our lives. Premenstrually, we are quite naturally more in tune with what is most meaningful in our lives. We're more apt to cry—but our tears are always related to something that holds meaning for us. The many studies of Dr. Katerina Dalton have documented that women are more emotional premenstrually, more apt to act out their anger, and more prone to headaches and fatigue, and they may even experience exacerbations of ongoing illnesses such as arthritis. To the extent that we are out of touch with the hidden parts of ourselves, we will suffer premenstrually. Years of personal and clinical experience have taught me that the painful or uncomfortable

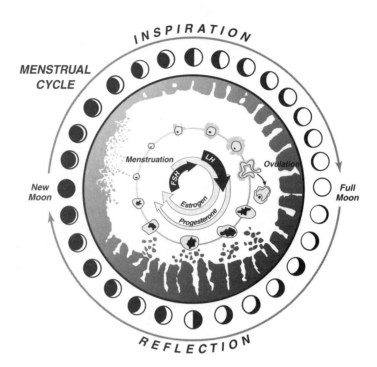

Figure 2

issues that arise premenstrually are always real and must be addressed.

10   Women need to believe in the importance of the issues that come up premenstrually. Even though our bodies and minds may not express these issues and concerns as they would in the first part of our cycle—on our so-called good days—our inner wisdom is clearly asking for our attention. One woman told me, for example, that whenever she becomes premenstrual, she worries that the house, car, and investments are in her husband's name only. When she mentions this to her husband, he replies, "What's wrong? Don't you trust me?" I'd call that a premenstrual reality check that needs attention! One husband reported that in the follicular phase of his wife's cycle, she was great, was always cheery, kept the house in order, and did the cooking. But after ovulation she "let herself go" and talked about wanting to go back to college and get out of the house more. I told him that these issues that arise premenstrually should be treated seriously, and I asked him to consider what his wife's needs were for her full personal development. I pointed out that her difficult behavior premenstrually was her way of expressing those needs.

11   There is an intimate relationship between a woman's psyche and her ovarian function throughout the menstrual cycle. Before we ovulate we are outgoing and upbeat, while ovulating we are very receptive to others, and after ovulation (premenstrually) we are more inward and reflective. An astounding study done in the 1930s supports my observations. The psychoanalyst Dr. Therese Benedek studied the psychotherapy records of a group of patients, while her colleague Dr. Boris Rubenstein studied the ovarian hormonal cycles of the same women. By looking at a woman's emotional content, Dr. Benedek was able to predict where she was in her menstrual cycle with incredible accuracy. The authors wrote, "We were pleased and surprised to find an exact correspondence of the

ovulative dates as independently determined by the two methods"–that is, psychoanalytic material compared with physiological findings. They found that before ovulation, when estrogen levels were at their highest, women's emotions and behavior were directed toward the outer world. During ovulation, however, women were more relaxed and content and quite receptive to being cared for and loved by others. During the post-ovulatory and premenstrual phase, when progesterone is at its highest, women were more likely to be focused on themselves and more involved in inward-directed activity. Interestingly, in women who had periods but did not ovulate, the authors saw similar cycles of emotions and behavior, except that around the time when ovulation should have occurred, these women missed not only ovulation but the accompanying emotions; that is, they were not relaxed, content, or receptive to being cared for by others.[12]

12 Given our cultural heritage and beliefs about illness in general and the menstrual cycle in particular, it is not difficult to understand how women have come to see their premenstrual phase not as a time for reflection and renewal but as a disease or a curse. In fact, the language that our culture uses regarding the uterus and ovaries has been experimentally shown to affect women's menstrual cycles. Under hypnosis, a woman who is given positive suggestions about her menstrual cycle will be much less apt to suffer from menstruation-related symptoms.[13] On the other hand, one study found that women who were led to believe that they were premenstrual when they weren't reported more adverse physical symptoms, such as water retention, cramps, and irritability, than another group who were led to believe they were not premenstrual.[14] These studies are excellent examples of how our thoughts and beliefs have the power to affect our hormones, our biochemistry, and our subsequent experience.

Healing Through Our Cycles

13 Once we begin to appreciate our menstrual cycle as part of our inner guidance system, we begin to heal both hormonally and emotionally. There is no doubt that premenstrually, many women feel more inward-directed and more connected to their personal pain and the pain of the world. Many such women are also more in touch with their own creativity and get their best ideas premenstrually, though they may not act on them until later. During the premenstrual phase, we need time to be alone, time to rest, and time away from our daily duties, but taking this time is a new idea and practice for many women. Premenstrual syndrome results when we don't honor our need to ebb and flow like the tides. This society likes action, so we often don't appreciate our need for rest and replenishment. The menstrual cycle is set up to teach us about the need for both the in-breath and the out-breath of life's processes. When we are premenstrual and feeling fragile, we need to rest and take care of ourselves for a day or two. In the Native American moon lodge, bleeding women came together for renewal and visioning and emerged afterward inspired and also inspiring to others. I think that the majority of PMS cases would disappear if every modern woman retreated from her duties for three or four days each month and had her meals brought to her by someone else.

14 I've personally found that simply and *unapologetically* stating my needs for a monthly slowdown to my husband is all that is needed. When I show respect for myself and the processes of my body, he shows respect as well, and my body responds with comfort and gratitude. Indeed, my experience of my own menstrual cycle began to change after I noticed that my most meaningful insights about myself, my life, and my writing came on the day or two just before my period. In my mid-thirties, I began to look forward to my periods, understanding them to be a sacred time that our culture didn't honor. When I am premenstrual, the things that make me feel teary are the things that are most important to me, things that I know tune me in to my power and my deepest truths. My increased sensitivity feels like a gift of insight. I don't become

angry, though if I did, I would pay attention and not chalk it up to "my stupid hormones." I like to keep track of the phases of the moon in my daily calendar to see if I'm ovulating at the full moon, the dark of the moon, or in between. When I ovulate at the full moon and menstruate at the dark of the moon, my inner reflective time is synchronized with the moon's darkness. Getting my period at the time of the full moon results in a more intense period: I am more emotionally charged than usual, and my bleeding is often heavier than normal. I've found that sometimes simply intending to bleed at the dark of the moon tends to move my cycles in this direction, though not always. (I don't "try" to control this.) Noting my individual cycle in relationship to the moon's cycle consciously connects me with the earth and helps me to feel connected with women past and present.

Notes

1. E. Hartman, "Dreaming Sleep (The D State) and the Menstrual Cycle," *Journal of Nervous and Mental Disease,* vol. 143 (1966), pp. 406–16; E. M. Swanson and D. Foulkes, "Dream Content and the Menstrual Cycle," *Journal of Nervous and Mental Disease,* vol. 145, no. 5 (1968): 358–63.
2. F. A. Brown, "The Clocks: Timing Biological Rhythms," *American Scientist,* vol. 60 (1972): pp. 756–66; M. Gauguelin, "Wrangle Continues over Pseudo-scientific Nature of Astrology," *New Scientist,* Feb. 25, 1978; W. Menaker, "Lunar Periodicity in Human Reproduction: A Likely Unit of Biological Time," *American Journal of Obstetrics and Gynecology,* vol. 77, no. 4 (1959): 905–14; E. M. Dewan, "On the Possibility of the Perfect Rhythm Method of Birth Control by Periodic Light Stimulation," *American Journal of Obstetrics and Gynecology,* vol. 99, no. 7 (1967): 1016–19.
3. R. P. Michael, R. W. Bonsall, and P. Warner, "Human Vaginal Secretion and Volatile Fatty Acid Content," *Science,* vol. 186 (1974): 1217–19.
4. Charles Wira, "Mucosal Immunity: The Primary Interface Between the Patient and the Outside World," in "The ABCs of Immunology," course syllabus, Dartmouth Hitchcock Medical Center, September 20–21, 1996.
5. E. Hampson and D. Kimura, "Reciprocal Effects of Hormonal Fluctuations on Human Motor and Perceptual Skills," *Behavioral Neuroscience,* vol. 102 (1988): 456–59.
6. Wira, "Mucosal Immunity" (see note 4).
7. Demetra George, *Mysteries of the Dark Moon: The Healing Power of the Dark Goddess* (Harper San Fransisco, 1992): 70–71.
8. W. Menaker, "Lunar Periodicity" (see note 2).
9. Lunar data adapted from Caroline Myss.
10. Hartman, "Dreaming Sleep," and Swanson and Foulkes, "Dream Content" (see note 1).
11. M. Altemus, B. E. Wexler, and N. Boulis, "Neuropsychological Correlates of Menstrual Mood Changes," *Psychosomatic Medicine,* vol. 51 (1989): 329–36.
12. Therese Benedek and Boris Rubenstein, "Correlations Between Ovarian Activity and Psychodynamic Processes: The Ovalutory Phase," *Psychosomatic Medicine,* vol. 1, no. 2 (1939): 247–70.
13. Bernard C. Gindes, "Cultural Hypnosis of the Menstrual Cycle," *New Concepts of Hypnosis* (London: George Allen Press, 1953).
14. Diane Ruble, "Premenstrual Symptoms: A Reinterpretation," *Science,* vol. 197 (July 15, 1977): 291–92.

Exploring Ideas

1. In your own words, write down how Northrup views the menstrual cycle. How does she encourage others to view it differently?

2. How do you view the menstrual cycle, or menstruation? How is your view different from Northrup's?

3. Interview others regarding their views on the menstrual cycle. How are their views similar to or different from Northrup's and your own?

4. How might the reader benefit by reading Northrup's essay? Who is her intended audience, and what is she trying to achieve?

5. In a paragraph or two, explain why the menstrual cycle is or is not appropriate reading material and an appropriate topic of discussion in this class.

6. Discuss your responses to #5 with classmates and others. How are their views on this subject similar to or different from your own? What is the strongest evidence others offer to support their views? What is the strongest evidence you offer to support your own?

Writing Strategies

1. Who is Northrup's intended reader? That is, to whom do you think she is writing? Explain. (Consider, for example, her opening sentence.)

2. What is the public resonance of Northrup's essay? That is, how might her essay matter to others? Who might benefit from reading it—and how? How does she convey the public resonance?

3. Describe Northrup's voice and how it is or isn't appropriate to her subject matter. Provide examples to support your opinion.

4. Identify three of Northrup's strongest points. What type of evidence does she use to support them? Would the points be as strong without the evidence? Explain.

5. Northrup chooses to begin with an excerpt from Judith Duerk's *Circle of Stones*. Why? What effect does this excerpt have as an opening?

Ideas for Writing

1. Northrup says, "In my mid-thirties, I began to look forward to my periods, understanding them to be a sacred time that our culture didn't honor." What time, place, or thing do you think is sacred but not honored by our culture?

2. Northrup believes that "replacing the harmful myths about our menstrual cycles with accurate information is part of women's healing." How might accurate information—education—help to heal some other situation?

> If responding to one of these ideas, go to the **Analysis** section of this chapter to begin developing ideas for your essay.

An Apology to Future Generations

Simon Benlow

Simon Benlow, whose writing also appears in Chapters 4 and 7, is a writer and composition teacher. As you read "An Apology to Future Generations," highlight things Benlow feels should be apologized for. Also, jot down any initial reactions you have to his ideas.

In the margins of this essay, a reader's comments point to key ideas and writing strategies. As you read the essay, consider how the comments might influence your own reading and writing.

Exploring Ideas

We can't see ourselves as well as others will see us later. We say this about earlier cultures.

Apology is not enough.

Personal extravagance and luxury.

We judge previous generations while letting our own generation off the hook.

Writing Strategies

Addresses the reader directly ("you") as someone in the future.

Thesis: We owe future generations an apology, though it cannot really suffice.

(The argument = Benlow's generation is guilty of spoiling the world for the future.)

Evidence for the argument = specific examples.

Using paragraphs as separate reasons for apology.

By now, you certainly know us better than we knew ourselves. You have shaken your heads in amazement. You have, no doubt, wondered at our disregard for you. You know how opulently we lived, how we gorged ourselves daily, how we lived beyond the means of ourselves and of following generations. You know that our desires extended in every direction in time and space, that our capacity to take was monstrous, and our restraint absent. Because we lived in our time, but irreparably harmed the world for those beyond it, I offer this unsatisfactory apology:

- For believing in a world of unlimited resources. We lived as though the water, the land, and the air would perpetually support our fetish with luxury items. We demanded personal extravagances of every imaginable (and entirely unimaginable) kind. Nearly every person of every town had his or her own internal combustion engine lawn mower, leaf blower, snow blower, hedge trimmer. Nearly every home and vehicle had air conditioners. And beyond these "utilities," we had hordes of trinkets, recreational instruments, and pleasure devices that all, eventually, had to lie in waste somewhere when our fickle appetites refocused on the new faster-smoother-quicker-shinier-more-interactive-more-believable gadget. We jet-skied, water-crafted, golf-carted, dune- and moon-buggied, sports-carred, and otherwise spark-plugged ourselves into a frenzy. We became enamored with the movement of machines and the repose of our own bodies.

- For allowing ourselves to be comforted by our own story of progress. The histories of our time kept us self-righteous. We looked back at the waste and pollution of the late nineteenth century—at the dawn of the industrial age. We sighed at the crass industrialists who unknowingly set out to run the entire world on fossil fuels. We denounced the bygone twentieth-century leaders who promoted hate and genocide. But, as you

Exploring Ideas

We celebrate science yet ignore scientists who call for restraint.

Our intellectual comfort helps create extreme materialism.

We celebrate decadence. Our homes are large. Why? Are we out of control?

Capriciousness = erratic, impulsive, flighty, inconstant.

know, our crimes of utter disinterest and self-absorption compete with even the most flagrant atrocities of our past.

- For ignoring our scientists who warned repeatedly that our way of life would have dire consequences. Even though we celebrated the role of science in our culture (that is, when it served our longing for increased convenience), we managed to dismiss an entire scientific community when it insisted that our hyperconsumptive lifestyle would ultimately damage the world around us. We branded them political zealots, and conjured up a pseudo anti-mainstream conspiracy so we could complacently dismiss their findings and promote the image of an apolitical, moderate (hence reasonable) population. Once such scientists were assigned to a political agenda (on the "Left"), the masses could be comforted in ignoring their warnings.

- For casting away criticisms of our lifestyle and foreign policies. While many peoples of the world (often the most destitute) insisted that our foreign policies promoted obscene degrees of inequity, we demonized or dismissed them. We ignored the lessons from eighteenth- and nineteenth-century revolutions: that absurd degrees of opulence coexist with (or even depend upon) equally absurd degrees of poverty, and even more importantly, that flagrant inequity eventually results in bloody retaliation.

- For celebrating the most opulent and decadent figures of our time. Our most honored people were those who flaunted their own degrees of comfort and disregard. Their homes, huge monuments to themselves, stretched over acres of private land and, for the most part, sat empty. In the race to mimic the wildly successful, our middle classes, everyday working men and women, sought to build inordinately large homes—with vaulted ceilings and multiple levels. We considered it normal for two adults to occupy vast domestic quarters with numerous empty rooms for storage or show. For holidays, we increased our parade of domestic performances by stringing thousands of electric lights inside and outside of our gargantuan homes and keeping them on for countless hours and days. In short, we measured our success and celebrated our piety with costly ornamentation.

- For fawning over our children and steeping them in layers of idle comfort, while ignoring, even crudely dismissing, the lives of their children's children. We bought them rooms full of trinkets to occupy their energy, and in so doing, we taught them to treasure petty extravagances that could be easily discarded in favor of new and more sophisticated ones. But we never considered the heaping mounds of discarded, out-of-favor junk—certificates of belonging in our age. We never considered how our self-indulgence would breed a nationalistic

Writing Strategies

The first phrase (stylistic fragment?) is always short.

Voice seems formal. (This is a *formal* apology!)

Provides evidence as support: middle class sought to build large homes "with vaulted ceilings" and strung "thousands of electric lights" inside and out.

The repetition of the opening structure creates formality.

Metaphor: "certificates of belonging."

capriciousness—a total disregard for others beyond our fenced-in, manicured, up-to-date, polished existence.

- For spreading into every last corner of every last region. We sought out the most pastoral, the most "untouched" land and infiltrated with no remorse. We occupied expanses of natural (what we called "virgin") areas, and transformed them from "undeveloped" terrain into overdeveloped sprawl. And we did it with utmost speed. We saw the land change before our own eyes. We watched our cities smear themselves into outlying rural areas; we saw wetlands, woods, and river flood plains blanketed by pavement, but drove happily over them. We said nothing when our fast-food chains (large corporate entities that sold a homogenous type of ready-to-consume "food") built locations in every remote corner of the map. We felt a comfortable familiarity in encountering the same foods, the same logos, the same containers, the same glowing buildings and signs throughout our land—and the world. And it was not only the corporate entities plowing and paving into virgin terrain. The average citizens cheerily built new, and increasingly bigger, homes despite the shrinking undeveloped space. In fact, we built homes faster than we could fill them—and left old empty ones in our wake.

- For perilously ignoring the deep connections among our lifestyles, our foreign policies, our governmental regulations, the environment, and other peoples of the world.

I imagine that you are breathing the exhaust fumes of our disregard. If large metropolitan areas are still inhabitable, your citizens must certainly deal with a plague of airborne toxins (brought on by war, pollution, or both). Perhaps you wear masks. Perhaps you figured out how to purify the air. Perhaps most of your income goes to such causes. (Perhaps you cannot even imagine what it is like to assume nothing about the air . . . to *not* consider it as daily routine.) I imagine that, in your time, the environment is a daily concern, and that you know the names and effects of toxins that only our most advanced scientists understood. No doubt, you must regard even the most basic food ingredients with scrutiny. I imagine that the sun is no longer personified in children's drawings with a gentle smile and happy radiant beams, but is, instead, something to avoid at all costs. (I imagine that you cannot possibly imagine how we once "bathed" in sun rays for recreation.)

I imagine that your everyday lives are filled with the consequences of our political naivety. Perhaps, the countries that provided our laborers, those we so boldly referred to as "Third World," have by now demanded a change in the world order. Perhaps they are now capable of responding to years of exploita-

---

"We" say nothing. Who is "we"? The majority?

Benlow is pointing to the most common parts of our culture—food, homes, cars, toys.

Urban areas are probably uninhabitable.

The constant use of "we" creates public resonance—but also involves the reader in the guilt.

Metaphor

Kind of a summary of all the above?

Metaphor: "breathing the exhaust fumes of our disregard."

He's not certain of the future—but assumes it'll be rough. (Qualifying here?)

Use of description to paint a picture.

Exploring Ideas

International policies/politics figure in, too.

We are all guilty. Even those who object to the current lifestyle contribute to it, participate in it. We must be a part of our culture while at the same time resisting it.

We are a young culture. America is a country like a child, without parental control. Our parents are children. Our leaders are like children in the world. We lack discipline and foresight—as a country.

tion; perhaps they have escaped the economic imperialism of the twentieth century; or, perhaps their numbers ultimately afforded them the ability to resist their tyrants—who served them up as objects to our "globally minded" leaders. Or perhaps our greed for oil became so great that we no longer concealed our desire to control entire regions of the world. Perhaps, the hidden global tensions of the late twentieth and early twenty-first centuries came to full realization, and you are living in the aftermath.

Every age has its dissonant voices. But as it shrinks into the past, its internal tensions and dissonant voices fade, and the telescopic lens of history sees it as a unity. And certainly, this fate will befall our time. The material conditions created by our time will frame us all as guilty, as complicit in the deterioration of a socially and environmentally uninhabitable world. And this is no defense of our dissonant voices—those who tried to warn us. They too enjoyed our opulence. As a collective mass of consumers, we all created the conditions that you presently endure—whatever they may be.

Although it is probably impossible, I hope you do not look back and characterize us as purely self-serving and wicked, but as trapped in our own enterprise. We were a young culture with no parents. In fact, we stumbled over ourselves to appear perpetually immature and restless. We packaged restlessness, and sold it in the form of hair dyes, fake breasts, and sexual stimulants. Like a mass of delirious adolescents, we made ourselves increasingly giddy, posing for ourselves and for one another, posing in every aspect of our lives: our homes, travel, clothes, food, water, and vacations. It was a mammoth parade of teenage delirium that began in New York, wormed through every tiny town of the Midwest, and wrapped around itself in dizzying perpetual circles on the beaches of California. As it came through every town, no one could resist it. It banged and clamored and woke everyone from dreamy isolation, and so even the most ascetic types found themselves playing along in some small way.

We grew outward and consumed everything because we told ourselves that we could, because our parents said we could, and because their parents said we should. Relentless growth was part of our mythology. It was hard-wired into our daily lives and our nightly dreams. Perhaps it was our conflated notion of private property that eclipsed our potential concern for those outside our fences or beyond our calendar years. Perhaps it was our bloated pride at overcoming nature; we were utterly smitten by the idea that nature could rarely infringe on our desires to move whimsically about the world. Perhaps it was some instinctual drive to outdo others—to surpass the luxuries of past generations. Perhaps it was all of these that blurred our collective vision of the future. Had we been able to look beyond our giant, ballooned notions of

Writing Strategies

Concession: dissonant voices (such as Benlow) enjoyed opulence too.

Figurative language: "we stumbled over ourselves"

Examples supporting the argument.

"Perhaps" shows Benlow's exploration of the issue.

Very formal language—seems like a funeral.

Exploring Ideas

We are guilty,
but nice, people.

. . . we're also
ridiculous.

self, property, and progress, perhaps we would have been able to foresee something or someone out there in the distance.

Although you cannot possibly imagine it, we were, generally, an agreeable people: we knew how to celebrate, how to have a parade, how to draw a crowd, how to break seating capacity records. And if you could return to our time, I would make a dubious wager that you, too, would find it difficult to resist the lure of our lifestyle, the attraction of our conveniences. And if we had been able to imagine you as real people, even as our own distant progeny, rather than a simple euphemism ("the future"), we certainly would have acted differently. Although we probably would not have relented in our give-it-to-me-now race for more, we would have taken a solemn moment to raise a toast and drink to your hardship.

Writing Strategies

Conclusion: any
humans tempted
by our times would
be likely to go
along, too.

Exploring Ideas

1. In a paragraph or two, describe how Benlow sees contemporary American culture.

2. How is the way that you see contemporary American culture similar to or different from the way Benlow sees it?

3. Consider your initial reactions to Benlow's essay. What points did you most agree or disagree with? What ideas did you not understand?

4. Choose three or four of your reactions (#3) and explore them further. Reread sections of Benlow's essay that you didn't understand and discuss them with others. If you disagree with Benlow, try accepting his point of view. If you agree with him, explore further the issue you agree on, trying to figure out how it came to be and/or where it might lead.

5. Ask others if they feel future generations deserve an apology and what for. Record their responses and compare them to Benlow's essay. How are their views similar to or different from Benlow's and your own?

Writing Strategies

1. Evaluate Benlow's introduction. How does or doesn't it invite the reader into the essay?

2. Describe Benlow's organization by dividing his apology into several major sections. What is the purpose of each major section?

3. Describe Benlow's voice as a writer and refer to several passages to support your description.

4. If workshopping Benlow's essay, what would you tell him? What do you like most about his apology? What one suggestion would you make?

5. Discuss your workshopping ideas (#4) with several classmates. How are your ideas similar to or different from your classmates' ideas?

Ideas for Writing

1. Imagine that Benlow's essay along with one of your own will be read by future generations. What would you like to say to future generations?

2. What idea of Benlow's might you expand on?

If responding to one of these ideas, go to the Analysis section of this chapter to begin developing ideas for your essay.

Outside Reading

F ind a written text that you believe illustrates radical thinking, and make a copy or print it out. While radical thinking sometimes appears in popular or general readership publications (*Time, Newsweek,* the *New York Times,* and so on), such periodicals usually appeal to conventional thinking. You might have better luck exploring less mainstream sources, such as academic journals in art, the sciences, communication, religion, political science, and so on. To conduct an electronic search of journals and magazines, go to your library's periodical database or to InfoTrac (http://infotrac.galegroup.com/itweb/). For your library database, perform a keyword search, or for InfoTrac, go to the main search box and choose "keywords." Enter word combinations such as *radical and ideas and science, innovative and business and ideas, revolutionary and medical and health, avant-garde and physics* (or any topic combined with synonyms for *radical*). (When performing keyword searches, avoid using phrases or articles such as *a, an, the*; instead, use nouns separated by *and.*) The search results will yield lists of journal and magazine articles.

You can also search the Internet. Try the search engine Lycos.com. Like most Internet search engines, Lycos.com combines words using *and*. In the search box, try various combinations, such as those above. Unlike periodical databases, the Internet search results will contain sources that are selling products and services. Be cautious of such sites.

As you will see, writers in many disciplines write and think on the edge of conventional wisdom and, as you will probably discover, any topic can be approached radically. Writing that transcends conventional thought varies widely in tone, style, length, and strategy. As you read through this chapter, keep the text you have discovered and notice the elements and strategies the writer uses. Depending on your instructor's suggestions, do one or more of the following:

1. Notice how the writer employs various rhetorical strategies. On the hard copy or photocopy:

   • Highlight the thesis if it is stated. If the thesis is implied, write it in your own words.
   • Highlight the most radical claims.
   • Highlight any passages in which the writer attempts to bridge conventional wisdom with radical thinking.
   • Identify any counterarguments (passages in which the writer anticipates and refutes opposition) or concessions (passages in which the writer grants value to another position).

2. Write an essay that discusses the strategies employed by the writer. The following questions may be helpful.

   • In what ways does the writer transcend or challenge conventional thinking?
   • How does the writer persuade the reader to see his or her vision?
   • Who is the audience for this text?
   • How does the audience impact the kinds of things said in the argument?
   • How would you describe the writer's voice?

3. Write at least three "Exploring Ideas" questions for the text you found.

4. Write at least three "Writing Strategies" questions for the text that you found.

5. Write two "Ideas for Writing," such as the ones following the essays in this book, for the text that you found.

INVENTION

Uncertainty can be your guiding light.

—U2

For this chapter, nothing is more important than the act of invention. Like in previous chapters, the writer should attempt to discover something particularly interesting or valuable—or even bizarre. Unlike previous chapters, the ultimate goal is to escape conventional thinking and to imagine something entirely outside of common intellectual activity. The following three sections are designed to help you through this process: specifically, to discover a topic (in **Point of Contact**), develop particular points about the topic (in **Analysis**), and make it relevant to a community of readers (in **Public Resonance**). The questions in each section may not provide language that fits directly into your final written assignment. However, answering them will help generate ideas. After you work through these three sections, the **Delivery** section, which immediately follows, will help you craft your ideas into a written text.

Point of Contact
Discovering a New Idea

O n the one hand, the focus of this chapter may seem rather abstract; we are, after all, attempting to imagine new intellectual ground. On the other hand, these ideas can have their beginnings in familiar, everyday terrain. While the goal may be to extend thinking beyond familiar ideas, we can still start with everyday life. The prompts on the next two pages are designed to generate possible writing topics. Fill in the blanks with as many possibilities as you can. As you explore each category, you might imagine particular situations or people to help you start exploring ideas. But do not confine yourself to practical situations or personal experiences. Imagine the possibilities beyond your experiences. And because you are searching for a topic to explore (not a simple question to answer), you should gravitate toward ideas that provoke an exploration (rather than an easy answer). Once you have decided on a topic, proceed to the **Analysis** section to develop the argument. (Also notice the responses Benlow gives for each section, which eventually led to the essay in this chapter.)

Imagining New Connections: Part of conventional thinking involves relationships. We are taught (directly and indirectly) to see some things as inherently related and others as entirely disconnected. But radical thinkers can see connections that are not normally seen. Radical thinkers might see an important connection between economy and nature, oceans and people, or music and politics. Imagine various possibilities and fill in the blanks to the following statements:

Most people do not see the connection between _____ and _____.

Even though it is not apparent, _____ and _____ are deeply connected.

Imagining Different Possibilities: The policies and procedures of society often blind us to a vast array of alternatives. Imagining those alternatives might reveal an entirely new way to live. For example, someone might imagine something even better than democracy, or a new way to fund college, or an alternative to war. Fill in the blanks with possible ideas:

Presently, most people _____, but they could _____.

Presently, the law requires that people must _____, but the law could state _____.

The usual policy for _____ is _____, but it could be _____.

Questioning Common Sense: Part of living everyday life means participating in common practices and beliefs. But commonality does not mean something is best. Simply because most people behave in some way or believe in some ideal does not mean that it is inherently correct. (In fact, the more common something is, the more likely it is to go without critique.) Imagine possibilities for the following and fill in the blanks:

Most people in my community want _____ without examining the underlying meaning.

I have always been taught to think _____, but now see a different way.

Exploring the Past and Future: Despite our advanced technology, we are still stuck in our own present perspective, and may be entirely disconnected from the realities of the past or future. A radical vision is one that sees beyond the confines of the present. A radical thinker might imagine what the world would be like if the American Revolution had not occurred, or how work in America will be defined in 50 years. As you imagine time beyond the present, fill in the blanks for the following:

> In the past, people's perspective of _____ may have been different from our present understanding.

> In the future, people will probably understand _____ differently than we do.

Going to the Root: The very act of living in our own skin can conceal the basic meaning of our lives, but radical thinking allows us to examine what we would otherwise overlook. In fact, the term *radical* comes from the Latin *radix*, which means *root* or *source*. Radical thinking might be seen as a process of finding the root or essence. For example, someone might explore the essence of womanhood or manhood, the true meaning of growing old, or the essence of education. Fill in the blanks to the following questions:

> What is the essence of _____?

> What is the most fundamental quality of _____?

Invention Activity: Now go beyond these questions. In groups or alone, use the categories in this section to ask more questions. After generating more questions within these categories, try to create more categories, and then create several questions for each category. Do not stop generating questions until everyone participating has encountered a potential topic.

Example: Simon Benlow's Notes for Point of Contact Questions

In the future, people will probably understand pollution differently than we do. If anything, future generations will suffer from our present overindulgence in land, gasoline, lumber, water. As we use up natural resources without any regard for future generations (or even other people of the world), we are (in a way) demanding that others after us go without—and pay for the consequences of our waste. We keep building/buying bigger and bigger vehicles, and consider our actions only (only!) when gas prices go up. In other words, the general trend in buying goods is to wrap ourselves in as much luxury as our wallets allow. Future generations will certainly feel the consequences of our consumption. The world only has so much clean water, clean air, and forested land.

Analysis

Exploring Theory

To a large degree, the intellectual activity in this chapter involves *theory*—reasoning that is divorced from practical or physical particulars. When people theorize, they explore the realm of ideas and assumptions and make claims that are usually generalized. For example, when Sigmund Freud theorized about the nature of the unconscious, he was not making guesses about his own mind, but that of *the human mind*. He theorized that psychological ailments emerge from childhood crises. His

theory, like all theories, could be applied to particular situations; he could use the general notion to help cure problems within specific patients.

Everyone has theories (general accounts or concepts that inform how we receive ideas and act on the world), but theories are usually not discussed openly. They most often lie undetected in our minds. For instance, many people might have a theory about knowledge acquisition; that is, they have a general account of how people come to know things. This theory may be fairly complicated and may involve memory, experience, and language use, but rarely do people examine such theories closely and ask hard questions: *how does language acquisition relate to knowledge acquisition?* Doing theory, then, is the act of examining and developing our concepts.

As you can imagine, theorists take little for granted. They ask why apples and bowling balls fall to the ground at the same speed. They wonder why the human body needs water to survive. They ask how television works on the mind. They are not willing to accept the answers they have been given, but look around them and imagine what other answers may be possible. For example, Wendell Berry does not accept the current mainstream practices for growing food in America. He imagines an entirely different strategy, divorced from the status quo. Michael Moore can envision a business model that runs contrary to most corporate practices today. Christiane Northrup imagines that the individual human body is not a closed system—that it is open to and influenced by stellar activity. And Simon Benlow foresees the hidden consequences in the most usual and seemingly harmless behaviors of our day. Although the ideas may initially seem outrageous, once the writers begin to develop their ideas, their radical visions become entirely logical.

Group Theory: Doing theory requires a degree of intellectual play, but also some deliberate and constructive probing. With several peers (on-line or in the classroom), choose one of the following topics:

- The difference between men and women
- When a child becomes an adult
- The relationship between individual and community
- The relationship between humans and nature

In your group, each participant should explain his or her theory about the topic in one minute—or one paragraph if using e-mail. After each participant has a turn, start again: everyone should take another turn and build upon or speak back to particular points made in the previous round. After the second round, start again. After three rounds, each participant should write a brief paragraph explaining how the theory session changed, developed, confirmed, expanded, or highlighted his or her ideas.

Now, theorize about your topic: the strategy here is to explore freely, beyond prior assumptions or quick answers. (We suggest pondering your topic for as long as possible before coming to any conclusions. Perhaps keep a notepad with you for a day or several days, and continue to re-think your ideas. Record even the most offbeat or seemingly irrelevant notions.) The following questions may help you discover meaning or make connections.

- What is the basic or essential quality of the topic?
- How does the topic affect or influence thinking?
- How does conventional thought or practice keep people from a radical perspective on this topic?
- What is the origin of the topic?
- What do people normally not consider about the topic?

Make certain to extend your thinking when answering these questions. In fact, you may not *answer* the questions at all, but begin a process of exploration that could continue in your writing. Imagine Linda, a business major, who has chosen to explore the *essence of business*. In a discussion with peers, she begins a true exploration of the topic:

What is the basic or essential quality of the topic?

Linda: Well, I wonder if this topic can even be thought about radically, but let's try it: I think the basic quality of business is competition.
Marcus: Competition with other people?
Linda: Yes . . . I think so. Other people or companies—or even countries.
Marcus: For that matter, what about towns and communities?
Linda: Yeah, I guess so. Towns and communities do compete for customers, for market, for tourism dollars.

Diana: So are all these people and communities competing for money?

Linda: Ultimately, yes. But at first, they are competing for more customers or clients.

Marcus: So . . . is it always about more customers? More money?

Linda: Well, I'd think so. Certainly, for retail stores, the daily goal is getting more people through the doors and to the cash register than the store across the street.

Diana: What if we looked at it like the companies are living organisms. I just saw something about bears on the Discovery Channel: every summer and fall, before hibernation, the bears try to consume as much food as possible. But they also need to conserve their strength. They don't want to exert a lot of energy while trying to eat all this food. The ultimate goal isn't the amount of food. It's survival. The bears are competing for food (like salmon), but the essence of their competing is survival.

Linda: So . . . back to business . . . companies are not necessarily competing for just money; they're competing for survival, for life.

Marcus: That makes a lot of sense. Surviving in business involves making a lot of money (more than others), but it also involves conserving. Think about it: companies that are out just to make a lot of money go down quickly because they didn't conserve.

Linda's thoughts on the essence of business are beginning to take flight. She is going beyond the quick, easy response and exploring some hidden dynamics of business. If she continues developing these ideas, she could transcend conventional wisdom and make valuable discoveries.

Overturning Conventional Wisdom: Everyday language is filled with sayings that suggest indisputable truths. They are often widely used and unexamined, and so often conceal more truth than they communicate. These sayings, sometimes called *clichés*, might even misguide our thinking. Consider the following: *What doesn't hurt you only makes you stronger. Bigger is better. Back to the basics. Boys will be boys.* Such clichés might get in the way of exploring your own topic. The following questions may help you work around conventional thinking:

- Can you think of any clichés related to your topic?
- How do they limit thinking?
- Might the opposite of the cliché be true?

Example: Simon Benlow's Response to Analysis Questions

What do people normally not consider about the topic? People do not normally consider the future because nothing in our popular culture invites us to, unless it's some silly movie inviting us to imagine a post–world war future. In general, we're not asked to consider how our present wants will influence anyone beyond ourselves. The presiding language of our culture is filled with provocations to be fulfilled, to be happy (i.e., buy lots of things and drive a new car).

Public Resonance

Connecting to Others

A topic that has public resonance taps into the concerns of many or makes a connection to public conditions or interests. In one sense, your topic may already have public resonance. Because you are theorizing (exploring more general ideas rather than particular situations), your topic may easily connect to others. However, radical thinking always runs the risk of alienating others. When a writer transcends conventional wisdom, he or she must also do the work of inviting others into the new vision, which is no small task (consider Galileo's fate!).

To some degree, writers who make radical (or new) claims are bound to the biases and prejudices of their contemporaries. They cannot simply dismiss the beliefs of others; instead, they must build an intellectual bridge between conventional thought and new thought. In a sense, this is the primary objective of the writing in this chapter. For example, in her essay, Christiane Northrup makes some radical claims about the biological processes of women's bodies, but she also acknowledges the possible gap between her understanding and more conventional views:

> The ebb and flow of dreams, creativity, and hormones associated with different parts of the [menstrual] cycle offer us a profound opportunity to deepen our connection with our inner knowing. This is a gradual process for most women, one that involves unearthing our personal history and then, day by day, thinking differently about our cycles and living with them in a new way.

In this passage Northrup hopes to illustrate a "profound opportunity" for her audience, but she also acknowledges the gradual progression toward such an understanding.

When making adventurous claims, it is especially important to make the connections so that your ideas have genuine significance and are more than spacey abstractions. Notice how Michael Moore makes a connection to his readers:

> I think it's time we applied the same attitudes we have about crack to corporate downsizing. It's simple: if it hurts our citizens, it should be illegal. We live in a democracy. We enact laws based on what we believe is right and wrong. Murder? Wrong, so we pass a law making it illegal. Burglary? Wrong, and we attempt to prosecute those who commit it.

Moore's broader point, about the injurious consequences of corporate downsizing, could be presented in rather abstract terms—and very few people would be engaged. But Moore attempts to make the issue about Americans, about people who live and work in this democracy.

Writers like Moore and Northrup (and all the other writers in this text) work to make a connection between their readers and the bigger social/political/natural world. When that connection is made, the writing gains a sense of purpose and significance. Use the following questions to help connect your ideas to your readers' concerns:

- What is conventional thought on the topic?
- What nonconventional claims have been made about the topic?
- What keeps people from understanding the thing/idea in nonconventional ways?
- How would a new understanding of the topic help people? (Who, particularly, would a new understanding help?)
- How might your particular understanding (your radical or adventurous thoughts) help people?

Example: Simon Benlow's Notes on Public Resonance Questions

What is conventional thought on the topic? The thing is . . . there is no conventional thought on this matter. People do not think about the future—in the specific and local sense. They don't imagine their lives affecting their grandchildren's world. People have been lulled into a present-tense-only mentality. Sure, most parents try to provide for their children . . . but they don't imagine how their lives (outside of creating a savings account) will affect the world that their children (and their children's children) will inhabit. In general, people in America spend most of their time thinking about their own *financial existence*, and the *future earning power* of their children. But they do not think about the air, the land, the water of the world 50 years, or 100 years, from now . . . and they don't imagine how present global politics might have consequences on the future.

Using Outside Sources:
Radical or adventurous claims do not exist in a vacuum; that is, they are often not entirely unique, but exist alongside other similar claims and discoveries. Notice Northrup's use of outside sources. She begins her writing with the words of Judith Duerk, and, later, refers to other doctors' work to illustrate points:

> An astounding study done in the 1930s supports my observations. The psychoanalyst Dr. Therese Benedek studied the psychotherapy records of a group of patients, while her colleague Dr. Boris Rubenstein studied the ovarian hormonal cycles of the same women. By looking at a woman's emotional content, Dr. Benedek was able to predict where she was in her menstrual cycle with incredible accuracy.

Northrup points to other voices not only to support her ideas, but also to imply that her own unconventional understanding of the menstrual cycle resonates with others' discoveries.

Exploring what has been said about your topic may be helpful in creating public resonance. Reading others' ideas on the topic can help to extend or complicate your initial thoughts, help to place your thoughts in a broader context, and/or help to show how your thoughts transcend convention. Finding interesting texts on your topic, however, may be challenging—especially if you are attempting to discover a novel connection. (See Chapter 12: Research and Writing for guidance in finding sources.)

Activities

1. Survey ten people (using e-mail, a class listserv, or personal interviews). Ask them their initial thoughts about your topic. Ask the same question that you used or wrote in the **Point of Contact** section, such as: *What is the relationship between nature and economy?* Write a brief summary of the responses and then explain how your peers' perceptions relate to your thoughts. The following questions may be helpful: How do the responses represent conventional or nonconventional thought? How can you make a connection between your peers' perceptions and the vision you would like to propose?

2. After your survey, write a brief summary of the responses. Do not evaluate or respond yourself. Send the summary to all the participants of your survey.

DELIVERY

> "Adventure is worthwhile in itself."
>
> —*Amelia Earhart*

When writers set out to make adventurous claims, they are bound to encounter some difficulties—and a good deal of uncertainty. Communicating radical or adventurous ideas involves a good deal of reflection and rethinking. Remember that the primary goal is to bring potential readers into your new vision, not to leave them behind. The following sections (**Rhetorical Tools, Organizational Strategies, Writer's Voice,** and **Revision Strategies**) are designed to help you build a sophisticated and engaging text—one that emerges from your particular ideas.

Rhetorical Tools

Developing your Thoughts

The primary objective for this writing is to communicate a new vision on your topic. This will take some sound explaining tactics. But you will also need to persuade your reader that your vision, your adventurous new way of thinking, is valuable, and this will take a broad range of tools.

Considering Your Thesis: Remember that a thesis provides focus for both writer and reader. For the kind of writing done in this chapter, a thesis is especially important; because the ideas are potentially abstract and far-reaching, a strong focus will keep the text from wandering. (While the goal may be to invite readers to *wonder*, a writer should keep readers from *wandering*.) However, do not be in a hurry to solidify your thesis. As you write and think, your ideas will certainly evolve.

Evolution of a Thesis	
The writer begins with a widely held understanding of her topic:	*The essence of business is money making.*
The writer develops a position different from conventional thinking:	*Like any organism, the essence of business is survival.*
The writer shapes the idea as she writes:	*Beneath the everyday affairs of making money, the essence of business is survival, which involves consuming and conserving.*

Using Narration: Narration draws readers into a set of events; a narrative or story can help writers illustrate a broader point; and when making adventurous claims, a narrative can help bridge the gap between conventional and radical ideas. You might also consider anecdotes or testimonials (brief and often personal accounts) that can be used to illustrate points. Notice Northrup's use:

> Indeed, my experience of my own menstrual cycle began to change after I noticed that my most meaningful insights about myself, my life, and my writing came on the day or two days before my period. In my mid-thirties, I began to look forward to my periods, understanding them to be sacred times that our culture didn't honor. When I am premenstrual, the things that make me feel teary are the things that are most important to me, things that I know tune me into my power and my deepest truths.

Using Description: Writers making adventurous or radical claims must consider the intellectual positions of their audience. Because readers may have no mental pictures of the ideas being put forth, it is up to the writer to sufficiently describe or characterize ideas. Notice Benlow's description, which helps the reader to see evidence of his claims:

> Nearly every person of every town had his or her own internal combustion engine lawn mower, leaf blower, snow blower, hedge trimmer. Nearly every home and vehicle had air conditioners. And beyond these "utilities," we had hordes of trinkets, recreational instruments, and pleasure devices that all, eventually, had to lie in waste somewhere when our fickle appetites refocused on the new faster-smoother-quicker-shinier-more-interactive-more-believable gadget.

Using Figurative Language: Sometimes literal description is simply insufficient to communicate the depth of an idea. That is when writers turn to figurative language, such as similes and metaphors, which help to represent complex or particularly abstract ideas. Notice Benlow's simile, which then develops into a metaphor:

> Like a mass of delirious adolescents, we made ourselves increasingly giddy, posing for ourselves and for one another, posing in every aspect of our lives: our homes, travel, clothes, food, water, and vacations. It was a mammoth parade of teenage delirium that began in New York, wormed through every tiny town of the Midwest, and wrapped around itself in dizzying perpetual circles on the beaches of California. As it came through every town, no one could resist it. It banged and clamored and woke everyone from dreamy isolation, and so even the most ascetic types found themselves playing along in some small way.

Using Definitions: Although radical thinking does not depend on dictionary definitions, writers can use definitions to communicate complex ideas. In fact, it might be said that defining and redefining terms is at the heart of radical thinking. Notice Moore's discussion of "democracy" and his application of the basic elements to his argument.

Argumentative Support: When making adventurous claims, writers must possess a broad range of support strategies.

Evidence

- **Statistics:** Information (often given numerical value) collected through experimentation, surveys, polls, and research.
- **Authorities:** References to published (most often written) sources.
- **Facts:** Agreed-upon events or truths, or conclusions drawn from investigation.
- **Examples:** Specific cases or illustrations of a phenomenon.
- **Allusion:** References to history, news events, films, television shows, science, nature, or literary texts.
- **Personal Testimonies/Anecdotes:** Individual accounts or experiences.
- **Scenarios:** Hypothetical or fictionalized accounts.

Appeals

- **Appeal to Logic:** Relates the argument to the audience's sense of reason.
- **Appeal to Emotion:** Relates the argument to the audience's emotional state or attempts to create a particular emotional state in the audience.
- **Appeal of Character:** Relates the argument to a quality of the author or speaker.
- **Appeal to Need:** Relates the argument to people's needs (spiritual, economic, physical, sexual, familial, political, etc.).
- **Appeal to Value:** Relates the argument to people's values (judgments about right and wrong, success, discipline, selflessness, moderation, honesty, chastity, modesty, self-expression, etc.).

Examine the appeals in Moore's "Why Doesn't GM Sell Crack?" Locate appeals to logic and value.

Appeal to Logic: Moore says if people really mean it when they argue that a company must do "whatever is necessary to create the biggest possible profit" then why don't they sell drugs, which make a bigger profit?

Appeal to Logic: Why is crack illegal? It harms lives. So does moving a major employer out of a community.

Appeal to Value: Says CEO salaries shouldn't be more than 30 times that of the workers and that if workers lose jobs, CEOs shouldn't prosper. The value of right and wrong, fairness, moderation.

Counterargument:
Counterarguments anticipate and refute claims or positions that oppose those being forwarded by the writer. Especially when their claims are nonconventional or challenging, writers must anticipate and account for positions outside of or opposed to their own. Because the writer has a whole set of intellectual conventions to contend with, counterargument is an important part of radical thinking. Wendell Berry, for example, uses counterargument throughout his essay:

> The people who benefit from this state of affairs have been at pains to convince us that the agricultural practices and policies that have almost annihilated the farming population have greatly benefited the population of food consumers. But more and more consumers are now becoming aware that our supposed abundance of cheap and healthful food is to a considerable extent illusory. They are beginning to see that the social, ecological, and even the economic costs of such "cheap food" are, in fact, great.

In a turnabout paragraph, Berry points to the opposing side, and then refutes the ideas—showing support for his position.

Depending on the position being taken and the kind of claims being put forth, some writers may need to counter many points. For example, we might say that Michael Moore is counterarguing throughout his essay. He is speaking directly back to the claim that corporations should be able to do whatever they deem necessary to generate profit.

Concession:
While counterarguments refute objections, concessions acknowledge the value of positions or claims other than those being forwarded by the writer. Even though a text making radical claims may not be openly argumentative, it still seeks to overturn conventional ideas. For this reason, concessions can be essential to engaging potentially apprehensive readers. Notice Benlow's concession:

> Although it is probably impossible, I hope you do not look back and characterize us as purely self-serving and wicked, but as trapped in our own enterprise. We were a young culture with no parents.

Most of Benlow's letter condemns his own generation, but he offers this small note that suggests that people were more weak than evil. Without such a concession, readers might reject Benlow's ideas as purely antagonistic.

Toulminian Analysis
(Claim, Warrant, Grounds): Stephen Toulmin's framework for analyzing arguments may be valuable for revealing the shortcomings of conventional thought. (See a more detailed explanation of Toulminian analysis on pp. 296–299.) Often the first step of revolutionary thinkers is to critique the logic of widely held beliefs. And Toulminian analysis allows writers to show previously unexamined assumptions. Notice how Moore's essay points to the basic assumptions beneath laws:

> I think it's time we applied the same attitudes we have about crack to corporate downsizing. It's simple: if it hurts our citizens, it should be illegal. We live in a democracy. We enact laws based on what we believe is right and wrong. Murder? Wrong, so we pass a law making it illegal. Burglary? Wrong, and we attempt to prosecute those who commit it. . . .
> As a society, we have a right to protect ourselves from harm. As a democracy, we have a responsibility to legislate measures to protect us from harm.

Moore's analysis reveals the assumptions (or what he calls "attitudes") beneath the laws of our society. Once he discovers that the basic motivation for enacting laws is to protect society from harm, he can apply that to corporate behavior.

Organizational Strategies

Addressing Special Concerns

How Should I Begin? The important point to remember in this chapter is that the writing must move the readers outside of their comfortable intellectual positions. The writing, in style and structure, should invite readers into a new way of thinking. In short, readers associate highly conventional writing structure with conventional thinking. So if writers want to move readers beyond conventional thinking, they might do well to explore alternative introduction strategies.

Following are some strategies for introductions. Consider an introductory strategy you would not typically use:

Anecdote: You might try a brief personal story that illustrates something significant and related to the topic.

Scenario: If you have not directly experienced something related to your topic, you can use a hypothetical or fictional situation that illustrates something significant and related to the topic.

Allusion: A reference to history, news, popular culture, or literature can create a powerful connection to your readers.

Figurative Language: A metaphor or simile that sheds new light on the topic can take the reader beyond conventional thinking.

Question: You might try an intense question, one that is impossibly difficult to answer or one that is seemingly easy to answer.

For any of these introduction strategies, remember that an opening paragraph should not only establish the tone of a text; it should also create an intellectual climate that is developed throughout the text.

> Examine the essays in this chapter and decide if or how the introductions help to invite the readers into a new way of thinking.

How Should I Make Connections to Conventional Thinking?

Conventional ideas are those you are trying to transcend or challenge. You might treat them in the same way you would in dealing with opposing arguments. In other words, you might use paragraphs to distinguish between conventional and radical ideas in the same way writers use paragraphs for counterargument (see pp. 246–249).

> Conventional thinking ¶
> New radical thinking ¶
> Conventional thinking ¶
> New radical thinking ¶

Or you might use the turnabout paragraph (see p. 257). For example, imagine Linda's topic (in the **Analysis** section), the essence of business. In making a connection to conventional thinking, she could use a paragraph that shifts to her new ideas:

> Money seems to be the thing that drives business. It seems to be the ultimate goal, the bottom line, the thing that is pursued every hour of every day. We might even say that money, itself, is the essence of business. It is, after all, the life source of every business enterprise—from the major international retail chain to the small-town Ma and Pa restaurant. **However,** money is merely the engine—the thing that sustains and develops business. It is not the essence. The essence of business is the same as the essence of a living organism: the struggle for survival. And when survival is the root of business, an exaggerated focus on money can actually put the nail in the coffin.

Notice the turnabout in the middle of the paragraph, where the direction shifts and the new way of thinking is introduced.

How Should I Conclude? Apprehensive readers might see radical claims

as irrelevant or even dangerous, and writers must be vigilant about connecting to readers. Conclusions are especially important places for making those connections, for making the claims in the text relevant and valuable to the world shared by the writer and readers. You might even say that a conclusion is where the writer uses *the most dramatic or direct means for connecting the idea to the reader*. Notice, for instance, Benlow's conclusion. Here, he offers a scenario and an image that reinforce the main idea of the essay:

> And if you could return to our time, I would make a dubious wager that you, too, would find it difficult to resist the lure of our lifestyle, the attraction of our conveniences. And if we had been able to imagine you as real people, even as our own distant progeny, rather than a simple euphemism ("the future"), we certainly would have acted differently. Although we probably would not have relented in our give-it-to-me-now race for more, we would have taken a solemn moment to raise a toast and drink to your hardship.

Examine the other conclusions of the essays in this chapter. Decide how each conclusion creates a connection to the shared world of the writer and reader.

Writer's Voice

Exploring Options

Inviting the Reader: The potential danger in this chapter is alienating the reader—creating unnecessary distance between the writer and reader. No matter how radical or challenging the ideas, a writer should attempt to bring the reader into a new vision. Even if the writer wants to overtly condemn conventional wisdom (and sometimes such a move is necessary), he or she should craft a voice that invites a reader into the ideas. Notice, too, that writers sometimes condemn ideas or actions, but are less inclined to attack people. After all, people should not necessarily be blamed because they think conventionally.

Moore, for instance, condemns conventional wisdom, but also avoids antagonizing or belittling the reader. Moore speaks to a collective *we*, presumably Americans who participate in democracy. Notice that he does not condemn people for allowing corporations to "downsize"; instead, he argues for what can be done: "Here's what I think we should do to protect ourselves."

Benlow, on the other hand, does appear to be condemning. He is, after all, pointing to the selfish acts of his generation. However, Benlow does not remove himself from blame, and even creates an alibi for him and us:

> Although it is probably impossible, I hope you do not look back and characterize us as purely self-serving and wicked, but as trapped in our own enterprise. We were a young culture with no parents.

Here, Benlow is careful not to simply scorn his generation—although he is insistent about the effects of its lifestyle.

Writers can also invite readers by making direct connections to their shared world. While Northrup makes rather adventurous claims, she also shows how her *ideas* give meaning to readers. She uses first-person plural pronouns (*we* and *us*), but also connects her *ideas* to her readers. This is apparent in the following Northrup passage:

> Given our cultural heritage and beliefs about illness in general and the menstrual cycle in particular, it is not difficult to understand how women have come to see their premenstrual phase not as a time for reflection and renewal but as a disease and a curse.

Even though Northrup's primary audience is women, men are not necessarily excluded or targeted. That is, men can easily read and engage the argument—that is, if they are willing to learn more about women's lives.

Considering Formality: While some writers tend toward a formal, sober tone, others use comedy or informality to connect with readers. While Northrup is more formal, more traditionally "academic" sounding, Moore is informal. (And his voice is probably appropriate because he traditionally does not write for an exclusively academic crowd. Instead, Moore attempts to engage large mainstream audiences.) He creates an informal tone with subtle jokes:

> If I had a nickel for every time I heard some guy in a suit tell me that "a company must do whatever is necessary to create the biggest profit possible," I would have a very big bottom line right now.

He also draws attention to his own situation:

> Two really big hairy guys from Gingrich's office pummel me after they read this book? Five to ten in Sing Sing.

And Moore addresses the audience directly (a move not usually made in more formal writing):

> For those of you free-marketers who disagree with these modest suggestions and may end up on a plane sitting next to me, screaming, "You can't tell a business how it can operate!"–I have this to say: Oh, yes, we can!

As you consider your own voice, remember to stay consistent throughout your text. If you are wondering about the degree to which you can explore levels of formality, ask your instructor about the range he or she deems appropriate.

Projecting Wonder: While writers need to create a sense of authority and credibility, they also need to project wonder or curiosity. If a writer is curious about the world, about the topic at hand, the reader will be inclined to explore with an open mind. Writers can invite exploration by suggesting possibilities–rather than forcing absolute statements or fixed answers. Notice Northrup's introduction:

> The ebb and flow of dreams, creativity, and hormones associated with different parts of the [menstrual] cycle offer us a profound opportunity to deepen our connection with our inner knowing. This is a gradual process for most women, one that involves unearthing our personal history and then, day by day, thinking differently about our cycles and living with them in a new way.

Her introduction is a call to, even a celebration of, what could be: a deeper understanding of "inner knowing." The claims themselves provide wonder and an engaging writerly presence. This is a powerful lesson for all writers: *drawing attention to the extraordinary creates interesting writing–and interesting writers!*

Revision Strategies

onveying a radical idea—one that steps outside of more conventional thinking—is likely to require serious revision. Explaining a new connection or possibility can be a challenge. The very nature of the radical subject matter means that writers must carefully consider the rhetorical moves they make; otherwise, readers may get left behind.

Consider the following revision strategies:

- Review this chapter, keeping your essay in mind. You might (1) explore your **Invention** notes, looking for helpful ideas and/or respond further in writing to relevant Invention questions; (2) review the **Rhetorical Tools, Organizational Strategies,** and **Writer's Voice** sections with an eye toward making appropriate changes; and (3) review several of the essays, noting the way the writers in this chapter approached this type of essay.

- Set aside at least as much time to revise as you took with invention and delivery.

- Create distance between you and your writing by getting away from it for a few days if possible or a few hours at least.

- Read your paper aloud to hear how it sounds or have someone else read it aloud to you.

- Print out a hard copy of your paper and read it carefully in a different place than where you wrote it.

- Figure out your writing strategy by noticing how the parts of your essay work together to support your main point. Consider making an outline of your essay to help you see this.

- Have someone else read and respond to your essay.

For help with **Peer Review,** see page 50.

Global Revision Questions

Invention (What have you learned by exploring your topic?)

- **Point of Contact:** What other ideas did you consider writing about before selecting this one? Why was this idea more worth pursuing than the others?

- **Analysis:** How has your exploration of this topic gone beyond your initial ideas and questions about it? In what ways have your ideas moved (radically) beyond your initial biases and perceptions—and beyond the common beliefs of your reader?

- **Public Resonance:** How might your essay be relevant to, or matter to, your reader? And what might be the consequence(s) of your essay? How might the reader think or act differently after reading it?

Delivery (What writing decisions have you made as part of your writing strategy?)

- **Rhetorical Tools:** Reexamine your rhetorical strategy for conveying a radical idea. What rhetorical tools discussed earlier in this chapter have you used to help get your point across? What other ones might be helpful?

  - What is the main idea of your essay, and how have you conveyed that main idea to the reader? What, besides your *intended* main idea, might the reader imagine your main idea to be? How might you help the reader to better hear what you are trying to say?

  - Where might you provide more evidence? Or where might a different type of evidence help the reader to better understand you? What might be the reader's likely responses to your claims and their support? How have you anticipated these responses and responded accordingly, making appropriate counterarguments and concessions? How have you provided background information and filled in gaps to help the reader follow along? How might your title, introduction, and conclusion provide more helpful information regarding the main point of your essay?

  - What information can you weed out of your essay to make it more focused? Where might the reader lose interest or get bogged down because you have over-explained or restated an idea?

- **Organizational Strategies:** Be sure that you understand how the structure of your essay works to help the reader understand you. How might you rearrange elements (claims; evidence; concessions; counterarguments) to allow the reader to better understand your ideas? How might you rearrange ideas within paragraphs? What ideas might be more helpful to the reader if placed earlier, or later, or near some other idea? How might connections and relationships between ideas be made more clear to the reader?

- **Writer's Voice:** Describe your writer's voice. Then explain why it is appropriate for this essay. What about your writer's voice is inviting to the reader? What about your writer's voice might alienate the reader? What changes might make your writer's voice more inviting?

■

CONSIDERING CONSEQUENCES

Questioning common sense and conventional thinking can have profound consequences. At some point, the idea of flying 500 miles an hour at 30,000 feet, driving down a highway at 65 miles an hour, or traveling on the back of a horse would have sounded absurd. A radical idea can influence government policy and thus many citizens, or it can influence the way an individual approaches an everyday issue, such as parenting, marriage, eating, health, and so on. Radical thinkers offer new ways to think, new ways to see the world in which we live, and new ways we might live in it. What might be the consequences of your essay for this chapter? That is, what effect might your ideas have on your reader's thoughts and actions? Consider these questions:

- Will the reader better understand the issue about which you wrote?
- Is the reader likely to think or behave differently?
- What might be the benefits to others? How might others be harmed?
- Who besides your instructor might benefit from your ideas?
- How might what you wrote about be affected?
- What might be the effect of these consequences on you, the writer?

Activities

The Consequences of Your Essay

1. List as many individuals as you can imagine whose thinking and/or actions might change if they were to read the essay you wrote for this chapter. For each individual you list, name the possible change in his or her thinking and/or action. (As you consider consequences upon your reader, consider the "ripple effect" of those consequences. If your reader thinks or behaves differently, what is the impact of that thinking or behavior on others?)

2. List three other forms of delivery that you might have used to express your idea (report, letter, poster, screenplay, Web site, speech, song, poem, action). How might the consequences of your message have been different if delivered by way of these other forms?

3. Discuss the possible consequences of your essay with others. Explain what your essay is about and then ask for feedback. You might ask the following questions: What impact might this essay have on the reader? How might this essay change the way someone thinks or acts? How did it make you think differently? How might it make you act differently?

4. In groups or alone, make a list of radical ideas and their consequences. Then select the one idea that you think has had the most important consequence and support your claim in a group discussion with several classmates, either on-line or in class.

The Consequences of the Chapter Readings

1. Which of the chapter readings did you find to be most interesting and why? How did the reading encourage you to think differently? What specific part(s) of the reading affected you the most?

2. How might *you* think and/or behave differently because of one of the readings? And, how might *others* benefit, or be harmed, by your new way of thinking and/or acting?

3. How might someone you know think or act differently after reading one of the essays in this chapter?

4. How might *the writers* in this chapter be influenced by what they write? How might they think or act differently? How might they be treated differently by others?

Considering Images

1. Explain how someone might view one of the images in this chapter differently after having read one of the essays in this chapter. What particular part of the written text might be most influential in changing the person's viewpoint?

2. Find an image not in this text and explain how someone might view it differently after having read one of the essays in this chapter.

3. Create an image and explain how someone might view it differently before and after reading one of the essays in this chapter.

The Consequences of Thinking Radically in Everyday Life

1. Alone or with others, write out a definition of "thinking radically." That is, what does it mean to "think radically"?

2. Read an encyclopedia article, trying to find out how a historical figure thought radically. Consider popular figures that you might like to know more about. After reading about the person, explain in writing why you think he or she thought radically.

3. Develop your definition for #1 above by providing examples of thinking radically. Refer to specific individuals who think, or have thought, radically.

4. Further explore the relationship between thought and action, ideas and matter. For example, explain how some radical thought has been manifested through action; explain how some radical idea has been manifested in the material world.

5. How has some particular instance of radical thinking benefited people? How has some particular instance of radical thinking harmed people?

6. Reconsider your response to #4 above.

Considering Images

1. Explain in writing how a particular image examines or challenges *common sense.*

2. Survey others, asking them to suggest images—photographs, paintings, and so on—that challenge common sense, or common thinking. Then, in writing, explain how one of the images does this. What way of thinking does it question and how?

EVERYDAY RHETORIC

Writing, Speech, and Action

The **Invention** and **Delivery** strategies discussed earlier in this chapter apply to other forms of communication as well. Radical ideas are conveyed through various forms of writing, speech, and action. For practice at applying this chapter's rhetorical tools and strategies to other forms, you might do one of the following activities. (For help, refer to Chapter 13.)

Write a Letter. Communicate your main idea and support in the form of a letter—either personal, business, or to the editor of a newspaper. Select a specific and appropriate individual to send your letter to. But don't merely put your essay in a letter format. Instead, revise it so that your content and style match the letter-writing situation in which the writer and reader share a somewhat different relationship than they do in an essay.

Make a Poster or Flyer. Create a poster that conveys your argument through a combination of words and images.

Give a Speech. Communicate the idea from your essay in the form of a speech to your classmates. Instead of merely reading your essay, which will bore the audience, prepare note cards and practice your delivery. Remember to provide verbal cues, use visual aids if helpful, and *present* the argument without arguing *with* or *at* your listeners.

Write (and Perform) a Skit, Poem, or Song. Artistic performances can be effective ways of communicating an idea. Of course, the idea may transform and evolve as it comes to life artistically. After performing or sharing your work of art, explain in writing how you used rhetorical tools and/or voice.

Take Action. In addition to speaking and writing, you might convey your idea by taking action. Then, in an essay, discuss the action you took and what its consequences were.

Exploring Visual Rhetoric

I t can be argued that images, too, use rhetoric. And by looking at how images "work," we can apply some of the important concepts of rhetoric, not just to writing and speaking, but to images as well. Looking at visual rhetoric can also help us to better understand how rhetoric is used in writing and speech.

Consider This Chapter's Opening Image: Describe the rhetoric of this chapter's opening image. Use the "Analyzing an Image" questions in Chapter 13 on page 694 to help you figure out how the image conveys an idea.

A. How is or isn't this chapter's opening image a good example of thinking radically?

B. What does this chapter's opening image suggest that thinking radically involves?

C. How does this chapter's opening image take on new meaning once it is combined with, or connected to, a chapter called "Thinking Radically"? How might the image communicate differently if not connected with this chapter?

D. Find another image that you think would work well as the opening image for this chapter. Write a memo, letter, or essay explaining how the image you found might encourage students to think about "Thinking Radically."

Find an Image That Relates to Your Essay: What image might you use in conjunction with the essay you wrote for this chapter?

A. Write a caption for the image.

B. Write an essay explaining the relationship between the image and your text. Consider the following questions as you develop your ideas:

- How does the image support or help to explain the text of the essay?
- What does the image argue? What claim does the image make?
- What specific elements of the image convey the main idea and the support for that idea?
- How might the reader view the image differently after having read your essay?
- How might the reader be confused by the relationship of your essay and image?

C. Write an essay in which you explain how your essay might influence the way others view the image. To do research for your essay, (1) show the image to several people, and (2) ask them how they view it. (Record their responses.) Then (3) ask them to read your essay and (4) explain how they now view the image differently.

D. Describe the rhetoric of your own photograph or image, using the "Analyzing an Image" questions on page 694.

Consider Other Images in This Chapter: Consider how the images in this chapter encourage people to think about thinking.

1. Using the "Analyzing an Image" questions on page 694, explain how key elements (such as focus, lighting, and so on) of one of the images in this chapter encourage the viewer to question common thinking.

2. Select the image from this chapter that least represents "thinking radically" to you. Then spend the next week looking at and writing about the image. Look at it several times each day, sometimes for only a few minutes, other times longer. Explore how you might be overlooking something. Imagine how the image might, in fact, be about "thinking radically." After one week, write an essay explaining how your ideas about the image changed.

3. Assign a classmate an image from this chapter, and have him or her do #2 above with it.

4. In groups, explore the image on page 555. How does the image relate to the nearby text? For example, what does it have to do with "the realm of ideas and assumptions" and what claim, if any, might it be making?

Thinking Radically in the World:
Review this chapter's introduction on pages 530–531, and then alone or with others, collect images that encourage radical ways of thinking. Find images from a variety of sources at school, work, and home, in the popular media, and on the street. Physically gather up the images as best you can in a folder so that you can study them and draw conclusions later.

1. Based on the images you have collected, who encourages thinking radically and who doesn't? For example, do images produced by the government, corporate America, local artists, or your college encourage radical thinking? Analyze the images you've collected and, in writing, explain who encourages or discourages radical thinking.

2. Based on the images you've collected, what type of radical thinking is encouraged? That is, what views are called into question, and what alternate ways of thinking are encouraged? Provide specific examples from the images you've collected to illustrate your ideas.

3. Based on the images you've collected, how are images used to encourage radical thinking? What elements of the image (content, composition, lighting, and so on) are most important, and how do these elements encourage the viewer to think differently?

4. Make a radical thinking collage or mobile. Admittedly, it's a flashback to junior high, but take the images you've collected and create a collage or a mobile. Then, in writing, explain how your collage or mobile encourages people to think.

Create a Visual Essay:
Combine 3–8 images into a visual essay that challenges common thinking. Use images that themselves are quite common—images that taken by themselves do not challenge common thinking—and make the relationship of the images be what creates the challenge to thinking.

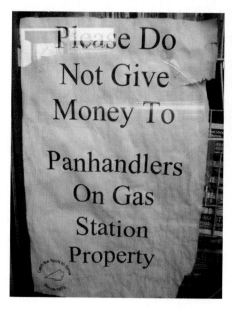

Create a visual essay by adding a third image (a fourth, fifth, etc.) to these two images. (The images need not contain words as these do.) Share your essay with others, exploring how the additional images create meaning.

12

Chapter Contents

Research and Writing: Gathering and Using Information from Sources

What does this image suggest about the nature of research and writing? How has technology changed research and writing?

Basic Concepts

Issues to Consider and Discuss

- When and why do people refer to sources in everyday life?
- How might sources contribute to a writer's credibility?
- Why should information gained from a source be documented?
- When is informal documentation acceptable?
- How can a researcher evaluate the reliability of information from a source?

Why Get Information from Sources?
How do you know what you know? Where did you learn it? In everyday life, we pick up information, use it, and pass it along to others when we think they might benefit from it. For example, we might tell a friend that we think she would enjoy using e-mail to keep in touch with her family, and to convince her of it we might provide some evidence for our claim. The evidence would not be formally documented: we might informally refer to an article we just read about the matter, or we might pass on anecdotal evidence based on personal experience. We are, in fact, basing our claim (our assertion or opinion) on something—and we can call that something *a source of information.*

In college and workplace writing, sources are used in the same basic way as in everyday life. While we use them in our writing to support claims, a source does not always have to agree with our opinion. Instead, a writer might provide information from a source and then respond to it by showing how he or she thinks the information is wrong. Or the writer might use the source in a variety of other ways—such as to provide necessary background information or to illustrate another interesting way of thinking about the matter.

When to Get Information from Sources:
Writers may do research throughout the writing process. For example, getting information from sources is helpful early in the process to explore the topic, as well as late in the process to develop certain points. Toward the end of the writing process, finding statistics, an appropriate quotation, or some other type of evidence to insert into the right place can be just the thing needed to "top off" a part of your essay. But sources are also helpful—more helpful, probably—early in the writing process when exploring an idea. Sources provide valuable new information that is likely to alter a writer/reader's early ideas about a topic and raise new and interesting questions. Many academic and workplace assignments require significant research *prior to any serious drafting.*

Where to Get Information from Sources:
A source can be an interview, a TV show, a movie, a newspaper, a magazine, a scholarly article in a professional journal, a book, and so on. Sources can be thought of as (1) primary—firsthand accounts—or (2) secondary—information from another, often primary, source of information. While primary sources (an interview; an experiment, survey, or study; an historical document; correspondence) are often useful and/or necessary, secondary sources save writers the trouble of reinventing the wheel—that is, of going out and conducting interviews or experiments (often a time-consuming and expensive process) when others have already done so. Using secondary sources means wisely taking advantage of research other people have already done. (See more about finding sources on p. 586.)

What Is Plagiarism? Plagiarism—failing to acknowledge, or give credit to, a source of information—is literary theft. It involves using either (1) an idea or (2) the manner of expression of another person as if it is the writer's own idea or manner of expression.

Plagiarism can take many forms and may be either intentional or unintentional. For example, knowingly turning in another person's paper and claiming it as one's own work is a serious form of academic dishonesty likely to have a serious consequence, such as damage to one's reputation and expulsion from school. Other times, however, writers plagiarize not because they are dishonest but because they are unaware of the rules. They do not know, for example, that the ideas taken from a source, even if not quoted directly, must be documented.

Just as it is every driver's responsibility to know and obey the rules of the road (for his or her own benefit as well as for the benefit of others), it is every writer's responsibility to know the rules of plagiarism. To avoid plagiarism, you must acknowledge your source (also referred to as "citing" or "crediting" the source) whenever you express someone else's idea, opinion, or theory or whenever you provide information—such as a fact or statistic—that is not common knowledge. If you use the exact words of the source, you must indicate that by putting them within quotation marks—and by crediting the source (quotation marks alone are not crediting the source). If you use information from a source but express it in your own words (called "paraphrasing" or "summarizing"), you should not put the information inside quotation marks, but you still must credit the source. (See more about plagiarism on p. 595.)

Why Document Sources: There are at least three good reasons for documenting sources:

- To be honest: When presenting others' opinions, research, or manner of expression, writers give credit to, or acknowledge, their sources.
- To gain credibility: If a source is credible (see Evaluating Sources, p. 592), then the writer's claims gain credibility, too. Many times writers are not experts on their subject matter; still, they can write confidently about their subjects as a result of sources. Also, writers are taken more seriously if they appear well-informed—as though they have "done their research."
- To provide readers with more information: Listing sources provides readers access to more information. This allows readers to explore the subject matter further.

Formal versus Informal Documentation: In academic and professional writing, information from sources can be documented formally or informally, depending upon the situation. Some writing requires in-text documentation that corresponds with a Works Cited page, while other writing does not. "My mother said it is raining," is an example of informal documentation. The information from the source is that *it's raining*. The source is *my mother*. In-text documentation and a Works Cited page would be unnecessary here. But more formal writing situations require more formal documentation. (See more about formal documentation of sources on p. 608.)

Observation, Interviews, Surveys

Academic writers do both *primary* and *secondary* research. In primary research, information is gathered firsthand by the researcher. That is, the researcher interacts directly with the subject(s) and is engaged in the activities and behavior of the thing being studied. A writer doing primary, or field, research makes observations or does experiments, interviews, and surveys. He or she participates in the original actions of gathering data.

Observation: In *detached observation*, the researcher attempts to stay removed or distant from the subject(s). In other words, the researcher tries to remain uninvolved so that his or her conclusions are not influenced by personal attachment to the subject(s). In detached, or what is sometimes called *scientific* observation, researchers attempt to generate conclusions that others would also generate in the same situation, under the same conditions. Findings generated from detached observation usually do not involve the personal situation or perspective of the researcher; therefore, the first-person pronouns *I* and *we* are usually absent from the writing.

In *participant observation*, on the other hand, the researcher interacts with the subject(s). The researcher acknowledges, and even draws attention to, that interaction and how it influences the information gathered. Here, the conclusions may even depend on the presence of the researcher. Annie Dillard's essay "Living Like Weasels" depends upon her interaction with the subject. What Dillard learns and ultimately communicates about weasels is a result of her brief participation in the weasel's existence:

> The weasel was stunned into stillness as he was emerging from beneath an enormous shaggy wild rose bush four feet away. I was stunned into stillness twisted backward on the tree trunk. Our eyes locked, and someone threw away the key.

Participant observation, however, must be carried out with a consideration for the subjects involved. A researcher must not attempt to change, or adversely affect, the subjects or the environment.

> Examine Jane Goodall's essay "Gombe" (in Chapter 3). Does the essay signal detached or participant observation?

Field Notes: Regardless of the type of observation, participant or detached, nothing is more important than good field notes. Good researchers do not rely on memory. After the initial observation, field notes become the primary source of interaction. Because researchers cannot return to the particular time and place of the observation and cannot re-live the experience itself, they must rely on ample notes that capture all possible details, nuances, and impressions. Field notes can be taken in a variety of ways, which may depend on the researcher and the research situation. Notice the range of details in the excerpts from field notes below. Also notice the observers' focus—and strategies for making connections between elements:

The Apartment
Second Fl.
June 1, 2002

The thermostat in the apartment reads 84 degrees (at 11 P.M.). The air conditioner is on, but produces only cool—not cold or air-conditioned—air. If turned on high, the air conditioner eventually blows a fuse. But if on high, it still only produces cool, not cold, air. Needs freon. A 20-inch box fan blows warm air around, not really cooling the place off much. If on medium or high, it makes too much noise. On low, as it is now, it is quiet, yet not very helpful. The television is loud, in order to be heard over the fan and air conditioner. Windows are closed. If open, street noise becomes a problem. Outside on the ground, it is much cooler, comfortable even, but this is a second-floor apartment with a poor, at best, air conditioner.

Sam's Diner
Palmer Street
May 18, 2002

At Sam's, the cooks (two men) are fully visible to the customers in the seating area. The grills, the cutting boards, the prep tables, the refrigerators, canisters, and utensils are all in plain view of customers. One of the two cooks, with a dark beard, is slicing meat (what appears to be ham), and the other is frying a sandwich. They are talking and laughing.

There are three servers, all women. One (wearing blue jeans) is standing behind the counter, by the cash register—occasionally joining in the conversation with the cooks, but also filling ketchup bottles. Another (with a long ponytail) is talking with a table of customers. She seems acquainted with them: she is kneeling and the three customers are all engaged in the conversation with her. The other server (with round glasses) is getting drinks for another table of customers (of four people). She is the only one of the staff moving throughout the diner. At 11:24 A.M., three tables are full. The remaining tables are empty.

Between 11:30 and 12:10 the dining area fills. All but two tables are taken by customers. The workers, servers, and cooks have stopped talking among themselves and are focused on different jobs.

12:14: Twelve tables are full and five people are seated at the counter. The first server (in blue jeans) attends to them, and seems to be exclusively in charge of the cash register. The other two (ponytail and round glasses) are both, now, moving quickly—from tables to the kitchen area.

The cooks are both at grills—their backs turned away from the customers (and servers) for long periods of time. (They only turn around quickly to place a finished plate on pick-up counter—and are not talking.)

Field notes allow the writer to return to the scene and find new connections or see meaning he or she did not see initially. Without field notes, an observer can only return to mental pictures, and because the human mind remembers selectively, those pictures will hold only details that have meaning initially, so the observer is left exploring a narrow and selective list of details—essentially, exploring his or her own memory. This significantly narrows the chances of discovering something. The surprising and valuable connections that *can* be made through observation occur because the observer notices a subtle connection or a hidden pattern—and these connections and patterns do not necessarily exist in an observer's selective memory.

Interviews: At a basic level, interviewing involves gathering information from a single person. But it can mean a great deal more. Good interviewers seek to engage interviewees in intensive conversations; they probe for knowledge and ideas, but they also allow interviewees to explore and develop ideas. A good interview, like a good essay, goes beyond basic knowledge; it provides insight.

Asking the Right Questions: Good interview questions create focus, yet allow interviewees to explore. While they may seek out specific information (data, facts, dates), interview questions can go beyond collecting basic knowledge. (In fact, asking interviewees basic information that can be retrieved through print sources undermines the interview process.) A more valuable strategy is to prompt interviewees to reflect on the meaning of issues or to make connections between ideas. Notice the difference between the following:

What's it like being a doctor?

How has working in the medical field influenced your personal life?

The first question does not focus attention on any particular issue; the interviewee could talk about anything related to the profession. The second question, however, draws attention to a particular issue, asking the interviewee to consider a particular relationship. It is more specific than the first question, but still calls for a certain degree of exploration.

Asking Follow-up Questions: Following up on answers is the interviewer's most powerful research tool. While a survey can only ask a list of preformulated questions, an interview can follow a line of thought that comes from an interviewee's response.
Imagine the following scenario in which a researcher is interviewing a civil engineer:

Interviewer: Is being a civil engineer interesting?
Engineer: Sure. I get to deal with all kinds of people and very real situations.
Interviewer: Is being a civil engineer hard?
Engineer: Well, some of the work can be difficult. Trying to figure in all the variables in a given project can be a mathematical nightmare.
Interviewer: What would you tell someone who wants to become a civil engineer?

Here, the interviewer comes up short in several ways. First, the questions are mundane. As worded here, such questions would probably not yield focused and insightful answers. That is, they prompt the engineer to respond in general terms. They are surface questions (the kind one might ask at a party), which yield short and uncomplicated answers. Also, the interviewer passes up opportunities to follow up. After the engineer's first responses, the interviewer could have asked about the "very real situations" or the "mathematical nightmare" but leaves both ideas and, instead, moves to the next question. This interview does not probe for insight or engage the thoughts of the interviewee, but merely poses a list of unrelated questions. However, notice the following example:

Interviewer: How is a civil engineer important to society?
Engineer: Well, civil engineers conceptualize living space for the public. They envision what it might be like to live in particular place, say a downtown area, and then lay out plans to make a park, an intersec-

Interviewer: tion, even an entire downtown livable—and they do it all while considering how an area will grow and how people's needs may change.

Interviewer: So, civil engineers have to be visionaries?

Engineer: Yes! They are not simply figuring formulas about buildings and zones and land; they are imagining what it might be like to live and work within a given area in the present and future.

Interviewer: And they do all this while accommodating the demands of city officials?

Here, the interviewer starts with a more insightful question; while the first interviewer depends on a vague concept ("interesting"), the second interviewer seeks out the meaning of a potential relationship (between civil engineers and society), and consequently receives an insightful response. Also, the interviewer in the second scenario springboards from the engineer's answers ("So, civil engineers have to be visionaries?"), thereby extending initial thoughts. The second interview evolves, even within a short amount of time.

Planning an Interview: When setting up an interview, be sure to respect the position and accommodate the schedule of the interviewee. Researchers should never impose themselves on potential interviewees. Use the following hints and strategies:

- Always request an interview well in advance of your own deadlines so that you can accommodate the interviewee's schedule.
- When making a request, introduce yourself and the reason for the interview: explain the nature of your research and how the interview will be integrated.
- Beforehand, negotiate a reasonable amount of time for the interview (such as 30 minutes) and stick to it so as not to impinge on the interviewee's time.
- Plan out the method of recording responses—writing, audiotaping, or videotaping. Ask the interviewee if his or her answers can be recorded, and if his or her name can be used in the research.
- At the end of the interview, thank the interviewee for his or her time, and leave promptly.

Using Interviews: Ideas from an interview can be incorporated into various writing situations and purposes. An interview can be used to support claims made in argument, to help explain an idea, or even to help explain the history or significance of some topic. In the following example, notice how the information helps support an idea:

Most often the water sewers can withstand the runoff from storms, but the past season has illustrated the inadequacy of the current sewer system. According to Harold Johnston, Director of Utilities, the sewer system was overwhelmed twice in the past three and a half months, and the result was that untreated sewage flowed out into Silver Lake. When an overflow occurs and untreated water spills into the natural water system, the high amounts of bacteria affect the wildlife and jeopardize the health of swimmers and water enthusiasts. In essence, anyone or anything in the lake for days after an overflow is swimming in sewage.

Here, the writer is trying to persuade readers that the water treatment system in her town is inadequate. The claim made by the Director of Utilities supports the idea. Although the writer probably collected extensive information about the treatment system, she only used one particular point in this paragraph because it directly supports the main idea. (Other information might be used in different passages.)

Surveys: While an interview is based on an individual's ideas and knowledge, a survey attempts to find public opinion on a topic. An interview is driven, in part, by the interviewee; his or her insights may influence the direction or emphasis of the interview. But with surveys, the researcher prearranges the direction and emphasis with carefully formulated questions.

Generating Questions: In generating survey questions, a researcher should consider three points.

1. Questions should not lead the respondent to an answer. Good survey questions avoid influencing the respondents' thinking about the issue. For instance, a question that asks: *Is our current president completely out of touch with public opinion?* leads the respondent toward a negative evaluation of the president. Such questions prompt respondents to take up a certain position even before answering. A better approach is to state the question without leading the respondent; for example: *Is the current president in touch with labor issues in America?*

2. Questions should narrow the focus of the respondents on a particular topic. While good survey questions should not influence the respondents' thinking on an issue, questions should create a particular focus. For instance, a question that asks: *Has the president taken an appropriate stance on international trade?* is more focused than *Do you like our current president?*

3. Questions should use common or unspecialized language. Because survey respondents may come from different walks of life, survey questions should avoid technical jargon or specialized terminology.

Choosing Respondents: Surveyors must consider the demographics (or particular human traits) of their potential respondents.

What is the age range in the respondent group?
What is the racial makeup of the respondent group?
What is the gender makeup of the respondent group?
What is the occupational makeup of the respondent group?
What is the geographical origin of the respondent group?

Recording Responses: Responses can be recorded in a variety of ways. Perhaps the easiest means is to elicit written responses by asking the respondents to write or check off their answers. But if that is not possible, the researcher must do the recording by writing or taping. (If you plan to tape answers, either on video or audio equipment, you should always ask the respondents' permission.)

Using Responses: Survey responses are most often used to show public opinion about a topic. A writer discussing water treatment in her hometown, for instance, might discover in a survey that most people are unaware of the issue:

> Although the failure of the water treatment system poses very real health risks to the community, most people are unaware, or entirely unconcerned. In an informal survey, twenty-four of thirty respondents claimed they had no idea that the untreated waste had spilled into Silver Lake twice this year. And of the six who did know, only two acknowledged it as a public health issue. One respondent put it bluntly: "If it doesn't affect my drinking water, I'm not that concerned."

Notice that the writer uses the information from the survey to enhance the significance, the public resonance, of her topic. In the first sentence, she sets up the idea and then plugs in the information from the survey.

Working Hours
Survey

Please respond to the following questions. Use the back if you need more space.

1) Do you currently hold a full-time job? What is the nature of the work?

2) If you work part-time, how many hours per week?

3) Are you paid salary or an hourly wage?

4) How many hours per week are you contracted to work? (Or how many hours per week are you supposed to work, according to the job description?)

5) How many hours per week do you normally work (at or away from the job site)? Do you work weekends?

6) How much time do you spend preparing for and/or traveling to and from work? (Feel free to give specifics.)

7) Is overtime mandatory or voluntary at your job? (What kinds of incentive are offered for overtime?)

8) Do you feel sufficiently compensated for the work you do? Why or why not?

This survey offers room for the respondents to write in answers—and to develop their thoughts. You could imagine someone responding to this survey fairly quickly because the questions are limited in number and fairly simple. While it could offer some valuable insights about working hours, it is also limited in its scope—like all surveys. Because this survey does not ask for personal information from the respondents (age, sex, education, etc.), the researcher should be careful not to make broad statements about salary and job satisfaction in America, but stay focused on the time people dedicate to their jobs.

Print and Electronic Sources

SECONDARY RESEARCH

In secondary research, the researcher explores the thoughts, theories, or findings of others in print and electronic sources. Examining print or electronic sources helps the researcher explore topics in detail and make points more convincingly. Whether a writer is arguing, explaining, or evaluating, sources can give depth and sophistication. However, sources should not replace other means of support and development (anecdotes, allusions, scenarios, appeals, examples, and so on). Instead, they should work in conjunction with these other strategies. Print and electronic sources should be thought of as another set of writerly tools for inventing, developing, and delivering ideas.

The entire research process should be seen as one of discovery. Good writers approach the process as an archeological journey in which each source is a potential link to some idea, some springboard, that might further develop their understanding and stance on a subject. They see each text, whether book, newspaper, or Web site, as a hypertextual connection to another idea. Good writers do not simply scan sources looking for information that fits into a particular subject; instead, they read with the thought of broadening their perspectives, of expanding their ideas, or of changing their opinions. Sources help to educate a writer about his or her particular subject and to develop a stance regarding that subject.

The first rule of finding secondary sources is: *don't give up.* Many writers are surprised to find how much information is out there. No matter how esoteric a topic, chances are that a great deal has been written about it. The key to doing research is finding the right path—or paths—to the information. And because of interconnected library resources, print reference guides, and electronic networks, the paths are many.

Searching the Library and the Internet

Books, periodicals, newspapers, government documents, reference books (such as dictionaries and encyclopedias), audiovisual materials, and Web sites can all be valuable sources of information, and all of these sources can be found by searching a library's catalog of holdings and/or the Internet. Knowing how to navigate through library catalogs and cyberspace is the first step in finding relevant, reliable, timely, and diverse sources.

The Library: You might begin by getting familiar with your library's Web site. Most likely, the Web site will explain all the library's resources, and it may provide links to other useful Web sites and databases.

When searching your library's catalog, you may be given the options of doing *an author search, a title search, a subject search,* or *a keyword search.* Do an *author search* if looking for works by a particular author, or a *title search* if you already know the title of the specific work. *Subject searches* are organized by headings (such as *agriculture, government, gender*), and will usually produce many sources for a particular topic. *Keyword* searches can be used to focus a search. For example, the keyword search for "weight" on one library's on-line catalog produced 804 entries. But narrowing the search by typing "weight and body" produced only 146. Thus, if you know you are looking for information about weight and the body, "weight and body" allows you to find the relevant sources without having to sort through all the others—

the computer does the sorting for you. Typing "weight *or* body" produced 3,993 entries. And typing "weight and body and media" produced just one entry. Typing "body weight" produced 93, and typing "bodyweight" produced none.

Searches can be made more efficient by using the following words (what are called *Boolean operators*):

> Using *and* between words narrows a search by finding documents containing multiple words—*weight and body.*

> Using *or* between words broadens a search by finding documents with either word in a multiword search—*weight or body.*

> Using *and not* between words finds documents excluding the word or phrase following "and not"—*weight and not body* (that is, weight only).

> Using *near* between words finds documents containing both words or phrases that are near, but not necessarily next to, each other—*weight near body.*

You may also want to become familiar with the physical layout of your library building before you use it. Many libraries offer tours; some tours are even on-line.

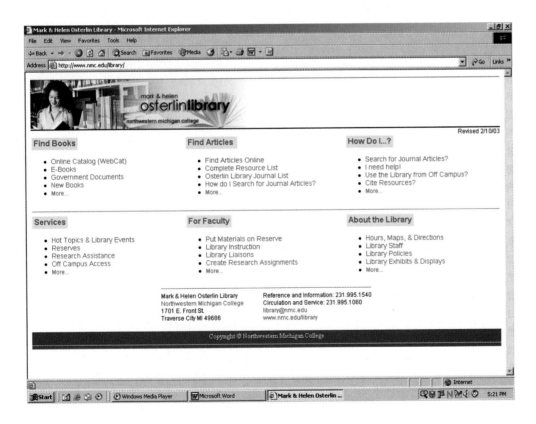

Most libraries have on-line catalogs, which list resources within their walls (such as Northwestern Michigan College's WebCat). Most libraries also have databases for finding articles beyond their walls—such as InfoTrac and EBSCOHOST.

Activities

1. Explore your library's home page, focusing on how it is a gateway to useful information. Describe how you get from the library home page to a book, journal, or newspaper; encyclopedias, maps, or almanacs; other useful Web sites; and so on.

2. Explore your library and take field notes. Describe (a) where each of the following are located, (b) what they look like, and (c) what they are for: circulation desk; computers for searching on-line library catalog; reading room or area; study rooms (for group or individual study); computer work stations; reference room or area; periodicals (journals and magazines); newspapers; books, maps, encyclopedias, and dictionaries; photocopiers; drinking fountains, restrooms, and clocks; a comfortable place for you to read and study. List and describe several other key features of your library not on this list.

The Internet: The Internet is an electronic communications network that connects computer networks and organizational computer facilities around the world. The World Wide Web is a part of the Internet designed to allow for easier navigation of the network through the use of graphical user interfaces and hypertext links between different addresses (definition from Merriam-Webster's on-line dictionary). The World Wide Web, or Web, is made up of many Web sites created and maintained by all types of organizations and individuals. Your school has a Web site, for example, as does your school's library, as may you. A home page, which greets the user upon arriving at a Web site, usually contains links to the other pages of that site or to other sites outside of it. Web sites can be found by (1) typing in the known address (or URL) of the site (such as www.whitehouse.gov) or (2) by doing a subject or keyword search.

Searching or surfing the Web is, basically, skimming through different Web sites using search engines. A search engine works like a keyword search on a library database. That is, you type in a word or phrase and the engine scans the World Wide Web for related sites. All search engines are not the same. Some, for example, attempt to be faster while others attempt to be more comprehensive. To read more about what search engines are and how they work, try doing a keyword search, or type in the following URL: http://www.monash.com/spidap.html. The *Composition of Everyday Life* Web site (http://english.heinle.com/maukmetz) has links to major search engines including the following:

http://www.google.com
http://www.altavista.com
http://www.allonesearch.com
http://dogpile.com
http://goto.com
http://www.monstercrawler.com
http://search.aol.com/

http://www.askjeeves.com/
http://www.ezgov.com/
http://yahoo.com
http://lawcrawler.lp.findlaw.com
http://www.lycos.com
http://www.webcrawler.com

Activities

1. Do several keyword searches, and in class compare your results with those of a classmate. Try different search engines and different keyword approaches for each question. For example, Google: *dogs* (6,890,000), *pets* (5,850,000), *dogs and pets* (991,000); Yahoo: *dogs* (5,666), and so on. Try several different keyword approaches for each question: In what ways might organized sports harm the young children who participate in them? What is the impact of people relocating to Western states on the environment? What novel written in the last half of the twentieth century has been influential?
2. List the different types of sponsors for Web sites that you found. For example, did you find government-sponsored Web sites? Web sites created and maintained by businesses? Individuals? Charitable organizations?

The Sources of Information: Secondary sources include books, periodicals (which are journals and magazines), newspapers, government documents, reference books (such as dictionaries and encyclopedias), audiovisual materials, and Web sites. They give a writer a broader understanding of a topic. In many ways, the process of reading and analyzing secondary sources is a process of invention: the writer is generating new ideas and perspectives, which, in turn, make writing more interesting and engaging (for both writer and reader).

When exploring a topic, it is helpful to use different types of sources—not *just* books, or not *just* Web sites. For example, books, although they contain a lot of information and are easy to find, can contain too much information to sort through, thus taking up a lot of the researcher's time. Books can also be outdated; whereas a journal or magazine article might be shorter, more current, and more focused on your particular topic. Web sites, too, are easy to find but are not always the most helpful source and may not always be up to date. An on-line article found through a library database can be more relevant and reliable even though, at first, it takes a bit more effort to find.

Books are found by searching a library's catalog. While most libraries have electronic catalogs (which allow for author, title, subject, or keyword searches), many academic libraries also have catalogs that are linked to other libraries so that people can check titles not only at that particular location but also in all other connected libraries. Through such services, library users can then order books to be delivered to a desired location.

When you have obtained a promising book, the best strategy is to read through the introductory and concluding chapters. (Introductions and conclusions most often give a broad understanding of the main argument and ideas of the text.) Also, consider edited books (a collection of chapters or articles by different authors) in your search. Edited books, which are very common in academia, often cover a very specific topic and offer many different perspectives from various authors.

Using On-line Catalogs: In a keyword search for books, adding words narrows a search while fewer words broadens the scope. For instance, in a keyword search, "economics" by itself tells the catalog to find any/all works with "economics" in the title or description. (At Northwestern Michigan College, this search yielded 1,387 works.) "Economics and consumers" narrows the search (and yielded 9 works—a much more reasonable number to browse.)

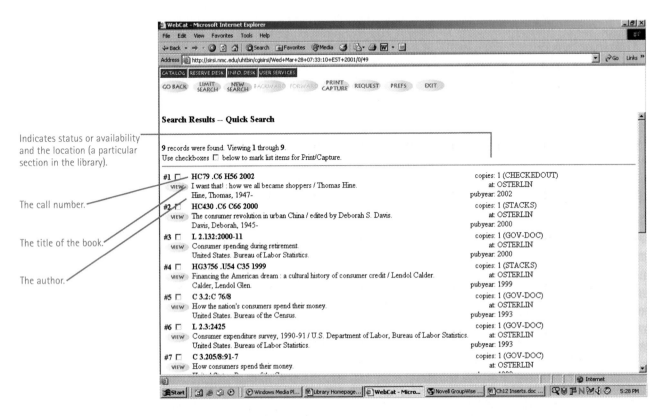

Indicates status or availability and the location (a particular section in the library).

The call number.

The title of the book.

The author.

Periodicals include magazines (for a general audience) or journals (for a specialized audience). (Some periodicals, such as *Ladies Home Journal* and the *Wall Street Journal*, are called journals, but are, in fact, magazines or newspapers.) Popular magazines, such as *People* or *Rolling Stone,* offer information about mainstream news or popular culture events, but rarely provide in-depth analysis of issues, and even more rarely deal with issues outside of major social and political topics.

Scholarly journals, which are usually specific to one discipline (such as English, writing, business, marketing, and so on), offer very detailed analyses and well-developed opinions on a seemingly endless range of topics. The writing in academic journals is most often well-researched and documented, so it tends to be more reliable than that of popular magazines.

Periodicals are listed on electronic databases, which are often available at public and academic libraries. Use searches (described above) to find articles by particular authors, about particular subjects, or in specific periodicals.

Newspapers are most valuable for highly publicized topics—those which are or have been highly visible to the public eye such as political events, controversial public figures, national or local disasters, and significant cultural events. Most academic and public libraries have newspaper databases (with access to past editions). Major newspapers also have Web sites. *USA Today*, for example, can be accessed on-line through a simple keyword search (*USA Today*) or by entering the URL www.USAtoday.com. Explore local newspapers for regional and local events, and national newspapers such as the following for national or world events: *Afro American, American Banker, Amsterdam News, Atlanta Constitution, Atlanta Journal, Boston Globe, Chicago Tribune, Christian Science Monitor, Denver Post, Detroit News, Houston Chronicle, Houston Post, Los Angeles Times, Muslim Journal, New York Times, San Francisco Chronicle, Sentinel [Los Angeles], St. Louis Post Dispatch, Times-Picayune, USA Today, Wall Street Journal [Eastern Edition], Washington Post.*

Government documents include reports, transcripts, pamphlets, articles, speeches, books, maps, films, and more. While the United States government is the nation's largest publisher, state and city governments publish, too. Such documents, which can be of great value in one's research, can be found on-line with keyword searches, or by going directly to the Government Printing Office (GPO) Web site at www. access.gpo.gov.

Reference books such as dictionaries, encyclopedias, and almanacs can be helpful, but should not be relied upon as one's only sources for a college research paper (doing so may indicate a researcher's inability to find a range of sources). Reference materials are usually found in a library's reference room or reference area and often cannot be checked out. They can be located, as with other library materials, by searching the library's catalog of holdings or by asking the reference librarian.

Audiovisual materials include videos, CDs, films, photographs, cassettes, records, microfilm, and microfiche, and are often used to supplement text resources. For example, for a project on fly-fishing, a video might supplement other sources such as books and magazine articles. Or, for a project on a poet, a CD or cassette of the poet reading his or her own work could be helpful. These materials are usually kept in a separate part of the library and can be found by searching the library's card catalog.

Web sites, as discussed earlier, can be found by typing in the Web site address (URL) or by doing a keyword search using your favorite search engine, such as Google, Yahoo, or Dogpile (see p. 586 for keyword searches). Much worthwhile information can be found on Web sites, yet researchers must beware. Because of the open nature of the Web, much information is likely to be unreliable. Thus, good evaluating skills (discussed on the next page) are essential. Also, remember that a simple keyword search can turn up thousands of Web sites. Narrowing one's focus by typing "weight and body and media," for example, will eliminate irrelevant sites found by typing just "weight."

Evaluating Sources:
Sources should be reliable, relevant, timely, and diverse. Just as good ingredients make good pizza, good sources make good papers. If your sources are weak or unreliable, you have just introduced weakness or unreliability into your writing. Thus, evaluating sources before using them is key.

Relevance: A source that is relevant is appropriately related to the writer's particular topic. A writer's first inclination may be to find those sources that directly support his or her thesis statement—that is, sources that speak directly about the writer's particular subject and that espouse his or her particular stance on it. However, this is very limiting—especially since the research process might, in fact, develop or change how a writer thinks about a subject. Sources do much more than back up someone's opinion. They might help to explain the complexities of the subject; explain the history of the subject; explain the writer's position; support the writer's position; show claims that oppose the writer's; show claims that are different from the writer's.

Because sources can be used in a variety of ways, a source that seems only remotely related to your project might, in fact, be extremely valuable in the long run. Consider the following example. A writer is researching voting practices in his community and wants to make a claim about low voter turnouts in recent elections. He finds a newspaper article about a local school, scheduled for demolition, that had previously been used as a voting location. This article at first might seem unhelpful. After all, how does this particular school relate to voting trends in the community? It may, in fact, suggest a great deal about voting. That is, one of the factors in voter turnout is proximity to voting locations. This article might, therefore, show a trend in declining number of voting locations. The same writer might find a government Web page about the history of voting in his state. At first this source may not seem valuable because the writer is primarily concerned with recent voter activity. However, the history may provide some clues about the system itself, about the reasons for establishing Tuesdays as election days, about the number of constituents in a given area—all potentially valuable factors in understanding the complexities of recent voter turnout.

Reliability: A reliable source offers valid claims and sound logic. Reliable sources also document the information they offer. That is, they prove that their claims are well-founded. For published books and academic journal articles, reliability may not be a significant concern because such sources (most often) endure a process of critical peer review. But every source should be put to the test. A reliable source:

- Documents claims involving statistics or data.
- Offers paths to other research that supports the claims being made.
- Admits its own biases and/or offers alternative points of view.
- Argues logically for particular biases or perspectives.

Remember that most popular magazines are guided by a primary force: money. Editorial policies are driven by the need to make information attractive to consumers. Therefore, claims are often inflated, mitigating details are often excluded, and generalizations are common. Also, magazines are funded, in large part, by corporate advertising, and so are not apt to publish articles that might compromise relationships with those advertisers. For these reasons, researchers should always be cautious about quoting popular magazines (or even news magazines) as unbiased truth.

Also, consider the author. Some authors have more credentials than others. However, a book or article by a well-known author should not necessarily outweigh another less public writer. Many academic and professional writers (who are not necessarily big names in the popular media) are well respected within small communities because they have spent years researching a particularly focused issue. For instance, Patricia Limerick, a highly respected scholar in history, has written a great deal about the American West. Although her name is not recognizable to the general public, it is often noted in history scholarship. It is relatively easy to check into authors. If you have found a text that looks promising, simply do an author search in various media (books, periodicals, newspapers) using his or her name. You might find that the author has written much about the subject, and in so doing, discover some additional sources for your project.

Timeliness: A significant concern in academic research is the date of the sources. It is important that claims are supported with sources that are not obsolete or behind the times. But this criterion depends upon the issue and the claim being made. Some claims require very current sources. For example, a writer making a claim about the state of cloning in America would be wise to consider sources published only within two to three years of her research. (Because the science of biotechnology evolves so rapidly and because each new advancement prompts significant public debate, claims that are ten years old might well be antiquated.) However, that same writer might also want to discuss the role of science in human development, and so discover a valuable text by a nineteenth-century philosopher, one who speaks about the role of machines in the evolution of the modern consciousness. In this case, the writer uses current texts to support claims about time-sensitive topics, and refers to an older source to express an issue that stretches beyond a particular era.

Writers should also remember that the most valuable source is not necessarily the most recent. For some topics, writers may find value in older sources, which may have had significant impact on the following writers and researchers. For instance, a writer focusing on contemporary political protests would certainly discover recent sources about protests against the World Trade Organization. However, she might also find texts by Henry David Thoreau, Martin Luther King, Jr., or Gandhi to be of value. Although such sources may be significantly older than a recent article on the Internet, they would offer much to any discussion about political protests. Of course, a hundred-year-old text would be used differently than a recent text. That is, a writer might use Thoreau to explain the importance of civic action as a general principle and use a recent source to articulate the present condition of political protest groups.

Diversity: Diversity refers to the variety of different sources a writer uses. Good writers seek to develop their projects and their perspectives with a variety of voices and media. Writers develop their views on a subject from a variety of sources—much in the same way people develop their views on religion or marriage or education from taking in and making sense of information from various sources. For example, our religious beliefs may have been influenced primarily by our parents, but other sources, such as childhood friends, books, movies, and music, also influence us. Even views that oppose our own are important, because they help us to define the borders of our beliefs. This process, making our own sense out of various pieces of information, is called *synthesis*, and it is what writers do when researching their topics. Writers need to consider and synthesize various sources about their topics; otherwise, their perspectives, and ultimately their positions, will be limited.

Evaluating Electronic Sources

In addition to the four criteria above, writers should be especially careful about Web pages. A particularly important criterion for Web pages is reliability. Because anyone with a computer (or access to a computer) can publish a Web page and make any claim he or she wishes, a researcher should be especially cautious of claims made on Web sites. In other words, much information on the World Wide Web is potentially bogus. Also, bias must be considered because the purpose of many sites is to sell something—and therefore they may provide information that is slanted. Of course, bias in itself is not bad. It is only negative when it is concealed. If a source is trying to sell something, its claims should not be accepted as unbiased truth. If the source asks for personal information, it may have an alternative agenda. Although some online sources (such as the *New York Times*) ask for registration to enter the site, many other sources may ask for personal information so they can market products or services to you. Be cautious about giving personal information (especially banking or social security numbers) to Web sites. If a source does not give author information, then you should be cautious with the claims being made. Here are some valuable questions to ask about Web pages:

- Who sponsors this site, and what credibility do they have for posting the information?
- Is the site attempting to sell something? If so, how might that impact the nature of the information?
- Does the site ask for personal information? (Does it state the purpose of this request?)
- Are statistics/data supported with appropriately documented sources?
- Is the information presented up to date? (When was the site last updated?)

For additional hints and strategies, check out the following sites:

http://gateway.lib.ohio-state.edu/tutor
http://www.ciolek.com/WWWVL-InfoQuality
http://www.library.cornell.edu/okuref/research/webeval
http://www.edtech.vt.edu/edtech/kmoliver/webeval/criteria

Taking Notes on Sources:
It may be tempting to photocopy or print out sources, and then underline or highlight the information you will transfer into your text. While this strategy works best when using just a little information from a source or two, taking notes in a journal or on note cards is a more efficient strategy, especially for a project involving several sources. The note-taking process gives the writer a chance to process information and consider how it relates to the goals of the project. Taking notes, then, is an early part of the writing process: the ideas crafted during the note-taking process can be transferred directly into a formal text. So as you take notes, imagine how that information might appear in your text.

As you read through sources, remain open to ideas and collect those that not only confirm your own opinions but also extend or even oppose your perspective. Remember that sources can serve many purposes in a research project. They can help to explain the complexities of the subject; explain the history of the subject; explain the writer's position; support the writer's position; show claims that oppose the writer's; show claims that are different from the writer's.

Imagine a writer is doing research on justice and political action, and discovers the following passage from Martin Luther King, Jr.:

> Human progress never rolls in on wheels of inevitability; it comes through the tireless efforts of men willing to be co-workers with God, and without this hard work, time itself becomes an ally of the forces of stagnation. We must use time creatively, in the knowledge that the time is always ripe to do right. Now is the time to make real the promise of democracy and transform our pending national elegy into a creative psalm of brotherhood. Now is the time to lift our national policy from the quicksand of racial injustice to the solid rock of human dignity.

The writer decides that this information is valuable because it adds complexity to her ideas. That is, it provides reasoning for political action. It may be *paraphrased, summarized*, or directly *quoted*.

A Note about Plagiarism

Most often, plagiarism occurs because writers are simply not going far enough in their paraphrasing. That is, they are not sufficiently rewording the ideas from the original source. A good paraphrase avoids using the same subjects and verbs as in the original text. To avoid this, read the original passage closely, but rather than writing down the ideas immediately, talk through them first. Remember that any one idea can be phrased in infinite ways.

Sometimes, writers plagiarize intentionally because they are desperate to complete an assignment or pass a class. They set out to steal (or buy) others' ideas. In this age of technology, students can easily download text from an on-line source, and they can even buy college essays from Web sites and on-line databases. However, such essays are pre-packaged, the topics are generalized, and the writing mundane—essentially, they are the opposite of what most college instructors want, and are contrary to the **Invention** strategies suggested throughout this book. Also, as Web sites featuring prewritten essays increase, so does the ability of instructors to detect plagiarism.

The consequences of plagiarism are more long reaching and destructive than what some students may assume. Besides failing an assignment, failing an entire class, or being expelled, students who plagiarize fail to learn essential writing and thinking skills—or even when and how to ask for help. They also establish a low standard for themselves, which is perhaps the worst result of plagiarizing.

Paraphrase is a rewording of the original source using your own words and expressions. It conveys the detail and complexity of the original text. A paraphrase of the King passage might read:

> Humanity doesn't progress without constant struggle of pious and committed individuals. Absence of such struggle means the lack of social and spiritual development. We have to use time to do what is right, to realize the idea of democracy, to change national sorrow into community and collaboration. We have to try to raise the nation up from racist practices into a place of shared honor and respect.

The paraphrase restates King's ideas, but does so without his particularly figurative language. The writer might find paraphrase valuable because she wants to share the nuances of the idea but does not want the tone of the original text (such as King's almost poetic voice) to interfere with or take over her own text.

Paraphrasing does not involve merely changing a word or two, or shifting around sentence parts. Inappropriate or lazy paraphrasing leads to *plagiarism*: the act of taking others' ideas or words without attributing proper credit. In the following example, the writer does not rephrase the ideas, but merely shifts words around and replaces others. If the following appeared in a text, it would be plagiarism.

> Human progress never rolls in on tires of inevitability; it comes by way of the tireless efforts of men willing to be co-workers with God, and without this hard work, time itself becomes an ally of the forces of stagnation. In the knowledge that the time is always ripe to do right, we must use time creatively.

Notice that in the first sentence, the note taker has only substituted one word for another here and there. In the second sentence, the note taker has just shifted sentence parts around. This is not paraphrasing because the note retains the original flavor and expression of the author.

Summary, like paraphrasing, involves expressing ideas from a source in your own words instead of using the words of the source. Unlike paraphrasing, summary removes much of the detail while still dealing with the complexity of the idea. Consider this well-taken summary note of the original King passage:

> Humanity progresses only by the struggle of spiritually motivated people, and those people must use time for social change and raise the country from racist oppression to shared honor and respect.

Notice that the idea of the passage is still represented, but that it has been shortened. Since summary leaves out detail while capturing the main idea, accuracy is essential. Be careful not to misinterpret the source, as the following summary does:

> Only people who go to church regularly can make the world a better place. Racism will thrive without their timely efforts.

Quotation, using the exact words of a source, allows you to add an especially important phrasing or passage to your own writing. The key, however, is to carefully select what ideas and manner of expression are worth quoting. Generally, writers avoid quoting more than 15 percent of their texts, though certain situations may call for more. When writing down quotes, keep in mind two points:

1. Quote sparingly. Quote only when a passage is particularly striking AND quote only the striking part. For example, do not quote an entire paragraph if you can quote just a sentence; do not quote an entire sentence if you can quote only three words from that sentence.

2. Put others' words within quotation marks. Consider the following well-taken quotation note from the original King passage:

   "Human progress never rolls in on wheels of inevitability; it comes through the tireless efforts of men willing to be co-workers with God, and without this hard work, time itself becomes an ally of the forces of stagnation."

The note is well taken (1) because it is word-for-word the same as the original, (2) because it is in quotation marks, and (3) because it is strikingly worded and worth quoting. Be certain not to change any wording or punctuation within a quotation.

Using Sources in Brief

Information can come from primary or secondary sources.

- Primary research is gathered firsthand: observation, interviews, surveys.
- Secondary research explores the primary research of others.

Sources should be evaluated for

- Relevance—appropriately related to your particular topic.
- Reliability—credible and trustworthy.
- Timeliness—not outdated or behind the times.
- Diversity—various sources providing different viewpoints.

Information from sources can be

- Paraphrased—expressed in your own words.
- Summarized—expressed in your own words, but with fewer details.
- Quoted—repeated exactly from the source.

Using Note Cards: While writing down ideas on note cards is initially more time consuming than highlighting or underlining, the extra time spent can pay off by saving *more* time later—in the writing stage. For example, if you write down ideas on 4" × 6" note cards, you can then arrange those note cards in the appropriate order and then write without having to sift through your many pages of highlighted text. Photocopying entire articles and printing out entire Web pages for an idea or two can create paperwork confusion. (It also costs money and wastes resources.)

Note cards contain four pieces of information: (1) the note, (2) the source, (3) the page number, (4) the topic.

The Source

Any time information from a source is used (summarized, paraphrased, or quoted) in a text, that source must be cited (acknowledged within the passage). Instead of going back later and having to find the source information (or worse, make it up), writing it down on the note card will save the time and trouble of having to go looking for it later. You need not write down complete bibliographic information, such as:

> King, Martin Luther, Jr. "Letter from Birmingham Jail." *A World of Ideas: Essential Readings for College Writers.* Ed. Lee A. Jacobus. Boston: St. Martin's, 1994. 121-37.

Instead, just write "King" or "Letter from Birmingham Jail" and make certain that you have recorded the complete bibliographic information for this source where you can easily find it—in a notebook, for example, with other sources.

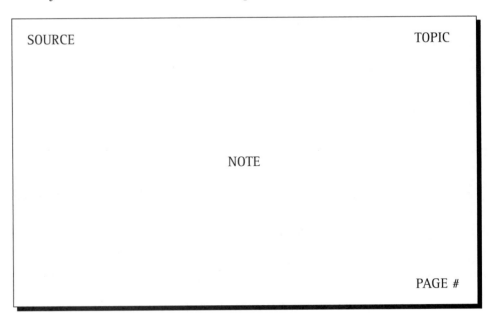

The Page Number

When sources are used in academic writing, the page numbers are included in the documentation, so writing down the page number while taking notes, like writing down the source, saves the time and trouble of having to go back and find it later on.

The Topic

Researchers also record the topic the source covers, or the way the source contributes to the overall project (*Cause of the Problem, Solutions, Taking Individual Action*, and so on). This is especially valuable in bigger projects, which may deal with many sources and various points. After indicating the subject matter on the card, you can then organize the cards by placing related ideas together. With more involved projects you can "play" with the cards, shuffling them about to determine what parts, or sections, your final text will have. Once you group the cards in general sections (background, problem, solution #1, solution #2, and so on), you can place each card within a section in order. Arranging each note card in the order it will appear in your text helps in two ways: (1) it allows you to arrive at an organization based on the ideas you discovered through your research, and (2) it allows the drafting process to go more smoothly because the ideas are laid out in front of you.

Working with Note Cards

- Each note card contains one idea.
- The source is indicated—either by a few key words or a symbol (such as A, B, C) that refers to a keyed list of sources.
- Sources are properly paraphrased, summarized, or quoted.
- The page number, if available, is listed.
- A topic heading helps the writer organize the information into logical sections.

*****

- Note cards are put in the order in which information will appear in the text.
- Additional notes are taken, on cards, to fill in gaps in the presentation.
- The writer develops a draft, referring to the note cards at hand.

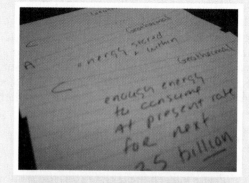

Integrating Information from Sources: Once information has been gathered from sources, the writer will likely integrate only some of the ideas into a final text; less relevant ideas will be discarded. Information from sources helps explain, develop, and support points, and it can provide credibility. Referring to good sources and documenting them appropriately tells the reader that the writer is aware of the world that surrounds us all; it tells the reader that the writer has conscientiously researched the subject and knows what others are saying and doing about it. However, writers should be careful not to allow sources to take over their writing—to move in and take charge of the ideas. Sources should be part of a broader set of strategies (such as personal anecdotes, allusions, scenarios, appeals, and so on) for supporting and developing ideas.

Organizing a text with sources may seem more difficult than organizing a text that is based exclusively on personal insights. However, the same principles apply: paragraphs must be coherent, and transitions must be made between points. Whether information is paraphrased, summarized, or directly quoted, it should be blended smoothly into the text so that the reader (1) understands its relationship to the writer's own ideas and (2) knows where the information came from. The challenge, then, is to maintain coherence and flow while integrating other voices and opinions. The best way to achieve coherence and flow is to develop an overall plan for your text without using outside sources. That is, develop a general strategy for your organization and then decide how the sources can help complete that plan. Perhaps the biggest mistake that writers make in working with sources is allowing the other texts, especially quotations, to take over the project. This can be avoided by making a general framework and using the sources to help fill in the points.

Activities

1. Browse through the essays in this text, noticing when sources are used. Then highlight three examples of each of the following: paraphrase, summary, quotation.
2. Consider the relevance of the information from each of the sources you identified in #1. How did the information help the reader to better understand the writer's main idea?
3. Notice how the information from each source you highlighted for #1 is integrated into the reading. For each source, explain how the writer lets the reader know the information is from a source.
4. Read through your own previous writing—essays, e-mails, and so on—identifying when you used sources. See if you can find several examples of each: paraphrase, summary, quotation. Then do #2 and #3 above for each source.
5. Share your study of sources (1–4 above) with a group of classmates, exploring the variety of ways in which information from sources can be integrated into your writing.

Integrating a paraphrase or summary is a relatively simple process. If a writer were developing an argument about justice and political action and wanted to include the ideas of Martin Luther King, Jr., he or she could include them as follows:

> Individuals must take action if positive change is to occur. In his "Letter from Birmingham Jail," Martin Luther King, Jr. explained that humanity does not progress without the constant struggle of pious and committed individuals. The absence of such struggle means the lack of social and spiritual development, so we must use time to do what it is right, to realize the idea of democracy, to change national sorrow into community and collaboration. We must seek to raise the nation up from racist practices and into a place of shared honor and respect (130). His words are as important today as they were in 1963.

Notice the in-text documentation (in MLA style) above. This reference refers the reader to a Works Cited page at the end of the essay, where complete bibliographic information allows the reader to locate the source. Here, only a page number is provided because the source–King's "Letter from Birmingham Jail"–is already referred to within the paragraph. Were King not mentioned earlier, the citation would read: (King 130). Remember, when you paraphrase or summarize you must give credit to (cite or document) your source because, even though you are not using the source's exact words, you are still using someone else's ideas. For a complete discussion of in-text citation, see pp. 608–609.

Or the writer could summarize King's ideas:

> Individuals must take action if positive change is to occur. In his "Letter from Birmingham Jail," Martin Luther King, Jr. explained that humanity progresses only by the struggle of spiritually motivated people, and those people must use time for social change and raise the country from racist oppression to shared honor and respect (130). His words are as important today as they were in 1963.

A writer may summarize because he or she simply wants to illustrate a point (made by the original text) and then move on to another idea. Usually, a summarized point is used to support a broader claim or to illustrate a stance, and the writer may have several other strategies for illustrating the claim or making the stance clear to the reader.

The writer may also quote directly. Writers quote sparingly. They more often rely on paraphrasing and summarizing ideas from a source, and when they do quote, they quote only the essential words, or phrases that are striking:

> In his "Letter from Birmingham Jail," Martin Luther King suggests that "human progress never rolls in on wheels of inevitability" (130).

Notice, here, the quotation marks before and after King's words. The quotation marks say to a reader, in effect, "these are someone else's words."

Special Considerations for Organizing Sources

Counterarguing Sources: Writers sometimes directly refer to sources because they oppose their own claims. That is, they counter the claims made in a source. (See Counterargument, p. 246.) In these cases, the writers directly refer to the source (by paraphrasing, summarizing, or quoting), and then respond directly to the idea. This can be done with a turnabout paragraph or by splitting the source's ideas from the writer's with a paragraph break. (See page 257 in Chapter 5: Making Arguments.)

Textual Cues: Whatever organizational strategy you use, make certain that you distinguish *your* ideas and claims from those of others so the reader can tell whose ideas are being explained or asserted. Also, make certain you show the relationships between and among sources. In other words, be sure to use appropriate *textual cues* (sentences, words, and phrases that explain the relationship between ideas, sources, or points in the paper) for the reader.

> Most music critics, *such as Smith, Castella, and Sanchez*, see the latest alternative genre as a collective response to the grunge scene of the early 90's.

Here, the critics listed are discussed prior to this sentence, and the writer simply reminds the reader about these voices and how they relate to the present point being made. Simple phrases (*such as*) cue the reader to make connections between passages in the text.

> Jones's ideas are often seen as radical. Alberta Slavik, *for example*, casts Jones aside as a "hyper-liberal" journalist: "William Jones has gone too far, simply parading his politics at the cost of facts" (76).

Again, the simple, short phrase *for example* helps the reader keep track of the names. The phrase tells the reader, even before he or she gets to the quotation, that Slavik sees Jones's ideas as radical. Textual cues become increasingly important as writers add names and sources to their texts.

Paragraph Transitions: Integrating outside sources can make a text more sophisticated, but can also create confusion if the writer does not make clear connections between points. Because outside sources often increase the complexity of a text, paragraph transitions (sentences and phrases that join the content of paragraphs AND show the logical connections) become vital to a coherent paper. Transition statements usually begin paragraphs and act as bridges from one paragraph to the next. The following sentences, which all begin paragraphs, act as bridges from previous points:

> Not all farmers, however, agree with Johnson's strategy.

> Despite this overwhelming amount of evidence, some teachers refuse to acknowledge the way gender and race figure into the classroom.

> But all of the discussion on war distracts voters from significant domestic issues that will impact everyday life in the present and future.

> Because of Smith's recent book, many researchers have begun focusing their attention on the ways technology will change our ability to communicate.

For more information on transitions, see p. 257.

Blending Information from a Source into Your Text: In the following paragraph, notice how Daniel Bruno blends together, or integrates, what he thinks and what his source says. He (1) states his main idea *(Sacks illustrates that all of today's college students cannot just be thrown in the same big barrel)*, (2) directs the reader to the source *(he spends; he says; he mentions)*, (3) provides the information from the source that supports, or explains, his idea (in this paragraph, Bruno both quotes and summarizes the source), and (4) concludes by commenting on the information. Writers need not include these four steps every time they use information from a source, but it can be helpful to frequently rely on these four elements: (1) the writer's main idea, (2) reference to the source, (3) information from the source, (4) the writer's commentary.

> In *Generation X Goes to College*, Peter Sacks illustrates that all of today's college students cannot just be thrown in the same big barrel. In describing the modern/post-modern clash in education, he spends the majority of his time talking about those students who are underprepared, who lack the basic study skills required in academic work, and who demonstrate little real commitment to their own education. Yet, he does not discuss this problem in isolation. He also mentions another type of student. For example, he introduces the reader to Marissa and Carol: "As very good students, [their views] were virtually excluded by The College in order to accommodate the whiners and complainers" (61). And he says they "suffered not only educationally" (63). In addition to discussing specific good students, an entire chapter presents survey results about students' attitudes toward education. While he makes claims such as "nearly a quarter of the students . . . harbored a disproportionate sense of entitlement," this very statement tells the reader that a full three quarters (that is, three out of four) students *do not* "harbor a disproportionate sense of entitlement" (54-59). He wraps up the book by focusing on another student, Andie, who he describes as "a good student, constantly picking [his] brain for information and feedback on her work" (186-7). His final paragraph, before the Epilogue, says, "Let's create a system that encourages people like Andie at least as much as the ones who don't give a damn" (187). Thus, Sacks shows that today's students are a more diverse group—in skill level, background, and attitude toward education—than has ever before been gathered together in the college classroom.

Notice how the references to sources cue the reader that the text is moving to an idea from a source. Writers use cues, also called *attributive phrases* (such as *according to, says, explains,* etc.), to help readers see when ideas are from a source. Notice Ann Marie Paulin's strategies:

> And most diets don't work. Psychologist Mary Pipher, in her book *Hunger Pains: The Modern Woman's Quest for Thinness*, cites a 1994 study which found that "90 percent of dieters regain all the weight they lost within five years" (32). The evidence is beginning to pile up out there that being fat may not be nearly as bad for a person's health as the crazy things people inflict upon their bodies to lose weight.

Notice that Paulin first makes a point about diets—they don't work. And then she offers the source and the quotation to support that point. In this case, the reader knows why the quotation is offered—to give credence to her claim about diets.

Punctuating Quotations:

Learning the three basic ways of punctuating quotations will be helpful when integrating the exact words of others into your text. Since readers are used to seeing quotations punctuated this way, if you follow these conventions your readers will more easily understand the relationship between your words and the words of your source.

Quotation Marks Only

And he says they "suffered not only educationally" (Sacks 63).

Emphasizing her point, Miller demands that "it is now time for something drastic to change here on campus" (43).

When the quoted matter blends directly into your sentence without a speaking verb (such as *say, says, said, exclaims, proclaims, states,* etc.) indicating a change in voice, no punctuation is required before the quotation. The sentence may be punctuated just as it would be if there were no quotation marks—*And he says they suffered not only educationally.*

Speaking Verb Followed by a Comma

His final paragraph, before the Epilogue, says, "Let's create a system that encourages people like Andie at least as much as the ones who don't give a damn" (Sacks 187).

Emphasizing her point, Miller suggests, "it is now time for something drastic to change here on campus" (43).

As Martin Luther King, Jr. explains, in his "Letter from Birmingham Jail," "One day the South will know that when these disinherited children of God sat down at lunch counters, they were in reality standing up for what is best in the American dream."

Speaking verbs (such as *say, says, suggests, exclaims, states,* etc.) indicate a shift in voice (from your voice to the voice of your source). In the third example above, *explains* (a speaking verb) tells the reader that the text is going to shift from the writer's voice to the voice of the source. A comma follows the speaking verb and precedes the quotation.

A speaking verb combined with a noun creates an attributive phrase that can be placed at the beginning, in the middle, or at the end of a sentence. Quoting involves crafting sentences carefully to create clear and natural sounding connections between the writer's own ideas and the words of the source. Here are some standard strategies:

Quotation at the Beginning of a Sentence

"All voting is a sort of gaming, like checkers or backgammon, with a slight moral tinge to it," explains Henry David Thoreau (56).

Quotation in the Middle of a Sentence

As Thoreau points out, "all voting is a sort of gaming, like checkers or backgammon, with a slight moral tinge to it" (56), and it is this moral issue that is often over-emphasized on ballots.

Quotation at the End of a Sentence

Henry David Thoreau claims that "voting is a sort of gaming, like checkers or backgammon, with a slight moral tinge to it" (56).

Quotation Divided by Your Own Words

"All voting," explains Thoreau, "is a sort of gaming."

> **Helpful Verbs for Attributing Quotes**
>
> says, argues, explains, suggests, emphasizes, insists, offers, claims, points out, considers, shows, demands, teaches, describes, tells, informs, instructs

Sentence Followed by a Colon

For example, he introduced the reader to Marissa and Carol: "As very good students, [their views] were virtually excluded by The College in order to accommodate the whiners and complainers" (Sacks 61).

As George Williams notes, protection of white privilege is critical to patterns of discrimination: "Whenever a number of persons within a society have enjoyed for a considerable period of time certain opportunities for getting wealth, for exercising power and authority, and for successfully claiming prestige and social deference, there is strong tendency for these people to feel that these benefits are theirs by 'right'" (727).

When the words to the left of a quotation (a list or explanation) are a complete thought consisting of an independent clause—that is, when those words alone could be followed by a period—a colon is used to connect the quotation (list or explanation) to the complete thought introducing it.

If an entire sentence is a quotation—that is, if it begins and ends with a quotation mark and contains no reference to the source in between—consider (1) connecting the quote, if appropriate, to the preceding sentence with a colon, or (2) adding a cue, or transition, as an introduction to the quote. For example, the quotation below might be integrated in the following two ways:

Not Integrated: Quote Not Connected to the Writer's Idea

For example, Sacks introduced the reader to Marissa and Carol. "As very good students, [their views] were virtually excluded by The College in order to accommodate the whiners and complainers" (Sacks 61).

Integrated: Quote Connected with a Colon

For example, Sacks introduced the reader to Marissa and Carol: "As very good students, [their views] were virtually excluded by The College in order to accommodate the whiners and complainers" (Sacks 61).

Integrated: Quote Connected with a Cue or Transitional Expression

For example, Sacks introduced the reader to Marissa and Carol. He said, "As very good students, [their views] were virtually excluded by The College in order to accommodate the whiners and complainers" (Sacks 61).

Special Conditions in Quoting

To integrate quotes smoothly into a text, writers sometimes find it helpful to omit or add certain words for clarity or cohesion. Standard guidelines exist for letting the reader know how the writer has altered a quotation. Of course the writer must be absolutely certain that he or she has not changed the source's intended meaning. Note also the standard approach to using long quotations.

Omitting Words: Occasionally, writers want to quote a passage but to leave out words or phrases. This is done with ellipses: . . . This construction tells the reader that words have been taken out of the original passage. Notice how one might quote a passage from Steven M. Richardson's essay (on page 169):

> Original: One of the best reasons to go to college is to find out what you're good at. Most people who become genetic engineers or metallurgists discover their calling after they enter college. Roughly a third of the undergraduate curriculum in most colleges involves General Education, a block of courses meant to encourage students to explore subjects that they might otherwise avoid.

> According to Steven M. Richardson, "one of the best reasons to go to college is to find out what you're good at. . . . Roughly a third of the undergraduate curriculum in most colleges involves General Education, a block of courses meant to encourage students to explore subjects that they might otherwise avoid."

The ellipses indicate the missing sentence from the quotation. The same strategy can be applied to cut any amount of text from a passage. For instance, in the sentence below, a passage has been cut from Richardson's passage:

> According to Richardson, "roughly a third of the undergraduate curriculum in most colleges involves General Education. . . ."

Adding Words: Sometimes it is valuable to add a note or comment within a quote. In this case, writers use brackets to set off their own words. For example, a writer may insert a word in a quoted passage to clarify a vague pronoun or to give a brief explanation:

> Original: After months of exhausting research, they had finally come to understand the problem with their design.

> Quotation: "After months of exhausting research, [the nuclear scientists] had finally come to understand the problem with their design" (Smith 82).

Here, the writer substitutes the actual noun for the pronoun *they*. Without the noun, the reader may not understand the meaning of the quotation. As in this example, inserting bracketed comments within quotes can clear up any potentially confusing information within a quote while maintaining the flow of the sentence.

Noting an Error: If a quotation is grammatically or syntactically flawed, a writer cannot simply change it. In such cases, the quotation must remain intact, and the writer must use brackets and the three-letter word *sic* to acknowledge the error. (Otherwise, a reader might assume that the error is on the part of the writer.)

Using Lengthy Quotes: When writers quote more than four lines, they must use a block quote. As in this passage from Ann Marie Paulin's essay, writers often use a colon before block quotes:

> Another example of this bullying someone thin comes from Pipher's book *Hunger Pains: The Modern Woman's Tragic Quest for Thinness*. Pipher recounts a conversation she overheard one day in a dress shop:
>
> > I overheard a mother talking to her daughter, who was trying on party dresses. She put on each dress and then asked her mother how she looked. Time after time, her mother responded by saying, "You look just awful in that, Kathy. You're so fat nothing fits you right." The mother's voice dripped with disgust and soon Kathy was crying. (89)
>
> Pipher goes on to suggest that Kathy's mother is a victim of the culture, too, because she realizes how hard the world will be on her fat daughter. Unfortunately, what she doesn't realize is how much better her daughter's quality of life would be if she felt loved by her mother. Any person surrounded by loving family members at home is much better equipped to deal with whatever the cruel world outside throws at her or him.

Double Quotes: Occasionally, writers quote a passage that contains a quotation or is itself a quotation. In this case, single quotation marks are used inside the double quotation marks:

> As Maria Gallagher has argued, "it is time that we turn the corner on the road of national energy policies and begin to take 'alternative energy' seriously" (23).

Activity: The following passage appears in Ann Marie Paulin's essay in Chapter 5: Making Arguments.

> For example, in one commercial for Slim Fast, the woman on the ad is prattling on about how she had gained weight when she was pregnant (seems to me, if you make a person, you ought to be entitled to an extra ten pounds) and how awful she felt. Then, there is a shot of this woman months later as a thin person with her toddler in her yard. She joyously proclaims that Slim Fast is "the best thing that ever happened to me!" The best thing that ever happened to her?! I thought I heard wrong. What about that little child romping by her heels? Presumably, there is a daddy somewhere for that little cherub. What about his role in her life? The thought that losing that weight is the most important thing that ever occurred in her life is sad and terrifying.

Divide the class into four groups and assign each group one of the following "special conditions": omitting words, adding words, using lengthy quotes, and double quotes. Each group should write a new passage that uses the Paulin quote and the assigned special condition. The groups then should share their passages with the class.

MLA Style

DOCUMENTING SOURCES

Different disciplines rely on different styles of documentation. The two most common styles are MLA (Modern Language Association) and APA (American Psychological Association). English and Humanities use MLA. Like other documentation styles, MLA depends on two basic components: (1) an in-text citation of a work and (2) a list of works at the end of the text. These two components function in the following ways:

- In-text (or parenthetical) citations provide unobtrusive documentation of specific information.
- In-text citations let a reader know that particular ideas come from a particular source.
- In-text documentation corresponds to the complete bibliographic information provided at the end of the text.
- In-text citations lead the reader directly to the corresponding Works Cited page.
- Done correctly, the in-text reference is the first word(s)—whether it be the author's name or an article title—of the alphabetized Works Cited page. This allows the reader to easily locate the source in the list of words.
- The Works Cited page provides complete information for finding the source.
- This complete information is provided only once and comes at the end of the entire text so that it doesn't interfere with ease of reading.
- This complete information should allow the reader to find the source easily.

In-Text Citation: In-text documentation involves referencing the original text in parentheses within the actual sentences of your text; because it uses parentheses, it is sometimes called *parenthetical citation*. An in-text citation must occur whenever a writer:

- Quotes directly from a source.
- Paraphrases ideas from a source.
- Summarizes ideas from a source.
- References statistics or data from a source.

In general, for MLA style, in-text citations should include the author's last name (unless it is given within the sentence) and page number of the source from which the cited material is taken (unless the source is electronic and lacks page numbers).

> "After months of exhausting research, they had finally come to understand the problem with their design" (Smith 82).

Only a space separates the name and the page number.

The end punctuation comes after the citation.

If the author is referred to in the sentence, his or her name can be omitted from the citation.

> Emphasizing her point, Miller demands that "it is now time for something drastic to change here on campus" (43).

If the source has no author, use the first word or phrase of the source's title and punctuate accordingly (quotation marks for an article and underlining for books).

> The oil had spread over much of the shoreline and had "already begun its death grip on a vast array of wildlife" ("Black Death").

If the source has two authors, use the last name of both authors.

> (Lunsford and Ede 158)

If you have more than one work by the same author, insert the title of the work after the author name and before the page number.

> (Faigley, Fragments of Rationality 43)

If you are citing material that is already quoted in the source, cite the source in which you found the quotation and add "qtd. in" before the author's name or title.

> (qtd. in Smith 82)

If you want to acknowledge more than one source for the same information, use a semicolon between citations within one set of parentheses.

> (Lunsford and Ede 158; Smith 82)

If you have an electronic source with no page numbers, simply exclude the page number from the citation. Do not add page numbers, and do not use those that a computer printer assigns.

Works Cited: Works Cited pages list the sources that are directly cited in the text. (Bibliographies or Works Consulted pages, on the other hand, list all the sources that a writer may have read and digested in the process of researching the project.) Entries in Works Cited pages must follow strict formatting guidelines, but the process is easy if you know the formulas involved. In general, the rule for in-text citation is that the information given should align with the first piece of information in the Works Cited. For example, notice the relationship between the in-text citation for King and the entire bibliographic information in the Works Cited page:

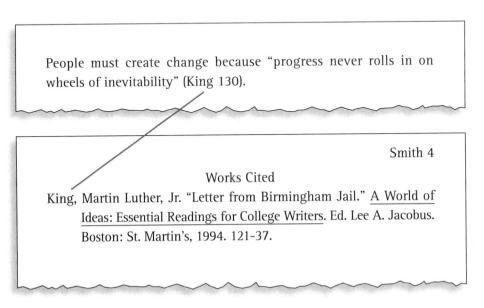

People must create change because "progress never rolls in on wheels of inevitability" (King 130).

Smith 4

Works Cited

King, Martin Luther, Jr. "Letter from Birmingham Jail." A World of Ideas: Essential Readings for College Writers. Ed. Lee A. Jacobus. Boston: St. Martin's, 1994. 121-37.

The following pages show specific formatting for different types of sources, but the following rules apply for all sources:

- Author name(s) comes first and is inverted (last name first) with a comma between first and last names.
- Title of the work comes directly after author name. In titles, all words except prepositions and articles (*a, an, the*) are capitalized.
- If no author appears, the title comes first.
- Article titles are in quotation marks (while the sources in which they appear, newspapers, journals and magazines, are underlined).
- Publication information follows the title of the source.
- Copyright or publication dates come last. But if the source is an article, then page numbers come last. If the source is electronic, the date of access and URL come last.
- Periods come after names of people (authors, editors, translators), after titles, the year of publication, and at the end of all entries.

Books

Bibliographic information for books is contained on the title page and the copyright page (the back side of the title page). The title page contains the full title of the book, the author(s), the publishing company and city. The copyright page contains date(s) and any edition numbers. Go to the title and copyright pages of this text and find all the information you would need to cite it as a source.

Author's name is inverted. For two or three authors, invert the first author's name and then list the next names, not inverted, directly after the first author. For more than three authors, add *et al.*, Latin for "and others," after the first name.

The title

Cook, Claire Kehrwald. Line by Line: How to Improve Your Own Writing. Boston: Houghton Mifflin, 1985. —— The date of publication.

City of publication. If the city is well-known, the name of the state can be omitted.

The publishing company

Corporate Author or Government Publication

Use the name of the corporation or the government agency for the author name.

American Automobile Association. Tour Book: New Jersey and Pennsylvania. Heathrow, FL: AAA, 2001.

If no publication information appears and the publication is a federal document, assume that it was published by the Government Printing Office in Washington, D.C.

Subsequent Editions

Place any edition information, found on the title page of a book, directly after the title. Use abbreviations: *2nd ed.*, *3rd ed.*, etc., or *Rev. ed.* for "Revised edition."

Tolkien, J. R. R. The Hobbit. Rev. ed. New York: Ballantine Books, 1982.

After the title of the book, add *Ed.* followed by the editor's name, not inverted.

Edited Book

Foucault, Michel. The Foucault Reader. Ed. Paul Rabinow. New York: Pantheon, 1984.

After the title of the book, add *Trans.* followed by the translator's name, not inverted.

Translated Book

Bakhtin, Mikhail. Problems of Dostoevsky's Poetics. Trans. Caryl Emerson. Minneapolis: University of Minnesota Press, 1984.

Articles

Articles appear in newspapers and periodicals (journals or magazines). While newspapers are usually published daily, magazines are usually published weekly or monthly, and journals are published quarterly or even biannually.

Article in Magazine

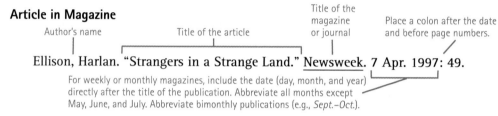

Ellison, Harlan. "Strangers in a Strange Land." <u>Newsweek</u>. 7 Apr. 1997: 49.

Author's name | Title of the article | Title of the magazine or journal | Place a colon after the date and before page numbers.

For weekly or monthly magazines, include the date (day, month, and year) directly after the title of the publication. Abbreviate all months except May, June, and July. Abbreviate bimonthly publications (e.g., *Sept.–Oct.*).

Article in a Journal Paginated by Volume

Most academic journals number the pages of each issue continuously through a volume. The second issue does not begin with page 1, but with the number after the last page of the previous issue.

Crow, Angela. "What's Age Got to Do with It? Teaching Older Students in the Computer-Aided Classrooms." <u>Teaching English in the Two-Year College</u> 27 (2000): 400-15.

The volume number comes directly after the title.

The year is in parentheses, followed by a colon and the page numbers.

Is It a Journal or a Magazine? At first glance, journals and magazines may look a lot alike. But closer inspection will reveal significant differences. Generally, journals are written for academic or highly specialized readers, and the articles put forward new theories or practices in a particular field of study (sociology, psychology, nursing, English, chemistry, history, etc.). Magazines are written for general readers, who may have a particular interest (cycling, running, gardening, and so on). If you are not certain what kind of periodical you have, use the following criteria:

Journals

- Seek to advance knowledge in a *field of study.*
- Deal with principles, theories, or core practices in an academic discipline.
- Associated with a particular discipline or field of academic study.
- Have few advertisements, which usually appear only at the beginning and end (not between or among articles).
- Have few colors and flashy pictures (unless they are related to a study or article).

Magazines

- Report information/news or offer how-to advice.
- Offer the latest technique in a hobby or sport.
- May appeal to readers with a particular *interest.*
- Have advertisements throughout the pages, even interrupting articles.
- Tend to have more colors and pictures.

Activity: Decide which type of periodical (magazine or journal) may have published the following articles, and in groups or as a class, discuss the reasoning behind your decisions:

"Heading for the Mountains: An Exciting Getaway for the Whole Family"
"Climactic Shifts in the Mountain Region"
"Coach Fired, Team Responds"
"Enzymes, Nutrition, and Aging: A Twenty-year Study"
"The Latest in Deep Water Bait"
"Re-inventing the Microscope"
"The Epistemology of Literature: Reading and Knowing"

Article in a Newspaper

If no author name appears, list the title first.

Add section letters before the page numbers.

"Bush: Shift Superfund Costs to Taxpayers." Blade [Toledo]. 24 Feb. 2002: A7.

Exclude articles (*a, an, the*) from publication titles, and add the city name in brackets if it does not appear in the title of the newspaper.

Scholarly Article Reprinted in an Anthology (such as a college textbook)
First, print the information for the article and then the information for the anthology in which the article appears.

Faigley, Lester. "Judging Writing, Judging Selves." College Composition and Communication 40 (1989): 395-412. Rpt. in Landmark Essays on Voice and Writing. Ed. Peter Elbow. Davis, CA: Hermagoras, 1994: 107–120.

Rpt. in (abbreviation for "Reprinted in")

The page numbers of the article

Encyclopedia Article

Author name (inverted) if one is given

The title (in quotation marks)

Esposito, Vincent J. "World War II: The Diplomatic History of the War and Post-War Period." Encyclopedia Americana. International ed., 2000.

The encyclopedia title (underlined)

The edition and year. (For familiar encyclopedias, you need not include volume number or city of publication.)

Other Sources

Pamphlet

Masonic Information Center. <u>A Response to Critics of Freemasonry</u>. Silver Spring, MD: Masonic Services Association: n.d.

Use abbreviations to indicate missing publication information: *n.p.* (no publisher or place), *n.d.* (no date), and *n.pag.* (no page numbers).

Personal Interview

The name of the interviewee, inverted

The date of the interview

Jackson, Lynn. Personal Interview. 4 Mar. 2002.

Personal Letter or Memo

The author name (inverted)

The title or description of the letter

Date

Bosley, Cindy. Letter to Leonard Kress. 15 Nov. 1999.

Published Letter

After the date of the letter, give the number of the letter if available.

Tolkien, J. R. R. "To Christopher Tolkien." 18 Jan. 1944. Letter 55 of <u>The Letters of J. R. R. Tolkien</u>. Eds. Humphrey Carpenter and Christopher Tolkien. New York: Houghton Mifflin, 2000: 67-68.

Information of the source in which the letter was published.

Television Program

Title of the episode or segment (in quotation marks)

Title of the program (underlined)

Name of the network (and call letters and city of the television station if appropriate)

"A Streetcar Named Marge." <u>The Simpsons</u>. Fox. 10 Oct. 1992.

The air date

Film

The title (underlined)

The director

<u>Monty Python's The Meaning of Life</u>. Dir. Terry Jones. Videocassette. Celandine Films, 1983.

The distributor   Year of release

The type of medium (DVD or videocassette)

Musical Composition

Composer's name (inverted)

Title of the work (underlined)

Do not underline the form, number, or key of a work

Strauss, Johann. <u>Tales from the Vienna Woods</u>, waltz op.325.

Sound Recording

Artist name

Title of a particular song or section (in quotation marks)

The collection title (underlined)

The recording company

The catalog number (if available)

Radiohead. "Karma Police." <u>OK Computer</u>. Capitol Records, 7 2438-55229-2 5, 1997.

The date of publication

Lecture or Speech

The speaker's name (inverted)

The title of presentation (in quotation marks)

Harkin, Patricia: "What's Wrong with This Picture? Teaching English in the Corporate Academy." Thirty-Third Annual CEA Conference. College English Association. The Westin Hotel, Cincinnati. 6 Apr. 2002.

The location of the lecture

The date

After the name of the meeting list the sponsoring organization.

Work of Art (painting, sculpture, photograph)

The artist's name (inverted)

The title of work (underlined)

The collector or institution that houses it

O'Keeffe, Georgia. <u>Evening Star No. VI</u>, The Georgia O'Keeffe Museum. Santa Fe, NM.

The city where it is held

Performance

The title (if applicable)

The author of the performed work (if applicable)

The performers

<u>A Christmas Carol</u>. By Charles Dickens. Perf. The Nebraska Theatre Caravan. Corson Auditorium, Interlochen, MI. 19 Nov. 2002.

The site of the performance

The date

Electronic Sources

Often, Web sites do not list authors. But when they do, author names should be documented as they are for print sources (inverted at the beginning of the entry). Like print sources, Web sites also have publication information, but it is different in nature: While a book, for instance, has a publishing company, a Web site is sponsored by an institution or organization (unless the site is a personal home page). Web site entries should include: the title of site (underlined), the date of publication or the date of the most recent update (if available), the name of the sponsoring institution or organization, the date when the researcher accessed the site, and the Uniform Resource Locator (URL)—which is often referred to, simply, as the "Internet address."

Often URLs can be excessively long and cumbersome. Rather than reproduce a URL that bleeds onto several lines of text, give the URL for the previous page in your search—if the reader can easily access the document by typing in the title or the author name. (When adding the URL to your citation, separate only after slashes [/] and do not add hyphens.) And with electronic sources especially, remember the basic principle behind citing sources: *to provide a guide for finding the sources you used.*

Web Site

Title of the site (underlined). If the site has no title, offer a description, such as *Homepage* (not underlined), in its place.

Pinsker, Sarah. Robin Flies Again: Letters Written by Women of Goucher College, Class of 1903. Goucher College. 29 May 2002 <http://goucher.edu/library/robin>.

Begin with the name of the Web site creator (inverted), if available.

The name of any sponsoring or supporting institution or organization

Date when you accessed the site

URL

Article in On-line Journal

Silva, Mary Cipriano and Ruth Ludwick. "Interstate Nursing Practice and Regulation: Ethical Issues for the 21st Century." Online Journal of Issues in Nursing 2 July 1999: 23 pars. 20 May 2002 <http://www.nursingworld.org/ojin/ethicol/ethics_1.htm>.

After the date of publication, give the range of pages or paragraphs (abbreviated as *pars.*). (In some instances, on-line journals will provide page numbers.)

On-line Book

If the book is part of an on-line scholarly project, include the sponsoring institution or director directly after the standard information for a print book.

Follow the format for print books.

McCreight, M. I. Chief Flying Hawk's Tales: The True Story of Custer's Last Fight. New York: Alliance Press Publishers, 1936. Online Books. Ed. John Mark Ockerbloom. University of Pennsylvania. 15 May 2002 <http://community-2.webtv.net/Wimz/CHIEFFLYINGHAWKS>.

Abstract

Use the format approriate for the type of source (book, article, etc.) and add the descriptor *Abstract* before the date of access and URL.

> Saline, Carol. "Are Philadelphia's Doctors Disappearing?" <u>Philadelphia Magazine</u>. 93.5 (2002): 88-91. Abstract. 29 May 2002 <http:// olc4.ohiolink. edu:20080/bin/gate.exe?f=doc&state=lqijnk.3.2>.

E-mail

Author of the e-mail | The title that appears in the subject line of the e-mail (in quotation marks) | Name of the recipient | Date the e-mail was sent. (If you are the recipient, write *E-mail to the author.*)

> Miller, Maria. "Changes to Physics Dept." E-mail to Dennis John. 23 Nov. 2000.

E-mail/Listserv Posting

Follow format for e-mail, but add the descriptor. | The name of the listserv or forum

> Brandywine, Jacob. "Raising Standards." Online posting. 19 Apr. 2001. Writing Program Committee. 23 May 2002 <hstrand@owens.edu>.

The electronic address of the listserv or the e-mail address of the moderator (in angle brackets)

CD-ROM

If no author is given, use the editor's, compiler's, or translator's name, with abbreviation (*ed., comp., trans.*) in its place. If none of these are listed, begin with the title.

> <u>The Trigonometry Explorer</u>. CD-ROM. Chevy Chase, MD: Cognitive Technologies Corp., 1996.

The label for the publication medium | Publication information (city, company, date)

On-line Encyclopedia

Title of the article | Title of the encyclopedia | Name of the on-line service | Date of access | If you found the source through a sequence of related topics, add *Path:* and then give the words in your search sequence, separated by semicolons.

> "India." <u>Encyclopedia Britannica</u>. Yahoo. 14 June 2002. Path: Reference; Encyclopedia; Encyclopedia Britannica; India; History. <http:// www.britannica.com/eb/article?eu=121168>.

Give the URL if available.

Sample Research Essay

Crofts wrote this essay for his English 112 class (a second-semester) composition course. As you read, take note of the strategies Crofts uses to integrate sources into his argument.

Chris Crofts

Professor John Mauk

English 112

May 10, 2002

Investigation of the Cyberspace Samurai

This is our world now . . . the world of the electron and the switch, the beauty of the baud. We make use of a service already existing without paying for what could be dirt-cheap if it wasn't run by profiteering gluttons, and you call us criminals. We explore . . . and you call us criminals. We seek after knowledge . . . and you call us criminals. We exist without skin color, without nationality, without religious bias . . . and you call us criminals. You build atomic bombs, you wage wars, you murder, cheat, and lie to us and try to make us believe it's for our own good, yet we're the criminals. Yes, I am a criminal. My crime is that of curiosity. My crime is that of judging people by what they say and think, not what they look like. I am a hacker, and this is my manifesto. You may stop this individual, but you can't stop us all . . . after all, we're all alike (Mentor).

The word seems to stir up dissension among those in the computer world: hacker. However, the possibility that hackers search out knowledge, instead of anarchy, is one quickly dismissed by the wave of media frenzy that accompanies the computer world. The media sometimes uses the word *hacker* instead of *cracker*. A cracker is a malicious person who uses password-guessing programs, packet sniffers, or other means to break into another person's computer account or otherwise defeat the security of a computer. There are three kinds of crackers, according to Steven Bellovin, a network security specialist for AT&T (Associated Press, February 17, 1995). The most common is the "cookbook" cracker. Cookbook crackers are not knowledgeable; they just collect tricks or "recipes" from other crackers and try them out. The second kind of cracker is the "creative show-off." These crackers use their own knowledge to break into computer systems, but only for fun, not for profit. The third kind of cracker is the "professional." These crackers use their knowledge to break into computer systems for profit or other serious purposes. The truth about hackers is known only by the select few who take the time to understand them. "Hacker" was originally a term of respect, given only to the most creative, clever computer users or programmers. Through misuse, the word now has derogatory meaning in the minds of the public (Barnet).

Crofts 2

Hackers have always tried to separate themselves from crackers. While the average cracker seeks destruction, hackers seek knowledge. The hacking community has devoted itself to solving problems. Often those problems occur in security systems. In many occasions, errors in computer hardware and software have no known solution. When this occurs, the usefulness of hacking comes into focus. When errors in computer systems occur, hackers invent ways to fix the errors. On occasion this means violating some computer laws. However, the countless instances of hackers breaking security codes and then quietly leaving seem too taboo among reporters who would rather research the cracker that accessed a credit card company's mainframe computer. There are indeed many laws against illegal access of private computing systems. However, do these acts of supposed terrorism by hackers who wish to improve security warrant the usually harsh sentences if they are caught? A person may be quick to assume the answer is "yes." However, these rulings are in many occasions based purely on the level of security breached, instead of the amount of damage done.

One example of this injustice took place in July of 1997. Hakuntla Devi Singla, the first woman convicted of computer hacking in the United States, penetrated a Coast Guard personnel database, the very database she constructed, from which she deleted information. However, under closer examination, we can obtain that Singla only accessed the Coast Guard database after being told her personnel records would not be forwarded to her new employer unless she dropped her Equal Employment Opportunity lawsuit against the Coast Guard. It is true that the accessing of the database by Singla did violate anti-hacking laws. However, this hack was only used to draw attention to the Coast Guard who blackmailed Singla after using her intelligence to build their database. Singla was sentenced to five months in prison, five months of house arrest, and ordered to pay a $35,000 fine. No action was taken against the Coast Guard for the allegations of sexual harassment by Singla (DiDio 72). This is hardly a just punishment without some form of investigation into the Coast Guard.

Unjust punishment is a subject weighed heavily by the minds and morals of those expressing their opinions. However, sheer logic would inform a person that a lawsuit by the Secure Digital Music Initiative in August of 1998 against Princeton Professor Edward Felten and his team of researchers lacked any warrant of illegal and/or unethical behavior. The controversy began when Felten's team, which also included researchers from Rice University and a Xerox research center, broke encryption technologies created by the SDMI. In a public challenge, the SDMI had been offering a $10,000 prize to anyone who could remove a digital water-mark from a music file in less than a month. The research team said they broke most of the encryption techniques within three weeks. Felten also noted that the team turned down the prize money so they wouldn't feel restrained in publishing their findings. But when the SDMI and the Recording Industry Association of America (RIAA) learned the researchers planned to present a paper at a conference in April, the RIAA sent a letter to Felten stating that "any disclosure of information gained from participating in the public challenge" could subject the researchers "to actions under the Digital Millennium Copyright Act" (Pack). With little examination one would quickly see the parody in this situation. However, perhaps it is a fair suit to sue a research team for publishing their findings resulting from a public contest held by those doing the prosecuting.

Despite the overwhelming evidence that hacking has been labeled inaccurately and often persecuted unjustly, the acting laws against hacking cry injustice more than do the past convictions. One such law states that no person shall "Produce, traffic in, or have device-making equipment." The punishment for violation of this law is a fine of $50,000 and/or a 15-year prison sentence. Repeat offenders receive a $100,000 fine and/or a 20-year prison sentence (Icove). Without comparison to other laws, one can easily observe the underlined injustice in the enforcement of this law. However, in comparing this law with others, the previous observation goes without saying. Rape of a person over the age of eighteen is punished only by a minimum sentence of three years (Young). Obviously there is something wrong here. The severity of these two crimes does not fit the punishment. It seems that we need to reexamine our views and values of acceptable and unacceptable behaviors. While neither crime may be acceptable, I would much rather live next to a person who spent time in prison for having a cloned cellular phone, instead of a rapist who got out early for good behavior.

Casting aside the negative views of hackers and the hacking community, one should also examine the positive results of hacking. Take for example the confession of a security manager who admitted to hiring a hacker. After being handed a piece of paper that would lead him to a page of customer names, addresses, phone numbers, and credit card numbers, the security manager decided to hire the young man who hacked his company's Web site. Following the incident the manager presented a statement to a journalist with *Computer-World* magazine.

Crofts 4

Most hackers, when faced with the opportunity to take advantage of a weakness and exploit it for some fiduciary gain, will shy away. Take a look at most of the "hacked" Web pages out there. The verbiage is that of an adviser: "This Web site hacked by [whomever]," or "Your security sucks. Your original home page is here [link to page]." Yeah, it's embarrassing and makes you feel violated, but most hackers will stop after they've hacked the Web page. I've got a fairly good sense about people, and I haven't made a hiring decision I've regretted. Anyway, that's my 2 cents on today's hackers and why I usually don't have a problem hiring them (Thurman).

This security manager has had the privilege of discovering what so many are still in the dark about; hackers have the means to fuel computer security for the years to come. Currently there seems to be an epidemic of security teams of hackers taking hold of the computer industry. The Houston-based Comsec Data Security, who claims to have three Fortune 500 companies for clients, credits its experienced hackers for giving it a unique perspective in developing better security systems (Steffora 43–46). When major companies like Microsoft or Compaq have new software they need checked for possible security weaknesses, they turn to elite teams of hackers. This hardly seems like the work of criminals.

If it were not for the curiosity and creativity of hackers, much of the business world would still be processed in filing cabinets and manual time clocks, which are manipulated easier than computer time clocks that require passwords to modify.

Hacking has also drawn the eye of the U.S. Government. Readily available encryption software easily turns e-mails and instant messages into strands of gobbledygook that can thwart even the pros at the National Security Agency. So agents for a time will have to resort to hacker-like methods. Bugging a computer let the FBI, in a 1999 investigation, listen in on a Mafia suspect. The FBI won't reveal how it did it, but defense lawyers suspect it was able to install software to capture each keystroke (Murphy). Perhaps the FBI won't reveal how it was able to bug the suspect's computer because they don't wish to reap the possible controversy that could result from an acknowledgment towards the usefulness of hacking. Then again, maybe that just goes without saying.

In light of the positive effect the hacking community has on the growth and development of the computer world, many still misconstrue what a hacker is. Instead of labeling hackers as "cyber-terrorists," we should look more closely at the purpose behind their activities. Vulnerabilities in networks exist, whether or not anyone knows about them. Hackers make these vulnerabilities known to the public. The process that hackers use in making these vulnerabilities known requires making sacrifices. Sometimes this means breaking the law. However, these laws are in place to deter any possible theft or malicious behavior. Punishing a hacker for exposing flaws in security is not an answer to the cracking problem. In fact it is just the opposite. Whether or not anyone will admit it, hackers help security professionals prevent damage to their systems at the hands of crackers. However, no matter how overwhelming the case for hacking is, there will always be people who blame hackers for the insecurities for which they are truthfully not responsible.

All bias aside, maybe hackers are to blame. Perhaps someone should be more outspoken and hold hackers accountable for what they have done. They are guilty of building and sustaining the World Wide Web. They are at fault for developing high-level encryption programs used by our government. They need to be punished for pushing current technologies to the very peak of their capabilities. They should be jailed for making it possible for people to communicate with each other over thousands of miles and for giving people access to a world of information simply by sitting at a computer with Internet access. But most of all, they need to be punished for seeking freedom, something well known by any United States citizen.

Hackers seek places without discrimination and stereotype. Places where what a person looks like does not reflect who they are in the minds of those they've never met. Is this view not similar to the views shared by those who founded the United States? Our founding fathers sought a place where men could worship freely, speak freely, and pursue a life of satisfaction and fulfillment. Hackers have discovered a place where knowledge is given without cost, where creativity, not conformity, is rewarded, and where the limits that a person can push themselves to are held only by the scope of their mind. We should all be so fortunate. There's a Biblical quotation etched on a stone wall in the CIA's lobby: "And ye shall know the truth, and the truth shall make ye free."

Knowledge is power because it allows you to make informed decisions based on how the world really is . . . and not on how you may otherwise believe it is (Scambray). According to Henry David Thoreau: "To know we know what we know, and know we don't know what we don't know is the only true knowledge." Hackers seek knowledge and understanding of a much greater magnitude than most would be willing to acknowledge. However, like those little security flaws, the knowledge is out there, whether or not we know about it.

Crofts 6

Works Cited

Barnet, Daniel J. <u>Bandits on the Information Superhighway</u>. Sebastopol, CA: O'Reilly
      & Associates Inc., 1996.

DiDio, Laura. "Behind the Hacking" <u>Computer World</u> 21 Sept. 1998. 19 Mar. 2002
      <http://olc4.ohiolink.edu/>.

Icove, David, Karl Seger, and William VonStorch. <u>Computer Crime: A Crimefighters</u>
      <u>Handbook</u>. Sebastopol, CA: O'Reilly & Associates Inc., 1995.

Mentor's Last Words. 16 Mar. 2002 <http://www.hackers.com/new/>.

Murphy, Victoria. "We Hack You." <u>Forbes</u>. Oct 2001: 50-51.

Pack, Thomas. "Legit Hack Creates Legal Controversy." <u>Econtent</u>. Oct. 2001: 9-10.

Scambray, Joel, Stuart McClure, and George Kurtz. <u>Hacking Exposed: Network Security</u>
      <u>Secrets and Solutions</u>. Berkeley, CA: Osborne/McGraw-Hill, 2001.

Steffora, Ann, and Martin Cheek. "Hacking Goes Legit." <u>Industry Week</u>. 7 Feb. 1994.
      19 Mar. 2002 <http://olc4.ohiolink.edu/>.

Thurman, Mathias. "'I Hired a Hacker': A Security Manager's Confession." <u>Computer World</u>.
      Feb. 2001: 50.

Young, Rudolph B. <u>Criminal Law: Codes and Cases</u>. New York: McGraw-Hill Book Co., 1972.

APA Style

The American Psychological Association (APA) documentation style is used in psychology, nursing, education, and related fields. But while the format is somewhat different from MLA, the strategies for finding, evaluating, and integrating sources remain the same. And even the basic principles of documentation remain the same across styles: the information in the in-text citation should correspond directly with the References page (the APA equivalent of a Works Cited page).

- In-text (or parenthetical) citations provide unobtrusive documentation of specific information.
- In-text citation lets a reader know that particular ideas come from a particular source.
- In-text citation corresponds to the complete bibliographic information provided at the end of the text.
- In-text citations lead the reader directly to the corresponding References page.
- Done correctly, the in-text citation is the first word(s)—whether it be the author's name or an article title—of the alphabetized References reference. This allows the reader to easily find the appropriate source on the References page.
- References page provides complete information for finding the source.
- This complete information is provided only once and comes at the end of the entire text so that it doesn't interfere with ease of reading.
- This complete information should allow the reader to find the source easily.

In-Text Citation: Like MLA style, in-text documentation for APA involves referencing the original text in parentheses within the actual sentences of your text. An in-text citation must occur whenever a writer:

- Quotes directly from a source.
- Paraphrases ideas from a source.
- Summarizes ideas from a source.
- References statistics or data from a source.

For direct quotes, APA in-text citations should include the author name, date (year only) of the source, and page number from which the cited material is taken. Include the author name in the citation unless it is given within the sentence.

"After months of exhausting research, they had finally come to understand the problem with their design" (Smith, 1998, p. 82).

Commas separate elements within the parentheses.

p. comes before the actual page number(s).

End punctuation comes after the parenthetical citation.

Writers using APA style often include the date directly after the author's name in the sentence.

Emphasizing her point, Miller (2000) demands that "it is now time for something drastic to change here on campus" (p. 43).

If the source has no author, use the first word or phrase of the source title and punctuate the title accordingly (either with quotation marks or italics).

"Even though most of the nation's coastal shorelines can no longer sustain a full range of sea life, the vast majority of Americans seem unconcerned" ("Dead Seas," 2001, p. 27).

If the source has two authors, use the last name of both authors. (Notice that APA style uses &, an ampersand.)

(Lunsford & Ede, 1984, p. 158)

If the cited material is quoted in another source, cite the source in which you found the quotation and add *as cited in* before the author name or title.

(as cited in Smith, 1998, p. 82)

If you want to acknowledge more than one source for the same information, use a semicolon between citations within one set of parentheses.

(Lunsford & Ede, 1984; Smith, 1998)

Electronic Sources: Many electronic sources (Web pages, for instance) do not have page numbers, but page numbers may appear on the hard copy. Unless the original source has page numbers, omit them from the in-text citation. Also, many electronic texts (especially Web pages) may lack authors; in that case, follow the same formula as with print sources and use the title of the source in the citation.

References: In general, the rule for in-text citation is that the information given should align with the first piece of information in the References list. The References list gives sources that are directly cited in the text. (Bibliographies or Works Consulted pages, on the other hand, list all the sources that a writer may have read and digested in the process of researching the project.) Entries in a References list must follow strict formatting guidelines, but the process is easy if you know the formulas involved.

The most basic idea in referencing sources is that the information in the in-text citation should correspond with the first piece of information given in the References list. For example, notice how the citation from Philips's essay (on p. 632) corresponds with the entry from her References list:

> In a recent survey in which 14,000 nurses responded, 41% said that they were dissatisfied with their job and 22% reported planning to quit within the next year (Freudenheim & Villarosa, 2001, p.17).

Nurse's Dilemma 9

References

Freudenheim, M., & Villarosa, L. (2001). Nursing shortage is raising worries on patients' care: Problem may get worse as more nurses join unions—complaints of long shifts and rising workloads. *Maine Nurse,* 3, 17. Retrieved Mar. 12, 2002, from http://www.ohiolink.edu/

The following pages show specific formatting for different types of sources, but the following rules apply for all sources:

- Author names come first. Last name first and first initial of first name (and middle name if given).
- Dates come in parentheses directly after the author names. If no author appears on the source, the title comes first.
- Title of the work comes directly after the date. Article titles are always in regular type, while the sources in which they appear, newspapers, magazines, and journals, are italicized. (Only the first letter of the title is capitalized unless there are proper nouns.)
- If no author appears, the title comes first.
- Publication information follows the title of the source.
- Cities of publication come last, but if the source is an article, then page numbers come last. If the source is electronic, the date of access and URL come last.

Books

All of the necessary information for books can usually be found on the title page, which is inside the front cover.

General Format for Books

Author last name and initials   Publication date in parentheses   Only the first word of the title is capitalized.   City of publication

   Cook, C. K. (1985). *Line by line: How to improve your own writing.* Boston: Houghton Mifflin.

Publishing company

Two or More Authors

Add all additional author names, also inverted, before the title.

   Vasta, R., Haith, M. M., & Miller, S. A. (1995). *Child psychology: The modern science.* New York: John Wiley & Sons, Inc.

Corporate Author

Use the name of the corporation for the author name. If the corporate author also published the text, write *Author* for the publisher.

   American Automobile Association. (2001). *Tour book: New Jersey and Pennsylvania.* Heathrow, FL: Author.

Subsequent Editions

Find the edition information on the title page of the book and place the information in the entry directly after the title. Use abbreviations: *2nd ed., 3rd ed.,* etc., or, as in the example below, use *Rev. ed.* for "Revised edition."

   Tolkien, J. R. R. (1982). *The hobbit.* (Rev. ed.). New York: Ballantine Books.

Edited Book

After the title, add the editor's name (first initial and last name) and *Ed.* (all in parentheses). Use *Eds.* if the book has more than one editor.

   Foucault, M. (1984). *The Foucault reader.* (P. Rabinow, Ed.). New York: Pantheon.

Translated Book

Add the translator's name (first initial and last name) and *Trans.* (all in parentheses) after the title of the book.

   Bakhtin, M. (1984). *Problems of Dostoevsky's poetics.* (C. Emerson, Trans.). Minneapolis: University of Minnesota Press.

Articles

Articles appear in newspapers and periodicals (journals or magazines). While newspapers are usually published daily, magazines are usually published weekly or monthly, and journals are published quarterly or even biannually.

Article in a Magazine

Include the date (year, month, day) directly after the author name. Do not abbreviate months.

Do not list volumes or issues.

Ellison, H. (1997, April 7). Strangers in a strange land. *Newsweek*, p. 49.

Article in a Newspaper

If no author appears, give the title of the article first, followed by the date.

After the title of the newspaper, add section letters before the page numbers.

Bush: Shift superfund costs to taxpayers. (2002, February 24). *The Blade*. p. A7.

Article in a Journal Paginated by Volume

Most academic journals number the pages of each issue continuously through a volume. The second issue does not begin with page 1, but with the number after the last page of the previous issue.

Crow, A. (2000). What's age got to do with it? Teaching older students in the computer-aided classrooms. *Teaching English in the Two-Year College, 27*, 400–415.

Place the volume number directly after the journal title, and before the page numbers.

Article or Chapter in an Edited Book

Mickelson, R. A., & Smith, S. S. (1991). Education and the struggle against race, class, and gender inequality. In E. Disch (Ed.), *Reconstructing gender: A multicultural anthology.* (pp. 303–317). Mountain View, CA: Mayfield.

Title of the book

Page numbers of the article or chapter (in parentheses)

Publication information

Encyclopedia Article

After author (if given) and date, give the title of the article.

Esposito, Vincent J. (2000). World War II: The diplomatic history of the war and post-war period. In *Encyclopedia Americana* (Vol. 29, pp. 364–367). Danbury, CT: Grolier Inc.

The name of the encyclopedia in italics

Volume number and page number(s) (in parentheses)

Other Sources

Brochure

Use abbreviations to indicate missing publication information: *n.p.* (no publisher or place), *n.d.* (no date), and *n.pag.* (no page numbers).

Masonic Information Center. (n.d.). *A response to critics of freemasonry.* [Brochure]. Silver Spring, MD: Masonic Services Association.

After the title, add the descriptor in brackets before the publication information.

Personal Interview or Letter

APA style recommends citing personal communications only with in-text citation—not in reference lists. In the in-text citation, give the name of the interviewee, the title *personal communication*, and the date.

(L. Jackson, personal communication, March 4, 2002)

Television Program

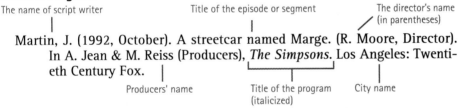

The name of script writer

Title of the episode or segment

The director's name (in parentheses)

Martin, J. (1992, October). A streetcar named Marge. (R. Moore, Director). In A. Jean & M. Reiss (Producers), *The Simpsons.* Los Angeles: Twentieth Century Fox.

Producers' name

Title of the program (italicized)

City name

Government Publication

If no author is given, use the government agency as the author, followed by the date and title (in italics), and the publication information that appears on the title page. If no publication information appears, and the publication is a federal document, you can assume that it was published by the Government Printing Office in Washington, D.C.

U.S. Census Bureau. (2002). *Statistical Abstract of the United Sates* (122nd ed.).

Electronic Sources

Like print sources, citations for electronic sources require author(s), date, title, and publication information. Authors and titles are formatted in the same manner as print sources. The difference occurs with publication information. The primary difference is that all entries for electronic sources require a Uniform Resource Locator (URL), or database name, and the date on which the source was accessed. After publication information, add *Retrieved,* the date, *from* and the name of sponsoring institution, the URL or the name of the database. (When adding the URL to your citation, separate only after slashes [/] and do not add hyphens.) Especially with electronic sources, remember the basic principle behind citing sources: *to provide a guide for finding the sources you used.* Therefore, the most direct route to the source should always be used in the entry.

Web Site

Name of the Web site creator (inverted), if available

Title of the site (italicized)

Pinsker, S. *Robin flies again: Letters written by women of Goucher College, class of 1903.* Retrieved May 29, 2002, from Goucher College: http:// goucher. edu/library/robin

The name of any sponsoring or supporting institution or organization

The URL

Article in On-line Journal

If the on-line journal is based on a print version (which is most common for academic journals), then follow the format for print articles, but after the article title, add the label [*Electronic version*] in brackets.

Crow, A. (2000). What's age got to do with it? Teaching older students in the computer-aided classrooms [Electronic version]. *Teaching English in the Two-Year College, 27,* 400–415.

Silva, M. C., & Ludwick, R. (1999, July 2). Interstate nursing practice and regulation: Ethical issues for the 21st century. *Online Journal of Issues in Nursing.* Retrieved May 20, 2002, from http://www.nursingworld.org/ojin/ethicol/ethics_1.htm

A Journal Article Retrieved from a Database

Boyd, Nancy G. (2002, March). Mentoring dilemmas: Developmental relationships within multicultural organizations. *Journal of Occupational & Organizational Psychology,* 123–125. Retrieved May 20, 2002, from Ohiolink database.

A Document within a Scholarly Database

Name of the designer/   The title   Any sponsoring institution
editor of the content   or organization

Hay, R. *Archive for the history of economic thought* [Electronic database]. Hamilton, Ontario: McMaster University. Retrieved May 14, 2002, from http://socserv2.socsci.mcmaster.ca/~econ/ugcm/3ll3/

On-line Book

Follow the format for print books, but exclude the original print publication information. After the title, insert *[Online]* and the sponsoring organization or institution.

McCreight, M. I. (1936). *Chief Flying Hawk's tales: The true story of Custer's last fight.* [Online]. University of Pennsylvania. Retrieved May 15, 2002, from http://community-2.webtv.net/Wimz/CHIEFFLYINGHAWKS

Activity: Make a References entry for the following article. (Consider the nature of the source in addition to the specific publication information.) Compare your entry with others in the class and discuss any differences.

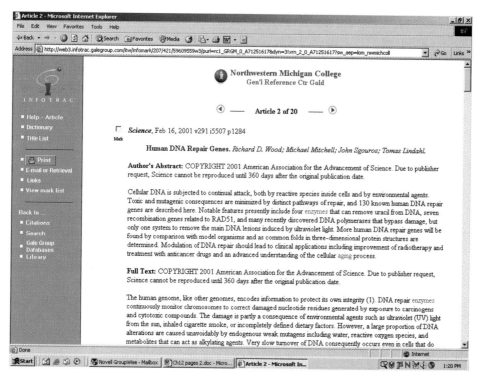

APA Format

The APA format requires a title page and an abstract.

Title Page: The title page includes the title, your name, course number, instructor's name, and date. You may arrange this information as shown below or present it all centered and in the top half of the title page. (For more information, refer to the APA Style Manual, 5th ed., or www.apastyle.org.) Also, include a shortened form of the title and the page number at the top of the title page and on all subsequent pages.

1/2" from top
shortened title and page
number

Title centered and double-
spaced if longer

Your name, in the center of
the page both vertically and
horizontally

Course title, instructor's name,
and date (double-spaced)

Nurse's Dilemma 1

Nurse's Dilemma: Fight or Flight

Gina Philips

English 112

Dr. John Mauk

May 10, 2002

Abstract: An abstract summarizes the main ideas of an essay in about 100 words. (If the project involves primary research, the abstract should also include research method, findings, and conclusions.) It goes on a page of its own, following your title page.

Nurse's Dilemma 2

Abstract

The current shortage of nurses was studied through secondary research. Retention of licensed RNs would be the most immediate cure. Many issues, including salary/benefits and working conditions contribute to current job dissatisfaction. Although research shows that nurses with bachelor's degrees have better critical thinking, leadership, and patient education skills, requiring more education at this time could backfire, helping to perpetuate the current shortage. Nurses must become activists, helping to "establish and maintain conditions of employment conducive to high quality nursing care" (Lindberg, Hunter, & Kruszewski, 1998, p. 44). Some states have recently passed legislation regarding nurse to patient ratios. These initiatives are the result of nurses standing up and fighting for themselves and for their patients.

1/2 inch
shortened title and page
number

Triple-space
center
no indentation

Double-space text

Sample Research Essay

Gina Philips wrote this essay for her English 112 class, a second-semester composition course. As you read, notice how Philips uses sources to develop ideas.

Nurse's Dilemma 3

Nurse's Dilemma: Fight or Flight

Few in the health care profession would deny that our country is in the midst of a nursing shortage. According to the California Healthcare Association vacancies average 20% in the state's 470 hospitals (Tieman, 2001). Joseph Boshart, president of Cross County Travcorps, one of the largest temporary nurse staffing companies in the country, says that there are currently 100,000 openings for registered nurses (Freudenheim & Villarosa, 2001, p. 17). The shortage has been purported to be a health care crisis that threatens the quality of care and patient safety. Peter Buerhaus, associate dean at the Vanderbilt University School of Nursing, has said that the nursing shortage is one of the dominant issues in health care today. He reports that in some cases the problem is so severe that hospital nursing floors have been shut and surgeries cancelled. "'This crisis has the potential to create a disaster scenario in terms of quality of care,'" Buerhaus said (as cited in Freudenheim & Villarosa, 2001, p. 17).

"Today's nursing shortage is a warning signal for tomorrow's healthcare organizations" (Coile, 2001). It looks like the situation is only going to get worse. At the present time there are still more nurses entering the field than are abandoning the profession, but according to a Buerhaus study published in *The Journal of the American Medical Association* last year, that trend will shift by the year 2006. At that time more nurses will be leaving than will be entering the field ("Coming up short," 2000).

So if quality of care and patient safety is an issue under the current circumstances, it's hard to imagine what's in store for those needing care four years from now. The time is now to address solutions to the nursing shortage. We need to look at why our country is in such dire need of nurses. Most experts agree that the reasons include nurses leaving the profession and college bound students avoiding the health care field (Atzori, Lupia & Tonges, 2002, p. 5).

Retention of licensed RNs would be the most immediate cure to the nursing shortage, but it's hard to make someone stay in a job that they aren't happy doing. In a recent survey in which 14,000 nurses responded, 41% said that they were dissatisfied with their job and 22% reported planning to quit within the next year (Freudenheim & Villarosa, 2001, p. 17). There are many issues that contribute to job dissatisfaction. These include: salary and benefits, practice environmental conditions, quality of care, professional autonomy and physical demands (King, 2000, p. 3).

Nurse's Dilemma 4

According to a February 2001 report by the Bureau of Health Professions in the federal Department of Health and Human Services, adjusted for inflation, average nurse salaries have hardly changed since 1992 (Freudenheim & Villarosa, 2001, p. 17). As one nurse explains it, "The industry is going to have to pay us significantly more and institute changes with us to support professional practice that is based on standards of care and quality" (as cited in King, 2000, p. 3). While salaries and professional autonomy are certainly viable complaints that perpetuate the feelings of dissatisfaction, the larger issues of mandatory overtime and unsafe nurse-to-patient ratios are more likely at the root of the problem.

Workloads need to be managed with increased support services and improved staffing (as cited in King, 2000, p. 3). In many hospitals, nurses are required to take care of ten or more medical and post-surgical patients who are often very ill. The numbers of patients per nurse are increasing and workloads in general are increasing. A nurse in California expresses that "the work is tremendously hard and stressful" (as cited in Freudenheim & Villarosa, 2001, p. 17). On top of the heavy workloads, because of short staffing, many nurses are forced to stay on the job when they are exhausted after a 12-hour shift. Mandatory overtime is a major concern. Nurses have an overwhelming fear of making mistakes when they are exhausted. It then becomes a patient safety issue (Freudenheim & Villarosa, 2001, p. 17).

It's no wonder that fewer younger Americans are choosing careers in health care and more specifically nursing. Why would a student choose a career that is "tremendously hard and stressful" when they have so many other professional choices? This is evidenced by the American Association of Colleges of Nurses report that enrollment of nursing students into entry level programs has fallen six consecutive years (Freudenheim & Villarosa, 2001, p. 17). The challenge then is to make nursing an attractive career choice for the younger generations. In the *Journal of Healthcare Management* Russell Coile (2001) states, "Health care organizations need to engage in long-term strategies that will restore the image and career potential of nursing as a profession" (pp. 224–227).

Many suggestions have been made as to how to make nursing a more attractive career choice. One that the American Nurses Association (ANA) supports is to reform nursing education and the licensure and certification mechanisms used to grant practice to RNs with different educational preparation. Entry level nursing education is currently offered in four year baccalaureate programs, two-year associate degree programs, and three-year hospital diploma programs. Each graduate receives the same license regardless of the degree program they pursued. Graduates of each program usually get the same entry-level positions and salaries as well ("Dramatic Reforms," 2001).

Under such a system there is no incentive to pursue a bachelor's degree because there is no return for the investment of extra time and money spent on additional education. Research has shown, however, that nurses with a bachelor's degree have better critical thinking, leadership, and patient education skills as compared to RNs with associate degree or diploma education. Although there is a perceived difference in skill level only 44% of surveyed institutions paid differentiated salaries based on education ("Dramatic Reforms," 2001).

Geraldine Bednash, PhD, RN, FAAN, Executive Director of the American Association of Colleges of Nursing, believes that the stability of the U.S. health care system depends on well-educated nursing personnel "with clearly defined roles that are sanctioned through a system of licensure and certification. Recognizing the contributions of RNs to the delivery of high-quality health care and to the well-being of those health systems will provide potential nursing students with an attractive and rewarding career option" (as cited in "Dramatic Reforms," 2001). She also says that without these dramatic reforms that the predicted shortages of 2006 will surely be a reality ("Dramatic Reforms," 2001).

This rationale does make some sense. It seems only fair that a person with additional education should have more responsibility and get paid more, but it doesn't seem like a solution to the nursing shortage in and of itself. These reforms would likely increase the numbers of students entering baccalaureate programs, but what about the students who choose to become RNs because licensing can be acquired in two years? How many of them wouldn't choose a career in nursing because they didn't have the time or money to get a four-year degree? It should also be noted that under the current system, no matter the degree program that the student follows the licensing exam they take is the same. So if an associate degreed nurse weren't well prepared, he/she wouldn't likely pass the licensing exam. I feel that the drastic reforms that Ms. Bednash supports could actually backfire and help perpetuate the problem rather than help fix it. I believe that the major reforms need to take place in the workplace. Why go to school for four years instead of two only to have mandatory overtime and inadequate staffing to look forward to?

Nurse's Dilemma 6

In order to increase RN retention and improve the image of nursing as to attract more college-bound students I propose that nurses become activists, lobbying with full force to bring about changes that will ensure patient safety and make nursing a profession which they can be proud to call their own. Nurses make up the largest percentage of the health care industry. Nurses need to be a force for change! If nurses are so significant to health care and in such short supply they need to stand up and make their voices heard (Hendrickson, 2001). It's time for those who spend their working hours helping others to help themselves before they become casualties of the nursing profession because of burnout and fatigue.

For some nurses this may be hard to do. In the past nursing has been degraded by feminists as "traditional women's work done by unassertive workers" (Lindberg, Hunter & Kruszewski, 1998, p. 407). While it is difficult to be branded so unfavorably, many nurses will agree that this has been true to some extent. Nurses have not banded together to use their personal power nor have they regularly demonstrated the use of coalition strategies to further their cause. "Individual and group strategies can and should be used by nurses of both genders to achieve personal self-actualization and to influence health care policy" (Lindberg, Hunter & Kruszewski, 1998, p. 407).

In actuality it is already the RN's responsibility to do this. According to the ANA's code for nurses, "The nurse participates in the profession's efforts to establish and maintain conditions of employment conducive to high quality nursing care." It goes on to say, "The nurse participates in the profession's efforts to implement and improve standards of care" (Lindberg, Hunter, & Kruszewski, 1998, p. 44). Each RN must choose to contribute something to the cause of their profession or accept the fact that their destiny will continue to be determined by those outside of nursing (Hendrickson, 2001). Each RN must decide whether nursing is just a job or a profession. "A professional insists on, promotes and supports the maintenance of standards of professional conduct and performance. A professional draws the line at what he or she will or won't do. A professional encourages and mentors those who follow him or her in their profession" (Hendrickson, 2001).

There are some nurses who are trying to be a force for change. More nurses are joining unions; an estimated 17%, or nearly 450,000, RNs belong to unions today, and the nurse's unions are becoming more active (Coile, 2001). Nurses have been getting increased attention from legislatures. Fifteen states including New York, Connecticut and Illinois are weighing

Nurse's Dilemma 7

bills that would prohibit forced overtime for nurses. Maine and New Jersey have already passed overtime measures.

The issues regarding unsafe nurse-to-patient ratios are also getting attention. Research has shown that when there are more nurses, there are lower morbidity rates, shorter lengths of stays, and fewer patient complaints (Robbins, 2001). Charles Idelson, spokesman for the California Nurses Association, representing 40,000 nurses, believes that nurses' working conditions can't be improved without safe staffing levels. He feels that mandated ratios would have a direct effect on employment rates as they have in Australia. Ratios were instituted there last year and they've had a 13% increase in the nursing workforce (Tieman, 2001, p. 10).

California has actually passed a nurse staffing law, becoming the first state to pass legislation requiring that nurses monitor only a certain number of patients. What they can't decide on is how many patients the law will allow for each nurse. While nurses, hospitals, unions and others have made recommendations, the California Nurses Association would like to see hospitals provide one RN for every three patients in med/surg units, the emergency room, and step-down/observation (Coile, 2001). At the present time they are considering emergency regulations that would require hospitals to operate under emergency ratios until the final ones can be evaluated and implemented (Tieman, 2001, p. 10). Although the laws will have California hospitals struggling to find more nurses in order to be in compliance with the mandated staffing, it does seem to be a step in the right direction for nurses.

Kentucky and Virginia are also in the process of setting standards for appropriate staffing, and legislatures have introduced less specific proposals in New York, Ohio, and Oregon (Freudenheim & Villarosa, 2001, p. 17). In Springfield, Illinois they had a Staff Nurse Political Action Day at the Capitol Building to promote "The Patient Safety Act." The Illinois Nurses Association believes that the "Act" will halt the further demise of quality care by proposing a qualified system to determine adequate staffing based on patient care needs (Robbins, 2001).

Nurses can be a force for change! All of these initiatives are the results of nurses standing up and fighting for themselves and for their patients. Improved working conditions for nurses doesn't just make their life easier; everyone benefits from a "healthy" nursing profession because we are all healthcare consumers. How many hours a nurse has been working and the number of patients that each nurse cares for affects each of us at some point in our lives. As for me, I'd rather be one of the three patients the nurse is taking care of rather than one of the ten.

Nurse's Dilemma 8

References

Atzori, M., Lupia, I. M., & Tonges, M. C. (2001). Nursing shortage: Nurses at Robert Wood
  Johnson University hospital say "It is time to do something about it!" [Electronic
  version]. *New Jersey Nurse, 31,* 1–5. Retrieved March 12, 2002, from
  http://www.ohiolink.edu/

Coile, Russell C. Jr. (2001). Future trends: Magnet hospitals use culture, not wages, to
  solve nursing shortage. *Journal of Healthcare Management, 46,* 224–227. Retrieved
  March 12, 2002, from http://www.ohiolink.edu/

Coming up short in the RN department. (2002). *New Jersey Nurse, 30,* 2. Retrieved March
  17, 2002, from http://www.ohiolink.edu/

Dramatic reforms required to head off cycles of nursing shortages, *JAMA* editorial
  recommends. (2001). *Maryland Nurse, 2,* 22. Retrieved March 3, 2002, from
  http://www.ohiolink.edu/

Freudenheim, M., & Villarosa, L. (2001). Nursing shortage is raising worries on patient's
  care: Problem may get worse as more nurses join unions—complaints of long shifts
  and rising workloads. *Maine Nurse, 3,* 17. Retrieved March 12, 2002, from
  http://www.ohiolink.edu/

Hendrickson, R. R. (2001). Where have all the nurses gone . . . ? *Maryland Nurse, 2,* 1–4.
  Retrieved March 12, 2002, from http://www.ohiolink.edu/

King, S. (2000). The future of nursing workforce. *Oregon Nurse, 65,* 3. Retrieved March
  17, 2002, from http://www.ohiolink.edu/

Lindberg, J. B. H., Love, M., & Kruszewski, A. Z. (1998). *Introduction to nursing.* 3rd ed.
  New York: Lippincott.

Robbins, P. E. & G.W. Update: RNs urge action in Springfield. *Chart, 98,* 2–3. Retrieved
  April 15, 2002, from http://www.ohiolink.edu/

Tieman, J. (2001). Counting down: California lawmakers face staffing ratio deadline.
  Modern Healthcare, 31, 10. Retrieved April 15, 2002, from http://www.ohiolink.edu/

Frequently Asked Questions

What If I Don't Know What Type of Source I Have? This question often comes up in researching electronic sources. Most on-line research methods lead to either periodicals (journals, magazines, and newspapers) or Web sites. (On-line books are generally not in the same search paths as periodicals.) If you have an electronic source and are not sure if it is a Web site or a periodical, check the top of the first page for publication information. If the text has a volume, issue, or date information, it is most likely a periodical. Also, an electronic article most often contains the title of the magazine or journal at the top of the first page.

How Do I Tell the Difference between a Journal and a Magazine? In general, a magazine is published more often than a journal. Magazines are published every week (*Time, Newsweek*), every other week, or even every month. Magazines are also written for nonspecialized, or *general*, readership, whereas journals are written for readers with a specialized field of knowledge (such as nursing, engineering, or pharmacology). While magazines attempt to inform or entertain the public about various (sometimes even eccentric) topics, journals attempt to investigate particular ideas, theories, or situations within a discipline or field of study. Check the publication information to see how often the periodical is published and look at the table of contents to see if the articles are written for general or specialized readers. (See p. 590.)

How Do I Find the Publication Information? Publication information for books can be found on the title page. The front of the page has the full title, the publisher, and the city of publication, and the reverse (or copyright page) includes the copyright dates and any edition information. For periodicals, the volume and issue number usually appear at the bottom of each page and are often printed on the first page inside the cover along with the table of contents. However, some periodicals fill the first few pages with advertisements. Web sites can be more tricky. If the author, last update, or sponsoring institution does not appear on the opening (or home) page, scroll down to the bottom of the page (or look on the menu for *Information* or *About Us*).

How Do I Know the Page Numbers of an Electronic Source? Generally, electronic sources do not have page numbers—and documentation styles do not require page numbers for Web sites or on-line journal articles. Sometimes, however, a print source will publish contents electronically and retain page numbers. (In other words, the source appears on-line exactly as it does in print.) In that case, simply use the page numbers as they appear.

Should I Use APA or MLA or What? MLA (or Modern Language Association) style is used by writers in languages and literature (such as English and communications). APA (or American Psychological Association) style is used by writers in the medical field, education, and, of course, psychology. CMS (or Chicago Manual of Style) is used by writers in humanities fields, such as religion, history, and philosophy. The sciences (such as physics and chemistry) have particular styles as well. When writing for an academic audience, you should always ask what style to use. Some instructors want their students to use a particular style, regardless of their major or field of study.

Why Are There Different Documentation Styles? The different styles have emerged over the course of years, and they have developed because different research techniques sometimes call for a particular type of documentation. As academic fields grow, they develop and reward particular research strategies—and one documentation style cannot always account for those strategies.

Standard Abbreviations

Ed. = Editor
Eds. = Editors
ed. = Edition, usually associated with a number (4th ed.)
Rev. ed. = Revised edition
n.d. = No date
n.p. = No publisher or no place
n.pag. = No page numbers
Trans. = Translator
p. = page number
pp. = page numbers
No. = Number
pars. = Paragraphs
Vol. = Volume

13

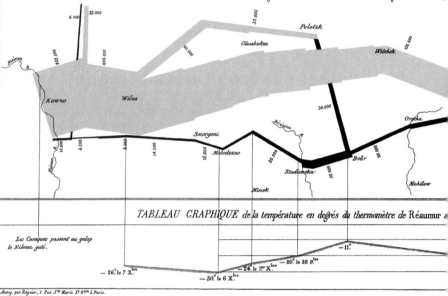

Chapter Contents

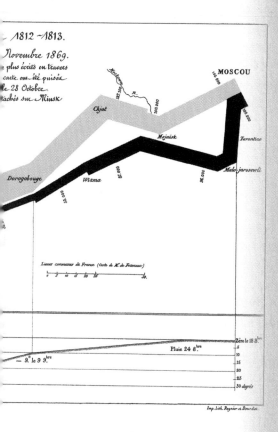

Everyday Rhetoric

*Research Charles Minard's graphic of
Napoleon's 1812 Russian campaign.
How many different types of information
(time, temperature, direction, and so on)
does Minard's graphic convey?*

■ **Verbal Communication**

Speeches

Briefings

Discussions

■ **Visual Communication**

Visuals: Analyzing an Image

Visuals and Written Text

> ## If I had a voice, hey, this is what I'd sing.
>
> —*Randall Bramblett*

The **Invention** and **Delivery** sections of Chapters 1–11 can be used not just to write essays, but for all types of communication—whether written, spoken, or visual. This chapter discusses some of those other types of communication, showing how the principles of invention and delivery apply, for example, to letters, memos, e-mail, Web sites, speeches, posters, and so on. It does not, however, teach you how to create a Web site, because that is beyond the scope of this text. Instead, this chapter looks at these non-essay forms of communication in the following ways: (1) it discusses the forms in general; (2) it shows, through a sample or two, what each form can look like; (3) it points out a few of the most important invention and delivery strategies from Chapters 1–11; (4) it provides opportunities for practice.

A look at letter writing illustrates this chapter's approach. Letters are so various that a comprehensive discussion of letter writing cannot be given here. But from rambling love letters to concise business letters, rhetoric is involved—the same rhetoric discussed in Chapters 1–11. The writer has a point of contact, does some analysis, and considers the public resonance of the writing situation. He or she considers what rhetorical tools will work best, determines organizational strategies, cultivates an appropriate writer's voice, revises, delivers the message, and consequences follow. Of course, the public resonance of a love letter is different from that of a business letter or a letter to the editor of a newspaper. And the public resonance of one business letter will be different from the public resonance of another business letter. This chapter invites you to think about what the difference is or might be, to consider each rhetorical situation you find yourself in, and to choose from the toolbox of strategies discussed in Chapters 1–11.

By *rhetorical situation* we mean any situation in which a person wants to communicate an idea to another person or group. It involves both the purpose in writing and the audience. Early on, communicators decide what form their communication will take. Will it be an essay, letter, brochure, flier, speech, discussion? For example, imagine you must miss the next two weeks of a class. How will you approach your professor about this? Will you discuss it after class, during office hours, or when you bump into him or her at the grocery store? Will you write an e-mail, a letter, or an essay? Or will you do nothing at all? Imagine another scenario: you work at a large company and have consistently been under-paid for working overtime. You have made phone calls and even talked to the payroll manager in person about this, yet the problem continues. Would a letter be appropriate, or is another face-to-face meeting necessary? Determining the form of communication is often a difficult decision that itself requires thoughtful analysis.

The form should be appropriate to the situation. And the form itself will influence the rhetorical decisions that you make. For example, creating a brochure calls for rhetorical decisions different from those used in writing an essay. The strategies and tools available have been discussed in Chapters 1–11; now it is a matter of applying them to the most appropriate form of communication. The essay is a good form for learning rhetorical strategies that can then be transferred to other everyday forms of communication.

WRITTEN COMMUNICATION

Consider a few everyday rhetorical situations. What form of communication might you choose and why? What specific circumstances would most influence your decision? For example, wrecking a friend's car would create a rhetorical situation: You need to tell him about it. You might discuss it with him, make a speech about it, e-mail him, write him a letter, draw a picture, and so on. Your decision would be influenced by various factors, such as the nature of your relationship and whether or not the two of you are physically near each other.

What form might you choose for each of the following rhetorical situations, and how might specific circumstances affect your decision?

Rhetorical Situations

- You must miss the next two weeks of this class.
- You have missed the last two weeks of this class.
- You broke your roommate's favorite coffee cup.
- The sales reps you manage are filling out monthly report forms incorrectly.
- The phone company has overcharged you for the fifth month in a row.
- A salesperson saved you $1,500 by advising you to buy a better and more reliable sailboat that you were not aware of.
- The street in front of your house has deep potholes.
- Your neighborhood has become full of stray dogs and cats.
- The airline lost your luggage.
- You suspect your neighbor of criminal activity.

1. Think of another rhetorical situation you have found yourself in lately. What created the situation? What form did you choose to address it? What other form might you have chosen? How did specific circumstances affect your decision? (That is, why did you choose that form instead of another?) How did the form you chose affect the rhetorical decisions you made? For example, how did the form affect the organization or the voice of the communication?

2. Think of rhetorical situations that you have not found yourself in yet, but that you can imagine might arise, and answer the above questions about them.

Letters

Perhaps the most significant difference between writing an essay and writing a letter is the relationship between the reader and the writer. The more general audience of an essay is usually replaced in letter writing by a more specific reader who has different expectations.

- To meet the reader's expectations, the letter writer must speak directly to the reader, usually about some particular situation, as opposed to an issue in general.

- The letter writer and letter reader might actually know each other or not. Even if one writes a love letter to a stranger, that stranger is a specific stranger and not "strangers in general." The same is true of a sales letter or a letter of application. While the writer may not personally know the potential client or employer, the letter can be crafted with a particular reader in mind.
- The relationship between reader and writer in a letter-writing situation affects the writing decisions made, thus influencing what is said, the way it is said, and the way it sounds to the reader.

Activities

1. List several situations in which a letter would be an appropriate form of communication. Use the following categories: personal, professional (or workplace), civic (or political), and academic.

2. Share your list (#1 above) with several other people, asking them to suggest other situations that would call for a letter to be written.

3. Write a real letter—not one for a class assignment. Don't make any writing decisions to improve your grade; instead, just write a letter with your only purpose being to convey an actual—not contrived—idea. Consider, but don't limit yourself to, the following situations:

   - to thank someone who has helped you
   - to suggest a better way of doing something
   - to solve a problem
   - to assure someone that you are doing well

4. Examine the letter you wrote for #3 above and identify the rhetorical tools you made use of. For example, did your letter have a main claim? What type of support, or evidence, did you provide? Did you include any counterarguments or concessions? Did you use any qualifiers? You might also look for logical fallacies (to be avoided), narration, description, and figurative language.

5. Examine an actual letter not written by you and identify the rhetorical tools it makes use of. (See #4 above.)

6. Consider the organizational strategy of a letter you wrote. Describe your opening strategy—that is, what were you trying to achieve in your opening paragraph(s)? Then describe your closing strategy. Explain the effectiveness of the arrangement—or order—of ideas. Identify several strategies you used to clearly show the relationship between ideas (such as transitional words, phrases, and sentences; grammatical structure; punctuation; etc.).

7. Consider the writer's voice of a letter you wrote. Describe in a few words the way you intended to sound (stern, friendly, silly, urgent, etc.). Then refer to several specific passages that illustrate your writer's voice.

8. Evaluate several letters. What was the writer trying to achieve? How successfully did he or she achieve it? Describe the strengths and weaknesses of the letter and refer specifically to rhetorical tools, organizational strategies, and writer's voice. Suggest how making different rhetorical, or writing, decisions would have improved the letter.

Professional Letter

Therese Cherry

This letter is based on the invention and delivery strategies that Therese Cherry used to write her essay "Beware of Drug Sales" in Chapter 5. As you read Cherry's letter, notice her writing decisions regarding rhetorical tools, organizational strategies, and writer's voice. You may want to compare those decisions to the ones she makes in her essay.

205 West 5th Street
Kenmore, OH 46904
(213) 555-9086
April 22, 2002

Ruth Weisheit, Public Affairs Specialist
Brunswick Resident Post
Food and Drug Administration
3820 Center Road
Brunswick, OH 44212

Dear Ms. Weisheit:

As a concerned citizen and patient, I have become very alarmed at the growing addiction to prescription drugs in the United States. Though the medical advancements of our time are to be applauded, it seems that stricter regulations on the marketing and prescribing of these drugs may be in order to help ensure public health.

According to the United Nations International Narcotics Control Board, advanced countries are overdosing on quick fix pills to ease non-medical problems like fat and stress. The INCB also reported that mood-altering drugs are often prescribed for social problems, such as unemployment or relationship problems. Not only are many of these drugs being prescribed unnecessarily, they are increasingly dangerous. According to Steven Pomper's May 2000 article "Drug Rush" in the *Washington Monthly On-line,* toxic reactions to marketed drugs are estimated to cost more than 30 billion dollars per year and to be among the ten leading causes of death in the U.S. Six new drugs approved since mid 1996 have been pulled off the market, and 150 deaths were linked to these drugs before they were pulled.

2

Although part of the problem involves unnecessary prescriptions being written, the aggressive marketing of these drugs appears to play a key role in this addiction issue. "Drug Rush" also reported that in 1997, the FDA loosened restrictions on the marketing of pharmaceutical companies, due in large part to heavy pressure from the pharmaceutical industry. This made it possible for drug companies to advertise on T.V. without spending huge chunks of time describing risks and side effects. And the 2000 Journal of the AMA has researched and shown findings that doctors are influenced to prescribe drugs that are marketed more heavily. Recent studies in Health Magazine stated that three-quarters of the respondents who saw one of these ads on T.V. and asked their doctors to prescribe it were successful.

Apparently, many factors have contributed to this growing epidemic, but none so fully or irresponsibly as the marketing companies that are pushing these drugs. The INCB stated in its 2000 report that there was a "continuing existence of aggressive sales methods and even some cases of financial support to various advocacy groups to foster sales" and appealed to the pharmaceutical industry to demonstrate social responsibility and voluntary cooperation. Even people in the industry will concede off the record that groups acting as advertising agents for manufacturers should be subject to FDA regulations. Since this voluntary cooperation does not seem likely, I would like to know what actions the FDA, as well as other organizations, are taking to curb the aggressive sales tactics of these pharmaceutical drugs.

The growing use of new and heavily marketed drugs for the ease of social conditions is not going to just go away. I am concerned about this issue and would like to learn how I can get involved with organizations that understand the importance of placing stronger restrictions on advertisers. Thank you for taking the time to address my concerns and I would appreciate any information you can send me.

Sincerely,

Therese Cherry

Therese Cherry

Letter to the Editor

Daniel Bruno

This letter to the editor is based on the invention and delivery strategies that Daniel Bruno used to write his essay "Entitlement Education" in Chapter 6. Notice the writing decisions Bruno makes (rhetorical tools, organizational strategies, writer's voice) and how his decisions for this letter are similar to and/or different from the decisions he makes for his essay.

—In Your Opinion—

Entitlement Education

The American education system is failing. But why? Today's student has what Peter Sacks, in his book *Generation X Goes to College*, calls a "sense of entitlement." Today's students, or many of today's students, think showing up entitles them to not just a passing grade, but to a B or better. And many parents support their children in this belief.

What these students and their parents need to know is that many other students do not expect A's and B's for just showing up, for putting forth a minimal effort, or for paying tuition. Instead they work hard and develop good attitudes and skills that prepare them for a competitive future. The students who feel entitled are the ones getting cheated because the gap between the more motivated and the less motivated students grows wider.

By the time they both graduate from college, the less motivated students are at a greater disadvantage than when they began college.

There is plenty of blame to go around. And, unfortunately, implementing the solution on a large scale seems impossible. Entire systems, educational and otherwise, are difficult to change. But a solution is possible: For their own benefit, the individual student and the individual parent must take action before it is too late. They must understand the reality of the situation. Yes, they can get good grades quite easily, but so what? Feeling entitled and sliding by can leave them severely disadvantaged. The entitlement mentality must be discouraged early in a child's life, or else by the time a student reaches college, it might be too late.

Daniel Bruno
Perrrysburg

For two weeks, read a different Letter to the Editor each day, preferably from different publications. Study the significance and the public resonance of each letter, along with the rhetorical tools, organizational strategies, and writer's voice. Write down how the writer's words do or do not go beyond the common beliefs of the reader, and how someone might think or act differently after reading the letter.

Personal Letter

Chester McCovey

This personal letter is based on the invention and delivery strategies that Chester McCovey used to write his essay "The Parting Breath of the Now Perfect Woman" in Chapter 10. Notice McCovey's writing decisions regarding rhetorical tools, organizational strategies, and writer's voice, and consider how—and why—his decisions are sometimes different and sometimes the same for this letter and his essay.

Nancy,

I finally read "The Birthmark" by Nathaniel Hawthorne. Thanks for recommending it! You're right! It's a great story, though the language is a little tough in places. I got used to that after a while, though, and actually enjoyed the poetry of Hawthorne's writing.

I like the story because it is put together so well. Rereading the story, you see that he laid it all out in the first paragraph, and there's plenty of excellent foreshadowing throughout. Can anyone deny that Hawthorne really is a masterful short story writer? And the theme is so relevant today: I guess you'd have to say the story is "timeless." Isn't it interesting that a story written in the eighteenth century is so relevant to what's going on today? Aylmer's attempt to make a beautiful woman perfect reminds me of our own faith in science, our own attempts to genetically engineer better tomatoes, "perfect" our chins and noses, and suck the fat out of our stomachs and thighs.

Of course I'm not against science altogether. I just wonder if we haven't lost perspective. Where do you draw the line? Once I say I'm "not against science altogether" I see how gray this area becomes. I can see the value of certain cosmetic surgery, but wonder if we as a culture are like Aylmer, trying to take something that's already naturally beautiful and make it perfect? Or, make it what we consider to be perfect? Good story! Hawthorne is talking about a very contemporary concern here.

How long, I wonder, have such stories been written or told? Do you know? The theme (man fiddling with nature) became very popular in the fifties, after the atom bombs were dropped on Japan (remember all those bad sci-fi movies), and I'm certain the theme was popular before that: There's Mary Shelley's "Frankenstein" which was written in the 1800s. Does this theme go back to the Greek classics, the Old Testament, and so on? How is this theme related to "original sin"? Wow. Let me know what you know about this. I'm interested. And by the way, how do you pronounce "Aylmer"?

Thanks again for the recommendation. Keep 'em coming, not that I'll be able to read them all.

Chet

Memos

Memos—short for "memorandums"—are a common type of everyday workplace communication. While letters are most often used to communicate with people outside of one's organization, memos are used among workers within an organization to deliver and receive information essential to doing their jobs.

- Memos vary in their degree of formality. Factors such as the seriousness of the subject matter and the relationship between the reader and the writer will determine the degree of formality.

- Memos are written to quickly convey essential workplace information. While an essay asks the reader to spend time carefully reading from beginning to end, a memo may use headings, bulleted lists, and other techniques that allow the reader to locate and take in the most relevant information. This strategy can also be applied to letters and essays.

- Memos are usually typed, rarely handwritten, and can be sent by e-mail.

Learning to Write Memos: Beyond Format

There is more to writing a memo than just learning how to format one. Notice how the memo format serves a *purpose*—namely, to help communicate important workplace information quickly. In addition to setting up the memo with **To, From, Subject,** and **Date** headings, the text of the memo should be made easy to read and understand.

Rhetorical tools, organizational strategies, and writer's voice issues discussed throughout this book will help you to write thorough and concise memos as you convey necessary work-related information.

Activity: Complete all six activities on the following page. Then, based on your experience, write a memo to a classmate explaining the most important things he or she needs to know to write a good memo. Be sure that you go well beyond describing the format of a memo, focusing instead on the rhetoric of workplace communication.

Activities

1. Interview several professionals—preferably in your field—to find out what role memos play in their work. How often do they write and receive memos? What sort of information do the memos convey? Are they sent on paper, via e-mail, or both ways?

2. Share the information gathered from interviews with professionals (#1 above) with your classmates, compiling a list of about ten situations that led to the writing of a memo (for example, to announce a new policy, to inform employees of an upcoming event, etc.). For each situation, what other form of communication might have been used to convey the information? Why was, or wasn't, a memo the best form to use?

3. Write a memo to a classmate who missed class. Don't make any writing decisions to improve your grade; instead, approach this as a real-life situation in which you want to inform the classmate of important information he or she needs to know. For example, did the professor talk about important concepts? Was there an assignment, and if so, what was it?

4. Evaluate the memo you wrote to a classmate (#3), looking at rhetorical tools, organization, and writer's voice.

   A. What rhetorical tools can you identify? For example, what was your memo's main claim or main idea? How did you support it? Where did you provide specific details? Where might you have been more specific?

   B. What organizational strategies did you employ to help the reader? Did you arrange ideas chronologically or did you put the most important ideas first? How might your arrangement—or ordering—of information help or hinder the reader's understanding? How did you connect ideas for the reader? Did you use headings, lists, or any other techniques to help the reader *see* information more easily?

   C. Describe the writer's voice of your memo. Was it formal, friendly, professional, dry, or something else? How did you hope to sound to the reader, and were you successful? Refer to several specific passages as support.

5. Rewrite a memo, going for a different writer's voice. Make it a little more casual or a little more formal. Then compare the two memos: which do you prefer and why?

6. Keep the same text of a memo, but lay it out differently. Try to make the memo more readable just by using headings, lists, underlining, boldface, and so on. Break paragraphs up in different places and indent differently. When you are done, explain how you have improved your memo's readability.

Memo to Michael Toth

Therese Cherry

This memo is based on the invention and delivery strategies that Therese Cherry used to write her essay "Beware of Drug Sales" in Chapter 5. Notice not just the formatting changes, but also the different rhetorical, or writing, decisions she makes, including rhetorical tools, organizational strategies, and writer's voice. Notice how the different writing situation influences Cherry's writing decisions (including format).

MEMORANDUM
National Council of Medical Practitioners

TO: Michael Toth, V.P. of Health Care Administration, Midwest Region
FROM: Therese Cherry, Assistant to the Secretary of Public Health
SUBJECT: Aggressive Marketing of Pharmaceutical Drugs
DATE: April 23, 2002

The United Nations International Narcotics Control Board (INBC) recently stated that advanced countries are overdosing on quick fix pills to ease "non-medical" problems like fat and stress (Dawn 1). It also reported that mood-altering drugs are often prescribed for social problems, such as unemployment or relationship problems (BBC 1).

These facts are not unknown to the NCMP, and due to the growing concern in the field of health care professionals, it is time to address this issue and determine any possible solutions.

Risks of Overprescribed Drugs

Not only are a rising number of patients taking prescription drugs to cure the normal stress that goes along with everyday life, the danger to public health is climbing too.

1. Toxic reactions to marketed drugs are estimated to cost more than 30 billion dollars per year and to be among the ten leading causes of death in the U.S. (Pomper 6).
2. Six new drugs approved since mid 1996 have been pulled off the market, and 150 deaths were linked to these drugs before they were pulled (Pomper 8).

Aggressive Marketing Partly to Blame

Pharmaceutical drugs are being advertised more widely and more frequently than ever before. The 2000 Journal of the AMA has shown findings that doctors are influenced to prescribe drugs that are marketed more heavily. And with all new drugs, there are some side effects and understudied long term results that are unknown.

2

1. In 1997, the FDA caved to heavy pressure from the industry and loosened restrictions, making it possible for drug companies to advertise on T.V. without spending huge chunks of time describing risks and side effects (Pomper 7).
2. As a result, recent studies in *Health Magazine* reported that three quarters of the respondents who saw one of these incomplete ads on television and asked their doctors to prescribe it were successful (Pomper).

Obviously, patients should have every possible benefit and opportunity to improve their health, but it is unethical and a disservice to say that an informed decision can be based solely on these ads. The fact is, some of the side effects of the newer drugs are unknown even to physicians.

A Call for Responsibility

The most obvious way to cope with this growing epidemic would be to leave health care between the physicians and their patients, and to advertise these pharmaceutical drugs with full disclosure. Unfortunately, marketing companies are in the business of selling products to make the money, not to cure the disease.

1. The INBC stated in its 2000 report that there was a "continuing existence of aggressive sales methods and even some cases of financial support to various advocacy groups to foster sales" and appealed to the pharmaceutical industry to demonstrate social responsibility and voluntary cooperation (Dawn 2).
2. "Even people in the industry will concede off the record that groups acting as advertising agents for manufacturers should be subject to FDA regulations" (Pomper 6).

Although the FDA has allowed restrictions to be lifted, physicians still bear the responsibility of the care of their patients and the prescription of medication. When prescribing these drugs, responsible physicians fully disclose all possible risks to the patient, including what is unknown. Along with more responsible dispensing of these drugs, the NCMP supports a lobby to the FDA to apply stronger restrictions on the marketing of pharmaceutical drugs.

As health care professionals, we must regard this crisis with utmost importance, and the Secretary of Health encourages and welcomes any insights or suggestions from you and your staff. Thank you for your time and concern for this important issue. Any questions or comments can be e-mailed to *tcNCMP@publichealth. com*, or you can call me directly at (216) 555-4351 ext. 366.

Memo to Faculty

Daniel Bruno

This memo is based on the invention and delivery strategies that Daniel Bruno used to write his essay "Entitlement Education" for Chapter 6. Notice how this writing situation calls for a different form of communication—a memo instead of an essay—and how this different situation and form require, or allow, Bruno to make different writing decisions regarding rhetorical tools, organizational strategies, and writer's voice.

To: All Faculty
From: Daniel Bruno, Vice-President for Academic Affairs
Re: Faculty Discussion on Entitlement Education
Date: August 20, 2002

Welcome back, Faculty. As we begin another academic year, I would like to encourage discussion regarding our responsibility to incoming and continuing students, particularly regarding what Peter Sacks describes in his book *Generation X Goes to College* as the students' "sense of entitlement."

Our first of several planned discussions will be Tuesday, September 10th at 10:30 a.m. in College Hall, Room 12.

We will begin our discussion by considering this question: Can students in today's American education system graduate from high school and some colleges with minimal effort and minimal learning? We will openly discuss this question, whether this happens at State College, and what might be the consequences for students and the community overall.

A particular concern of mine is that such students would ultimately find themselves severely disadvantaged because so many other students do not possess an entitlement mentality. These students grow and develop a great deal during their time at college. If this is true, the gap between the more-motivated and the less-motivated students grows even wider, leaving some college-educated students at a greater disadvantage than when they entered college.

What is our responsibility as faculty and what action can we take to best serve our students? I hope you can join me to discuss these important issues. If you have any questions or comments before September 10th, you can reach me at 555-5151 or at dbruno@ statecollege.edu.

Memo to Vice President

John F. Kennedy

This memo from President Kennedy to Vice President Johnson is a historical document, as it eventually led to the United States sending astronauts to the moon. According to the National Aeronautics and Space Administration's (NASA) History Office, the memo was written April 20, 1961, after a week of discussion about how the United States should respond to the April 12 orbital flight of Soviet cosmonaut Yuri Gagarin. Vice President Johnson responded to this memo with a memo of his own on April 28. That memo and others can be found at NASA's History Office Web site (http://www.hq.nasa.gov/office/pao/History/Apollomon/docs.htm). As you read, consider Kennedy's purpose and how he achieves it. What different writing decisions might he have made if speaking or if writing an essay?

THE WHITE HOUSE

WASHINGTON

April 20, 1961

MEMORANDUM FOR

VICE PRESIDENT

In accordance with our conversation I would like for you as Chairman of the Space Council to be in charge of making an overall survey of where we stand in space.

1. Do we have a chance of beating the Soviets by putting a laboratory in space, or by a trip around the moon, or by a rocket to land on the moon, or by a rocket to go to the moon and back with a man. Is there any other space program which promises dramatic results in which we could win?

2. How much additional would it cost?

3. Are we working 24 hours a day on existing programs. If not, why not? If not, will you make recommendations to me as to how work can be speeded up.

4. In building large boosters should we put out emphasis on nuclear, chemical or liquid fuel, or a combination of these three?

5. Are we making maximum effort? Are we achieving necessary results?

I have asked Jim Webb, Dr. Weisner, Secretary McNamara and other responsible officials to cooperate with you fully. I would appreciate a report on this at the earliest possible moment.

News Releases

An activist who wants exposure for a cause might send a news release to a local media outlet, such as a newspaper, radio, or TV station. The goal of a news release—to get media exposure—should be kept in mind when making writing decisions.

- Media outlets receive far more news releases than they have time to report on. So sending the release to an appropriate outlet, getting to the point quickly, and providing complete and accurate information in a concise and coherent manner are all key to writing a successful news release.

- News releases are short announcements—only a page or two. Because they compete for attention with many other news releases, they follow a standard format, style, and structure that allows an editor to process their information quickly.

- News releases generally begin with an opening sentence that answers the questions *who, what, when, where*, and *why*. The story itself is often arranged in a pyramid structure, with ideas being presented from most to least important.

- The style of a news release is objective and straightforward. Sentences are fairly short, figurative language is rare, and personal reflections are generally avoided.

Activities

1. List several situations in which a news release would be an appropriate form of communication. To help you generate ideas, think in the following categories: personal, professional (workplace), civic (or political), and academic.

2. Who on your campus might send out a news release?

3. Write a news release announcing one of the following:

   - a campus organization will be holding a protest
   - a campus organization will be holding a fundraiser
   - you alone will be holding a protest or a fundraiser

   Play it straight. That is, practice writing an actual news release, even though you may have fabricated the writing situation for this assignment.

4. Exchange news releases with as many classmates as you can, looking carefully at their rhetorical tools, organizational strategies, and writer's voice. Select the one or two news releases you think would most likely get media exposure. Explain why you think so. That is, why did you select them? Consider their content as well as the rhetorical decisions the writers made in presenting the information.

5. Write a letter—see Letters, pp. 646–651—to a local journalist, inviting him or her to talk to your class about the similarities and differences among journalism and other styles of writing.

6. What rhetorical strategies that apply to writing a news release apply to other forms of communication as well? How might writing a good news release help you to develop valuable skills for essay or letter writing?

1999 Nobel Peace Prize News Release

Nobel Foundation

Each year the Nobel Foundation awards prizes in Physics, Chemistry, Physiology or Medicine, Literature and Peace. This press, or news, release announces the Nobel Peace Prize for 1999. Other releases can be found at the Foundation's official Web site. As you read this news release, consider its purpose and how rhetorical tools, organizational strategies, and writer's voice are used to achieve that purpose.

DEN NORSKE
NOBELKOMITE
The Norwegian
Nobel Committee

THE NORWEGIAN NOBEL COMMITTEE

The Nobel Peace Prize 1999

The Norwegian Nobel Committee has decided to award the Nobel Peace Prize for 1999 to **Médecins Sans Frontières** in recognition of the organization's pioneering humanitarian work on several continents.

Since its foundation in the early 1970s, Médecins Sans Frontières has adhered to the fundamental principle that all disaster victims, whether the disaster is natural or human in origin, have a right to professional assistance, given as quickly and efficiently as possible. National boundaries and political circumstances or sympathies must have no influence on who is to receive humanitarian help. By maintaining a high degree of independence, the organization has succeeded in living up to these ideals.

By intervening so rapidly, Médecins Sans Frontières calls public attention to humanitarian catastrophes, and by pointing to the causes of such catastrophes, the organization helps to form bodies of public opinion opposed to violations and abuses of power.

In critical situations, marked by violence and brutality, the humanitarian work of Médecins Sans Frontières enables the organization to create openings for contacts between the opposed parties. At the same time, each fearless and self-sacrificing helper shows each victim a human face, stands for respect for that person's dignity, and is a source of hope for peace and reconciliation.

Oslo, October 15, 1999

Brochures

Brochures, or pamphlets, come in different forms but are often a single sheet of paper folded twice to create six panels, three on the front and three on the back. The physical characteristics of brochures influence the rhetorical decisions a writer makes.

- A brochure unfolds—as does the information within it. Whereas writing an essay involves dividing information into categories (sections, paragraphs, sentences), writing a brochure involves the additional concern of fitting that information into fixed spaces—the panels of the brochure.

- Writing brochures requires both good organization and conciseness.

- Brochures are used to advertise a product, service, program, policy, or idea. A brochure might inform you—or attempt to persuade you—about a particular brand of lawnmower, how to stretch before working out, a college program, and so on.

- Brochures, like essays, have a main idea and support for that idea. They are clearly organized, and the information is carefully arranged. Ideas are connected through transitions, grammatical consistency, and visual elements. As with other forms of writing, the writer's voice should not alienate the reader, and the brochure must be carefully revised and edited before being made public.

Activities

1. Brochures are all over your campus. Make note of them as you walk through offices and hallways, and take two or three brochures that grab your attention. Make a study of the ones you took, considering the following questions:

   A. How important is the visual element to the brochure's success?

   B. How is the brochure organized? Does one of the panels act as a title page or an introduction? Does the brochure have a conclusion? Is information arranged chronologically or by order of importance?

   C. What do you find confusing—or hard to follow—about the brochure? Is anything about the brochure unappealing or troubling?

2. Create a six-panel brochure "advertising" a particular grammatical concept, such as "How to Avoid Sentence Fragments" or "Four Basic Comma Rules."

3. Give a draft of your brochure to a classmate (or several classmates) and ask for help. Guide your classmate with specific questions. For example, you might ask about your use of rhetorical tools: What does your classmate think is your main idea? What support did he or she find most convincing? What other support might be helpful? Also ask about your organizational strategy (the arrangement and connection of ideas) and your writer's voice (how the way you sounded affected the reader). Consider the peer advice you received and revise your brochure.

How to Make a Six-Panel Brochure

Brochures come in different shapes and sizes, but anyone can make a six-panel brochure using regular 8½ × 11 paper. To understand the relationship among panels, make two folds in a sheet of paper, as illustrated below, and notice which panel acts as the front, the back, and so on.

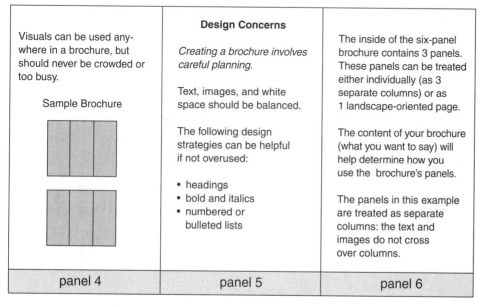

side 1

	Back Cover	**Front Cover**
The six-panel brochure is designed to lay flat and be folded. The panels in this illustration are numbered 1, 2, 3, 4, 5, and 6 for easy reference. Panel 1 is opposite panel 6. Panel 2 is opposite panel 5 Panel 3 is opposite panel 4. Before designing a brochure on a computer, try sketching out some ideas on folded sheet of paper.	When opened and laid flat, this middle panel sits next to the front cover, but when folded, it acts as the back cover. It often includes concluding information such as a summary of main points, publication and contact information such as addresses, and a key image or two. copyright 2004 Sample Brochures	This panel acts as brochure cover and may include a title, an image, and text conveying main ideas. Image
panel 1	panel 2	panel 3

side 2

	Design Concerns	
Visuals can be used anywhere in a brochure, but should never be crowded or too busy. Sample Brochure	*Creating a brochure involves careful planning.* Text, images, and white space should be balanced. The following design strategies can be helpful if not overused: • headings • bold and italics • numbered or bulleted lists	The inside of the six-panel brochure contains 3 panels. These panels can be treated either individually (as 3 separate columns) or as 1 landscape-oriented page. The content of your brochure (what you want to say) will help determine how you use the brochure's panels. The panels in this example are treated as separate columns: the text and images do not cross over columns.
panel 4	panel 5	panel 6

Posters and Fliers

Posters and fliers concisely present information on one page. Posters, which vary in size, are meant to be "posted" on a vertical surface (wall, window, etc.), while fliers, which are smaller, are meant to be handed out.

- Like essays, posters have a main idea and probably make an argument—that is, they provide evidence, or support, for that idea. A poster advertising a film, for example, is arguing that you should see that film. More specifically, it might be arguing that you should see the film because it is an exciting thriller or a really wacky comedy.

- Both posters and fliers use visual layouts to get the reader's attention, and then deliver main points with supporting material.

- Images are often used and may even play a more prominent role than words. While some posters and fliers do rely on text to develop an idea, others rely more on images or figurative language.

- In some fields, poster presentations are used at conferences to convey complex information quickly.

Activities

1. Collect at least three posters or fliers and consider what argument each one is making. Write down its main claim in one complete sentence (not just a phrase), and then describe in a paragraph how the claim is supported. Refer to specific rhetorical tools, organizational strategies, and writer's voice.

2. Exchange posters and fliers (from #1) with classmates and write down the main claim and its support for each one. Then discuss. Did classmates disagree about what some posters or fliers were claiming? What was the reason for the disagreement?

3. Find at least one poster or flier that you think is not making a claim. Show it to several people to see what they think it is claiming.

4. Create a class collection of posters and fliers promoting local bands. Which ones are most successful and why? Consider (1) what each one communicates about the band, and (2) how successfully it encourages the intended audience to support the band. If you can't find many posters or fliers about different bands, collect ones about local talks or other events.

5. Create a poster or flier for any claim you want to make. After completing it, write an essay explaining why a poster or flier is an appropriate form of communication for that situation. What is it about the poster or flier form that makes it a good way to communicate that message? What other forms might you have chosen? What would have been their advantages and disadvantages? How did the poster or flier form affect your writing decisions—rhetorical tools, organizational strategies, and writer's voice?

6. Create a poster or flier for an appropriate situation. Consider, but do not limit yourself to, the following situations:

   - inviting others to participate in something
   - asking for assistance
   - offering assistance

What visual elements combine to create a sign or poster?
What elements combine to create an effective image?

How do visual elements that occur naturally
become strategies for communicating?

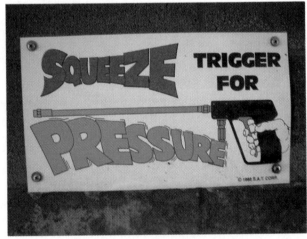

Poster Rhetoric

Location: Posters usually work better in high traffic areas, where people are more likely to notice them. This poster is placed on a door and will be noticed many times by people entering the stairwell.

Information: Key words on the poster are more prominent. The poster to the right announces itself to fans of Jazz! The rest of the poster provides important information quickly.

Some posters provide long sections of text, as do some ads in magazines, based on the theory that some people will stop and read the small print.

Time: Posters frequently convey timely information—an upcoming concert, for example. The poster above is actually two posters, the blue one promoting a Dick Hyman concert, and the red and white one drawing attention to the poster's timeliness—Tonight. The original poster has been on the door for several days; the additional poster, added the day of the concert, focuses solely on time.

Visual Elements: Posters, like fishing lures, attempt to catch the audience's interest. Posters do this visually, with colors, pictures, and layout. The poster above illustrates several important visual elements: It is colorful, it has a picture of a piano keyboard, and key words (Jazz, Dick Hyman, and Tonight) stand out.

Posters, fliers, signs, and notes are members of the same family. Location, information, time, and visual elements all contribute to their rhetorical effectiveness. Additionally, the physical element—an egg—contributes to the poster, or sign, to the left.

From notes on refrigerators to neon signs in Times Square, common rhetorical strategies apply.

Leaflet from the War in Iraq (2003). Notice how the leaflet appeals to the readers' values. It engages their sense of hope, family, community. Rather than merely telling the Iraqi soldiers to lay down their arms, it invites them to reflect on their lives beyond the military struggle. (For more leaflets, visit http://www.iwar.org.uk/psyops/resources/iraq.)

With posters, it's all about impact!

- Posters and signs are written to be "read" quickly.
- Short word bursts should be large and legible.
- A poster should not be cluttered with a lot of intricate graphics.
- Bold, contrasting colors are useful.

E-mail

Because it can be written and sent quickly, before the writer has had time to reflect and revise, e-mail poses special concerns. E-mail is a good example of how particular forms of communication affect the rhetorical decisions that must be made. For example, revising and considering consequences are always important, but *because* e-mail is such a convenient way to communicate, sometimes they are overlooked. Thus, writers must focus on revision and consequences. Consider the following examples, each sent by a student to her composition instructor:

> Professor peace, my name is michele grier I am in your 12:00 m.w.f class. i just wanted to let you no I will be not be able to attned class tonight. Because I'am required to have to attend a jaazz concernt for a history of jazz class I am taking. I care very much about class attnedance and don't like to miss it. I will turn in tonighs writing assignment next class period if you will except it I hope you will please let me know if we did naything important class today. thank you, michele

> . . .

> Professor Walker,

> I will be absent from class tonight because I have to attend a jazz concert for my History of Jazz class. I will put a copy of tonight's homework in your mailbox this afternoon. And I will get an update on tonight's class from Pete and Racquel. If there's anything else you can tell me, please do.

> Thank you,
> Kelly Birdsong (12:00–1:50 M/W/F)

While both e-mails express the same basic thoughts, they impress the reader in different ways.

Sending an e-mail prematurely is like saying something you should not have said. Because of the spontaneous nature of speech, most people have at some time said something they wish they could take back. E-mail allows time for revision, but also allows the writer to click "send" *before* he or she has adequately revised or reflected on consequences. Consider another e-mail, this one sent in the heat of the moment:

> I am very upset with my grade. I worked hard on my paper and you ripped it apart. You rip all my papers apart and I'm sick of it. I have never gotten bad grades before like this. I tried to ask you about my paper after class but you were to busy. I think if your not going to help me when I have a question you shouldn't grade so hard. Everyone around me feels the same way. My paper deserved an A not the B you gave me. I think you should change it and reconsider the way you teach and grade.

Although this student has expressed herself clearly and may have made legitimate points about the class, her writer's voice is not inviting and might even be alienating to the reader. The rhetorical tools, organizational strategies, and writer's voice sections of Chapters 1–11 apply to e-mails as well as to essays.

Activities

1. Reflect on your own e-mail use. In what situations do you send e-mail? What forms of communication might you use instead, and why do you choose e-mail?

2. Review several old e-mails you have sent, focusing on rhetorical tools, organizational strategies, and writer's voice. How do you express main ideas and support them? How else might you have done so? Describe your organizational strategy—the arrangement of ideas and how they are connected—and point out other ways you might have organized your e-mail. Describe your writer's voice and how it might influence the reader.

3. Rewrite an old e-mail you have sent and discuss the improvements you made in terms of rhetorical tools, organizational strategies, and writer's voice.

4. Copy and paste several excellent e-mail passages you have received, and then explain why you think each one is excellent writing.

5. Write an e-mail for the following situation: your car broke down and you missed a final exam. Print out your e-mail and exchange it with a group of classmates. Then decide which rhetorical tools, organizational strategies, and writer's voice are most effective.

Activity: Evaluate Robin's e-mail response to John's request for directions. What rhetorical tools and organizational strategies does she use to communicate more clearly? How helpful do you think Robin's response would be and why?

Hi Robin. Are you getting this email at work? My questions for you is: If I park on 80th St in Brooklyn, what block should I park on (that is, what streets should I park between)?
AND, what train do I take to the Edison Hotel?

Hi John,

Park between 3rd and 4th Avenue. It runs one way from 4th to 3rd. You may have difficulty finding a spot. You can go to other blocks if necessary to find a spot. The subway is on 4th Avenue at 77th St.

When do you expect to arrive? If I am going to be home, you could come to my house and I could then accompany you to the city. If that is not the case, get on the Manhattan-bound "R" train. Take it to 36th in Brooklyn. Get off the train. Stay on that same platform. A Manhattan-bound "W" train will arrive directly across the platform. Get on that train. It is an express train and it will get you where you are going much faster. It also goes over the Manhattan Bridge so you get a nice view. The "R" train goes through a tunnel. It will take you to exactly the same stop in Manhattan but at about double the travel time. Get out at 49th St. in Manhattan. Your hotel is on 47th St. between Broadway and 8th Ave. It is very close to the subway stop. Make sure you have a map of the city. When you get on the subway, ask the guy in the booth for a subway map. They are free.

So, let me know when exactly you plan to arrive. I would like to be home. It will make your trip into the city much more pleasant if I am with you.

Robin

Web Sites

Most Web sites rely on *hypertext*, unlike an essay, which is presented linearly. Hypertext allows the writer to present an idea without stopping at that moment to develop it further. Instead a link is provided to the supporting or related information. A Web site's homepage "greets" visitors, letting them know what the site is about and providing links to other Web pages. Those other pages can either be other pages of the site or other Web sites.

The nature of the Internet itself influences the rhetorical decisions a writer must make.

- As with other forms of communication, writers must be aware of (1) what they are trying to achieve, (2) what their readers expect, and (3) what the form of communication allows them to do, requires them to do, or prevents them from doing.

- Purposeful writing, accurate and up-to-date information, effective organization, and conciseness are all important when creating a Web site. Since people tend to skim text quickly on the Internet, a Web site must have a point and be strategically organized, featuring main ideas and allowing for easy navigation from one idea to another. Sentences should be concise.

- Visual elements such as colors (for background and fonts) should allow for easy reading, as should other design elements, such as spacing and images. A conservative approach often allows for easier reading.

- Since the Web makes it easy to include visuals, most Web sites include them—thus, readers expect them. Visual elements (such as photographs, icons, artwork, and animation) should be kept simple, and Web sites can be successful without them.

- Pages that take too long to download are likely to be skipped over by most Web users; thus, the size of an image, video, and sound files should not be too large.

Activity: Visit the Web sites for your school, your school's library, and this book, and do the following:

1. Write down what you consider to be the strengths and weaknesses for each site, and why.
2. Share the strengths and weaknesses you wrote down with a group of classmates, discussing how their ideas are similar to or different from your own.
3. Draw conclusions, based on your group discussion, about each Web site. What are its strengths and weaknesses, and why?
4. Write a letter, memo, or essay evaluating the sites and proposing changes for improvement.

Activities

1. What rhetorical situations (such as selling a product) call for a Web site? Surf the Internet to discover as many different situations as you can.

2. Find at least three Web sites you think are effective. Identify the purpose of the site and explain how the site achieves that purpose. Refer to rhetorical tools (such as how main ideas are expressed and supported), organizational strategies (such as the arrangement and connection of ideas), and writer's voice. Also, discuss other design elements such as colors, spacing, the use of visuals, and hypertext.

3. Create a Web site with at least four links: two to other pages you have created for your Web site and two to other Web sites. Then write an essay explaining how effectively you used rhetorical tools, organizational strategies, and writer's voice on your site.

4. Ask a classmate to look at your Web site (#3) and explain how effectively you used rhetorical tools, organizational strategies, and writer's voice.

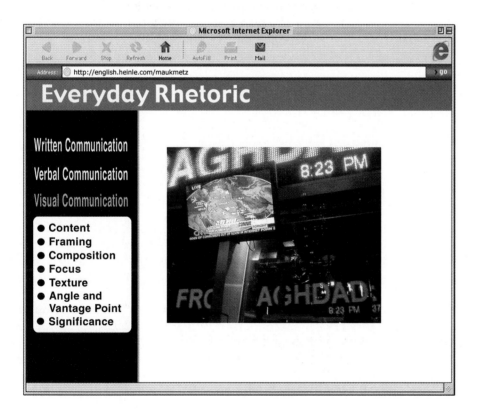

This Web page is about everyday rhetoric. Clicking on "Visual Communication" shows an example to the right, and links to further information about visuals appear in the box below.

VERBAL COMMUNICATION

Because verbal communication—speeches, discussions, briefings, and so on—is spoken, not written down, certain rhetorical strategies get special attention.

- Speakers provide verbal cues that help the reader follow along. Transitions between ideas and explicit explanations of how one idea relates to another are often helpful.

- Volume, pronunciation, and pace are important. Going too quickly or too slowly, speaking too softly or too loudly, or failing to distinctly pronounce words makes hearing and ultimately comprehension difficult for the audience. Speakers should also consider how their physical appearance might affect the listener.

- As with written communication, good content is the key. Sound ideas presented logically are essential—thus, the invention and delivery strategies from Chapters 1–11 should be used to invent and present one's ideas.

- Speakers get nervous and some people's greatest fear is public speaking. The secret here is preparation—a prepared speaker is going to be more confident. Experience is also important. Many people who can't imagine themselves speaking in front of others become confident public speakers over time.

Speeches

Speeches vary from formal (such as the president's State of the Union address) to informal (such as someone saying a few words off-the-cuff at a picnic). In a speech, the speaker is distinct from the audience; in a discussion, the speaker and audience merge. Speeches may be memorized, read, off-the-cuff (without preparation), or extemporaneous.

- Memorizing a speech takes work, and if you lose your place, you may have trouble finding it again. Shorter speeches are better candidates for memorization. Some public speakers memorize their speeches, even delivering them in dramatic fashion.

- Reading a speech is sometimes appropriate. For example, some political speakers read their entire speech off a teleprompter. But reading a speech runs the risk of boring and alienating the audience, especially if read in a flat or monotone voice or too rapidly.

- Off-the-cuff speeches can be powerful. They can also become uncomfortable quickly. Certain situations call for an off-the-cuff speech—for example, a basketball coach during a fourth quarter time-out urging his or her team to play harder. If the situation allows for preparation, however, a well-prepared and practiced speech is likely to be more successful.

- Extemporaneous speaking has the advantage of allowing the speaker to thoroughly prepare and then deliver the speech in a natural speaking voice, without having to memorize, read, or develop off-the-cuff ideas along the way. This type of delivery often works best. Of course, one part of a speech might be extemporaneous, another part memorized, another part read, with off-the-cuff comments inserted throughout.

Activities

1. Interview a variety of people until you find several whose attitudes about their own public speaking have changed. How have their attitudes changed and why? Has anyone gone from being uncomfortable speaking in public to enjoying it? Has anyone gone from enjoying it to being uncomfortable? Draw conclusions from your interview and prepare a two- to five-minute speech with a main idea and support.

2. Write and deliver a short speech. Consider, but don't limit yourself to, the following occasions: paying tribute to, or honoring, someone; informing others of an important issue; calling others to take action; announcing a change.

   A. Write out three versions of your speech, expressing the same ideas but trying different organizational strategies (opening, closing, arrangement of ideas, verbal cues). Practice delivering your speech, recording it and playing it back if you can, and then write a final speech.

   B. Explain the major ways that the text of your speech is different from the text of an essay. Refer specifically to rhetorical tools, organizational strategies, and writer's/speaker's voice.

3. In small groups or as a class, deliver an off-the-cuff speech.

   A. Develop a list of topics, such as "The Importance of College Football," "How to Get All A's," "The Best Thing about College," and so on.

   B. Select a person to speak.

   C. Give the speaker a topic and ten seconds to begin giving a two-minute speech.

   D. Take turns until each member has delivered a speech.

4. Take the same topic you spoke on for #3 above and write out the complete text of a two-minute speech. Deliver it in class.

5. Find a copy of Lou Gehrig's Farewell Speech, and read through it several times, studying Gehrig's rhetoric with a group of friends. Respond to the following prompts:

   A. What is the purpose of Gehrig's speech? That is, what is he trying to achieve?

   B. What rhetorical tools and organizational strategies does Gehrig use to achieve his purpose?

   C. Does Gehrig use any of the following: metonymy, hyperbole, anaphora, synecdoche, antithesis, anastrophe?

   D. Gehrig is dealing with sensitive subject matter—he is dying. Which of his rhetorical strategies are particularly helpful, considering the circumstances of his speech?

Do We Live in a Democracy?

Mike Ferner

Mike Ferner delivered this speech at the "Democracy Rising" rally held in Toledo, Ohio, on December 15, 2001. As you read, consider the rhetorical decisions Ferner makes (rhetorical tools, organizational strategies, writer's/speaker's voice), and how those decisions might have been different had he used some other form of communication.

With your permission tonight I would like to provoke us with this question: do we live in a democracy? Do "we the people," listed right up front in our Constitution's preamble, really form the basis of government power and policy?

"Well, of course," you might say. After all, we are taught that from our earliest days in school. Millions of advertising images equate freedom with everything from 7-11 stores to Calvin Klein jeans. And of course President Bush repeats daily that we are fighting the terrorist foes of democracy and freedom.

Even though the media and every aspect of our dominant culture daily reinforce the notion that America is a democracy—that we always fight on the side of the angels—there have always been courageous voices that question and challenge.

One such voice came from a most unusual source, a Major General in the U.S. Marine Corps, named Smedley Butler. Just before he retired in 1934, and for the rest of his life, he questioned out loud what he'd done in the military.

He concluded that in his words "War is a racket. It always has been. . . . A racket is best described as something that is not what it seems to the majority of people. Only a small 'inside' group knows what it is about. It is conducted for the benefit of the very few, at the expense of the very many."

Butler admitted that "he helped make Mexico safe for American oil interests in 1914. . . . I brought light to the Dominican Republic for the American sugar interests in 1916. . . . I helped make Honduras right for American fruit companies in 1903. . . . In China in 1927 I helped see to it that Standard Oil went its way unmolested." He acknowledged that he'd spent most of his 33 years in the Marines as "a high-class muscle man for Big Business, Wall Street, and the bankers. In short, I was a racketeer, a gangster for capitalism."

If America was a democracy in Butler's day, how could such things happen?

If we live in a democracy today, how could our government get away with bombing one of the poorest nations on earth, killing thousands of civilians who had absolutely nothing to do with the criminal, inexcusable attacks of September 11?

If we live in a democracy, how is it that UNOCAL Corp. executives are counting the days until, as General Butler might say, Afghanistan is made safe for American oil interests?

If we live in a democracy, where "we the people" are sovereign citizens from whom all political power flows, by what authority does Daimler-Chrysler Corporation extort $89 million dollars in tax abatements, and then our elected school board submits a funding request to the company's foundation for a technical training school?

If we live in a democracy, by what authority do our elected officials impoverish our sacred democratic institutions, like our public schools, and force them to beg for corporate charity?

If we live in a democracy, why do our school officials implore the Coca-Cola Co. to please cut back on how many hours a day its machines beckon to students, creating lifelong "brand loyalty," and rotting their health?

Do we in fact live in a democracy, or is it more accurately a plutocracy, defined by Webster's as "a government in which the wealthy class rules"? Or as Smedley Butler put it, a "racket . . . conducted for the benefit of the very few, at the expense of the very many."

Brothers and sisters, we don't have unlimited time to use our humanity and our hearts to build a democratic society, and with its power create a world where we are at peace with ourselves, other species, and the planet. Tonight we are privileged to be here with hundreds of our fellow citizens who care deeply. In a few minutes we will hear from Ralph Nader, one of America's most stalwart believers in the power of people. This is a golden opportunity. Let us make the most of it.

Briefings

Briefings are short, often informal speeches that concisely convey the most relevant information. The speaker may draw conclusions and make recommendations, or just report information. Because a briefing focuses on main ideas, questions that probe into specifics are likely to follow. Briefings may be carefully planned and somewhat formal, or they can be impromptu. Heads of government and business routinely receive briefings, as do lower-level employees. One cannot be sure when a co-worker or teacher might ask for a briefing on a particular situation. In fact, briefings are common throughout everyday life: parents, spouses, and children routinely brief each other on family matters. Briefings are both routine and essential for conducting business.

1. Recall an everyday briefing you recently delivered. Describe the situation. What did you brief someone on? Was the briefing requested or did you initiate it? How long was the briefing and what was its result? Was there a question and answer period afterward?

2. Do your best to write down the text of a briefing you recently gave (#1), including questions and answers. What rhetorical tools did you use? For example, did you make counterarguments or concessions? Describe your organizational strategy—the way you arranged and connected ideas—and writer's/speaker's voice.

3. Prepare a briefing for a situation in your everyday life. For example, you might have to update a professor on a class project, inform your boss about your schedule, or explain to a customer how a product works. Practice briefing the audience and then deliver the briefing.

4. In thirty seconds, explain an essay you wrote for this class. Rehearse your briefing at home, and then deliver it in class without any text.

5. Prepare three briefings of an essay you wrote: thirty seconds, one minute, and two minutes long. Practice delivering the briefings at home, and then deliver them in class without any text.

Activity: Study any two pages in this text, taking notes and going over them until you can recall the information well enough to give a briefing. Then brief a classmate on the information the pages cover. Or, go over your notes from a previous class, then brief classmates on the information. Or, prepare carefully, then brief classmates on the next major assignment due in this course.

Press Briefing

Ari Fleischer, White House Press Secretary

Each day the president's press secretary, in this case Ari Fleischer, briefs the press on important White House news. This briefing, given to a pool of reporters aboard Air Force One en route to Andrews Air Force Base, is from September 11, 2001, and is followed by questions from the press along with Mr. Fleischer's responses. This press briefing, including questions and answers, along with other White House briefings can be found on-line at http://www.whitehouse.gov/news/briefings/. Keep in mind the purpose of a briefing as you notice Mr. Fleischer's use of rhetorical tools, organizational strategies, and voice.

5:30 P.M. EDT

MR. FLEISCHER: The President will address the nation tonight, upon his return to the White House. He met this afternoon for one hour and five minutes with his national security team via live tele-conference from Offutt Air Force Base in Nebraska.

Among the things the President said were, "We will find these people and they will suffer the consequence of taking on this nation. We will do what it takes," and he continued, "No one is going to diminish the spirit of this country."

The President has also heard today from countless world leaders either who are calling to—back to Washington or have sent him directly communiques. He's heard from Britain, France, Germany, Russia—a host of nations, all of whom have expressed their outrage at this attack, and who have assured the American people that the international community stands with America.

That's what I've got.

Q: The message tonight, do you know how soon after he gets back to the White House he'll be able to do that?

MR. FLEISCHER: Can't indicate yet.

Q: And when he does, the message is to the American people, as he said earlier, and to foreign countries?

MR. FLEISCHER: It will be a message of resolve and reassurance. It will be a reassuring message that our nation has been tested before, our nation has always prevailed.

Q: Does the President have any information about the source of the violence and the mastermind behind it?

MR. FLEISCHER: I'm not going to discuss any of the intelligence information that's been provided to the President.

Q: Can you give us some idea of why the stops that we made today were made? I understand the nature of the tragedy that we're dealing with, but why these particular locations?

MR. FLEISCHER: For security purposes that involve the President.

(To read the additional questions and answers that followed, go to the White House Web site.)

Briefing Paper:
Drug Testing in the Workplace

American Civil Liberties Union

Briefings can be written as well as spoken. This briefing paper can be found at the American Civil Liberties Union Web site (www.aclu.org). Notice the rhetorical tools, organizational strategies, and writer's voice of the briefing, and consider how the writer might have made different rhetorical decisions if using some other form of communication—an essay, for example.

There was a time in the United States when your business was also your boss's business. At the turn of the century, company snooping was pervasive and privacy almost nonexistent. Your boss had the right to know who you lived with, what you drank, whether you went to church, or to what political groups you belonged. With the growth of the trade union movement and heightened awareness of the importance of individual rights, American workers came to insist that life off the job was their private affair not to be scrutinized by employers.

But major chinks have begun to appear in the wall that has separated life on and off the job, largely due to the advent of new technologies that make it possible for employers to monitor their employees' off-duty activities. Today, millions of American workers every year, in both the public and private sectors, are subjected to urinalysis drug tests as a condition for getting or keeping a job.

The American Civil Liberties Union opposes indiscriminate urine testing because the process is both unfair and unnecessary. It is unfair to force workers who are not even suspected of using drugs, and whose job performance is satisfactory, to "prove" their innocence through a degrading and uncertain procedure that violates personal privacy. Such tests are unnecessary because they cannot detect impairment and, thus, in no way enhance an employer's ability to evaluate or predict job performance.

Here are the ACLU's answers to some questions frequently asked by the public about drug testing in the workplace.

Q: Don't employers have the right to expect their employees not to be high on drugs on the job?

A: Of course they do. Employers have the right to expect their employees not to be high, stoned, drunk, or asleep. Job performance is the bottom line: If you cannot do the work, employers have a legitimate reason for firing you. But urine tests do not measure job performance. Even a confirmed "positive" provides no evidence of present intoxication or impairment; it merely indicates that a person may have taken a drug at some time in the past.

Q: Can urine tests determine precisely when a particular drug was used?

A: No. Urine tests cannot determine when a drug was used. They can only detect the "metabolites," or inactive leftover traces of previously ingested substances. For example, an employee who smokes marijuana on a Saturday night may test positive the following Wednesday, long after the drug has ceased to have any effect. In that case, what the employee did on Saturday has nothing to do with his or her fitness to work on Wednesday. At the same time, a worker can snort cocaine on the way to work and test negative that same morning. That is because the cocaine has not yet been metabolized and will, therefore, not show up in the person's urine.

Q: If you don't use drugs, you have nothing to hide—so why object to testing?

A: Innocent people do have something to hide: their private life. The "right to be left alone" is, in the words of the late Supreme Court Justice Louis Brandeis, "the most comprehensive of rights and the right most valued by civilized men." Analysis of a person's urine can disclose many details about that person's private life other than drug use. It can tell an employer whether an employee or job applicant is being treated for a heart condition, depression, epilepsy or diabetes. It can also reveal whether an employee is pregnant.

Q: Are drug tests reliable?

A: No, the drug screens used by most companies are not reliable. These tests yield false positive results at least 10 percent, and possibly as much as 30 percent, of the time. Experts concede that the tests are unreliable. At a recent conference, 120 forensic scientists, including some who worked for manufacturers of drug tests, were asked, "Is there anybody who would submit urine for drug testing if his career, reputation, freedom or livelihood depended on it?" Not a single hand was raised. Although more accurate tests are available, they are expensive and infrequently used. And even the more accurate tests can yield inaccurate results due to laboratory error. A survey by the National Institute of Drug Abuse, a government agency, found that 20 percent of the labs surveyed mistakenly reported the presence of illegal drugs in drug-free urine samples. Unreliability also stems from the tendency of drug screens to confuse similar chemical compounds. For example, codeine and Vicks Formula 44-M have been known to produce positive results for heroin, Advil for marijuana, and Nyquil for amphetamines.

Q: Still, isn't universal testing the best way to catch drug users?

A: Such testing may be the easiest way to identify drug users, but it is also by far the most un-American. Americans have traditionally believed that general searches of innocent people are unfair. This tradition began in colonial times, when King George's soldiers searched everyone indiscriminately in order to uncover those few people who were committing offenses against the Crown. Early

Americans deeply hated these general searches, which were a leading cause of the Revolution. After the Revolution, when memories of the experience with warrantless searches were still fresh, the Fourth Amendment was adopted. It says that the government cannot search everyone to find the few who might be guilty of an offense. The government must have good reason to suspect a particular person before subjecting him or her to intrusive body searches. These longstanding principles of fairness should also apply to the private sector, even though the Fourth Amendment only applies to government action.

Urine tests are body searches, and they are an unprecedented invasion of privacy. The standard practice, in administering such tests, is to require employees to urinate in the presence of a witness to guard against specimen tampering. In the words of one judge, that is "an experience which even if courteously supervised can be humiliating and degrading." Noted a federal judge, as he invalidated a drug-testing program for municipal fire-fighters, "Drug testing is a form of surveillance, albeit a technological one."

Q: But shouldn't exceptions be made for certain workers, such as airline pilots, who are responsible for the lives of others?

A: Obviously, people who are responsible for others' lives should be held to high standards of job performance. But urine testing will not help employers do that because it does not detect impairment. If employers in transportation and other industries are really concerned about the public's safety, they should abandon imperfect urine testing and test performance instead. Computer-assisted performance tests already exist and, in fact, have been used by NASA for years on astronauts and test pilots. These tests can actually measure hand-eye coordination and response time, do not invade people's privacy, and can improve safety far better than drug tests can.

Q: Drug use costs industry millions in lost worker productivity each year. Don't employers have a right to test as a way of protecting their investment?

A: Actually, there are no clear estimates about the economic costs to industry resulting from drug use by workers. Proponents of drug testing claim the costs are high, but they have been hard pressed to translate that claim into real figures. And some who make such claims are manufacturers of drug tests, who obviously stand to profit from industry-wide urinalysis. In any event, employers have better ways to maintain high productivity, as well as to identify and help employees with drug problems. Competent supervision, professional counseling and voluntary rehabilitation programs may not be as simple as a drug test, but they are a better investment in America.

Our nation's experience with cigarette smoking is a good example of what education and voluntary rehabilitation can accomplish. Since 1965, the proportion of Americans who smoke cigarettes has gone down from 43 percent to 32 percent.

This dramatic decrease was a consequence of public education and the availability of treatment on demand. Unfortunately, instead of adequately funding drug clinics and educational programs, the government has cut these services so that substance abusers sometimes have to wait for months before receiving treatment.

Q: Have any courts ruled that mandatory urine testing of government employees is a violation of the Constitution?

A: Yes. Many state and federal courts have ruled that testing programs in public workplaces are unconstitutional if they are not based on some kind of individualized suspicion. Throughout the country, courts have struck down programs that randomly tested police officers, fire-fighters, teachers, civilian army employees, prison guards and employees of many federal agencies. The ACLU and public employee unions have represented most of these victorious workers.

In Washington, D.C., for example, one federal judge had this to say about a random drug testing program that would affect thousands of government employees: "This case presents for judicial consideration a wholesale deprivation of the most fundamental privacy rights of thousands upon thousands of loyal, law-abiding citizens. . . ." In 1989, for the first time, the U. S. Supreme Court ruled on the constitutionality of testing government employees not actually suspected of drug use. In two cases involving U. S. Customs guards and railroad workers, the majority of the Court held that urine tests are searches, but that these particular employees could be tested without being suspected drug users on the grounds that their Fourth Amendment right to privacy was outweighed by the government's interest in maintaining a drug-free workplace.

Although these decisions represent a serious setback, the Court's ruling does not affect all government workers, and the fight over the constitutionality of testing is far from over.

Q: If the Constitution can't help them, how can private employees protect themselves against drug testing?

A: Court challenges to drug testing programs in private workplaces are underway throughout the country. These lawsuits involve state constitutional and statutory laws rather than federal constitutional law. Some are based on common law actions that charge specific, intentional injuries; others are breach of contract claims. Some have been successful, while others have failed. Traditionally, employers in the private sector have extremely broad discretion in personnel matters. In most states, private sector employees have virtually no protection against drug testing's intrusion on their privacy, unless they belong to a union that has negotiated the prohibition or restriction of workplace testing. One exception to this bleak picture is California, in which the state constitution specifies a right to privacy that applies, not only to government action, but to actions by private business as well.

In addition to California, seven states have enacted protective legislation that restricts drug testing in the private workplace and gives employees some measure of protection from unfair and unreliable testing: Montana, Iowa, Vermont and Rhode Island have banned all random or blanket drug testing of employees (that is, testing without probable cause or reasonable suspicion), and Minnesota, Maine and Connecticut permit random testing only of employees in "safety sensitive" positions. The laws in these states also mandate confirmatory testing, use of certified laboratories, confidentiality of test results and other procedural protections. While they are not perfect, these new laws place significant limits on employers' otherwise unfettered authority to test and give employees the power to resist unwarranted invasions of privacy.

The ACLU will continue to press other states to pass similar statutes and to lobby the U.S. Congress to do the same.

Discussions

In discussion, speaker and audience merge. That is, the person speaking is also part of the audience. Of course discussion is common in all walks of life: college classes, the workplace, our personal lives, and so on. Since discussion involves responding to others, *listening* is the key to a good discussion. If one person is not listening or if one person is talking too much, the discussion suffers. And the larger the discussion group, the more one must be willing to listen. Discussion thrives on a fairly balanced back-and-forth exchange of ideas; imbalance in discussions is not productive.

Imagine the following verbal exchange: You walk up to a clerk in a store and say, "I bought this VCR here yesterday, and it doesn't work," and the clerk responds, "Today I had a hot dog for lunch." Or you call a friend on the telephone and say, "I just saw the most interesting movie about UFOs last night," and your friend responds, "My mother baked a chocolate cake for my 10th birthday." Imagine that you approach your history professor after class and say, "I've been having a lot of personal problems lately and wondered if I could have an extension on my next assignment," and your professor replies, "The Civil War was fought between the North and the South, the Union and the Confederacy." In these examples, the second person's comment is not a response to the first person's comment.

When we discuss, we listen and respond to what others are saying. Through discussion, we will get our problem with the VCR solved, explore the issue of UFOs or movies about UFOs, and come to some understanding with our professor about our work in the class.

In each of the examples above, discussion is subverted: the clerk, for example, does not respond to what you, the customer, say, but instead says something else apparently unrelated to your concern. When we discuss, we listen and respond to what others are saying. And we do it in a way that adds to the conversation. You might, for example, contribute a strong point; ask a question that helps the group to probe the issue further; provide an example to illustrate what someone else has said; or keep quiet, listening to others who have a lot to say about the topic, then contributing an important point at just the right moment. The best discussers don't necessarily say or write the most. Discussion is not all about quantity.

As you can see, there's more to discussion than you might think at first. In classroom discussions, teachers work to keep the discussion on track and moving forward. Political discussions sometimes have moderators who serve the same purpose. When discussing with friends or classmates, it is often important to keep in mind the purpose of the discussion so as not to get sidetracked. Most students have been in a small group or class discussion that has gotten off track and ended up being not very fruitful. These discussions are entertaining for some, frustrating for others, but generally do not serve the purpose for which they were intended.

We can judge a discussion by whether or not it is fruitful. A good apple tree produces many apples. It is fruitful. A good discussion produces ideas. When you begin a discussion, you think certain things. When the discussion is over, you should ask yourself how your ideas have changed. Of course, some discussions are not meant to be fruitful in this way. A social exchange with a friend, family member, or co-worker is not necessarily supposed to change the way you think (although it might). When we talk about the weather, we are having a different sort of discussion. It helps to understand the difference between these two kinds of discussion—one meant to explore an idea and understand it better, the other meant "only" to socialize (which is quite important in itself). You know you are truly discussing if you are trying to find truth in or understand what other people are saying. If you learn something, think differently, change your mind, or seriously consider a different point of view, the discussion can be considered a fruitful one.

Activity: After discussing, explore further, noticing important points that might not be so obvious. Seek them out. Discover them! In writing, explain the most significant way(s) that your thinking changed. The following questions may be helpful:

- How do you think differently now than you did before the discussion? What new ideas did you consider that you had not thought about before?
- How does your thinking now go beyond your initial ideas, biases, perceptions, beliefs? How does your thinking now go beyond the common beliefs of others?
- How might you explore some idea further?

Activities

1. Think of a discussion you participated in that was fruitful. What did you learn or think differently about? What was, is, or might be the consequence of what you learned or how you think differently?

2. Take notes on a class discussion. Make sure it is a discussion, in which the audience members are also the speakers, and not a lecture, in which the audience listens while the lecturer does most of the speaking. How fruitful was the discussion and why? Explain how new ideas or ways of thinking emerged from the discussion. What comments or questions were especially helpful in the discussion? What were they in response to and what did they lead to?

3. Have a fruitful discussion. Select any topic that several people are generally interested in, begin discussing, and see where the discussion leads. Take notes so that you can trace the development of the discussion.

   A. What direction(s) did the discussion develop in? What fruit did it produce?
   B. Did the discussion evolve or fizzle out? Or evolve, then fizzle out? What ended the discussion?
   C. What comments or questions were especially helpful in the discussion? What were they in response to and what did they lead to?
   D. How did participants' views differ regarding the fruitfulness of the discussion? What did they think was the discussion's value?
   E. Which participants were most valuable to the discussion and why?

4. Think about the role of rhetorical tools, organizational strategies, and writer's/speaker's voice in one particular discussion (#3 above, for example). How were claims, or main ideas, expressed and supported? How were ideas arranged and connected to each other? In what ways was voice important?

■ VISUAL COMMUNICATION

Visuals

Analyzing an Image

This section discusses how visuals can be used alone and with written text. The first part talks about how to analyze images in order to better understand how they communicate ideas alone–that is, separate from words. The second part focuses on using visuals to supplement written text, the way they are often used in textbooks, magazine articles, reports, and so on.

Visual images cannot always be separated from written text. The image to the right, for example, *contains* written text ("God Bless the Freaks"), which is an important part of the image. Although the image below, a snowy road, contains no words, it too can be *read*. Certain elements of the image combine to convey an idea or emotion to the reader/viewer. The elements listed below and discussed on the following pages will help you to read–or analyze–images.

Analyzing an image involves carefully studying various elements and noticing how each element contributes to the overall effect. Elements to consider include the following:

- Content–the subject, information, or objects that are pictured
- Framing–what has been placed within the boundaries of the image
- Composition–the way the visual elements of the image are arranged
- Focus–the degree to which some areas of the image are sharp (or clear) and other areas are blurry
- Lighting–the degree to which some areas of the image appear to be in bright light and other areas are in low light or in shadows
- Texture–how the image, or certain objects in the image, look like they would feel if you could touch them
- Angle, vantage point, and perspective–the angle at which the image is presented or the vantage point or perspective from which a photograph, for example, is taken

You may, in your analysis, consider other elements as well. Colors, for example, may be subdued or bright and splashy. And certain colors or combinations of colors (such as red, white, and blue) communicate ideas.

The list of elements above is not exhaustive, but instead tries to help you focus on important elements that might otherwise be overlooked.

Visuals and Text: What is the relationship between visuals and text? We know that

- Some visuals contain written text and some do not.

- Visuals can be influenced by the written text near them.

- Words (and letters for that matter) are themselves a type of visual, as illustrated by the *Peace* comic below.

- Images, even if they do not contain words, can still be read by making sense of their visual elements.

The American flag on this page, for example, communicates to us in a way similar to how written text might. Various ingredients—such as colors, design, and context—combine to create meaning for the viewer. The colors red, white, and blue alone mean something to most Americans. And those colors arranged in a particular pattern—of *stars* and *stripes*—probably mean something more specific. For example, we imagine a person is more likely to salute the flag than a red, white, and blue flower arrangement. Of course the meaning of the colors or the flag varies somewhat from person to person—for example, from a patriot to a traitor. The *context* in which the image (made up of colors and shapes arranged in a certain pattern) appears also influences how we read, or make meaning out of, the image. The flag pictured here is surrounded by black. And, as you have noticed, the blue is missing and the red and white appear to be torn or tattered. All of these elements combined communicate an idea, just as this paragraph of writing communicates an idea.

Images are also influenced by the text they are near. The American flag shown above might communicate a different idea (or be interpreted differently) depending on whether it is near writing about the lack of respect for the United States throughout the world, or writing about how the United States has often stood alone on the side of truth and justice, persevering through difficult challenges.

PEACE

P	E
A	CE

"Peace" is a comic strip made up of images, like any comic strip. Only we recognize the images in this comic strip as letters, and we combine (or read) them into a word—"Peace."

The letters might have been made more colorful, or more comical, or been combined with images of people, for example, to create a more traditional-looking comic strip. This word comic strip illustrates how words and letters are images and it helps to show how images without words can be read the way written text is.

Images in Context: When analyzing an image such as a movie poster, for example, you may focus on just the poster, without paying attention to what is outside its borders. Or you may look beyond the actual poster and include its context in your analysis. For example, is the poster hanging on a movie theater wall (and if so, what kind of theater is it?), or is the poster hanging in a college dorm room? Is the poster lying on the ground? Does it have a footprint on it? Perhaps the poster has been vandalized by graffiti,

or perhaps it still has the price tag on it. Many of the images in this text are, in fact, images of images in context. This is to encourage you to consider not just the original image, but the image and its context. Also, remember that all of these images can be considered within yet another context: they are all purposely placed within a college writing textbook. Notice as you read how the nearby written text influences the image, and vice versa.

The images on this page are all affected by the context in which they appear. The Sunday NFL Countdown image is in the context of a television screen, which is in the larger context of a living room. The American flag is actually an image of the American flag placed within the context of another flag, one that includes an eagle, stars, and a blue sky with clouds. And from the background of the photograph we can identify a larger context—that of a neighborhood. The image of the poster is lying on the ground, not hung on a wall, and it is covered with leaves. The context seems to be outdoors in autumn. The tepee is placed in context by a single background image—stadium lights. We doubt, then, that Native Americans are using it to live in. Each image is affected by the context in which it appears.

Accident and Intent:
A streak of sunlight through an image creates an effect, whether the artist intended it or not. Whether it's a streak of sunlight or the way an image is framed, composed, focused, and so on, you may, depending upon the nature of your analysis, decide to consider the creator's intent. Remember that while many images are carefully created, others occur more by accident. However, intended or accidental, the particular elements of an image work together to convey meaning.

Viewer Interpretation:
Just as two people can read the same essay and come away with different ideas, two people can view the same image and interpret it differently. That image might be a photograph in a college textbook or a sunset on the Gulf of Mexico. Whether creating an image or reacting to one, analysis involves not just explaining one's own reaction to the image, but understanding how the elements of the image help to create that reaction and how those same elements might create a different reaction in someone else.

The sticker in the window of the vehicle above says "city mpg 12" and "highway mpg 16." Either on purpose, or by accident, the American flag is reflected in the window, suggesting a relationship. Similarly, the words "Soup & Bread" with the reflection of a person on a bicycle with garbage bags strapped on back either purposely or accidentally suggests an idea. In the first case, the image asks the viewer to consider the relationship between gas-guzzling vehicles and the United States; in the second case, the image, by drawing on certain basic concepts (soup, bread, bicycle, garbage bags), invites the reader to consider issues of homelessness, poverty, and so on. Of course, the viewer may interpret these images in various ways. A person's political views, for example, are just one factor that will influence how he or she interprets the "Elect Bush" bumper sticker or the "Please Take a Number" sign.

Analyzing an Image: Analyzing an image involves carefully noting the content of the image, and then considering its formal elements, such as shapes, lines, colors, contrasts (between lights and darks), and so on. Imagine watching a movie and altering the image on the screen so that the picture is no longer in color but is black and white. Then imagine eliminating the background music and sound effects, leaving you with a black-and-white image and characters speaking. Then imagine that the characters begin speaking Latin and subtitles appear on the screen. As the elements you are familiar with (color, music, English) are stripped away, your viewing experience changes. You might analyze still images in this way, mentally stripping away certain elements by focusing on one—or a few—at a time.

Content: Analyzing images involves considering how various elements combine to communicate ideas. You will naturally begin by noticing the content of the image. When analyzing, it is important to notice everything that is pictured, perhaps even listing the individual elements on a sheet of paper.

Framing: After noticing what is pictured, you can focus on other elements, such as how the different objects are framed. Whether by choice, by accident, or by necessity, certain objects are included in an image while other objects are left out. As you analyze images, consider what has been placed within the frame of the image, what has been left out, and why.

Composition: Next, you might consider how the image is composed—that is, how the various elements are arranged within the frame. What is in the foreground of the image? What is in the background? What is off to the side? How does the spatial relationship of these objects convey meaning? Are certain objects above or below each other? Are they touching, close to each other, or far apart? These spatial relationships can be both aesthetic—that is, pleasing to the eye—and meaningful. Composition also includes matters of light and darkness, lines, shapes, focus, and so on.

Focus: Some images are sharp (or in focus) while others are blurry (or out of focus). And some objects within the same image are in focus while others are not. How does the focus convey meaning? And how does the spatial relationship of these elements contribute to the image's overall meaning?

Lighting: Lighting is also important. An entire image may be dark or light, or some parts of the image may be in shadows or in bright light. While shadows and light may be a natural consequence of a sunny day or a tall building blocking a photographer's light, the way the elements are lit creates an effect. Strong images can be produced by accident or by careful planning.

Texture: Images can suggest, or appear to have, texture. Just as tree bark and a marble countertop look as if they would feel different, visual images can suggest the way they might feel if you touched them. While other elements, such as content, framing, and composition, may be all the same, a smooth or rough texture may suggest a different idea about what is being pictured.

Angle and Vantage Point: Every image suggests a perspective. That is, the objects are shown from a particular angle and vantage point. A photograph of a politician speaking with a crowd of supporters suggests one meaning, while a shot of the same politician from behind and speaking to a mere handful of people suggests something else. A low-angle shot, looking up at the politician, might suggest power; a high-angle shot, looking down on the politician, might suggest weakness. Of course angle and vantage point must ultimately be considered along with the other elements of the image.

Individual Elements Combined:

As we focus on these individual elements, we must keep in mind that our goal is to understand how all these elements work together to express an idea, just as the elements of an essay, novel, poem, or movie work together. When analyzing, we focus on one element at a time, but we are always looking at more than one element. For example, when we consider how an image is framed or composed, we are also considering the image's content. When we talk about composition, we are looking at how these various formal elements work together. So we must also consider other formal elements, such as focus, lighting, and angle.

Notice the content of the images on this page. What is pictured? Carefully note everything you see. Then consider how the elements are composed. For example, the image above shows an elephant, a shopping cart, and some people. The viewer is likely to make some connection between the shopping cart in the foreground and the elephant in the background. What might the content and composition of this image be suggesting?

Consider other elements as well. How do focus, lighting, and angle or vantage point help to communicate an idea? The four images on this page, for example, are all of an elephant in a store; but each image encourages the viewer to think something different. How do they do this? What particular elements of each image suggest a unique idea?

Significance: Simply describing the details of an image is not analysis. Instead, analysis involves understanding how particular details work together to convey an idea. All elements of an image must be considered, yet some elements will have more impact than others.

Consider the significance of the images on this page (and throughout this book). What point might each image be making? Remember, you may interpret the image differently than someone else, but you should be able to explain how you arrived at your interpretation by discussing the various elements of the image—content, framing, composition, focus, lighting, texture, angle and vantage point, and so on.

Analyzing an Image: The "Analyzing an Image" questions below will help you analyze how and why the image affects you (and others) as it does.

Content

What content (subject, topic, or information) is captured in the photograph? What are the main objects or elements in the photograph? Of the main elements, which appear to be most prominent? Which are less prominent?

Framing

How is the image framed? What has been placed within the boundaries of the photograph, and what has not been included? Why might the photographer have framed the image this way?

Composition

How are the various elements of the image arranged? Are visual elements symmetrical (distributed evenly) or asymmetrical (not distributed evenly)? Are elements touching, overlapping, close together or far apart, above or below each other, or to the left or to the right of each other? What is in the background? How does the arrangement of elements affect the relationship of one element to another, and how might this relationship encourage someone to think about the image?

Focus

How is the image focused? That is, what objects or areas appear most clear or sharp and what objects or areas are less clear? Is there anything unusual or striking about the focus? How does the way the image is focused affect the other elements of the image? What does it draw attention to or away from? How does it affect the relationship of certain elements?

Lighting

How is the image lit? That is, what objects or areas are well-lit and what areas are dark, or in shadow? Is the light harsh or soft? Is there a contrast of tones from light to dark? What is darkest and what is lightest, and how does the lighting affect what is pictured? How might different lighting change the image?

Texture

What is the texture of the image? If you could touch what is pictured, how would it feel? How does the photograph's texture relate to its content?

Angle and Vantage Point

From what angle is the photograph taken? Is it straight on or from above, below, or some other angle? Is the angle exaggerated? How does the angle affect the composition of the image? That is, are some elements more in the foreground or background? Are some more prominent?

Significance and Public Resonance

What seems to be the main idea of the image? How do content, framing, composition, focus, lighting, texture, angle, and vantage point help to convey the idea? What public concern does the image speak to? To whom might this matter? How might people benefit by exploring the image's possible meanings?

Reading Images Together: Practice answering the "Analyzing an Image" questions, and then discuss your reading, or analysis, of the image with a group of classmates or friends.

1. Choose an image in this book and write out responses for each "Analyzing an Image" question.

   A. Discuss your written responses, exploring interesting areas of agreement and disagreement. For help, see "Discussions" on pages 682–683.
   B. In a paragraph or two, explain how your understanding of the image changed through discussion.

2. Find an image in an art book or magazine and answer the "Analyzing an Image" questions about it. Then discuss it with others, and write a paragraph or two about how your understanding of the image changed.

3. Find an image from an advertisement and answer the "Analyzing an Image" questions about it. Then discuss it with others and write a paragraph or two about how your understanding of the image changed.

Focusing on Context: By taking an image and placing it in a slightly different context, explore how context influences an image's meaning.

1. Choose an image in this book and explain how the written text near the image affects its meaning. Then place the same image in a slightly different context in this book and explain how its meaning changes.

2. Choose an image not in this book and explain how the written text near the image affects its meaning. Then place the same image in a context in this book and explain how its meaning changes.

3. Choose an image either in this book or not and explain how the written text near the image affects its meaning. Then write new text of your own that, combined with the image, changes its meaning.

Note: It would be quite easy to place the image in a different context and then claim, for example, that the image doesn't make sense. Instead, place the image effectively, where it works well with the new text.

Crop an Image: Take a photo of your own, or take one from a magazine, newspaper, or Web site, and re-frame—or crop—the image to give it new meaning. After cropping the image, explain in a paragraph or two how the way you cropped the image changed its meaning.

Create Your Own Word Comic: Create four versions of your own word comic, such as the one on page 685.

- In one version, use only simple images of the letters—for example, Times New Roman 12-point font.
- In another version, use colorful, comic-like letters that you have created yourself.
- In a third, combine letters with other images, such as drawings of people and things.
- Finally, create a comic without the use of any letters.

Try to convey the same idea each time.

Visuals and Written Text

Visuals—such as photographs, diagrams, and charts—are often used to supplement a written text. When using visuals with text, it is helpful to keep in mind the following points:

- Visuals allow the reader to see—or visualize—ideas more easily.
- Photographs, drawings, charts, graphs, and diagrams can all be used to present ideas *visually*.
- Visuals can be used to supplement a larger written or spoken presentation, such as an essay, a speech, or a Web site. An essay or memo, for example, may include a pie chart or some other visual as an aid to the reader.
- Visual aids are often helpful in making a speech or briefing clearer and more interesting: they provide another way besides listening for the reader to take in and process information.
- Visuals are often used to present complex information quickly when placed close to and after the first reference to them in a text.
- Visuals are usually expanded upon, or talked about, in the text.

Some visuals are not used to supplement a written text, such as an essay, but are used along with words to illustrate an idea. Consider this chapter's opening image, Charles Joseph Minard's famous graphic illustrating Napoleon's Russian campaign of 1812. Minard (1781–1870) provides information—such as movement and army size—visually, not just with words. Words and images work together to "tell a story"—in this case, the story of an unsuccessful military campaign.

There are many different kinds of visuals, and while they vary in nearly every way imaginable, Edward R. Tufte, in *The Visual Display of Quantitative Information*, gives the following five "Principles of Graphical Excellence":

- Graphical excellence is the well-designed presentation of interesting data—a matter of substance, of statistics, and of design.
- Graphical excellence consists of complex ideas communicated with clarity, precision, and efficiency.
- Graphical excellence is that which gives to the viewer the greatest number of ideas in the shortest time with the least ink in the smallest space.
- Graphical excellence is nearly always multivariate.
- And graphical excellence requires telling the truth about the data.

Telling the Truth about Data: If visuals claim to represent some truth, they should do so accurately. For example, a line graph should not be distorted to make stockholders think a company lost little money when in fact it lost a lot. Such a misrepresentation could have serious consequences. A visual is a representation of something. Except in rare situations (such as obvious satire), the audience expects the visual representation to be accurate.

Visuals Make Arguments: Visuals are interesting in subtle ways. Florence Nightingale (1820–1910) studied Napoleon's Russian campaign of 1812 and concluded that most of the 390,000 deaths were because of disease. Because Minard's graphic provides data about *temperature* and *deaths* but says nothing about *disease*, does it argue or suggest that the men died not because of disease, but instead froze or starved to death? A graphic, like an essay, makes a particular argument through the particular strategies its creator employs. Minard's graphic and Nightingale's response provide us with an interesting example to consider as we explore the possibilities visuals offer us.

Testing a Visual: You can test a visual by asking this question: Will it help the reader better understand the information? Considering the following questions will also be helpful when creating visuals:

- Is the visual useful? Does it help the audience better understand the information?
- Is the visual over-designed or overly complex? A visual should convey information, not draw attention to its own design. Data ink (ink that conveys information) should be more prominent than non-data ink (ink used to create borders, gridlines, etc.).
- Could the information be presented in some other visual way? For example, might information expressed in a bar chart be better expressed in a table?
- Does the visual accurately represent the information? Poorly designed visuals can distort information and mislead the reader, resulting in serious consequences. Such visuals are at least likely to call into question the author's credibility.
- If used to supplement a written text, is the visual referred to in the text—that is, does the actual text in some way discuss the information presented in the visual? Is the visual appropriately placed in the text? Visuals usually work best near to and following the first textual reference to the information.
- In more formal writing situations, visuals are referred to by a number and title. For example, a table might be referred to as "Table 2: Breeds of Cattle in Louisiana." Any visual that is not a table would be referred to as a figure, such as "Figure 4: Increase in Movie-Making Cost from 1970–2000." When referring to the table in the written text, the writer might say, "In Table 2: Breeds of Cattle in Louisiana," "According to Table 2: Breeds of Cattle in Louisiana," and so on.

Activities

1. Create a visual to supplement the text of an essay you wrote. Do not use the visual as a substitute for the text, but as another way to help the reader understand an idea.

2. For your next essay, create a cover page that includes a visual.

3. Explain the rhetoric of the visual that you created for Activity #1 or #2. For example, how does it express or support a main idea? What information does it convey or in what way does it convey information the text does not convey?

4. Find a good visual and write it out in essay form. What argument is it making? What evidence does it offer? Say it all in words.

5. Evaluate Minard's Napoleon campaign graphic. How many different types of information does it convey? Is the graphic successful? Compare it to several other graphics from recent newspapers, magazines, or scholarly publications.

6. Watch the national news on several different networks, focusing on the visuals. What purpose do they serve? Do they convey important information clearly? Could any visuals be eliminated? Do they supplement or support the anchorperson's text?

7. Find a visual from the local newspaper and describe how it makes an argument. A simple grocery store advertisement for meat or a department store advertisement for slacks will work fine. Discuss its main claim, support, any counterarguments or concessions it makes, its organization, and voice.

8. Find a visual that you think misrepresents reality and explain why.

9. Create a visual that accurately represents something about yourself, and then alter that visual to misrepresent reality. Consider, but don't limit yourself to, the following visuals: pie chart, bar chart, line graph, flow chart, diagram, photograph. Then write an essay explaining what visual elements created the misrepresentation.

Notice how the following three graphics, or visuals (all line graphs representing the same data), can be used to make the profits and losses of ABC (a fictional company) look either larger or smaller. Graphic 2 makes the profits and losses look smaller because points on the vertical axis are closer together and points on the horizontal axis are further apart. Graphic 3 does the opposite. Information can be distorted in other ways as well—for example, by making a particular line or mark much darker or brighter (see Graphic 4). Graphic designers consider how such decisions accurately portray information.

Graphic 1

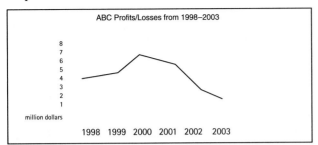

Graphic 2

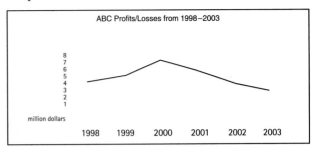

Graphic 3

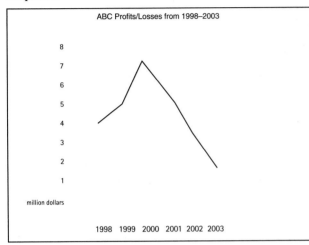

Graphic 4

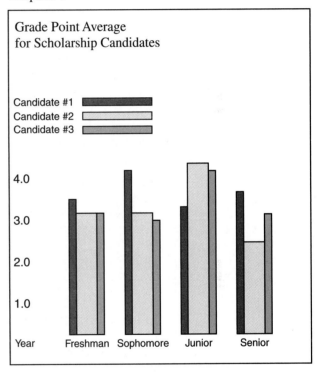

In Graphic 4, the color and size of the bar draw attention to Candidate #2. If done more subtly, the audience might be misled to favor Candidate #2—not because of the data, but because of the way it is presented. As it is done here (quite blatantly), the graphic designer is more likely to call into question his or her own credibility.

The Gap Widens

Daniel Bruno

The visual "The Gap Widens" is based on the invention and delivery strategies that Daniel Bruno used to write his essay "Entitlement Education" in Chapter 6. As you read this visual, consider its rhetoric. What decisions (regarding rhetorical tools, organizational strategies, and voice) does Bruno make? For example, how is the main claim expressed and supported? Then read Bruno's analysis of his visual.

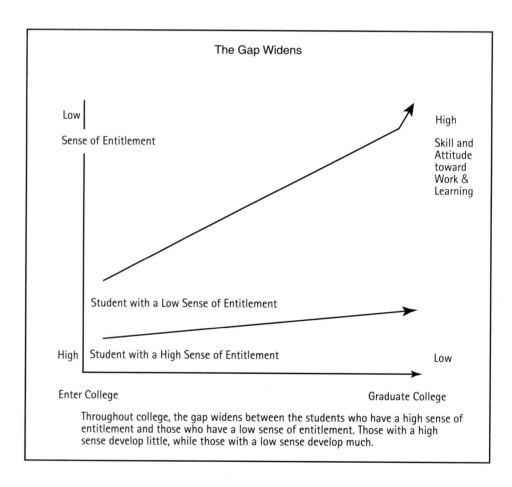

The Gap Widens

Low
Sense of Entitlement

High
Skill and Attitude toward Work & Learning

Student with a Low Sense of Entitlement

High | Student with a High Sense of Entitlement

Low

Enter College

Graduate College

Throughout college, the gap widens between the students who have a high sense of entitlement and those who have a low sense of entitlement. Those with a high sense develop little, while those with a low sense develop much.

Analysis of "The Gap Widens": A Graphic Illustration of "Entitlement Education"

Daniel Bruno

"The Gap Widens" attempts to graphically illustrate the main idea of my essay "Entitlement Education," which claims that students with a high sense of entitlement learn less (including less about how to learn) than students with a low sense of entitlement do. Because of this, the student who enters college at a lower academic level remains not just at a lower level compared to the student who enters at a higher level, but "the gap widens" as the student at the higher level develops and grows.

Emphasis on Two Main Lines: The graphic is moderately successful. I attempted to keep it simple, using ink to illustrate key information and avoiding ink that just drew attention to how pretty or fancy the graphic itself was. I felt, however, that to be clear I needed to use more ink than I had originally imagined. In a sense, all I really wanted to do was draw two lines illustrating a widening gap. See below.

I felt, however, that I must label the lines: Students with a Low Sense of Entitlement (top line); and Students with a High Sense of Entitlement (bottom line).

Horizontal Axis: I also had to deal with the vertical and horizontal axes. What does each represent? The horizontal was quite simple: I labeled the far left "Enter College" and the far right "Graduate College." I used an arrow to indicate that "Graduate College" was not the end. And I did not use a vertical line on the right side for the same reason. The student, I wanted to suggest, will be affected for life, and not just in college.

Vertical Axis: The vertical axis was more challenging. I wanted to make clear that the two lines began on the left representing two things: the student's "sense of entitlement" (from low at the top to high at the bottom) as well as the student's academic skills and attitude level (from high at the top to low at the bottom). This visual is not statistical, so things get a little muddy here. Because it is illustrating a concept, an abstract idea, and not, let's say, the number of truck sales over the past five years, the visual might, I am afraid, get confusing. The "sense of entitlement" and the "skills and attitude toward learning" are supposed to be represented across the entire line. For example, when sense of entitlement is high, learning is low; and when sense of entitlement is low, learning is high.

Yet the visual emphasizes "sense of entitlement" on the left axis and "skills and attitude" on the right axis. This is what I meant to do, but to some it may be confusing. I labeled the left axis "Sense of Entitlement" and indicated "Low" at the top and "High" at the bottom; and I labeled the right axis "Skill and Attitude toward Work & Learning" (a label I am not completely happy with).

Font and Line Features: I gave the visual a simple title, "The Gap Widens," and used thin lines and a thin, clean-looking font (Arial). The lines representing the students are thicker because they are the main visual element: everything else in the visual exists to support or explain those two lines. I used arrows at the end of each line, again to indicate an ongoing process or consequence. I felt that the top line being straight was not quite right. Instead, it might bend upward indicating an exponential growth. I was unable to figure this out on my computer, so I added a more-upward line "Graduate College" that tried to suggest this element. I kept all fonts and lines uniform, making only the title and the two major lines heavier than all the others.

How Big a Gap? A major decision was how big a gap the visual would suggest. Too big and the visual would not be credible. The audience would think the visual was lying. Too small and it wouldn't seem to matter. I took the Goldilocks approach (not too big, not too small) and just eyed-up what seemed appropriate. A curving line, showing the gap growing exponentially, would have helped here.

Finally, I included a brief explanation of the visual at the bottom so that it would not be too intrusive. I had hoped the visual would stand on its own, without this explanation, but was not confident that it could. Creating this visual was challenging and time-consuming. I think it is moderately successful. I am not sure how else this information might have been expressed visually, but it seems that the type of argument I was making required a fair amount of labeling (and perhaps the little explanation at the bottom). Less labeling and explanation (words/text) could also be successful, but would be open, I think, to more misinterpretation. On the opposite page there are a couple examples of simpler visuals, ones that might be included on a poster, bumper sticker, T-shirt, for example.

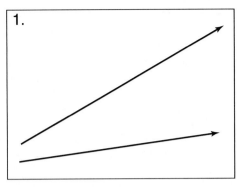

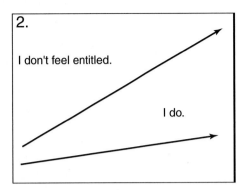

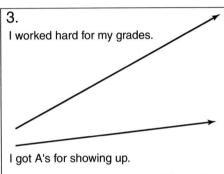

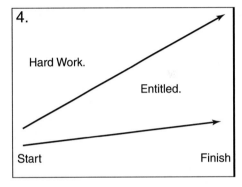

14

Twelve Common Concerns

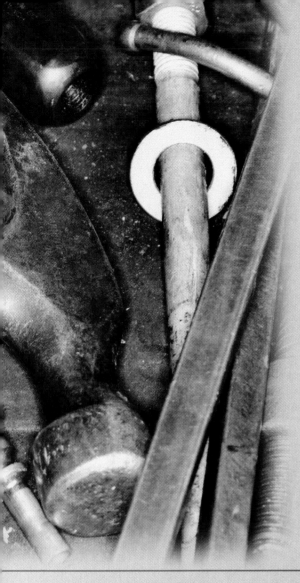

Rhetorical Handbook

What is grammar?
Why is it important?

Where to Find It

How Sentences Work

A Look at Basic Grammar

Every sentence is made up of words that cluster into related groups. If a group has a subject and a verb, it is called a *clause*; if it doesn't, it is called a *phrase*. When a noun (such as *dog*) and a verb (such as *sleeps* or *eats* or *barks* or *bites*) group together, a sort of chemical reaction occurs. Other words group together around *dog* and *sleeps* to fill in the story. Some words describe the dog *(big, black, furry, stray)*, while others describe the sleeping *(soundly, restlessly, peacefully)*. Still others connect, explaining the relationship between one word or word group and another. And, as you know, words change their forms to express number and time, so that instead of "one dog sleeps" we can say "two dogs slept" or "two big dogs slept soundly" and so on.

Thus, sentences consist of clauses and phrases placed together in a way that allows one person's idea to be understood, in one way or another, by someone else. What happens when a group of sentences communicates an idea from one person to another is both truly magical and absolutely ordinary. Should we be astonished that one person can write down an idea and another person can read and understand it so easily, and that we can also speak and hear and comprehend those sentences more or less instantaneously, and that those sentences are spoken and understood every day by three-year-olds?

Perhaps what is most astonishing is how ordinary all this is. The brief explanation of words, phrases, and clauses that follows is basically how it works.

How Sentences Work (in Brief)

Words—Parts of Speech

1. **Noun**—A noun names a person, place, or thing.

2. **Pronoun**—A pronoun takes the place of a noun.

3. **Verb**—A verb expresses an action or a state of being.

4. **Adjective**—An adjective modifies a noun or pronoun.

5. **Adverb**—An adverb modifies a verb, adjective, or adverb.

6. **Conjunction**—A conjunction connects words, phrases, and clauses and shows a relationship.

7. **Preposition**—A preposition, placed before a noun and its modifiers, creates a modifying phrase.

8. **Interjection**—An interjection expresses surprise or strong emotion.

Words (parts of speech) are combined into phrases and clauses to create sentences (see next page).

Phrases

1. **Prepositional**—Consisting of a preposition, modifiers, and a noun, the prepositional phrase functions most often as an adjective or adverb.

2. **Participial**—Consisting of a participle, modifiers, and a noun, the participial phrase functions as an adjective.

3. **Gerund**—Consisting of a gerund, modifiers, and a noun, the gerund phrase functions as a noun.

4. **Infinitive**—Consisting of an infinitive, modifiers, and a noun, the infinitive phrase functions as a noun, adjective, or adverb.

5. **Appositive**—An appositive (which may also be a single noun) describes or restates a noun.

6. **Absolute**—Consisting of a noun, modifiers, and often a participle, the absolute phrase modifies an entire clause.

Clauses

1. **Independent**—An independent clause (main clause) contains a subject and a verb not preceded by a subordinating conjunction.

2. **Dependent**—A dependent clause (subordinate clause) contains a subject and a verb and is preceded by a subordinating conjunction or a relative pronoun.

   - **Noun Clause**—Noun clauses function as subjects, objects, or complements.
   - **Adjective Clause**—Adjective clauses modify nouns or pronouns.
   - **Adverb Clause**—Adverb clauses modify verbs, adjectives, or adverbs.

Sentences—Classified by Structure

1. **Simple**—A simple sentence contains one independent clause.

2. **Compound**—A compound sentence contains two independent clauses.

3. **Complex**—A complex sentence contains one independent and one dependent clause.

4. **Compound-complex**—A compound-complex sentence contains at least two independent clauses and at least one dependent clause.

How Parts of Speech Function in a Sentence

Words may function in different ways in a sentence. For example, *fish* can be a noun or a verb. *(Fish are fun to watch. I fish at my grandma's lake.)* Parts of speech may also function in different ways in a sentence. For example, a noun—such as *fish*—may be the subject of a sentence or the object of a sentence. *(Fish are fun to watch. I saw a fish.)*

1. **Subject**—The subject of a sentence is a noun (or noun phrase, noun clause, or pronoun), normally precedes the verb (predicate), and names who or what the sentence is about.

2. **Verb (Predicate)**—The predicate of a sentence (a verb and the words that complete its meaning) usually follows the subject and expresses what the subject does, what it is, or what has been done to it.

3. **Object**—Objects are nouns (or noun phrases, noun clauses, or pronouns), usually follow the verb, and can be direct objects or indirect objects.

4. **Complement**—Complements are nouns (or noun phrases, noun clauses, or pronouns) but can also be adjectives (or adjective phrases), usually follow a subject, verb, and any objects, and can be subject complements, object complements, predicate nouns, or predicate adjectives.

5. **Adverbials**—Adverbials are adverbs (or adverb phrases or adverb clauses) that refer to the verb.

Sentences—Classified by Purpose

1. **Declarative**—A sentence that makes a statement and ends with a period.

2. **Imperative**—A sentence that expresses a command.

3. **Interrogative**—A sentence that asks a question.

4. **Exclamatory**—A sentence that expresses an emphatic statement and ends with an exclamation mark.

Nine Ways of Combining Simple Sentences (Independent Clauses)

1. Subject + verb. Subject + verb.

2. Subject + verb; subject + verb.

3. Subject + verb, coordinating conjunction subject + verb.

4. Subject + verb; conjunctive adverb, subject + verb.

5. Subject + verb subordinating conjunction subject + verb.

6. Subordinating conjunction subject + verb, subject + verb.

7. Subject + relative clause (relative pronoun + verb) + verb.

8. Subject + verb + verb.

9. Phrase, subject + verb.

How Sentences Work (Expanded)

Words—Parts of Speech

Noun: A noun names a person, place, thing, idea, quantity, or condition. Nouns can be proper, common, collective, abstract, or concrete.

Proper nouns name specific people, places, and things. They are always capitalized.

Jane
Eatonton, Georgia
John Kenneth Galbraith
Gutenberg College
Star Wars

Zaire
the Red Cross
Mexican American
English
the Middle East

Common nouns name people, places, and things by general type. They are not capitalized.

woman
town
economist
college
movie

nation
organization
people
language
region

Collective nouns name groups of people or things and are treated as singular, not plural.

jury
congress
committee
band
public

Abstract nouns name ideas, qualities, and conditions.

patriotism
hatred
love
integrity
joy

despair
freedom
perfection
respect

Concrete nouns name things or qualities that are perceptible by the senses.

reporter
ball
cricket
letter
check

book
hot dog
flower
bed

Pronoun: A pronoun takes the place of a noun. Pronouns can be personal, possessive, reflexive, interrogative, demonstrative, indefinite, or relative.

Personal pronouns refer to specific persons or things.

	Subject Form		**Object Form**	
	Singular	*Plural*	*Singular*	*Plural*
first person	I	we	me	us
second person	you	you	you	you
third person	he		him	
	she	they	her	them
	it		it	

Possessive pronouns indicate ownership.

	Singular	*Plural*
first person	my, mine	our, ours
second person	your, yours	your, yours
third person	his, his	
	her, hers	their, theirs
	its, its	

Reflexive pronouns show that someone or something is acting for or on itself.

	Singular	*Plural*
first person	myself	ourselves
second person	yourself	yourselves
third person	himself	
	herself	themselves
	itself	

Interrogative pronouns are used to ask questions.

Subject	*Object*	*Other*
who / whoever	whom / whomever	what / which / whose

Demonstrative pronouns point out particular persons or things.

Singular	*Plural*
this / that	these / those

Indefinite pronouns serve as general subjects or objects in a sentence.

Singular	*Plural*
another / any / anybody / anyone / anything	all / both / few
each / either / everybody / everyone / everything	many / several
neither / nobody / no one / nothing / one	some
somebody / someone / something	

Relative pronouns connect adjective clauses to nouns or pronouns.

Refer to People	*Refer to Things*	*Refer to People or Things*
who / whom	that / what / whatever	that / whose
whoever / whomever	which / whichever	

Verb: A verb expresses an action or a state of being. The three types of verbs are *action, linking,* and *auxiliary.* Verbs can take other forms and become *verbals*—words formed from verbs that do not function as verbs. (See "Verbals" at the end of this section.)

Action verbs express action, either physical or mental. Action verbs are either transitive or intransitive.

Transitive verbs require direct objects to complete their meaning.

> Joe sold . . .
> (*Joe*/subject *sold*/verb)

> Joe sold the boat.
> (*boat* is the direct object; it names who or what)

> Joe finally sold Tom the old sailboat in the backyard.
> (Other words fill out the sentence. *Tom* is an indirect object—it names who was indirectly affected by the action of the verb. *Finally* modifies *sold. Old* modifies *sailboat,* as does the prepositional phrase *in the backyard.*)

> I love . . .
> (*I*/subject *love*/verb)

> I love baseball.
> (*baseball* is the direct object; it names who or what)

> I still love baseball after all these years.
> (Other words fill out the sentence. *Still* modifies *love,* as does the prepositional phrase *after all these years.*)

Intransitive verbs do not require direct objects to complete their meaning.

> The ship sank.
> Chelsea skipped.
> Scott flipped.

> None of the verbs above *(sank, skipped, flipped)* require an object to complete their meaning. Other words—such as modifiers—can be added to the sentences, but as long as no object is required, the verb is considered to be intransitive.

> The ship sank off the coast of South America.
> (*Off the coast of South America* is two prepositional phrases.)

> Chelsea, the little girl next door, skipped down the sidewalk.
> (*The little girl next door* is an appositive that describes *Chelsea; down the sidewalk* is a prepositional phrase.)

> Scott flipped. (intransitive)
> Scott flipped a pancake. (transitive)
> (If Scott did a flip, then *flipped* requires no object and is intransitive. But if Scott flipped a pancake, then *flipped* has a direct object, *a pancake,* and the verb is therefore transitive. Thus, the same verb can be intransitive or transitive, depending upon whether or not an object is required to complete its meaning.)

Linking verbs express a state of being or a condition—not an action.

> The consumer is king. (Juliet Schor)
>
> Punctuation, then, is a prop, a pillar that holds society upright. (Pico Iyer)
>
> The hyphenated modifier is the meat and potatoes of journalese. (John Leo)
>
> She smells clean, like cucumbers and watermelon. (Jessie Thuma)
>
> My heart feels terrible. (Alice Walker)
>
> The biggest problem as I see it is that although students are able to graduate from high school (and even some colleges) with minimal effort, those students may find themselves cheated in the long run. (Daniel Bruno)

Common Linking Verbs—Forms of To Be

is	am	are	was
were	be	being	been

Common Linking Verbs—Other Forms

appear	feel	grow	look	become
make	seem	smell	taste	sound

Auxiliary verbs (also called **helping verbs**) work with other verbs to create verb tenses or form questions.

> As Albert Schweitzer has said, "Man can hardly even recognize the devils of his own creation." (Rachel Carson)
>
> The verb consists of two words: *has* (a helping verb) and *said* (a past participle).
>
> He had so little breath that, during his last years, he was always leaning on something. (Alice Walker)
>
> The verb of the second clause consists of three words: *was* (a helping verb), *always* (a modifier), and *leaning* (a present participle). The verb of the first clause is *had*, a past tense linking verb.
>
> If parents are entitled to put their needs and interests before those of their own children, why should they or any other adults feel an obligation to help somebody else's children? (Barbara Dafoe Whitehead)
>
> The verb consists of two words: *are* (a helping verb) and *entitled* (a past participle).

Common Auxiliary Verbs—Forms of To Be

is	am	are	was
were	being	been	

Common Auxiliary Verbs—Other Forms

can	do	has	might	should	would
could	does	have	must	will	
did	had	may	ought to		

Verb Forms

Verbs take different forms that can be categorized as infinitive, third-person singular present, past, present participle, and past participle.

Infinitive: The base form of a verb, often used with the word *to*, the infinitive (the form one would look up in the dictionary) indicates action that occurs in the present, occurs habitually, or is generally true.

Third-Person Singular Present: Frequently ending in *–s* or *–es*, the third-person singular indicates action that occurs in the present, occurs habitually, or is generally true.

Past: Ending in *–d* or *–ed* (except in irregular verbs), the past tense indicates that something happened before now.

Present Participle: Ending in *–ing*, the present participle with an auxiliary forms a verb; with an auxiliary verb, it functions as an adjective or a noun.

Past Participle: Usually ending in *–d* or *–ed* (the same as the past tense except in irregular verbs), the past participle with an auxiliary forms a verb; without an auxiliary, it functions as an adjective.

infinitive	(I, you, we) walk	say, sing, care
third-person singular present	(he, she, it) walks	says, sings, cares
past	(I, she, they) walked	said, sang, cared
present participle	(am, was) walking	saying, singing, caring
past participle	(have, has, was) walked	said, sung, cared

Verb Talk

- **Action verbs** express action, either physical or mental.
- **Intransitive verbs** show action that is limited to the subject.
- **Transitive verbs** transfer the action from an actor to a direct object.
- **Linking verbs** allow the word or words following them to complete the meaning of the subject.
- **Auxiliary**, or **helping**, **verbs** combine with the base or a participle form of another verb to create tense, mood, and voice (active or passive).
- **Verbals** are formed from verbs and act as adjectives, adverbs, and nouns.
- **Verb tense** indicates when an action or state of being occurs.
- **Verb mood** expresses whether the speaker considers a thing to be a fact, a command, or an unreal or hypothetical condition contrary to fact.
- **Voice** can be active or passive, depending upon whether the grammatical subject is doing the action or being acted upon.

Many common English verbs are irregular and form their past tense and participle forms in unpredictable ways. Below is a partial list.

	Infinitive	*Past Tense*	*Past Participle*
Regular Verbs (most verbs in English are regular verbs)	walk	walked	walked
	jump	jumped	jumped
	follow	followed	followed
Irregular Verbs (many verbs in English are irregular verbs)	be	was/were	been
	begin	began	begun
	bite	bit	bitten
	blow	blew	blown
	break	broke	broken
	come	came	come
	cost	cost	cost
	do	did	done
	draw	drew	drawn
	drink	drank	drunk
	drive	drove	driven
	eat	ate	eaten
	fly	flew	flown
	freeze	froze	frozen
	give	gave	given
	go	went	gone
	read	read	read
	ring	ring	rung
	see	saw	seen
	shoot	shot	shot
	spring	sprang	sprung
	swear	swore	sworn
	swim	swam	swum
	take	took	taken
	tear	tore	torn
	throw	threw	thrown
	wear	wore	worn
	write	wrote	written

Verbals

Verbals are formed from verbs but do not function as verbs. There are three types: *participles* (verbals that function as modifiers or as part of the verb), *gerunds* (verbals that function as nouns), and *infinitives* (verbals that function as nouns or modifiers). Notice how a verb, such as *fish*, can be used as a participle, gerund, or infinitive.

I fish with cousin Dan.
(*Fish* is a verb in this sentence. We might have used any other action verb: *swim, work, play, argue, eat*, etc.)

Participles look like verbs and are formed from verbs but cannot function as verbs in a sentence. Participles can be present or past (present participles end in *–ing*, and past participles end in *–ed* or an irregular past tense form). Participles are used (1) in participial phrases that modify other sentence parts, (2) as modifying words, or (3) with a helping word or words to create a verb.

Participial Phrase
   Fishing with cousin Dan, I lost my wallet.
   While fishing with cousin Dan, I lost my wallet.
   I lost my wallet fishing with cousin Dan.

Participal as Modifier
   Cousin Dan is my fishing guru.
   I am cousin Dan's favorite fishing partner.
   Cousin Dan and I both enjoy the fishing life.

Participal as Part of a Verb
   I go fishing with cousin Dan.
   I am fishing with cousin Dan.
   I have never been fishing with cousin Dan.

Gerunds are verbals that act as nouns.

   Fishing is fun.
   No one likes fishing like I do.
   You can watch TV shows about cooking, painting, hunting, and fishing.

Infinitives, like gerunds, can act as nouns.

   To fish is fun.
   No one likes to fish like I do.

Verb Tense

Tense indicates time. Verbs have three simple tenses (present, past, and future) along with three perfect tenses (present perfect, past perfect, and future perfect) and six progressive tenses, one corresponding to each simple and perfect tense.

present	I dance. She sings.
past	I danced. She sang.
future	I will dance. She will sing.
present perfect	I have danced. She has sung.
past perfect	I had danced. She had sung.
future perfect	I will have danced. She will have sung.
present progressive	I am dancing. She is singing.
past progressive	I was dancing. She was singing.
future progressive	I will be dancing. She will be singing.
present perfect progressive	I have been dancing. She has been singing.
past perfect progressive	I had been dancing. She had been singing.
future perfect progressive	I will have been dancing. She will have been singing.

Tenses are indicated by a form of the main verb (*dance* and *sing* in the examples above) and auxiliary verbs. Notice that *dance* is a regular verb: *dance, danced, danced*. And *sing* is an irregular verb: *sing, sang, sung*.

Verb Mood

Mood reflects a writer's attitude towards a statement.

Indicative mood expresses a declarative statement or question.

Another trait of the creative person is idle curiosity. (S. I. Hayakawa)
The whole process of spraying seems caught up in an endless spiral. (Rachel Carson)
Many terms in journalese come from sportswriting. (John Leo)
I crouched low to avoid destroying a jewelled spider's web that stretched, exquisite and fragile, across the trail. (Jane Goodall)

Imperative mood expresses a command or a direct request.

Vote.
Stand up.
Sit down.
Help yourself to another burger.
Make yourself comfortable.
Take the less usual side. (Paul Roberts)
Don't get me wrong: there is no shame in that. (Daniel Bruno)

Subjunctive mood expresses a conditional situation, a hypothetical, a wish, or some statement contrary to fact.

If I were the president, I would make some changes around here.
I wish I were the president.

Adjective: An adjective modifies a noun or pronoun. The three articles—*a*, *an*, and *the*—mark, or precede, certain nouns and, therefore, function as a special type of adjective.

An adjective answers one of the following questions:

What kind?   How many?
Which one?   Whose?

Adjectives Modifying Nouns

red balloon   Orwellian partyspeak
big river   skulking rhetoric
little women   bright, doomed city
recent layoffs   endless, obsessive preoccupation
practical goal   pure elation
blatant manipulation   everyday lives
amusing instance   simple euphemism

Adverb: An adverb modifies a verb, adjective, or adverb.

Adverbs frequently end in *–ly* and answer the following questions:

How?   How often?
When?   To what extent?
Where?

Adverbs Modifying Verbs

clearly said   reluctantly explained
jump quickly   suddenly stopped
constantly sang   replied sheepishly
will happily move   land smoothly
willingly applauded   dropped instantly

Interjection: An interjection expresses surprise or strong emotion.

Hey!   Oh!   Okay!   Wow!
Wow! This cheesecake is delicious.
Hey! Let's go to the coffeehouse and get a bagel.

Good and Well

In casual, or nonstandard, speech, you often hear the adjective *good* instead of the adverb *well* used to modify a verb. For example, you might hear one of the following sentences:

"I did good at bowling last night."
Or
"I bowled good."

Or, if asked, "How did you bowl?" someone might respond,

"I did good."
Or, someone might just say,
"Good."

Yet *good* is an adjective, and *well* is an adverb; adjectives modify nouns and pronouns while adverbs modify verbs, adjectives, and adverbs.

1. Do you consider *good* to be incorrect in the sentences above? Why or why not?

2. Why should, or shouldn't, you avoid using *good* as an adverb?

3. Interview several classmates and others outside of class to get their views on using *good* and *well* correctly.

4. Consider the following sentences. Would you say *good* or *well,* and why?

   Lisa does _____ at whatever she does.
   She hasn't felt _____ about New England since she left.
   Lorenzo is _____ at playing the spoons.
   Diamonds don't look _____ in that ring.
   I don't feel _____.

5. *Bad* and *badly* pose a similar problem. Which word would you use in the sentences below and why?

   Martha golfed _____ (bad, badly).
   I have never done so _____ (bad, badly) on a math test.
   The _____ (bad, badly) thing about it is the grinding sound.
   Dan is _____ (bad, badly) at being on time.
   I feel _____ (bad, badly) when it rains.

6. What word would you use below and why? Did you use an adjective or adverb?

   Jefferson _____ explained his reason for leaving early.
   Georgia told a _____ story that helped me to understand.
   Next month we are _____ driving to Detroit.
   My head was _____ spinning after my second time on the Tilt-a-Whirl.
   Did you hear about the _____ strike at the refinery?

Conjunction: A conjunction connects words, phrases, and clauses and shows a relationship. Conjunctions may be coordinating, subordinating, or correlative.

Coordinating conjunctions link sentence parts of equal grammatical rank. There are only seven coordinating conjunctions.

> I went, and she stayed.
> She and I went to dinner and a movie.
> We went to a movie but not to dinner.

and	or	nor	for	yet	but	so

Subordinating conjunctions link clauses, making one clause dependent on, or subordinate to, the other. Many words act as subordinating conjunctions.

> Because I went, she stayed.
> I went although she stayed.
> Even though I went and she stayed, we still had fun.

after	however	that
although	if	though
as	in case	till
as if	in order that	unless
as far as	in that	until
as soon as	no matter how	when
as though	now that	whenever
because	once	where
before	since	wherever
even if	so that	whether
even though	supposing that	while
how	than	why

Correlative conjunctions work in pairs to link sentence parts.

> Whether it rains or not, I am washing my pickup truck tomorrow.
> I could go for either a bath or a shower right now.

both . . . and	either . . . or	whether . . . or
neither . . . nor	not only . . . but also	

Preposition: A preposition placed before a noun and its modifiers creates a prepositional phrase. Prepositional phrases function as either adverbs or adjectives.

Paul left his umbrella <u>by the door</u>.
The woman <u>at the counter</u> said the bus leaves <u>at noon</u>.
Who said the majority <u>of customers</u> <u>in the carryout</u> were buying emergency supplies?

Common One-Word Prepositions

about	by	outside
above	concerning	over
across	despite	past
after	down	since
against	during	through
along	except	throughout
among	for	till
around	from	to
at	in	toward
before	inside	under
behind	into	underneath
below	like	until
beneath	near	up
beside	of	upon
besides	off	with
between	on	within
beyond	onto	without
but	out	

Common Multiple-Word Prepositions

according to	by way of	instead of
ahead of	due to	on account of
along with	except for	out of
apart from	in addition to	up to
as for	in case of	with regard to
as to	in front of	with respect to
as well as	in spite of	with the exception of
because of	inside of	

Phrases

A phrase is a group of related words without a subject and a verb. Phrases can be categorized as prepositional, participial, gerund, infinitive, appositive, or absolute.

Prepositional: Consisting of a preposition, modifiers, and a noun, the prepositional phrase functions most often as an adjective or adverb.

> Barney chased a rabbit <u>under the porch</u>.
> The top executives met <u>in the conference room</u> <u>for about two hours</u>.

Participial: Consisting of a participle, modifiers, and a noun, the participial phrase functions as an adjective.

> <u>Running after the rabbit</u>, Barney disappeared under the porch.
> <u>While meeting in the conference room</u>, the executives voted to study the issue further.

Gerund: Consisting of a gerund, modifiers, and a noun, the gerund phrase functions as a noun.

> <u>Running after a rabbit</u> is hard work for a small dog.
> <u>Meeting in the conference room</u> is convenient for everyone except Mary.

Infinitive: Consisting of an infinitive, modifiers, and a noun, the infinitive phrase functions as a noun, adjective, or adverb.

> <u>To run after a rabbit all day</u> is good exercise.
> The most convenient place <u>to meet the new employee</u> is the conference room.

Appositive: An appositive (which may also be a single noun) describes or restates a noun.

> Barney, <u>a short-haired terrier</u>, chased a wild rabbit under the porch.
> Mary, <u>the only executive with an office across the street</u>, didn't mind meeting in the conference room.

Absolute: Consisting of a noun, modifiers, and often a participle, the absolute phrase modifies an entire clause.

> <u>The rabbit hiding under the porch</u>, Barney barked at the screen door.
> Mary arrived at the meeting late, <u>her office being across town</u>.

Clauses

A clause is a group of words with a subject and a verb (or predicate). The two types of clauses are *independent* (or main) and *dependent* (or subordinate).

Independent: An independent (main) clause contains a subject and a verb not preceded by a subordinating conjunction.

> Joe passed his math test.
> Subject/*Joe*   Verb/*passed*

> To see *Star Wars* again after 20 years is to revisit a place in the mind. (Roger Ebert)
> Subject/*To see*   Verb/*is*

Dependent: A dependent (subordinate) clause contains a subject and a verb and is preceded by a subordinating conjunction or a relative pronoun. Dependent clauses can function as subjects, objects, or complements (noun clauses), as adjectives modifying nouns or pronouns, or as adverbs modifying verbs, adjectives, or adverbs.

> Because Joe passed his math test, he ordered a pizza with all the toppings.
> Subordinating conjunction/*Because*

> It's possible, however, that as we grow older, we retain the tastes of our earlier selves. (Roger Ebert)
> Subordinating conjunction/*that*   Subject/*we*   Verb/*retain*
> (*that* makes the clause *we retain* dependent)
> Subordinating conjunction/*as*   Subject/*we*   Verb/*grow*
> (*as* makes the clause *we grow* dependent)

> Now it was adults who were the emotionally fragile ones and thus had to be protected against adversity while children were the resilient ones and could take it. (Barbara Dafoe Whitehead)
> Relative pronoun/*who*   Verb/*were*
> (The relative clause *who were the emotionally fragile ones and thus had to be protected against adversity* modifies the noun *adults*. Other relative pronouns include *that* and *which* and are either followed by a subject and a verb or just a verb. In either case, the relative clause modifies the noun before it.)

Examples of Relative Clauses

> the lion that roared at Dorothy . . .
> the band that the club owner hired . . .
> the woman who won the marathon . . .

Sentences—Classified by Structure

Simple: A simple sentence contains one independent clause.

> Bobby played the banjo on the back step.
> Subject/*Bobby*   Verb/*played*

> My daughter doesn't ask for $42 pants from the Gap or $38 shirts from Abercrombie & Fitch. (Jessie Thuma)
> Subject/*daughter*   Verb/*doesn't ask*

Compound: A compound sentence contains two independent clauses.

> Bobby played the banjo on the back step, and he made a musical dent in the night.
> Subject/*Bobby*   Verb/*played*   Subject/*he*   Verb/*made*

> This bipartisan consensus has been politically expedient, but it has taken an enormous toll on our public commitment to children. (Barbara Dafoe Whitehead)
> Subject/*consensus*   Verb/*has been expedient*
> Subject/*it*   Verb/*has taken*

Complex: A complex sentence contains one independent and one dependent clause.

> When Bobby played the banjo on the back step, he made a musical dent in the night.
> Dependent clause: Subordinating conjunction/*When*   Subject/*Bobby*
>   Verb/*played*
> Independent clause: Subject/*he*   Verb/*made*

> If you want the reader to believe that college football is bad for the players, you have to do more than say so. (Paul Roberts)
> Dependent clause: Subordinating conjunction/*If*   Subject/*you*   Verb/*want*
> Independent clause: Subject/*you*   Verb/*have*

Compound-complex: A compound-complex sentence contains at least two independent clauses and at least one dependent clause.

> When Bobby played the banjo on the back step, he made a musical dent in the night, and the neighbors complained.
> Dependent clause: Subordinating conjunction/*When*   Subject/*Bobby*   Verb/*played*
> Independent clause: Subject/*he*   Verb/*made*
> Independent clause: Subject/*neighbors*   Verb/*complained*

> Now this is a way to go about reaching five hundred words, and if you are content with a "D" grade, it is as good a way as any. (Paul Roberts)
> Independent clause: Subject/*this*   Verb/*is*
> Dependent clause: Subordinating conjunction/*if*   Subject/*you*   Verb/*are*
> Independent clause: Subject/*it*   Verb/*is*

How Parts of Speech Function in a Sentence

Words may function in different ways in a sentence. For example, *fish* can be a noun or a verb. *(Fish are fun to watch. I fish with cousin Dan at Carpenter Lake.)* Parts of speech may also function in different ways in a sentence. For example, a noun—such as *fish*—may be the subject of a sentence or the object of a sentence. *(Fish are fun to watch. I saw a fish.)*

1. **Subject**—The subject of a sentence is a noun (or noun phrase, noun clause, or pronoun), normally precedes the verb (predicate), and names who or what the sentence is about.

2. **Verb (Predicate)**—The predicate of a sentence (a verb and the words that complete its meaning) usually follows the subject and expresses what the subject does, what it is, or what has been done to it.

3. **Objects**—Objects are nouns (or noun phrases, noun clauses, or pronouns), usually follow the verb, and can be direct objects or indirect objects.

4. **Complement**—Complements are nouns (or noun phrases, noun clauses, or pronouns) but can also be adjectives (or adjective phrases), usually follow a subject, verb, and any objects, and can be subject complements, object complements, predicate nouns, or predicate adjectives.

5. **Adverbials**—Adverbials are adverbs (or adverb phrases or adverb clauses) that refer to the verb.

Activity: Identify parts of speech, particularly subjects and verbs, in the following sentences.

1. As health care professionals, we must regard this crisis with the utmost importance.
2. I like the story because it is put together so well.
3. As a concerned citizen and patient, I have become very alarmed at the growing addiction to prescription drugs in the United States.
4. At the same time, each fearless and self-sacrificing helper shows each victim a human face, stands for respect for that person's dignity, and is a source of hope for peace and reconciliation.
5. The President will address the nation tonight, upon his return to the White House.

Sentences—Classified by Purpose

Declarative: A sentence that makes a statement and ends with a period.

> My daughter smokes. (Alice Walker)

> Up in the trees the other chimpanzees of the group were moving about, getting ready for the new day. (Jane Goodall)

> We ourselves may never see this cottonwood reach maturity, probably will never take pleasure in its shade or birds or witness the pale gold of its autumn leaves. (Edward Abbey)

Imperative: A sentence that expresses a command.

> Get rid of obvious padding. (Paul Roberts)

> Please keep a copy of this notice with your tax records. (IRS Tax Relief Notice)

Interrogative: A sentence that asks a question.

> What if you don't know what you want to do? (Steven M. Richardson)

> Does he feel like something is missing from his life, but he's not sure what it is? And worst of all, does he blame me for what is missing? (Dave Hawes)

Exclamatory: A sentence that expresses an emphatic statement and ends with an exclamation mark.

> She was no good! Why did *she* win? What were those judges thinking! (Cindy Bosley)

> "I don't care," my daughter says, tossing her hair. "I want to suffer!" (Jessie Thuma)

> If there was a crack house in your neighborhood, what would you do? You would try to get rid of it! (Michael Moore)

Combining sentences sometimes helps the reader see the relationship between ideas. For example, "I went. She stayed." can mean "I went because she stayed" or "I went although she stayed." Combining the sentences with a subordinating conjunction clarifies the relationship. The strategies on the following page can be helpful for combining sentences, and for eliminating fused sentences and comma splices. For example, the comma splice "I went, she stayed." can be rewritten using 1, 2, 3, 4, 5, or 6 on the opposite page.

Nine Ways of Combining Simple Sentences (Independent Clauses)

1. Subject + verb. Subject + verb. (Two simple sentences)

Mary was relaxing in the meadow. Mary saw a dragonfly.
Larry had never flown a plane before. He landed the 747 safely.
A nickel isn't worth much anymore. George gave Susie a dime.

2. Subject + verb; subject + verb. (One compound sentence)

Mary was relaxing in the meadow; Mary saw a dragonfly.
Larry had never flown a plane before; he landed the 747 safely.
A nickel isn't worth much anymore; George gave Susie a dime.

3. Subject + verb, coordinating conjunction subject + verb. (One compound sentence)

Mary was relaxing in the meadow, and she saw a dragonfly.
Larry had never flown a plane before, yet he landed the 747 safely.
A nickel isn't worth much anymore, so George gave Susie a dime.

4. Subject + verb; conjunctive adverb, subject + verb. (One compound sentence)

Mary was relaxing in the meadow; therefore, she saw a dragonfly.
Larry had never flown a plane before; nevertheless, he landed the 747 safely.
A nickel isn't worth much anymore; hence, George gave Susie a dime.

5. Subject + verb subordinating conjunction subject + verb. (One complex sentence)

Mary was relaxing in the meadow when she saw a dragonfly.
Larry had never flown a plane before until he landed the 747 safely.
A nickel isn't worth much anymore though George gave Susie a dime.

6. Subordinating conjunction subject + verb, subject + verb. (One complex sentence)

Since Mary was relaxing in the meadow, she saw a dragonfly.
Although Larry had never flown a plane before, he landed the 747 safely.
Now that a nickel isn't worth much anymore, George gave Susie a dime.

7. Subject + relative clause (relative pronoun + verb) + verb. (One complex sentence)

Mary, who was relaxing in the meadow, saw a dragonfly.
Larry, who had never flown a plane before, landed the 747 safely.
A nickel isn't worth much anymore. George gave Susie a dime. [relative clause will not work]

8. Subject + verb + verb. (One simple sentence)

Mary was relaxing in the meadow and saw a dragonfly.
Larry had never flown a plane before and landed the 747 safely.
A nickel isn't worth much anymore. George gave Susie a dime. [compound verb will not work]

9. Phrase, subject + verb. (One simple sentence)

Relaxing in the meadow, Mary saw a dragonfly.
Never having flown a plane before, Larry landed the 747 safely.
A nickel not being worth much anymore, George gave Susie a dime.

Organization

The essays in this text illustrate just how different essays can be. But every essay has a structure, or organization—the same way we might say every house, garage, or chicken coop has a structure. Organization—like word choice, content, voice, and so on—is determined by considering one's purpose in writing, the reader, and the overall writing situation. But it is also determined by those very ideas that are being presented.

What Is Organization?

Controlling Idea: Looking at organization in general terms, we can say that an essay (or any piece of writing) is about *one thing*. Sometimes that one thing is quite general and includes many parts; other times it is more specific. Shorter pieces, such as the ones usually written in college writing courses, tend to benefit from having a narrower focus. Since the piece is relatively short, there isn't time or space to deal with a larger topic. Essays of 10, 20, or more pages may have a broader main idea—though even an essay of this length can benefit from having an extremely narrow focus. This focus or controlling idea (sometimes called a "main idea" or a "thesis") provides the basis for the organization of the essay. The support for this main idea, as well as its introduction and conclusion, are hung on, or based upon, the main idea.

Beginning, Middle, and End: To keep most readers' interest, a person must get to the main idea pretty quickly, and once it is adequately discussed, cannot just drop it. Thus, an essay (letter, report, etc.) has a beginning, middle, and end. The beginning (or introduction) leads the reader into the meat of the essay. The bulk of an essay supports the main idea (the essays in this text illustrate the various strategies that can be used). The ending (or conclusion) of the essay brings it all to a close in one of various ways. While a conclusion might merely summarize the main points, this summary is often unnecessary. Instead, a conclusion probably asks the reader to seriously consider the writer's main point. This is often done subtly. Conclusions lead the reader out of the essay and back to the larger world. They try to answer the reader's main question: "So what? (What is the point of this essay?)" They encourage (again, often subtly) the reader to think or act differently.

Activity: Study the organization of several essays in this text. Describe, by writing in the margin, what each paragraph is about and how it functions in the overall scheme—or organization—of the essay. Describe how the introduction and conclusion lead the reader into and out of the essay. How, for example, does the introduction effectively get the reader to the point of the essay? What does the conclusion attempt to do? How does it help the reader to think or act differently?

Theme Writing:

One typical organization, often helpful but ultimately limited, is the five-paragraph essay. It includes a brief introduction, three supporting paragraphs (each developing a different point), and a conclusion (usually one fairly brief paragraph). The five-paragraph essay may be altered—for example, to include only two or as many as four or five supporting paragraphs. Regardless of the number of paragraphs, one can see the need eventually to develop beyond the five-paragraph, or theme-writing, approach. Just as most writing tasks challenge the limitation of the introduction/three paragraphs/conclusion format, they also challenge an expanded version of this format. In short, much can be learned by writing themes organized in this way, but writers should be able to identify when this format is not suitable to the complexity of their ideas. Organization is a writing tool used for improving communication; it should never become a limitation.

Five-Paragraph Essay: The five-paragraph essay—because it is simple—allows one to better understand the basics of organization. Five-paragraph essays contain a clear beginning, middle, and end: the main idea is often stated in the beginning; three distinct, though related, ideas support or develop the main idea; and a conclusion follows. Notice in the example below how each paragraph develops or supports a clearly stated main idea. Notice also how key terms from the controlling idea are repeated, word for word or with synomyms, in the topic sentences (or main ideas for the supporting paragraphs). These characteristics of essay organization should be kept in mind without becoming a limitation.

Controlling Idea: Myrtle Beach is a great place to go on vacation.

Supporting Paragraph #1: Myrtle Beach has a lot of nice golf courses.
Supporting Paragraph #2: Myrtle Beach has a beautiful long beach.
Supporting Paragraph #3: Myrtle Beach has plenty of good night life.

One can see much potential here for going beyond the five-paragraph essay. By narrowing the essay's focus, dealing with counterarguments and concessions, or establishing a purpose beyond merely describing some positive aspects of Myrtle Beach, the essay will naturally desire a more complex (and less limiting) organization.

Beyond the Five-Paragraph Essay: Instead of explaining three nice things about Myrtle Beach, a writer might show why Myrtle Beach is preferable to Daytona Beach, Panama City, Acapulco, or the Jersey shore. This approach would likely include making more counterarguments and concessions. Or the writer might narrow his or her focus to just *the beach*. Such an approach might deal briefly with golf courses, night life, and other matters in the introduction or elsewhere, then focus more specifically on the virtues of the beach. Going beyond the five-paragraph approach generally requires more analysis and is likely to produce a more engaging essay.

Beyond Theme Writing: This textbook is full of essays and other writing, each piece organized to help the reader more easily follow the writer's ideas. Each piece has a beginning, middle, and end—and each beginning, middle, and end works a little differently than any other. Writers impose structure upon their ideas, but the very nature of those ideas influences the structure that can be imposed. The writer, then, is not only working with ideas, but also with the fluid way in which all those ideas can interact to become an organized piece of writing. You should not feel that you must figure out the *right* organization, but instead that you must figure out one that engages readers, directs them through the ideas, and leaves them reflective at the end. Many possibilities exist.

Analyzing the organization of Steven M. Richardson's essay "College? What's in It for Me?" helps us to see what Richardson is up to. He begins with a brief introduction; then he states reasons for not going to college; he then transitions (in one paragraph) to reasons *for* going to college; then he states his *main* reason for going to college (one he feels many people overlook); finally, he concludes his essay by leaving the reader with a main point. Analyzing other essays in this text as well as your own essays will help you to better understand how writers use overall organization to help readers follow along.

The Organization of Steven M. Richardson's Essay "College? What's in It for Me?"

Introduction Leading into the Main Idea

- Introduces the idea that there are reasons for attending and for not attending college; establishes credibility as (1) college administrator and (2) parent of two college-age children (paragraph 1)

Reasons Not to Attend College

- Reason #1 for not going to college: cost (paragraph 2)
- Reason #1 continued: even though college is not as expensive as some say, it still isn't cheap (paragraph 3)
- Reason #2 for not going to college: when the economy is good, you can get a job (paragraph 4)
- Reason #3 for not going to college: seems like a waste of time if you don't know what you want to study (paragraph 5)
- Reason #4 for not going to college: a lot of people just don't like school (paragraph 6)

Transitional Paragraph from Reasons Not to Attend to Reasons to Attend

- Transitional paragraph taking the reader from reasons not to go to college to reasons to go to college (paragraph 7)

Reasons to Attend College

- Reason #1 for going to college: while you can get a good job without a college education, the jobs with highest salaries tend to require a college education (paragraph 8)
- Concession: you can earn a good salary without a college education, though most jobs with high salaries do require a college education (paragraph 9)
- Reason #2: one of the best reasons for going to college is to find out what you want to do (paragraph 10)
- In fact, college is all about discovering who you are and what you can do (paragraph 11)

Conclusion Wrapping Up the Main Idea and Leading the Reader out of the Essay

- While college is not right for everybody, it is an investment in your future and a door to a career and personal growth for many (paragraph 12)

Activities

1. To make sure you understand your own essay's organization, label each paragraph. You might (1) state the paragraph's main idea and/or (2) explain how the paragraph functions (which involves not just stating its main idea, but also explaining the paragraph's main idea in relationship to the overall piece—don't just describe a spark plug, but explain its role in the running of the automobile). When reading another writer, do the same thing—especially if the piece is important and you need to understand it well.
2. Examine theme writing (the five-paragraph essay). Make two lists, one naming the advantages of the five-paragraph essay structure, and one naming the disadvantages. Then, consider yourself as writer and your relationship to the five-paragraph essay. When does it suit your needs? When doesn't it? Can you benefit at this point in your career from learning the five-paragraph approach, from utilizing aspects of it when useful, or from avoiding it altogether?

Document Design

While a writer's ideas are of primary concern, those ideas must be delivered in a way that facilitates their being understood. Thus, a writer's organization, word choice, and sentence structure are all important—as is document design. Memos, for example, follow a certain general design that varies from workplace to workplace. So do letters, news releases, and other documents. (Chapter 12 provides examples of document design for non-essay writing.) While a particular professor may require a title page or a certain font type or size, professors (and readers) in general will expect you to follow certain general formatting guidelines. Following these guidelines—and modifying them as appropriate according to a particular professor's instructions—should help to create a more readable document. The instructions below generally use MLA style.

Title Page: Some professors prefer a title page; some don't. If preparing a title page, include the following: title (centered about one-third of the way down the page); your name; course information (course, section, and instructor's name); and the date. A professional-looking title page will create a good first impression on the reader.

Identification: If you have no title page, include identification information (name, course, professor, date) in the upper left-hand corner of the first page. Identify pages in the upper right-hand corner with an appropriate header (your name and page number).

Title: Do not put your title in quotation marks, underline it, or end it with a period. The first and last words should be capitalized, as should all other words except for articles (*a, an, the*), prepositions, and conjunctions.

Paper: Use white, unlined $8\frac{1}{2} \times 11$ paper.

Print Job: Use a good quality printer and black ink.

Margins: Use one inch margins (and do not justify the right margin).

Spacing: Double-space.

Font Size and Type: Use a standard font type such as Times New Roman, 12 point. Do not use sans serif fonts or fonts that look like handwriting.

Page Numbers: Number each page.

Paragraphs: Indent, and do not double-space between, paragraphs.

Documentation: Document all sources either formally or informally, depending upon the writing situation. If using formal documentation, follow standard guidelines. There are four commonly used styles:

- MLA (Modern Language Association) is generally used in English, foreign languages, and other fields in the humanities.
- APA (American Psychological Association) is generally used in the social sciences.
- CSE (Council of Science Editors) is generally used in the natural sciences.
- CMS (Chicago Manual of Style) is generally used in history, and sometimes in the humanities and sciences.

Mechanics: Follow standards of capitalization, spacing, spelling, and punctuation.

Visuals: If using visuals, such as tables or figures (which includes charts, graphs, diagrams, maps, and photos), place the visual near and following the reference to it in the text. In more formal writing, label the visual by title and number (Table 1: Election Results by State; or Figure 1: Pickup Truck Sales for 2004).

Sample Document Design (MLA)

Bruno 1

Daniel Bruno
Composition I
Dr. Fritz Strisky
November 5, 2001

Entitlement Education

  In his book Generation X Goes to College, Peter Sacks describes, among other things, the sense of entitlement that some students in today's consumerist culture have toward a college education. One entire chapter explores this issue alone, providing examples of this "sense" and looking into its "humble beginnings." Sacks shows how consumerism has invaded education, leading some students to expect good grades for little effort. But he fails, it seems, to emphasize enough a most harmful effect of this sense of entitlement. The biggest problem, as I see it, is that although students are able to graduate from high school (and even some colleges) with minimal effort, those students may find themselves cheated in the long run.

  How might they be cheated? One might argue that students get cheated because entitlement doesn't go on forever. At some point it stops. For example, a college graduate with a marketing degree, but especially weak thinking or writing skills, may find himself disadvantaged on the job. It is not that his boss puts her foot down; instead, the job does. Our student finds himself not well prepared for it. He gets cheated because he is disadvantaged at his job--a job that he paid money to learn how to do. Of course the point isn't about marketing majors. The same is true of students in any field. (Marketing is just what came to mind.)

  One might also claim that students will be cheated because their lives will somehow *be less*. This argument claims that a person's intelligence contributes to his quality of life. Here we must remember that "intelligence" is not just "knowledge." Instead, it is being able to use knowledge, to make connections and figure things out, to see causes and solve problems. A person may have much knowledge--that is, he may have accumulated a lot of facts--but not have much intelligence . . . or so the argument goes. As one goes from first grade to twelfth, from twelfth grade to college, and from freshman to senior, education shifts focus from mere accumulation of information (knowledge) to application of information (intelligence). And while we may accumulate more knowledge as a senior in college than we did as a senior in high school, the focus in college has (or should have) shifted from mere knowledge to intelligence--that is, to the ability to make good use of one's knowledge.

If no title page, include identification information (name, course, professor, date) in the upper left-hand corner of the first page.

Give your essay an interesting title. Do not put it in quotation marks, underline it, or end it with a period. The first and last words should be capitalized as should all other words except for articles (*a, an, the*), prepositions, and conjunctions.

Identify all pages in the upper right-hand corner with an appropriate header including your name (the essay's title is used in APA).

Unless otherwise instructed, type your essay and print it out on 8½ × 11 white paper, with one-inch margins.

Unless otherwise instructed, double-space your essay.

To make reading easier, be sure to use a good quality printer and black ink.

Use a standard font type such as Times New Roman, 12 point. Do not use sans serif fonts or fonts that look like handwriting.

Indent, and do not add an additional double-space between, paragraphs when a document is double-spaced. (If a document is to be single-spaced, double-space between paragraphs.) Number each page.

Document all sources either formally or informally, depending upon the writing situation.

Bruno 2

Other standard arguments claim other ways students might be cheated. For example, we might feel sorry for someone who doesn't get a joke--or a reference. Allusions to literature, history, philosophy and so on allow us to say much in few words. But does the listener understand? If a person is unaware of common references--the Battle of the Bulge, Normandy, Existentialism, T. S. Eliot, World War I, Rasputin, John the Baptist, Gandhi, apartheid, Jonas Salk, Johnny Appleseed, Lewis and Clark, the Trail of Tears, slavery, the Donner Party, and so on--he misses out on conversations, on meaning, on *connecting with his fellow inmates*. Of course, here one might counter that you don't need to know all of these things. And, I agree, you don't. People tend to hang out with people who have similar interests and tastes.

One more argument claims that because we live in a democracy, we must be well-educated. Since all the citizens are responsible for the government, our forefathers promoted public education so that all citizens--not just the wealthy and elite--would know how to read and write. Thomas Jefferson wrote,

> I know no safe depository of the ultimate powers of society but the people themselves; and if we think them not enlightened enough to exercise their control with a wholesome discretion, the remedy is not to take it from them, but to inform their discretion by education. This is the true corrective of abuses of constitutional power. (The Writings 15:278)

In what ways can educated citizens correct abuses in a democracy? A person's way of life, his purchases and activities--not just a person's vote or protest march--is part of the responsibility. Thus, consumers and neighbors and co-workers and so on should behave responsibly and think intelligently. It is our responsibility as citizens of a democracy.

True enough, these are all ways that students who are allowed to just slide by end up getting cheated. But another way (and one less talked about) strikes me as being far more offensive. This reason hinges on the fact that many students are not just sliding by.

In Generation X Goes to College, Peter Sacks illustrates that all of today's college students cannot just be thrown in the same big barrel. In describing the modern/post-modern clash in education, he spends the majority of his time talking about those students who are underprepared, who lack the basic study skills required in academic work, and who demonstrate little real commitment to their own

Bruno 3

education. Yet, he does not discuss this problem in isolation. He also mentions another type of student. For example, he introduces the reader to Marissa and Carol: "As very good students, [their views] were virtually excluded by The College in order to accommodate the whiners and complainers" (61). And he says they "suffered not only educationally" (63). In addition to discussing specific good students, an entire chapter presents survey results about students' attitudes toward education. While he makes claims such as "nearly a quarter of the students . . . harbored a disproportionate sense of entitlement," this very statement tells the reader that a full three quarters (that is, three out of four) students *do not* "harbor a disproportionate sense of entitlement" (54-59). He wraps up the book by focusing on another student, Andie, who he describes as "a good student, constantly picking [his] brain for information and feedback on her work" (186-7). His final paragraph, before the Epilogue, says, "Let's create a system that encourages people like Andie at least as much as the ones who don't give a damn" (187). Thus, Sacks shows that today's students are a more diverse group--in skill level, background, and attitude toward education--than has ever before been gathered together in the college classroom.

Bruno 4

Works Cited

"Almanac." *The Chronicle of Higher Education.* 18 Oct. 2000. http://chronicle.com/
    free/almanac/2000/almanac.htm.

Jefferson, Thomas. *The Writings of Thomas Jefferson.* Ed. Andrew Adgate
    Lipscomb and Albert Ellery Bergh. 20 vols. Washington, D.C.: 1903-4.

Sacks, Peter. *Generation X Goes to College.* Open Court: Chicago and LaSalle,
    Illinois, 1996.

If using formal documentation, follow standard guidelines for the appropriate style: MLA, APA, or another style required by the situation.

If using MLA style, as shown here, include in-text references that correspond to a Works Cited page that lists complete bibliographic information for sources.

With in-text documentation, periods go after the parentheses and quotation marks go before them.

Include a Works Cited page that corresponds to the in-text references throughout the essay.

List sources in alphabetical order. (For more information, see Chapter 12.)

Begin a long Works Cited list on a separate page. If including only a few sources and if space permits, you may be permitted to list them immediately following the essay. Include all works on the same page if possible.

Writing Style

C hapters 1–11 discuss the writer's voice as the presence of the writer within the text. Style can be thought of as the way a writer treats his or her readers; more specifically, *style* is a term that characterizes the words and phrases that a writer decides to use in communicating with readers.

Many different styles can be considered "good writing." But an effective style in one situation may not work as well in another (for example, writing a letter to a friend vs. writing a college essay; writing an initial response to a video shown in class vs. writing a final lab report in biology class; writing a thank-you note to a professor vs. writing a letter to the college newspaper). The same writer is able to write X and Y depending upon the particular situation.

Consider Daniel Bruno's writing style in "Entitlement Education." He writes:

> In our competitive world, the sad truth is that even some of the very good students, though their college dreams were to be doctors and lawyers and pharmacists and engineers, will be waiting tables.

In an e-mail to a friend—a less formal writing situation—Bruno might have written:

> Wake up! It's a dog-eat-dog world. Even a lot of good students won't get the job they're after.

Writing style is influenced by a variety of factors including word choice, sentence structure, paragraph length, punctuation, figurative expressions, writing purpose, and so on. For example, deciding to elevate one's vocabulary, use fewer commas, or make the reader laugh will affect a writer's style.

Describe the writing style of each of the following passages. You might also consider these passages in context by referring to the entire essay's overall subject matter and purpose. How does each style match (or not match) the particular writing situation? And how do the writers vary their styles within essays?

- The rapidity of change and the speed with which new situations are created follow the impetuous and heedless pace of man rather than the deliberate pace of nature. (Rachel Carson)

- One reason for this shift to "upscale emulation" is the decline of the neighborhood as a focus of comparison. Economically speaking, neighborhoods are relatively homogeneous groupings. In the 1950's and 60's, when Americans were keeping up with the Joneses down the street, they typically compared themselves to other households of similar incomes. Because of this focus on neighbors, the gap between aspirations and means tended to be moderate. (Juliet Schor)

- The woman put her keys in her purse, slammed the car door, took one step toward the gentleman and advocated for herself (loudly), "LISTEN, BUCKO!", she said, "I've had two heart attacks and five bypass surgeries in the last three years. I CAN PARK HERE!" (Dan Wilkins)

The Circle of Good Writing: Because language is shared, and because our purpose in writing is to communicate information from one person to another, we can judge writing by the degree to which it achieves its purpose. Thus, we must consider our purpose in writing and then assess how successfully the writing is likely to achieve that purpose. Of course, no two writers' styles are identical, and some will vary in interesting ways. But if a writer's word choice, organization, voice, and so on somehow interfere with the reader's understanding of the message, the writing (or the style of writing) might be considered problematic, unhelpful, difficult, or even "bad."

Thus, the shared nature of language requires that in most writing situations, a writer's style fall within a certain area—we can call this area the Circle of Good Writing. Your writing need not be the same as your instructor's or anyone else's (in fact, it could not be exactly the same), but it should not vary significantly from the usual conventions that others such as professors, employers, and clients employ in their own writing.

Diagram: Circle of Good Writing
Because language is shared, writing style should fall within a common area.

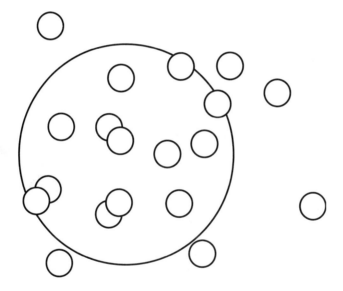

While you need not have the same writing style as your employer, your instructor, or Ernest Hemingway, because you share language and written communication with others, you will communicate more effectively if your writing style falls within not outside of the Circle of Good Writing.

Problems with Style: Appropriate writing style helps a writer communicate with a reader. More complex topics generally require more complex-sounding style. To students, college textbooks or scholarly articles sometimes sound elevated because the subject matter is complex and requires a technical vocabulary and complex sentence structure. But writing style should not make a topic sound more complex than it actually is.

Some writers stretching to sound educated or professional dress up simple ideas in unnecessarily complex or fancy language. This can make reading more difficult, just because of the writer's style. Writing style should be focused on clearly expressing the ideas of the writer without drawing much attention to itself. Style that does not call attention to itself (but that instead focuses on the ideas being expressed) is usually the most effective.

Consider the following passage from Daniel Bruno's essay "Entitlement Education."

> The problem, of course, is that the two students have entered college on different academic levels and the one on the higher level has graduated on an *even higher* level while the one on the lower level has remained pretty much the same.

Bruno might have expressed the same idea in different ways, some of which might sound too elevated or too chatty to his reader:

Elevated Writing

Upon careful study it appears that the problem, per se, is at the time of matriculation two collegians embarked upon higher education at dissimilar academic levels and the first such student ultimately graduated on a higher academic level of learning whereas the second such student continually resided upon the lower of the two academic levels.

Too Chatty

Well, the problem is two students go off to college and one is already better off school-wise than the other. And the better-off one graduates even better off, and the other one doesn't do so hot.

Not Thoughtful

Simply put, smart students learn a lot and dumb ones don't.

Wishy-Washy

It seems to me that perhaps the problem might be that two students could have entered college on different academic levels and, in my opinion, the one on the higher level might graduate on an *even higher level* while the one on the lower level might possibly not have learned as much.

Pig-Headed

Wake up! The problem is so simple I can't imagine why no one has done anything about it. Obviously, two students have entered college on different academic levels and the one on the higher level is bound to graduate on an *even higher* level. The one on the lower level gets what he deserves. Got it?

Formulaic

The problem is two students have entered college on different academic levels. The one on the higher level has graduated on an even higher level. The lower one has remained the same.

Take other sentences—either from your own writing or from the essays in this text—and rewrite them in different styles. Consider how you might express the same ideas to different readers in different writing situations.

Activities

1. Create or find three examples of different writing styles. Explain why each does or does not fall within the Circle of Good Writing. Explain in what situation each might or might not be appropriate.
2. Describe your writing style. It may help to read through old essays, letters, e-mails, and so on. How does your writing style vary from one situation to another? How would you describe the writing style you use for college essays, and why do you use that style?
3. Read just the opening paragraphs of at least five essays in this text. Describe the writing style of each and how it relates to the content of the essay.

Paragraphs

Ｇeneral advice about paragraphs is that they should be about one thing, and not be too long or too short. A quick look at paragraphs in this text illustrates their varying lengths. Long paragraphs can be uninviting to the reader. They also run the danger of being an unorganized dumping ground for the various ideas the writer came up with while drafting. But stringing together many short paragraphs (two or three sentences) can also create problems for the reader. Both long and short paragraphs are acceptable, but writers generally group related ideas into paragraphs to help the reader take in one manageable unit of thought before moving on to another. Having many short paragraphs fails to help the reader see the relationship between ideas.

Supporting Paragraphs: Writers think about (1) how each paragraph functions within the overall essay and (2) how each paragraph is organized within itself. Read through several essays in this book, noticing how paragraphs function and are organized. Paragraphs are often organized deductively—stating the main idea first, then supporting it. They are also organized inductively—giving support first, then the main idea. Some paragraphs (called "turnabout paragraphs" in this text) begin with a point and then pivot, or move, the reader to another somehow-related point. And other paragraphs serve as transitions between the preceding and following paragraphs or sections of text.

Deductive: If information is organized deductively, the main idea is presented first and the support for that idea follows. Stating the main idea first often helps the reader to more readily understand the point of the paragraph.

> Sadly, the gap between these two groups grows even wider. The motivated student with good study skills (the one who has had at least an adequate high school education) attends class, takes notes, understands reading assignments, follows instructions, develops even better habits of mind, gains even more knowledge, and learns ways of making that knowledge work for his and her fellow humans. But in a system where B's are average and C's might indicate that although a student "tried" he did not demonstrate understanding or skill, the poorer students continue to advance through the system while remaining trapped at the bottom. Their level of thinking does not change much while that of their better-prepared peers does.

The opening sentence of the preceding paragraph expresses a main idea—that the gap between two groups of students grows wider. The rest of the paragraph explains *why*.

Activity: Find three deductive paragraphs in this book.

Inductive: If information is organized inductively, the main idea is presented following the support. The deductive paragraph above can be reorganized by placing the main idea last.

> The motivated student with good study skills (the one who has had at least an adequate high school education) attends class, takes notes, understands reading assignments, follows instructions, develops even better habits of mind, gains even more knowledge, and learns ways of making that knowledge work for his and her fellow humans. But in a system where B's are average and C's might indicate that although a student "tried" he did not demonstrate understanding or skill, the poorer students continue to advance through the system while remaining trapped at the bottom. Their level of thinking does not change much while that of their better-prepared peers does. **Sadly, the gap between these two groups grows even wider.**

Activity: Find three inductive paragraphs in this book.

Turnabout: Writers often find it helpful to pivot from one idea to another within the same paragraph—the second idea being a major point that plays off of the first idea. The pivot—or turnabout—is usually signaled by a transition word or expression, such as *but, however, on the other hand, still, yet,* and so on.

> In his book *Generation X Goes to College,* Peter Sacks describes, among other things, the sense of entitlement that some students in today's consumerist culture have toward a college education. One entire chapter explores this issue alone, providing examples of this "sense" and looking into its "humble beginnings." Sacks shows how consumerism has invaded education, leading some students to expect good grades for little effort. But he fails, it seems, to emphasize enough a most harmful effect of this sense of entitlement. The biggest problem, as I see it, is that although students are able to graduate from high school (and even some colleges) with minimal effort, those students may find themselves cheated in the long run.

Notice how the above paragraph turns on the word *But*, thus building on the previous point and moving in a different, yet appropriate, direction. The first half of the paragraph says what Peter Sacks describes; the second half turns on *but* and says what he *doesn't* do.

Activity: Find three turnabout paragraphs in this book.

Transition: Some paragraphs, especially in longer pieces, function as transitions that take the reader from one idea (usually a section of an essay) to another idea (another section of the essay).

> True enough, these are all ways that students who are allowed to just slide by end up getting cheated. But another way (and one less talked about) strikes me as being far more offensive. This reason hinges on the fact that many students are not just sliding by.

The above paragraph moves the reader from the previously mentioned ways students are cheated to a far more offensive way students are cheated. Then the rest of the essay develops this point.

Activity: Find three transition paragraphs in this book.

Unity, Development, and Coherence: Paragraphs (and essays) can be considered in terms of their unity, development, and coherence.

Unity means that each paragraph is about one thing—that is, it has a purpose and it goes about achieving that purpose without significant digression.

Development means that the paragraph is sufficiently thorough—a matter that can only be determined by considering that paragraph's purpose and what must be done to achieve that purpose.

Coherence means that the relationship between ideas is clear to the reader—that the writing flows. The writer assists the reader by arranging ideas in an appropriate order and by providing transitions, repeating key terms, and following conventions of grammar.

In revision, working toward a more unified, developed, and coherent essay should help to create more readable writing.

Opening and Closing Paragraphs: Shorter essays often have an opening paragraph, several supporting paragraphs, and a closing paragraph. Opening paragraphs bring the reader into the essay, introducing the subject and setting the tone. Closing paragraphs take the reader out of the essay, back to the outside world. The possibilities are limitless for ways of beginning and ending essays. In general, readers are likely to respond well to a sincere and purposeful introduction that seems to be moving toward something interesting. And while conclusions work in a myriad of ways, a good conclusion probably makes some sort of final point that a reader might actually consider. Openings and closings are also discussed briefly in this chapter under "Organization."

Strategies for Introductions

1. Begin with a statistic, quotation, or anecdote.
2. Ask a question.
3. Create a strong visual image.
4. Provide necessary background.
5. Make a comparison.
6. Briefly explain what the essay is responding to.
7. Allude to the public resonance of the essay.
8. Create a tone for the essay.

Test the approach you take by asking yourself if you think it will engage the reader.

Strategies for Conclusions

1. Suggest or emphasize the public resonance.
2. State and explain the main idea.
3. Create a strong image.
4. Ask an important question.
5. Relate back to a point from the introduction.
6. Call the reader to thought or action.
7. Make a recommendation.
8. Suggest a consequence.

Test the approach you take by asking yourself if it leaves the reader with your essay's main point.

Activities

1. Read one essay in this book as a study of paragraphs. Note each paragraph's organization (deductive, inductive, turnabout) and function (transition, support). Explain why you think each paragraph is unified, developed, and coherent.

2. To revise an essay, write out a main idea for each of your paragraphs. Try placing the main idea in different places.

3. Study introductions by reading just the introductions of several essays in this book. Describe the way they work. Do they fit into one of the strategies listed above, or do they use a different strategy? Describe how each introduces the essay. How does it engage the reader?

4. Read just the conclusions of several essays. Can you describe the way they work? Do they seem to be leaving the reader with something to ponder? (While reading conclusions, keep in mind that some may be more than one paragraph long.)

5. Analyze one introduction and one conclusion, either from an essay in this book or elsewhere. Describe the strategies they used. How did the introduction attempt to engage the reader? How did it introduce the topic? Was it successful? Did the conclusion emphasize the main point of the essay? Was it successful? Report your findings in a brief report or on-line discussion.

6. Rewrite your introduction with an eye towards getting into the essay quickly. Cut anything that unnecessarily delays getting to main points or that takes away from the essay's forward momentum.

Sentence Vitality

Writing appeals to a reader for various reasons, one of which is sentence vitality. *Vitality* can be defined as "the peculiarity distinguishing the living from the nonliving." Some sentences are more alive than others. For sentences to have vitality, they should be clear, concise, coherent, and complete. Consider the following sentences. Which ones seem more alive—and why?

The Gods, they say, give breath, and they take it away. But the same could be said—could it not?—of the humble comma. (Pico Iyer)

Once he stamped so hard on my head that my neck was nearly broken. (Jane Goodall)

Still, the city creeps closer, day by day. (Edward Abbey)

She smells clean, like cucumbers and watermelon. (Jessie Thuma)

Sadly, the gap between these two groups grows even wider. (Daniel Bruno)

So here's what I don't understand: if profit is supreme, why doesn't a company like General Motors sell crack? (Michael Moore)

Perhaps we can liberate tobacco from those who have captured and abused it, enslaving the plant on large plantations, keeping it from freedom and its kin, and forcing it to enslave the world. (Alice Walker)

I imagine you are breathing the exhaust fumes of our disregard. (Simon Benlow)

The menstrual cycle itself mirrors how consciousness becomes matter and how thought creates reality. (Christianne Northrup)

Situated on a lake, the Sea World I visited features a water show with ski jumps and corny skits. (Jaime Stayer)

Clarity: If a sentence is clear, it is free from obscurity or ambiguity. It is easily understood. Since one purpose of writing is to clearly communicate an idea to another person, writers focus on the clarity of their expression.

Conciseness: When a sentence is concise, its idea has been expressed without unnecessary words. It is free of ornamentation and superfluous details and makes its point in few words. Good writing is usually fairly concise. While every unnecessary word need not be eliminated, cutting most of them will add vitality to one's writing. Good writing is "economical"—there is little waste.

Coherence: Coherence involves connecting ideas for the reader in a systematic and logical way. If a sentence is coherent, it is logically or aesthetically ordered. It is clear and understandable. One can see how a systematic and consistent method of relating words to each other within and across sentences helps to make one's writing more intelligible, or understandable, to the reader. This systematic and consistent method involves grammar. Matters such as agreement in number (singular or plural) and tense (past, present, future) as well as other grammatical concerns contribute to a piece of writing's coherence.

Strategies to Create Clear, Concise, and Coherent Writing

The following strategies help to achieve clear, concise, and coherent writing:

Rely on Active (not Passive) Sentences

While both active and passive sentences are useful, active sentences tend to express ideas more directly and thus contribute to sentence vitality. In an active sentence, the grammatical subject does the action; in a passive sentence, the grammatical subject is acted upon. Consider how these two sentences both express the same idea:

> The farmer milked the cow.
> The cow was milked by the farmer.

The first sentence is active because the grammatical subject—*the farmer*—is doing the action. The second sentence is passive because the grammatical subject—*the cow*—is being acted upon. To recognize passive sentences, look for the following: (1) the grammatical subject is being acted upon, (2) the verb requires a helping word (*was milked*, for example, instead of *milked*), (3) the noun doing the action is expressed in a prepositional phrase beginning with *by*, and this *by*-phrase could be eliminated from the sentence. Consider two more sentences (one active and one passive). Each could be used to express the same idea.

> The CEO made millions while employees lost their life savings.
> Mistakes were made.

The first sentence consists of two clauses: (1) *The CEO* (subject) *made* (verb) and (2) *while* (subordinating conjunction) *employees* (subject) *lost* (verb). Both clauses are active because the grammatical subject is doing the action. To express these ideas in a passive construction, one would write: *Millions were made by the CEO while their life savings was lost by the employees.* Notice the *by*-phrase and verb form of the passive construction. Also notice how the passive constructions in this example are wordy and cumbersome. The second sentence—*Mistakes were made*—is passive and might also be used to say *The CEO made millions while employees lost their life savings.* It focuses not on who made the mistakes, but on the fact that mistakes were made.

When to Use the Passive Voice: Both active and passive sentences are important in writing. If focusing on the cow, the passive construction—*The cow was milked by the farmer*—may be more appropriate than the active sentence that features the farmer. Similarly, the newspaper headline *Kennedy Shot* is passive, yet more appropriate than an active expression of the same idea: *Oswald Shoots*. And in certain situations, it may be appropriate to avoid placing blame (or seeking praise) by saying *Mistakes were made* or *The cow was milked*.

Writers rely more on active sentences because they are more direct. Check to see if too many passive sentences have crept into your writing—and rewrite any sentences that you decide work better in the active voice. As you do, remember that active and passive voice refers to grammatical structure. Consider two more sentences:

> The finch ate a sunflower seed.
> The house was destroyed by a furious hurricane.

The first sentence above is active, though it may seem the idea conveys little action. The second sentence is passive even though it describes a lot of activity.

Eliminate Wordiness

Early drafts tend to contain unnecessary words that slow the pace of the reading and often distract the reader. Writers weed sentences of unnecessary words, the way a gardener removes unwanted weeds from a flower garden, thus featuring the flowers. Notice the clear and concise sentences below and the fabricated wordier versions a writer might find in a rough draft. For some, developing an eye toward eliminating wordiness takes time. The first step is going through rough drafts and deleting unnecessary repetition and wordy expressions.

Concise: Still, the city creeps closer, day by day. (Edward Abbey)
Wordy: In the final analysis, the city is still creeping a little bit closer each and every day.

Concise: She smells clean, like cucumbers and watermelon. (Jessie Thuma)
Wordy: She is a clean-smelling girl. She has the smell of vegetables like cucumbers and watermelon. But not carrots.

Concise: Sadly, the gap between these two groups grows even wider. (Daniel Bruno)
Wordy: It is sad that the gap between the first group of students and the second group of students continues to grow wider and wider.

Concise: So here's what I don't understand: if profit is supreme, why doesn't a company like General Motors sell crack? (Michael Moore)
Wordy: I'm a little puzzled about something. If profit is really what is supreme, why wouldn't General Motors decide to sell something like crack instead of selling cars, trucks, SUVs, etc.?

Commonly Used Wordy Expressions and What They Mean

black in color	means	black
square in shape	means	square
due to the fact that	means	because
in this day and age	means	today (or now)
at the present time	means	now
for the most part	means	mostly
in the final analysis	means	finally
in the event that	means	if
frank and honest	means	honest
revert back	means	revert

Avoid Unnecessary Expletives

Expletives—consisting of *there* or *it* plus a form of *to be*—often sneak into early drafts of our writing. While expletives are sometimes helpful and even necessary, eliminating some expletives can add to a piece of writing's sentence vitality. Consider the following two ways of expressing the same idea:

Idea expressed using an expletive:
There are laws that we can enact that will prevent companies from doing anything to hurt us.

Michael Moore's actual statement without the expletive construction:
We can enact laws to prevent companies from doing anything to hurt us.

In the example above, the expletive construction seems unnecessary and requires the sentence to be a little wordy. A few expletives, even if not absolutely essential, are not likely to bother the reader. But using a lot of expletives takes away from a piece of writing's vitality. In the example above, the writer can (1) simply eliminate the expletive, (2) eliminate the word *that*, and then (3) make a few adjustments to the rest of the sentence. The result is that the subject *(we)* and the verb *(can enact)* have been moved to the front of the sentence, and a few unhelpful words have been deleted. The same could be done in the following sentence: *It was Joe who paid for the tickets.* Eliminating the expletive *(it was)* allows the writer to eliminate the relative pronoun *who* and write *Joe paid for the tickets.*

Not all expletives are so easy to avoid (and not all expletives should be avoided). In many cases, instead of rewriting a single sentence, the writer will be able to combine several sentences, thus being even more concise. Before you consider a draft to be complete, highlight all the expletives so that you become aware of how many you use. If you use several per paragraph, consider combining and restructuring sentences to add more vitality to your writing.

Compare an actual paragraph from Jessie Thuma's "The Ring of Truth: My Child Is Growing Up" to one she might have written that contains unnecessary expletives:

Paragraph Containing Expletives

It isn't like my daughter asks for $42 pants from the Gap or $38 shirts from Abercrombie & Fitch. She doesn't wear makeup. There are, however, about a dozen pots of flavored lip gloss that rattle around the bottom of her orange book bag. She gets straight A's. My daughter doesn't have a boyfriend. It isn't that she is obsessed with boys. She dreams about meeting a "totally hot guy" when we go camping for a week at a deserted state forest, but there isn't a problem if she doesn't meet a boy. She is prepared to settle for reading a stack of books next to the lake. When she is rebellious it is to sneak into the occasional R-rated movie. There is much that I have to be grateful for.

Thuma's Actual Paragraph (without Expletives)

My daughter doesn't ask for $42 pants from the Gap or $38 shirts from Abercrombie & Fitch. She doesn't wear makeup, unless you count the dozen pots of flavored lip gloss that rattle around the bottom of her orange book bag. She gets straight A's. My daughter doesn't have a boyfriend; she isn't obsessed with boys. She dreams about meeting a "totally hot guy" when we go camping for a week at a deserted state forest, but she is prepared to settle for reading a stack of books next to the lake if the boy thing doesn't work out. The extent of her rebellion is to sneak into the occasional R-rated movie. I have much to be grateful for.

Rely on Subjects and Verbs to Convey Meaning

Subjects that state what a sentence is about and verbs that clearly express what the subject does or is or what was done to the subject bring sentences to life. Notice how in the examples below the writers rely on few modifying words, and instead convey their meaning through clear subjects *(Gods, he, we, menstrual cycle, Sea World)* and vivid—or lively—verbs *(give, stamped, can liberate, mirrors, features).*

> The Gods, they say, give breath, and they take it away. But the same could be said—could it not?—of the humble comma. (Pico Iyer)

> Once he stamped so hard on my head that my neck was nearly broken. (Jane Goodall)

> Perhaps we can liberate tobacco from those who have captured and abused it, enslaving the plant on large plantations, keeping it from freedom and its kin, and forcing it to enslave the world. (Alice Walker)

> The menstrual cycle itself mirrors how consciousness becomes matter and how thought creates reality. (Christianne Northrup)

> Situated on a lake, the Sea World I visited features a water show with ski jumps and corny skits. (Jaime Stayer)

Make a study of how the writers in this book use clear and accurate subjects along with vivid or lively verbs to convey their ideas. Also, notice the way your favorite writers, not included in this book, use subjects and verbs.

Show Relationships (Subordination and Coordination, Parallelism, Agreement, and Word Order)

Writers (and speakers) don't just express ideas; they also show the reader the relationship between those ideas. For example, *John sang, and Julie left* can mean various things: that is, the relationship between John's singing and Julie's leaving is not necessarily clear. Subordinating one idea to another often makes the relationship clearer. Consider the following: *John sang because Julie left. John sang even though Julie left. John sang when Julie left. John sang before Julie left. John sang after Julie left. Because John sang, Julie left. Although John sang, Julie left.* The subordinating conjunctions *(because, even though, when, before, after, although)* express a more specific relationship than the coordinating conjunction *and.*

Notice the various strategies Cindy Bosley takes advantage of in the lengthy sentence below (subordination, coordination, parallelism, agreement, word order).

> If your parents are crazy <u>and</u> poor, <u>and if</u> you can't win the Junior Miss Pageant, <u>and if</u> it's the kind of town <u>where</u> you stay or they don't ever want you coming back, <u>you get</u> <u>married</u>, <u>you move</u> to Texas where your husband sells drugs, <u>you hide away</u> from the world <u>until</u> your self grows enough to break you out, <u>and then</u> <u>you leave</u> <u>and</u> <u>you pray</u> for your mother's loneliness <u>and</u> <u>you spend</u> <u>your</u> life learning to come to terms with <u>your own,</u> <u>and</u> <u>you are</u> smart <u>and</u> <u>willful</u> <u>and</u> <u>strong,</u> <u>and</u> <u>you don't</u> ever have to draw another chart before the Pageant begins. (Cindy Bosley)

If Bosley had not worked to make relationships clear, her sentence might have read as follows:

Your parents are crazy. Poor. You can't win the Junior Miss Pageant. The kind of town where you stay. They don't ever want you coming back. You get married. You move to Texas. Your husband sells drugs. You hide away from the world. Your self grows enough to break out. You leave. You pray. Your mother's loneliness. You spend your life learning to come to terms. Your loneliness. You are smart. Willful. Strong. You don't ever have to draw another chart. The Pageant begins.

Write Complete Sentences

Complete sentences are discussed on pages 754–755. In brief, because language is shared, readers expect sentences to begin and end in certain places determined by the grammatical structure of the ideas being expressed. For example, Joan Didion writes,

> And once it comes, now that I am wise in its ways, I no longer fight it.

Didion's sentence contains three clauses—two dependent *(once it comes; that I am)* and one independent *(I no longer fight)*. Didion and her readers view this group of clauses as one sentence. Were she to punctuate it as *And once it comes. Now that I am wise in its ways. I no longer fight it.* the reader would be at least slightly thrown off by the writer's sense of sentence boundaries. The intended meaning might be unclear to the reader. Certainly, the reader would be a little distracted.

Activities

1. Find several lifeless sentences from your own writing and bring them to life. Make sure that your new, more vital sentences are clear, concise, coherent, and complete. Make them shorter, not longer, than their lifeless predecessors if you can.

2. Find a paragraph of your own writing in which you use several expletives (*there* or *it* plus a form of *to be*). Rewrite the entire paragraph, combining sentences and communicating main ideas with lively subjects and verbs.

3. Photocopy or print out a passage of at least 1,000 words by any writer you enjoy reading. Identify several lively sentences and on a separate page explain specifically why you think those sentences are lively. Then, exchange passages with a classmate (or classmates) and see if you agree on which sentences are lively and why.

4. Go through your next essay, subordinating less important ideas to more important ones. For example, locate facts and observations—ideas your reader is well aware of—next to claims or opinions of your own. Then attempt to subordinate one idea to the other. For example, Christianne Northrup might have written, "Women sometimes live together in natural settings, and their ovulations tend to occur at the time of the full moon, with menses and self-reflection at the dark of the moon." Instead she subordinates the more obvious idea to the main idea: "When women live together in natural settings, their ovulations tend to occur at the time of the full moon, with menses and self-reflection at the dark of the moon." Or Jessie Thuma might have written, "Knowledge and experience are hard to shed once they have been acquired." Instead, she writes, "Once acquired, knowledge and experience are hard to shed."

5. Along with your next essay, turn in at least three sentences from that essay in which you subordinated a less important idea to a more important idea. Type out each subordinated sentence as well as a version of the sentence in which the less important idea is not subordinated.

6. Keep a journal of lively sentences. Write down any lively sentences you read or hear throughout this school term. Underneath each one explain what gives it its vitality.

Coherence and Conciseness

Coherence and conciseness have been discussed regarding sentence vitality—but paragraphs and essays (as well as letters, reports, and such) should also be coherent and concise.

- Coherence involves connecting ideas for the reader in a systematic and logical way. If a piece of writing is coherent, it is logically or aesthetically ordered. It is clear and understandable. It flows.
- If a piece of writing is concise, its idea has been expressed without unnecessary words, sentences, or paragraphs. Concise writing is free of ornamentation and superfluous details. It makes its point economically, with little waste.

Matters ranging from purpose in writing to in-text documentation contribute coherence and conciseness to a piece of writing. Notice how the following strategies combine to create coherence and conciseness in the sample essay "Entitlement Education":

- A title that expresses the focus of the essay
- Purposeful writing
- A purposeful introduction moving steadily towards a main point
- Accurate word choice
- Sentence vitality (eliminating wordiness, using strong subjects and verbs, etc.)
- Explicit statements (including statements of main ideas and statements of support)
- Summary of appropriate information
- Consistent verb tense
- Conventional punctuation (commas, colons, quotation marks, etc.)
- Transitional words, expressions, sentences, and paragraphs
- Pronouns
- Pronoun/antecedent agreement
- Subject/verb agreement
- Parallelism
- Parenthetical information
- Subordination/coordination
- Relevant use of sources
- Integration of borrowed material
- In-text documentation and a corresponding Works Cited page

Bruno 1

Daniel Bruno
Composition I
Dr. Fritz Strisky
November 5, 2001

<u>Entitlement Education</u>

  In his book <u>Generation X Goes to College</u>, Peter Sacks describes, among other things, the sense of entitlement that some students in today's consumerist culture have toward a college education. One entire chapter explores this issue alone, providing examples of this "sense" and looking into its "humble beginnings." Sacks shows how consumerism has invaded education, leading some students to expect good grades for little effort. But he fails, it seems, to emphasize enough a most harmful effect of this sense of entitlement. The biggest problem, as I see it, is that although students are able to graduate from high school (and even some colleges) with minimal effort, those students may find themselves cheated in the long run.

  How might they be cheated? One might argue that students get cheated because entitlement doesn't go on forever. At some point it stops. For example, a college graduate with a marketing degree, but especially weak thinking or writing skills, may find himself disadvantaged on the job. It is not that his boss puts her foot down; instead, the job does. Our student finds himself not well prepared for it. He gets cheated because he is disadvantaged at his job--a job that he paid money to learn how to do. Of course the point isn't about marketing majors. The same is true of students in any field. (Marketing is just what came to mind.)

  One might also claim that students will be cheated because their lives will somehow *be less.* This argument claims that a person's intelligence contributes to his quality of life. Here we must remember that "intelligence" is not just "knowledge." Instead, it is being able to use knowledge, to make connections and figure things out, to see causes and solve problems. A person may have much knowledge--that is, he may have accumulated a lot of facts--but not have much intelligence . . . or so the argument goes. As one goes from first grade to twelfth, from twelfth grade to college, and from freshman to senior, education shifts focus from mere accumulation of information (knowledge) to application of information (intelligence). And while we may accumulate more knowledge as a senior in college than we did as a senior in high school, the focus in college has (or should have) shifted from mere knowledge to intelligence--that is, to the ability to make good use of one's knowledge.

Title provides coherence by providing the reader with an overall focus.

Clear reference to Sacks's book provides coherence—the rest of the essay is about this.

Consistent verb tense—present—provides coherence.

Transitional expressions such as "for example" provide coherence by clarifying the relationship between ideas.

"Also" indicates a relationship between this claim and the previous one.

Pronouns such as "this" provide coherence by connecting ideas.

Parallelism provides coherence (to use; to make; to see OR may have much knowledge; but not have much intelligence.).

"Other," "for example," "but," "of course," and "and" show the relationship between ideas.

Other standard arguments claim other ways students might be cheated. For example, we might feel sorry for someone who doesn't get a joke--or a reference. Allusions to literature, history, philosophy and so on allow us to say much in few words. But does the listener understand? If a person is unaware of common references--the Battle of the Bulge, Normandy, Existentialism, T. S. Eliot, World War I, Rasputin, John the Baptist, Gandhi, apartheid, Jonas Salk, Johnny Appleseed, Lewis and Clark, the Trail of Tears, slavery, the Donner Party, and so on--he misses out on conversations, on meaning, on *connecting with his fellow inmates*. Of course, here one might counter that you don't need to know all of these things. And, I agree, you don't. People tend to hang out with people who have similar interests and tastes.

Items in a series (on conversations, on meaning, on connecting) expressed in equal grammatical form contribute to coherence.

One more argument claims that because we live in a democracy, we must be well-educated. Since all the citizens are responsible for the government, our forefathers promoted public education so that all citizens--not just the wealthy and elite--would know how to read and write. Thomas Jefferson wrote,

Explicit statements of main ideas, followed with support for that idea, contribute to coherence.

Smoothly integrating appropriate outside information and documenting correctly contribute to coherence.

> I know no safe depository of the ultimate powers of society but the people themselves; and if we think them not enlightened enough to exercise their control with a wholesome discretion, the remedy is not to take it from them, but to inform their discretion by education. This is the true corrective of abuses of constitutional power. (The Writings 15:278)

The quoted material is discussed.

In what ways can educated citizens correct abuses in a democracy? A person's way of life, his purchases and activities--not just a person's vote or protest march--is part of the responsibility. Thus, consumers and neighbors and co-workers and so on should behave responsibly and think intelligently. It is our responsibility as citizens of a democracy.

True enough, these are all ways that students who are allowed to just slide by end up getting cheated. But another way (and one less talked about) strikes me as being far more offensive. This reason hinges on the fact that many students are not just sliding by.

This entire paragraph provides coherence between two sections by taking the reader from the previous ideas to "another way."

Main ideas at the beginning of paragraphs provide coherence by letting the reader know the reason for the information that follows.

In Generation X Goes to College, Peter Sacks illustrates that all of today's college students cannot just be thrown in the same big barrel. In describing the modern/post-modern clash in education, he spends the majority of his time talking about those students who are underprepared, who lack the basic study skills required in academic work, and who demonstrate little real commitment to their own

Bruno 3

education. Yet, he does not discuss this problem in isolation. He also mentions another type of student. For example, he introduces the reader to Marissa and Carol: "As very good students, [their views] were virtually excluded by The College in order to accommodate the whiners and complainers" (61). And he says they "suffered not only educationally" (63). In addition to discussing specific good students, an entire chapter presents survey results about students' attitudes toward education. While he makes claims such as "nearly a quarter of the students . . . harbored a disproportionate sense of entitlement," this very statement tells the reader that a full three quarters (that is, three out of four) students *do not* "harbor a disproportionate sense of entitlement" (54-59). He wraps up the book by focusing on another student, Andie, who he describes as "a good student, constantly picking [his] brain for information and feedback on her work" (186-7). His final paragraph, before the Epilogue, says, "Let's create a system that encourages people like Andie at least as much as the ones who don't give a damn" (187). Thus, Sacks shows that today's students are a more diverse group--in skill level, background, and attitude toward education--than has ever before been gathered together in the college classroom.

A properly used colon— to introduce a quote with words that could be punctuated as a sentence— provides coherence. The reader knows immediately the relationship of the words on the left and right of the colon.

Quotation marks provide coherence by making clear that the words inside them are from a source.

In-text documentation that corresponds to a Works Cited page provides coherence by being inobtrusive while at the same time providing important information.

Bruno 4

Works Cited

"Almanac." *The Chronicle of Higher Education.* 18 Oct. 2000. http://chronicle.com/ free/almanac/2000/almanac.htm.

Jefferson, Thomas. *The Writings of Thomas Jefferson.* Ed. Andrew Adgate Lipscomb and Albert Ellery Bergh. 20 vols. Washington, D.C.: 1903-4.

Sacks, Peter. *Generation X Goes to College.* Open Court: Chicago and LaSalle, Illinois, 1996.

Activities

1. Check your own essay for coherence and conciseness by referring to the strategies above. For example, ask yourself, "How does my title help the reader to focus on my main idea?" or "How does my purpose in writing help to make my essay coherent and concise?"

2. Take a reader-based, not a writer-based, approach to revision. That is, as you revise, imagine both likely and possible areas where a reader might not make a connection that you intended. Consider the various coherence and conciseness strategies and fill in such gaps as you see fit.

3. Weed your writing of unnecessary words. If your essay then fails to meet a length requirement for the assignment, return to the appropriate invention section in the text and explore your topic further, developing interesting ideas worth discussing in your essay.

4. Using the table of contents of this book, make a study of essay titles. What strategies do the authors seem to use when titling their essays? Which titles are most intriguing and why? Which ones do you and your classmates want to read based on just the title? Describe how a few successful titles help to focus the reader on the writer's purpose in writing.

Complete Sentences

Identifying, Understanding, and Revising Sentence Fragments and Run-On Sentences:
Writers and readers share ideas about what constitutes a sentence or what constitutes a part of a sentence. In standard written English (or edited American English), sentences generally contain at least one independent clause. Sometimes they contain more. A group of words lacking an independent clause is a **sentence fragment**. A group of words made up of two independent clauses not connected by either a coordinating conjunction (*and, or, nor, for, yet, but, so*) or a semicolon is a **run-on sentence**. There are two kinds of run-on sentences: **fused sentence** and **comma splices**.

Fragment: A sentence fragment, since it contains no independent clause, can be a single word, a phrase, a dependent clause, or any combination of the three *without an independent clause*. Writers sometimes purposely use fragments for effect. Such as here, for example. This strategy is acceptable and can be effective, though fragments should not creep into one's writing by accident.

Phrases Are Not Complete Sentences

Falling off his horse and getting right back on it.
The neighbor's new Siamese kitten, Lorenzo.

Dependent Clauses Are Not Complete Sentences

When Joe passed his algebra test.
As long as you and Susie are going to the game.

Combinations of Phrases and Dependent Clauses Are Not Complete Sentences

Running to catch the bus so that I won't be late for class.
George Washington who was the first president of the United States and general of the Continental army.

Run-On Sentence: In a run-on sentence, the two independent clauses are "run together" with a comma (a comma splice) or with no punctuation at all (a fused sentence).

Comma Splice

I went home, she stayed at the party.
I am tired of reading, I am going to bed now.
Joe flew the 767, he had never landed a plane before.
There is a mouse in the closet, we need a better mousetrap.

Fused Sentence

I went home she stayed at the party.
I am tired of reading I am going to bed now.
Joe flew the 767 he had never landed the plane before.
There is a mouse in the closet we need a better mousetrap.

How to Identify Sentence Fragments and Run-On Sentences

1. Identify the independent clauses in your sentence.

   - If there are no independent clauses, the sentence is a fragment.
   - If there is only one independent clause, the sentence is a complete sentence.
   - If there are two or more independent clauses, go to step 2.

2. If you found two or more independent clauses, how are they connected?

   - If with a coordinating conjunction *(and, or, nor, for, yet, but, so)*, you have a complete sentence.
   - If with a semicolon, you have a complete sentence.
   - If with a comma, you have a comma splice.
   - If with no punctuation, you have a fused sentence.

3. If you have a fragment, comma splice, or a fused sentence, you may revise your sentence in several ways.

How to Revise Fragments

Some writers use fragments sparingly to achieve a desired effect. But fragments should not occur by accident. Most sentence fragments should be identified and revised to read as complete sentences. While this can be done in various ways, the objective is always to either (1) attach the fragment to an independent clause, (2) add an independent clause to the fragment, or (3) restructure the sentence to create an independent clause.

Revising Fragments That Are Phrases
(A phrase is a group of related words without a subject and a verb.)

Falling off his horse and getting right back on it.
(a fragment because it is only a phrase and has no independent clause)

Joe fell off his horse and got right back on it.
(a complete sentence because an independent clause—*Joe* (subject) *fell and got* (verb)—has been added)

Falling off his horse and getting right back on it, Joe joined the posse and captured the bandits.
(a complete sentence because the phrase has been connected to an independent clause—*Joe* [subject] *joined and captured* [verb])

Revising Fragments That Are Dependent Clauses
(A dependent clause is a clause preceded by a subordinating conjunction.)

When Joe passed his algebra test.
(a fragment because it is only a dependent clause and has no independent clause)

Joe passed his algebra test.
(a complete sentence because the subordinating conjunction—*when*—has been eliminated, thus creating an independent clause)

When Joe passed his algebra test, he let out a sigh of relief.
(a complete sentence because the dependent clause has been attached to an independent clause)

Agreement

Agreement—the grammatical relationship between a subject and a verb or between a pronoun and its antecedent—contributes to coherence, or the way a piece of writing flows smoothly from one idea to another. For example, a writer will decide whether to write in a particular tense—such as past or present—and then stick to that tense until there is a good reason to change. Unnecessary shifts in tense can be confusing or distracting.

> One thing that contributes to coherence—or the way a piece of writing flows smoothly from one idea to another—was agreement.

In the sentence above, the verbs do not agree in tense. The sentence shifts from present tense *(contributes)* to past tense *(was)*. The shift is unnecessary and distracting.

Verb Tense Agreement: Shifts in verb tense indicate important changes in time (past, present, future). A piece of writing generally has one controlling tense—that is, most of the verb tenses are the same. Verb tense may then shift to indicate an actual change in time.

> Liz left the football game early and went to a movie. She is not a big fan of the game. I doubt that she will ever enjoy football.

The first sentence above uses a past tense verb *(left)*. But the follow-up sentence is written in present tense because it's not that she *was* not a fan of the game. She still *is* not. The third sentence used a present tense verb *(doubt)* and a future tense verb *(will enjoy)*. These shifts in tense accurately express the time relationship among several ideas; thus, there is a good reason to change tense. Some shifts, however, are less purposeful and thus may be confusing or distracting.

> Liz left the football game early and goes to a movie.

This shift is unnecessary. It is hard to imagine why the writer shifts from past tense *(left)* to present tense *(goes)*. While the meaning still seems clear, the shift is distracting. If further unnecessary shifts were to occur or if the passage were to deal with a more complex concept, the reader would become confused.

Unnecessary tense shifts sometimes occur when the writer shifts unexpectedly to the present tense after beginning in the past tense. This often occurs when narrating. Consider the following example:

> When I first got off the plane in Belgrade, I noticed how cool and crisp the air felt. I see the mountains in the distance and want to drive out to them and begin climbing.

The verb *see* in the second sentence marks an unnecessary shift from past tense to present. Because the verb tense is not consistent and because the change does not express an actual change in time, the shift is likely to distract the reader.

Shifts in Person: In addition to shifts in tense, writers can shift person.

> When I first got off the plane in Belgrade, I noticed how cool and crisp the air felt. You see the mountains in the distance and want to drive out to them and begin climbing.

The passage above now shifts not only from past tense to present, but from first person to second—from *I* to *you*. An unnecessary shift in person may distract or confuse the reader.

Pronouns can be first, second, or third person. First-person pronouns refer to the person speaking *(I, me, mine; we, our, ours);* second-person pronouns refer to the person being spoken to *(you, your, yours);* and third-person pronouns refer to the person or thing being talked about *(he, him, his; she, her, hers; it, its; they, them, theirs).* In the example above, the writer refers to himself in the first person *(I)*, then shifts unnecessarily to the second person *(you)*. The passage below is consistent in tense (past) and person (first).

> When I first got off the plane in Belgrade, I noticed how cool and crisp the air felt. I saw the mountains in the distance and wanted to drive out to them and begin climbing.

Activities

1. After studying pronoun/antecedent agreement (on the following page), study Bruno's pronoun/antecedent choices throughout "Entitlement Education." Notice what decisions he makes and what decisions he might have made instead. When does he use masculine singular, feminine singular, and plural pronouns? What might be the effect of his choices on the reader? If workshopping Bruno's essay, what suggestions might you make regarding his pronoun decisions?
2. Study Bruno's verb tense throughout "Entitlement Education." What is the controlling tense? When does he shift to a different tense and why? If workshopping Bruno's essay, what suggestions might you make regarding verb tense?
3. Write a paragraph in which you shift for good reason among past, present, and future tenses. What would you say is the controlling tense of your paragraph? Did you use any tenses besides simple past, present, and future? That is, did you use a perfect or progressive tense?
4. Write a paragraph with a controlling tense. Then try to distract and confuse the reader by shifting verb tenses unnecessarily.
5. Before turning in your next essay, check your pronoun/antecedent agreement carefully. Study it. First, go through what you have written and circle every "they," "their," and "them." Then identify the word to which the pronoun refers (draw a line from the circled word to the word it replaces). Since "they," "their," and "them" are plural, the antecedent must also be plural. If it is not, revise the sentence accordingly.
6. Exchange papers with a classmate, doing #5 before turning in your paper.

Pronoun/Antecedent Agreement

Pronouns take the place of (or refer back to) nouns; the nouns they replace (or refer back to) are called their antecedents.

> The little girl enjoyed her ride on the giant Ferris wheel.

In the sentence above, *her* takes the place of *the little girl*—that is, it allows the writer to not have to repeat *the little girl*. Since *girl* is (1) singular, (2) feminine, and (3) in the third person, so is the pronoun that replaces (or refers back to) it.

Pronoun/antecedent agreement can be tricky in sentences more complex than the example above. When several sentences work together to form a paragraph or several paragraphs, more vigilance is required to make sure pronouns and antecedents agree. Consider how Daniel Bruno deals with pronoun/antecedent agreement in "Entitlement Education":

> Students should do well to look around them, at the room full of fellow classmates. They should imagine that many of those students will be graduating one day. And they should imagine the students in the classroom next door and across the hall and in all the other buildings on campus. They will be graduating too.

In the example above, Bruno consistently uses the third-person plural pronoun *they*. Pronouns and antecedents require special attention when it comes to the third-person singular. In the example below, Bruno decided to use the feminine pronoun *she* to refer to both men and women.

> The injustice, then, has been done to the students (as Sacks says, the students are the victims). While the student has happily skipped (or unhappily slogged) along through sixteen years of formal education, she is allowed, if she wants, to come away with very little in terms of education. She is allowed, unfortunately, to escape practically unscathed by learning.

What other decisions might Bruno have made instead? Consider the following:

1. While the student has happily skipped along, he is allowed, if he wants, to come away with very little in terms of education. (These disadvantages also hold for use of "she" to imply both genders, as Bruno does.)

   Advantage: Concise.
   Disadvantage: Can be misleading or offensive. Is exclusive, not inclusive.

2. While the student has happily skipped along, he or she is allowed, if he or she wants, to come away with very little in terms of education.

   Advantage: Explicitly refers to both genders.
   Disadvantage: Possibly wordy, especially if *he or she* is repeated.

3. While the student has happily skipped along, she or he is allowed, if she or he wants, to come away with very little in terms of education.

   Advantage: Explicitly refers to both genders.
   Disadvantage: Possibly wordy, especially if *she or he* is repeated.

4. While the student has happily skipped along, he/she is allowed, if he/she wants, to come away with very little in terms of education.

   Advantage: Explicitly refers to both genders and is more concise than *he or she*.
   Disadvantage: May sound unnatural.

5. While the student has happily skipped along, she/he is allowed, if she/he wants, to come away with very little in terms of education.

   Advantage: Explicitly refers to both genders and is more concise than *she or he*.
   Disadvantage: May sound unnatural.

6. While the student has happily skipped along, s/he is allowed, if s/he wants, to come away with very little in terms of education.

   Advantage: Explicitly refers to both genders and is very concise.
   Disadvantage: May sound unnatural.

7. While students have happily skipped along, they are allowed, if they want, to come away with very little in terms of education.

   Advantage: Concise and natural sounding.
   Disadvantage: Plural may not work for a particular idea.

8. While the student has happily skipped along, serious learning has not been required.

   Advantage: Concise.
   Disadvantage: Eliminating the pronoun may create an awkward expression.

9. While a student has happily skipped along, they are allowed, if they want, to come away with very little in terms of education.

   Advantage: Often sounds natural and is easily understood.
   Disadvantage: Has traditionally been considered to be incorrect because the pronoun *(they)* is plural and the noun *(student)* is singular.

All of the above are options to choose from, though using the masculine or feminine pronoun to refer to both men and women is generally not acceptable because it is exclusive, not inclusive. A writer might first try recrafting the sentence to either make the pronoun and antecedent both plural or to eliminate the need for a pronoun altogether. If that doesn't work, he or she must choose between one of the other options, carefully considering the pros and cons of each strategy.

Subject/Verb Agreement:
In addition to indicating tense (past, present, future), verbs indicate number—they can be singular or plural. Nouns, too, can indicate number (*dog* is singular; *dogs* is plural). Thus, singular nouns take singular verbs; and plural nouns take plural verbs.

> My sister takes the train to work.
> My sisters take the train to work.

A singular noun *(sister)* with a plural verb *(take)* conveys the same meaning as when the subject and verb agree. Yet in edited American English (or standard written English), subjects and verbs generally agree in number.

In the following sentence, the subject and verb do not agree in number: *My sister take the train to work. Sister* is singular, and *take* is plural. Consider the following questions: How important is it that subjects and verbs agree? In what situations would you consider the above sentence to be acceptable? Unacceptable? How might an employer, colleague, classmate, teacher, English teacher, client, boyfriend, or girlfriend react to sentences in which subjects and verbs do not agree?

Other Subject/Verb Agreement Issues

Phrases or clauses that act as subjects take singular verbs.

> Having a kennel full of hungry puppies and no dog food is Marcia's biggest fear.

In American English, collective nouns take singular verbs.

> The government is taxing the citizens more now than in previous years.
> (Other collective nouns to look for include *team, class, congress, orchestra,* and *administration.*)

Compound subjects joined by "and" take a plural verb; some other compound subjects take plural or singular verbs, depending upon the meaning.

> Bob and Sue share a common interest in painting by numbers. (*share* is plural—two people *share*)
> Bob shares a common interest with Sue. (*shares* is singular—one person *shares*)
> Either Bob or Sue shares a common interest with Sally.
> Neither Bob nor Sue shares a common interest with Sally. (*shares* is singular—one or the other *shares*)

Indefinite pronouns—such as everyone, everybody, all, and anybody—usually take a singular verb (and pronoun).

> Everyone in our family goes to the annual ice cream social at the volunteer fire department. (*goes* is a singular verb—one person *goes*; two people *go*)

Parallelism

P arallelism (like agreement) contributes to a piece of writing's coherence, or how it flows. Parallel structure means using the same grammatical form (noun, verb, participial phrase, etc.) to help indicate that ideas are related.

Herbert ate a big dinner, sat down in his favorite chair, and put on his slippers.
(We see that Herbert did three things. Each is expressed in the same grammatical form—a verb phrase).

Herbert ate a big dinner, sat down in his favorite chair, and putting on his slippers.
(Here, the third thing, *putting on his slippers*, is expressed in a different grammatical form—a participial phrase instead of a verb.)

Parallel items have two things in common. They are related in both grammatical form and meaning. Combining form and meaning in this way contributes both clarity and coherence to one's writing. Sentence parts connected with coordinating conjunctions should be equal grammatically, as should comparisons, listed items, and headings.

Instead, it is being able to use knowledge, to make connections and figure things out, to see causes and solve problems.
(Each of the three items in this list is expressed in equal grammatical form—*to use, to make, to see.*)

One can read with either more intelligence or less intelligence—noticing or missing the logical fallacies that others use to sell them laundry soap, SUVs, political leaders, and a general way of living.
(Notice that the sentence parts connected by *or* and *and* are grammatically equal—*more intelligence/less intelligence; noticing/missing; laundry soap/SUVs/ political leaders/a general way of living.*)

Now when we connect two things—the present grade-inflated, entitlement-driven education system that has got a foothold in most of America's high schools and colleges and the diversity in skill and attitude toward education of today's college students—two problems appear.
(Above, the first *and* connects two nouns—*high schools and colleges;* the second connects two noun phrases.)

Parallelism with Coordinating Conjunctions: Since *and* connects parallel (or coordinate) sentence parts, the words, phrases, or clauses connected by *and* take the same grammatical form, which helps the reader to more easily pick up on the relationship between the ideas. One way to ensure better parallelism is to identify all coordinating conjunctions *(and, or, nor, for, yet, but, so)* and then to make sure the sentence parts they connect are grammatically equal.

> Bob went fishing **and** fell into the lake.
> (*And* connects two verbs—*went* and *fell.*)

> The man in the green hat **and** the woman with the umbrella are old friends.
> (*And* connects two nouns—*man* and *woman.*)

> I went to the market **and** to the bookstore before it rained.
> (*And* connects two prepositional phrases—*to the market* and *to the bookstore.*)

> The doctor was two hours behind schedule, **and** all the patients had to wait.
> (*And* connects two independent clauses—*The doctor was . . .* and *all the patients had. . . .*)

> It was raining, yet everyone had fun.
> (*Yet* connects two independent clauses—*It was raining* and *everyone had fun.*)

> We finished cleaning the garage, but not the basement.
> (*But* connects two nouns—*the garage* and *not the basement.*)

Other Parallel Situations: Semicolons, Comparisons/Contrasts, Lists, and Headings:

Focusing on parallelism is a good way to write more coherently as well as to understand how sentence parts relate to each other. Elements that function equally should be grammatically equal.

Semicolons

> For example, one might argue that students find themselves cheated because upon graduation they will not be prepared to do their jobs: engineers will build defective bridges; doctors will botch their operations; and marketers will have no clue how to market.

Semicolons express a coordinate relationship, just as coordinating conjunctions do—in fact, we might call them "coordinate-colons." The sentence parts joined, or separated, by a semicolon should be grammatically equal because that's what a semicolon does: it connects sentence parts that are grammatically equal.

Comparisons/Contrasts

> The problem, of course, is that the two students have entered college on different academic levels and **the one on the higher level** has graduated on an even higher level while **the one on the lower level** has remained pretty much the same.

The parallel grammatical structure of the comparison/contrast helps the reader to more easily notice the relationship between the ideas.

Lists

> They have at least three options: (1) take advantage of the easy system and learn a little along the way; (2) motivate themselves, working harder (and learning more) than the system requires them to; and (3) attend a more academically rigorous school (of course such schools still exist though they are likely to cost more to attend).
>
> We bought eggs, cheese, butter, and milk.
>
> *Grocery List*
> eggs, cheese, butter, bagels, cookies, sauce, milk, bread, beans, soap, a light bulb, sister

A grocery list provides a good example of how form and meaning work in conjunction. When meaning is parallel or equal (all things we can pick up at a grocery store) then form tends to also be parallel or equal (all nouns). Notice with our grocery list that things we can't pick up (or do) at the grocery store are not parallel. We can pick up our sister if she is at the grocery store, but if she appears on our list just because we were thinking about her, "sister" is not parallel because of the meaning, not because of the form.

Headings

Notice the parallel structure of the headings in Paul Roberts's essay "How to Say Nothing in Five Hundred Words." They are all imperative statements. But headings need not be imperative statements. Any grammatical form can be used. For example, Juliet Schor uses noun phrases to list the seven basic elements of "A Politics of Consumption."

Headings from "How to Say Nothing in Five Hundred Words" Are Imperative Statements
> Avoid the Obvious Content
> Take the Less Usual Side
> Slip Out of Abstraction
> Get Rid of Obvious Padding

Headings under "A Politics of Consumption" Are Noun Phrases
> A right to a decent standard of living
> Quality of life rather than quantity of stuff
> Ecologically sustainable consumption
> Democratize consumption practices
> A politics of retailing and the "cultural environment"
> Expose commodity "fetishism"
> A consumer movement and governmental policy

Activities

1. Before turning in an essay, check for parallel structure.

    A. Identify all coordinating conjunctions (*and, or, nor, for, yet, but, so*) and make sure that the words or group of words they connect are the same grammatical form. (Note: *for* most often functions as a prepositional phrase and not a coordinating conjunction.) This includes items in a series, such as *bread, cheese, butter, and milk.*

    B. Find semicolons and make sure that the words or group of words they connect are the same grammatical form.

2. Exchange essays with a classmate and check for parallel structure.

Word Choice

Mark Twain said, "The difference between the almost right word & the right word is really a large matter—it's the difference between the lightning bug and the lightning" (Letter to George Bainton, 10/15/1888). The right word will be accurate and appropriate for the audience. To choose the right word, writers consider their purpose in writing, the reader, and the overall writing situation.

Accurate: Accuracy in word choice begins with understanding language as something that is shared. For example, people generally agree on what a cat is, and on what to call it. Thus, the word *cat* accurately expresses the idea "cat" (which corresponds to the material reality of a cat). This simple example illustrates how we share language. What I call a cat, you, too, call a cat. And we not only share the word *cat*—we also share the concept *"cat."* Other, more abstract, concepts—such as *patriotism, honesty, love, service,* and so on—can vary more in meaning from one person to another.

This look at language shows us how we share not only words but categories of thoughts. We group various animals into *cats, dogs, rabbits* or various people into *holy, heathen, pagan,* or *successful, struggling, washed up.* When we refer to a category of thought *(cat, love, rest, white, struggling)* we try to choose a word that will accurately express our thought to others—and thus allow us to be heard.

When choosing words, consider the following questions:

- Am I using this word in the way that it is usually understood?
- If I am using this word in an unusual sense, will my reader understand it that way? Or should I define the word and/or illustrate it with an example?
- Could I replace this word with one that more accurately expresses my meaning?
- Have I used unusual words in an attempt to impress my reader with my vocabulary? If so, should I replace these words with plain, straightforward language?
- Am I comfortable with my word choice? How does it make me sound?

Imagine the Reader: Your reader must understand your words to mean roughly what you meant by them. Thus, you must imagine how your intended reader is likely to understand a particular term.

Appropriate: Language can be accurate, but still not appropriate. For example, word choice might be too casual or too formal for a particular writing situation; it might be gender-biased, overly technical, insensitive, or archaic. Writers determine whether or not words are appropriate by sizing up each particular writing situation and considering how their word choice is likely to influence the reader.

Imagine the Reader Imagining the Writer: When you write, you project a persona—that is, you come across to the reader in a certain way. Thus, you should imagine how you will sound to the reader—what this text calls your "writer's voice." When you write, ask yourself: What writing voices are appropriate in this particular writing situation? How do I want to sound to my reader?

Casual, Middle-Level, and Formal Word Choice: Formality in word choice—or diction—varies, depending upon the writing situation. An e-mail to a friend would be quite casual, a scientific report more formal. In most cases, a middle-level word choice is appropriate. In all cases, the writer makes word choice decisions based on (1) the purpose in writing, (2) the nature of the subject, and (3) the writer's relationship to the reader.

- Slang can be used effectively in an essay; but slang used indiscriminately often indicates a lack of serious thought or a lack of sensitivity for the reader.
- Archaic (old and outdated) language strikes some modern readers as insincere, and thus if used at all should be used cautiously.
- Flowery writing draws attention to itself, not to the ideas being expressed. This type of writing can make for slow and difficult reading.

Gender Bias and Sensitivity in Language: Writers must be aware of the consequences of gender-biased language. A job ad that states "the candidate must own his own tools" appears to be excluding women candidates. Thus, third-person singular pronouns (such as *he, she, he/she, s/he,* etc.) should be chosen carefully. Words once common, such as *congressman, policeman, chairman,* have been replaced with gender-neutral terms, such as *representative, officer, chair.* Nurses are no longer assumed to be women, and CEOs are not assumed to be men. Showing awareness and sensitivity through one's choice of words invites the reader to listen—whereas showing insensitivity gives the reader a reason for tuning out.

Jargon: Jargon—the technical language of a field—must be used carefully with a person who is not an expert in that field. Experts use jargon to "talk shop." But non-experts do not share the same language. Writers must be careful not to frustrate readers by talking too far over their heads. Some readers become suspicious of technical vocabulary, wondering why the writer cannot explain the idea more simply and directly. Good communicators are able to explain complex ideas in plain language.

General and Specific Language: Specific word choice usually enlivens one's writing and therefore better engages the reader. But using general, or abstract, language is also important. When choosing the right word, the writer must decide upon the appropriate level of abstraction. This is done by considering the purpose in writing, the reader, and the writing situation.

Some words are abstract—that is, they express general qualities but do not provide specific detail about those qualities. Notice that each of the lists below moves from general to specific.

Levels of Abstraction

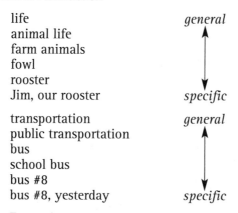

life	*general*
animal life	
farm animals	
fowl	
rooster	
Jim, our rooster	*specific*

transportation	*general*
public transportation	
bus	
school bus	
bus #8	
bus #8, yesterday	*specific*

Every time you move to a more specific term, possibilities of meaning are eliminated. For example, *farm animals* includes cows, pigs, mules, goats, sheep, ducks, chickens, and geese. But *fowl* eliminates cows, pigs, mules, and goats as options. *Fowl* can mean ducks, chickens, or geese—but *rooster* eliminates these. *Jim, our rooster* is specific. He is one particular rooster—though we can refer to "Jim" *generally* over the course of his life or more *specifically*, such as "Jim" when he was a chick, "Jim" the day we got him, or "Jim" the day he died.

Writers must consider what level of abstraction to use. When we provide examples and statistics and colors, for example, we are being specific. But specifics are not always desirable—the reader can get bogged down in too much detail or sidetracked by irrelevant detail. A more specific word choice can be more accurate, but at times you will want to speak more generally. It is good to keep in mind two things about levels of abstraction:

- move back and forth between general and specific information
- consider replacing general language with more specific language

Many examples throughout this book illustrate the ways in which paragraphs (and essays) provide an appropriate balance of general and specific information. Consider the following examples from Alice Walker's "My Daughter Smokes" and Pico Iyer's "In Praise of the Humble Comma":

But, finally, one must feel empathy for the tobacco plant itself. For thousands of years, it has been venerated by Native Americans as a sacred medicine. They have used it extensively—its juice, its leaves, its roots, its (holy) smoke—to heal wounds and cure diseases, and in ceremonies of prayer and peace. And though the plant as most of us know it has been poisoned by chemicals and denatured by intensive mono-cropping and is therefore hardly the plant it was, still, to some modern Indians it remains a plant of positive power. I learned this when my Native American friends, Bill Wahpepah and his family, visited with me for a few days and the first thing he did was sow a few tobacco seeds in my garden. (Alice Walker)

Punctuation thus becomes the signature of cultures. The hot-blooded Spaniard seems to be revealed in the passion and urgency of his doubled exclamation points and question marks (*"¡Caramba! ¿Quién sabe?"*), while the impassive Chinese traditionally added to his so-called inscrutability by omitting all directions from his ideograms. The anarchy and commotion of the sixties were given voice in the exploding exclamation marks, riotous capital letters, and Day-Glo italics of Tom Wolfe's spray-paint prose; and in Communist societies, where the State is absolute, the dignity—and divinity—of capital letters is reserved for Ministries, Subcommittees, and Secretariats. (Pico Iyer)

Each paragraph above states a general idea first, and then develops that idea with specific information. Walker gets specific about the history of the tobacco plant and even refers to a particular individual, her friend Bill Wahpepah (she even gives his name), to support her claim that one "must feel empathy for the tobacco plant."

Iyer supports his general claim that "punctuation thus becomes the signature of cultures" by providing specific examples (Spanish and Chinese punctuation, Tom Wolfe's "spray-paint prose," and capitalization in Communist societies). Notice how other writers throughout this text move back and forth from general ideas to specific support.

Activities

1. Read through some of your own previous writing and identify words that may be inaccurate. How might a different word choice allow the reader a better chance of understanding what you meant?
2. Read through some of your own previous writing and identify words that may be accurate, yet inappropriate. Explain why the word choice might be inappropriate and how a different word choice might be better.
3. Take one paragraph from your own previous writing and rewrite it two different ways: using more formal diction and using less formal diction. Do not make your changes too drastic—instead, experiment with fine adjustments in your writer's voice.
4. Find three paragraphs in this book that include both general and specific information. How many levels of abstraction can you identify? How does the writer move from one level to another?
5. Study one essay in this book in terms of how it presents general and abstract information. Consider highlighting general statements with one color and specific information with another color. Describe how the writer moves back and forth throughout the essay from general to specific.

Punctuation

Commas, Colons, Semicolons, Dashes, Hyphens, and Parentheses

Punctuation is nothing to be afraid of. You already know a lot of the basics, and over time, as you continue to write, you will learn even more. You already know that periods end most sentences, and you know that question marks end sentences that ask a question. You also know that periods are used not only at the ends of certain sentences (ones that make statements or mild commands), but that they are also used after many abbreviations (such as *Dr., Mrs.,* or *a.m.*). Yes, punctuation involves learning rules—many of which you already know—but punctuation involves more: once you understand the rules, you can more purposefully apply them to have a rhetorical effect.

We can illustrate the rhetorical effect of punctuation by looking at how the basic end punctuation marks affect the following three sentences:

- Have a seat, George.
- Have a seat, George!
- Have a seat, George?

Notice how, because of punctuation, each sentence speaks to you differently. The same point could be illustrated, in a less obvious way, by looking at how commas, dashes, and parentheses can be used to set off a sentence part. We might say that each of these sentences speaks to you differently, perhaps in a very slight way, because of how punctuation is used.

- Notice how, because of punctuation, each sentence speaks to you differently.
- Notice how—because of punctuation—each sentence speaks to you differently.
- Notice how (because of punctuation) each sentence speaks to you differently.

Setting off a sentence part with dashes (—) means something different than setting off a sentence part with parentheses ( ). Just as knowing what words mean, or suggest, allows you to communicate with others more effectively, knowing what different forms of punctuation mean, or suggest, does the same. Understanding punctuation allows you to more clearly and concisely communicate your ideas. Many readers know that when a writer places ideas within dashes, he or she means to emphasize those ideas and that ideas placed within parentheses are thought to be less important. Understanding these subtleties, which can be learned through reading about punctuation rules as well as by being more attentive to how others punctuate, can be helpful to you both as a writer and as a reader.

Commas: Commas are little signals indicating a break in thought. While we know where one word ends and another begins because someone puts a space between the words, the comma tells us something more. It separates certain parts of a sentence, and by doing so—some words to the left and some words to the right—the comma subtly indicates the relationship between the parts of a sentence.

While I was talking on the phone, I was watering my plants.

The comma above separates the two main parts of the sentence: *While I was talking on the phone* (a dependent clause) and *I was watering my plants* (an independent clause).

Mike Easler, left-handed power hitter for the Pirates, slugged one out of the park.

The two commas above, looking like bookends, stand at the beginning and ending of a sentence part *(a left-handed power hitter for the Pirates)* that interrupts the main part of the sentence *(Mike Easler slugged one out of the park)*. The interrupting part, an appositive, restates the noun that it follows (Mike Easler = left-handed power hitter for the Pirates). Commas separate ideas for the reader, who quickly makes sense of the relationship.

QUICK GUIDE TO COMMAS

Commas are generally used to indicate that an independent clause is beginning.

> After the party at Jake's house, we sang Calypso songs for days.
> Although they were tired from hunting, the hounds chased the children around the backyard.
> We drove down to see if the river was flooded, and our pickup truck got stuck in the mud.

Commas are generally used to separate items in a series.

> Alice gave Ralph a necktie, a bottle of cologne, and some chocolates.
> We ate good food, drank some tasty apple cider, and sang songs around the campfire.
> The Big Reds were moving the ball down the field, scoring touchdowns, and taking all the fun out of the game for the Spartans.

Commas are generally used between coordinate modifiers.

> Suzette is a lovely, intelligent girl.
> Some large, purple birds swooped down from above.

Commas are generally used to set off an interrupting element.

> The rest of our group, for example, is going home tomorrow.
> The parking on campus, though it doesn't bother me, has become a hot topic.
> Ella Fitzgerald, the famous jazz singer, was born in Newport News, Virginia.

Commas are also used in dates, addresses, place names, and long numbers.

> We drove through Whitley City, Kentucky, on August 16, 1972.
> John's truck has 124,618 miles on it.
> Please mail my refund to 35 Flarton Place, Burton, Maine 00178.

Commas are also used when a quotation follows a speaking verb.

> She said, "Are you coming?"
> After it rained for three days straight, Mrs. Merriweather asked, "Who wants to mop up all this water?"

Commas Are Often Used in the Following Ways

Before Independent (or Main) Clauses

When a main clause is preceded by a single word, a phrase, a dependent clause, or another independent clause, a comma is often used to help the reader negotiate the sentence parts. The comma can be viewed as "setting off" the introductory part or as signaling that a main clause is about to begin.

Going down the road, the truck stopped to pick up the hitchhiker.
Phrase, Independent Clause

While I was talking on the phone, I was watering my plants.
Dependent Clause, Independent Clause

The fire was burning brightly, and the rain was beginning to fall.
Independent Clause, Coordinating Conjunction Independent Clause

Sadly, the Comets came out flat for the second half.
Word, Independent Clause

Before Coordinating Conjunctions When They Join Two Independent Clauses

Commas usually appear before coordinating conjunctions connecting two independent clauses. But when coordinating conjunctions connect two dependent clauses, phrases, or words, commas are not used.

The fire was burning brightly, and the rain was still falling gently.
(*and* connects two independent clauses)

The Rangers were sitting around and talking.
(*and* connects two participles—*sitting around* and *talking*)

Herbert felt awful after the firefighters' cookout and called his sister for advice.
(*and* connects two verbs—*felt* and *called*)

Not before Dependent (or Subordinate) Clauses

Commas don't usually precede subordinating conjunctions *(because, since, although,* etc.) the way they do coordinating conjunctions *(and, or, nor, for, yet, but, so).* The sentence parts (an independent clause and a dependent clause) are distinct because of the subordinating conjunction and thus don't require a comma. At times, however, a comma may be used to build an even stronger distinction between the two clauses. For example, S. I. Hayakawa writes, "All new ideas sound foolish at first, because they are new." Writers size up the situation and decide whether or not inserting a comma before a dependent clause will help the reader to better see the intended relationship between ideas.

Activities

1. Scan the essays in this textbook, noticing how commas are used. Find at least three examples of the following: (1) a comma before a main clause (or setting off an introductory element), (2) two commas to set off an interrupting element, (3) a comma between items in a series, (4) a comma between coordinate modifiers.
2. Scan your own writing—an essay, letter, e-mail—and notice how commas are used. Find at least three examples of the following: (1) a comma before a main clause (or setting off an introductory element), (2) two commas to set off an interrupting element, (3) a comma between items in a series, (4) a comma between coordinate modifiers.

To Set off Interrupting Elements

Some sentence parts interrupt, in one way or another, the next-door relationship of two sentence parts. The sentence *The dog, for example, barked* can be viewed as having two parts: the main clause *(The dog barked)* and an interrupting element *(for example)*. Interrupting elements can be one word, a phrase, or a clause.

> French fries, although I haven't had any for a while, sure do taste good.
> French fries, an American classic, are sold all around the world.
> French fries, yum, are my favorite kind of potatoes.

Interrupting elements can also be set off with parentheses or dashes. In general, parentheses suggest that the inserted information is somehow less important compared to the main point being made. Yet (because this information is still included) it is somehow important and possibly interesting. Dashes—unlike parentheses—draw attention to the interrupting bit of information. Dashes and parentheses are stronger separators than the comma.

Consider the following examples, and look through *CEL* to see the various ways writers use commas, dashes, and parentheses to set off interrupting sentence parts.

Dashes

> Given time—time not in years but in millennia—life adjusts, and a balance has been reached. (Rachel Carson)

> The Gods, they say, give breath, and they take it away. But the same could be said—could it not?—of the humble comma. (Pico Iyer)

> College is lots of work and—let's be honest—it's sometimes boring, too. (Steven Richardson)

Comma

> A sadder truth, I am afraid, is that because of skills and attitudes developed in high school, for some students the reality of genuine learning (as opposed to just getting by) might already be too late. (Daniel Bruno)

> Soon, I predict, they and other companies will not be able to sell us out. (Michael Moore)

> I crouched low to avoid destroying a jewelled spider's web that stretched, exquisite and fragile, across the trail. (Jane Goodall)

Parentheses

> After my mother's never-subtle hints that if I'd just lose twenty pounds, boys would like me and I might even win a beauty contest, it was my friend Bridget who wanted us to enter the Ottumwa (pronounced Uh-TUM-wuh) Junior Miss Pageant together. (Cindy Bosley)

> Doubtless, my sense of education at that time (as well as my sense of what constituted good writing) was more than mildly seasoned by a huge dose of the Beats—Allen Ginsburg, Gregory Corso, William Burroughs, Kenneth Patchen, Leroi Jones, and, of course, Jack Kerouac. (Leonard Kress)

> When I am in a migraine aura (for some people the aura lasts fifteen minutes, for others several hours), I will drive through red lights, lose the house keys, spill whatever I am holding, lose the ability to focus my eyes or frame coherent sentences, and generally give the appearance of being on drugs, or drunk. (Joan Didion)

To Separate Items in a Series

Placing a comma between each item in a series helps the reader know where one item stops and another begins. Thus, we punctuate the following sentence as shown: *As individuals in a society, we conform to laws, clothing styles, hairstyles, and even culinary tastes (most Americans like French fries but not raw oysters).* Punctuating the list as *laws clothing styles hairstyles and even culinary tastes* would have been at the least distracting to the reader. The comma before *and* in a list is optional, though in some cases it may help to clarify meaning.

> Just go to any pet store and look at the vast array of foods, toys, beds, and treats, not to mention the shampoos and skin treatments. (David Hawes)

> If a person is unaware of common references—the Battle of the Bulge, Normandy, Existentialism, T. S. Eliot, World War I, Rasputin, John the Baptist, Gandhi, apartheid, Jonas Salk, Johnny Appleseed, Lewis and Clark, the Trail of Tears, slavery, the Donner Party, and so on—he misses out on conversations, on meaning, on *connecting with his fellow inmates.*

> Three, four, sometimes five times a month, I spend the day in bed with a migraine headache, insensible to the world around me. (Joan Didion)

To Separate Coordinate Modifiers

When side-by-side modifiers modify the same word independently of each other, the modifiers are usually separated with a comma.

the big, black dog

The dog is big. And the dog is black. Each modifier (*big* and *black*) modifies the dog independently of the other.

> What happened was that I took a bite of honey and then I joined my sister and brother, two and ten years younger, watching Saturday morning cartoons together on the black, brown, white carpet, patterned in such a wild way that it was quickly making my head ache. (Cindy Bosley)

Hyphens: Another type of modifier, the compound modifier, is punctuated with a hyphen. Compound modifiers are more than one word combined to function as one modifier.

We had thirty-five minutes to write an in-class essay.

The words *in* and *class* combine to modify *essay*. Notice also that numbers from twenty-one through ninety-nine are also hyphenated. Scan the pages of this text looking for hyphenated words. Describe, based on your observations, how hyphens seem to be used. Begin with these examples.

> Students who come to campus with the single-minded goal of preparing for a career just don't get it. (Steven M. Richardson)

> Although we probably would not have relented in our give-it-to-me-now race for more, we would have taken a solemn moment to raise a toast and drink to your hardship. (Simon Benlow)

> One of the largest land-holding families in California took its richest holdings by a trick: By law a man could take up all the swamp or water-covered land he wanted. (John Steinbeck)

Colons: Colons are useful for connecting a list, explanation, or quotation to the statement introducing it. For example, in the following sentence from "The Tucson Zoo," Lewis Thomas uses a colon to connect an explanation, or description, of a sensation to the statement that introduces it: "As I now recall it, there was only one sensation in my head: pure elation mixed with amazement at such perfection." Properly used colons can save time while connecting ideas clearly.

So here's what I don't understand: if profit is supreme, why doesn't a company like General Motors sell crack? (Michael Moore)

It was a long time before I began thinking mechanistically enough to accept migraine for what it was: something with which I would be living, the way some people live with diabetes. (Joan Didion)

Punctuation, one is taught, has a point: to keep up law and order. (Pico Iyer)

Semicolons: Semicolons are stronger than commas and weaker than periods. They are used to connect sentence parts that are equal grammatically, such as two independent clauses, two dependent clauses, two phrases, or two words—but not a clause and a phrase or an independent clause and a dependent clause.

Ovulation represents mental and emotional creativity at its peak; the FSH-LH surge that accompanies ovulation may be the biological basis for this. (Christianne Northrup)

The sky is clear and blue; however, the game has been postponed.

Last summer I drove through Bangor, Maine; Hanover, New Hampshire; and Halifax, Nova Scotia.

Activities

Commas

1. Create a comma quiz for your classmates by removing the commas from one page of recent writing you have produced. Allow your classmate(s) ten minutes to punctuate the text, and then discuss how their punctuation compares to the original.
2. Find or create at least one example of the following: (1) a sentence that is clearer to the reader because it is punctuated one way instead of another, (2) a sentence that is clear but distracting to the reader punctuated one way instead of another.
3. Prepare and then deliver a five-minute presentation on commas, attempting to make some important aspect of commas clearer to your audience.

Colons, Semicolons, and Dashes

4. Scan the essays in this textbook, noticing how colons and semicolons are used. Carefully study several examples of each. How is the colon or semicolon used? What two sentence parts are being connected? Read enough examples to give yourself a chance to get a feel for the colon and the semicolon.
5. Use a colon, a semicolon, and a dash in your class notes, essay, e-mail, homework, etc.
6. Write a one-page essay on any topic, using at least one semicolon, colon, and dash.

Index